PHILOSOPHY 101

Selections from the Works of the
Western World's Greatest Thinkers

Books by Stanley Rosen

PHILOSOPHY 101

Selections from the Works of the
Western World's Greatest Thinkers

Edited by
STANLEY ROSEN

GRAMERCY BOOKS
NEW YORK

Previously published under the title *The Philosopher's Handbook*

This 2007 edition is published by Gramercy Books, an imprint of Random House Value Publishing, by arrangement with Random House Reference, divisions of Random House, Inc., New York.

Previously published in hardcover as *The Examined Life: Readings from Western Philosophers from Plato to Kant* and in paperback as *The Philosopher's Handbook*.

Gramercy is a registered trademark and the colophon is a trademark of Random House, Inc.

Random House
New York • Toronto • London • Sydney • Auckland
www.valuebooks.com

Interior page design by Shonna Dowers

A catalog record for this title is available from the Library of Congress.

ISBN: 978-0-517-22987-3

Printed and bound in the United States of America

10 9 8 7 6 5 4 3 2 1

To the memory of Gian-Carlo Rota

CONTENTS

Contents

PART FIVE: EPISTEMOLOGY

PART SIX: PHILOSOPHY OF SCIENCE

I wish to acknowledge the great contribution made to the completion of this volume by my research assistant, Lawrence Horsburgh. His energy and dedication, as well as his good sense, were indispensable in all phases of the preparation of this manuscript.

INTRODUCTION

by

STANLEY ROSEN

Aristotle begins his treatise on metaphysics with the assertion that all human beings have the desire to acquire knowledge. By this, he means that we value knowledge for its own sake, entirely apart from its utility. As evidence, Aristotle cites the delight that we take in sense perception, and in particular, in vision, the sense that discriminates the largest number of intelligible forms. His teacher, Plato, expressed the delight in vision in a still more radical way in the *Symposium* by attributing it to a demonic force, Eros, which raises human beings up from the world of everyday life to the domain of pure intelligible structure. In these two great founding fathers of the Western philosophical tradition, one sees a poetical and a sober or prosaic statement of the universality of philosophical love.

Implicit in both statements, but perhaps more clearly in that of Plato, is the claim that we desire not merely knowledge, in the sense of a system of true propositions about the world, but a kind of knowledge that satisfies our most fundamental desire for happiness or blessedness. In the mythical language of the doctrine of Eros, human beings strive for a completeness in the vision of the truth that is the philosophical version of the completeness of sexual love. Otherwise stated, sexual love desires the satisfaction of the body, of which the most radical form is the overcoming of personal finitude through the act of procreation, whereas the love of the soul can be satisfied only through a vision of the order of the whole of human experience.

In short, the Platonic dialogues present us with a poetical account of the philosophical nature of the human being. They also raise the following question: what kind of knowledge is characteristically philosophical? The same question lies at the heart of contemporary philosophy. In the Greek texts, the philosophical appetite seeks to replace opinions with knowledge. But some forms of knowledge are more satisfactory than others. Plato and Aristotle both place general truths higher than particular ones, and they define knowledge in the strict sense as precise and unchangeable. In the contemporary world, the precision and the reliability of mathematics and the experimental sciences seem to make these the definitive types of knowledge, even though it would be difficult to say that such knowledge is unchangeable. Are we then to assume that mathematical and scientific knowledge is philosophical knowledge par excellence, or, in other words, that philosophy is either the same as science or the analysis of scientific method?

This assumption is unsatisfactory because it leaves out all reference to human life in any sense other than that of the pursuit of scientific, that is, theoretical, truth. If the love of truth is the desire for completeness or happiness, then a purely scientific conception of philosophy is at odds with human life. For who could honestly claim that scientific knowledge alone is both the necessary and sufficient prerequisite for happiness? Furthermore, if we look a bit more closely at what is meant by scientific knowledge, we find that it cannot itself be explained purely theoretically, that is, simply by the assertion of true propositions about the state of things. The propositions in which we describe "the state of things" themselves depend upon a host of assumptions about scientific procedure, assumptions which cannot themselves be fully verified by that procedure.

In other words, science is saturated with philosophy in the form of theories about how to conduct the scientific enterprise, in particular about what things are, and how they become, accessible to scientific investigation. Still more fundamentally, questions arise as to the extent of the applicability of scientific methods, the use to which we should put scientific knowledge, and even how far we should push our inquiry into the secrets of nature. None of these questions entails the conclusion that science is defective. The questions rather illuminate the difference between science and philosophy, or let us say that they remind us of the many kinds of knowledge and the various senses of *true*.

Such a difference is already visible at the level of the arts and crafts, that is, in any activity defined generally as "technical." By this, I mean a methodical procedure, whether simple or complex, that can be taught to others in a step-by-step way, and which is then practiced in accord with rules. A purely technical or objective explanation of any art or science is impossible. The choice of technical materials, their arrangement, an exposition of the purposes of the art or science, are all an expression of a more general interpretation of the activity in question. In sum, the intrinsic utility of the technique and the intentions of its practitioners are not accessible in a description based upon the methodology of science. Political, ethical, social, aesthetic, and even religious considerations enter into the picture. For that matter, there is not one universal scientific method, but a multiplicity of procedures, assumptions, hypotheses, and so on, all of them chosen on the basis of varying philosophical convictions about the nature of reality.

The similarity in the problem of explaining any human activity, whether or not it qualifies as "technical," to that of explaining philosophy is itself a sign of the universality of philosophy. As soon as we go beyond a "merely technical" account of some procedure (assuming that "merely technical" accounts are possible), we are philosophizing. It is not only insufficient, but also impossible, to find out "the facts" without reflecting upon what counts as a fact, how to determine facts of different kinds, and why we should be concerned with them. Those who believe themselves to dislike philosophy, or to be of a purely "practical" nature, are therefore deluding themselves. They fail to see that "practical" already designates a philosophical position or doctrine. We can escape philosophy only by escaping from our very humanity.

If this is so—and I am firmly convinced that it is—then the task of an introduction to philosophy is to show the intelligent reader that he or she has already been philosophizing. This cannot be done by providing a condensed history of the views of other philosophers, or even a survey of the parts of the discipline as it is conceived by specialists. Such information is of course important, but its acquisition is not the first step. We have to be motivated to acquire that information. When Aristotle says that all human beings have the desire to know, he does not mean that all human beings are professional philosophers, but rather that our delight in sense perception, our curiosity about the change of seasons and foliage, our wonder at the regular movement of the stars, are all evidence of an innate appetite for knowledge.

But he also means something more than this. Aristotle holds that it is good for human beings to know rather than to be ignorant. Let us say for the moment that there are two main types of knowledge. One type is of how things are; the other type is more complicated and includes knowledge of good and evil as well as the beautiful and the ugly. We often refer today to these two types as knowledge of facts and values. In the Bible, the latter kind of knowledge is more fundamental than the former. This is illustrated by the story of the Garden of Eden, in which God forbids Adam and Eve to taste of the fruit of the knowledge of good and evil. God is silent about knowledge of truth and falsity, but this knowledge comes only after expulsion from the Garden of Eden. It depends upon our fallen condition, which in turn is brought about by knowledge of good and evil. Knowledge of both kinds is thus presented in the biblical account as a consequence of human disobedience, or, in other words, of our imperfection.

For Aristotle, however, who is representative of the tradition of Western philosophy, the two kinds of knowledge are an expression of two kinds of human excellence or perfection. Furthermore, Aristotle clearly makes the theoretical life, or the contemplation of how things are, higher than the practical life, or the pursuit of moral and political virtue. Let us say that these two lives express two types of perfection, that is, two ways of achieving the characteristically human excellence, one through wisdom or a grasp of truth and the other through moderation, which is best represented by the virtue of justice. The highest form of human existence would then be characterized by the possession of both types of goodness.

Whether or not we agree with Aristotle about the difference between and relative ranking of wisdom and moderation, he illustrates for us the more general philosophical conception of the good life as dependent upon knowledge and sound judgment. Called *phronesis* in Greek, sound judgment is not the same as ethical virtue but is closely connected with it. It is impossible to have *phronesis* if one is not good, and it is impossible to exercise the ethical virtues without *phronesis*. Contrary to the biblical tradition, then, the good life is a consequence of intellectual activity, whether one contemplates how things are, or deliberates about the actions that are requisite to the good or virtuous life. In the latter case, it is we human beings who calculate the goodness or evil intrinsic to deeds. We do not make this determination on the basis of divine revelation, but through our own intelligence. In this sense, despite their historical and geographic separation, one could say that Aristotle, and through him the tradition of philosophical rationalism, represents the repudiation of the deepest part of the biblical religious tradition. For Aristotle, expulsion from the Garden of Eden is the condition of human goodness. But mankind save themselves; they do not await salvation as a gift of God.

We seem to have arrived at a sharp distinction between philosophy and religion. But this distinction cannot be unambiguously preserved, for a very simple reason. The commands of God, that is, the contents of divine revelation, are sufficiently ambiguous that they require interpretation. There is so much disagreement about the correct sense of Holy Scripture that the claim that this sense is manifest is itself an interpretation, and so subject to rejection. Prophets, preachers, and scholars alike all attempt to derive the genuine will of God from the revealed text. They may themselves appeal to divine revelation, but this simply moves the problem back a step. How do we decide which interpretation is based upon the genuine revelation? The result of this problem is theology, or the application of philosophical, historical, rhetorical, and philological types of reasoning to the task of biblical interpretation.

I raise this issue not to reject religion or even to insist upon its inferiority to philosophy, but rather as a crucial illustration of the universality of philosophy. The connection between philosophy and the good life is nowhere more evident than in the domain of religion, even though, and perhaps precisely because, religion differs essentially from philosophy. As we have already seen, a similar point obtains with respect to modern science. Our very conception of science, as well as our decision concerning the sovereignty of science over philosophy, and so of the value of science, are all philosophical rather than scientific decisions. I will come back to this point shortly. Meanwhile, let us say only that philosophy is not itself intelligible on the model of the particular arts and sciences, any more than it can be reduced to a form of religion. I therefore disagree with those who deny that terms like *good* or *perfection* can be rationally applied to human life. On the contrary, it is my thesis that the deepest and most universal sense of philosophy is precisely that of the pursuit of the good life, and so of whatever degree of perfection is available to members of our species. And I hold that we are compelled to pursue the good life by the very nature of human existence. Unfortunately, this compulsion does not guarantee success.

It is very important to understand that the preceding remarks are not intended as a logical or scientific proof of the claim that philosophy constitutes the perfection of human existence. The claim is itself philosophical, not logical or scientific; it expresses an interpretation of the facts of human existence, not a fact. The statement that human beings have the desire to know is much closer to being a fact than is the claim that philosophy is the perfection of human nature. One can also offer the following simple argument on behalf of the universality of philosophy: since every interpretation of the presence or absence of meaning and value in life is a philosophical thesis, so too is the denial of the significance of philosophy.

To say this in another way: proofs rest not simply upon laws of inference but also upon conceptions of the nature of those laws, the principles of evidence, and so on. We cannot prove something except on the basis of certain assumptions. I claim that the assumptions about the universality of philosophy, or still more immediately, about the natural inclination of human beings to reflect about the meaning and value of life, are more evident than any argument that could be constructed to prove the opposite. The very effort to prove the opposite is itself a demonstration of the assumption. It is of course not a proof that every human being is thoughtful to the same degree as the most accomplished philosophers.

A corollary of the previous conclusion is that philosophy, or the inclination to philosophize, must be visible in everyday life. To be sure, we move far beyond the everyday in our pursuit of the structure of intelligibility or the sources of value, but that movement is initiated by common human desires, by the delights and the sorrows of ordinary experience, which is of course the standard by which we define the extraordinary. In the next section of this introduction, I shall spell out this corollary by examining two models or conceptions of philosophy, my own and one that is radically opposed to it. In keeping with the impossibility of introducing philosophy except by philosophizing, I shall argue for the superiority of my own view, but not, I hope, at the price of refuting a caricature of its rival. My purpose is not so much to persuade the reader that I am right as that one should, and indeed, must, engage in the argument.

The word *philosophy* is of Greek origin and means literally "love of or friendship for wisdom." This simple linguistic fact shows us at once that philosophy is an intrinsic expression of human nature.

Like all such expressions, however, it is subject to two kinds of distortion. On the one hand, we can trivialize the word by applying it to virtually any human activity, as is illustrated by references to "my philosophy of investment" or even "the offensive philosophy" of a football coach. On the other hand, we can ignore or reject the significance of the original meaning of the term and replace it with a technical definition, such as "conceptual analysis" or "the methodology of science."

The popular use of the term *philosophy* is in a way closer to its original sense than is the second or (as I shall call it) the technical use. This is evident from the fact that *wisdom* refers traditionally to a kind of general intelligence or capacity for judging effectively in diverse circumstances. Wisdom is the mark of a well-ordered life that has achieved the kind of perfection available to human beings. We could call it understanding rather than knowledge, since it is concerned not with technical mastery of this or that art or science, but with how the ends or purposes of the arts and sciences fit together in the unity of existence. We normally associate wisdom with the happiness that arises from the successful pursuit of the noble and the good.

The popular contemporary use of the term *philosophy* as a general understanding of how effectively to perform virtually any activity whatsoever is thus a debased but still perceptible reflection of the original sense of wisdom. Investing in the stock market and playing football are two quite distinct skills, each with its own repertoire of techniques. In both cases, there is a general conception of how to do something that is not itself a technique but rather a criterion by which techniques are chosen, and so too a goal toward which they are applied. In these and all analogous cases, "how to do something" is inseparable from "why we are doing it." One could of course object that the purpose of football is to win, and that this purpose, although it regulates one's choices of techniques, has nothing to do with wisdom. But this objection misses the point. What counts for us in the present discussion is not the degree to which the end of an activity exhibits wisdom, but rather the use of *philosophy* to designate the general pattern of choices directed toward that end. Equally important, the word *philosophy* can be applied in its popular use to the general considerations underlying the pursuit of any end whatsoever.

It should be clear that the popular use of *philosophy* is rooted in the immediate and pretheoretical conviction that human activity is purposive. We act not simply to accomplish some immediate goal, like the satisfaction of a desire or the production of a tool, but to fulfill certain ends that regulate our conception of a proper or good human life. There are of course many different interpretations of what constitutes a good life, just as people disagree about how to achieve happiness. But this does not change the fact that we all pursue what we take to be the good. Stated somewhat more cautiously, every normal person wishes to be happy rather than sad, and to acquire good rather than bad things. We are entitled to use the term *normal* on the basis of our experience, that is, on the basis of the common agreement of our fellow human beings. And this entitles us to use the term *wisdom* to refer to knowledge of the good life. Furthermore, the disagreement concerning the content of the good life is not so great that we are entirely unable to distinguish between the wise and the foolish.

To summarize the previous reflection: Everyday human life teaches us that speeches and deeds are both directed toward the satisfaction of general or regulative ends. We are all, the reflective and the unreflective alike, moved by the desire for happiness, and we tend to understand as "good" those things that make us happy. But we are unlike in our conception of what makes us happy, and so what is good. The more we reflect upon this disagreement, the more we tend to doubt that we possess wisdom in the full sense of the term. But this doubt does not automatically lead us to repudiate the pursuit of wisdom, or for that matter to deny our capacity to distinguish degrees of wisdom. It serves instead to accentuate the desirability of wisdom. We are aware of, and so in a kind of anticipatory sense can be said to "know," what we do not, but long to, possess. And so we come to understand ourselves as lovers of wisdom or philosophers.

The preceding remarks are intended to illustrate the contention that the human being is by nature a philosophical animal. This is of course not to deny that philosophy manifests itself in different degrees within different individuals. The contention is rather that the structure of human life is defined by the need for wisdom. This need can be blocked or perverted in countless ways, but it will always shine through in our perception and analysis of human motives. A perverted conception of the good, and so of happiness, is nevertheless a conception of the good, and so it is a desire for happiness. There is, however, a quite different, or at least apparently quite different, conception of human life, and so of philosophy, which is rooted in the previously noted disagreement concerning what is good, and so what makes us happy. And to this conception I now turn.

Everyday life testifies to the fact that human activity is intentional or purposive. We do x for the sake of y. Life also shows us that we regard some intentions or purposes as better than others. This is the basis of such distinctions as those between good and evil, noble and base, beautiful and ugly. But the mere fact that I judge something to be good does not make it good. Differently stated, if the goodness of a speech or deed depends upon my opinion of its merits, then I cannot appeal to the intrinsic goodness of the speech or deed in order to demonstrate that my assessment is correct, and thus better than the assessment of those who disagree with me. Speaking very generally, we can verify whether a deed has occurred, just as we can understand the content of speeches if we know the language and are familiar with the topics discussed. But there seems to be a discontinuity between our perception of the fact and our estimation of its goodness. In contemporary language, there seems to be a disjunction of facts and values.

Accepting this disjunction does not require us to deny the existence or intelligibility of values. What happens is that the concept of an intrinsic good—that is, a degree of goodness that is visible within an act or event as independent of the opinion of the person who esteems it—is replaced by the concept of the good as equivalent to the fact of estimation. Values become facts, but in so becoming, they lose their value. By this, I mean that the value lies renowned not in the act or event, but in your or my estimation of the goodness of that act or event. The value becomes a matter of opinion. It is no longer, properly speaking, regarded as part of knowledge.

From this standpoint, the traditional conception of wisdom as a unity of knowledge is substantially modified, if not rejected. Knowledge is now defined as a grasp of what is the case, or how things are; it is thus closely associated with the technical arts and sciences. Competent observers can arrive at agreement about how thing are in a way that is verifiable through observation or logical argument. Otherwise stated, how things are is in principle open to public scrutiny, or still better, it can be decided by techniques that are universally applicable. But no such techniques exist by which to determine which conception of good or assignment of value is the correct one.

It should be stated here that this sketch is an introductory and therefore oversimplified account of the alternative to my version of the traditional conception of wisdom. Arguments can be constructed to show that difficulties analogous to those involved in "evaluating values" are also present in the determination of how things are. Factual knowledge depends upon sense perception, and sensory apparatus varies from species to species. We now know that there are alternative conceptions of geometry, logic, and physics; that is, we can modify our conception of the scientific tools by which to determine how things are. It has even been claimed that scientific and technical knowledge is a social construction, dependent upon cultural or historical opinions, and so it reflects the same type of subjectivity or relativism as do our conceptions of goodness and happiness. Claims of this sort lead directly to a reversal of the treatment of values as facts. Facts are now said to be values, that is, expressions of how things look to us or consequences of social preference of one kind or another.

For our present purposes, the main point of these difficulties is the following. The attempt to replace the traditional conception of wisdom with one that is more precise, more conceptually sophisticated, or closer to the procedures of the mathematical and natural sciences, carries with it two fundamental defects. In the first place, every step forward in the pursuit of logical and scientific sophistication is a step away from the understanding of wisdom as a unity of knowing what is the case and how we shall live. Despite various attempts to conceive of the unity of science, scientific progress has in fact been associated with the increasing fragmentation of human existence, and in the extreme case, with the inability to attribute any genuine value or significance to it. If human experience is indeed a kind of secondary result of the motion of matter in the void, then it would seem to be "a tale told by an idiot, full of sound and fury, signifying nothing," to borrow a line from William Shakespeare.

This last observation has already introduced the second defect of the rejection of the traditional conception of wisdom. Whereas it was intended to rectify the ostensible subjectivity of commonsense or pretheoretical doctrines of goodness, and to replace the ostensibly arbitrary conception of happiness with a precise and objective conception of knowledge, what I am calling the technical conception of wisdom has led instead to the triumph of subjectivity and the rejection of the objective status of values. In a purely theoretical doctrine of philosophy, which depends upon logic and scientific procedures to define rationality, it is impossible to attribute rationality to the claim that we ought to be rational. In other words, the statement "reason is good" is itself rhetorical or purely subjective. And the problem is intensified by the progressive reduction of conscious human experience to fluctuations in our neurophysiological system. This development leads to the depreciation, or indeed to the denial, of the very existence of subjectivity. From this standpoint, what is today called "postmodernism"—the celebration of difference, change, the multiplicity of viewpoints, and the absence of a unified central consciousness or personal identity as well as of any hierarchy of purposes or ends—is simply an ideological adaptation of the results of the scientific rationalism of the modern Enlightenment.

In short, the rejection of the popular or traditional conception of wisdom cannot itself be regarded as an unambiguous advance in precision and sophistication of conceptual analysis. It is in no sense a repudiation of logic or science to observe that both logic and science can be used wisely or foolishly. But there are fundamental differences between logical analyses and the technical procedures of science, on the one hand, and the purposes for which we employ these analyses and procedures, on the other. If the purposes are not themselves rational, then neither are the instruments. A similar argument applies to all attempts, whether partial or total, to "deconstruct" or dissolve the unity of consciousness, and with it, our attempts to live wisely, or to pursue goodness as well as truth, that is to say, to pursue the truth because it is good.

One might offer a counterargument here: It could be humanly unsatisfactory, and even finally disastrous, to discover the truth about how things are. Still, this does not alter how things are, nor does it in any way invalidate the superiority of technical, logically valid, scientifically regulated rationalism to the imaginary speculations of traditional philosophy. I myself fail to perceive the force of this line of reasoning. My failure is rooted in a lack of appreciation not for logic and science, but instead for the philosophical misuse of the prestige of logic and science. In the first place, if the philosophical doctrine, or what one may call the ideology of scientism, were correct, it could still be detached from science and replaced by an edifying or "noble" lie, to employ an expression from Plato. This is essentially the recommendation of Friedrich Nietzsche, and it is what he means when he says that art is worth more than the truth. Simply stated, the truth acquires worth or value only from the noble lies of art, that is, from procedures that enhance life rather than robbing it of vitality. In short, if scientism were true, it should on this argument be rejected anyhow because it is destructive of the human spirit.

It is, however, not necessary to reply to the ideology of scientism by invoking Nietzsche. The aforementioned ideology is in fact in agreement with Nietzsche on the basic presupposition, namely, that life is an illusion, or that, in the wonderful desolation of Shakespeare's line, "We are such stuff as dreams are made on, and our little lives are rounded with a sleep." Nietzsche, as it were, recommends the preservation of the illusion that we are awake, whereas scientism recommends that the illusion be dissipated by knowledge that we are asleep. There is, however, another possibility. We can hardly imagine that we exist, as was noted by thinkers like Augustine and René Descartes, if *imagine* is taken here to exclude our actual existence. Gottfried Wilhelm Leibniz once observed that if life is a dream, it must still possess structure. I would like to expand that observation by adding that there are good and bad dreams, or, in still more forceful words, that the problem of human existence, and the rational methods for addressing those problems, are exactly the same, whether we are awake or dreaming.

In fact, of course, it makes no sense to speak of life as a dream. Such a comparison is possible only because we already know the difference between waking and dreaming life. Otherwise stated, it makes no sense to reduce experience to a side effect of matter in motion, especially since materialism is a philosophical doctrine, and science itself is the product of the activity intrinsic to human experience. The only sensible procedure is to take our bearings by human experience, which is the expression of our nature, and therefore of our attempts to modify nature where possible, in order to live the best possible life. And this means that we must philosophize as fully and as perfectly as possible.

Let me now summarize the entire argument to this point: The traditional view of philosophy that stems from Socrates identifies it as the perfection of human nature, and so as the essential component of the good life. There are two main opposing views, which rest primarily upon mathematical science in the first case and history or temporality on the other. The first view holds that nature is independent of, and provides no rationally valid support for, values in general or the rank-ordering of activities and types of life. The second view insists that "custom is the king of all men," or, in other words, that judgments of good and evil, nobility and baseness, justice and injustice, are opinions that vary from country to country and from one historical period to another.

For the sake of convenience, let us call these two views "scientism" and "historicism." It is important to understand that they eventually come together, and the core of their agreement lies in a rejection of the classical or Socratic conception of nature. Representatives of the first view conceive of nature as fundamentally extension, motion, or energy, and knowledge as the formulation of the laws that express (usually mathematically) the behavior of the primary particles (or fields) constituting extension (or energy). On this view, we acquire knowledge of human behavior, and so of the values that are held by human societies, through the application of scientific procedures: observation, description, and quantification. One may then arrive at laws of human behavior, but these tell us what is the case, not what ought to be.

Whether or not representatives of scientism insist upon the complete reduction of human experience to the equations of physics, or only to an intermediate science of neurophysiology, evaluations of all kinds lose their natural status and are reduced to the level of opinion. But opinions vary from epoch to epoch. And in particular, our views on the nature and purpose of science also vary. But even if they were invariant, they would lack any basis in nature, and so could not be regarded as anything other than opinions or the expressions of a historical perspective, namely, our own. There would be no scientific way to prove the superiority of scientific to nonscientific cultures. Any attempt to do so would rest upon claims about the utility of science, but the useful is not the same as the good. Utility is in the eye of the beholder; that is, something is useful depending upon our intentions, purposes, and so, upon our *values*.

In a word, on the view being discussed, values, and thus opinions about the good life, are either illusions or prejudices. Or, in the language of the theory of evolution, those views have come to prevail that are "useful" for the preservation of the species. Even assuming that this could actually be shown, the preservation of existence is a biological drive, not a value. It states how things are, not what we ought to do. And indeed, the extraordinary progress of science in the last century opens the real prospect that we can change our evolutionary destiny. But should we do this? And if we should, in what way? Plainly, the dreams initiated by science leave references to self-preservation incomplete and unsatisfactory.

In the last analysis, there is a difference between science and philosophy, but not a radical separation. The devastating consequences of the attempt to enforce this separation are often concealed by the rhetoric of success. We celebrate our triumph over nature, the extension of human life, the increase in health, wealth, and all forms of material power. But the rhetoric by which we indulge in self-congratulatory celebrations of the expansion of scientific knowledge is itself an implicit claim to some standard of value, some conception of the good, that differs from the standards of scientific methodology. The appeal to power is in itself meaningless; power corrupts and destroys as well as enriches and exalts. What counts is the uses of power, and by *count*, of course, I am not referring to the operations of arithmetic. This is why the most thoughtful scientists look to philosophy, in one form or another, not simply for the justification of their miraculous power but for insight into its legitimate purposes, and also, perhaps, its wise limitations.

Thus, not only is the love of wisdom compatible with the value of science, but it endorses our pursuit of the basis of that value. If, as some would claim, there are no bases or foundations in human life other than opinions or subjective viewpoints, whether of the individual or some social or historical collective, then, in the words of Nietzsche and Fyodor Dostoyevsky, "everything is permitted" because it makes no difference what we do. To this last expression of irresponsibility, we give the name nihilism, literally, "nothing-ism." Some respond to the doctrine of nihilism with good cheer, even with enthusiasm, on the grounds that it signals a new wave of human creativity, uninhibited by traditional prejudices. Others reject the very concept as a disease imported from the European continent that has infected the spirit of "Anglo-Saxon" philosophy and so must be extirpated by the medicine of scientific rationalism. The question is therefore whether we can live a genuinely human life on the assumption that all values, including truth itself, are human opinions, and so neither valuable nor true in themselves.

This introduction to philosophy started with everyday life and moved from the time of Socrates to that of the present generation. We noted the difference as well as the relation between philosophy and religion, plus the challenge to and the transformation in the nature of philosophy initiated by modern science and technology. The cycle of philosophy in the history of Western civilization can be described as an evolution in the self-conception of humanity. The crucial philosophical questions are "who am I?" and "what is the good life?" Whereas these questions were regarded at the beginning of our philosophical tradition as amenable to rational response, that conviction has been steadily diminished, thanks primarily to the influence of modern science, or, still more precisely, the modern "scientific worldview" that developed during the English and French Enlightenment. The extraordinary optimism of the Enlightenment, which was already visible in the seventeenth century, and its enthusiastic anticipation of the coming age of universal reason and happiness, or salvation on Earth, has not perhaps entirely disappeared from our midst. But if I am not mistaken, it is restricted among philosophers to the most technically oriented thinkers, for whom the preferred answers to the two philosophical questions are "I am a machine" and "the very question about the good life is meaningless."

So much for our panoramic summary. My intention has been to introduce the intelligent nonspecialist to the universality, but also to the urgency, of philosophy. In so doing, I have referred to what I take to be the most pervasive dimensions of the Western philosophical tradition. A discussion and examples of the particular subdivisions of philosophy are provided in the body of this volume, which is divided into six parts. Let me emphasize that the editors of each part have been selected because of their expertise, not because they endorse my conception of philosophy. Their introductory essays constitute additional perspectives on the issues I have raised. I want to stress once more that my distinction between philosophy and science is not motivated by any kind of antiscientific or reactionary desire to return to a wiser and safer past. On the contrary, I share the admiration of my contemporaries for the extraordinary discoveries of science and for their life-giving and life-enhancing practical consequences. But just as science is not philosophy, so one should not confuse an endorsement of science for allegiance to "scientism" or the ideological use of science to reduce the traditional desire for the good life to the level of ideology. To this, I add that it is entirely unphilosophical to wish to return to the past. We have no choice but to move into the future. If this voyage is to be philosophical, then it must be convinced of its own significance. Such a conviction is rooted in our everyday lives, in particular in our desire to know the truth. I have tried to keep the connection between knowledge and goodness from being concealed by the hypnotic effects of technical prowess.

The six parts of this volume are devoted to the major and traditional subdivisions of philosophy: social and political philosophy, the philosophy of religion, the philosophy of art and culture, metaphysics, epistemology, and the philosophy of science. This approach is superior, in my opinion, to a purely historical one. Each part is introduced by a philosopher with a special interest and competence in the particular branch of philosophy. The authors of these essays have selected a small but representative number of texts from important philosophical works, and have tried to strike a balance between a multiplicity of short excerpts and a failure to provide a sense of the variety of philosophical doctrines. This is not a dictionary or an encyclopedia but an attempt to give a fair portrait of the aforementioned variety in a way that encourages the reader to philosophize, not to look up famous names or definitions of technical terms. Facts about philosophy are worthless, except to the philosopher. And we are all philosophers by nature.

PHILOSOPHY 101

Selections from the Works of the
Western World's Greatest Thinkers

PART ONE
SOCIAL AND POLITICAL PHILOSOPHY

INTRODUCTION

by

PAUL RAHE

It was Socrates who first summoned philosophy down from the heavens, settled it in the cities, introduced it into the homes of men, and forced it to make inquiry into life and morals and things evil and good. Such is the testimony of the Roman philosopher-statesman Marcus Tullius Cicero. As this claim suggests, the emergence of moral and political philosophy was not coeval with that of philosophy itself. Thales, Anaximander, Anaximenes, and their successors had focused their attention more narrowly on the natural world. But if these pre-Socratics neglected the human things, it would be wrong to suppose that politics was of no pertinence to their concerns as philosophers.

To begin with, there is the question of philosophy's origins within the first self-governing civic polities known to man. It is revealing that the word *kosmos* and its cognates were used in the political realm well before they were appropriated by the philosophers. The army described in the Catalogue of Ships in the second book of Homer's *Iliad* was arranged in its appropriate ranks by a *kosmetor*; the annually elected magistrates of the city on Crete that appears to have pioneered constitutional forms were called *kosmoi*. Put simply, the ancient Greek city (*polis*) was configured as a *kosmos* before the philosophers adopted the pertinent term and used it to assert that the natural world is likewise an intelligible and ordered whole.

This coincidence is revealing because it points to and reflects something more fundamental. The presumption that Gottfried Wilhelm Leibniz much later dubbed the Principle of Sufficient Reason—the presumption that there is a fit between reason and the world such that the latter is intelligible to the former—was a political principle before it became the hypothesis underpinning philosophy. The republicanism of the ancient Greeks was predicated on the assumption that rational speech, which they called *logos*, is adequate to political reality; it was grounded on the conviction that by means of public deliberation human thinking can be refined and made to comprehend the issues that arise in the conduct of political affairs. The philosophers merely extended this presumption to the natural world. In the process, they universalized and made explicit what their fellow citizens had tacitly assumed. With Leucippus of Abdera, they asserted that "no thing comes into being at random but all takes place in accord with *logos* and by necessity."

Phusis and *Nomos*

It was inevitable that philosophy's debt to politics be repaid. From speculation about the natural world one can all too easily draw conclusions about matters of more immediate concern to man. Aristotle intimates that Anaximander of Miletus and the first *phusiologoi*—"those exercising *logos* regarding nature"—espoused a species of monotheism; this was in keeping with their presumption that the natural world reflects a single ordering principle. In this spirit, Xenophanes of Colophon dismisses the Olympian gods outright. "One god there is," he contends, "greatest among gods and humankind, in no way like mortals in body or in the thought of his mind. In his entirety, he sees; in his entirety, he thinks; in his entirety, he hears. Always in the same place, he remains, moving not at all; it is not fitting that he should shift about now here and, then, elsewhere." But, holding aloof from toil, he sets all things aquiver with the thought of his mind.

Xenophanes knew perfectly well that "mortal men believe that gods are begotten, and that they have the dress, voice, and body of mortals." He was familiar with Hesiod's Theogony, a poetic treatment of the origin of the gods and the cosmos, and he knew something of the beliefs of the barbarians. But for the opinions of mankind he had little, if any, respect. "If oxen, horses, or lions had hands with which to sketch and fashion works of art as men do," he remarked, "then horses would draw the forms of gods like horses, oxen like oxen, and they would each make their gods' bodies similar in frame to the bodies that they themselves possess." Indeed, he observed, "the Ethiopians claim that their gods are snub-nosed and black; the Thracians, that theirs are blue-eyed and red-headed." The critical element in Xenophanes' analysis is the supposition that the divine must conform to the dictates of Leibniz's Principle of Sufficient Reason—that god can do only that which it is "fitting" that he do. In consequence, Xenophanes finds offensive the fact that "Homer and Hesiod have attributed to the gods everything which is deemed shameful and blameworthy among humankind: theft, adultery, and deceiving one another." The god of the philosophers conforms to reason—if he is not, in fact, reason itself.

This posed a political problem. The philosophers' fellow citizens took it for granted that the fate of the community depended upon propitiating ancestral gods, who could be relied on to come to the defense of the people; so the philosophers' critique of the received religion as irrational and ethnocentric was not just unsettling but impious, and it seemed likely to provoke divine wrath. The Theban poet Pindar spoke for the cities when he charged the *phusiologoi* with "plucking wisdom's fruit unripe." The poets are said to have reviled philosophy as a "bitch yelping and baying at her master," to have charged her with "being great in the empty speech of fools," to have spoken of her disciples as a "mob of overly clever men holding sway," and to have dismissed these "subtle ponderers" on the grounds that they were, if truth be told, "very poor indeed."

These attacks might have been more easily deflected had the early philosophers managed to articulate an account of politics that made sense of the convictions of ordinary men concerning justice and the common good. In fact, however, Xenophanes and his successors seem only to have cast doubt on these convictions. Their subversion of inherited norms was not without consequence. The result is starkly visible in the speeches given by various Athenians in the period of the Peloponnesian War and reported by the historian Thucydides. These provide evidence for the influence of the sophists and of the distinction that they drew between nature (*phusis*) and convention, custom, or law (*nomos*). The "realism" that the Athenians consistently display when they articulate the relationship between justice and self-interest or necessity is grounded in the conviction that man is by nature erotic, that his *eros* finds its fulfillment in the pursuit of self-interest and everlasting fame, and that *nomos* can never for long hold *phusis* in check.

The same themes dominate in the comedy *The Clouds*, which Aristophanes wrote and saw produced in the midst of Thucydides' great war. The play turns on the problems of its protagonist Strepsiades, who is unable to pay the debts he incurred while indulging his son Pheidippides' taste for horses. For help, he turns to

Socrates, who is represented as being devoted to the study of natural science and who is said to be able to teach the rhetorical skills that a man needs if he is to win his case in court when, in fact, he has the weaker argument. Strepsiades is old, uneducated, and obtuse (except with regard to his own material interests), and he proves to be unable to learn the winning argument. In his place, he enlists his spirited young son Pheidippides, whose innate love of victory renders him more capable of learning. To entice the initially reluctant Pheidippides, Socrates stages a rollicking debate between a pious, conventional defender of justice and a philosophical opponent. The upshot of their exchange is that convention, custom, and law (*nomos*) are contrary to nature (*phusis*), which dictates erotic self-indulgence; that they cannot be sustained against nature's demands; and that only a fool or a weakling would prefer a life lived in accord with *nomos* to the pleasures associated with *phusis* unleashed. Predictably, the Pheidippides who returns from Socrates' school no longer defers to his elders; in fact, to his father's horror and dismay, he is willing to contemplate thrashing not just his father but his mother as well. To Strepsiades, then, poetic justice is done—but not to him alone. For Socrates is also hoisted by his own petard; at the end of the play, an enraged Strepsiades burns the philosopher's school to the ground.

None of this would be of philosophical interest were it not for the fact that the debate between the defender of justice and the philo-sophical libertine is restaged between Strepsiades and his son at the end of the play. The first time that this debate is presented, the just or better argument is forced by his antagonist the unjust argument to concede that *eros* is irresistible when he himself and everyone in the audience is proven to be a pederast. When it is restaged, Pheidippides justifies beating his father by making an appeal to nature. "Consider the chickens and the other beasts," he suggests. "They defend themselves against their fathers. Yet how do they dif-fer from us, except that they do not write decrees?" Strepsiades then blurts out a reply: "Why, then, since you imitate the chickens in everything, won't you eat dung and sleep on a perch?" This response gains comic force from the fact that Socrates first appears in the play seated on a perch, purporting to tread on air and look down on the sun in the manner of a god, and from the fact that he is said by a disciple to have been caught unawares, gawking at the heavens, by a lizard who defecated into his mouth. Pheidippides does not grasp the force of Strepsiades' retort any more than his father does, but he is reduced to a pathetic appeal to authority nonetheless. "It's not the same," he tells his father, "and it wouldn't seem so to Socrates either."

This comic and vulgar exchange between father and son charts philosophy's political turn, for Strepsiades' unwitting refutation of the unjust argument in the form advanced by his son points out the path followed by the Socrates we encounter when reading Xenophon's *Memorabilia,* which contains his memories of his teacher, and the dialogues authored by Plato. Like Strepsiades, this Socrates enlists *phusis* in defense of *nomos* by reflecting on what is revealed by the fact that human beings are by nature quite different from chickens and the other animals; like Strepsiades, he concludes that this crucial difference consists in the fact that human beings know shame and possess a sense of what is fitting, that they write decrees and adopt laws, that they impose on themselves customs and conventions, and that these reflect a conviction on their part that a life of mere self-indulgence is not just ignoble but ultimately repulsive as well.

Whether Aristophanes' comic depiction of Socrates as a natural philosopher and a sophist did him a grave injustice we cannot say. But both Xenophon and Plato affirm that Socrates turned away from the natural science that had engaged him in his youth and that he brought philosophy down from its contemplation of the heavens, caused it to enter into the cities and houses of men, and made it concern itself with human things. On the available evidence, we must assume that Socrates did so under the persuasion that Aristophanes had exposed a chink in all prior philosophy's armor—its inability to account for the qualities within human beings that made philosophy's pursuit possible in the first place. If Socrates adopted self-knowledge as his goal, it was because he had come to recognize that the philosopher had hitherto been inclined to forget himself.

Plato

Such is the Socrates whom we meet when we read the Platonic dialogues. He is not a dogmatist; he is in the grips of wonder, which, in the *Theaetetus,* he calls "a very philosophical passion." He begins his inquiries with the opinions entertained by ordinary men or by those whom they think wise; though he nearly always finds these opinions wanting, he presumes that they are the appropriate starting point for philosophical reflection because they contain an intimation of the truth. This Socrates is characteristically distinguished from his inter- locutors by an awareness of his own ignorance; generally the dialogues end with an admission on his part that the process of critical examina- tion has left him at a loss. It would, however, be a mistake to conclude from this that there is nothing to the Socratic disposition other than an unbridled and destructive skepticism. As we can infer from the image of the divided line that Socrates offers for our contemplation in Plato's *Republic*, he is no René Descartes, he is convinced that knowledge begins with trust.

One cannot claim to be aware of one's own ignorance, as Socrates does, if one is persuaded that there is nothing to know; indeed, one cannot so be aware unless one has a sufficient inkling of the truth to be able to discern what is false. Like the Ionian philosophers, Socrates takes as a given the Principle of Sufficient Reason; unlike them, he has reflected on the preconditions of their shared pre- sumption that knowledge is possible. His conclusions in this regard are most clearly presented in his discussion of *eros* in the *Symposium*—for whereas Aristophanes, in the speech given him in that dialogue by Plato, treats *eros* as the desire for completion and wholeness, Socrates counters that man's sense of his own incom- pleteness is rooted in his desire for the beautiful and ultimately the good.

Eros, as Socrates depicts it, is like a philosopher; if the latter were wise, he would not long for wisdom; if he were so ignorant as to be unaware of the degree of his ignorance, he would not long for wis- dom. Reason and *eros* are treated as inseparable. The ordinary human desire for beautiful bodies, for offspring, for immortal fame; the admi- ration that men feel for the beautiful and the noble; their eagerness to secure for themselves that which is good and to accomplish that which is worthy—these "lesser mysteries of *eros*" point beyond themselves to the greater mystery: what is the nature of the beautiful and the good? If philosophy cannot achieve the detachment from human concerns sought by the Socrates of *The Clouds*, it is because, properly under- stood, the longing for wisdom is ordinary human *eros* followed through to its end. If it is worthwhile for the philosopher to examine the opinions widely held by ordinary men or espoused by those reputed to be wise, it is because, confused though it may be, ordinary human desire points in the direction of the truth concerning that which is. The fact that we can sometimes recognize our errors as such reflects the fact that we all have an inkling of what is true.

This, the starting point for his reflection, enables Socrates to articulate a critique of injustice. In the *Gorgias*, he is quickly able to dispose of the sophist Gorgias and his assistant Polus—for their professional pride in benefiting their students renders these two teachers of rhetoric vulnerable to shame. Kallikles (Callicles), the Athenian who seeks to learn rhetoric from them, is in this particular invulnerable, and he restates the unjust argument of Aristophanes' *Clouds* with great force, contending that the laws are a conspiracy of the weak to contain the strong, that natural justice dictates that the strong get the better of the weak, and that it would be ignoble for a man of real strength to be deterred by *nomos* and the conventional understanding of justice and moderation from a ruthless pursuit of the pleasures pointed out by *phusis*. To dissuade him, Socrates must demonstrate that even if he is entirely successful in his project, even if he becomes a tyrant and his command of rhetoric enables him to escape punishment for the harm he does his fellow man, he will be miserable. This he achieves by meeting Kallikles on his own ground: he shows him that he has misunderstood the dictates of nature; that the conventional understanding of justice and moderation, for all its limitations, better reflects nature's dictates; and that the pleasures associated with a life of self-indulgence are nothing if not preceded by an equivalent pain. The key to this argument is that there is a hierarchy of pleasures corresponding to the erotic hierarchy sketched out in the *Symposium* and that satisfying the baser desires is no more pleasant and no more noble than scratching an itch.

The same themes reappear in Plato's greatest dialogue, the *Republic*. Socrates' defeat of the sophist Thrasymachus early on corresponds with his silencing of Gorgias and Polus. The speech that Plato's older brother Glaucon delivers after expressing reservations about Socrates' refutation of Thrasymachus is an elaboration of Kallikles' restatement of the unjust argument. Socrates' reply to the challenge leveled by Glaucon and seconded by Plato's other older brother Adeimantus ultimately takes the form of a demonstration that the life of the philosopher is superior in both dignity and pleasure to the life of the successful tyrant, and this demonstration is grounded in an account of the erotic hierarchy within the human soul. The two dialogues differ chiefly in the fact that, in the interval between Glaucon's challenge and his own reply, Socrates explores at length with Plato's brothers just what would be required if one were to establish a truly well ordered city.

Given that human beings are restless, ambitious, and unlikely to be satisfied with rustic simplicity, they conclude that the city that they are constructing in speech will require policing and defense. Given that the Guardians entrusted with this responsibility will themselves be a threat to its well-being, they will need to be educated in public spiritedness. For this to be effective, not only will they have to be thoroughly indoctrinated, but they will have to be deprived of property and family lest private concerns lead them to neglect the common good. At every turn, the demands become more radical, and the prospect that such a city could actually be established becomes less plausible—until Socrates sets the most preposterous precondition of all, contending that there will be "no respite from evils for the cities . . . nor for mankind nor will the polity we have now described in speech ever emerge from nature" until "the philosophers rule as kings."

This claim provokes Adeimantus, the more conventional of the two brothers, to restate Aristophanes' and Kallikles' critique of philosophy, and this in turn forces Socrates to come to its defense. Socrates begins by distinguishing philosophy from sophistry, then he articulates what philosophy is and what causes it unjustly to be condemned in ordinary cities, and finally he intimates that philosophy is of greater dignity than the city itself. It is as a consequence of his need to clarify what philosophy is and to indicate the education that must be provided if philosopher-kings are to be produced that Socrates then elaborates the images of the sun, line, and cave. What began as a dialogue concerning justice becomes a discussion of education and ultimately an account of philosophy and its pursuit of the good. In the end, two conclusions emerge: first, that just rule is unlikely unless the rulers are as indifferent to the rewards on offer to rulers as are the philosophers described by Socrates; and second, that the political community is to be judged for its contribution to philosophy and not vice versa.

By means of the last of the three images, that of the cave, Socrates articulates the limits of politics. The cave is the city itself; the chains that bind its inhabitants are the more or less arbitrary customs and laws of the community; and the puppet-handlers are the poets, the sophists, and the demagogues who fashion its governing illusions. Most of what the citizens take to be true is inference from the shadows cast by these artifacts on the wall of the cave. The discovery that all of this is illusory is at first quite painful. But, according to Socrates, the initial shock of liberation opens the way for an exceptionally gifted individual's emergence from the cave, for his gradual habituation to the light, and for his discovery of that which truly is. The process by which this takes place is the education of a philosopher.

There is no suggestion here that the city itself can be enlightened. Those whom Socrates calls "the true Guardians" are, in fact, to be distinguished from those he now describes as mere Auxiliaries— Guardians who are subjected to the initial indoctrination but do not receive the higher education. As for the multitude, he contends that it can never become philosophic. The cave then represents the human condition; only the handful blessed with a divine, philosophical disposition can ever hope to escape. If the city is to be well governed, those who have made their escape must eventually be forced to return to the cave and to put their wisdom to use. In the ordinary city, however, which has not seen to their education, Socrates argues that philosophers have no such obligation.

Plato's *Republic* is not a blueprint for utopia. It exploits the political idealism of the young, represented by Plato's brothers, for the sake of an exploration of the limits of politics, the nature of the human soul, and the superiority of the philosophical life. Its implausibility as an actual project owes less to the unlikelihood that one can indoctrinate a class of Auxiliaries and deny them property and family ties than to the requirement that wisdom rule. Plato's Socrates never claims that he is himself wise—only that he has encountered no one wiser than himself. The wisdom that he attributes to the philosopher in the *Republic* is possessed by no one he knows—and arguably for good reason. To apprehend the Idea of the Good as such is to understand the whole as a whole; the attempt to do so is comparable, as Socrates suggests, to looking directly at the sun. But as he himself remarked elsewhere, according to both Xenophon and Plato, looking directly at the sun produces only blindness.

Aristotle

Like his teacher Plato, Aristotle published dialogues. While these have not survived, we do have a collection of writings more like lecture notes than formal treatises, which were apparently intended for use within the school that Aristotle founded. Nowhere in these works does Aristotle provide us with an elaborate argument concerning human *eros*; nowhere does he give us an extended critique of the baser pleasures. But there can be no doubt that the arguments he advances presuppose something of the sort. That there is a human good which men in their confusion pursue he does not doubt, and he is in no way hesitant to argue the superiority of the philosophical life.

There is, however, one crucial difference between Aristotle's account and Plato's: the former is prepared to concede considerable dignity to ordinary human life. This concession has two, closely related dimensions. On the one hand, Aristotle asserts what Plato tacitly denies: that man is by nature a political animal. On the other, where Plato had spoken of political or demotic and of philosophical virtue, Aristotle contends that there is also such a thing as moral virtue.

Aristotle acknowledges that the political community owes its existence to private concerns—to the need for common defense against attack and to the desire for economic cooperation. But he is too respectful of the convictions of ordinary men to be willing to suppose that such an account of the origins of the city would explain its true nature. If the desire for mere life brought the *polis* into being, he observes, it is the desire to live nobly and well that sustains it. Thus, when he describes man as a political animal, he is not simply asserting that human beings are gregarious. Such a claim would fail to distinguish mankind from the ants and the bees. He is contending, instead, that ordinarily it is in and through the life of the *polis* that gregarious beings of this sort "have a share in the good life."

To understand what Aristotle means by the good life, we must take careful note of those faculties that distinguish man from the beasts. In Aristotle's view, human beings are set apart from the other animals by their capacity for rational speech (*logos*). This capacity enables the human being to perform as no other animal can; it makes it possible for him to perceive and make clear to others through reasoned discourse the difference between what is advantageous and what is harmful, between what is just and what is unjust, and between what is good and what is evil. It is the sharing of these things, Aristotle insists, that constitutes the household and the *polis* each as a community.

This analysis of human nature explains why Aristotle singles out as mankind's greatest benefactor the human being who first organized the *polis*, and it accounts as well for his assertion that someone who, by nature, belongs outside the political community must be either a god or a hunted animal alone and at war with the world. It matters little whether the individual lives in solitude, in slavery, as a resident alien, or under the rule of a tyrant or king. Human beings (other than philosophers) are rendered servile and virtually subhuman by the circumstances or fully conscious choices that deny them participation in the political life. They are rendered servile and virtually subhuman because they are prevented from developing fully those faculties of rational argument (*logos*) and cooperative action (*praxis*) that men possess and the other nonpolitical animals lack entirely. We exclude slaves from the political community, Aristotle explains, because some men lack the capacity for prudential deliberation regarding the advantageous, the just, and the good; we exclude women, though they possess this capacity, because it has no authority over them; and we exclude children because they possess it in incomplete form. For all but the handful of men capable of that quasi-divine existence devoted to philosophy, the fully human life is a life of *praxis* conducted in accord with the dictates of *logos*.

Aristotle's account of moral virtue follows from this understanding of human nature. The political and demotic virtue mentioned by Plato is purely instrumental; it is the excellence of the citizen, not that of man, and it requires a sacrifice of that which is best in humankind. In the *Republic* it is fully possessed by those among the Guardians who come to be called Auxiliaries as opposed to true Guardians and philosophers—men who give up not just property and family but all freedom of thought for the sake of serving a communal good that they do not themselves enjoy. For Plato, human excellence is philosophical virtue—the rare set of qualities that enables a man to leave the confines of the cave and see things as they are in the light of the sun. In contrast, Aristotle's account of moral virtue presupposes the existence of a class of human beings who are neither fully outside nor simply confined to the cave, and who pursue a way of life that is both admirable and, on balance, pleasurable: the class of gentlemen, who may dabble in philosophy; the exemplars in every age of taste, decorum, and public spiritedness; the mainstay of every decent polity. Aristotle's description of the great-souled or high-minded man suggests that there is something vaguely comic about the gentleman, but that he is worthy and estimable we need not doubt.

Challenge and Response

Plato and Aristotle were by no means the only political philosophers who appeared in antiquity, but that they towered over Socrates' Stoic and Epicurean disciples no one need doubt. It was, in any case, their arguments concerning politics and morality, especially those of Aristotle, that were reshaped in Latin for an audience of Roman gentlemen and given a Stoic tone by Cicero and that remained thereafter the common possession of educated men until very near to our own time. Moreover, in late antiquity, Plato was baptized by Augustine: philosophy was subordinated to theology and reason to revelation; the Christian God was substituted for the Idea of the Good; and Plato's erotic hierarchy was now said to end in the beatific vision. Thomas Aquinas eventually did something of the same sort for Aristotle, and the latter's moral and political thinking directly informed Christian political and moral theology from the thirteenth century on.

It was not until the second decade of the sixteenth century that a challenge emerged to the Platonic-Aristotelian consensus. The Florentine Niccolò Machiavelli's assault on the moral teachings of the classical philosophers and their Christian successors was grounded in a straightforward rejection of their claim that ordinary human desire points beyond its immediate objects to the Idea of the Good or even to God—that human *eros* is by nature directed to a definable, discoverable, and ultimately satisfying end. "All the things of men are in motion," he wrote. "They cannot remain fixed." By this, he meant to convey something closely akin to what Thomas Hobbes would have in mind when he subsequently asserted that reason is the slave of the passions. As Machiavelli put it in *The Prince* by way of explanation, "the human appetites" are "insatiable"; "by nature" human beings "desire everything" while "by fortune they are allowed to secure little"; and since "nature has created men in such a fashion" that they are "able to desire everything" but not "to secure everything," their "desire is always greater than the power of acquisition."

As a consequence of accepting this doctrine, the Florentine dismissed as utopian the moral and political teachings advanced by his classical and Christian predecessors; under its guidance, he rejected the Aristotelian doctrine of the mean, arguing that the pursuit of moderation is a species of folly and contending that in a world in constant flux there simply is not and cannot be "a middle road." One must take one's political bearings, he asserted, from a fact putatively admitted by "all who reason concerning civic life": that anyone intent on setting up a republic and ordaining its laws must "presuppose that all men are wicked and that they will make use of the malignity of their spirit whenever they are free and have occasion to do so." Machiavelli does, of course, trace "good examples" to "good education." But that education is not, as it was for Aristotle, a process of moral training and habituation, and it is in no way aimed at liberating men from the dominion of their passions. Its goal is to shape, direct, and fortify the spirited passions, and it arises from "good laws"—such as those, spawned in early Rome by the strife between the Senate and the people and "those tumults that many inconsiderately condemn." These tumults had enabled "the people to vent their ambition" and had thereby given rise to the predatory *virtù* that impelled that city to conquer the world.

In the *Republic*, Plato had linked his analysis of the different political regimes with his account of the erotic hierarchy of the soul, suggesting that a different passion and, therefore, a different kind of man are dominant in each. In the *Politics*, Aristotle had combined structural and moral analysis, acknowledging the validity of the traditional division between polities dominated by the one, the few, and the many; further distinguishing kingship from tyranny, aristocracy from oligarchy, and well-ordered popular government from democracy; and articulating these juxtapositions chiefly with an eye to the moral character of the ruling individual or group. Machiavelli dismisses all such moral distinctions as illusory and speaks of principalities and republics only, while intimating that the difference between the two is negligible since, directly or indirectly, princes rule both.

The reasoning that underpins this rejection of the received moral and political teaching, Machiavelli outlines in the fifteenth chapter of *The Prince*, where he parodies the discussion of moral virtue in Aristotle's *Nicomachean Ethics*, explicitly devoting his attention, as

Aristotle had, to "qualities for which human beings . . . are general-ly praised or condemned," and then producing, again in imitation of the Peripatetic, an eleven-member catalog of juxtaposed virtues and vices. He adds only, in that chapter's title, that he has in mind the praise and blame awarded "princes in particular," and in his cat-alog he so confuses the qualities listed that one is left wondering which is a virtue, which a vice, and even whether there is an intrin-sic distinction between the two. Before confronting his readers with this quandary, however, Machiavelli explicitly repudiates the man-ner in which Plato, Aristotle, and their many Christian admirers had approached the apportioning of praise and blame.

In preparing the ground for the shocking conclusion to this chap-ter—his suggestion that virtue and vice have to be distinguished solely with an eye to "security and well-being"—Machiavelli out-lines a critique of the moral imagination. His intention of writing "a thing useful for him who understands it" renders it "more prof-itable," he asserts, for him "to go behind to the effectual truth of the matter rather than to that matter as represented in the imagination." With this as his premise, he dismisses as worthless the efforts of the "many," such as Plato, Aristotle, Augustine, and Aquinas, who "have imagined republics and principalities which have been seen never and are not known in truth to exist." There is, he explains, so great "a distance between how one lives and how," one is taught, "one ought to live" that "he who leaves aside that which is done in favor of that which ought to be done studies rather his ruin than his preservation." He therefore concludes that "it is necessary for a prince, if he would maintain himself, to study to be able to be not good," as that term is conventionally understood, "and to use this knowledge or not as necessity demands." Such are "the modes and governance" that are appropriate for dealing not just with enemies but "with subjects" and "friends."

At first glance, Machiavelli's attack on morality looks like a restatement of the argument of Kallikles. It differs from it, however, in one particular: Machiavelli claims to be public spirited; his aim is to liberate mankind from the tyranny of a priestcraft that requires as its underpinning a utopian moral teaching of the sort first sketched by Plato and Aristotle; and he points the way to a positive moral and political teaching grounded on the unjust argument of Aristophanes' *Clouds*.

In the mid–seventeenth century, Thomas Hobbes rose to the challenge—seeking, in the midst of the great civil war that shook Christendom in the wake of the Reformation, to refute Machiavelli's republican defense of popular tumults by making explicit the Florentine's denial that reason is itself erotic and by tracing out the consequence of its being a mere instrument of what Plato and Aristotle had considered the baser passions. Hobbes traces the moral, political, and theological cacophony of his own day to a failure on the part of the multitudes in thrall to the classical philosophers and their Christian admirers to recognize the imbecility of moral reason and the moral imagination.

There is a lust of mind that distinguishes Hobbesian man from the beasts, but it is not the idle curiosity of the contemplative; like the longing for riches and honor, this lust "may be reduced to . . . Desire of Power." Moreover, because human consciousness is above all else the awareness of consequences, man quite naturally conceives of himself first and foremost as the cause of future effects, as a creature endowed with power. In fact, for him, "all conception of future, is conception of power able to produce something." In short, his subjectivity is itself constituted by a "perpetuall solicitude of the time to come. . . . So that man, which looks too far before him, in the care of future time, hath his heart all the day long, gnawed on by feare of death, poverty, or other calamity; and has no repose, nor pause of his anxiety, but in sleep."

The absence of a *summum bonum*, a definable and final good for man, adds a further complication: because the human being is insatiable and human felicity is a haphazard progress of desire from one more or less whimsically selected object to another, as a hunter of causes and consequences, man longs first and foremost not for any particular end, but rather for the means "to assure for ever, the way of his future desire." In short, he experiences a "perpetuall and restlesse desire of Power after power." The resulting quest for power eventually brings him face-to-face with his fellow human beings. Inevitably, given the incapacity of *logos* to provide a foundation for community, he treats these men, like everything else he encounters, simply as instruments for dominating nature. Just as inevitably, they treat him likewise. The consequence is a struggle in which "felicity" loses its close connection with bodily need and comes to be a species of progressive conquest in which each individual strives "continually to out-go the next before." Vanity is unleashed, and all the passions of man come to be reduced to feelings of *relative* power and powerlessness. Since "every man looketh that his companion should value him, at the same rate he sets upon himselfe," men squabble, come to blows, and then kill one another not only or even primarily because their material interests clash but "for trifles, as a word, a smile, a different opinion, and any other signe of undervalue."

The only escape from this perpetual self-destructive war of all against all is an abandonment of all moral principles, all speculative opinions, and all grounds of quarrel and a submission to the dictates of a sovereign and representative prince or assembly authorized to impose peace, empowered to settle all disputes, entrusted with the determination of principles, and thereby made strong enough to enforce its every command. In this fashion, Hobbes explained to men in general and to rulers in particular the "dictates of Reason" concerning morals and politics, which turn out to be nothing other than "Conclusions, or Theoremes concerning what conduceth to the conservation and defence of themselves." For Hobbes and for the many who adopted and adapted his teaching, morality is material self-interest rightly understood.

Liberalism and Its Enemies

In the aftermath of the English civil war, Hobbes's preference for absolute monarchy had a certain vogue in circles not overly given to piety. When, however, it was discovered that Charles II and his heir apparent James, the duke of York, were exponents of the species of priestcraft exposed by Machiavelli, figures such as John Locke turned back to the Florentine and embraced his defense of tumults. Like Machiavelli and Hobbes, the author of *An Essay Concerning Human Understanding* believes "that the Philosophers of old did in vain enquire, whether *summum bonum* consisted in Riches, or bodily Delights, or Virtue, or Contemplation," observing that "they might have as reasonably disputed, whether the best Relish were to be found in Apples, Plumbs, or Nuts; and have divided themselves into Sects upon it." It is all, he suggests, a matter of taste. What men have in common is not an erotic orientation toward the good defined in any concrete way but "a constant succession of *uneasinesses*" such that "very litle part of our life is so vacant from these *uneasinesses*, as to leave us free to the attraction of remoter absent good."

The predominance of uneasiness gives rise to the desire for the means to relieve that uneasiness—which for most men most of the time is not political power but labor and the property it produces, and it is on Locke's analysis of the origin of property in human labor and ingenuity that his correction of Hobbes turns. Like Hobbes, who had served Sir Francis Bacon, Locke was a proponent of scientific and technological progress; he was distinctive, however, in his insistence that such progress was contingent on the security of property rights—for men would only improve that which they could securely own. The centerpiece of the argument that he presents in his *Two Treatises of Government* is, in fact, his claim that "God gave the World . . . to the use of the Industrious and Rational, (and *Labour* was to be *his Title* to it;) not to the Fancy or Covetousness of the Quarrelsom and Contentious." It was by portraying man as what Benjamin Franklin later dubbed "a tool-making animal" that Locke sought to make sense of the emergence and development of civil society as an association for the protection of the laboring man's right to the fruits of his own labor.

Locke was perfectly prepared to acknowledge the horrors of anarchy, but he doubted very much that they so exceeded those of tyranny that human beings could be persuaded to give up the right to organized self-defense. A well-ordered government would include a monarchical executive armed with a prerogative enabling him to execute the laws, defend the realm, and respond to emergencies; it would include a representative assembly empowered to lay taxes, make laws, and examine the conduct of the executive's ministers. But it would rest ultimately on an enlightened citizenry prepared, in the face of executive and legislative abuse, to take up arms in defense of the right to life, liberty, and property.

Locke's argument laid the foundations for the kind of society that we now live in—one oriented not toward the pursuit of honor and glory or the saving of souls, but toward a provision of basic human wants through the marriage of commerce and technology. Many embraced this project, and figures of real stature, such as Bernard Mandeville, David Hume, Adam Smith, the baron de Montesquieu, and James Madison, refined Locke's arguments. But there were others on what came to be called the left and the right who came to regard commercial society as repulsive. The first and most influential of these was an expatriate from Geneva named Jean-Jacques Rousseau.

Like Hobbes and Locke, Rousseau embraces Machiavelli's critique of the classical understanding of human desire; like them as well, he grounds his account of politics and morality in a conjectural history of man's emergence from the state of human nature. He differs from his predecessors in insisting, in his *Discourse on the Origin and Foundations of Inequality Among Men*, that man's natural state was not, at first, a state of war and in suggesting that human nature underwent a transformation both within the state of nature and in leaving it. Rousseau's point is that the destructive passions attributed to man by Hobbes and Locke are acquired. In the beginning, man exhibited only pity and an instinct for self-preservation; he was distinguished from the other animals only by his perfectibility—the tool-making capacity, so celebrated by Locke, that enabled him to bring his needs and resources back into equilibrium when accidents upset it. In the beginning, because his needs and desires were circumscribed and he was able to provide for his preservation without doing harm to others, pity for the most part dictated his relations with his fellows, for he was in this sense by nature good, and he was both free from dependence on others and content with his lot. There was a stage in man's development, Rousseau suggests, when this set of qualities provided the underpinning for a primitive, prepolitical society.

In time, however, the equilibrium broke down and scarcity of food emerged. Organized agriculture was then invented as a response, and with it, as Locke had pointed out, came private property and the division of labor. This in turn, Rousseau adds, dictated a fatal dependence of the weak and dull on the talented and strong and gave rise to an inequality in wealth and status that was in no way just. Civil society was a tool subsequently devised by the rich; it originated in a contract to end the suicidal war of all against all that erupted when the poor rebelled against their subjection, but it did nothing to alleviate the injustice that had given rise to that war in the first place.

There is no hint in Rousseau's argument that man can or should return to his natural state. He suggests, instead, a reform of civil society. In his estimation, apart from outright despotism, the worst form of human association is the commercial or bourgeois society envisaged by Locke, for the cutthroat competition that it engenders and the intensification of the division of labor occasioned by the technological progress that it encourages serve only to magnify in rich and poor alike the very propensity for comparing oneself with others that had bedeviled man ever since the origins of the division of labor. This disposition, which Hobbes had called vanity and Rousseau calls *amour propre*, inspires much in the way of human accomplishment but is incompatible with the happiness of man.

For the political problem posed by inequality, Rousseau suggests, in *The Social Contract*, a political solution, exemplified by ancient Sparta and Rome. These republics effected a further transformation of human nature by educating their citizens in such a manner as to reshape *amour propre* into a virtue—constituted by patriotism, public spiritedness, and a love of equality—which gives rise to a political consensus that Rousseau dubbed "the general will." Short of the creation of such a community, the only relief for man within civil society would be a moral education designed to liberate the individual from *amour propre* and to render him happy as well as just and good—an education of just the sort sketched out by Rousseau in his *Emile*.

History

Rousseau was the last great philosopher to ground his moral and political philosophy in an appeal to nature. Even Immanuel Kant, who was otherwise one of Rousseau's fiercest admirers, refrained from following him in this particular. Kant was far more impressed by the doctrine of "the general will," and he elected to dislodge it from its political context—and thus, by means of what he called "the categorical imperative," to liberate ethics from its traditional subordination to the dictates of political prudence. Where Hobbes and Locke had, in effect, reduced the good to the useful, Kant not only reasserted the centrality of the noble and beautiful but cut it loose from the good. If one adopts as a principle "to act only in such a way that one can also will that one's maxim should become a universal law," he contended, one will have put duty before interest in a manner revelatory of the dignity and freedom possessed by rational beings endowed with a capacity to legislate for themselves.

Rousseau's conjectural history and his suggestion that human nature is plastic were, in the long run, even more influential than his doctrine of "the general will." They led Kant to reflect on the question whether, within civil society, there is a logic of development, comparable to that discerned by Rousseau in man's prepolitical state, leading in the fullness of time to the emergence of a league of liberal democracies. They inspired Georg Wilhelm Friedrich Hegel to treat all of human history as the unfolding of such a logic—so that particular moral codes and particular political systems are seen not only to be linked to particular times but to succeed one another in a natural progression; his own time and the political forms and moral outlook distinctive of it he regarded as history's completion. In similar fashion, Rousseau's thinking in these two regards enabled Karl Marx to envisage technological progress and its revolutionizing of the means of production as a motor driving the series of changes in class structure and in ideological outlook that constitute human history, and it encouraged him to imagine a time when scarcity would end, when the subjection engendered by the division of labor would dissolve, and when men would be restored to a sociability not unlike that achieved by man in Rousseau's prepolitical state—while nonetheless enjoying all of the material advantages awarded by modern technology.

The historicist propensity exemplified by Hegel and Marx elicited another response from Friedrich Nietzsche, who was skeptical about their claim to have discovered in history the unfolding of an inexorable logic. Nietzsche suggested, instead, that since it was recognized that man had repeatedly refashioned himself in the course of past history, he could and should now do so again—in full consciousness of what he was about. Nietzsche's elaboration of his doctrine of the Will to Power, as well as his attempt to make sense of man's past history and future prospects on this basis, was arguably the last great attempt by a philosopher to provide moral and political guidance on the basis of an appeal to the things that are.

Philosophy's End

The modern project began as an attempt to establish philosophical rule. Thomas Hobbes spoke for his mentor Sir Francis Bacon, for his contemporary René Descartes, and for the Enlightenment that followed upon their efforts when, after comparing himself with the author of the *Republic*, he set as the philosopher's preeminent task a conversion of the "Truth of Speculation, into the Utility of Practice." This project, which these three figures initiated and their successors in the eighteenth and nineteenth centuries strove to complete, eventuat-ed in a highly self-conscious campaign aimed at accomplishing what Plato's Socrates had considered impossible: the enlightenment of the multitude and their liberation from the cave. By the middle of the twen-tieth century, however, this project seemed to have run its course. For in the preceding decades, in the name of science and with support and applause from many of the most distinguished intellectual offspring of Bacon, Descartes, and Hobbes, tyrants such as Adolf Hitler and Joseph Stalin established totalitarian regimes, authored massive tomes, and paraded as philosopher-kings—all as if in an unconscious parody in deeds of the city limned in speech by Socrates, Glaucon, and Adeimantus. The totalitarian interlude was as great a disaster for phi-losophy as it was for politics, and it has had a sobering effect on those inclined to pursue the life of the mind.

In our various academies, students of philosophy still discuss the advantageous and the harmful, the just and the unjust, and good and evil, but they nearly all do so within the frameworks sketched out by the great figures of the past; with rare exceptions, they tend to confine their speculation within limits provided by the liberal democratic norms now predominant. It is as if, in a world at last made safe for democracy, there is no longer any prospect for an escape from the cave. The great tradi-tion of moral and political speculation seems to have come to an end. We are saddled with a science reminiscent in its reductionism of that of the pre-Socratics and similarly forgetful of its origins in ordinary human concerns, and there is no one to awaken us from our dogmatic slumber.

Martin Heidegger, the greatest philosopher of the twentieth centu-ry, eventually repudiated metaphysics, abandoned all appeal to *logos*, and, after a profoundly embarrassing flirtation with national socialism, resorted to a vatic prose reminiscent of that deployed by the ancient poets. Ludwig Wittgenstein, Heidegger's only serious rival, came in the end to the conviction that human thinking is unable to escape the con-fines of linguistic convention. Neither developed a philosophical teaching concerning politics and morality, for neither believed this pos-sible. We stand in need of an Aristophanes to inspire in some twenty-first-century Socrates a recovery of the crucial distinction between *nomos* and *phusis* and a proper appreciation of its significance. Only then can philosophy be summoned back down from the heav-ens, settled in the cities and homes of men, and forced to make inquiry into life and morals and things evil and good.

SYMPOSIUM
by
PLATO

Socrates is at a symposium (a drinking party) with several prominent Greeks, including Aristophanes the comic poet and Agathon the tragedian, in whose honor the symposium is being held, in celebration of Agathon's first victory as a tragic poet. At the symposium, the celebrants elect to do away with the flute girls, the most common form of entertainment at such gatherings. Instead, each man will present a speech in honor of a god who never receives proper adulation—Eros. Agathon has just spoken, and though his speech was well received, he now finds himself engaged in a discussion with Socrates about some of the points he has made.

Then now, said Socrates, let us recapitulate the argument. First, is not love of something, and of something too which is wanting to a man?

Yes, he replied.

Remember further what you said in your speech, or if you do not remember I will remind you: you said that the love of the beautiful set in order the empire of the gods, for that of deformed things there is no love—did you not say something like that?

Yes, said Agathon.

Yes, my friend, and the remark was a just one. And if this is true, love is the love of beauty and not of deformity?

He assented.

And the admission has been already made that love is of that which a man wants and has not?

True, he said.

Then love wants and has not beauty?

Certainly, he replied.

And would you call that beautiful which wants and does not possess beauty?

Certainly not.

Then would you still say that love is beautiful?

Agathon replied: I fear that I did not understand what I was saying.

Yet you made a fair speech, Agathon, replied Socrates; but once more say:—Is not the good also the beautiful?

Yes.

Then in wanting the beautiful, love wants also the good?

I cannot refute you, Socrates, said Agathon. And let us suppose that what you say is true.

Say rather, dear Agathon, that you cannot refute the truth; for Socrates is easily refuted.

And now I will take my leave of you, and rehearse the tale of love which I heard from Diotima of Mantineia, a woman wise in this and many other kinds of knowledge, who in the days of old, when the Athenians offered sacrifice before the coming of the plague, delayed the disease ten years. She was my instructress in the art of love, and I shall repeat to you what she said to me, beginning with the admissions made by Agathon, which are nearly if not quite the same which I made to the wise woman when she questioned me: I think that this will be the easiest way, and I shall take both parts myself as well as I can. Like Agathon, she spoke first of the being and nature of love, and then of his works. And I said to her in nearly the same words which he used to me, that love was a mighty god, and likewise fair; and she proved to me as I proved to him that, by my own showing, love was neither fair nor good. "What do you mean, Diotima," I said, "is love then evil and foul?" "Hush," she cried; "is that to be deemed foul which is not fair?" "Certainly," I said. "And is that which is not wise, ignorant? Do you not see that there is a mean between wisdom and ignorance?" "And what may that be?" I said. "Right opinion," she replied; "which, as you know, being incapable of giving a reason, is not knowledge (for how can knowledge be devoid of reason? nor again, ignorance, for neither can ignorance attain the truth), but is clearly something which is a mean between ignorance and wisdom." "Quite true," I replied. "Do not then insist," she said, "that what is not fair is of necessity foul, or what is not good evil; or infer that because love is not fair and good he is therefore foul and evil; for he is in a mean between them." "Well,"

I said, "love is surely admitted by all to be a great god." "By those who know or by those who do not know?" "By all." "And how, Socrates," she said with a smile, "can love be acknowledged to be a great god by those who say that he is not a god at all?" "And who are they?" I said. "You and I are two of them," she replied. "How can that be?" I said. "That is very intelligible," she replied; "for you yourself would acknowledge that the gods are happy and fair—of course you would—would you dare to say that any god was not?" "Certainly not," I replied. "And you mean by the happy, those who are the possessors of things good and fair?" "Yes." "And you admitted that Love, because he was in want, desires those good and fair things of which he is in want?" "Yes, I admitted that." "But how can he be a god who has no share in the good or the fair?" "That is not to be supposed." "Then you see that you also deny the divinity of Love."

"What then is love?" I asked; "Is he mortal?" "No." "What then?" "As in the former instance, he is neither mortal nor immortal, but in a mean between the two." "What is he then, Diotima?" "He is a great spirit and like all spirits he is intermediate between the divine and the mortal." "And what," I said, "is his power?" "He interprets," she replied, "between gods and men, conveying to the gods the prayers and sacrifices of men, and to men the commands and replies of the gods; he is the mediator who spans the chasm which divides them, and in him all is bound together, and through him the arts of the prophet and the priest, their sacrifices and mysteries and charms, and all prophecy and incantation, find their way. For God mingles not with man; but through Love all the intercourse and speech of God with man, whether awake or asleep, is carried on. The wisdom which understands this is spiritual; all other wisdom, such as that of arts and handicrafts, is mean and vulgar. Now these spirits or intermediate powers are many and diverse, and one of them is Love." "And who," I said, "was his father, and who his mother?" "The tale," she said, "will take time; nevertheless I will tell you. On the birthday of Aphrodite there was a feast of the gods, at which the god Poros or Plenty, who is the son of Metis or Discretion, was one of the guests. When the feast was over, Penia or Poverty, as the manner is on such occasions, came about the doors to beg. Now Plenty, who was the worse for nectar (there was no wine in those days), went into the garden of Zeus and fell into a heavy sleep; and Poverty considering her own straitened circumstances, plotted to have a child by him, and accordingly she lay down at his side and conceived Love, who partly because he is naturally a lover of the beautiful, and because Aphrodite is herself beautiful, and also because he was born on her birthday, is her follower and attendant. And as his parentage is, so also are his fortunes. In the first place he is always poor, and anything but tender and fair, as the many imagine him; and he is hard-featured and squalid, and has no shoes, nor a house to dwell in; on the bare earth exposed he lies under the open heaven, in the streets, or at the doors of houses, taking his rest; and like his mother he is always in distress. Like his father too, whom he also partly resembles, he is always plotting against the fair and good; he is bold, enterprising, strong, a hunter of men, always weaving some intrigue or other, keen in the pursuit of wisdom, and never wanting resources; a philosopher at all times, terrible as an enchanter, sorcerer, sophist; for as he is neither mortal nor immortal, he is alive and flourishing at one moment when he is in plenty, and dead at another moment, and again alive by reason of his father's nature. But that which is always flowing in is always flowing out, and so he is never in want and never in wealth; and, further, he is in a mean between ignorance and knowledge. The truth of the matter is as follows: No god is a philosopher or seeker after wisdom, for he is wise already; nor does any man who is wise seek after wisdom. Neither do the ignorant seek after wisdom. For herein is the evil of ignorance, that he who is neither good nor wise is nevertheless satisfied: he has no desire for that of which he feels no want." "But who then, Diotima," I said, "are the lovers of wisdom, if they are neither the wise nor the foolish?" "A child may answer that question," she replied; "they are those who, like love, are in a mean between the two. For wisdom is a most beautiful thing, and love is of the beautiful; and therefore love is also a philosopher or lover of wisdom, and being a lover of wisdom is in a mean between the wise and the ignorant. And this again is a quality which Love inherits from his parents; for his father is wealthy and wise, and his mother poor and foolish. Such, my dear Socrates, is the nature of the spirit Love. The error in your conception of him was very natural, and as I imagine from what you say, has arisen out of a confusion of love and the beloved, which made you think that love was all beautiful. For the beloved is truly beautiful, and delicate, and perfect, and blessed; but the principle of love is of another nature, and is such as I have described."

I said: "O thou stranger woman, thou sayest well, and now, assuming love to be such as you say, what is the use of him to us men?" "That, Socrates," she replied, "I will proceed to unfold: of his nature and birth I have already spoken; and you acknowledge that love is of the beautiful. But some one will say: Of the beautiful in what, Socrates and Diotima?—or rather let me put the question more clearly, and ask: When a man loves the beautiful, what does he desire?" I answered her, "That the beautiful may be his." "Still," she said, "the answer suggests a further question: What is given by the possession of beauty?" "To what you have asked," I replied, "I have no answer ready." "Then," she said, "let me put the word 'good' in the place of the beautiful, and repeat the question once more: He who loves the good loves; what does he love?" "The possession of the good," I said. "And what does he gain who possesses the good?" "Happiness," I replied; "there is no difficulty in answering that." "Yes," she said, "the happy are made happy by the acquisition of good things. Nor is there any need to ask why a man desires happiness; the answer is already final." "You are right," I said. "And is this wish and this desire common to all? And do all men always desire their own good, or only some men?—What say you?" "All men," I replied; "the desire is common to all." "Why, then," she rejoined, "are not all men, Socrates, said to love, but only some of them? Whereas you say that all men are always loving the same things." "I myself wonder," I said, "why that is." "There is nothing to wonder at," she replied; "the reason is that one part of love is separated off and receives the name of the whole, but the other parts have other names." "Give an illustration," I said. She answered me as follows: "There is poetry, which, as you know, is complex and manifold. All creation or passage of non-being into being is poetry or making, and the processes of all art are creative; and the masters of arts are all poets or makers." "Very true." "Still," she said, "you know that they are not called poets, but have other names; the specific term, poetry, is confined to that portion of the art which is separated off from the rest of poetry, and is concerned with music and metre; and this is what is called poetry, and they who possess this kind of poetry are called poets." "Very true," I said. "And the same holds of love. For you may say generally that all desire of good and happiness is only the great and subtle power of love; but those who turn towards him by any other path, whether the path of money-making or gymnastics or philosophy, are not called lovers—the name of the genus is reserved for those whose affection takes one form only—they alone are said to love, or to be lovers." "I dare say," I replied, "that you are right." "Yes," she added, "and you hear people say that lovers are seeking for their other half; but I say that they are seeking neither for the half of themselves, nor for the whole, unless the half or the whole be also a good. And they will cut off their own hands and feet and cast them away, if they are evil; for they love not what is their own, but what is another's, unless indeed by the words 'good' and 'their own' and 'bad' and 'another's' they mean the same thing. For there is nothing which men love but the good. Do you think that there is?" "Certainly, I should say, that there is nothing." "Then," she said, "the conclusion of the whole matter is, that men love the good." "Yes," I said. "To which may be added that they love the possession of the good?" "Yes, that may be added." "And not only the possession, but the everlasting possession of the good?" "That may be added too." "Then love," she said, "may be described generally as the love of the everlasting possession of the good?" "That is most true."

"Then if this be the nature of love, can you tell me further," she said, "what is the manner of the pursuit? What are they doing who show all this eagerness and heat which is called love? Answer me." "Nay, Diotima," I replied, "if I had known, I should not have wondered at your wisdom, neither should I have come to you to learn about this very matter." "Well," she said, "I will teach you;—love is only birth in beauty, whether of body or soul." "The oracle requires an explanation," I said; "I do not understand you." " I will make my meaning clearer," she replied. "I mean to say, that all men are bringing to the birth in their bodies and in their souls. There is a certain age at which human nature is desirous of procreation—procreation which must be in beauty and not in deformity; and this procreation is the union of man and woman, and is a divine thing; for conception and generation are an immortal principle in the mortal creature, and in the inharmonious they can never be. But the deformed is always inharmonious with the divine, and the beautiful harmonious. Beauty, then, is the destiny or goddess of parturition who presides at birth, and therefore when approaching beauty the conceiving power is propitious, and diffuse, and benign, and begets and bears fruit: at the sight of ugliness it frowns and contracts in pain, and is averted and morose, and shrinks up, and not without a pang refrains from conception. And this is the reason why, when the hour of conception arrives, and the teeming nature is full, there is such a flutter and ecstasy about beauty whose approach is the alleviation of the pain of travail. For love, Socrates, is not, as you imagine, the love of the beautiful only." "What then?" "The love of generation and birth in beauty." "Yes," I said. "Yes, indeed," she replied. "But why of generation?" I said. "Because to the mortal, generation is a sort of eternity and immortality," she replied; "and if, as has been already admitted, love is of the everlasting possession of the good, all men will necessarily desire immortality together with the good. Wherefore love is of immortality."

All this she taught me at various times when she spoke of love. And I remember that she once said to me, "What is the cause, Socrates, of love, and the attendant desire? See you not how all animals, birds as well as beasts, in their desire of procreation, are in agony when they take the infection of love, which begins with the desire of union; whereto is added the care of offspring, on behalf of whom the weakest are ready to battle against the strongest even to the uttermost, and to die for them, and will let themselves be tormented with hunger or suffer anything in order to maintain their offspring. Man may be supposed to act thus from reason; but why should animals have these passionate feelings? Can you tell me why?" Again I replied, that I did not know. She said to me: "And do you expect ever to become a master in the art of love, if you do not know this?" "But that, Diotima, is the reason why I come to you; as I have told you already, I am aware that I want a teacher, and I wish that you would explain to me the cause of this and of the other mysteries of love." "Marvel not," she said, "if you believe that love is of the immortal, as we have already several times acknowledged; for here again, and on the same principle too, the mortal nature is seeking as far as is possible to be everlasting and immortal: and this is only to be attained by generation, because generation always leaves behind a new existence in the place of the old. Nay even in the life of the same individual there is succession and not absolute unity: a man is called the same, and yet in the short interval which elapses between youth and age, and in which every animal is said to have life and identity, he is undergoing a perpetual process of loss and reparation—hair, flesh, bones, blood, and the whole body are always changing. Which is true not only of the body, but also of the soul, whose habits, tempers, opinions, desires, pleasures, pains, fears, never remain the same in any one of us, but are always coming and going; and equally true of knowledge, which is still more surprising—for not only do the sciences in general come and go, so that in respect of them we are never the same; but each of them individually experiences a like change. For what is implied in the word 'recollection,' but the departure of knowledge, which is ever being forgotten and is renewed and preserved by recollection, and appears to be the same although in reality new, according to that law of succession by which all mortal things are preserved, not absolutely the same, but by sub-stitution, the old worn-out mortality leaving another new and similar existence behind—unlike the divine, which is always the same and not another? And in this way, Socrates, the mortal body, or mortal anything, partakes of immortality; but the immortal in another way. Marvel not then at the love which all men have of their offspring; for that universal love and interest is for the sake of immortality."

I was astonished at her words, and said: "Is this really true, O thou wise Diotima?" And she answered with all the authority of a sophist: "Of that, Socrates, you may be assured;—think only of the ambition of men, and you will wonder at the senselessness of their ways, unless you consider how they are stirred by the love of an immortality of fame. They are ready to run risks greater far than they would have run for their children, and to spend money and undergo any sort of toil, and even to die for the sake of leaving behind them a name which shall be eternal. Do you imagine that Alcestis would have died to save Admetus, or Achilles to avenge Patroclus, or your own Codrus in order to preserve the kingdom for his sons, if they had not imagined that the memory of their virtues, which is still retained among us, would be immortal? Nay," she said, "I am persuaded that all men do all things, and the better they are the more they do them, in hope of the glorious fame of immortal virtue; for they desire to be immortal.

"They whose bodies only are creative, betake themselves to women and beget children—this is the character of their love; their offspring, as they hope, will preserve their memory and give them the blessedness and immortality which they desire in the future. But creative souls—for there certainly are men who are more creative in their souls than in their bodies—conceive that which is proper for the soul to conceive or retain. And what are these conceptions?—wisdom and virtue in general. And such creators are poets and all artists who are deserving of the name inventor. But the greatest and fairest sort of wisdom by far is that which is concerned with the ordering of states and families, and which is called temperance and justice. And he who in youth has the seed of these implanted in him and is himself inspired, when he comes to maturity desires to beget and generate. He wanders about seeking beauty that he may beget offspring—for in deformity he will beget nothing—and naturally embraces the beautiful rather than the deformed body; above all when he finds a fair and noble and well-nurtured soul, he embraces the two in one person, and to such a one he is full of speech about virtue and the nature and pursuits of a good man; and he tries to educate him; and at the touch of the beautiful which is ever present to his memory, even when absent, he brings forth that which he had conceived long before, and in company with him tends that which he brings forth; and they are married by a far nearer tie and have a closer friendship than those who beget mortal children, for the children who are their common offspring are fairer and more immortal. Who, when he thinks of Homer and Hesiod and other great poets, would not rather have their children than ordinary human ones? Who would not emulate them in the creation of children such as theirs, which have preserved their memory and given them everlasting glory? Or who would not have such children as Lycurgus left behind him to be the saviours, not only of Lacedaemon, but of Hellas, as one may say? There is Solon, too, who is the revered father of Athenian laws; and many others there are in many other places, both among Hellenes and barbarians. All of them have given to the world many noble works, and have been the parents of virtue of every kind, and many temples have been raised in their honour for the sake of their children; which were never raised in honour of any one, for the sake of his mortal children.

"These are the lesser mysteries of love, into which even you, Socrates, may enter; to the greater and more hidden ones which are the crown of these, and to which, if you pursue them in a right spirit, they will lead, I know not whether you will be able to attain. But I will do my utmost to inform you, and you do follow if you can. For he who would proceed aright in this matter should begin in his youth to visit beautiful forms; and first, if he be guided by his instructor aright, to love one such form only—out of that he should create fair thoughts; and soon he will of himself perceive that the beauty of one form is akin to the beauty of another; and then if beauty of form in general is his pursuit, how foolish would he be not to recognize that the beauty in every form is one and the same! And when he perceives this he will abate his violent love of the one, which he will despise and deem a small thing, and will become a lover of all beautiful forms; in the next stage he will consider that the beauty of the mind is more honourable than the beauty of the outward form. So that if a virtuous soul have but a little comeliness, he will be content to love and tend him, and will search out and bring to the birth thoughts which may improve the young, until he is compelled to contemplate and see the beauty of institutions and laws, and to understand that the beauty of them all is of one family, and that personal beauty is a trifle; and after laws and institutions he will go on to the sciences, that he may see their beauty, being not like a servant in love with the beauty of one's own youth or man or institution, himself a slave mean and narrow-minded, but drawing towards and contemplating the vast sea of beauty, he will create many fair and noble thoughts and notions in boundless love of wisdom; until on that shore he grows and waxes strong, and at last the vision is revealed to him of a single science, which is the science of beauty everywhere. To this I will proceed; please to give me your very best attention.

"He who has been instructed thus far in the things of love, and who has learned to see the beautiful in due order and succession, when he comes toward the end will suddenly perceive a nature of wondrous beauty (and this, Socrates, is the final cause of all our former toils)—a nature which in the first place is everlasting, not growing and decaying, or waxing and waning; in the next place not fair in one point of view and foul in another, or at one time or in one relation or at one place fair, at another time or in another relation or at another place foul, as if fair to some and foul to others, or in the likeness of a face or hands or any other part of the bodily frame, or in any form of speech or knowledge, or existing in any other being; as for example, in an animal or in heaven or in earth or in any other place, but beauty only; absolute, separate, simple, and everlasting, which without diminution and without increase, or any change, is imparted to the ever-growing and perishing beauties of all other things. He who under the influence of true love rising upward from these begins to see that beauty, is not far from the end. And the true order of going or being led by another to the things of love, is to use the beauties of earth as steps along which he mounts upwards for the sake of that other beauty, going from one to two, and from two to all fair forms, and from fair forms to fair practices, and from fair practices to fair notions, until from fair notions he arrives at the notion of absolute beauty, and at last knows what the essence of beauty is. This, my dear Socrates," said the stranger of Mantineia, "is that life above all others which man should live, in the contemplation of beauty absolute; a beauty which if you once beheld, you would see not to be after the measure of gold, and garments, and fair boys and youths, whose presence now entrances you; and you and many a one would be content to live seeing only and conversing with them without meat or drink, if that were possible— you only want to be with them and to look at them. But what if man had eyes to see the true beauty—the divine beauty, I mean, pure and clear and unalloyed, not clogged with the pollutions of mortality, and all the colours and vanities of human life—thither looking, and holding converse with the true beauty divine and simple? Do you not see that in that communion only, beholding beauty with the eye of the mind, he will be enabled to bring forth, not images of beauty, but realities (for he has hold not of an image but of a reality), and bringing forth and nourishing true virtue to become the friend of God and be immortal, if mortal man may. Would that be an ignoble life?"

Such, Phaedrus—and I speak not only to you, but to all of you— were the words of Diotima; and I am persuaded of their truth. And being persuaded of them, I try to persuade others, that in the attainment of this end human nature will not easily find a better helper than love. And therefore, also, I say that every man ought to honour him as I myself honour him, and walk in his ways, and exhort others to do the same, and praise the power and spirit of love according to the measure of my ability now and ever.

The words which I have spoken, you, Phaedrus, may call an encomium of love, or anything else which you please.

GORGIAS
by
PLATO

Socrates is speaking to the famous sophist Gorgias, attempting to discover what it is that Gorgias teaches. During the discussion, Gorgias and his student Polus have both been forced to relent that it is better to suffer harm than to do harm to others. At this, Callicles enters the conversation and chastises Socrates for making such foolish claims seem probable through verbal trickery and intimidation.

allicles: For by the rule of nature, to suffer injustice is the greater disgrace because the greater evil; but conventionally, to do evil is the more disgraceful. For the suffering of injustice is not the part of a man, but of a slave, who indeed had better die than live; since when he is wronged and trampled upon, he is unable to help himself, or any other about whom he cares. The reason, as I conceive, is that the makers of laws are the majority who are weak; and they make laws and distribute praises and censures with a view to themselves and to their own interests; and they terrify the stronger sort of men, and those who are able to get the better of them, in order that they may not get the better of them; and they say, that dishonesty is shameful and unjust; meaning, by the word injustice, the desire of a man to have more than his neighbours; for knowing their own inferiority, I suspect that they are too glad of equality. And therefore the endeavour to have more than the many, is conventionally said to be shameful and unjust, and is called injustice, whereas nature herself intimates that it is just for the better to have more than the worse, the more powerful than the weaker; and in many ways she shows, among men as well as among animals, and indeed among whole cities and races, that justice consists in the superior ruling over and having more than the inferior. For on what principles of justice did Xerxes invade Hellas, or his father the Scythians? (not to speak of numberless other examples). These are the men who act according to nature; yes, by Heaven, and according to the law of nature: not, perhaps, according to that artificial law, which we forge and impose upon our fellows, of whom we take the best and strongest from their youth upwards, and tame them like young lions,—charming them with the sound of the voice, and saying to them, that with equality they must be content, and that the equal is the honourable and the just. But if there were a man who had sufficient force, he would shake off and break through, and escape from all this; he would trample under foot all our formulas and spells and charms, and all our laws, sinning against nature: the slave would rise in rebellion and be lord over us, and the light of natural justice would shine forth. And this I take to be the sentiment of Pindar, in the poem in which he says, that

> Law is the king of all, mortals as well as immortals;

this, as he says,

> Makes might to be right, and does violence with
> high hand; as I infer from the deeds of Heracles, for
> without buying them—

—I do not remember the exact words, but the meaning is, that without buying them, and without their being given to him, he carried off the oxen of Geryon, according to the law of natural right, and that the oxen and other possessions of the weaker and inferior properly belong to the stronger and superior. And this is true, as you may ascertain, if you will leave philosophy and go on to higher things: for philosophy, Socrates, if pursued in moderation and at the proper age, is an elegant accomplishment, but too much philosophy is the ruin of human life. Even if a man has good parts, still, if he carries philosophy into later life, he is necessarily ignorant of all those things which a gentleman and a person of honour ought to know; he is inexperienced in the laws of the State, and in the language which ought to be used in the dealings of man with man, whether private or public, and utterly ignorant of the pleasures and desires of mankind and of human character in general. And people of this sort, when they betake themselves to politics or business, are as ridiculous as I imagine the politicians to be, when they make their appearance in the arena of philosophy. For, as Euripides says,

> Every man shines in that and pursues that, and
> devotes the greatest portion of the day to that in
> which he thinks himself to excel most,

and anything in which he is inferior, he avoids and depreciates, and praises the opposite from partiality to himself, and because he thinks that he will thus praise himself. The true principle is to unite them. Philosophy, as a part of education, is an excellent thing, and there is no disgrace to a man while he is young in pursuing such a study; but when he is more advanced in years, the thing becomes ridiculous, and I feel towards philosophers as I do towards those who lisp and imitate children. For I love to see a little child, who is not of an age to speak plainly, lisping at his play; there is an appearance of grace and freedom in his utterance, which is natural to his childish years. And when I hear some small creature carefully articulating his words, I am offended; the sound is disagreeable, and has to my ears the twang of slavery. But when I see a man lisping as if he were a child, that appears to me ridiculous and unmanly and worthy of stripes. And I have the same feeling about students of philosophy; when I see a youth so engaged,—that I consider to be quite in character, and becoming a man of a liberal education, and him who neglects philosophy I regard as an inferior man, who will never aspire to anything great or noble. But if I see him continuing the study in later life, and not leaving off, I think that he ought to be beaten, Socrates; for as I was saying, such an one, even though he have good natural parts, becomes effeminate. He flies from the busy centre and the market-place, in which, as the poet says, men become distinguished; he creeps into a corner for the rest of his life, and talks in a whisper with three or four admiring youths, but never speaks out like a freeman in a satisfactory manner. Now I, Socrates, am very well inclined towards you, and my feeling may be compared with that of Zethus towards Amphion, in the play of Euripides, of which I was just now speaking: for I am disposed to say to you much what Zethus said to his brother, that you, Socrates, are careless when you ought to be careful;

> Having a soul so noble, are remarkable for a puerile exterior;
> Neither in a court of justice could you state a case, or
>   give any reason or proof,
> Or offer valiant counsel on another's behalf.

And you must not be offended, my dear Socrates, for I am speaking out of good-will towards you, if I ask whether you are not ashamed of being thus defenseless; which I affirm to be the condition not of you only but of all those who will carry the study of philosophy too far. For suppose that some one were to take you, or any one of your sort, off to prison, declaring that you had done wrong when you had done no wrong, you must allow that you would not know what to do:—there you would stand giddy and gaping, and not having a word to say; and when you went up before the Court, even if the accuser were a poor creature and not good for much, you would die if he were disposed to claim the penalty of death. And yet, Socrates, what is the value of

> An art which converts a man of sense into a fool,

who is helpless, and has no power to save either himself or others, when he is in the greatest danger and is going to be despoiled by his enemies of all his goods, and deprived of his right to citizenship?—he being a man who, if I may use the expression, may be boxed on the ears with impunity. Then, my good friend, take my advice, and refute no more:

> Learn the arts of business, and acquire the reputation
>   of wisdom.
> But leave to others these niceties,

whether they are to be described as follies or absurdities:

> For they will only
> Give you poverty for the inmate of your dwelling.

Cease, then, emulating these paltry splitters of words, and emulate only the man of substance and honour, who is well to do. . . .

. . . Quite so, Socrates; and they are really fools, for how can a man be happy who is the servant of anything? On the contrary, I plainly assert, that he who would truly live ought to allow his desires to wax to the uttermost, and not to chastise them; but when they have grown to their greatest he should have courage and intelligence to minister to them and to satisfy all his longings. And this I affirm to be natural justice and nobility. To this the many cannot attain; and they blame the strong man because they are ashamed of their own weakness, which they desire to conceal, and hence they say that intemperance is base. As I was saying before, they enslave the nobler natures, and being unable to satisfy their pleasures, they praise temperance and justice out of cowardice. For if a man had been originally the son of a king, or had a nature capable of acquiring an empire or a tyranny of exclusive power, what could be more truly base or evil than temperance—to a man like him, I say, who might freely be enjoying every good, and has no one to hinder him, and yet has admitted custom and reason and the opinion of other men to be lords over him?—must not he be in a miserable plight whom the reputation of justice and temperance hinders from giving more to his friends than to his enemies, even though he be a ruler in his city? Nay, Socrates, for you profess to be a votary of the truth, and the truth is this:—that luxury and intemperance and licence, if they are duly supported, are happiness and virtue—all the rest is a mere bauble, custom contrary to nature, fond inventions of men nothing worth. . . .

Socrates: Well, I will tell you another image, which comes out of the same school:—Let me request you to consider how far you would accept this as an account of the two lives of the temperate and the intemperate:—There are two men, both of whom have a number of casks; the one man has his casks sound and full, one of wine, another of honey, and a third of milk, besides others filled with other liquids, and the streams which fill them are few and scanty, and he can only obtain them with a great deal of toil and difficulty; but when his casks are once filled he has no need to feed them any more, and has no further trouble with them or care about them. The other, in like manner, can procure streams, though not without difficulty; but his vessels are leaky and unsound, and night and day he is compelled to be filling them, and if he pauses for a moment, he is in an agony of pain. Such are their respective lives:—And now would you say that the life of the intemperate is happier than that of the temperate? Do I not convince you that the opposite is the truth?

Callicles: You do not convince me, Socrates, for the one who has filled himself has no longer any pleasure left; and this, as I was just now saying, is the life of a stone: he has neither joy nor sorrow after he is once filled; but the life of pleasure is the pouring in of the stream.

Socrates: And if the stream is always pouring in, must there not be a stream always running out, and holes large enough to admit of the discharge?

Callicles: Certainly.

Socrates: The life, then, of which you are now speaking, is not that of a dead man, or of a stone, but of a cormorant; you meant that he is to be hungering and eating?

Callicles: Yes.

Socrates: And he is to be thirsting and drinking?

Callicles: Yes, that is what I mean; he is to have all his desires about him, and to be able to live happily in the gratification of them.

Socrates: Capital, excellent; go on as you have begun, and have no shame; I, too, must disencumber myself of shame: and first, will you tell me whether you include itching and scratching, provided you have enough of scratching and continue scratching through life, in your notion of happiness?

Callicles: What a strange being you are, Socrates! a regular clap-trap speaker.

Socrates: That was the reason, Callicles, why I scared the modesty out of Polus and Gorgias; but your modesty will not be scared, for you are a brave man. And now, answer my question.

Callicles: I answer, that the scratcher would live pleasantly.

REPUBLIC
by
PLATO

Socrates, having been to the Piraeus (the port of Athens) to see a festival, has been detained by several friends. A conversation has ensued about the nature of justice, in which Thrasymachus has told Socrates that justice is the advantage of the stronger, and that just acts are never performed voluntarily. Socrates has refuted Thrasymachus, but not to his own satisfaction. Now, he finds himself in discussion with Glaucon and Adeimantus, who press him further on the issue.

Glaucon attempts to elucidate the issue.

I wish, he [Glaucon] said, that you would hear me as well as him, and then I shall see whether you and I agree. For Thrasymachus seems to me, like a snake, to have been charmed by your voice sooner than he ought to have been; but to my mind the nature of justice and injustice have not yet been made clear. Setting aside their rewards and results, I want to know what they are in themselves, and how they inwardly work in the soul. If you please, then, I will revive the argument of Thrasymachus. And first I will speak of the nature and origin of justice according to the common view of them. Secondly, I will show that all men who practise justice do so against their will, of necessity, but not as a good. And thirdly, I will argue that there is reason in this view, for the life of the unjust is after all better far than the life of the just—if what they say is true, Socrates, since I myself am not of their opinion. But still I acknowledge that I am perplexed when I hear the voices of Thrasymachus and myriads of others dinning in my ears; and, on the other hand, I have never yet heard the superiority of justice to injustice maintained by any one in a satisfactory way. I want to hear justice praised in respect of itself; then I shall be satisfied, and you are the person from whom I think that I am most likely to hear this; and therefore I will praise the unjust life to the utmost of my power, and my manner of speaking will indicate the manner in which I desire to hear you too praising justice and censuring injustice. Will you say whether you approve of my proposal?

Indeed I do; nor can I imagine any theme about which a man of sense would oftener wish to converse.

I am delighted, he replied, to hear you say so, and shall begin by speaking, as I proposed, of the nature and origin of justice.

They say that to do injustice is, by nature, good; to suffer injustice, evil; but that the evil is greater than the good. And so when men have both done and suffered injustice and have had experience of both, not being able to avoid the one and obtain the other, they think that they had better agree among themselves to have neither; hence there arise laws and mutual covenants; and that which is ordained by law is termed by them lawful and just. This they affirm to be the origin and nature of justice;—it is a mean or compromise, between the best of all, which is to do injustice and not be punished, and the worst of all, which is to suffer injustice without the power of retaliation; and justice, being at a middle point between the two, is tolerated not as a good, but as the lesser evil, and honoured by reason of the inability of men to do injustice. For no man who is worthy to be a man would ever submit to such an agreement if he were able to resist; he would be mad if he did. Such is the received account, Socrates, of the nature and origin of justice.

Now that those who practice justice do so involuntarily and because they have not the power to be unjust will best appear if we imagine something of this kind: having given both to the just and the unjust power to do what they will, let us watch and see whither desire will lead them; then we shall discover in the very act the just and unjust man to be proceeding along the same road, following their interest, which all natures deem to be their good, and are only diverted into the path of justice by the force of law. The liberty which we are supposing may be most completely given to them in the form of such a power as is said to have been possessed by Gyges the ancestor of Croesus the Lydian. According to the tradition, Gyges was a shepherd in the service of the king of Lydia; there was a great storm, and an earthquake made an opening in the earth at the place where he was feeding his flock. Amazed at the sight, he descended into the opening, where, among other marvels, he beheld

a hollow brazen horse, having doors, at which he stooping and looking in saw a dead body of stature, as appeared to him, more than
human, and having nothing on but a gold ring; this he took from
the finger of the dead man and reascended. Now the shepherds met
together, according to custom, that they might send their monthly
report about the flocks to the king; into their assembly he came having the ring on his finger, and as he was sitting among them he
chanced to turn the collet of the ring inside his hand, when instantly he became invisible to the rest of the company and they began to
speak of him as if he were no longer present. He was astonished at
this, and again touching the ring he turned the collet outwards and
reappeared; he made several trials of the ring, and always with the
same result—when he turned the collet inwards he became invisible,
when outwards he reappeared. Whereupon he contrived to be chosen one of the messengers who were sent to the court; where as soon
as he arrived he seduced the queen, and with her help conspired
against the king and slew him, and took the kingdom. Suppose now
that there were two such magic rings, and the just put on one of
them and the unjust the other; no man can be imagined to be of
such an iron nature that he would stand fast in justice. No man
would keep his hands off what was not his own when he could safely take what he liked out of the market, or go into houses and lie
with anyone at his pleasure, or kill or release from prison whom he
would, and in all respects be like a God among men. Then the
actions of the just would be as the actions of the unjust; they would
both come at last to the same point. And this we may truly affirm
to be a great proof that a man is just, not willingly or because he
thinks that justice is any good to him individually, but of necessity,
for wherever any one thinks that he can safely be unjust, there he is
unjust. For all men believe in their hearts that injustice is far more
profitable to the individual than justice, and he who argues as I have
been supposing, will say that they are right. If you could imagine
any one obtaining this power of becoming invisible, and never
doing any wrong or touching what was another's, he would be
thought by the lookers-on to be a most wretched idiot, although
they would praise him to one another's faces, and keep up appearances with one another from a fear that they too might suffer
injustice. Enough of this.

Now, if we are to form a real judgment of the life of the just and unjust, we must isolate them; there is no other way; and how is the isolation to be effected? I answer: Let the unjust man be entirely unjust, and the just man entirely just; nothing is to be taken away from either of them, and both are to be perfectly furnished for the work of their respective lives. First, let the unjust be like other distinguished masters of craft; like the skilful pilot or physician, who knows intuitively his own powers and keeps within their limits, and who, if he fails at any point, is able to recover himself. So let the unjust make his unjust attempts in the right way, and lie hidden if he means to be great in his injustice (he who is found out is nobody): for the highest reach of injustice is: to be deemed just when you are not. Therefore I say that in the perfectly unjust man we must assume the most perfect injustice; there is to be no deduction, but we must allow him, while doing the most unjust acts, to have acquired the greatest reputation for justice. If he have taken a false step he must be able to recover himself; he must be one who can speak with effect, if any of his deeds come to light, and who can force his way where force is required by his courage and strength, and command of money and friends. And at his side let us place the just man in his nobleness and simplicity, wishing, as Aeschylus says, to be and not to seem good. There must be no seeming, for if he seem to be just he will be honoured and rewarded, and then we shall not know whether he is just for the sake of justice or for the sake of honours and rewards; therefore, let him be clothed in justice only, and have no other covering; and he must be imagined in a state of life the opposite of the former. Let him be the best of men, and let him be thought the worst; then he will have been put to the proof; and we shall see whether he will be affected by the fear of infamy and its consequences. And let him continue thus to the hour of death; being just and seeming to be unjust. When both have reached the uttermost extreme, the one of justice and the other of injustice, let judgment be given which of them is the happier of the two.

Heavens! my dear Glaucon, I [Socrates] said, how energetically you polish them up for the decision, first one and then the other, as if they were two statues.

I do my best, he [Glaucon] said. And now that we know what they are like there is no difficulty in tracing out the sort of life which awaits either of them. This I will proceed to describe; but as you may think the description a little too coarse, I ask you to suppose,

Socrates, that the words which follow are not mine.—Let me put them into the mouths of the eulogists of injustice: They will tell you that the just man who is thought unjust will be scourged, racked, bound—will have his eyes burnt out; and, at last, after suffering every kind of evil, he will be impaled: Then he will understand that he ought to seem only, and not to be, just; the words of Aeschylus may be more truly spoken of the unjust than the just. For the unjust is pursuing a reality; he does not live with a view to appearances— he wants to be really unjust and not to seem only:—

> His mind has a soil deep and fertile,
> Out of which spring his prudent counsels.

In the first place, he is thought just, and therefore bears rule in the city; he can marry whom he will, and give in marriage to whom he will; also he can trade and deal where he likes, and always to his own advantage, because he has no misgivings about injustice; and at every contest, whether in public or private, he gets the better of his antagonists, and gains at their expense, and is rich, and out of his gains he can benefit his friends, and harm his enemies; moreover, he can offer sacrifices, and dedicate gifts to the gods abundantly and magnificently, and can honour the gods or any man whom he wants to honour in a far better style than the just, and therefore he is likely to be dearer than they are to the gods. And thus, Socrates, gods and men are said to unite in making the life of the unjust better than the life of the just.

Socrates and his companions have been led by the discussion to erect a city in speech, hoping that if they can describe a perfectly just city they will have a better understanding of justice in the human soul. While discussing the education fit for the Guardians of their city, Socrates begins to speak. All replies are made by Glaucon.

And now, I said, let me show in a figure how far our nature is enlightened or unenlightened:—Behold! human beings living in an underground den, which has a mouth open towards the light and reaching all along the den; here they have been from their childhood, and have their legs and necks chained so that they cannot move, and can only see before them, being prevented by the chains from turning round their heads. Above and behind them a fire is blazing at a distance, and between the fire and the prisoners there is a raised way; and you will see, if you look, a low wall built along the way, like the screen which marionette players have in front of them, over which they show the puppets.

I see.

And do you see, I said, men passing along the wall carrying all sorts of vessels, and statues and figures of animals made of wood and stone and various materials, which appear over the wall? Some of them are talking, others silent.

You have shown me a strange image, and they are strange prisoners.

Like ourselves, I replied; and they see only their own shadows, or the shadows of one another, which the fire throws on the opposite wall of the cave?

True, he said; how could they see anything but the shadows if they were never allowed to move their heads?

And of the objects which are being carried in like manner they would only see the shadows?

Yes, he said.

And if they were able to converse with one another, would they not suppose that they were naming what was actually before them?

Very true.

And suppose further that the prison had an echo which came from the other side, would they not be sure to fancy when one of the passers-by spoke that the voice which they heard came from the passing shadow?

No question, he replied.

To them, I said, the truth would be literally nothing but the shadows of the images.

That is certain.

And now look again, and see what will naturally follow if the prisoners are released and disabused of their error. At first, when any of them is liberated and compelled suddenly to stand up and turn his neck round and walk and look towards the light, he will suffer sharp pains; the glare will distress him, and he will be unable to see the realities of which in his former state he had seen the shadows;

and then conceive some one saying to him, that what he saw before was an illusion, but that now, when he is approaching nearer to being and his eye is turned towards more real existence, he has a clearer vision,—what will be his reply? And you may further imagine that his instructor is pointing to the objects as they pass and requiring him to name them,—will he not be perplexed? Will he not fancy that the shadows which he formerly saw are truer than the objects which are now shown to him?

Far truer.

And if he is compelled to look straight at the light, will he not have a pain in his eyes which will make him turn away to take refuge in the objects of vision which he can see, and which he will conceive to be in reality clearer than the things which are now being shown to him?

True, he said.

And suppose once more, that he is reluctantly dragged up a steep and rugged ascent, and held fast until he is forced into the presence of the sun himself, is he not likely to be pained and irritated? When he approaches the light his eyes will be dazzled, and he will not be able to see anything at all of what are now called realities.

Not all in a moment, he said.

He will require to grow accustomed to the sight of the upper world. And first he will see the shadows best, next the reflections of men and other objects in the water, and then the objects themselves; then he will gaze upon the light of the moon and the stars and the spangled heaven; and he will see the sky and the stars by night better than the sun or the light of the sun by day?

Certainly.

Last of all he will be able to see the sun, and not mere reflections of him in the water, but he will see him in his own proper place, and not in another; and he will contemplate him as he is.

Certainly.

He will then proceed to argue that this is he who gives the season and the years, and is the guardian of all that is in the visible world, and in a certain way the cause of all things which he and his fellows have been accustomed to behold?

Clearly, he said, he would first see the sun and then reason about him.

And when he remembered his old habitation, and the wisdom of the den and his fellow-prisoners, do you not suppose that he would felicitate himself on the change, and pity them?

Certainly, he would.

And if they were in the habit of conferring honours among themselves on those who were quickest to observe the passing shadows and to remark which of them went before, and which followed after, and which were together; and who were therefore best able to draw conclusions as to the future, do you think that he would care for such honours and glories, or envy the possessors of them? Would he not say with Homer,

> Better to be the poor servant of a poor master,

and to endure anything, rather than think as they do and live after their manner?

Yes, he said, I think that he would rather suffer anything than entertain these false notions and live in this miserable manner.

Imagine once more, I said, such an one coming suddenly out of the sun to be replaced in his old situation; would he not be certain to have his eyes full of darkness?

To be sure, he said.

And if there were a contest, and he had to compete in measuring the shadows with the prisoners who had never moved out of the den, while his sight was still weak, and before his eyes had become steady (and the time which would be needed to acquire this new habit of sight might be very considerable) would he not be ridiculous? Men would say of him that up he went and down he came without his eyes; and that it was better not even to think of ascending; and if any one tried to loose another and lead him up to the light, let them only catch the offender, and they would put him to death.

No question, he said.

This entire allegory, I said, you may now append, dear Glaucon, to the previous argument; the prisonhouse is the world of sight, the light of the fire is the sun, and you will not misapprehend me if you interpret the journey upwards to be the ascent of the soul into the intellectual world according to my poor belief, which, at your desire, I have expressed—whether rightly or wrongly God knows. But, whether true or false, my opinion is that in the world of knowledge the idea of good appears last of all, and is seen only with an effort;

and, when seen, is also inferred to be the universal author of all things beautiful and right, parent of light and of the lord of light in this visible world, and the immediate source of reason and truth in the intellectual; and that this is the power upon which he who would act rationally either in public or private life must have his eye fixed.

I agree, he said, as far as I am able to understand you.

Moreover, I said, you must not wonder that those who attain to this beatific vision are unwilling to descend to human affairs; for their souls are ever hastening into the upper world where they desire to dwell; which desire of theirs is very natural, if our allegory may be trusted.

Yes, very natural.

And is there anything surprising in one who passes from divine contemplations to the evil state of man, misbehaving himself in a ridiculous manner; if, while his eyes are blinking and before he has become accustomed to the surrounding darkness, he is compelled to fight in courts of law, or in other places, about the images or the shadows of images of justice, and is endeavouring to meet the conceptions of those who have never yet seen absolute justice?

Anything but surprising, he replied.

Anyone who has common sense will remember that the bewilderments of the eyes are of two kinds, and arise from two causes, either from coming out of the light or from going into the light, which is true of the mind's eye, quite as much as of the bodily eye; and he who remembers this when he sees any one whose vision is perplexed and weak, will not be too ready to laugh; he will first ask whether that soul of man has come out of the brighter life, and is unable to see because unaccustomed to the dark, or having turned from darkness to the day is dazzled by excess of light. And he will count the one happy in his condition and state of being, and he will pity the other; or, if he have a mind to laugh at the soul which comes from below into the light, there will be more reason in this than in the laugh which greets him who returns from above out of the light into the den.

That, he said, is a very just distinction.

But then, if I am right, certain professors of education must be wrong when they say that they can put a knowledge into the soul which was not there before, like sight into blind eyes.

They undoubtedly say this, he replied.

Whereas, our argument shows that the power and capacity of learning exists in the soul already; and that just as the eye was unable to turn from darkness to light without the whole body, so too the instrument of knowledge can only by the movement of the whole soul be turned from the world of becoming into that of being, and learn by degrees to endure the sight of being, and of the brightest and best of being, or in other words, of the good.

Very true.

And must there not be some art which will effect conversion in the easiest and quickest manner; not implanting the faculty of sight, for that exists already, but has been turned in the wrong direction, and is looking away from the truth?

Yes, he said, such an art may be presumed.

And whereas the other so-called virtues of the soul seem to be akin to bodily qualities, for even when they are not originally innate they can be implanted later by habit and exercise, the virtue of wisdom more than anything else contains a divine element which always remains, and by this conversion is rendered useful and profitable; or, on the other hand, hurtful and useless. Did you never observe the narrow intelligence flashing from the keen eye of a clever rogue—how eager he is, how clearly his paltry soul sees the way to his end; he is the reverse of the blind, but his keen eyesight is forced into the service of evil, and he is mischievous in proportion to his cleverness?

Very true, he said.

But what if there had been a circumcision of such natures in the days of their youth; and they had been severed from those sensual pleasures, such as eating and drinking, which, like leaden weights, were attached to them at their birth, and which drag them down and turn the vision of their souls upon the things that are below— if, I say, they had been released from these impediments and turned in the opposite direction, the very same faculty in them would have seen the truth as keenly as they see what their eyes are turned to now.

Very likely.

Yes, I said; and there is another thing which is likely, or rather a necessary inference from what has preceded, that neither the uneducated and uninformed of the truth, nor yet those who never make an end of their education, will be able ministers of State; not the former, because they have no single aim of duty which is the rule of all their actions, private as well as public; nor the latter, because they will not act at all except upon compulsion, fancying that they are already dwelling apart in the islands of the blest.

Very true, he replied.

Then, I said, the business of us who are the founders of the State will be to compel the best minds to attain that knowledge which we have already shown to be the greatest of all—they must continue to ascend until they arrive at the good; but when they have ascended and seen enough we must not allow them to do as they do now.

What do you mean?

I mean that they remain in the upper world: but this must not be allowed; they must be made to descend again among the prisoners in the den, and partake of their labours and honours, whether they are worth having or not.

But is not this unjust? he said; ought we to give them a worse life, when they might have had a better?

You have again forgotten, my friend, I said, the intention of the legislator, who did not aim at making any one class in the State happy above the rest; the happiness was to be in the whole State, and he held the citizens together by persuasion and necessity, making them benefactors of the State, and therefore benefactors of one another; to this end he created them, not to please themselves, but to be his instruments in binding up the State.

True, he said, I had forgotten.

Observe, Glaucon, that there will be no injustice in compelling our philosophers to have a care and providence of others; we shall explain to them that in other States, men of their class are not obliged to share in the toils of politics: and this is reasonable, for they grow up at their own sweet will, and the government would rather not have them. Being self-taught, they cannot be expected to show any gratitude for a culture which they have never received. But we have brought you into the world to be the rulers of the hive, kings of yourselves and of the other citizens, and have educated you far better and more perfectly than they have been educated, and you are better able to share in the double duty. Wherefore each of you, when his turn comes, must go down to the general underground abode, and get the habit of seeing in the dark. When you have acquired the habit, you will see ten thousand times better than the inhabitants of the den, and you will know what the several images are, and what they represent, because you have seen the beautiful and just and good in their truth. And thus our State which is also yours will be a reality, and not a dream only, and will be administered in a spirit unlike that of other States, in which men fight with one another about shadows only and are distracted in the struggle for power, which in their eyes is a great good. Whereas the truth is that the State in which the rulers are most reluctant to govern is always the best and most quietly governed, and the State in which they are most eager, the worst.

Quite true, he replied.

And will our pupils, when they hear this, refuse to take their turn at the toils of State, when they are allowed to spend the greater part of their time with one another in the heavenly light?

Impossible, he answered; for they are just men, and the commands which we impose upon them are just; there can be no doubt that every one of them will take office as a stern necessity, and not after the fashion of our present rulers of State.

Yes, my friend, I said; and there lies the point. You must contrive for your future rulers another and a better life than that of a ruler, and then you must have a well-ordered State; for only in the State which offers this, will they rule who are truly rich, not in silver and gold, but in virtue and wisdom, which are the true blessings of life. Whereas if they go to the administration of public affairs, poor and hungering after their own private advantage, thinking that hence they are to snatch the chief good, order there can never be; for they will be fighting about office, and the civil and domestic broils which thus arise will be the ruin of the rulers themselves and of the whole State.

Most true, he replied.

And the only life which looks down upon the life of political ambition is that of true philosophy. Do you know of any other?

Indeed, I do not, he said.

And those who govern ought not to be lovers of the task? For, if they are, there will be rival lovers, and they will fight.

No question.

Who then are those whom we shall compel to be Guardians? Surely they will be the men who are the wisest about affairs of State, and by whom the State is best administered, and who at the same time have other honours and another and a better life than that of politics.

They are the men, and I will choose them, he replied.

Socrates and his companions have now begun to speak about the various possible forms of the state, and Socrates has been asked to give an account of the regimes that do not attain to the perfection of the state they have described in their speech.

And must not the tyrannical man be like the tyrannical State, and the democratical man like the democratical State; and the same of the others?

Certainly.

And as State is to State in virtue and happiness, so is man in relation to man?

To be sure.

Then comparing our original city, which was under a king, and the city which is also under a tyrant, how do they stand as to virtue?

They are the opposite extremes, he said, for one is the very best and the other is the very worst.

There can be no mistake, I said, as to which is which, and therefore I will at once enquire whether you would arrive at a similar decision about their relative happiness and misery. And here we must not allow ourselves to be panic-stricken at the apparition of the tyrant, who is only a unity and may perhaps have a few retainers about him; but let us go as we ought into every corner of the city and look all about, and then we will give our opinion.

A fair invitation, he replied; and I see, as every one must, that a tyranny is the wretchedest form of government, and the rule of a king the happiest.

And in estimating the men, too, may I not fairly make a like request, that I should have a judge whose mind can enter into and see through human nature? He must not be like a child who looks at the outside and is dazzled at the pompous aspect which the tyrannical nature assumes to the beholder, but let him be one who has a clear insight. May I suppose that the judgment is given in the hearing of us all by one who is able to judge, and has dwelt in the same place with him, and been present at his daily life and known him in his family relations, where he may be seen stripped of his tragedy attire, and again in the hour of public danger—he shall tell us about the happiness and misery of the tyrant when compared with other men?

That again, he said, is a very fair proposal.

Shall I assume that we ourselves are able and experienced judges and have before now met with such a person? We shall then have some one who will answer our enquiries.

By all means.

Let me ask you not to forget the parallel of the individual and the State; bearing this in mind, and glancing in turn from one to the other of them, will you tell me their respective conditions?

What do you mean? he asked.

Beginning with the State, I replied, would you say that a city which is governed by a tyrant is free or enslaved?

No city, he said, can be more completely enslaved.

And yet, as you see, there are freemen as well as masters in such a state?

Yes, he said, I see that there are—a few; but the people, speaking generally, and the best of them are miserably degraded and enslaved.

Then if the man is like the State, I said, must not the same rule prevail? His soul is full of meanness and vulgarity—the best elements in him are enslaved; and there is a small ruling part, which is also the worst and maddest.

Inevitably.

And would you say that the soul of such an one is the soul of a freeman, or of a slave?

He has the soul of a slave, in my opinion.

And the State which is enslaved under a tyrant is utterly incapable of acting voluntarily?

Utterly incapable.

And also the soul which is under a tyrant (I am speaking of the soul taken as a whole) is least capable of doing what she desires; there is a gadfly which goads her, and she is full of trouble and remorse?

Certainly.

And is the city which is under a tyrant rich or poor?

Poor.

And the tyrannical soul must be always poor and insatiable?

True.

And must not such a State and such a man be always full of fear?

Yes, indeed.

Is there any State in which you will find more of lamentation and sorrow and groaning and pain?

Certainly not.

And is there any man in whom you will find more of this sort of misery than in the tyrannical man, who is in a fury of passions and desires?

Impossible.

Reflecting upon these and similar evils, you held the tyrannical State to be the most miserable of States?

And I was right, he said.

Certainly, I said. And when you see the same evils in the tyrannical man, what do you say of him?

I say that he is by far the most miserable of all men.

There, I said, I think that you are beginning to go wrong.

What do you mean?

I do not think that he has as yet reached the utmost extreme of misery.

Then who is more miserable?

One of whom I am about to speak.

Who is that?

He who is of a tyrannical nature, and instead of leading a private life has been cursed with the further misfortune of being a public tyrant.

From what has been said, I gather that you are right.

Yes, I replied, but in this high argument you should be a little more certain, and should not conjecture only; for of all questions, this respecting good and evil is the greatest.

Very true, he said.

Let me then offer you an illustration, which may, I think, throw a light upon this subject.

What is your illustration?

The case of rich individuals in cities who possess many slaves: from them you may form an idea of the tyrant's condition, for they both have slaves; the only difference is that he has more slaves.

Yes, that is the difference.

You know that they live securely and have nothing to apprehend from their servants?

What should they fear?

Nothing. But do you observe the reason of this?

Yes; the reason is, that the whole city is leagued together for the protection of each individual.

Very true, I said. But imagine one of these owners, the master say of some fifty slaves, together with his family and property and slaves, carried off by a god into the wilderness, where there are no freemen to help him—will he not be in an agony of fear lest he and his wife and children should be put to death by his slaves?

Yes, he said, he will be in the utmost fear.

The time has arrived when he will be compelled to flatter divers of his slaves, and make many promises to them of freedom and other things, much against his will—he will have to cajole his own servants.

Yes, he said, that will be the only way of saving himself.

And suppose the same god, who carried him away, to surround him with neighbours who will not suffer one man to be the master of another, and who, if they could catch the offender, would take his life?

His case will be still worse, if you suppose him to be everywhere surrounded and watched by enemies.

And is not this the sort of prison in which the tyrant will be bound—he who being by nature such as we have described, is full of all sorts of fears and lusts? His soul is dainty and greedy, and yet alone, of all men in the city, he is never allowed to go on a journey, or to see the things which other freemen desire to see, but he lives in his hole like a woman hidden in the house, and is jealous of any other citizen who goes into foreign parts and sees anything of interest.

Very true, he said.

And amid evils such as these will not he who is ill-governed in his own person—the tyrannical man, I mean—whom you just now decided to be the most miserable of all—will not he be yet more miserable when, instead of leading a private life, he is constrained by fortune to be a public tyrant? He has to be master of others when he is not master of himself: he is like a diseased or paralytic man who is compelled to pass his life, not in retirement, but fighting and combating with other men.

Yes, he said, the similitude is most exact.

Is not his case utterly miserable? And does not the actual tyrant lead a worse life than he whose life you determined to be the worst?

Certainly.

He who is the real tyrant, whatever men may think, is the real slave, and is obliged to practise the greatest adulation and servility, and to be the flatterer of the vilest of mankind. He has desires which he is utterly unable to satisfy, and has more wants than any one, and is truly poor, if you know how to inspect the whole soul of him: all his life long he is beset with fear and is full of convulsions, and distractions, even as the State which he resembles: and surely the resemblance holds?

Very true, he said.

Moreover, as we were saying before, he grows worse from having power: he becomes and is of necessity more jealous, more faithless, more unjust, more friendless, more impious, than he was at first; he is the purveyor and cherisher of every sort of vice, and the consequence is that he is supremely miserable, and that he makes everybody else as miserable as himself.

No man of any sense will dispute your words.

Come then, I said, and as the general umpire in theatrical contests proclaims the result, do you also decide who in your opinion is first in the scale of happiness, and who second, and in what order the others follow: there are five of them in all—they are the royal, timocratical, oligarchical, democratical, tyrannical.

The decision will be easily given, he replied; they shall be choruses coming on the stage, and I must judge them in the order in which they enter, by the criterion of virtue and vice, happiness and misery.

Need we hire a herald, or shall I announce, that the son of Ariston [the best] has decided that the best and justest is also the happiest, and that this is he who is the most royal man and king over himself; and that the worst and most unjust man is also the most miserable, and that this is he who being the greatest tyrant of himself is also the greatest tyrant of his State?

Make the proclamation yourself, he said.

And shall I add, "whether seen or unseen by gods and men"?

Let the words be added.

Then this, I said, will be our first proof; and there is another, which may also have some weight.

What is that?

The second proof is derived from the nature of the soul: seeing that the individual soul, like the State, has been divided by us into three principles, the division may, I think, furnish a new demonstration.

Of what nature?

It seems to me that to these three principles three pleasures correspond; also three desires and governing powers.

How do you mean? he said.

There is one principle with which, as we were saying, a man learns, another with which he is angry; the third, having many forms, has no special name, but is denoted by the general term appetitive, from the extraordinary strength and vehemence of the desires of eating and drinking and the other sensual appetites which are the main elements of it; also money-loving, because such desires are generally satisfied by the help of money.

That is true, he said.

If we were to say that the loves and pleasures of this third part were concerned with gain, we should then be able to fall back on a single notion; and might truly and intelligibly describe this part of the soul as loving gain or money.

I agree with you.

Again, is not the passionate element wholly set on ruling and conquering and getting fame?

True.

Suppose we call it the contentious or ambitious—would the term be suitable?

Extremely suitable.

On the other hand, every one sees that the principle of knowledge is wholly directed to the truth, and cares less than either of the others for gain or fame.

Far less.

"Lover of wisdom," "lover of knowledge," are titles which we may fitly apply to that part of the soul?

Certainly.

One principle prevails in the souls of one class of men, another in others, as may happen?

Yes.

Then we may begin by assuming that there are three classes of men—lovers of wisdom, lovers of honour, lovers of gain?

Exactly.

And there are three kinds of pleasure, which are their several objects?

Very true.

Now, if you examine the three classes of men, and ask of them in turn which of their lives is pleasantest, each will be found praising his own and depreciating that of others: the money-maker will contrast the vanity of honour or of learning if they bring no money with the solid advantages of gold and silver?

True, he said.

And the lover of honour—what will be his opinion? Will he not think that the pleasure of riches is vulgar, while the pleasure of learning, if it brings no distinction, is all smoke and nonsense to him?

Very true.

And are we to suppose, I said, that the philosopher sets any value on other pleasures in comparison with the pleasure of knowing the truth, and in that pursuit abiding, ever learning, not so far indeed from the heaven of pleasure? Does he not call the other pleasures necessary, under the idea that if there were no necessity for them, he would rather not have them?

There can be no doubt of that, he replied.

Since, then, the pleasures of each class and the life of each are in dispute, and the question is not which life is more or less honourable, or better or worse, but which is the more pleasant or painless—how shall we know who speaks truly?

I cannot myself tell, he said.

Well, but what ought to be the criterion? Is any better than experience and wisdom and reason?

There cannot be a better, he said.

Then, I said, reflect. Of the three individuals, which has the greatest experience of all the pleasures which we enumerated? Has the lover of gain, in learning the nature of essential truth, greater experience of the pleasure of knowledge than the philosopher has of the pleasure of gain?

The philosopher, he replied, has greatly the advantage; for he has of necessity always known the taste of the other pleasures from his childhood upwards: but the lover of gain in all his experience has not of necessity tasted—or, I should rather say, even had he desired, could hardly have tasted—the sweetness of learning and knowing truth.

Then the lover of wisdom has a great advantage over the lover of gain, for he has a double experience?

Yes, very great.

Again, has he greater experience of the pleasures of honour, or the lover of honour of the pleasures of wisdom?

Nay, he said, all three are honoured in proportion as they attain their object; for the rich man and the brave man and the wise man alike have their crowd of admirers, and as they all receive honour they all have experience of the pleasures of honour; but the delight which is to be found in the knowledge of true being is known to the philosopher only.

His experience, then, will enable him to judge better than any one?

Far better.

And he is the only one who has wisdom as well as experience?

Certainly.

Further, the very faculty which is the instrument of judgment is not possessed by the covetous or ambitious man, but only by the philosopher?

What faculty?

Reason, with whom, as we were saying, the decision ought to rest.

Yes.

And reasoning is peculiarly his instrument?

Certainly.

If wealth and gain were the criterion, then the praise or blame of the lover of gain would surely be the most trustworthy?

Assuredly.

Or if honour or victory or courage, in that case the judgment of the ambitious or pugnacious would be the truest?

Clearly.

But since experience and wisdom and reason are the judges—

The only inference possible, he replied, is that pleasures which are approved by the lover of wisdom and reason are the truest.

And so we arrive at the result, that the pleasure of the intelligent part of the soul is the pleasantest of the three, and that he of us in whom this is the ruling principle has the pleasantest life.

Unquestionably, he said, the wise man speaks with authority when he approves of his own life.

And what does the judge affirm to be the life which is next, and the pleasure which is next?

Clearly that of the soldier and lover of honour; who is nearer to himself than the money-maker.

Last comes the lover of gain?

Very true, he said.

Twice in succession, then, has the just man overthrown the unjust in this conflict; and now comes the third trial, which is ded-

icated to Olympian Zeus the saviour: a sage whispers in my ear that
no pleasure except that of the wise is quite true and pure—all others are a shadow only; and surely this will prove the greatest and
most decisive of falls?

Yes, the greatest; but will you explain yourself?

I will work out the subject and you shall answer my questions.

Proceed.

Say, then, is not pleasure opposed to pain?

True.

And there is a neutral state which is neither pleasure nor pain?

There is.

A state which is intermediate, and a sort of repose of the soul
about either—that is what you mean?

Yes.

You remember what people say when they are sick?

What do they say?

That after all nothing is pleasanter than health. But then they
never knew this to be the greatest of pleasures until they were ill.

Yes, I know, he said.

And when persons are suffering from acute pain, you must have
heard them say that there is nothing pleasanter than to get rid of
their pain?

I have.

And there are many other cases of suffering in which the mere
rest and cessation of pain, and not any positive enjoyment, is
extolled by them as the greatest pleasure?

Yes, he said; at the time they are pleased and well content to be
at rest.

Again, when the pleasure ceases, that sort of rest or cessation will
be painful?

Doubtless, he said.

Then the intermediate state of rest will be pleasure and will also
be pain?

So it would seem.

But can that which is neither become both?

I should say not.

And both pleasure and pain are motions of the soul, are they not?

Yes.

But that which is neither was just now shown to be rest and not motion, and in a mean between them?

Yes.

How, then, can we be right in supposing that the absence of pain is pleasure, or that the absence of pleasure is pain?

Impossible.

This then is an appearance only and not a reality; that is to say, the rest is pleasure at the moment and in comparison of what is painful, and painful in comparison of what is pleasant; but all these representations, when tried by the test of true pleasure, are not real but a sort of imposition?

That is the inference.

Look at the other class of pleasures which have no antecedent pains and you will no longer suppose, as you perhaps may at present, that pleasure is only the cessation of pain, or pain of pleasure.

What are they, he said, and where shall I find them?

There are many of them: take as an example the pleasures of smell, which are very great and have no antecedent pains; they come in a moment, and when they depart leave no pain behind them.

Most true, he said.

Let us not, then, be induced to believe that pure pleasure is the cessation of pain, or pain of pleasure.

No.

Still, the more numerous and violent pleasures which reach the soul through the body are generally of this sort—they are reliefs of pain.

That is true.

And the anticipations of future pleasures and pains are of a like nature?

Yes.

Shall I give you an illustration of them?

Let me hear.

You would allow, I said, that there is in nature an upper and lower and middle region?

I should.

And if a person were to go from the lower to the middle region, would he not imagine that he is going up; and he who is standing in the middle and sees whence he has come, would imagine that he is already in the upper region, if he has never seen the true upper world?

To be sure, he said; how can he think otherwise?

But if he were taken back again would he imagine, and truly imagine, that he was descending?

No doubt.

All that would arise out of his ignorance of the true upper and middle and lower regions?

Yes.

Then can you wonder that persons who are inexperienced in the truth, as they have wrong ideas about many other things, should also have wrong ideas about pleasure and pain and the intermediate state; so that when they are only being drawn towards the painful they feel pain and think the pain which they experience to be real, and in like manner, when drawn away from pain to the neutral or intermediate state, they firmly believe that they have reached the goal of satiety and pleasure; they, not knowing pleasure, err in contrasting pain with the absence of pain, which is like contrasting black with grey, instead of white—can you wonder, I say, at this?

No, indeed; I should be much more disposed to wonder at the opposite.

Look at the matter thus:—Hunger, thirst, and the like, are inanitions of the bodily state?

Yes.

And ignorance and folly are inanitions of the soul?

True.

And food and wisdom are the corresponding satisfactions of either?

Certainly.

And is the satisfaction derived from that which has less or from that which has more existence the truer?

Clearly, from that which has more.

What classes of things have a greater share of pure existence in your judgment—those of which food and drink and condiments and all kinds of sustenance are examples, or the class which contains true opinion and knowledge and mind and all the different kinds of virtue? Put the question in this way:—Which has a more pure being—that which is concerned with the invariable, the immortal, and the true, and is of such a nature, and is found in such natures; or that which is concerned with and found in the variable and mortal, and is itself variable and mortal?

Far purer, he replied, is the being of that which is concerned with the invariable.

And does the essence of the invariable partake of knowledge in the same degree as of essence?

Yes, of knowledge in the same degree.

And of truth in the same degree?

Yes.

And, conversely, that which has less of truth will also have less of essence?

Necessarily.

Then, in general, those kinds of things which are in the service of the body have less of truth and essence than those which are in the service of the soul?

Far less.

And has not the body itself less of truth and essence than the soul?

Yes.

What is filled with more real existence, and actually has a more real existence, is more really filled than that which is filled with less real existence and is less real?

Of course.

And if there be a pleasure in being filled with that which is according to nature, that which is more really filled with more real being will more really and truly enjoy true pleasure; whereas that which participates in less real being will be less truly and surely satisfied, and will participate in an illusory and less real pleasure?

Unquestionably.

Those then who know not wisdom and virtue, and are always busy with gluttony and sensuality, go down and up again as far as the mean; and in this region they move at random throughout life, but they never pass into the true upper world; thither they neither look, nor do they ever find their way, neither are they truly filled with true being, nor do they taste of pure and abiding pleasure. Like cattle, with their eyes always looking down and their heads stooping to the earth, that is, to the dining-table, they fatten and feed and breed, and, in their excessive love of these delights, they kick and butt at one another with horns and hoofs which are made of iron; and they kill one another by reason of their insatiable lust. For they fill themselves with that which is not substantial, and the part of themselves which they fill is also unsubstantial and incontinent.

Verily, Socrates, said Glaucon, you describe the life of the many like an oracle.

Their pleasures are mixed with pains—how can they be otherwise? For they are mere shadows and pictures of the true, and they are coloured by contrast, which exaggerates both light and shade, and so they implant in the minds of fools insane desires of themselves; and they are fought about as Stesichorus says that the Greeks fought about the shadow of Helen at Troy in ignorance of the truth.

Something of that sort must inevitably happen.

And must not the like happen with the spirited or passionate element of the soul? Will not the passionate man who carries his passion into action, be in the like case, whether he is envious and ambitious, or violent and contentious, or angry and discontented, if he be seeking to attain honour and victory and the satisfaction of his anger without reason or sense?

Yes, he said, the same will happen with the spirited element also.

Then may we not confidently assert that the lovers of money and honour, when they seek their pleasures under the guidance and in the company of reason and knowledge, and pursue after and win the pleasures which wisdom shows them, will also have the truest pleasures in the highest degree which is attainable to them, inasmuch as they follow truth; and they will have the pleasures which are natural to them, if that which is best for each one is also most natural to him?

Yes, certainly; the best is the most natural.

And when the whole soul follows the philosophical principle, and there is no division, the several parts are just, and do each of them their own business, and enjoy severally the best and truest pleasures of which they are capable?

Exactly.

But when either of the two other principles prevails, it fails in attaining its own pleasure, and compels the rest to pursue after a pleasure which is a shadow only and which is not their own?

True.

And the greater the interval which separates them from philosophy and reason, the more strange and illusive will be the pleasure?

Yes.

And is not that farthest from reason which is at the greatest distance from law and order?

Clearly.

And the lustful and tyrannical desires are, as we saw, at the greatest distance?

Yes.

And the royal and orderly desires are nearest?

Yes.

Then the tyrant will live at the greatest distance from true or natural pleasure, and the king at the least?

Certainly.

But if so, the tyrant will live most unpleasantly, and the king most pleasantly?

Inevitably.

Would you know the measure of the interval which separates them?

Will you tell me?

There appear to be three pleasures, one genuine and two spurious: now the transgression of the tyrant reaches a point beyond the spurious: he has run away from the region of law and reason, and taken up his abode with certain slave pleasures which are his satellites, and the measure of his inferiority can only be expressed in a figure.

How do you mean?

I assume, I said, that the tyrant is in the third place from the oligarch; the democrat was in the middle?

Yes.

And if there is truth in what has preceded, he will be wedded to an image of pleasure which is thrice removed as to truth from the pleasure of the oligarch?

He will.

And the oligarch is third from the royal; since we count as one royal and aristocratical?

Yes, he is third.

Then the tyrant is removed from true pleasure by the space of a number which is three times three?

Manifestly.

The shadow then of tyrannical pleasure determined by the number of length will be a plane figure.

Certainly.

And if you raise the power and make the plane a solid, there is no difficulty in seeing how vast is the interval by which the tyrant is parted from the king.

Yes; the arithmetician will easily do the sum.

Or if some person begins at the other end and measures the interval by which the king is parted from the tyrant in truth of pleasure, he will find him, when the multiplication is complete, living 729 times more pleasantly, and the tyrant more painfully by this same interval.

What a wonderful calculation! And how enormous is the distance which separates the just from the unjust in regard to pleasure and pain!

Yet a true calculation, I said, and a number which nearly concerns human life, if human beings are concerned with days and nights and months and years.

Yes, he said, human life is certainly concerned with them.

Then if the good and just man be thus superior in pleasure to the evil and unjust, his superiority will be infinitely greater in propriety of life and in beauty and virtue?

Immeasurably greater.

Well, I said, and now having arrived at this stage of the argument, we may revert to the words which brought us hither: Was not some one saying that injustice was a gain to the perfectly unjust who was reputed to be just?

Yes, that was said.

Now then, having determined the power and quality of justice and injustice, let us have a little conversation with him.

What shall we say to him?

Let us make an image of the soul, that he may have his own words presented before his eyes.

Of what sort?

An ideal image of the soul, like the composite creations of ancient mythology, such as the Chimera or Scylla or Cerberus, and there are many others in which two or more different natures are said to grow into one.

There are said to have been such unions.

Then do you now model the form of a multitudinous, many-headed monster, having a ring of heads of all manner of beasts, tame and wild, which he is able to generate and metamorphose at will.

You suppose marvelous powers in the artist; but as language is more pliable than wax or any similar substance, let there be such a model as you propose.

Suppose now that you made a second form as of a lion, and a third of a man, the second smaller than the first, and the third smaller than the second.

That, he said, is an easier task; and I have made them as you say.

And now join them, and let the three grow into one.

That has been accomplished.

Next fashion the outside of them into a single image, as of a man, so that he who is not able to look within, and sees only the outer hull, may believe the beast to be a single human creature.

I have done so, he said.

And now, to him who maintains that it is profitable for the human creature to be unjust, and unprofitable to be just, let us reply that, if he is right, it is profitable for this creature to feast the multitudinous monster and strengthen the lion and lion-like qualities, but to starve and weaken the man, who is consequently liable to be dragged about at the mercy of either of the two; and he is not to attempt to familiarize or harmonize them with one another—he ought rather to suffer them to fight and bite and devour one another.

Certainly, he said; that is what the approver of injustice says.

To him the supporter of justice makes answer that he should ever so speak and act as to give the man within him in some way or other the most complete mastery over the entire human creature. He should watch over the many-headed monster like a good husbandman, fostering and cultivating the gentle qualities, and preventing the wild ones from growing; he should be making the lion-heart his ally, and in common care of them all should be uniting the several parts with one another and with himself.

Yes, he said, that is quite what the maintainer of justice will say.

And so from every point of view, whether of pleasure, honour, or advantage, the approver of justice is right and speaks the truth, and the disapprover is wrong and false and ignorant.

Yes, from every point of view.

from
POLITICS
by
ARISTOTLE

Now if any one would watch the parts of a state from the very first as they rise into existence, as in other matters, so here he would gain the truest view of the subject. In the first place, then, it is requisite that those should be joined together, which cannot exist without each other, as the male and the female, for the business of propagation; and this not through deliberate choice, but by that natural impulse which acts both in plants and in animals, namely, the desire of leaving behind them others like themselves. By nature too some beings command, and others obey, for the sake of mutual safety; for a being endowed with discernment and forethought is by nature the superior and governor; whereas he who is merely able to execute by bodily labour, is the inferior and a natural slave; and hence the interest of master and slave is identical. But there is a natural difference between the female and the slave; for nature does nothing meanly, like artists who make the Delphic swords; but she has one instrument for one end; for thus her instruments are most likely to be brought to perfection, being made to contribute to one end, and not to many. Yet, among Barbarians, the female and the slave are upon a level in the community; the reason for which is, that they are not fitted by nature to rule; and so their relationship becomes merely that between slaves of different sexes. For which reason the poets say,

> Tis meet that barbarous tribes to Greeks should bow.

as if a barbarian and a slave were by nature one and the same. Now of these two societies the domestic tie is the first, and Hesiod is right when he says,

> First house, then wife, then oxen for the plough;

for the ox is to the poor man in the place of a household slave. That society, then, which nature has established for daily support, is a family (οἰκοζ), and those who compose it are called by Charondas Ομοσίπνοι, and by Epimenides the Cretan Ομόκαπνοι. But the society of many families, which was instituted for lasting and mutual advantage, is called a village (κώμη), and a village is most naturally composed of the emigrant members of one family, whom some persons call Ομογάλακτεζ, the children and the children's children. And hence, by the way, states were originally governed by kings, as the Barbarians now are; for they were composed of those who always were under kingly government. For every family is governed by the elder, as are its branches, on account of their relationship; and this is what Homer says,

> Then each his wife and child doth rule,

for in this scattered manner they formerly lived. And the general opinion which makes the gods themselves subject to kingly government, arises from the fact that most men formerly were, and many are so now; and as they hold the gods to be like themselves in form, so they suppose their manner of life must needs be the same. But when many villages join themselves perfectly together into one society, that society is a state (πόλιζ), and contains in itself, if I may so speak, the perfection of independence; and it is first founded that men may live, but continued that they may live happily. For which reason every state is the work of nature, since the first social ties are such; for to this they all tend as to an end, and the nature of a thing is judged by its tendency. For what every being is in its perfect state, that certainly is the nature of that being, whether it be a man, a horse, or a house; besides, its own final cause and its end must be the perfection of any thing; but a government complete in itself constitutes a final cause and what is best. Hence it is evident, that a state is one of the works of nature, and that man is naturally a political animal, and that whosoever is naturally, and not accidentally, unfit for society, must be either inferior or superior to man, just as the person reviled in Homer,

> No tribe, nor state, nor home hath he.

For he whose nature is such as this, must needs be a lover of strife, and as solitary as a bird of prey. It is clear, then, that man is truly a more social animal than bees, or any of the herding cattle; for nature, as we say, does nothing in vain, and man is the only animal who has reason. Speech indeed, as being the token of pleasure and pain, is imparted to other beings also, and thus far their nature extends; they can perceive pleasure and pain, and can impart these sensations to others; but speech is given to us to express what is useful or hurtful to us, and also what is just and unjust; for in this particular man differs from other animals, that he alone has a perception of good and evil, of justice and injustice, and it is the interchange of these common sentiments which forms a family and a city. And further, in the order of nature, the state is prior to the family or the individual; for the whole must necessarily be prior to the parts; for if you take away the whole body you cannot say a foot or a hand remains, unless by equivocation, as if any one should call a hand made of stone, a hand; for such only can it have when mutilated. But everything is defined according to its effects and inherent powers, so that when these no longer remain such as they were, it cannot be said to be the same, but something of the same name. It is plain, then, that the state is prior to the individual, for if an individual is not complete in himself, he bears the same relation to the state as other parts do to a whole; but he that is incapable of society, or so complete in himself as not to want it, makes no part of a state, but is either a beast or a god. There is then in all persons a natural impetus to associate with each other in this manner, and he who first established civil society was the cause of the greatest benefit; for as man, thus perfected, is the most excellent of all living beings, so without law and justice he would be the worst of all; for nothing is so savage as injustice in arms; but man is born with a faculty of gaining himself arms by prudence and virtue; arms which yet he may apply to the most opposite purposes. And hence he who is devoid of virtue will be the most wicked and cruel, the most lustful and gluttonous being imaginable. Now justice is a social virtue for it is the rule of the social state, and the very criterion of what is right.

from
THE PRINCE
by
NICCOLÒ MACHIAVELLI

Concerning the Qualities for Which Men and Especially Princes Are Praised or Blamed

It remains then to look at what should be the modes and governance of a prince with regard to subjects or friends. And because I know that many have written of this, I doubt not that, in writing of it again, I shall be held presumptuous—mostly for departing, in my disputation concerning this matter, from the orders of the others. But given that my intention is to write a thing useful for him who understands it, it has seemed to me more profitable to go behind to the effectual truth of the matter rather than to that matter as represented in the imagination. And many there are who have imagined republics and principalities which have been seen never and are not known in truth to exist; for there is such a distance between how one lives and how one ought to live that he who leaves aside that which is done in favor of that which ought to be done studies rather his ruin than his preservation: for a man who wishes in all particulars to make a profession of good comes to ruin among so many who are not good. Whence it is necessary that a prince, if he wishes to maintain himself, study to be able to be not good and to use this knowledge or not as necessity demands.

Leaving aside, then, the things imagined with regard to a prince and discussing those which are true, I say that all men, whenever they are spoken of, and princes most of all, because they are placed higher, are noted for some of these qualities which earn them either blame or praise. And this is the reason that someone is held to be liberal, someone miserly (using a Tuscan term because *avaro* in our language is still he who desires to possess by means of rapine, *misero* we call one who holds back too much from using his own); someone is held to be a donor, someone rapacious; someone cruel, someone given to pity; the one a breaker of trust, the other trustworthy; the one effeminate and pusillanimous, the other ferocious and spirited; the one humane, the other proud; the one lustful, the other chaste; the one a man of integrity, the other astute; the one harsh, the other easygoing; the one grave, the other light; the one religious, the other disinclined to belief; and similarly. And I know that everyone will confess that it would be a most praiseworthy thing for there to be found in a prince all of the qualities written out above that are considered good; but because they cannot be possessed nor with integrity be observed since human circumstances do not consent to this, it is necessary for him to be prudent in such a manner as to know how to flee the infamy of those vices that would lose him his estate and, with regard to those that would not, to be on his guard—if it is possible. But if this is not possible, one can with less hesitation let them proceed. And he should not even care about incurring infamy for those vices without which it is difficult for him to save his estate: for, if everything is well considered, there will be found something seeming to be virtue which, if followed, would be his ruin, and there will be found something else seeming to be vice which, if followed, would produce his security and well-being.

How Faith Is to Be Observed by Princes

How praiseworthy it is in a prince to keep faith and to live with integrity and not by astuteness—this everyone understands. Nevertheless one sees, by experience in our times, which princes have done great things, what little attention they have paid to the demands of good faith, and how they have known by their astuteness to work their way around the brains of men; and they have, in the end, overcome those who have sought a foundation for themselves in loyalty. . . .

To a prince, then, it is not necessary to have the qualities written of above, but it is necessary to seem to have them. No, I will be bold to say this—for the one having them and always observing them, they are damaging, and for the one seeming to have them they are useful: useful it is to seem compassionate, trustworthy, humane, endowed with integrity, religious, and to be such, but to be in such a condition, with one's spirit so constructed, that, when you need to not possess these qualities, you are prepared and know how to shift to the contrary qualities. And this must be understood—that a

prince, and a new prince most of all, cannot observe all the qualities
for which men are considered good since he is frequently subject to
the necessity to maintain his estate, to maneuver in a manner contrary to the dictates of faith, charity, humanity, and religion. And
then it is requisite that he possess a spirit disposed to shift as the
winds of fortune and the variability of things command; and, as
noted above, not to depart from the good, whenever possible, but to
know to enter into evil, whenever necessary.

A prince ought, then, to take great care lest anything ever escape
his mouth that is not full of the five qualities written of above and
that to one seeing and hearing he be all pity, all trustworthiness, all
integrity, all humanity, all religion—and there is no greater necessity than to seem to possess this last quality. Universally men judge
more by the eyes than by the hands since seeing touches everyone
while sensing touches few. Everyone sees what you seem, few sense
what you are, and these few are not so bold as to oppose the opinions of the many, who have the majesty of his estate for their
defense; and in the actions of all men, and princes most of all, where
there is no tribunal to which to make appeal, one focuses on the
results. Let, then, a prince act in such a manner as to conquer and
maintain his estate, and the means will always be judged honorable,
and they will be praised by everyone—since the crowd is always
going to be taken in by appearances and results, and in the world
there is no one but the crowd. . . .

Of Reason and Science

. . . I have said before that a man did excel all other animals in this faculty: that when he conceived anything whatsoever, he was apt to inquire the consequences of it, and what effects he could do with it. And now I add this other degree of the same excellence: that he can by words reduce the consequences he finds to general rules, called *theorems*, or *aphorisms*; that is, he can reason, or reckon, not only in number, but in all other things whereof one may be added unto or subtracted from another. . . .

. . . By this it appears that reason is not, as sense and memory, born with us, nor gotten by experience only, as prudence is, but attained by industry, first in apt imposing of names, and secondly by getting a good and orderly method in proceeding from the elements, which are names, to assertions made by connexion of one of them to another, and so to syllogisms, which are the connexions of one assertion to another, till we come to a knowledge of all the consequences of names appertaining to the subject in hand; and that is it men call SCIENCE. And whereas sense and memory are but knowledge of fact, which is a thing past and irrevocable, *Science* is the knowledge of consequences, and dependence of one fact upon another, by which, out of that which we can presently do, we know how to do something else when we will, or the like, another time; because when we see how anything comes about, upon what causes, and by what manner, when the like causes come into our power, we see how to make it produce the like effects. . . .

. . . To conclude, the light of human minds is perspicuous words, but by exact definitions first snuffed and purged from ambiguity; *reason* is the *pace*; increase of *science*, the *way*; and the benefit of mankind, the *end.* And on the contrary, metaphors, and senseless and ambiguous words, are like *ignes fatui* [a fool's fire], and reasoning upon them is wandering amongst innumerable absurdities; and their end, contention and sedition, or contempt. . . .

Of the Virtues, Commonly
Called Intellectual; and Their Contrary Defects

. . . The causes of this difference of wits are in the passions; and the difference of passions proceedeth, partly from the different constitution of the body, and partly from different education. For if the difference proceeded from the temper of the brain and the organs of sense, either exterior or interior, there would be no less difference of men in their sight, hearing, or other senses, than in their fancies and discretions. It proceeds therefore from the passions, which are different, not only from the difference of men's complexions, but also from their difference of customs and education.

The passions that most of all cause the differences of wit are principally: the more or less desire of power, of riches, of knowledge, and of honour. All which may be reduced to the first, that is, desire of power. For riches, knowledge, and honour are but several sorts of power.

And therefore, a man who has no great passion for any of these things, but is, as men term it, indifferent, though he may be so far a good man as to be free from giving offence, yet he cannot possibly have either a great fancy or much judgment. For the thoughts are to the desires as scouts and spies, to range abroad and find the way to the things desired; all steadiness of the mind's motion, and all quickness of the same, proceeding from thence; for as to have no desire is to be dead, so to have weak passions is dullness; and to have passions indifferently for every thing, GIDDINESS and *distraction*; and to have stronger and more vehement passions for anything that is ordinarily seen in others is that which men call MADNESS. . . .

Of the Difference of Manners

By *manners* I mean not here decency of behaviour, as how one man should salute another, or how a man should wash his mouth or pick his teeth before company, and such other points of the *small morals*, but those qualities of mankind that concern their living together in peace and unity. To which end we are to consider that the felicity of this life consisteth not in the repose of a mind satisfied. For there is no such *Finis ultimus* (utmost aim) nor *Summum Bonum* (greatest good) as is spoken of in the books of the old moral philosophers. Nor can a man any more live, whose desires are at an end, than he whose senses and imaginations are at a stand. Felicity is a continual progress of the desire, from one object to another, the attaining of the former being still but the way to the latter. The cause whereof is that the object of man's desire is not to enjoy once only, and for one instant of time, but to assure forever the way of his future desire. And therefore the voluntary actions and inclinations of all men tend, not only to the procuring, but also to the assuring of a contented life, and differ only in the way; which ariseth partly from the diversity of passions in divers men, and partly from the difference of the knowledge or opinion each one has of the causes which produce the effect desired.

So that in the first place, I put for a general inclination of all mankind, a perpetual and restless desire of power after power, that ceaseth only in death. And the cause of this is not always that a man hopes for a more intensive delight than he has already attained to, or that he cannot be content with a moderate power, but because he cannot assure the power and means to live well, which he hath present, without the acquisition of more. And from hence it is that kings, whose power is greatest, turn their endeavours to the assuring it at home by laws or abroad by wars; and when that is done, there succeedeth a new desire, in some of fame from new conquest, in others of ease and sensual pleasure, in others of admiration or being flattered for excellence in some art or other ability of the mind. . . .

Of the Natural Condition of Mankind, As Concerning Their Felicity, and Misery

Nature hath made men so equal in the faculties of body and mind as that, though there be found one man sometimes manifestly stronger in body or of quicker mind than another, yet when all is reckoned together the difference between man and man is not so considerable as that one man can thereupon claim to himself any benefit to which another may not pretend as well as he. For as to the strength of body, the weakest has strength enough to kill the strongest, either by secret machination, or by confederacy with others that are in the same danger with himself.

And as to the faculties of the mind—setting aside the arts grounded upon words, and especially that skill of proceeding upon general and infallible rules called science (which very few have, and but in few things), as being not a native faculty (born with us), nor attained (as prudence) while we look after somewhat else—I find yet a greater equality amongst men than that of strength. For prudence is but experience, which equal time equally bestows on all men in those things they equally apply themselves unto. That which may perhaps make such equality incredible is but a vain conceit of one's own wisdom, which almost all men think they have in a greater degree than the vulgar, that is, than all men but themselves and a few others whom, by fame or for concurring with themselves, they approve. For such is the nature of men that howsoever they may acknowledge many others to be more witty, or more eloquent, or more learned, yet they will hardly believe there be many so wise as themselves. For they see their own wit at hand, and other men's at a distance. But this proveth rather that men are in that point equal, than unequal. For there is not ordinarily a greater sign of the equal distribution of anything than that every man is contented with his share.

From this equality of ability ariseth equality of hope in the attaining of our ends. And therefore, if any two men desire the same thing, which nevertheless they cannot both enjoy, they become enemies; and in the way to their end, which is principally their own conservation, and sometimes their delectation only, endeavour to destroy or subdue one another. And from hence it comes to pass that, where an invader hath no more to fear than another man's single power, if one plant, sow, build, or possess a convenient seat, others may probably be expected to come prepared with forces united, to dispossess and deprive him, not only of the fruit of his labour, but also of his life or liberty. And the invader again is in the like danger of another.

And from this diffidence of one another, there is no way for any man to secure himself so reasonable as anticipation, that is, by force or wiles to master the persons of all men he can, so long till he see no other power great enough to endanger him. And this is no more than his own conservation requireth, and is generally allowed. Also, because there be some that taking pleasure in contemplating their own power in the acts of conquest, which they pursue farther than their security requires, if others (that otherwise would be glad to be at ease within modest bounds) should not by invasion increase their power, they would not be able, long time, by standing only on their defence, to subsist. And by consequence, such augmentation of dominion over men being necessary to a man's conservation, it ought to be allowed him.

Again, men have no pleasure, but on the contrary a great deal of grief, in keeping company where there is no power able to over-awe them all. For every man looketh that his companion should value him at the same rate he sets upon himself, and upon all signs of contempt, or undervaluing, naturally endeavours, as far as he dares (which amongst them that have no common power to keep them in quiet, is far enough to make them destroy each other), to extort a greater value from his contemners, by damage, and from others, by the example.

So that in the nature of man we find three principal causes of quarrel: first, competition; secondly, diffidence; thirdly, glory.

The first maketh men invade for gain; the second, for safety; and the third, for reputation. The first use violence to make themselves masters of other men's persons, wives, children, and cattle; the second, to defend them; the third, for trifles, as a word, a smile, a different opinion, and any other sign of undervalue, either direct in their persons, or by reflection in their kindred, their friends, their nation, their profession, or their name.

Hereby it is manifest that during the time men live without a common power to keep them all in awe, they are in that condition which is called war, and such a war as is of every man against every man. For WAR consisteth not in battle only, or the act of fighting, but in a tract of time wherein the will to contend by battle is sufficiently known. And therefore, the notion of *time* is to be considered in the nature of war, as it is in the nature of weather. For as the nature of foul weather lieth not in a shower or two of rain, but in an inclination thereto of many days together, so the nature of war consisteth not in actual fighting, but in the known disposition thereto during all the time there is no assurance to the contrary. All other time is PEACE.

Whatsoever therefore is consequent to a time of war, where every man is enemy to every man, the same is consequent to the time wherein men live without other security than what their own strength and their own invention shall furnish them withal. In such condition there is no place for industry, because the fruit thereof is uncertain, and consequently, no culture of the earth, no navigation, nor use of the commodities that may be imported by sea, no commodious building, no instruments of moving and removing such things as require much force, no knowledge of the face of the earth, no account of time, no arts, no letters, no society, and which is worst of all, continual fear and danger of violent death, and the life of man, solitary, poor, nasty, brutish, and short.

It may seem strange, to some man that has not well weighed these things, that nature should thus dissociate, and render men apt to invade and destroy one another. And he may, therefore, not trusting to this inference made from the passions, desire perhaps to have the same confirmed by experience. Let him therefore consider with himself—when taking a journey, he arms himself, and seeks to go well accompanied; when going to sleep, he locks his doors; when even in his house, he locks his chests; and this when he knows there be laws, and public officers, armed, to revenge all injuries shall be done him—what opinion he has of his fellow subjects, when he rides armed; of his fellow citizens, when he locks his doors; and of his children and servants, when he locks his chests. Does he not there as much accuse mankind by his actions, as I do by my words? But neither of us accuse man's nature in it. The desires and other passions of man are in themselves no sin. No more are the actions that proceed from those passions, till they know a law that forbids them—which till laws be made they cannot know. Nor can any law be made, till they have agreed upon the person that shall make it.

It may peradventure be thought, there was never such a time nor condition of war as this; and I believe it was never generally so, over all the world. But there are many places where they live so now. For the savage people in many places of *America* (except the government of small families, the concord whereof dependeth on natural lust) have no government at all, and live at this day in that brutish manner as I said before. Howsoever, it may be perceived what manner of life there would be where there were no common power to fear, by the manner of life which men that have formerly lived under a peaceful government use to degenerate into, in a civil war.

But though there had never been any time wherein particular men were in a condition of war against another, yet in all times kings and persons of sovereign authority, because of their independency, are in continual jealousies and in the state and posture of gladiators, having their weapons pointing and their eyes fixed upon one another, that is, their forts, garrisons, and guns upon the frontiers of their kingdoms, and continual spies upon their neighbours, which is a posture of war. But because they uphold thereby the industry of their subjects, there does not follow from it that misery which accompanies the liberty of particular men.

To this war of every man against every man, this also is consequent: that nothing can be unjust. The notions of right and wrong, justice and injustice, have there no place. Where there is no common power, there is no law; where no law, no injustice. Force and fraud are in war the two cardinal virtues. Justice and injustice are none of the faculties neither of the body, nor mind. If they were, they might be in a man that were alone in the world, as well as his senses and passions. They are qualities that relate to men in society, not in solitude. It is consequent also to the same condition that there be no propriety, no dominion, no *mine* and *thine* distinct, but only that to be every man's that he can get, and for so long as he can keep it. And thus much for the ill condition which man by mere nature is actually placed in, though with a possibility to come out of it, consisting partly in the passions, partly in his reason.

The passions that incline men to peace are fear of death, desire of such things as are necessary to commodious living, and a hope by their industry to obtain them. And reason suggesteth convenient articles of peace, upon which men may be drawn to agreement. These articles are they which otherwise are called the Laws of Nature, whereof I shall speak more particularly in the two following chapters.

Of the First and Second Natural Laws and of Contracts

The RIGHT OF NATURE, which writers commonly call *jus naturale*, is the liberty each man hath to use his own power, as he will himself, for the preservation of his own nature, that is to say, of his own life, and consequently of doing anything which, in his own judgment and reason, he shall conceive to be the aptest means thereunto.

By LIBERTY is understood, according to the proper signification of the word, the absence of external impediments, which impediments may oft take away part of a man's power to do what he would, but cannot hinder him from using the power left him, according as his judgment and reason shall dictate to him.

A LAW OF NATURE (*lex naturalis*) is a precept or general rule, found out by reason, by which a man is forbidden to do that which is destructive of his life or taketh away the means of preserving the same, and to omit that by which he thinketh it may be best preserved. For though they that speak of this subject use to confound *jus* and *lex* (*right* and *law*), yet they ought to be distinguished, because RIGHT consisteth in liberty to do or to forbear, whereas LAW determineth and bindeth to one of them; so that law and right differ as much as obligation and liberty, which in one and the same matter are inconsistent.

And because the condition of man (as hath been declared in the precedent chapter) is a condition of war of everyone against everyone (in which case everyone is governed by his own reason and there is nothing he can make use of that may not be a help unto him preserving his life against his enemies), it followeth that in such a condition every man has a right to everything, even to one another's body. And therefore, as long as this natural right of every man to everything endureth, there can be no security to any man (how strong or wise soever he be) of living out the time which nature ordinarily alloweth men to live. And consequently it is a precept, or general rule, of reason *that every man ought to endeavour peace, as far as he has hope of obtaining it, and when he cannot obtain it, that he may seek and use all helps and advantages of war*. The first branch of which rule containeth the first and fundamental law of nature, which is *to seek peace, and follow it*. The second, the sum of the right of nature, which is *by all means we can, to defend ourselves*.

From this fundamental law of nature, by which men are commanded to endeavour peace, is derived this second law: *that a man be willing when others are so too, as far-fourth as for peace and defence of himself he shall think it necessary, to lay down this right to all things, and be contented with so much liberty against other men, as he would allow other men against himself*. For as long as every man holdeth this right of doing anything he liketh, so long are all men in the condition of war. But if other men will not lay down their right as well as he, then there is no reason for anyone to divest himself of his; for that were to expose himself to prey (which no man is bound to), rather than to dispose himself to peace. This is the law of the Gospel: "whatsoever you require that others should do to you, that do ye to them." And that law of all men: *quod tibi fieri non vis, alteri ne fecerisi.* . . .

Of Other Laws of Nature

. . . These dictates of reason men use to call by the name of laws, but improperly; for they are but conclusions or theorems concerning what conduceth to the conservation and defence of themselves, whereas law, properly, is the word of him that by right hath command over others. But yet if we consider the same theorems, as delivered in the word of God, that by right commandeth all things, then are they properly called laws.

THE FIRST AND
SECOND DISCOURSES
by
JEAN-JACQUES ROUSSEAU

This selection is excerpted from "The Second Discourse," also known as "Discourse on the Origin and Foundations of Inequality Among Men."

The first person who, having fenced off a plot of ground, took it into his head to say *this is mine* and found people simple enough to believe him, was the true founder of civil society. What crimes, wars, murders, what miseries and horrors would the human race have been spared by someone who, uprooting the stakes or filling in the ditch, had shouted to his fellow-men: Beware of listening to this impostor; you are lost if you forget that the fruits belong to all and the earth to no one! But it is very likely that by then things had already come to the point where they could no longer remain as they were. For this idea of property, depending on many prior ideas which could only have arisen successively, was not conceived all at once in the human mind. It was necessary to make much progress, to acquire much industry and enlightenment, and to transmit and augment them from age to age, before arriving at this last stage of the state of nature. Therefore let us start further back in time and attempt to assemble from a single point of view this slow succession of events and knowledge in their most natural order.

Man's first sentiment was that of his existence, his first care that of his preservation. The products of the earth furnished him with all the necessary help; instinct led him to make use of them. Hunger and other appetites making him experience by turns various manners of existing, there was one appetite that invited him to perpetuate his species; and this blind inclination, devoid of any sentiment of the heart, produced only a purely animal act. This need satisfied, the two sexes no longer recognized each other, and even the child no longer meant anything to his mother as soon as he could do without her.

Such was the condition of nascent man; such was the life of an animal limited at first to pure sensations and scarcely profiting from the gifts nature offered him, far from dreaming of wresting anything from it. But difficulties soon arose; it was necessary to learn to conquer them. The height of trees, which prevented him from reaching their fruits, the competition of animals that sought to nourish themselves with these fruits, the ferocity of those animals that wanted to take his very life, all obliged him to apply himself to bodily exercises. It was necessary to become agile, fleet in running, vigorous in combat. Natural arms, which are branches of trees and stones, were soon discovered at hand. He learned to surmount nature's obstacles, combat other animals when necessary, fight for his subsistence even with men, or make up for what had to be yielded to the stronger.

In proportion as the human race spread, difficulties multiplied along with men. Differences of soil, climate, and season could force them to admit differences in their ways of life. Barren years, long and hard winters, and scorching summers which consume everything required of them new industry. Along the sea and rivers they invented the fishing line and hook, and became fishermen and eaters of fish. In forests they made bows and arrows, and became hunters and warriors. In cold countries they covered themselves with the skins of beasts they had killed. Lightning, a volcano, or some happy accident introduced them to fire, a new resource against the rigor of winter. They learned to preserve this element, then to reproduce it, and finally to prepare with it meats they previously devoured raw.

This repeated utilization of various beings in relation to himself, and of some beings in relation to others, must naturally have engendered in man's mind perceptions of certain relations. Those relationships that we express by the words large, small, strong, weak, fast, slow, fearful, bold, and other similar ideas, compared when necessary and almost without thinking about it, finally produced in him some sort of reflection, or rather a mechanical prudence that indicated to him the precautions most necessary to his safety.

The new enlightenment that resulted from this development increased his superiority over the other animals by making him aware of his superiority. He practiced setting traps for them; he tricked them in a thousand ways; and although several surpassed him in strength at fighting, or in speed at running, of those which might serve him or hurt him he became with time the master of the former, and the scourge of the latter. Thus the first glance he directed upon himself produced in him the first stirring of pride; thus, as yet scarcely knowing how to distinguish ranks, and considering himself in the first rank as a species, he prepared himself from afar to claim first rank as an individual.

Although his fellow-men were not for him what they are for us, and although he scarcely had more intercourse with them than with other animals, they were not forgotten in his observations. The conformities that time could make him perceive among them, his female, and himself led him to judge of those which he did not perceive; and seeing that they all behaved as he would have done under similar circumstances, he concluded that their way of thinking and feeling conformed entirely to his own. And this important truth, well established in his mind, made him follow, by a premonition as sure as dialectic and more prompt, the best rules of conduct that it was suitable to observe toward them for his advantage and safety.

Taught by experience that love of well-being is the sole motive of human actions, he found himself able to distinguish the rare occasions when common interest should make him count on the assistance of his fellow-men, and those even rarer occasions when competition should make him distrust them. In the first case he united with them in a herd; or at most by some kind of free association that obligated no one and lasted only as long as the passing need that had formed it. In the second case, everyone sought to obtain his own advantage, either by naked force if he believed he could, or by cleverness and cunning if he felt himself to be the weaker.

That is how men could imperceptibly acquire some crude idea of mutual engagements and of the advantages of fulfilling them, but only insofar as present and perceptible interest could require; for foresight meant nothing to them, and far from being concerned about a distant future, they did not even think of the next day. Was it a matter of catching a deer, everyone clearly felt that for this purpose he ought faithfully to keep his post; but if a hare happened to pass within reach of one of them, there can be no doubt that he pursued it without scruple, and that having obtained his prey, he cared very little about having caused his companions to miss theirs.

It is easy to understand that such intercourse did not require a language much more refined than that of crows or monkeys, which group together in approximately the same way. For a long time inarticulate cries, many gestures, and some imitative noises must have composed the universal language; by joining to this in each country a few articulated and conventional sounds—the institution of which, as I have already said, is not too easy to explain—there were particular languages, but crude imperfect ones, approximately like those which various savage nations still have today.

I cover multitudes of centuries like a flash, forced by the time that elapses, the abundance of things I have to say, and the almost imperceptible progress of the beginnings; for the more slowly events followed upon one another, the more quickly they can be described.

These first advances finally put man in a position to make more rapid ones. The more the mind was enlightened, the more industry was perfected. Soon, ceasing to fall asleep under the first tree or to withdraw into caves, they discovered some kinds of hatchets of hard, sharp stones, which served to cut wood, scoop out earth, and make huts from branches they later decided to coat with clay and mud. This was the epoch of a first revolution, which produced the establishment and differentiation of families, and which introduced a sort of property—from which perhaps many quarrels and fights already arose. However, as the stronger were probably the first to make themselves lodgings they felt capable of defending, it is to be presumed that the weak found it quicker and safer to imitate them than to try to dislodge them; and as for those who already had huts, each man must seldom have sought to appropriate his neighbor's, less because it did not belong to him than because it was of no use to him, and because he could not seize it without exposing himself to a lively fight with the family occupying it.

The first developments of the heart were the effect of a new situation, which united husbands and wives, fathers and children in common habitation. The habit of living together gave rise to the sweetest sentiments known to men: conjugal love and paternal love. Each family became a little society all the better united because reciprocal affection and freedom were its only bonds; and it was then that the first difference was established in the way of life of the two sexes, which until this time had had but one. Women became more sedentary and grew accustomed to tend the hut and the children, while the man went to seek their common subsistence. The two sexes also began, by their slightly softer life, to lose something of their ferocity and vigor. But if each one separately became less suited to combat savage beasts, on the contrary it was easier to assemble in order to resist them jointly.

In this new state, with a simple and solitary life, very limited needs, and the implements they had invented to provide for them, since men enjoyed very great leisure, they used it to procure many kinds of commodities unknown to their fathers; and that was the first yoke they imposed on themselves without thinking about it, and the first source of the evils they prepared for their descendants. For, besides their continuing thus to soften body and mind, as these commodities had lost almost all their pleasantness through habit, and as they had at the same time degenerated into true needs, being deprived of them became much more cruel than possessing them was sweet; and people were unhappy to lose them without being happy to possess them.

At this point one catches a slightly better glimpse of how the use of speech was established or perfected imperceptibly in the bosom of each family; and one can conjecture further how particular causes could have spread language and accelerated its progress by making it more necessary. Great floods or earthquakes surrounded inhabited cantons with water or precipices; revolutions of the globe detached and broke up portions of the continent into islands. One conceives that among men thus brought together and forced to live together, a common idiom must have been formed sooner than among those who wandered freely in the forests on solid ground. Thus it is very possible that after their first attempts at navigation, islanders brought the use of speech to us; and it is at least very probable that society and languages came into being on islands and were perfected there before they were known on the continent.

Everything begins to change its appearance. Men who until this time wandered in the woods, having adopted a more fixed settlement, slowly come together, unite into different bands, and finally form in each country a particular nation, unified by customs and character, not by regulations and laws but by the same kind of life and foods and by the common influence of climate. A permanent proximity cannot fail to engender at length some contact between different families. Young people of different sexes live in neighboring huts; the passing intercourse demanded by nature soon leads to another kind no less sweet and more permanent through mutual frequentation. People grow accustomed to consider different objects and to make comparisons; imperceptibly they acquire ideas of merit and beauty which produce sentiments of preference. By dint of seeing one another, they can no longer do without seeing one another again. A tender and gentle sentiment is gradually introduced into the soul and at the least obstacle becomes an impetuous fury. Jealousy awakens with love; discord triumphs, and the gentlest of the passions receives sacrifices of human blood.

In proportion as ideas and sentiments follow upon one another and as mind and heart are trained, the human race continues to be tamed, contacts spread, and bonds are tightened. People grow accustomed to assembling in front of the huts or around a large tree; song and dance, true children of love and leisure, became the amusement or rather the occupation of idle and assembled men and women. Each one began to look at the others and to want to be looked at himself, and public esteem had a value. The one who sang or danced the best, the handsomest, the strongest, the most adroit, or the most eloquent became the most highly considered; and that was the first step toward inequality and, at the same time, toward vice. From these first preferences were born on one hand vanity and contempt, on the other shame and envy; and the fermentation caused by these new leavens eventually produced compounds fatal to happiness and innocence.

As soon as men had begun to appreciate one another, and the idea of consideration was formed in their minds, each one claimed a right to it, and it was no longer possible to be disrespectful toward anyone with impunity. From this came the first duties of civility, even among savages; and from this any voluntary wrong became an outrage, because along with the harm that resulted from the injury, the offended man saw in it contempt for his person which was often more unbearable than the harm itself. Thus, everyone punishing the contempt shown him by another in a manner proportionate to the importance he accorded himself, vengeances became terrible, and men bloodthirsty and cruel. This is precisely the point reached by most of the savage peoples known to us, and it is for want of having sufficiently distinguished between ideas and noticed how far these peoples already were from the first state of nature that many have hastened to conclude that man is naturally cruel, and that he needs civilization in order to make him gentler. On the contrary, nothing is so gentle as man in his primitive state when, placed by nature at equal distances from the stupidity of brutes and the fatal enlighten-ment of civil man, and limited equally by instinct and reason to protecting himself from the harm that threatens him, he is restrained by natural pity from harming anyone himself, and noth-ing leads him to do so even after he has received harm. For, according to the axiom of the wise Locke, *where there is no property, there is no injury*.

But it must be noted that the beginnings of society and the rela-tions already established among men required in them qualities different from those they derived from their primitive constitution; that, morality beginning to be introduced into human actions, and each man, prior to laws, being sole judge and avenger of the offens-es he had received, the goodness suitable for the pure state of nature was no longer that which suited nascent society; that it was neces-sary for punishments to become more severe as the occasions for offense became more frequent; and that it was up to the terror of revenge to take the place of the restraint of laws. Thus although men had come to have less endurance and although natural pity had already undergone some alteration, this period of development of human faculties, maintaining a golden mean between the indolence of the primitive state and the petulant activity of our vanity, must have been the happiest and most durable epoch. The more one thinks about it, the more one finds that this state was the least sub-ject to revolutions, the best for man (*p*), and that he must have come out of it only by some fatal accident, which for the common good ought never to have happened. The example of savages, who have almost all been found at this point, seems to confirm that the human race was made to remain in it always; that this state is the veritable prime of the world; and that all subsequent progress has been in appearance so many steps toward the perfection of the indi-vidual, and in fact toward the decrepitude of the species.

As long as men were content with their rustic huts, as long as they were limited to sewing their clothing of skins with thorns or fish bones, adorning themselves with feathers and shells, painting their bodies with various colors, perfecting or embellishing their bows and arrows, carving with sharp stones a few fishing canoes or a few crude musical instruments; in a word, as long as they applied themselves only to tasks that a single person could do and to arts that did not require the cooperation of several hands, they lived free, healthy, good, and happy insofar as they could be according to their nature, and they continued to enjoy among themselves the sweetness of independent intercourse. But from the moment one man needed the help of another, as soon as they observed that it was useful for a single person to have provisions for two, equality disappeared, property was introduced, labor became necessary; and vast forests were changed into smiling fields which had to be watered with the sweat of men, and in which slavery and misery were soon seen to germinate and grow with the crops.

Metallurgy and agriculture were the two arts whose invention produced this great revolution. For the poet it is gold and silver, but for the philosopher it is iron and wheat which have civilized men and ruined the human race. Accordingly, both of these were unknown to the savages of America, who therefore have always remained savage; other peoples even seem to have remained barbarous as long as they practiced one of these arts without the other. And perhaps one of the best reasons why Europe has been, if not earlier, at least more constantly and better civilized than the other parts of the world is that it is at the same time the most abundant in iron and the most fertile in wheat. It is very difficult to guess how men came to know and use iron; for it is not credible that by themselves they thought of drawing the raw material from the mine and giving it the necessary preparations to fuse it before they knew what would result. From another point of view, it is even harder to attribute this discovery to some accidental fire, because mines are formed only in arid spots, stripped of both trees and plants; so that one would say that nature had taken precautions to hide this deadly secret from us. There only remains, therefore, the extraordinary circumstance of some volcano which, by throwing up metallic materials in fusion, would have given observers the idea of imitating this operation of nature. Even so, it is necessary to suppose in them much courage and foresight to undertake such difficult labor and to envisage so far in advance the advantages they could gain from it: all of which hardly suits minds that are not already more trained than theirs must have been.

With regard to agriculture, its principle was known long before its practice was established, and it is hardly possible that men, constantly occupied with obtaining their subsistence from trees and plants, did not rather promptly have an idea of the ways used by nature to grow plants. But their industry probably turned in that direction only very late, either because trees, which along with hunting and fishing provided their food, did not have need of their care; or for want of knowing how to use wheat; or for want of implements to cultivate it; or for want of foresight concerning future need; or, finally, for want of means to prevent others from appropriating the fruit of their labor. Once they became industrious, it is credible that, with sharp stones and pointed sticks, they began by cultivating a few vegetables or roots around their huts long before they knew how to prepare wheat and had the implements necessary for large-scale cultivation. Besides, to devote oneself to that occupation and seed the land, one must be resolved to lose something at first in order to gain a great deal later: a precaution very far from the turn of mind of savage man, who, as I have said, has great difficulty thinking in the morning of his needs for the evening.

The invention of the other arts was therefore necessary to force the human race to apply itself to that of agriculture. As soon as some men were needed to smelt and forge iron, other men were needed to feed them. The more the number of workers was multiplied, the fewer hands were engaged in furnishing the common subsistence, without there being fewer mouths to consume it; and since some needed foodstuffs in exchange for their iron, the others finally found the secret of using iron in order to multiply foodstuffs. From this arose husbandry and agriculture on the one hand, and on the other the art of working metals and multiplying their uses.

From the cultivation of land, its division necessarily followed; and from property once recognized, the first rules of justice. For in order to give everyone what is his, it is necessary that everyone can have something; moreover, as men began to look to the future and as they all saw themselves with some goods to lose, there was not one of them who did not have to fear reprisals against himself for wrongs he might do to another. This origin is all the more natural as it is impossible to conceive of the idea of property arising from anything except manual labor; because one can not see what man can add, other than his own labor, in order to appropriate things he has not made. It is labor alone which, giving the cultivator a right to the product of the land he has tilled, gives him a right to the soil as a consequence, at least until the harvest, and thus from year to year; which, creating continuous possession, is easily transformed into property. When the ancients, says Grotius, gave Ceres the epithet of legislatrix, and gave the name of Thesmaphories to a festival celebrated in her honor, they thereby made it clear that the division of lands produced a new kind of right: that is, the right of property, different from the one which results from natural law.

Things in this state could have remained equal if talents had been equal, and if, for example, the use of iron and the consumption of foodstuffs had always been exactly balanced. But this proportion, which nothing maintained, was soon broken; the stronger did more work; the cleverer turned his to better advantage; the more ingenious found ways to shorten his labor; the farmer had greater need of iron or the blacksmith greater need of wheat; and working equally, the one earned a great deal while the other barely had enough to live. Thus does natural inequality imperceptibly manifest itself along with contrived inequality; and thus do the differences among men, developed by those of circumstances, become more perceptible, more permanent in their effects, and begin to have a proportionate influence over the fate of individuals.

Things having reached this point, it is easy to imagine the rest. I shall not stop to describe the successive invention of the other arts, the progress of languages, the testing and use of talents, the inequality of fortunes, the use or abuse of wealth, nor all the details that follow these, and that everyone can easily fill in. I shall simply limit myself to casting a glance at the human race placed in this new order of things.

Behold all our faculties developed, memory and imagination in play, vanity aroused, reason rendered active, and the mind having almost reached the limit of the perfection of which it is susceptible. Behold all the natural qualities put into action, the rank and fate of each man established, not only upon the quantity of goods and the power to serve or harm, but also upon the mind, beauty, strength, or skill, upon merit or talents. And these qualities being the only ones which could attract consideration, it was soon necessary to have them or affect them; for one's own advantage, it was necessary to appear to be other than what one in fact was. To be and to seem to be became two altogether different things; and from this distinction came conspicuous ostentation, deceptive cunning, and all the vices that follow from them. From another point of view, having formerly been free and independent, behold man, due to a multitude of new needs, subjected so to speak to all of nature and especially to his fellow-men, whose slave he becomes in a sense even in becoming their master; rich, he needs their services; poor, he needs their help; and mediocrity cannot enable him to do without them. He must therefore incessantly seek to interest them in his fate, and to make them find their own profit, in fact or in appearance, in working for his. This makes him deceitful and sly with some, imperious and harsh with others, and makes it necessary for him to abuse all those whom he needs when he cannot make them fear him and does not find his interest in serving them usefully. Finally, consuming ambition, the fervor to raise one's relative fortune less out of true need than in order to place oneself above others, inspires in all men a base inclination to harm each other, a secret jealousy all the more dangerous because, in order to strike its blow in greater safety, it often assumes the mask of benevolence: in a word, competition and rivalry on one hand, opposition of interest on the other; and always the hidden desire to profit at the expense of others. All these evils are the first effect of property and the inseparable consequence of nascent inequality.

PART TWO
PHILOSOPHY OF RELIGION

INTRODUCTION

by

WILLIAM DESMOND

I

Philosophy of religion, considered as a distinct philosophical specialty, seems to be a relatively recent invention. Perhaps it might be dated from around the end of the eighteenth century. An analogous invention might be "aesthetics," considered also as a distinct philosophical specialty (commonly attributed to the eighteenth-century philosopher Alexander Baumgarten). Not that philosophers were previously silent about art and beauty, or about the divine or God. Quite to the contrary, there is hardly a philosopher who did not in some way or other talk about God, even though none would have thought of themselves as specialists in the philosophy of religion. Similarly there is no aesthetics, say, in Plato, though he is deeply concerned with image and art and things aesthetic, and all of this in light of the pedagogic, psychological, metaphysical, political implications of art.

There is something striking about the invention of philosophy of religion as a speciality; this seems to have occurred around the time that religion itself was coming under unprecedented assault by some of the leading "avant-garde" intellectuals of the West. As intellectuals staked their claim for autonomy from theological supervision, and, on a scale hitherto unknown, took atheism as a respectable, indeed necessary position, philosophy of religion was born among the intellectuals. People fell out of love with the divine and their loss was reborn as theory about what they had lost, and perhaps its impossibility in the first place. Out of this was born a diversity of academic intellectual approaches toward the religious.

There is this further peculiarity about the philosophy of religion. One might think that if religion has any significance, it must have something to do with the whole of life. It cannot be constrained by the limits of a mere speciality. Is it possible, then, to have a speciality about something that potentially infiltrates the whole of our attitudes toward the meaning of being? One might well wonder if previous philosophers knew this, not primarily as a theme for reflection, but in their bones, so to say. Hence the impossibility of avoiding addressing, in some form or other, the enigma of the divine. Now one might well claim to be interested in philosophy of religion as an intellectual affair, and not hold to any religious belief about God, indeed be an atheist. Or one could be interested in religion as a human form, not in the divine or God as the ostensible "reality" addressed in that form, or addressing us through it. Once again: how can this more "holistic" implication or reference be squared with the limiting and determining frame imposed by any speciality?

Perhaps the question is analogous to one that might be put to philosophy itself. Though philosophy may have splintered into diverse academic specialities, is there not something about its quest that seeks to address our sense of the whole? How, then, can it be a specialty? Indeed does not such a "holistic" sense of philosophy show its affiliation with something similar to the religious as lived in full existential seriousness? If there is a genuine philosophical thinking on religion, can it be the specialty philosophy of religion?

Suppose one made a distinction, purely strategic I add, between two kinds of philosophers: call them the lovers and the theorists. Some philosophers will show more the character of lovers; others of theorists; still others will show complex minglings of the two. (Recall the word *theory* has its roots in the Greek *theoria,* which contains reference to those delegates sent to watch the sacred games at the religious festivals; this is the premodern sense of theory: celebrating vigilance at the sacred play of being. The modern *theory* is neutralized of these meanings.) The lovers are passionate in their search and speech; the theorists dispassionate and sober. The lovers love singularity and show it themselves; the theorists value universality and selfless understanding. Among the lovers one might number Plato, Augustine, Bonaventure, Blaise Pascal, Søren Kierkegaard, Friedrich Nietzsche; among theorists, Aristotle, Thomas Aquinas, René Descartes, Immanuel Kant, and Georg Wilhelm Friedrich Hegel. Of course, this distinction always needs qualification: thinkers without love are sterile, lovers without thought mindless. Philosophy is both: *philia* and *sophia*. Plato was a great thinker yet a philosopher of *eros*; Hegel, a great champion of systematic reason, was not devoid of a certain reverence.

And suppose something like this distinction is reflected in approaches to the philosophy of religion. When philosophy becomes concerned with religion without God, is this talk about love, without talk of the beloved? We are in love; analysis seems to petrify the passion; maybe the passion is already dead by the time analysis rears its head. When I am in love, I sing the beloved. When I analyze and ask if I am in love, I am no longer in love. I may even think I am now in a superior position, for after all, now I am in charge, putting the question. I am no longer intoxicated with my love. Am I in a better situation? Perhaps when I loved, then I was home. Now I am loveless, but I think I am in a better place. We search for clarity against ambiguity, but the search for clarity is itself ambiguous, so it drags its own lack of clarity with itself, lack of clarity about itself.

Think again of the analogy with art/aesthetics. I am inspired and sing great poems. I am no longer inspired, so I analyze. I might even come up with a theory that singing songs is impossible because it does not comport itself in accord with my logic. My song is degraded to a mistake, if not an impossibility. Again I am in love and in my love something is generated. I am not in love, and I make a theory to show that love is a mistake, an impossibility even. I am the eunuch preaching in the harem of the impossibility of *eros*. Is it so with some philosophers? Eunuchs for theory, eunuchs of theory? Think of religion as an intoxication with the divine. The feast is in full swing. The police knock on the door. What happens? Either the feast envelops them and they cease to be police. Or their presence induces a sobriety in which the festivity vanishes. Was the vanished festivity unreal? Truer to being as full, hyperbolic being, being as agape? Now in the vacancy, we spin our theories. Or in compensation we begin to conceive of ourselves as creators: think of aesthetics as the discipline that now creates new gods but these are called "creativity" or "genius" (in ethics "autonomy" is the god). But have we just made a false double of God? Our god, false, because without God? Our love, loveless, because without the beloved? Our thought, thoughtless, because bereft of, or tangential to, the fullness of being?

II

Let us now consider some of the influences shaping the place of religion in Western modernity. This discussion is not meant to be Eurocentric. The West, in some respects, is anomalous relative to the rest of the human family, and indeed relative to its own traditions. But the arm of its influence extends globally, and it is an important question to what extent the exportation of the characteristic ethos of science and technology, and the attitudes going with them, will not create elsewhere difficulties, certainly discomforts for religious orientations to being.

One might say that Western modernity shows a progressive process of stripping the world of the signs of the divine and its ambiguous communication to man. As being becomes more objectified, the less it provides the nurturing matrix for religious reverence. In tandem with this, we find an increasing recourse to our own powers to deal with this world in its qualitative poverty. We understand ourselves as seeking to be masters who can overcome its equivocal thereness. Once again, this our ascendancy seems to issue in a stifling of the communications of the divine. Whichever way we turn, the world seems to mirror back our own face to ourselves. Thus results what might be termed an ethos of humanistic autonomy, itself resulting then in deep difficulties in our being open to any transcendence as other to us.

In an earlier time, Augustine described his own journey to God in terms of a double movement: *ab exterioribus ad interiora, ab inferioribus ad superiora.* The soul moves from the exterior to the interior; then it must move from inferior to superior. We might improvise on this thought. Suppose we make the first move to ourselves in order to move beyond the lack of hard evidences in the outer world. Yet the inner to which we turn is itself equivocal. This turn to ourselves or the innerness of soul is indeed one of the major recourses of religion. The religious way says: in the deepest intimacy of the soul, the soul finds itself with a radical other: God. This is the superior. But now note: this turn to self might also seem to be the turn to our own power, which feels itself irritated with any acknowledgment of anything superior to itself. And so the seeds of a kind of usurpation are here contained also—even though the usurpation will call itself the release of genuine freedom and creativity. We make the claim to be both autonomous and transcending; we are autonomous transcendence itself. No man and no God above me, as Nietzsche exclaimed.

I illustrate this way by Descartes, who is considered by many to be the father of modern philosophy, and is famous for his turn to self in the argument: *cogito ergo sum* (I think, therefore I exist). The argument was already formulated by Augustine relative to the skeptics: *dubito ergo sum* (I doubt, therefore I exist). At one level, Descartes looks similar to Augustine, for in addition to proving the self in the *cogito* argument, he goes on to prove the existence of God. Is not this the movement from the inferior to the superior? But then we ask: which is the real foundation, or ultimate—self or God? Our suspicions are aroused when Descartes seems to use God as a means to certify our epistemological/cognitive confidence in a new mathematical science of nature/externality. When Augustine was asked what he sought to know, he said: God and the soul. *Nihilne plus* (nothing more)? Answer: *Nihil omnino* (nothing at all). In other words, the knowing of God was the *ne plus ultra*. With Descartes, we seem now to have God on our side as knowers, and so are emboldened to make ourselves "masters and possessors of nature," secure in a foundation grounding the new science as project to be completed through a myriad of experiments, and to yield tremendous practical benefits. We today are the beneficiaries of the success of that dream. But one still asks: Can God be used thus? Have we taken a fateful or fatal step outside fitting reverence, when God is thus used? And is not the self-perfection of our own power not then the superiority we project? Not God as the superior, but ourselves as creating ourselves at a higher level as superior being. *Voilà* the apparition of a kind of *Ubermensch*! The pious Descartes and the impious Nietzsche appear as blood brothers.

Misgiving were felt from the start. I cite the witness of a great mathematician and scientist, and great explorer of the labyrinth of the human heart. Thus Pascal: I cannot forgive Descartes; all he wanted from God was to give a little fillip to the world, and then he had no more need of God. Pascal should know. He could have been a greater Cartesian than the great Descartes himself, but he suspected the erosion of attention to the divine. And the result? Is it the hollow earth on which we have constructed a variety of crystal palaces, as Fyodor Dostoyevsky might suggest? Our hollow earth, in whose hollowness Nietzsche's shout about the death of God echoes and reechoes, until it becomes mere white noise, humming in the background of our postmodern chatter?

III

This double movement from exterior to interior, and from inferior to superior, is also reflected in attitudes toward the traditional proofs of God's existence. I speak here of a tradition often referred to as natural theology. The suggestion is that while our access to the supernatural is primarily through revelation, human beings might also make use of natural reason without any reference to revelation. The unaided use of reason is called upon to establish rationally the existence of God, regardless of our specific religious affiliation, or lack of it. Aquinas's five ways, or arguments, are perhaps the most well known: (1) from change in the world to the first unchanged mover; (2) from causality to the first uncaused cause; (3) from possibility or contingency in finite being to God as necessary being; (4) from gradations of perfection in the world to absolute perfection; (5) from the teleogy of things in nature to God as ultimate governance. Among the proofs Anselm's ontological way has also been of great interest. It has supposedly been refuted again and again, and yet also defended again and again by strong thinkers, and indeed reinvented in new guises, for instance by Benedict de Spinoza and Hegel.

Generally the first set of proofs is a posteriori, and dependent on evidences from the external world. By contrast, the second is a priori, at least in this sense of not being beholden to an evidentiary source external to ourself. The first look to the evidences of externality for signs that communicate some sense of a divine source. The second claims that the way is through what is most intensive in inwardness itself: what I would call the hyperbolic thought of God—the being greater than which none can be conceived. The claim is something like this: we come upon this hyperbolic thought in our immanent exploration of thought, and at its limit of self-knowing. The ontological proof is a way that, having turned toward interiority, seeks to make a transition from the inferior to the superior. We are the inferior, even in the inward infinity of our thinking; within that interiority there is an inescapable reference to what is more than us, infinitely more than us: God.

I am putting the point in a manner that might not always be granted about this proof. I mean the ontological argument is treated as a logical puzzle; in question is the logical validity of the deduction from the concept of God to God's existence, purely on the basis of the concept of God alone. But when Anselm first formulates the proof, very clearly he does so in an ethos of religious meditation: logic is embedded in a milieu of prayer. Anselm is a lover first and a theorist second. This is not quite so in the modern reformulation, say in Descartes and Kant. The ethos of thought now is more geometrical, mathematical, rather than meditative prayer. Not surprisingly, the concept of God is considered on the analogy to the triangle. Inherent in the definition of a triangle is the necessary truth that its three angles together constitute 180 degrees; from the concept it cannot be otherwise. So with the concept of God: it cannot be other than that God must exist; for the concept of the most perfect being must necessarily include existence. Once we understand the concept either of a triangle or God, we know what is necessarily implied by this. God as the necessary being or the perfect being is similar: once we understand the concept of absolute necessity or perfection, it follows it must exist.

Kant claims that all we here have is an analysis of a concept. Such an analysis will always deal with possibility; it will not get you to existence; there is a gap between concept and existence that cannot be bridged by mere conceptual analysis. The ontological proof provides us with a conceptual analysis of the idea of God. If God exists, then he is necessary; but it gives us no rationally necessary evidence that he does exist. Indeed in the world we cannot find such evidence, for God is not a finite and determinate object. God transcends possible experience; and we are not allowed so to transcend it—at least not transcend and claim rational cognitive certainty for claims made about what is beyond experience. A hundred possible thalers and a hundred real thalers do not differ in concept; but there is a world of a difference between the two, which cannot be bridged by concepts alone. Kant claims that since all the other proofs, seemingly a posteriori, reduce to the ontological, they too lack the rational cogency claimed.

Kant is often seen as a destroyer, but mainly he seems intent on destroying the self-certainty of rationalist metaphysicians and with instruments he learned to perfection in the school of the rationalists. He offers us a different way to God—through our moral being. The version of the ontological proof he attacks can be seen as a version of a kind of logicist inner way; but might one take the moral way also as a variant of the "inner" way? It too suggests an effort to move from the inferior to the superior—on the basis of what is implied by our moral being. Something unconditional comes to emergence in our moral being, something not to be found in the evidences of externality; on the basis of this moral unconditional, a way can be found to affirm God as a postulate demanded by our moral being.

This suggests a noncognitive approach to God. Dare to know! exclaims the enlightener Kant. But then it turns out we cannot know very much! Does the bang then become a whimper? For it is not quite that Kant finally becomes a lover rather than a theorist. For moral duty surpasses theory and love for him, and he resists the abandon of love as perhaps too equivocal, too dangerous to the rationalistic conscience in his intellectual blood. His Enlightenment motto Dare to know! does not become Dare to love!

Kant's critique of the traditional proofs has been taken as definitive. But is this so? Not quite. As formulated in the ethos of modernity, it conceives of nature in terms of Newtonian mechanism, where at most we might make a plausible inference from the machine to the machine maker. In his *Third Critique* Kant moves in a somewhat different direction to rethink nature in some qualified teleological terms. But as I said, the ethos of his thought lies quite far from Anselm. As it is also from the ethos of thought of Aquinas. I will confine myself to one major point. Nature here is not a machine. The scholastic philosophers argued like forensic lawyers; but beneath the surface of disputatious univocity, there often is more at work. Aquinas's attunement to the being of the world is redolent, though hesitantly named so, of the glory of creation. The world is a creation and communicates the glorious, albeit initially ambiguous, signs of the creator. His third way, the way from possible being, later called the proof from contingency, hangs on the fact that the world is a happening that carries no self-explanation. It is, but it might not be; there is no inherent necessity that it must be. It is a happening that happens to be, but the happening as happening points to being beyond contingency that is the source or ground of happening. This he names God.

One might say that if this has any power, it is not just as a logical argument, but presupposes openness to the ontological enigma of the "that it is" of beings. Astonishment at the sheer being there of the world, its givenness as given into being; not the "what" of beings, but the that of being at all. This is at the edge of determinate science and more akin to religious reverence or aesthetic appreciation—perhaps a kind of unknowing love. What can we say about Aquinas the theorist? His theories might seem as thin as the arguments of forensic lawyers, when we have no sense of the living concern at stake, and this last has to do with secret loves. Pascal suggests something like this: when we are reflecting on the arguments, we might be intellectually engaged, but a few minutes later they are out of mind and we forget them. But this is also to forget the love that remains secret in the arguments.

And don't the proofs, or better "ways," have their own source in a variety of different forms of metaphysical astonishment? Consider the argument from design: does it not grow out of metaphysical astonishing at the aesthetic marvel of the happening of the world? Or consider our great perplexity at the great anomaly of the excess of human transcending. We are self-surpassing beings; but is this an excess overreaching into emptiness or into something other? Consider the way Kant tried to canonize our moral being; isn't this seeded in the great wonder of our sense of unconditional good? These all suggest what one might call hyperboles of being: happenings excessive to complete finite determination, and yet about which we must think as philosophers, and in whose excess perhaps our unknowing love of being already moves.

Kant wanted to avoid both materialism and pantheism. Hence his desire to retain the gap between God and the world. Inevitably, the ways to God were conceived as a bridging inference or deduction that would get you from the immanent world to a transcendent deity. The ontological proof claimed to do this by deduction; the other proofs by evidential inference from being as here given, or from significant aspects of the world. The gap remains on both approaches: the first cannot move from concept to existence by means of concepts alone; the second might establish some persuasive case, but no necessarily compelling proof. At most we might establish that God is the architect of the world (physico-theological proof), but this falls short of the full reality attributed to the absolute God of monotheism, including of course God's goodness. The moral way offers us the immanence of something unconditional: the moral law. On this basis a move to the divine as unconditional is charted.

Already in Kant's time, reaction to the mechanical worldview was strong enough to demand a way of immanence that was more than moral. So we find the upsurgence of pantheism and also concern with the sublime. This latter concern is also a very postmodern one, though its earlier religious resonances are now aestheticized, hence stripped of something of its previous spiritual seriousness. Does this interest in the sublime reflect a crossing of the divide between lovers and theorists? Does pantheism, and its more current variant panentheism, try to unite both? Think of Spinoza as reflecting the doubleness. He claimed to philosophize more geometrically, and initially was excoriated as an atheist or materialist; though he spoke of the one substance as God or nature. And then in the revival of Spinozism later in the eighteenth century, he was baptized anew by Novalis as the God-intoxicated man. Pan(en)theism and philosophies of the sublime reject the merely quantitative world of mechanism for the more qualitative world of organism. The organism shows signs of immanent life and vitality and becoming. Think of God thus, and we do not have the anorexic transcendence of mechanism and deism. We have an immanent vitalizing principle, a more inherent principle of life such as we find within the organism. So the world seems more like an organism, a living totality. (Something like this is resurrected today, say, in the Gaia hypothesis.) We do not need "proofs"; there is no gulf of immanence and transcendence to be negotiated by inference or deduction. We need the exploration of the divine in immanence itself. Hence we find the resurgence of the ontological proof, but now it is transformed from merely rational deduction from a concept into an exemplification of what is said to be most fundamental in all being.

Thus we come to Hegel: against the mechanical sign that points to an external machine maker, we are to think the God of the whole. The sign of God is the absolute organism as a living totality that contains its own principle of becoming within itself. Beyond external dualism, we are asked to see the immanence of God in the whole. Pantheism is often associated with a nature that is outside history. By contrast, Hegel incorporates the emphasis on time and history we find in the biblical religions: the story has a beginning and an end, and it is in the end that we will find the fullness. Hegel gives us a kind of historicist panentheism (not any simple pantheism, but the view that everything is contained in God). This more general panentheism continues to be popular in postevolutionary times, as in, say, process philosophy (shorn of Hegel's grander vision). After the chastening of Kantian critique, philosophical thought is emboldened to reach out to the whole; and why not if we can determine the meaning of what is other to ourselves?

Nevertheless, such an overreaching of reason, such as we find in Hegel, seems to have produced a different chastening that leads all the way from Kierkegaard to different forms of postmodernism. In the contrast of Hegel and Kierkegaard, have we again the difference of theorist and lover? Yes and no. Hegel will affirm the ontological argument, and generalize it by saying that thinking and being cannot be sundered. Kierkegaard will demur, and most passionately relative to God: to think God philosophically, and to be religious, are not one and the same. To be religious requires more than thought; it requires the singularity of an adventure that takes us to the limits of thought, and indeed beyond, insofar as God is more than the measure of human intelligibility.

There is also the fact that these chastenings after the overreaching of idealism also produced other forms of nonrational overreachings. While we find an anti-idealist but religious chastening in Kierkegaard, we find an anti-idealist and, in certain respects, an antireligious chastening in Nietzsche. We also find a different overreaching, which veers in the direction of a more rhapsodic amoral pantheism. If Nietzsche seems to be the progenitor of the postmodern self, the old God may be said to be dead, but a new god dances toward the empty throne, or slouches.

IV

The distinction between the lovers and theorizers has a point relative to the excess of evil. Passionately the lovers cry out: the waters rise to our necks; show us your face; if not, curse the darkness. Calmly the theorists seek to restore order, to rationalize the appearance of scandal and transform it into a harmonious whole. Justifications of God by the rationalizers in the face of evil are often identified with the theodicies. Yet the lovers too seek their theodicy, in the living sense of seeking the justice of divine ways in a world often dark.

If there are evidences of God, they are not univocal. The hyperboles of being are also perilously equivocal. And there are negative hyperboles—most evident in our involvement with evil. Think, for instance, how David Hume turns around the argument from design. The arguments suggests: as the artwork is to the artist, or the watch to the watchmaker, so is the world to God. But if the artwork or watch or world is badly made, what does this say about the maker? Bad pot, bad potter. Chaotic world, what god? Malign deity? Or perhaps benign but incompetent? Or a mere apprentice? Or a deity who expired a long time ago, but his botched work outlives him and here we sit in the mess? Sometimes we are so overwhelmed by the presence of evil that we wonder if it is Descartes's malign genius that rules and confuses the sublunary world.

Evil is a great enigma, and yet it is incontrovertible. One might even wonder if our time, having a diminished sense of the mysterious otherness of the good, of God, turns to evil as a last frontier of mystery. For whatever evil is, it is something resisting easy conceptualization or rationalization. Often it has been seen as the great stumbling block to trust in God, or faith. But perhaps the perplexity actually becomes more enigmatic and intractable for those who strain to hold on to this trust.

There are complications also in an age dominated by science and technology, such as ours. If we love, we seem to inhabit one world, one charged with signs of the beloved; if we rationalize, we stand over against another world, a colder, seemingly more neutral thereness. Consider: Earlier peoples have been said to inhabit a world that was not a neutral "It" but more like a "Thou"—peopled with divine or sometimes malign powers that were more or less like us, only more powerful. Now we are supposed to inhabit the world as neutrally there. I am sick, but I go to my doctor, not my shaman; my sickness is scientific, not expiatory. The crops fail or an earthquake convulses the country, but we do not accuse our political leaders of degeneracy; instead we calculate it as the outcome of indifferent forces. Even if we call a catastrophe an Act of God, we mean nothing religious. We mean something incalculable, yes, but indifferently incalculable, not charged with the meaning of religious punishment. Nature is an organization of univocal, impersonal forces, not an ambiguous community of personalized powers. But if the universe thus loses some of its terror, it also loses its mysterious intimacy. It ceases to arouse religious reverence and is made an object of scientific curiosity and technological exploitation.

What, then, of evil? Scientifically now we seem to inhabit this world of an "It." But do we live it thus, can we? Is there still, so to say, the submerged archaic self? And traces of the old tangle of chaos and terror and mystery? I am subjected to unmerited misfortune or senseless sickness. At a certain extreme I buckle and utter a question that is senseless, scientifically speaking: "Why me?" Can we make sense scientifically of the fact that we humans are the only animals who knowingly shake our fists at the empty sky? Let science have its full say; but does the battered heart still reach farther, or stretch out only to a heartless universe?

This is an elemental question. Must we make some reference to the religious heart to make any sense of it? But even were that so, does it not also show the worm of doubt stirring within the heart of religion itself? What follows? One might call it a dialectic of trust and distrust. Even then, the matter can be approached differently by what broadly we might term the realist and the idealist. The realist claims not to flinch before the brute resistance of things; the idealist takes pride in not being arrested by the same resistance. The idealist wistfully yearns: "Perhaps, perhaps. It is not yet, but it ought to be! I dream, I dream . . ." The realist rudely retorts: "This is so! Wake up, you wistful innocent! I told you so!" The idealist points us beyond to a hidden heaven; the realist reminds us with sweet glee that life here is hell.

Of course, the realist swaggers like the metaphysical tough, but doesn't the idealist have a more difficult part? It is easier to deflate every extravagant desire, to jibe at every "ought" not yet realized, to prick every intimation of unseen otherness. The realist points out our descent from apes but does not help us take wing with angels. But are not many religions different ways of gathering up our idealistic zeal? Each has its glimpse of paradise, its picture of perfection, its anticipation of Elysian fields, its *Tir na nOg.* "God" sometimes names an extremity in our efforts to picture perfection. True, idealism becomes saccharine without the realistic principle. To be credible, a religion needs its devil's advocate. And so it is inevitably shaped in the tension between realism and idealism. Besides heaven, there is hell; besides salvation, sin; besides Eden, the sticky jungle of the lapsed world. Indeed many religions, in trying to incorporate the realistic principle, have difficulty in preserving the divine unstained.

So we come round to evil again. The most radical form of the difficulty is this: if God is good, why does evil seem rampant? Religions have tried various ways, theodicies again, of giving God an "alibi." Is any completely convincing? We seem caught in conflict between the idealistic and realistic ways. Sometimes the realistic principle will win: we postpone the ideal to an always elsewhere heaven; meanwhile the world remains defiled, to be dominated with contempt. Without the bitter savor of salt, an untempered idealism cannot win; defeat is part of our lot, an episode in our education. But a cynical realism too is defeat, passing itself off as the voice of weary experience. An enduring idealism must endure defeat.

Religions respond to evil by seeking to transcend the condition of metaphysical distrust by a deeper or higher trust. We know the precariousness of our finitude in the middle. The love of being in our own being, when threatened, can turn into opposition to being in the being of the other. The lamb does not trust the lion, the hen the fox, the fly the spider. Animals betray this distrust either by fleeing their enemies or devouring their prey. In the animal kingdom there are no idealists, hence no religions. But with us religion is one of the most crucial ways of responding to metaphysical distrust. Some religious attitudes just give vent to this distrust; they hate the earth, realistically recognized, for not being their ideal heaven, dreamed of unrealistically. Other religious attitudes seek to overcome the distrust not by fleeing the real but by trying to realize the ideal, loving the earth for its promise, even in the frailty of its grandeur. The human being alone has religion, for it alone mindfully contends against metaphysical distrust, struggles against this condition of its own being, to transmute it into its opposite.

This dialectic of trust and distrust can be expressed in more abstract philosophical form or in mythic terms. By way of illustration, consider the thought of Gottfried Wilhelm Leibniz. Here we find a metaphysical "idealism," not without a certain plausibility in logic, producing unparalleled theological optimism. Leibniz held that God, in his infinite wisdom, and out of all the possibilities open to him, created the best of all possible worlds. Given God's goodness and omnipotence, what God made must be good. Even though we cannot see as God sees, from God's vantage point the world must be maximally good. What seems evil to us is like the shadow in a beautiful painting—necessary to the light, contrast, and harmony of the whole, and so from the standpoint of the whole (God's standpoint), good. Leibniz's *Theodicy* became one of the most celebrated works of its time. But in 1756 there occurred an Act of God: the famous earthquake of Lisbon, the great catastrophe that shook the satisfied minds of the time. Later Voltaire was to contemplate this disaster in juxtaposition with Leibniz's optimal assessment of things. The famous results was *Candide*, another work that attained celebrated status. This dual celebrity of *Theodicy* and *Candide* underscores our double nature: we dream the absolute dream that is God and doubt that same dream. The best of all possible worlds contains incalculable suffering, the grief of which no idealistic metaphysical theory can conjure away. We try to comfort someone in distress, but there are times when to say, "All is for the best, God knows," borders on the blasphemous. And yet we struggle to say, "It is good."

The difficulty is traditionally put this way. Is there a lack of congruence between God's goodness and power? God is held to be both omnipotent and absolutely good. Yet the persistent recalcitrance of evil causes us to wonder if God is impotent to prevent what to us is so appalling. Since he is omnipotent, how can he tolerate the evil so opposite to his nature? If he is all-good, he seems powerless; if all-powerful, he seems heartless.

This is an abstract way of putting the problem. There are older, more imaginative ways. Thus earlier peoples, naming the perplexing mixture of power and goodness, named the Wrath of God. We sup on a milkier diet, think of sweet goodness, and forget the awful majesty of incomprehensible power. Our ancestors tasted acid. Even the highest power has a terrible, dark side. This they called the Wrath of God. Just and unjust seem indiscriminately destroyed, without any reckoning of merits. In the Lisbon earthquake many perished in the churches, while those in the brothels were preserved. Must we choose, then, between power without goodness and goodness without power?

The traditional theodicies tried to think God in terms of the unity of power and goodness. In modernity generally, power has often been dissociated from the good, and indeed the inherent hospitality of being to goodness has not often been granted. We then risk an image of God as all-powerful but with a face perhaps too uncomfortably close to unlitateral, arbitrary power, that is, to the tyrant. So with natural catastrophes we sometimes speak of the "tyranny of things." And then there are those human beings who will themselves to become the Wrath of God: they willfully pursue sheer power and end up as rulers lacking in justice, that is, tyrants. Indeed a contributing factor to modern skepticism concerning religion is a perceived likeness of tyranny and God's power. A domineering heteronomy seems to squash our claim to autonomy. We choose our own self-transcendence over divine transcendence as other.

I will mention two responses to this difficulty of power and goodness. One is the Kantian response that tries to moralize God: our experience of the moral unconditional points a way to God as ground of the moral law. Despite the calm surface of reason, Kant was engaged with evil in the scandalous disjunction between virtue and happiness. The other is the Nietzschean response: the Kantian moral world order is rejected as an idealistic superimposition of the amoral flux of things, what Nietzsche calls the innocence of becoming. We must move beyond good and evil. But then Nietzsche's name for the ultimate is will to power. Thus we end up with power without inherent goodness, and at most, the values we impose on the flux, values themselves ultimately groundless. The cure of nihilism seems itself another mutant of nihilism.

It seems we must rethink the dialectic of trust and mistrust. How? Revisit the hospitality of being to the good, and the ground of affiliation of goodness and power. How revisit? Perhaps with new philosophical openness to religious reverence. For reverence is a happening of love before the worthy other; in it we are given some intimation of the hospitality of being and the goodness of power.

V

Where does that leave us? Theorists or lovers? If theorists, we may perhaps retain a certain equilibrium, but at the cost of forgetting something of the urgency of ultimacy at issue in being religious. If lovers, we remember the urgency but risk forfeiting sober lucidity. The best thinkers seek the point of balance of both: mindfulness of the urgency of ultimacy.

Is it a bit outdated to mention thinkers like Kant, Hegel, Nietzsche? Do we not inhabit postmodern times? But the seeds of our times are in these thinkers. My point is not to endorse them, but to recall something of their spiritual and intellectual seriousness, and the impasses their thinking suggests. To some postmoderns, Nietzsche is almost a saint. It is true that his cry of the death of God has crossed a mutation barrier of familiarity, and passed over into the limbo zone of postmodern kitsch. But we should ask ourselves: is this because we are lovers or rationalizers; or perhaps neither? The passionate spirit of a Nietzsche is to be honored, as is the passion of thought of the great heros of reason. We seem neither able to give ourselves over to the passion of reason, for we distrust it; nor able to give ourselves over to a love of what exceeds us, because we suspect it of being too grand, or unworthy of us. The superiority of our being blasé might be our inferiority. Both seem too much for us. Nietzsche speaks of the last men: "what is longing?" asks the last man and blinks; "what is a star?" asks the last man and blinks. What do we say now? In the modest spiritual lowlands of our times, has the last man triumphed? And triumphed by reading Nietzsche? Do we need a divine madness to wake us from the enchantments he has cast?

Of course, in many respects the atheist is a very modern phenomenon, possible only after the biblical religions depopulated the world of gods. There are no gods; there is only the One God. The One God is everywhere and nowhere, and in Christianity incarnated as a singular self—at once, absolute pure spirit and a paradoxical fleshed absolute. What if nature is depopulated of gods, and the remaining One cannot be imaged? Divinity loses its intimacy with the external world. And while divinity may instead take up dwelling in the inner self, the outside world seems silenced and an uncanny emptiness comes to reign. It is only a few steps from this depopulation of the world of gods to the ascetic Christian war on dedivinized nature. It is only a few more steps from a Christian war on the world to an un-Christian war. If there is nothing to be reverenced in external otherness, what is to hold the human self back from unleashing its brutal impulses on it? Christianity did restrain, not by a god in the external world but by a God superior to the world and self. It also restrained because the superior spoke to the interior self and could take up abode in the inner temple. What happens if the inner God is felt to vanish like the outer? The inner self ceases to be a temple and goes the same way as the pagan gods previously conquered. The self becomes a cold, abandoned sanctuary. We are left with the dark gropings of the psyche inside, the blind forces of an indifferent nature outside, and the meaningless collision of the two. The technological hubris of a secular will to power pillages the disenchanted earth, unmindful of any piety of the whole. We lack this redeeming feature of the religious—its reverence.

Religions are not themselves guiltless. At the beginnings of modernity the war of Christians with each other did much to make thoughtful persons wonder whether the urgency of ultimacy had turned into madness, and whether we ought to turn away from its religious form or make antireligious war on it. In the Enlightenment and its wake, Christianity has come under strong criticism, some of which involves it own self-deconstruction. Some thinkers, like Karl Marx, repudiate its supposedly otherworldly side, and more recently they have been joined by some Christians, under the banner of liberation theology. Other thinkers, rationalists not revolutionaries, have fought Christianity's resistance to modern science. Others have struggled with its ascetic spirit and its suspicions of things bodily. Still others have taken issue with its sometimes ambivalent attitude toward art, and in neopagan fashion tried to reinstate the poet as a kind of priest; the aestheticism of modernity harbors a not so secret religious strain. And again ironically, it has been the sons of German pastors, Nietzsche especially, who have done the most to disturb Christianity, especially Protestantism in its self-assurance. No mingling of pagan and Christian, but rather war on the Christian; Dionysus versus the Crucified! He reminded us of an old pagan truth: gods without tie with the earth become anemic and wither away.

Must we then endorse some new paganism? It is not so simple, for we know there are other reversals. The same energy of our transcending that moves us in the space of the holy is also the source of our restless questioning. We eat of the tree promising knowledge, and eventually come to wonder about the reverse possibility. We spread our wings for a new flight, daring to pride ourselves, like the modern Prometheans, with being the absolute original; but in turning away from the originating experience of the holy, we risk the dying of the light though we call this death Enlightenment. Is postmodernity now waking up to this death?

If there is no simple going back to the first immediate thereness of the sacred, can one pass through Ezekiel's valley of dry bones? Can one be returned to being as sign of the divine, but at a different level of intermediated mindfulness? If so, such mindfulness would not be any debunking humanism that now tires us. Nor any nostalgic return behind complexly differentiated self-consciousness that would sacrifice its troubled mind for thoughtless immersion in the flow of images. Does some presentiment of ultimacy disclose itself, ambiguously but plurivocally, in this flow? Patient mindfulness here is no unreflective immersion in images of the sacred but finesse in reading the signs of their flow. With their grand flowerings of profound sacred images, great religions are born, develop, and die. But ontological perplexity is perennial. The sense of sacred mystery gives religious expression to this perplexity, which, though mythic imagination ages, always cries for reawakening to a deeper metaphysical mindfulness.

This also demands alertness to the anemia of being religious in technological societies. The cry "God is dead" is a poignant ejaculation in a vanishing, or amnesia, centuries old. We forget that what such plaints concentrate has also long had an essentially religious meaning: the necessity of passing through forsakenness, abandonment, nothingness to become properly mindful of the divine. The twentieth century has known repeatedly the harrowing of hell, so deeply it seems we have lost the hope of it as a penitential prelude. Distrust dominates in the dialectic with trust. But we are not pioneers in the dark born of religious destitution. And yet we seem to have lost the memory of such night symbols. Like the bemused spectators sniggering at bewilderment of Nietzsche's Madman, we become blandly, even chirpily at ease with the desolation. There is no desolation. We are having a nice day, though it might be the dead of night. Though the times may not be ripe, can mindfulness ready itself? In bleak times religious mindfulness will still break out. Its dissidence in our univocalized, instrumentalized world cannot be entirely ground under. Be we theorists or lovers, do we have to be just foolish virgins?

CONFESSIONS
AUGUSTINE

L et me know Thee, O Lord, who knowest me; let me know Thee, as I am known. Power of my soul, enter into it, and fit it for Thee, that Thou mayest have and hold it without spot or wrinkle. This is my hope, therefore do I speak, and in this hope do I rejoice, when I rejoice healthfully. Other things of this life are the less to be sorrowed for, the more they are sorrowed for; and the more to be sorrowed for, the less men sorrow for them. For behold, Thou lovest the truth, and he that doth it, cometh to the light. This would I do in my heart before Thee in confession: and in my writing, before many witnesses.

And from Thee, O Lord, unto whose eyes the abyss of man's conscience is naked, what could be hidden in me though I would not confess it? For I should hide Thee from me, not me from Thee. But now, for that my groaning is witness, that I am displeased with myself, Thou shinest out, and art pleasing, and beloved, and longed for; that I may be ashamed of myself, and renounce myself, and choose Thee, and neither please Thee nor myself, but in Thee. To Thee therefore, O Lord, am I open, whatever I am; and with what fruit I confess unto Thee, I have said. Nor do I it with words and sounds of the flesh, but with the words of my soul, and the cry of the thought which Thy ear knoweth. For when I am evil, then to confess to Thee is nothing else than to be displeased with myself; but when holy, nothing else than not to ascribe it to myself: because Thou, O Lord, blessest the godly, but first Thou justifiest him when ungodly. My confession then, O my God, in Thy sight, is made silently, and not silently. For in sound, it is silent; in affection, it cries aloud. For neither do I utter any thing right unto men, which Thou has not before heard from me; nor dost Thou hear any such thing from me, which Thou has not first said unto me . . .

Not with doubting, but with assured consciousness, do I love Thee, Lord. Thou hast stricken my heart with Thy word, and I loved Thee. Yea also heaven and earth, and all that therin is, behold on every side they bid me love Thee; nor cease to say so unto all, that they may be without excuse. But more deeply wilt Thou have mercy on whom Thou wilt have mercy, and wilt have compassion on whom Thou hast had compassion: else in deaf ears do the heaven and the earth speak Thy praises. But what do I love, when I love Thee? Not beauty of bodies, nor the fair harmony of time, nor the brightness of the light, so gladsome to our eyes, nor sweet melodies of varied songs, nor the fragrant smell of flowers, and ointments, and spices, not manna and honey, not limbs acceptable to embracements of flesh. None of these I love, when I love my God; and yet I love a kind of light, and melody, and fragrance, and meat, and embracement when I love my God, the light, melody, fragrance, meat, embracement of my inner man: where there shineth unto my soul what space cannot contain and there soundeth what time beareth not away, and there smelleth what breathing disperseth not, and there tasteth what eating diminisheth not, and there clingeth what satiety divorceth not. This is it which I love when I love my God.

And what is this? I asked the earth, and it answered me, "I am not He"; and whatsoever are in it confessed the same. I asked the sea and the deeps, and the living creeping things, and they answered, "We are not Thy God, seek above us." I asked the moving air; and the whole air with his inhabitants answered, "Anaximenes was deceived, I am not God." I asked the heavens, sun, moon, stars, "Nor (say they) are we the God whom thou seekest." And I replied unto all the things which encompass the door of my flesh: "Ye have told me of my God, that ye are not He; tell me something of Him." And they cried out with a loud voice, "He made us." My questioning them, was my thoughts on them: and their form of beauty gave the answer. And I turned myself unto myself, and said to myself, "Who art thou?" And I answered, "A man." And behold, in me there present themselves to me soul, and body, one without, the other within. By which of these ought I to seek my God? I had sought Him in the body from earth to heaven, so far as I could send messengers, the beams of mine eyes. But the better is the inner, for to it as presiding and judging, all the bodily messengers reported the answers of heaven and earth, and all things therein, who said, "We are not God, but He made us." These things did my inner man know by the ministry of the outer: I the inner knew them; I, the mind, through the senses of my body. I asked the whole frame of the world about my God; and it answered me, "I am not He, but He made me."

Is not this corporeal figure apparent to all whose senses are perfect? Why then speaks it not the same to all? Animals small and great see it, but they cannot ask it: because no reason is set over their senses to judge on what they report. But men ask, so that the invisible things of God are clearly seen, being understood by the things that are made; but by love of them, they are made subject unto them: and subjects cannot judge. Nor yet do the creatures answer such as ask, unless they can judge: nor yet do they change their voice (i.e., their appearance), if one man only sees, another seeing asks, so as to appear one way to this man, another way to that; but appearing the same way to both, it is dumb to this, speaks to that; yea rather it speaks to all; but they only understand, who compare its ovice received from without, with the truth within. For truth saith unto me, "Neither heaven, nor earth, nor any other body is thy God." This, their very nature saith to him that seeth them: "They are a mass; a mass is less in a part thereof than in the whole." Now to thee I speak, O my soul, thou art my better part: for thou quickenest the mass of my body, giving it life, which no body can give to a body: but thy God is even unto thee the Life of thy life.

What then do I love, when I love my God? Who is He above the head of my soul? By my very soul will I ascend to Him. I will pass beyond that power whereby I am united to my body, and fill its whole frame with life. Nor can I by that power find my God; for so horse and mule that have no understanding, might find Him; seeing it is the same power, whereby even their bodies live. But another power there is, not that only whereby I animate, but that too whereby I imbue with sense my flesh, which the Lord hath framed for me: commanding the eye not to hear, and the ear not to see; but the eye, that through it I should see, and the ear, that through it I should hear; and to the other senses severally, what is to each their own peculiar seats and offices; which, being divers, I the one mind, do through them enact. I will pass beyond this power of mine also; for this also have the horse and mule, for they also perceive through the body.

I will pass then beyond this power of my nature also, rising by degrees unto Him who made me. And I come to the fields and spacious palaces of my memory, where are the treasures of innumerable images, brought into it from things of all sorts perceived by the senses. There is stored up, whatsoever besides we think, either by enlarging or diminishing, or any other way varying those things which the sense hath come to; and whatever else hath been committed and laid up, which forgetfulness hath not yet swallowed up and buried. When I enter there, I require what I will to be brought forth, and something instantly comes; others must be longer sought after, which are fetched, as it were, out of some inner receptacle; others rush out in troops, and while one thing is desired and required, they start forth, as who should say, "Is it perchance I?" These I drive away with the hand of my heart, from the face of my remembrance; until what I wish for be unveiled, and appear in sight, out of its secret place. Other things come up readily, in unbroken order, as they are called for; those in front making way for the following; and as they make way, they are hidden from sight, ready to come when I will. All which takes place when I repeat a thing by heart.

There are all things preserved distinctly and under general heads, each having entered by its own avenue: as light, and all colours and forms of bodies by the eyes; by the ears all sorts of sounds; all smells by the avenue of the nostrils; all tastes by the mouth; and by the sensation of the whole body, what is hard or soft; hot or cold; smooth or rugged; heavy or light; either outwardly or inwardly to the body. All these doth that great harbour of the memory receive in her numberless secret and inexpressible windings, to be forthcoming, and brought out at need; each entering in by his own gate, and there laid up. Nor yet do the things themselves enter in; only the images of the things perceived are there in readiness, for thought to recall. Which images, how they are formed, who can tell, though it doth plainly appear by which sense each hath been brought in and stored up? For even while I dwell in darkness and in silence, in my memory I can produce colours, if I will, and discern betwixt black and white, and what others I will: nor yet do sounds break in and disturb the image drawn in by my eyes, which I am reviewing, though they also are there, lying dormant, and laid up, as it were, apart. For these too I call for, and forthwith they appear. And though my tongue be still, and my throat mute, so can I sing as much as I will; nor do those images of colours, which notwithstanding be there, intrude themselves and interrupt, when another store is called for, which flowed in by the ears. So the other things, piled in and up by the other senses, I recall at my pleasure. Yea, I discern the breath of lilies from violets, though smelling nothing; and I prefer honey to sweet wine, smooth before rugged, at the time neither tasting nor handling, but remembering only.

These things do I within, in that vast court of my memory. For there are present with me, heaven, earth, sea, and whatever I could think on therein, besides what I have forgotten. There also meet I with myself, and recall myself, and when, where, and what I have done, and under what feelings. There be all which I remember, either on my own experience, or others' credit. Out of the same store do I myself with the past continually combine fresh and fresh likenesses of things which I have experienced, or, from what I have experienced, have believed: and thence again infer future actions, events and hopes, and all these again I reflect on, as present. "I will do this or that," say I to myself, in that great receptacle of my mind, stored with the images of things so many and so great, "and this or that will follow." "O that this or that might be!" "God avert this or that!" So speak I to myself; and when I speak, the images of all I speak of are present, out of the same treasury of memory; nor would I speak of any thereof, were the images wanting.

Great is this force of memory, excessive great, O my God; a large and boundless chamber! who ever sounded the bottom thereof? Yet is this a power of mine, and belongs unto my nature; nor do I myself comprehend all that I am. Therefore is the mind too strait to contain itself. And where should that be, which it containeth not of itself? Is it without it, and not within? How then doth it not comprehend itself? A wonderful admiration surprises me, amazement seizes me upon this. And men go abroad to admire the heights of mountains, the mighty billows of the sea, the broad tides of rivers, the compass of the ocean, and the circuits of the stars, and pass themselves by; nor wonder that when I spake of all these things, I did not see them with mine eyes, yet could not have spoken of them, unless I then actually saw the mountains, billows, rivers, stars, which I had seen, and that ocean which I believe to be, inwardly in my memory, and that, with the same vast spaces between, as if I saw them abroad. Yet did not I by seeing draw them into myself, when with mine eyes I beheld them; nor are they themselves with me, but their images only. And I know by what sense of the body each was impressed upon me. . . .

Great is the power of memory, a fearful thing, O my God, a deep and boundless manifoldness; and this thing is the mind, and this am I myself. What am I then, O my God? What nature am I? A life various and manifold, and exceeding immense. Behold in the plains, and caves, and caverns of my memory, innumerable and innumerably full of innumerable kinds of things, either through images, as all bodies; or by actual presence, as the arts; or by certain notions or impressions, as the affections of the mind, which, even when the mind doth not feel, the memory retaineth, while yet whatsoever is in the memory is also in the mind—over all these do I run, I fly; I dive on this side and on that, as far as I can, and there is no end. So great is the force of memory, so great the force of life, even in the mortal life of man. What shall I do then, O Thou my true life, my God? I will pass even beyond this power of mine which is called memory: yes, I will pass beyond it, that I may approach unto Thee, O sweet Light. What sayest Thou to me? See, I am mounting up through my mind towards Thee who abidest above me. Yea, I now will pass beyond this power of mine which is called memory, desirous to arrive at Thee, whence Thou mayest be arrived at; and to cleave unto Thee, whence one may cleave unto Thee. For even beasts and birds have memory; else could they not return to their dens and nests, nor many other things that they are used unto; nor indeed could they be used to any thing, but by memory. I will pass then beyond memory also, that I may arrive at Him who hath separated me from the four-footed beasts and made me wiser than the fowls of the air, I will pass beyond memory also, and where shall I find Thee, Thou truly good and certain sweetness? And where shall I find Thee? If I find Thee without my memory, then I do not retain Thee in my memory. And how shall I find Thee, if I remember Thee not?

For the woman that had lost her groat, and sought it with a light; unless she had remembered it, she had never found it. For when it was found, whence should she know whether it were the same, unless she remembered it? I remember to have sought and found many a thing; and this I thereby know, that when I was seeking any of them, and was asked, "Is this it?" "Is that it?" so long said I "No," until that were offered me which I sought. Which had I not remembered (whatever it were) though it were offered me, yet should I not find it, because I could not recognize it. And so it ever is, when we seek and find any lost thing. Notwithstanding, when any thing is by chance lost from the sight, not from the memory (as any visible body), yet its image is still retained within, and it is sought until it be restored to sight; and when it is found, it is recognized by the image which is within: nor do we say that we have found what was lost, unless we recognize it; nor can we recognize it, unless we remember it. But this was lost to the eyes, but retained in the memory. . . .

How then do I seek Thee, O Lord? For when I seek Thee, my God, I seek a happy life. I will seek Thee, that my soul may live. For my body liveth by my soul; and my soul by Thee. How then do I seek a happy life, seeing I have it not, until I can say, where I ought to say it, "It is enough"? How seek I it? By remembrance, as though I had forgotten it, remembering that I had forgotten it? Or, desiring to learn it as a thing unknown, either never having known, or so forgotten it, as not even to remember that I had forgotten it? Is not a happy life what all will, and no one altogether wills it not? Where have they known it, that they so will it? Where seen it, that they so love it? Truly we have it, how, I know not. Yea, there is another way, wherein when one hath it, then is he happy; and there are, who are blessed in hope. These have it in a lower kind, than they who have it in very deed; yet are they better off than such as are happy neither in deed nor in hope. Yet even these, had they it not in some sort, would not so will to be happy, which that they do will, is most certain. They have known it then, I know not how, and so have it by some sort of knowledge, what, I know not, and am perplexed whether it be in the memory, which if it be, then we have been happy once; whether all severally, or in that man who first sinned, in whom also we all died, and from whom we are all born with misery, I now enquire not; but only, whether the happy life be in the memory? For neither should we love it, did we not know it. We hear the name, and we all confess that we desire the thing; for we are not delighted with the mere sound. For when a Greek hears it in Latin, he is not delighted, not knowing what is spoken; but we Latins are delighted, as would he too, if he heard it in Greek; because the thing itself is neither Greek nor Latin, which Greeks and Latins, and men of all other tongues, long for so earnestly. Known therefore it is to all, for could they with one voice be asked, "would they be happy?" they would answer without doubt, "they would." And this could not be, unless the thing itself whereof it is the name were retained in their memory. . . .

See what a space I have gone over in my memory seeking Thee,

O Lord; and I have not found Thee, without it. Nor have I found any thing concerning Thee, but what I have kept in memory, ever since I learnt Thee. For since I learnt Thee, I have not forgotten Thee. For where I found Truth, there found I my God, the Truth Itself; which since I learnt, I have not forgotten. Since then I learnt Thee, Thou residest in my memory; and there do I find Thee, when I call Thee to remembrance, and delight in Thee. These be my holy delights, which Thou hast given me in Thy mercy, having regard to my poverty.

But where in my memory residest Thou, O Lord, where residest Thou there? What manner of lodging hast Thou framed for Thee? What manner of sanctuary hast Thou builded for Thee? Thou hast given this honour to my memory, to reside in it; but in what quarter of it Thou residest, that I am considering. For in thinking on Thee, I passed beyond such parts of it as the beasts also have, for I found Thee not there among the images of corporeal things; and I came to those parts to which I committed the affections of my mind, nor found Thee there. And I entered into the very seat of my mind (which it hath in my memory, inasmuch as the mind remembers itself also), neither wert Thou there: for as Thou art not a corporeal image, nor the affection of a living being (as when we rejoice, condole, desire, fear, remember, forget, or the like); so neither art Thou the mind itself; because Thou art the Lord God of the mind; and all these are changed, but Thou remainest unchangeable over all, and yet hast vouchsafed to dwell in my memory, since I learnt Thee. And why seek I now in what place thereof Thou dwellest, as if there were places therein? Sure I am, that in it Thou dwellest, since I have remembered Thee ever since I learnt Thee, and there I find Thee, when I call Thee to remembrance.

Where then did I find Thee, that I might learn Thee? For in my memory Thou wert not, before I learned Thee. Where then did I find Thee, that I might learn Thee, but in Thee above me? Place there is none; we go backward and forward, and there is no place. Every where, O Truth, dost Thou give audience to all who ask counsel of Thee, and at once answerest all, though on manifold matters they ask Thy counsel. Clearly dost Thou answer, though all do not clearly hear. All consult Thee on what they will, though they hear not always what they will. He is Thy best servant who looks not so much to hear that from Thee which himself willeth, as rather to will that which from Thee he heareth.

Too late I loved Thee, O Thou Beauty of ancient days, yet ever new! Too late I love Thee! And behold, Thou wert within, and I abroad, and there I searched for Thee; deformed I, plunging amid those fair forms which Thou hadst made. Thou wert with me, but I was not with Thee. Things held me far from Thee, which, unless they were in Thee, were not at all. Thou calledst and shoutedst, and burstest my deafness. Thou flashedst, shonest, and scatteredst my blindness. Thou breathedst odours, and I drew in breath and pant for Thee. I tasted, and hunger and thirst. Thou touchedst me, and I burned for Thy peace.

THE GUIDE FOR THE PERPLEXED
MOSES MAIMONIDES

Attributes of God

Know that the negative attributes of God are the true attributes: they do not include any incorrect notions or any deficiency whatever in reference to God, while positive attributes imply polytheism, and are inadequate, as we have already shown. It is now necessary to explain how negative expressions can in a certain sense be employed as attributes, and how they are distinguished from positive attributes. Then I shall show that we cannot describe the Creator by any means except by negative attributes. An attribute does not exclusively belong to the one object to which it is related; while qualifying one thing, it can also be employed to qualify other things, and is in that case not peculiar to that one thing. E.g., if you see an object from a distance, and on enquiring what it is, are told that it is a living being, you have certainly learnt an attribute of the object seen, and although that attribute does not exclusively belong to the object perceived, it expresses that the object is not a plant or a mineral. Again, if a man is in a certain house, and you know that something is in the house, but not exactly what, you ask what is in that house, and you are told, not a plant or a mineral. You have thereby obtained some special knowledge of the thing; you have learnt that it is a living being, although you do not yet know what kind of a living being it is. The negative attributes have this in common with the positive, that they necessarily circumscribe the object to some extent, although such circumscription consists only in the exclusion of what otherwise would not be excluded. In the following point, however, the negative attributes are distinguished from the positive. The positive attributes, although not peculiar to one thing, describe a portion of what we desire to know, either some part of its essence or some of its accidents; the negative attributes, on the other hand, do not, as regards the essence of the thing which we desire to know, in any way tell us what it is, except it be indirectly, as has been shown in the instance given by us.

After this introduction, I would observe that,—as has already been shown—God's existence is absolute, that it includes no composition, as will be proved, and that we comprehend only the fact that He exists, not His essence. Consequently it is a false assumption to hold that He has any positive attribute; for He does not possess existence in addition to His essence; it therefore cannot be said that the one may be described as an attribute [of the other]; much less has He [in addition to His essence] a compound essence, consisting of two constituent elements to which the attribute could refer; still less has He accidents, which could be described by an attribute. Hence it is clear that He has no positive attribute whatever. The negative attributes, however, are those which are necessary to direct the mind to the truths which we must believe concerning God; for, on the one hand, they do not imply any plurality, and, on the other, they convey to man the highest possible knowledge of God; e.g., it has been established by proof that some being must exist besides those things which can be perceived by the senses, or apprehended by the mind; when we say of this being, that it exists, we mean that its non-existence is impossible. We then perceive that such a being is not, for instance, like the four elements, which are inanimate, and we therefore say that it is living, expressing thereby that it is not dead. We call such a being incorporeal, because we notice that it is unlike the heavens, which are living, but material. Seeing that it is also different from the intellect, which, though incorporeal and living, owes its existence to some cause, we say it is the first, expressing thereby that its existence is not due to any cause. We further notice, that the existence, that is the essence, of this being is not limited to its own existence; many existences emanate from it, and its influence is not like that of the fire in producing heat, or that of the sun in sending forth light, but consists in constantly giving them stability and order by well-established rule, as we shall show: we say, on that account, it has power, wisdom, and will; i.e., it is not feeble or ignorant, or hasty, and does not abandon its creatures; when we say that it is not feeble, we mean that its existence is capable of producing the existence of many other things; by saying it is not ignorant, we mean "it perceives," or "it lives," for everything that perceives is living; by saying "it is not hasty, and does not abandon its creatures," we mean that all these creatures preserve a certain order and arrange-ment; they are not left to themselves; they are not produced aimlessly, but whatever condition they receive from that being is given with design and intention. We thus learn that there is no other being like unto God, and we say that He is One, i.e., there are not more Gods than one.

It has thus been shown that every attribute predicated of God either denotes the quality of an action, or—when the attribute is intended to convey some idea of the Divine Being itself, and not of His actions—the negation of the opposite. Even these negative attributes must not be formed and applied to God, except in the way in which, as you know, sometimes an attribute is negatived in reference to a thing, although that attribute can naturally never be applied to it in the same sense, as, e.g., we say, "This wall does not see." Those who read the present work are aware that, notwith-standing all the efforts of the mind, we can obtain no knowledge of the essence of the heavens—a revolving substance which has been measured by us in spans and cubits, and examined even as regards the proportions of the several spheres to each other and respecting most of their motions—although we know that they must consist of matter and form; but the matter not being the same as sublunary matter, we can only describe the heavens in terms expressing nega-tive properties, but not in terms denoting positive qualities. Thus we say that the heavens are not light, not heavy, not passive and there-fore not subject to impressions, and that they do not possess the sensations of taste and smell; or we use similar negative attributes. All this we do, because we do not know their substance. What, then, can be the result of our efforts, when we try to obtain a knowledge of a Being that is free from substance, that is most simple, whose existence is absolute, and not due to any cause, to whose perfect essence nothing can be superadded, and whose perfection consists, as we have shown, in the absence of all defects. All we understand is the fact that He exists, that He is a Being to whom none of His crea-tures is similar, who has nothing in common with them, who does not include plurality, who is never too feeble to produce other beings, and whose relation to the universe is that of a steersman to a boat; and even this is not a real relation, a real simile, but serves only to convey to us the idea that God rules the universe; that is, that He gives it duration, and preserves its necessary arrangement.

This subject will be treated more fully. Praised be He! In the contemplation of His essence, our comprehension and knowledge prove insufficient; in the examination of His works, how they necessarily result from His will, our knowledge proves to be ignorance, and in the endeavour to extol Him in words, all our efforts in speech are mere weakness and failure!

On Prophecy

Prophecy is, in truth and reality, an emanation sent forth by the Divine Being through the medium of the Active Intellect, in the first instance to man's rational faculty, and then to his imaginative faculty; it is the highest degree and greatest perfection man can attain; it consists in the most perfect development of the imaginative faculty. Prophecy is a faculty that cannot in any way be found in a person, or acquired by man, through a culture of his mental and moral faculties; for even if these latter were as good and perfect as possible, they would be of no avail, unless they were combined with the highest natural excellence of the imaginative faculty. You know that the full development of any faculty of the body, such as the imagination, depends on the condition of the organ, by means of which the faculty acts. This must be the best possible as regards its temperament and its size, and also as regards the purity of its substance. Any defect in this respect cannot in any way be supplied or remedied by training. For when any organ is defective in its temperament, proper training can in the best case restore a healthy condition to some extent, but cannot make such an organ perfect. But if the organ is defective as regards size, position, or as regards the substance and the matter of which the organ is formed, there is no remedy. You know all this, and I need not explain it to you at length.

Part of the functions of the imaginative faculty is, as you well know, to retain impressions by the senses, to combine them, and chiefly to form images. The principal and highest function is performed when the senses are at rest and pause in their action, for then it receives, to some extent, divine inspiration in the measure as it is predisposed for this influence. This is the nature of those dreams which prove true, and also of prophecy, the difference being one of quantity, not of quality. Thus our Sages say, that dream is the sixtieth part of prophecy; and no such comparison could be made between two things of different kinds, for we cannot say the perfection of man is so many times the perfection of a horse. In *Bereshit Rabba* (sect. xvii.) the following saying of our Sages occurs, "Dream is the *nobelet* (the unripe fruit) of prophecy." This is an excellent comparison, for the unripe fruit (*nobelet*) is really the fruit to some extent, only it has fallen from the tree before it was fully developed and ripe. In a similar manner the action of the imaginative faculty during sleep is the same as at the time when it receives a prophecy, only in the first case it is not fully developed, and has not yet reached its highest degree. But why need I quote the words of our Sages, when I can refer to the following passage of Scripture: "If there be among you a prophet, I, the Lord, will make myself known unto him in a vision, in a dream will I speak to him" (Num. xii. 6). Here the Lord tells us what the real essence of prophecy is, that it is a perfection acquired in a dream or in a vision (the original *mareb* is a noun derived from the verb *raab*); the imaginative faculty acquires such an efficiency in its action that it sees the thing as if it came from without, and perceives it as if through the medium of bodily senses. These two modes of prophecy, vision and dream, include all its different degrees. It is a well-known fact that the thing which engages greatly and earnestly man's attention whilst he is awake and in the full possession of his senses forms during his sleep the object of the action of his imaginative faculty. Imagination is then only influenced by the intellect in so far as it is predisposed for such an influence. It would be quite useless to illustrate this by a simile, or to explain it fully, as it is clear, and every one knows it. It is like the action of the senses, the existence of which no person with common sense would ever deny. After these introductory remarks you will understand that a person must satisfy the following conditions before he can become a prophet: The substance of the brain must from the very beginning be in the most perfect condition as regards purity of matter, composition of its different parts, size and position; no part of his body must suffer from ill-health; he must in addition have studied and acquired wisdom, so that his rational faculty passes from a state of potentiality to that of actuality; his intellect must be as developed and perfect as human intellect can be; his passions pure and equally balanced; all his desires must aim at obtaining a knowledge of the hidden laws and causes that are in force in the Universe; his thoughts must be engaged in lofty matters; his attention directed to the knowledge of God, the consideration of His works, and of that which he must believe in this respect. There must be an absence of the lower desires and appetites, of the seeking after pleasure in eating, drinking, and cohabitation; and, in short, every pleasure connected with the sense of touch. (Aristotle correctly says that this sense is a disgrace to us, since we possess it only in virtue of our being animals; and it does not include any specifically human element, whilst enjoyments connected with other senses, as smell, hearing, and sight, though likewise of a material nature, may sometimes include [intellectual] pleasure, appealing to man as man, according to Aristotle. This remark, although forming no part of our subject, is not superfluous, for the thoughts of the most renowned wise men are to a great extent affected by the pleasures of this sense, and filled with a desire for them. And yet people are surprised that these scholars do not prophesy, if prophesying be nothing but a certain degree in the natural development of man.) It is further necessary to suppress every thought or desire for unreal power and dominion; that is to say, for victory, increase of followers, acquisition of honour, and service from the people without any ulterior object. On the contrary, the multitude must be considered according to their true worth; some of them are undoubtedly like domesticated cattle, and others like wild beasts, and these only engage the mind of the perfect and distinguished man in so far as he desires to guard himself from injury, in case of contact with them, and to derive some benefit from them when necessary. A man who satisfies these conditions, whilst his fully developed imagination is in action, influenced by the Active Intellect according to his mental training,—such a person will undoubtedly perceive nothing but things very extraordinary and divine, and see nothing but God and His angels. His knowledge will only include that which is real knowledge, and his thought will only be directed to such general principles as would tend to improve the social relations between man and man.

We have thus described three kinds of perfection: mental perfection acquired by training, perfection of the natural constitution of the imaginative faculty, and moral perfection produced by the suppression of every thought of bodily pleasures, and of every kind of foolish or evil ambition. These qualities are, as is well known, possessed by the wise men in different degrees, and the degrees of prophetic faculty vary in accordance with this difference. Faculties of the body are, as you know, at one time weak, wearied, and corrupted, at others in a healthy state. Imagination is certainly one of the faculties of the body. You find, therefore, that prophets are deprived of the faculty of prophesying when they mourn, are angry, or are similarly affected. Our Sages say, Inspiration does not come upon a prophet when he is sad or languid. This is the reason why Jacob did not receive any revelation during the period of his mourning, when his imagination was engaged with the loss of Joseph. The same was the case with Moses, when he was in a state of depression through the multitude of his troubles, which lasted from the murmurings of the Israelites in consequence of the evil report of the spies, till the death of the warriors of that generation. He received no message of God, as he used to do, even though he did not receive prophetic inspiration through the medium of the imaginative faculty, but directly through the intellect. We have mentioned it several times that Moses did not, like other prophets, speak in similes. There were also persons who prophesied for a certain time and then left off altogether, something occurring that caused them to discontinue prophesying. The same circumstance, prevalence of sadness and dulness, was undoubtedly the direct cause of the interruption of prophecy during the exile; for can there be any greater misfortune for man than this: to be a slave bought for money in the service of ignorant and voluptuous masters, and powerless against them as they unite in themselves the absence of true knowledge and the force of all animal desires? Such an evil state has been prophesied to us in the words, "They shall run to and fro to seek the word of God, but shall not find it" (Amos viii. 12); "Her king and her princes are among the nations, the law is no more, her prophets also find no vision from the Lord" (Lam. ii. 9). This is a real fact, and the cause is evident; the pre-requisites [of prophecy] have been lost. In the Messianic period—may it soon commence—prophecy will therefore again be in our midst, as has been promised by God.

It is necessary to consider the nature of the divine influence, which enables us to think, and gives us the various degrees of intelligence.

For this influence may reach a person only in a small measure, and in exactly the same proportion would then be his intellectual condition, whilst it may reach another person in such a measure that, in addition to his own perfection, he can be the means of perfection for others. The same relation may be observed throughout the whole Universe. There are some beings so perfect that they can govern other beings, but there are also beings that are only perfect in so far as they can govern themselves and cannot influence other beings. In some cases the influence of the [Active] Intellect reaches only the logical and not the imaginative faculty; either on account of the insufficiency of that influence, or on account of a defect in the constitution of the imaginative faculty, and the consequent inability of the latter to receive that influence: this is the condition of wise men or philosophers. If, however, the imaginative faculty is naturally in the most perfect condition, this influence may, as has been explained by us and by other philosophers, reach both his logical and his imaginative faculties: this is the case with prophets. But it happens sometimes that the influence only reaches the imaginative faculty on account of the insufficiency of the logical faculty, arising either from a natural defect, or from a neglect in training. This is the case with statesmen, lawgivers, diviners, charmers, and men that have true dreams, or do wonderful things by strange means and secret arts, though they are not wise men; all these belong to the third class. It is further necessary to understand that some persons belonging to the third class perceive scenes, dreams, and confused images, when awake, in the form of a prophetic vision. They then believe that they are prophets; they wonder that they perceive visions, and think that they have acquired wisdom without training. They fall into grave errors as regards important philosophical principles, and see a strange mixture of true and imaginary things. All this is a consequence of the strength of their imaginative faculty, and the weakness of their logical faculty, which has not developed, and has not passed from potentiality to actuality.

It is well known that the members of each class differ greatly from each other. Each of the first two classes is again subdivided, and contains two sections, namely, those who receive the influence only as far as it is necessary for their own perfection, and those who receive it in so great a measure that it suffices for their own perfection and that of others. A member of the first class, the wise men, may have his mind influenced either only so far, that he is enabled to search, to understand, to know, and to discern, without attempting to be a teacher or an author, having neither the desire nor the capacity; but he may also be influenced to such a degree that he becomes a teacher and an author. The same is the case with the second class. A person may receive a prophecy enabling him to perfect himself but not others; but he may also receive such a prophecy as would compel him to address his fellow-men, teach them, and benefit them through his perfection. It is clear that, without this second degree of perfection, no books would have been written, nor would any prophets have persuaded others to know the truth. For a scholar does not write a book with the object to teach himself what he already knows. But the characteristic of the intellect is this: what the intellect of one receives is transmitted to another, and so on, till a person is reached that can only himself be perfected by such an influence, but is unable to communicate it to others, as has been explained in some chapters of this treatise. It is further the nature of this element in man that he who possesses an additional degree of that influence is compelled to address his fellow-men, under all circumstances, whether he is listened to or not, even if he injures himself thereby. Thus we find prophets that did not leave off speaking to the people until they were slain; it is this divine influence that moves them, that does not allow them to rest in any way, though they might bring upon themselves great evils by their action. E.g., when Jeremiah was despised, like other teachers and scholars of his age, he could not, though he desired it, withhold his prophecy, or cease from reminding the people of the truths which they rejected. "For the Word of the Lord was unto me a reproach and a mocking all day, and I said, I will not mention it nor will I again speak in His name; but it was in mine heart as a burning fire, enclosed in my bones, and I was wearied to keep it, and did not prevail" (Jer. xx. 8, 9). This is also the meaning of the words of another prophet, "The Lord God hath spoken, who shall not prophesy?" (Amos iii. 8).

Every man possesses a certain amount of courage, otherwise he would not stir to remove anything that might injure him. This psychical force seems to me analogous to the physical force of repulsion. Energy varies like all other forces, being great in one case and small in another. There are, therefore, people who attack a lion, whilst others run away at the sight of a mouse. One attacks a whole army and fights, another is frightened and terrified by the threat of a woman. This courage requires that there be in a man's constitution a certain disposition for it. If man, in accordance with a certain view, employs it more frequently, it develops and increases, but, on the other hand, if it is employed, in accordance with the opposite view, more rarely, it will diminish. From our own youth we remember that there are different degrees of energy among boys.

The same is the case with the intuitive faculty; all possess it, but in different degrees. Man's intuitive power is especially strong in things which he has well comprehended, and in which his mind is much engaged. Thus you may yourself guess correctly that a certain person said or did a certain thing in a certain manner. Some persons are so strong and sound in their imagination and intuitive faculty that, when they assume a thing to be in existence, the reality either entirely or partly confirms their assumption. Although the causes of this assumption are numerous, and include many preceeding, succeeding, and present circumstances, by means of the intuitive faculty the intellect can pass over all these causes, and draw inferences from them very quickly, almost instantaneously. This same faculty enables some persons to foretell important coming events. The prophets must have had these two forces, courage and intuition, highly developed, and these were still more strengthened when they were under the influence of the Active Intellect. Their courage was so great that, e.g., Moses, with only a staff in his hand, dared to address a great king in his desire to deliver a nation from his service. He was not frightened or terrified, because he had been told, "I will be with Thee," (Exod. iii. 12). The prophets have not all the same degree of courage, but none of them have been entirely without it. Thus Jeremiah is told: "Be not afraid of them," etc. (Jer. i. 8), and Ezekiel is exhorted, "Do not fear them or their word" (Ezek. ii. 6). In the same manner, you find that all prophets possessed great courage. Again, through the excellence of their intuitive faculty, they could quickly foretell the future, but this excellence, as is well known, likewise admits of different degrees.

The true prophets undoubtedly conceive ideas that result from premises which human reason could not comprehend by itself; thus they tell things which men could not tell by reason and ordinary imagination alone; for [the action of the prophets' mental capacities is influenced by] the same agent that causes the perfection of the imaginative faculty, and that enables the prophet thereby to foretell a future event with such clearness as if it was a thing already perceived with the senses, and only through them conveyed to his imagination. This agent perfects the prophet's mind, and influences it in such a manner that he conceives ideas which are confirmed by reality, and are so clear to him as if he deduced them by means of syllogisms.

This should be the belief of all who choose to accept the truth. For [all things are in a certain relation to each other, and] what is noticed in one thing may be used as evidence for the existence of certain properties in another, and the knowledge of one thing leads us to the knowledge of other things. But [what we said of the extraordinary powers of our imaginative faculty] applies with special force to our intellect, which is directly influenced by the Active Intellect, and caused by it to pass from potentiality to actuality. It is through the intellect that the influence reaches the imaginative faculty. How then could the latter be so perfect as to be able to represent things not previously perceived by the senses, if the same degree of perfection were withheld from the intellect, and the latter could not comprehend things otherwise than in the usual manner, namely, by means of premiss, conclusion, and inference? This is the true characteristic of prophecy, and of the disciplines to which the preparation for prophecy must exclusively be devoted. I spoke here of true prophets in order to exclude the third class, namely, those persons whose logical faculties are not fully developed, and who do not possess any wisdom, but are only endowed with imaginative and inventive powers. It may be that things perceived by these persons are nothing but ideas which they had before, and of which impressions were left in their imaginations together with those of other things; but whilst the impressions of other images are effaced and have disappeared, certain images alone remain, are seen and considered as new and objective, coming from without. The process is analogous to the following case: A person has with him in the house a thousand living individuals; all except one of them leave the house: when the person finds himself alone with that individual, he imagines that the latter has entered his house now, contrary to the fact that he has only not left the house. This is one of the many phenomena open to gross misinterpretations and dangerous errors, and many of those who believed that they were wise perished thereby.

There were, therefore, men who supported their opinion by a dream which they had, thinking that the vision during sleep was independent of what they had previously believed or heard when awake. Persons whose mental capacities are not fully developed, and who have not attained intellectual perfection, must not take any notice of these [dreams]. Those who reach that perfection may, through the influence of the divine intellect, obtain knowledge independent of that possessed by them when awake. They are true prophets, as is distinctly stated in Scripture, *ve nabi lebab hokmah* (Ps. xc. 12), "And the true prophet possesseth a heart of wisdom." This must likewise be noticed.

Greatness

105. If an animal did rationally what it does by instinct, and if it spoke rationally what it speaks by instinct when hunting, or warning its fellows that the prey has been lost or found, it would certainly go on to talk about matters which affect it more seriously, and it would say, for instance: "Bite through this cord; it is hurting me and I cannot reach it."

106. *Greatness.* Causes and effects show the greatness of man in producing such excellent order from his own concupiscence.

107. The parrot wipes its beak although it is clean.

108. What part of us feels pleasure? Is it our hand, our arm, our flesh, or our blood? It must obviously be something immaterial.

109. *Against Scepticism.* It is odd that we cannot define these things without making them obscure; we talk about them all the time. We assume that everyone conceives of them in the same way, but that is a quite gratuitous assumption, because we have no proof that it is so. I see indeed that we apply these words on the same occasions; every time two men see a body change its position they both use the same word to express what they have seen, each of them saying that the body has moved. Such conformity of application provides a strong presumption of conformity of thought, but it lacks the absolute force of total conviction, although the odds are that it is so, because we know that the same conclusions are often drawn from different assumptions.

   That is enough to cloud the issue, to say the least, though it does not completely extinguish the natural light which provides us with certainty in such matters. The Platonists would have wagered on it, but that makes the light dimmer and upsets the dogmatists, to the glory of the sceptical clique which stands for ambiguous ambiguity, and a certain dubious obscurity from which our doubts cannot remove every bit of light any more than our natural light can dispel all the darkness.

[Verso] The least thing is of this kind. God is the beginning and the end. Eccl.

Reason

110. We know the truth not only through our reason but also through our heart. It is through the latter that we know first principles, and reason, which has nothing to do with it, tries in vain to refute them. The sceptics have no other object than that, and they work at it to no purpose. We know that we are not dreaming, but, however unable we may be to prove it rationally, our inability proves nothing but the weakness of our reason, and not the uncertainty of all our knowledge, as they maintain. For knowledge of first principles, like space, time, motion, number, is as solid as any derived through reason, and it is on such knowledge, coming from the heart and instinct, that reason has to depend and base all its argument. The heart feels that there are three spatial dimensions and that there is an infinite series of numbers, and reason goes on to demonstrate that there are no two square numbers of which one is double the other. Principles are felt, propositions proved, and both with certainty though by different means. It is just as pointless and absurd for reason to demand proof of first principles from the heart before agreeing to accept them as it would be absurd for the heart to demand an intuition of all the propositions demonstrated by reason before agreeing to accept them.

Our inability must therefore serve only to humble reason, which would like to be the judge of everything, but not to confute our certainty. As if reason were the only way we could learn! Would to God, on the contrary, that we never needed it and knew everything by instinct and feeling! But nature has refused us this blessing, and has instead given us only very little knowledge of this kind; all other knowledge can be acquired only by reasoning.

That is why those to whom God has given religious faith by moving their hearts are very fortunate, and feel quite legitimately convinced, but to those who do not have it we can only give such faith through reasoning, until God gives it by moving their heart, without which faith is only human and useless for salvation.

111. I can certainly imagine a man without hands, feet, or head, for it is only experience that teaches us that the head is more necessary than the feet. But I cannot imagine a man without thought; he would be a stone or an animal.

112. Instinct and reason, signs of two natures.

113. *Thinking reed.* It is not in space that I must seek my human dignity, but in the ordering of my thought. It will do me no good to own land. Through space the universe grasps me and swallows me up like a speck; through thought I grasp it.

114. Man's greatness comes from knowing he is wretched: a tree does not know it is wretched.

Thus it is wretched to know that one is wretched, but there is greatness in knowing one is wretched.

115. *Immateriality of the soul.* When philosophers have subdued their passions, what material substance has managed to achieve this?

116. All these examples of wretchedness prove his greatness. It is the wretchedness of a great lord, the wretchedness of a dispossessed king.

117. *Man's greatness.* Man's greatness is so obvious that it can even be deduced from his wretchedness, for what is nature in animals we call wretchedness in man, thus recognizing that, if his nature is today like that of the animals, he must have fallen from some better state which was once his own.

Who indeed would think himself unhappy not to be king except one who had been dispossessed? Did anyone think Paulus Emilius was unhappy not to be consul? On the contrary, everyone thought he was happy to have been so once, because the office was not meant to be permanent. But people thought Perseus so unhappy at finding himself no longer king, because that was meant to be a permanent office, that they were surprised that he could bear to go on living. Who would think himself unhappy if he had only one mouth and who would not if he had only one eye? It has probably never occurred to anyone to be distressed at not having three eyes, but those who have none are inconsolable.

118. Man's greatness even in his concupiscence. He has managed to produce such a remarkable system from it and make it the image of true charity.

Contradictions

119. *Contradictions.* (After showing how vile and how great man is.) Let man now judge his own worth, let him love himself, for there is within him a nature capable of good; but that is no reason for him to love the vileness within himself. Let him despise himself because this capacity remains unfilled; but that is no reason for him to despise this natural capacity. Let him both hate and love himself; he has within him the capacity for knowing truth and being happy, but he possesses no truth which is either abiding or satisfactory.

I should therefore like to arouse in man the desire to find truth, to be ready, free from passion, to follow it wherever he may find it, realizing how far his knowledge is clouded by passions. I should like him to hate his concupiscence which automatically makes his decisions for him, so that it should not blind him when he makes his choice, nor hinder him once he has chosen.

120. We are so presumptuous that we should like to be known all over the world, even by people who will only come when we are no more. Such is our vanity that the good opinion of half a dozen of the people around us gives us pleasure and satisfaction.

121. It is dangerous to explain too clearly to man how like he is to the animals without pointing out his greatness. It is also dangerous to make too much of his greatness without his vileness. It is still more dangerous to leave him in ignorance of both, but it is most valuable to represent both to him.

Man must not be allowed to believe that he is equal either to animals or to angels, nor to be unaware of either, but he must know both.

122. APR [At Port Royal] *Greatness and wretchedness.* Since

wretchedness and greatness can be concluded each from the other, some people have been more inclined to conclude that man is wretched for having used his greatness to prove it, while others have all the more cogently concluded that he is great by basing their proof on wretchedness. Everything that could be said by one side as proof of greatness has only served as an argument for the others to conclude he is wretched, since the further one falls the more wretched one is, and vice versa. One has followed the other in an endless circle, for it is certain that as man's insight increases so he finds both wretchedness and greatness within himself. In a word man knows he is wretched. Thus he is wretched because he is so, but he is truly great because he knows it.

123. *Contradictions.* Contempt for our existence, dying for nothing, hatred of our existence.

124. *Contradictions.* Man is naturally credulous, incredulous, timid, bold.

125. What are our natural principles but habitual principles? In children it is the principles received from the habits of their fathers, like hunting in the case of animals.

A change of habit will produce different natural principles, as can be seen from experience, and if there are some principles which habit cannot eradicate, there are others both habitual and unnatural which neither nature nor a new habit can eradicate. It all depends on one's disposition.

126. Fathers are afraid that their children's natural love may be eradicated. What then is this nature which is liable to be eradicated?

Habit is a second nature that destroys the first. But what is nature? Why is habit not natural? I am very much afraid that nature itself is only a first habit, just as habit is a second nature.

127. Man's nature may be considered in two ways; either according to his end, and then he is great and beyond compare, or according to the masses, as the nature of horses and dogs is judged by the masses from seeing how they run or ward off strangers, and then man is abject and vile. These are the two approaches which provoke such divergent views and such argument among philosophers, because

each denies the other's hypothesis.

One says: "Man was not born for this end, because everything he does belies it." The other says: "He is falling far short of his end when he acts so basely."

128. Two things teach man about his whole nature: instinct and experience.

129. *Trade. Thoughts.* All is one, all is diversity.

How many natures lie in human nature! How many occupations! How fortuitously in the ordinary way each of us takes up the one that he has heard others praise. A well-turned heel.

130. If he exalts himself, I humble him.
    If he humbles himself, I exalt him.
    And I go on contradicting him
    Until he understands
    That he is a monster that passes all understanding.

131. The strongest of the sceptics' arguments, to say nothing of minor points, is that we cannot be sure that these principles are true (faith and revelation apart) except through some natural intuition. Now this natural intuition affords no convincing proof that they are true. There is no certainty, apart from faith, as to whether man was created by a good God, an evil demon, or just by chance, and so it is a matter of doubt, depending on our origin, whether these innate principles are true, false, or uncertain.

Moreover, no one can be sure, apart from faith, whether he is sleeping or waking, because when we are asleep we are just as firmly convinced that we are awake as we are now. As we often dream we are dreaming, piling up one dream on another, is it not possible that this half of our life is itself just a dream, on to which the others are grafted, and from which we shall awake when we die? That while it lasts we are as little in possession of the principles of truth and goodness as during normal sleep? All this passage of time, of life, all these different bodies which we feel, the different thoughts which stir us, may be no more than illusions like the passage of time and vain phantoms of our dreams. We think we are seeing space, shape, movement, we feel time pass, we measure it, in fact we behave just as we do when we are awake. As a result, since half our life is spent in sleep, on our own admission and despite appearances we have no idea of the truth because all our intuitions are simply illusions during that time. Who knows whether the other half of our lives, when we think we are awake, is not another sleep slightly different from the first, on to which our dreams are grafted as our sleep appears, and from which we awake when we think we are sleeping? And who can doubt that, if we dreamed in the company of others and our dreams happened to agree, which is common enough, and if we were alone when awake, we should think things had been turned upside-down?

These are the main points on each side, to say nothing of minor arguments, like those the sceptics direct against the influences of habit, education, local customs, and so on, which the slightest puff of scepticism overturns, though they convince the majority of ordinary people, who have only this vain basis for their dogmas. You have only to look at their books; if you are not sufficiently persuaded you soon will be, perhaps too much so.

I pause at the dogmatists' only strong point, which is that we cannot doubt natural principles if we speak sincerely and in all good faith.

To which the sceptics reply, in a word, that uncertainty as to our origin entails uncertainty as to our nature. The dogmatists have been trying to answer that ever since the world began.

(Anyone wanting ampler information about scepticism should look at their books; he will soon be persuaded, perhaps too much so.)

This means open war between men, in which everyone is obliged to take sides, either with the dogmatists or with the sceptics, because anyone who imagines he can stay neutral is a sceptic *par excellence*. This neutrality is the essence of their clique. Anyone who is not against them is their staunch supporter, and that is where their advantage appears. They are not even for themselves; they are neutral, indifferent, suspending judgment on everything, including themselves.

What then is man to do in this state of affairs? Is he to doubt everything, to doubt whether he is awake, whether he is being pinched or burned? Is he to doubt whether he is doubting, to doubt whether he exists?

No one can go that far, and I maintain that a perfectly genuine sceptic has never existed. Nature backs up helpless reason and stops it going so wildly astray.

Is he, on the other hand, to say that he is the certain possessor of truth, when at the slightest pressure he fails to prove his claim and is compelled to loose his grasp?

What sort of freak then is man! How novel, how monstrous, how chaotic, how paradoxical, how prodigious! Judge of all things, feeble earthworm, repository of truth, sink of doubt and error, glory and refuse of the universe!

Who will unravel such a tangle? This is certainly beyond dogmatism and scepticism, beyond all human philosophy. Man transcends man. Let us then concede to the sceptics what they have so often proclaimed, that truth lies beyond our scope and is an unattainable quarry, that it is no earthly denizen, but at home in heaven, lying in the lap of God, to be known only in so far as it pleases him to reveal it. Let us learn our true nature from the uncreated and incarnate truth.

If we seek truth through reason we cannot avoid one of these three sects. You cannot be a sceptic or a Platonist without stifling nature, you cannot be a dogmatist without turning your back on reason.

Nature confounds the sceptics and Platonists, and reason confounds the dogmatists. What then will become of you, man, seeking to discover your true condition through natural reason? You cannot avoid one of these three sects nor survive in any of them.

Know then, proud man, what a paradox you are to yourself. Be humble, impotent reason! Be silent, feeble nature! Learn that man infinitely transcends man, hear from your master your true condition, which is unknown to you.

Listen to God.

Is it not as clear as day that man's condition is dual? The point is that if man had never been corrupted, he would, in his innocence, confidently enjoy both truth and felicity, and, if man had never been anything but corrupt, he would have no idea either of truth or bliss. But unhappy as we are (and we should be less so if there were no element of greatness in our condition) we have an idea of happiness but we cannot attain it. We perceive an image of the truth and possess nothing but falsehood, being equally incapable of absolute ignorance and certain knowledge; so obvious is it that we once enjoyed a degree of perfection from which we have unhappily fallen.

Let us then conceive that man's condition is dual. Let us conceive that man infinitely transcends man, and that without the aid of faith he would remain inconceivable to himself, for who cannot see that unless we realize the duality of human nature we remain invincibly ignorant of the truth about ourselves?

It is, however, an astounding thing that the mystery furthest from our ken, that of the transmission of sin, should be something without which we can have no knowledge of ourselves.

Without doubt nothing is more shocking to our reason than to say that the sin of the first man has implicated in its guilt men so far from the original sin that they seem incapable of sharing it. This flow of guilt does not seem merely impossible to us, but indeed most unjust. What could be more contrary to the rules of our miserable justice than the eternal damnation of a child, incapable of will, for an act in which he seems to have so little part that it was actually committed 6000 years before he existed? Certainly nothing jolts us more rudely than this doctrine, and yet, but for this mystery, the most incomprehensible of all, we remain incomprehensible to ourselves. The knot of our condition was twisted and turned in that abyss, so that it is harder to conceive of man without this mystery than for man to conceive of it himself.

This shows that God, in his desire to make the difficulties of our existence intelligible to us, hid the knot so high, or more precisely, so low, that we were quite unable to reach it. Consequently it is not through the proud activity of our reason but through its simple submission that we can really know ourselves.

These fundamental facts, solidly established on the inviolable authority of religion, teach us that there are in faith two equally constant truths. One is that man in the state of his creation, or in the state of grace, is exalted above the whole of nature, made like unto God and sharing in his divinity. The other is that in the state of corruption and sin he has fallen from that first state and has become like the beasts. These two propositions are equally firm and certain.

Scripture openly declares this when it says in certain places: *My delights were with the sons of men—I will pour out my spirit upon all flesh—Ye are gods,* while saying in others: *All flesh is grass—Man is like the beasts that perish—I said in my heart concerning the estate of the sons of men.*

Whence it is clearly evident that man through grace is man like unto God and shares in his divinity, and without grace he is treated like the beasts of the field.

Transition from Knowledge of Man to Knowledge of God

193. *Prejudice leading to error.* It is deplorable to see everybody debating about the means, never the end. Everyone thinks about how he will get on in his career, but when it comes to choosing a career or a country it is fate that decides for us.

It is pitiful to see so many Turks, heretics, unbelievers follow in their fathers' footsteps, solely because they have all been brought up to believe that this is the best course. This is what makes each of us pick his particular career as locksmith, soldier, etc.

That is why savages do not care about Provence.

194. Why have limits been set upon my knowledge, my height, my life, making it a hundred rather than a thousand years? For what reason did nature make it so, and choose this rather than that mean from the whole of infinity, when there is no more reason to choose one rather than another, as none is more attractive than another?

195. *Little of everything.* As we cannot be universal by knowing everything there is to be known about everything, we must know a little about everything, because it is much better to know something about everything than everything about something. Such universality is the finest. It would be still better if we could have both together, but, if a choice must be made, this is the one to choose. The world knows this and does so, for the world is often a good judge.

196. Some fancy makes me dislike people who croak or who puff while eating. Fancy carries a lot of weight. What good will that do us? That we indulge it because it is natural? No, rather that we resist it.

197. There is no better proof of human vanity than to consider the causes and effects of love, because the whole universe can be changed by it. Cleopatra's nose.

198. . . . When I see the blind and wretched state of man, when I survey the whole universe in its dumbness and man left to himself with no light, as though lost in this corner of the universe, without knowing who put him there, what he has come to do, what will become of him when he dies, incapable of knowing anything, I am moved to terror, like a man transported in his sleep to some terrify-

ing desert island, who wakes up quite lost and with no means of escape. Then I marvel that so wretched a state does not drive people to despair. I see other people around me, made like myself. I ask them if they are any better informed than I, and they say they are not. Then these lost and wretched creatures look around and find some attractive objects to which they become addicted and attached. For my part I have never been able to form such attachments, and considering how very likely it is that there exists something besides what I can see, I have tried to find out whether God has left any traces of himself.

I see a number of religions in conflict, and therefore all false, except one. Each of them wishes to be believed on its own authority and threatens unbelievers. I do not believe them on that account. Anyone can see that. Anyone can call himself a prophet, but I see Christianity, and find its prophecies, which are not something that anyone can do.

199. . . . *Disproportion of man.* This is where unaided knowledge brings us. If it is not true, there is no truth in man, and if it is true, he has good cause to feel humiliated; in either case he is obliged to humble himself.

And, since he cannot exist without believing this knowledge, before going on to a wider inquiry concerning nature, I want him to consider nature just once, seriously and at leisure, and to look at himself as well, and judge whether there is any proportion between himself and nature by comparing the two.

Let man then contemplate the whole of nature in her full and lofty majesty, let him turn his gaze away from the lowly objects around him; let him behold the dazzling light set like an eternal lamp to light up the universe, let him see the earth as a mere speck compared to the vast orbit described by this star, and let him marvel at finding this vast orbit itself to be no more than the tiniest point compared to that described by the stars revolving in the firmament. But if our eyes stop there, let our imagination proceed further; it will grow weary of conceiving things before nature tires of producing them. The whole visible world is only an imperceptible dot in nature's ample bosom. No idea comes near it; it is no good inflating our conceptions beyond imaginable space, we only bring forth atoms compared to the reality of things. Nature is an infinite sphere whose centre is everywhere and circumference nowhere. In short it is the greatest perceptible mark of God's omnipotence that our imagination should lose itself in that thought.

Let man, returning to himself, consider what he is in comparison with what exists; let him regard himself as lost, and form this little dungeon, in which he finds himself lodged, I mean the universe, let him learn to take the earth, its realms, its cities, its houses and himself at their proper value.

What is a man in the infinite?

But, to offer him another prodigy equally astounding, let him look into the tiniest things he knows. Let a mite show him in its minute body incomparably more minute parts, legs with joints, veins in its legs, blood in the veins, humours in the blood, drops in the humours, vapours in the drops: let him divide these things still further until he has exhausted his powers of imagination, and let the last thing he comes down to now be the subject of our discourse. He will perhaps think that this is the ultimate of minuteness in nature.

I want to show him a new abyss. I want to depict to him not only the visible universe, but all the conceivable immensity of nature enclosed in this miniature atom. Let him see there an infinity of universes, each with its firmament, its planets, its earth, in the same proportions as in the visible world, and on that earth animals, and finally mites, in which he will find again the same results as in the first; and finding the same thing yet again in the others without end or respite, he will be lost in such wonders, as astounding in their minuteness as the others in their amplitude. For who will not marvel that our body, a moment ago imperceptible in the universe, itself imperceptible in the bosom of the whole, should now be a colossus, a world, or rather a whole, compared to the nothingness beyond our reach? Anyone who considers himself in this way will be terrified at himself, and, seeing his mass, as given him by nature, supporting him between these two abysses of infinity and nothingness, will tremble at these marvels. I believe that with his curiosity changing into wonder he will be more disposed to contemplate them in silence than investigate them with presumption.

For, after all, what is man in nature? A nothing compared to the infinite, a whole compared to the nothing, a middle point between all and nothing, infinitely remote from an understanding of the extremes; the end of things and their principles are unattainably hidden from him in impenetrable secrecy.

Equally incapable of seeing the nothingness from which he emerges and the infinity in which he is engulfed.

What else can he do, then, but perceive some semblance of the middle of things, eternally hopeless of knowing either their principles or their end? All things have come out of nothingness and are carried onwards to infinity. Who can follow these astonishing processes? The author of these wonders understands them: no one else can.

Because they failed to contemplate these infinities, men have rashly undertaken to probe into nature as if there were some proportion between themselves and her.

Strangely enough they wanted to know the principles of things and go on from there to know everything, inspired by a presumption as infinite as their object. For there can be no doubt that such a plan could not be conceived without infinite presumption or a capacity as infinite as that of nature.

When we know better, we understand that, since nature has engraved her own image and that of her author on all things, they almost all share her double infinity. Thus we see that all the sciences are infinite in the range of their researches, for who can doubt that mathematics, for instance, has an infinity of infinities of propositions to expound? They are infinite also in the multiplicity and subtlety of their principles, for anyone can see that those which are supposed to be ultimate do not stand by themselves, but depend on others, which depend on others again, and thus never allow of any finality.

But we treat as ultimate those which seem so to our reason, as in material things we call a point indivisible when our senses can perceive nothing beyond it, although by its nature it is infinitely divisible.

Of these two infinities of science, that of greatness is much more obvious, and that is why it has occurred to few people to claim that they know everything. "I am going to speak about everything," Democritus used to say.

But the infinitely small is much harder to see. The philosophers have much more readily claimed to have reached it, and that is where they have all tripped up. This is the origin of such familiar titles as *Of the principles of things, Of the principles of philosophy*, and the like, which are really as pretentious, though they do not look it, as this blatant one: *Of all that can be known.*

We naturally believe we are more capable of reaching the centre of things than of embracing their circumference, and the visible extent of the world is visibly greater than we. But since we in our turn are greater than small things, we think we are more capable of mastering them, and yet it takes no less capacity to reach nothingness than the whole. In either case it takes an infinite capacity, and it seems to me that anyone who had understood the ultimate principles of things might also succeed in knowing infinity. One depends on the other, and one leads to the other. These extremes touch and join by going in opposite directions, and they meet in God and God alone.

Let us then realize our limitations. We are something and we are not everything. Such being as we have conceals from us the knowledge of first principles, which arise from nothingness, and the smallness of our being hides infinity from our sight.

Our intelligence occupies the same rank in the order of intellect as our body in the whole range of nature.

Limited in every respect, we find this intermediate state between two extremes reflected in all our faculties. Our senses can perceive nothing extreme; too much noise deafens us, too much light dazzles; when we are too far or too close we cannot see properly; an argument is obscured by being too long or too short; too much truth bewilders us. I know people who cannot understand that 4 from 0 leaves 0. First principles are too obvious for us; too much pleasure causes discomfort; too much harmony in music is displeasing; too much kindness annoys us; we want to be able to pay back the debt with something over. *Kindness is welcome to the extent that it seems the debt can be paid back. When it goes too far gratitude turns into hatred.*

We feel neither extreme heat nor extreme cold. Qualities carried to excess are bad for us and cannot be perceived; we no longer feel them, we suffer them. Excessive youth and excessive age impair thought; so do too much and too little learning.

In a word, extremes are as if they did not exist for us nor we for them; they escape us or we escape them.

Such is our true state. That is what makes us incapable of certain knowledge or absolute ignorance. We are floating in a medium of vast extent, always drifting uncertainly, blown to and fro; whenever we think we have a fixed point to which we can cling and make fast, it shifts and leaves us behind; if we follow it, it eludes our grasp, slips away, and flees eternally before us. Nothing stands still for us. This is our natural state and yet the state most contrary to our inclinations.

We burn with desire to find a firm footing, an ultimate, lasting base on which to build a tower rising up to infinity, but our whole foundation cracks and the earth opens up into the depth of the abyss.

Let us then seek neither assurance nor stability; our reason is always deceived by the inconsistency of appearances; nothing can fix the finite between the two infinities which enclose and evade it.

Once that is clearly understood, I think that each of us can stay quietly in the state in which nature has placed him. Since the middle station allotted to us is always far from the extremes, what does it matter if someone else has a slightly better understanding of things? If he has, and if he takes them a little further, is he not still infinitely remote from the goal? Is not our span of life equally infinitesimal in eternity, even if it is extended by ten years?

In the perspective of these infinities, all finites are equal and I see no reason to settle our imagination on one rather than another. Merely comparing ourselves with the finite is painful.

If man studied himself, he would see how incapable he is of going further. How could a part possibly know the whole? But perhaps he will aspire to know at least the parts to which he bears some proportion. But the parts of the world are all so related and linked together that I think it is impossible to know one without the other and without the whole.

There is, for example, a relationship between man and all he knows. He needs space to contain him, time to exist in, motion to be alive, elements to constitute him, warmth and food for nourishment, air to breathe. He sees light, he feels bodies, everything in short is related to him. To understand man therefore one must know why he needs air to live, and to understand air one must know how it comes to be thus related to the life of man, etc.

Flame cannot exist without air, so, to know one, one must know the other.

Thus, since all things are both caused or causing, assisted and assisting, mediate and immediate, providing mutual support in a chain linking together naturally and imperceptibly the most distant and different things, I consider it as impossible to know the parts without knowing the whole as to know the whole without knowing the individual parts.

The eternity of things in themselves or in God must still amaze our brief span of life.

The fixed and constant immobility of nature, compared to the continual changes going on in us, must produce the same effect.

And what makes our inability to know things absolute is that they are simple in themselves, while we are composed of two opposing natures of different kinds, soul and body. For it is impossible for the part of us which reasons to be anything but spiritual, and even if it were claimed that we are simply corporeal, that would still more preclude us from knowing things, since there is nothing so inconceivable as the idea that matter knows itself. We cannot possibly know how it could know itself.

Thus, if we are simply material, we can know nothing at all, and, if we are composed of mind and matter, we cannot have perfect knowledge of things which are simply spiritual or corporeal.

That is why nearly all philosophers confuse their ideas of things, and speak spiritually of corporeal things and corporeally of spiritual ones, for they boldly assert that bodies tend to fall, that they aspire towards their centre, that they flee from destruction, that they fear a void, that they have inclinations, sympathies, antipathies, all things pertaining only to things spiritual. And when they speak of minds, they consider them as being in a place, and attribute to them movement from one place to another, which are things pertaining only to bodies.

Instead of receiving ideas of these things in their purity, we colour them with our qualities and stamp our own composite being on all the simple things we contemplate.

Who would not think, to see us compounding everything of mind and matter, that such a mixture is perfectly intelligible to us? Yet this is the thing we understand least; man is to himself the greatest prodigy in nature, for he cannot conceive what body is, and still less what mind is, and least of all how a body can be joined to a mind. This is his supreme difficulty, and yet it is his very being. *The way in which minds are attached to bodies is beyond man's understanding, and yet this is what man is.*

Finally to complete the proof of our weakness, I shall end with these two considerations. . . .

200. . . . Man is only a reed, the weakest in nature, but he is a thinking reed. There is no need for the whole universe to take up arms to crush him: a vapour, a drop of water is enough to kill him. But even

if the universe were to crush him, man would still be nobler than his slayer, because he knows that he is dying and the advantage the universe has over him. The universe knows none of this.

Thus all our dignity consists in thought. It is on thought that we must depend for our recovery, not on space and time, which we could never fill. Let us then strive to think well; that is the basic principle of morality.

201. The eternal silence of these infinite spaces fills me with dread.

202. Be comforted; it is not from yourself that you must expect it, but on the contrary you must expect it by expecting nothing from yourself.

LECTURES ON THE PHILOSOPY OF RELIGION
by
GEORG WILHEM FRIEDRICH HEGEL

Introduction to the Philosophy of Religion

It has appeared to me to be necessary to make religion by itself the object of philosophical consideration, and to add on this study of it, in the form of a special part, to philosophy as a whole. By way of introduction I shall, however, first of all (A) give some account of the severance or division of consciousness, which awakens the need our science has to satisfy, and describe the relation of this science to philosophy and religion, as also to the prevalent principles of the religious consciousness. Then, after I have (B) touched upon some preliminary questions which follow from those relations, I shall give (C) the division of the subject.

To begin with, it is necessary to recollect generally what object we have before us in the Philosophy of Religion, and what is our ordinary idea of religion. We know that in religion we withdraw ourselves from what is temporal, and that religion is for our consciousness that region in which all the enigmas of the world are solved, all the contradictions of deeper-reaching thought have their meaning unveiled, and where the voice of the heart's pain is silenced—the region of eternal truth, of eternal rest, of eternal peace. Speaking generally, it is through thought, concrete thought, or, to put it more definitely, it is by reason of his being Spirit, that man is man; and from man as Spirit proceed all the many developments of the sciences and arts, the interests of political life, and all those conditions which have reference to man's freedom and will. But all these manifold forms of human relations, activities, and pleasures, and all the ways in which these are intertwined; all that has worth and dignity for man, all wherein he seeks his happiness, his glory, and his pride, finds its ultimate centre in religion, in the thought, the consciousness, and the feeling of God. Thus God is the beginning of all things, and the end of all things. As all things proceed from this point, so all return back to it again. He is the centre which gives life and quickening to all things, and which animates and preserves in existence all the various forms of being. In religion man places himself in a relation to this centre, in which all other relations concentrate themselves, and in so doing he rises up to the highest level of consciousness and to the region which is free from relation to what is other than itself, to something which is absolutely self-sufficient, the unconditioned, what is free, and is its own object and end.

Religion, as something which is occupied with this final object and end, is therefore absolutely free, and is its own end; for all other aims converge in this ultimate end, and in presence of it they vanish and cease to have value of their own. No other aim can hold its ground against this, and here alone all find their fulfillment. In the region where the spirit occupies itself with this end, it unburdens itself of all finiteness, and wins for itself final satisfaction and deliverance; for here the spirit relates itself no longer to something that is other than itself, and that is limited, but to the unlimited and infinite, and this is an infinite relation, a relation of freedom, and no longer of dependence. Here its consciousness is absolutely free, and is indeed true consciousness, because it is consciousness of absolute truth. In its character as feeling, this condition of freedom is the sense of satisfaction which we call blessedness, while as activity it has nothing further to do than to manifest the honour of God and to reveal His glory, and in this attitude it is no longer with himself that man is concerned—with his own interests or his empty pride—but with the absolute end. All the various peoples feel that it is in the religious consciousness they possess truth, and they have always regarded religion as constituting their true dignity and the Sabbath of their life. Whatever awakens in us doubt and fear, all sorrow, all care, all the limited interests of finite life, we leave behind on the shores of time; and as from the highest peak of a mountain, far away from all definite view of what is earthly, we look down calmly upon all the limitations of the landscape and of the world, so with the spiritual eye man, lifted out of the hard realities of this actual world, contemplates it as something having only the semblance of existence, which seen from this pure region bathed in the beams of the spiritual sun, merely reflects back its shades of colour, its varied tints and lights, softened away into eternal rest. In this region of spirit flow the streams of forgetfulness from which Psyche drinks, and in which she drowns all sorrow, while the dark things of this life are softened away into a dream-like vision, and become transfigured until they are a mere framework for the brightness of the Eternal.

This image of the Absolute may have a more or less present vitality and certainty for the religious and devout mind, and be a present source of pleasure; or it may be represented as something longed and hoped for, far off, and in the future. Still it always remains a certainty, and its rays stream as something divine into this present temporal life, giving the consciousness of the active presence of truth, even amidst the anxieties which torment the soul here in this region of time. Faith recognises it as the truth, as the substance of actual existing things; and what thus forms the essence of religious contemplation, is the vital force in the present world, makes itself actively felt in the life of the individual, and governs his entire conduct. Such is the general perception, sensation, consciousness, or however we may designate it, of religion. To consider, to examine, and to comprehend its nature is the object of the present lectures.

We must first of all, however, definitely understand, in reference to the end we have in view, that it is not the concern of philosophy to produce religion in any individual. Its existence is, on the contrary, presupposed as forming what is fundamental in every one. So far as man's essential nature is concerned, nothing new is to be introduced into him. To try to do this would be as absurd as to give a dog printed writings to chew, under the idea that in this way you could put mind into it. He who has not extended his spiritual interests beyond the hurry and bustle of the finite world, nor succeeded in lifting himself above this life through aspiration, through the anticipation, through the feeling of the Eternal, and who has not gazed upon the pure ether of the soul, does not possess in himself that element which it is our object here to comprehend.

It may happen that religion is awakened in the heart by means of philosophical knowledge, but it is not necessarily so. It is not the purpose of philosophy to edify, and quite as little is it necessary for it to make good its claims by showing in any particular case that it must produce religious feeling in the individual. Philosophy, it is true, has to develop the necessity of religion in and for itself, and to grasp the thought that Spirit must of necessity advance from the other modes of its will in conceiving and feeling to this absolute mode; but it is the universal destiny of Spirit which is thus accomplished. It is another matter to raise up the individual subject to this height. The self-will, the perversity, or the indolence of individuals may interfere with the necessity of their universal spiritual nature; individuals may deviate from it, and attempt to get for themselves a standpoint of their own, and hold to it. This possibility of letting oneself drift, through inertness, to the standpoint of untruth, or of lingering there consciously and purposely, is involved in the freedom of the subject, while planets, plants, animals, cannot deviate from the necessity of their nature—from their truth—and become what they ought to be. But in human freedom what is and what ought to be are separate. This freedom brings with it the power of free choice, and it is possible for it to sever itself from its necessity, from its laws, and to work in opposition to its true destiny. Therefore, although philosophical knowledge should clearly perceive the necessity of the religious standpoint, and though the will should learn in the sphere of reality the nullity of its separation, all this does not hinder the will from being able to persist in its obstinacy, and to stand aloof from its necessity and truth.

There is a common and shallow manner of arguing against cognition or philosophical knowledge, as when, for instance, it is said that such and such a man has a knowledge of God, and yet remains far from religion, and has not become godly. It is not, however, the aim of knowledge to lead to this, nor is it meant to do so. What knowledge must do is to know religion as something which already exists. It is neither its intention nor its duty to induce this or that person, any particular empirical subject, to be religious if he has not been so before, if he has nothing of religion in himself, and does not wish to have.

But the fact is, no man is so utterly ruined, so lost, and so bad, nor can we regard any one as being so wretched that he has no religion whatever in him, even if it were only that he has the fear of it, or some yearning after it, or a feeling of hatred towards it. For even in this last case he is inwardly occupied with it, and cannot free himself from it. As man, religion is essential to him, and is not a feeling foreign to his nature. Yet the essential question is the relation of religion to his general theory of the universe, and it is with this that philosophical knowledge connects itself, and upon which it essentially works. In this relation we have the source of the division which arises in opposition to the primary absolute tendency of the spirit toward religion, and here, too, all the manifold forms of consciousness, and their most widely differing connections with the main interest of religion, have sprung up. Before the Philosophy of Religion can sum itself up in its own peculiar conception, it must work itself through all those ramifications of the interests of the time which have at present concentrated themselves in the widely-extended sphere of religion. At first the movement of the principles of the time has its place outside of philosophical study, but this movement pushes on to the point at which it comes into contact, strife, and antagonism with philosophy.

from
FEAR AND TREMBLING
by
SØREN KIERKEGAARD

Problema 1
Is there a Teleological Suspension of the Ethical?

The ethical as such is the universal, and as the universal it applies to everyone, which from another angle means that it applies at all times. It rests immanent in itself, has nothing outside itself that is its τέλοξ [end, purpose] but is itself the τέλοξ for everything outside itself, and when the ethical has absorbed this into itself, it goes not further. The single individual, sensately and psychically qualified in immediacy, is the individual who has his τέλοξ in the universal, and it is his ethical task continually to express himself in this, to annul his singularity in order to become the universal. As soon as the single individual asserts himself in his singularity before the universal, he sins, and only by acknowledging this can he be reconciled again with the universal. Every time the single individual, after having entered the universal, feels an impulse to assert himself as the single individual, he is in a spiritual trial [*Anfægtelse*], from which he can work himself only by repentantly surrendering as the single individual in the universal. If this is the highest that can be said of man and his existence, then the ethical is of the same nature as a person's eternal salvation, which is his τέλοξ forevermore and at all times, since it would be a contradiction for this to be capable of being surrendered (that is, teleologically suspended), because as soon as this is suspended it is relinquished, whereas that which is suspended is not relinquished but is preserved in the higher, which is its τέλοξ.

If this is the case, then Hegel is right in "The Good and Conscience," where he qualifies man only as the individual and considers this qualification as a "moral form of evil" (see especially *The Philosophy of Right*), which must be annulled [*ophævet*] in the teleology of the moral in such a way that the single individual who remains in that stage either sins or is immersed in spiritual trial. But Hegel is wrong in speaking about faith; he is wrong in protesting loudly and clearly against Abraham's enjoying honor and glory as a father of faith when he ought to be sent back to a lower court and shown up as a murderer.

Faith is namely this paradox that the single individual is higher than the universal—yet, please note, in such a way that the movement repeats itself, so that after having been in the universal he as the single individual isolates himself as higher than the universal. If this is not faith, then Abraham is lost, then faith has never existed in the world precisely because it has always existed. For if the ethical—that is, social morality—is the highest and if there is in a person no residual incommensurability in some way such that this incommensurability is not evil (i.e., the single individual, who is to be expressed in the universal), then no categories are needed other than what Greek philosophy had or what can be deduced from them by consistent thought. Hegel should not have concealed this, for, after all, he had studied Greek philosophy.

People who are profoundly lacking in learning and are given to clichés are frequently heard to say that a light shines over the Christian world, whereas a darkness enshrouds paganism. This kind of talk has always struck me as strange, inasmuch as every more thorough thinker, every more earnest artist still regenerates himself in the eternal youth of the Greeks. The explanation for such a statement is that one does not know what one should say but only that one must say something. It is quite right to say that paganism did not have faith, but if something is supposed to have been said thereby, then one must have a clearer understanding of what faith is, for otherwise one falls into such clichés. It is easy to explain all existence, faith along with it, without having a conception of what faith is, and the one who counts on being admired for such an explanation is not such a bad calculator, for it is as Boileau says: *Un sot trouve toujours un plus sot, qui l'admire* [One fool always finds a bigger fool, who admires him].

Faith is precisely the paradox that the single individual as the single individual is higher than the universal, is justified before it, not as inferior to it but as superior—yet in such a way, please note, that it is the single individual who, after being subordinate as the single individual to the universal, now by means of the universal becomes the single individual who as the single individual is superior, that the single individual as the single individual stands in an absolute relation to the absolute. This position cannot be mediated, for all mediation takes place only by virtue of the universal; it is and remains for all eternity a paradox, impervious to thought. And yet faith is this paradox, or else (and I ask the reader to bear these consequences *in mente* [in mind] even though it would be too prolix for me to write them all down) or else faith has never existed simply because it has always existed, or else Abraham is lost.

It is certainly true that the single individual can easily confuse this paradox with spiritual trial [*Anfægtelse*], but it ought not to be concealed for that reason. It is certainly true that many persons may be so constituted that they are repulsed by it, but faith ought not therefore to be made into something else to enable one to have it, but one ought rather to admit to not having it, while those who have faith ought to be prepared to set forth some characteristics whereby the paradox can be distinguished from a spiritual trial.

The story of Abraham contains just such a teleological suspension of the ethical. There is no dearth of keen minds and careful scholars who have found analogies to it. What their wisdom amounts to is the beautiful proposition that basically everything is the same. If one looks more closely, I doubt very much that anyone in the whole wide world will find one single analogy, except for a later one, which proves nothing if it is certain that Abraham represents faith and that it is manifested normatively in him, whose life not only is the most paradoxical that can be thought but is also so paradoxical that it simply cannot be thought. He acts by virtue of the absurd, for it is precisely the absurd that he as the single individual is higher than the universal. This paradox cannot be mediated, for as soon as Abraham begins to do so, he has to confess that he was in a spiritual trial, and if that is the case, he will never sacrifice Isaac, or if he did sacrifice Isaac, then in repentance he must come back to the universal. He gets Isaac back again by virtue of the absurd. Therefore, Abraham is at no time a tragic hero but is so something entirely different, either a murderer or a man of faith. Abraham does not have the middle term that saves the tragic hero. This is why I can understand a tragic hero but cannot understand Abraham, even though in a certain demented sense I admire him more than all others.

In ethical terms, Abraham's relation to Isaac is quite simply this: the father shall love the son more than himself. But within its own confines the ethical has various gradations. We shall see whether this story contains any higher expression for the ethical that can ethically explain his behavior, can ethically justify his suspending the ethical obligation to the son, but without moving beyond the teleology of the ethical.

When an enterprise of concern to a whole nation is impeded, when such a project is halted by divine displeasure, when the angry deity sends a dead calm that mocks every effort, when the soothsayer carries out his sad task and announces that the deity demands a young girl as sacrifice—then the father must heroically bring this sacrifice. He must nobly conceal his agony, even though he could wish he were "the lowly man who dares to weep" and not the king who must behave in a kingly manner. Although the lonely agony penetrates his breast and there are only three persons in the whole nation who know his agony, soon the whole nation will be initiated into his agony and also into his deed, that for the welfare of all he will sacrifice her, his daughter, this lovely young girl. 0 bosom! 0 fair cheeks, flaxen hair (v. 687). And the daughter's tears will agitate him, and the father will turn away his face, but the hero must raise the knife. And when the news of it reaches the father's house, the beautiful Greek maidens will blush with enthusiasm, and if the daughter was engaged, her betrothed will not be angry but will be proud to share in the father's deed, for the girl belonged more tenderly to him than to the father.

When the valiant judge who in the hour of need saved Israel binds God and himself in one breath by the same promise, he will heroically transform the young maiden's jubilation, the beloved daughter's joy to sorrow, and all Israel will sorrow with her over her virginal youth. But every freeborn man will understand, every resolute woman will admire Jephthah, and every virgin in Israel will wish to behave as his daughter did, because what good would it be for Jephthah to win the victory by means of a promise if he did not keep it—would not the victory be taken away from the people again?

When a son forgets his duty, when the state entrusts the sword of judgment to the father, when the laws demand punishment from the father's hand, then the father must heroically forget that the guilty one is his son, he must nobly hide his agony, but no one in the nation, not even the son, will fail to admire the father, and every time the Roman laws are interpreted, it will be remembered that many interpreted them more learnedly but no one more magnificently than Brutus.

But if Agamemnon, while a favorable wind was taking the fleet under full sail to its destination, had dispatched that messenger who fetched Iphigenia to be sacrificed; if Jephthah, without being bound by any promise that decided the fate of the nation, had said to his daughter: Grieve now for two months over your brief youth, and then I will sacrifice you; if Brutus had had a righteous son and yet had summoned the lictors to put him to death—who would have understood them? If, on being asked why they did this, these three men had answered: It is an ordeal in which we are being tried [*forsøges*]—would they have been better understood?

When in the crucial moment Agamemnon, Jephthah, and Brutus heroically have overcome the agony, heroically have lost the beloved, and have only to complete the task externally, there will never be a noble soul in the world without tears of compassion for their agony, of admiration for their deed. But if in the crucial moment these three men were to append to the heroic courage with which they bore the agony the little phrase: But it will not happen anyway—who then would understand them? If they went on to explain: This we believe by virtue of the absurd—who would understand them any better, for who would not readily understand that it was absurd, but who would understand that one could then believe it?

The difference between the tragic hero and Abraham is very obvious. The tragic hero is still within the ethical. He allows an expression of the ethical to have its τέλος in a higher expression of the ethical; he scales down the ethical relation between father and son or daughter and father to a feeling that has its dialectic in its relation to the idea of moral conduct. Here there can be no question of a teleological suspension of the ethical itself.

Abraham's situation is different. By his act he transgressed the ethical altogether and had a higher τέλος outside it, in relation to which he suspended it. For I certainly would like to know how Abraham's act can be related to the universal, whether any point of contact between what Abraham did and the universal can be found other than that Abraham transgressed it. It is not to save a nation, not to uphold the idea of the state that Abraham does it; it is not to appease the angry gods. If it were a matter of the deity's being angry, then he was, after all, angry only with Abraham, and Abraham's act is totally unrelated to the universal, is a purely private endeavor. Therefore, while the tragic hero is great because of his moral virtue, Abraham is great because of a purely personal virtue. There is no higher expression for the ethical in Abraham's life than that the father shall love the son. The ethical in the sense of the moral is entirely beside the point. Insofar as the universal was present, it was cryptically in Isaac, hidden, so to speak, in Isaac's loins, and must cry out with Isaac's mouth: Do not do this, you are destroying everything.

Why, then, does Abraham do it? For God's sake and—the two are wholly identical—for his own sake. He does it for God's sake because God demands this proof of his faith; he does it for his own sake so that he can prove it. The unity of the two is altogether correctly expressed in the word already used to describe this relationship. It is an ordeal, a temptation. A temptation—but what does that mean? As a rule, what tempts a person is something that will hold him back from doing his duty, but here the temptation is the ethical itself, which would hold him back from doing God's will. But what is duty? Duty is simply the expression for God's will.

Here the necessity of a new category for the understanding of Abraham becomes apparent. Paganism does not know such a relationship to the divine. The tragic hero does not enter into any private relationship to the divine, but the ethical is the divine, and thus the paradox therein can be mediated in the universal.

Abraham cannot be mediated; in other words, he cannot speak. As soon as I speak, I express the universal, and if I do not do so, no one can understand me. As soon as Abraham wants to express himself in the universal, he must declare that his situation is a spiritual trial [*Anfægtelse*], for he has no higher expression of the universal that ranks above the universal he violates.

Therefore, although Abraham arouses my admiration, he also appalls me. The person who denies himself and sacrifices himself because of duty gives up the finite in order to grasp the infinite and is adequately assured; the tragic hero gives up the certain for the even more certain, and the observer's eye views him with confidence. But the person who gives up the universal in order to grasp something even higher that is not the universal—what does he do? Is it possible that this can be anything other than a spiritual trial? And if it is possible, but the individual makes a mistake, what salvation is there for him? He suffers all the agony of the tragic hero, he shatters his joy in the world, he renounces everything, and perhaps at the same time he barricades himself from the sublime joy that was so precious to him that he would buy it at any price. The observer cannot understand him at all; neither can his eye rest upon him with confidence. Perhaps the believer's intention cannot be carried out at all, because it is inconceivable. Or if it could be done but the individual has misunderstood the deity—what salvation would there be for him? The tragic hero needs and demands tears, and where is the envious eye so arid that it could not weep with Agamemnon, but where is the soul so gone astray that it has the audacity to weep for Abraham? The tragic hero finishes his task at a specific moment in time, but as time passes he does what is no less significant: he visits the person encompassed by sorrow, who cannot breathe because of his anguished sighs, whose thoughts oppress him, heavy with tears. He appears to him, breaks the witchcraft of sorrow, loosens the bonds, evokes the tears, and the suffering one forgets his own sufferings in those of the tragic hero. One cannot weep over Abraham. One approaches him with a *horror religiosus*, as Israel approached Mount Sinai. What if he himself is distraught, what if he had made a mistake, this lonely man who climbs Mount Moriah, whose peak towers sky-high over the flatlands of Aulis, what if he is not a sleepwalker safely crossing the abyss while the one standing at the foot of the mountain looks up, shakes with anxiety, and then in his deference and horror does not even dare to call to him?—Thanks, once again thanks, to a man who, to a person overwhelmed by life's sorrows and left behind naked, reaches out the words, the leafage of language by which he can conceal his misery. Thanks to you, great Shakespeare, you who can say everything, everything, everything just as it is—and yet, why did you never articulate this torment? Did you perhaps reserve it for yourself, like the beloved's name that one cannot bear to have the world utter, for with his little secret that he cannot divulge the poet buys this power of the word to tell everybody else's dark secrets. A poet is not an apostle; he drives out devils only by the power of the devil.

But if the ethical is teleologically suspended in this manner, how does the single individual in whom it is suspended exist? He exists as the single individual in contrast to the universal. Does he sin, then, for from the point of view of the idea, this is the form of sin.

Thus, even though the child does not sin, because it is not conscious of its existence as such, its existence, from the point of view of the idea, is nevertheless sin, and the ethical makes its claim upon it at all times. If it is denied that this form can be repeated in such a way that is not sin, then judgment has fallen upon Abraham. How did Abraham exist? He had faith. This is the paradox by which he remains at the apex, the paradox that he cannot explain to anyone else, for the paradox is that he as the single individual places himself in an absolute relation to the absolute. Is he justified? Again, his justification is the paradoxical, for if he is, then he is justified not by virtue of being something universal but by virtue of being the single individual.

How does the single individual reassure himself that he is legitimate? It is a simple matter to level all existence to the idea of the state or the idea of a society. If this is done, it is also simple to mediate, for one never comes to the paradox that the single individual as the single individual is higher than the universal, something I can also express symbolically in a statement by Pythagoras to the effect that the odd number is more perfect than the even number. If occasionally there is any response at all these days with regard to the paradox, it is likely to be: One judges it by the result. Aware that he is a paradox who cannot be understood, a hero who has become a σχάνδαλον [offense] to his age will shout confidently to his contemporaries: The result will indeed prove that I was justified. This cry is rarely heard in our age, inasmuch as it does not produce heroes—this is its defect—and it likewise has the advantage that it produces few caricatures. When in our age we hear these words: It will be judged by the result—then we know at once with whom we have the honor of speaking. Those who talk this way are a numerous type whom I shall designate under the common name of assistant professors. With security in life, they live in their thoughts: they have a *permanent* position and a *secure* future in a well-organized state. They have hundreds, yes, even thousands of years between them and the earthquakes of existence; they are not afraid that such things can be repeated, for then what would the police and the newspapers say? Their life task is to judge the great men, judge them according to the result. Such behavior toward greatness betrays a strange mixture of arrogance and wretchedness—arrogance because they feel called to pass judgement, wretchedness because they feel that their lives are in no way allied with the lives of the great. Anyone with even a smattering *erectioris ingenii* [of nobility of nature] never becomes an utterly cold and clammy worm, and when he approaches greatness, he is never devoid of the thought that since the creation of the world it has been customary for the result to come last and that if one is truly going to learn something from greatness one must be particularly aware of the beginning. If the one who is to act wants to judge himself by the result, he will never begin. Although the result may give joy to the entire world, it cannot help the hero, for he would not know the result until the whole thing was over, and he would not become a hero by that but by making a beginning.

Moreover, in its dialectic the result (insofar as it is finitude's response to the infinite question) is altogether incongruous with the hero's existence. Or should Abraham's receiving Isaac by a *marvel* be able to prove that Abraham was justified in relating himself as the single individual to the universal? If Abraham actually had sacrificed Isaac, would he therefore have been less justified?

But we are curious about the result, just as we are curious about the way a book turns out. We do not want to know anything about the anxiety, the distress, the paradox. We carry on an esthetic flirtation with the result. It arrives just as unexpectedly but also just as effortlessly as a prize in a lottery, and when we have heard the result, we have built ourselves up. And yet no manacled robber of churches is so despicable a criminal as the one who plunders holiness in this way, and not even Judas, who sold his Lord for thirty pieces of silver, is more contemptible than someone who peddles greatness in this way.

It is against my very being to speak inhumanly about greatness, to make it a dim and nebulous far-distant shape or to let it be great but devoid of the emergence of the humanness without which it ceases to be great, for it is not what happens to me that makes me great but what I do, and certainly there is no one who believes that someone became great by winning the big lottery prize. A person might have been born in lowly circumstances, but I would still require him not to be so inhuman toward himself that he could imagine the king's castle only at a distance and ambiguously dream of its greatness, and destroy it at the same time he elevates it because he elevated it so basely. I require him to be man enough to tread confidently and with dignity there as well. He must not be so inhuman that he insolently violates everything by barging right off the street into the king's hall—he loses more thereby than the king. On the contrary, he should find a joy in observing every bidding of propriety with a happy and confident enthusiasm, which is precisely what makes him a free spirit. This is merely a metaphor, for that distinction is only a very imperfect expression of the distance of spirit. I require every person not to think so inhumanly of himself that he does not dare to enter those palaces where the memory of the chosen ones lives or even those where they themselves live. He is not to enter rudely and foist his affinity upon them. He is to be happy for every time he bows before them, but he is to be confident, free of spirit, and always more than a charwoman, for if he wants to be no more than that, he will never get in. And the very thing that is going to help him is the anxiety and distress in which the great were tried, for otherwise, if he has any backbone, they will only arouse his righteous envy. And anything that can be great only at a distance, that someone wants to make great with empty and hollow phrases—is destroyed by that very person.

Who was as great in the world as that favored woman, the mother of God, the Virgin Mary? And yet how do we speak of her? That she was the favored one among women does not make her great, and if it would not be so very odd for those who listen to be able to think just as inhumanly as those who speak, then every young girl might ask: Why am I not so favored? And if I had nothing else to say, I certainly would not dismiss such a question as stupid, because, viewed abstractly, vis-à-vis a favor, every person is just as entitled to it as the other. We leave out the distress, the anxiety, the paradox. My thoughts are as pure as anybody's, and he who can think this way surely has pure thoughts, and, if not, he can expect something horrible, for anyone who has once experienced these images cannot get rid of them again, and if he sins against them, they take a terrible revenge in a silent rage, which is more terrifying than the stridency of ten ravenous critics. To be sure, Mary bore the child wondrously, but she nevertheless did it "after the manner of women," and such a time is one of anxiety, distress, and paradox. The angel was indeed a ministering spirit, but he was not a meddlesome spirit who went to the other young maidens in Israel and said: Do not scorn Mary, the extraordinary is happening to her. The angel went only to Mary, and no one could understand her. Has any woman been as infringed upon as was Mary, and is it not true here also that the one whom God blesses he curses in the same breath? This is the spirit's view of Mary, and she is by no means—it is revolting to me to say it but even more so that people have inanely and unctuously made her out to be thus—she is by no means a lady idling in her finery and playing with a divine child. When, despite this, she said: Behold, I am the handmaid of the Lord—then she is great, and I believe it should not be difficult to explain why she became the mother of God. She needs worldly admiration as little as Abraham needs tears, for she was no heroine and he was no hero, but both of them became greater than these, not by being exempted in any way from the distress and the agony and the paradox, but became greater by means of these.

It is great when the poet in presenting his tragic hero for public admiration dares to say: Weep for him, for he deserves it. It is great to deserve the tears of those who deserve to shed tears. It is great that the poet dares to keep the crowd under restraint, dares to discipline men to examine themselves individually to see if they are worthy to weep for the hero, for the slop water of the snivellers is a debasement of the sacred.—But even greater than all this is the knight of faith's daring to say to the noble one who wants to weep for him: Do not weep for me, but weep for yourself.

We are touched, we look back to those beautiful times. Sweet sentimental longing leads us to the goal of our desire, to see Christ walking about in the promised land. We forget the anxiety, the distress, the paradox. Was it such a simple matter not to make a mistake? Was it not terrifying that this man walking around among the others was God? Was it not terrifying to sit down to eat with him? Was it such an easy matter to become an apostle? But the result, the eighteen centuries—that helps, that contributes to this mean deception whereby we deceive ourselves and others. I do not feel brave enough to wish to be contemporary with events like that, but I do not for that reason severely condemn those who made a mistake, nor do I depreciate those who saw what was right.

But I come back to Abraham. During the time before the result, either Abraham was a murderer every minute or we stand before a paradox that is higher than all mediations.

The story of Abraham contains, then, a teleological suspension of the ethical. As the single individual he became higher than the universal. This is the paradox, which cannot be mediated. How he entered into it is just as inexplicable as how he remains in it. If this is not Abraham's situation, then Abraham is not even a tragic hero but a murderer. It is thoughtless to want to go on calling him the father of faith, to speak of it to men who have an interest only in words. A person can become a tragic hero through his own strength —but not the knight of faith. When a person walks what is in one sense the hard road of the tragic hero, there are many who can give him advice, but he who walks the narrow road of faith has no one to advise him—no one understands him. Faith is a marvel, and yet no human being is excluded from it; for that which unites all human life is passion, and faith is a passion.

PART THREE
PHILOSOPHY OF ART AND CULTURE

INTRODUCTION

by

ROBERT PIPPIN

E ver since human beings became distinct sorts of creatures, they
have taken pleasure in imitating the natural world and the
events of their fellow humans. Such imitators often concentrated on
a kind of formal perfection in their objects, and in a certain grand-
ness in the actions they represented; they strove in their
representations for the "beautiful." Although all civilizations worthy
of the name have pointed to the achievements of their artists as typical of, indeed, definitive of, such a civilized life, the fact of there
being art at all and the nature of its importance have also always
been puzzling. Why there should be such an activity at all, what sort
of pleasure this might be, and whether the activity and our enjoyment of it are important or worthwhile in a human community are
among the earliest questions raised by the first philosophers, especially by Plato and Aristotle. The fact that human beings like to
gather in the dark and watch other human beings pretend to be
characters who often do horrible or hilarious things to each other;
the presence of marble versions of gods and animals and humans in
public spaces (why reproduce something when the originals are all
over the place?), the delight taken in highly artificial and unusual
arrangement of words and in their metric and aural properties, and
the efforts made by human beings to produce sounds in various har-
monic (and even dissonant) relations to each other are all on the face
of it, and in the light of how much effort the great struggle for existence itself costs, rather mysterious.

Since there is a natural human pleasure in learning, and since we
often learn by imitation, Aristotle suggested that this link with
learning and human nature might guide reflection about the function and value of art. Since we seem especially interested in
representing the beautiful, and in dramatic depictions of very great,
heroic, and thereby beautiful (fine, noble) men and women and
their beautiful deeds, and since the power of the beautiful to sway

our judgment and move our emotions is so great (and has seemed to many linked somehow with our sexual desire and erotic natures), it seemed reasonable to Plato to try to understand (and to assess) this pleasure and its importance by understanding the role of the emotions (especially the role of the erotic) in human life.

The fact that we desire the beautiful, both in art and in natural and romantic contexts, reveals something about our basic erotic nature, according to Plato, about what we want by nature. The desire for the beautiful reveals, it was claimed, that desire is not satisfiable in a wholly sensible way or by sensible particulars, that what we finally want to possess is not just a beautiful body but the beauty manifested by other bodies and in even "higher," more perfect forms. There might also be a great deal that anyone needs to know in living a life, but which is so elusive and difficult that such knowledge could not be formulated in philosophical claims and arguments, but which could be presented more intuitively, indirectly, and experientially in aesthetic experience. (Although Plato's and Aristotle's views are quite different, this link between our interest in the beautiful and what both understood to be the fundamental human desire—for wisdom—unites them, even if Plato seemed to worry in the *Republic* more about the dangerous political effects of art's emotional power.) The idea that our love of beauty manifests something fundamental about human nature itself will play a recurring role in reflections on the aesthetic dimension of life.

Moreover, since the role of human emotions can be very powerful, and since artists and poets can be extremely effective at exciting and directing such emotions, such artists and poets might be quite powerful or politically influential in a community. If such skill at imitating and reproducing is *so* great that the observer can even be made to forget that he is seeing a particular perspective and believes that the poet's view of human life, the family, the gods' and human beings' place in the cosmos, is simply true, then that power is all the greater. Epic and tragic poets might assume the role of the moral educators in a community, powerfully swaying audiences to admire or reject various human individuals and types.

Such assumptions set the stage for a great controversy or ancient "quarrel," when one begins to worry about our being led so effectively by those who know more how to lead than where they should lead us. Could it even be possible that an ideal human city might be better off without artists and poets, that they should be banned? Could Socrates have been serious about such a famous proposal in Plato's *Republic*?

It is worthy of note that the earliest philosophical discussion of the arts had so much to do with such concerns about the putative *danger* of the arts, its role in education, its effects on the emotions and allegiances of citizens. Such issues have obviously not gone away (although provincial libraries now go after J. D. Salinger rather than Homer) and frame the discussion even for some who oppose Plato's views. Aristotle, for example, may have mounted a kind of indirect defense of the tragic poets against such Platonic charges (arguing that the emotional experience felt in viewing tragic drama was "cathartic," a kind of release, and thereby useful, that the experience of such pity and fear could be politically moderating or humbling, not dangerous or excessive), but his account was also framed as an element of a political philosophy, or even a political psychology, as if the city-state were the appropriate, all-encompassing context. He still took seriously the question: is art really good for us?

But these early controversies raised a number of issues besides the political and generally evaluative one. As the political issue already demonstrates, one important general consideration concerns the relation between artistic and other activities, especially whether such aesthetic activities and reactions always (or never) serve some other-than-aesthetic purpose, whether it is political, or religious, or social (like a "class interest"). Is art, and the artist's ability to direct and excite emotions through imitation and expression, more like a tool with which other ends might be achieved—political, morally educative, or religious—or is there something distinctly aesthetic that we seek in such experiences, for its own sake? Plato and Aristotle might want to consider the role of the tragic poets as a vital element in the political (and especially educational) life of a city-state, and perhaps that was how art (including public monuments, temples, and statues) was experienced by the ancient Greeks, but it could also be claimed that such a context might distort more than it reveals about art's true function in human life, and even Plato and Aristotle might be misreading and so misreporting the actual, classical experience of art (as Friedrich Nietzsche would later argue).

The general controversy about the relative dependence or independence of aesthetic experience became as important and contested an issue as the question that remained at the core of aesthetic reflection: what is art? And the two are obviously related issues. Since for most of the postclassical and premodern period, the function of art was to be subservient to religion, especially in architecture and music, the nature of such aesthetic experience seemed relatively unproblematic. Distinctions between art and craft were not paramount; imitative success and either pleasure (at the majesty and beauty of divine creation) or a certain sort of pain (awe at the majesty and power of God; anxiety about salvation) seemed clearly the way in which art functioned in its subservient, essentially religious role. But the emergence of a radically new historical period in European civilization, first with the Italian and German and then English Renaissance, and then with the discoveries of the new natural science and the political project of the Enlightenment, also began to affect profoundly the experience of the beautiful and the artistic, and reflective attempts to understand the nature and function of art. With the modern world, the aesthetic dimension came to be understood more and more as essentially *independent*, and as having a distinct sort of *importance* in human life.

To understand fully the altered status of the beautiful in general in modernity, and the different ways in which art came to be appreciated in the modern world, one would have to understand something like the nature of the modern revolution itself, a topic still hotly debated. There is, at least, not much controversy that, at the beginning of the modern period, a settled, aristocratic, hierarchical social and political order based on inherited position and tradition came to an end, that the temporal and spiritual power of organized religion diminished, fragmented, and changed, that a new form of production and economic distribution began to flourish, that democratic control over political institutions and public power grew rapidly, and that human beings, armed with a new scientific method modeled on mathematical physics, began to be able to improve the conditions of their existence and to master nature in ways unimaginable in antiquity. There is certainly still great controversy, though, over how to understand the significance of such wrenching change, what it meant and still means that human history could, in effect, break apart like this (if indeed it did). It would certainly be very surprising if, in the midst of this altered context, human beings would not come to experience the world and their own productions in some different aesthetic way, but the nature of those differences and the meaning of the beginnings of a genuinely "modern art" are still contested.

For one thing, it is clear enough that the new and ever more authoritative scientific understanding of the natural world would have to alter a great deal in any attempt to understand our delight in the naturally beautiful. If there really is no "great chain of being" or hierarchy of less to more perfect or better being, if the natural world is a stable, eternal world of form that we are inclined by nature to know, then the traditional understanding of the significance of the beautiful—much of which certainly survived and flourished in the Platonism of the Italian Renaissance—could not be defended. If nature was better understood as matter in motion, subject to necessary causal laws, what new explanation could there be for our various and apparently common affective reactions to the natural world in some of its manifestations rather than others?

The first systematic, ambitious, and widely influential attempt to rethink the meaning of the aesthetic in the altered context of modernity was presented in the extraordinary book written by the German philosopher Immanuel Kant, *Critique of Judgment,* published in 1790. Several of the deep and largely permanent alterations in the modern Western conception of the aesthetic dimension were introduced and defended in that work. In the first place, Kant insisted on the subjective nature of such experience. He argued that although the form of an aesthetic judgment, "this is beautiful," appears to express a standard affirmative assertion ascribing a predicate to an object, beauty cannot possibly be understood as an objective predicate. The new mechanistic natural world of causally interacting particles, which Kant himself had already defended so powerfully as the only sort of objective world we could make true or false claims about, cannot contain "the beautiful" as a natural predicate. Instead, "this is beautiful" must be understood to have as its true or deep grammatical structure, "I am experiencing a certain sort of pleasure in the presence of this object." Beauty must be understood as a distinct *result* of the interaction between the world and our particular cognitive equipment, not as a predicate like "has mass" or "moves at thirty-two feet per second." To experience the beautiful is not to have learned anything about nature; therefore there are not some appreciators who know more than others. To claim that an object is beautiful is only to claim that it gives me pleasure, produces a pleasurable sensation.

But Kant hardly left his analysis at such a subjective and potentially relativistic point. At such a point, one person might find something beautiful, another not, and that would be it; one might express delight at a sunset or a bird's song, another at the smell of cabbage cooking, another at the sight of a dead cow, and given the vast range of individual preferences, backgrounds, and dispositions, "everything would be subjective." But Kant proceeded to argue that even though the ultimate source of aesthetic experience is our own faculties and their interaction, not the nature of the world, this new source has its own kind of authority and claim to legitimacy. One could show, Kant argued, that an aesthetic judgment, if it is a proper aesthetic judgment, possesses a certain claim on all other human beings. Since that claim is not tied to something "in the world" that a person would "miss" by not appreciating the beautiful, the nature of this claim to universality has to be expressed differently. "I am experiencing a distinct sort of pleasure, and aesthetic pleasure" expresses a general claim on the reaction of all others: "*All ought to feel such a pleasure* in the presence of such an object." With great ingenuity and his usual bold originality, Kant proceeded to attempt a "deduction" or general justification of the possibility of such a claim on all others.

The details of such an argument are complex and still much contested. (Kant argued that an aesthetic pleasure is not dependent on any particular sensible constitution or particular interests. It depends only on the disinterested free play of the kind of faculties that *any* human subject must be assumed to possess and so is a reaction that can be rationally expected from any such subject.) But the direction in which Kant sent reflection on aesthetics, what he expressed about how we might understand the beautiful in the altered situation of modernity and why it might still be a profoundly important dimension of human experience, remain influential to this day. First, aside from his most important formulation, about the subjectivity of the beautiful (a claim itself shared in other ways by more empirical, sensualist theories of beautiful, like Francis Hutcheson's, Edmund Burke's, and Lord Kames's), Kant advanced several theses that were to affect a great deal of what came after him. According to Kant, certain natural experiences occasion a kind of delight because we discover that the immediately given sensible elements of our experience present themselves to us in what seems a kind of *purposive* form, as if somehow the directly sensible world is "suited" to our intellectual need and indeed demand for order and harmony in the world. But this order and harmony must not be a result or function of the application of a normal empirical concept like "flower" or "landscape" or a result of our *making*, that is, imposing order. Our ordering concepts can be satisfied in any number of humdrum ways; but the fact that the independent sensible elements of our experience can occasion a kind of "free play" of our imagination, not directly guided or ordered by a concept, but falling into a kind of free order on their own, is all, in a word, delightful. Such a pleasure, moreover, is not linked to the satisfaction of any clear goal nor tied to any specific interest. (If we do try to make use of some object "for the sake of pleasure" or a specific interest, we will not be experiencing the beautiful, but rather a mere repeatable sensible pleasure, Kant argued.) The world as we directly take it in sensibly seems to fit and suits "on its own" for our intellectual purposes. Nature could have been colorless and monotonous and simply dull. The fact that it isn't so ugly is quite pleasurable and thus, in a distinct sort of way, of great importance for our sense of ourselves.

For Kant also formulated what would be the greatest problem for modern philosophy, the largest question to be answered in the situation created by the scientific revolution. According to that new science, we are just as much parts of the natural world as anything else, subject to necessary causal laws regulating, and rendering in principle predictable, all alteration in time. This new principle makes it exceedingly hard to understand the special sort of respect we want to accord human beings, the dignity we believe that each individual is owed just by being a human being. A great dualism appears to have been bequeathed to us by modernity, between our natural and sensible being on the one hand, and our free, morally responsible being on the other. Kant did not believe a philosophical solution for such a dilemma was possible, but he also insisted that we could not leave the issue as simply a great mystery. Holding ourselves to a standard of individual moral responsibility must make some kind of overall sense, must fit into some sort of whole or general view of things, if we are to be able to keep faith with such a moral destiny.

At this point in his reasoning, the experience of the beautiful emerges as a crucial dimension of Kant's overall philosophy. As we have seen, Kant located our delight in the beautiful in the fact that the sensible apprehensible natural world is not merely apprehensible as bit and chunks of material wholes. "Apart" from our intellectual ordering and regulating, it exhibits some sort of suitability "for us," for our nonsensible purposes and goals. Kant thought that this was experienced by virtue of the delight occasioned by formal regularities exhibited in our imaginative "free" apprehension. But the most important point he was making involved the dual claim that our capacity to appreciate the beautiful is not subservient to some other sensible end or concrete interest—the beautiful is not a manifestation of something else or reducible to some other sort of pleasure or interest; it is autonomous; and second, this capacity demonstrates that our moral and nonsensible natures are not absurdly adrift in some material, meaningless cosmos. We were in effect demonstrating our transcendence of our material and corporeal natures by such a capacity to appreciate, take such a delight in, such formal, non-material aspects of the natural world.

Such claims about the *subjectivity* of aesthetic experience, and such insistence on the *autonomy of the aesthetic,* came to play essential roles in almost all later modern reflection on the aesthetic dimension. The beautiful was not meant to be understood as a mere means in the service of something else, or a simple psychological pleasure, manifested in a variety of ways by a variety of individuals. The newly liberated bourgeois individual came to consider himself entitled to a pleasure not subservient to the religious or the political or even the sensible, and he could now experience an equally liberated aesthetic dimension. And such an experience came to be quite important: our capacity to appreciate the beautiful could be said to evince a certain *dignity,* moral significance, and even transcendence of the material (and later the commercialized, bourgeois) world.

To be sure, Kant's position would often be left far behind. For one thing, Kant was much more interested in the naturally beautiful; he relegated artworks to a decidedly secondary significance and even seemed slightly suspicious, on moral grounds, of artistic activity not directly linked to the (for him) "original" natural experience of the beautiful. Art*works* of all kinds would quickly assume much more importance than that afforded them by Kant. (Indeed, the Kantian and traditional emphasis on the beautiful in nature would soon lose its hold on the imagination of European modernity.

Perhaps the idea of such a holistic, comprehensive harmony with the natural world began to look naive in the era of modern science and technology. It began to look difficult enough to feel at home with our won constructions and productions. Reconciliation with ourselves and with each other loomed as even more pressing problems.) Pleasure would not long hold pride of place in explanations of the aesthetic, as the experience of the sublime—and a much greater interest in aesthetic reactions of shock, the painful, the uncanny, the mysterious, the horrifying—would come to occupy more central roles in the public life of art, and the political and social function of artworks would come back into prominence as great questions, supplanting to some extent the more metaphysical concerns evident in Kant. Nevertheless, the link that Kant tried to establish between the aesthetic dimension of experience and human freedom, its role in manifesting the fact of our not being sensible, determined creatures, would begin a style of thought and introduce a set of issues that would be constitutive of modern reflections on the significance of the aesthetic.

This was immediately obvious in the extremely influential post-Kantian manifesto written in 1793 by the German poet and playwright Friedrich Schiller, *On the Aesthetic Education of Man in a Series of Letters*. In Schiller's hands, many of Kant's ideas were presented without all of the complex links to the general Kantian project in critical philosophy, and were developed and expanded in ways that revealed a great deal about both the aspirations and the anxieties of the new age. For the modern age had announced itself as the age of liberation, and the great persistent question of modernity thus concerned what was also the most important Kantian theme: freedom itself, its nature and the conditions of its realization. The question obviously provoked a number of pressing political responses, and both Kant and Schiller were living through the age of the French Revolution as they wrote their important works. But the familiar idea (persistent despite so much criticism and even what seems to many such manifest implausibility) that the aesthetic dimension of life could make us better people (or could reveal the presence of our better qualities) took a distinct shape in Schiller's work, one greatly influenced by the Kantian understanding of what makes us worthwhile in the first place, or our freedom. It is "through beauty," Schiller was bold enough to say, that "we arrive at freedom," and so can realize our "noblest destiny" as moral beings. The idea that the creation of and participation in art could count as the achievement of freedom (by contrast, could establish a kind of resistance to natural and social experiences of necessity) would have a long and complex history thereafter.

Kant had borrowed from Jean-Jacques Rousseau the idea that would become one of the most historically influential ever uttered by a philosopher—that all human beings are worthy of a kind of unqualified respect by virtue of a capacity they all share: the ability to set the course of their own lives as individuals, to be self-determining or autonomous beings. They are entitled to such respect for that reason. Because they have that capacity, no one can be treated as a mere means for anyone else; they are all "ends in themselves." More specifically, such subjects can be considered free because they can deliberate and choose what to do; they can set their ends on the basis of reason, not merely pursue ends set by nature or society. Human reason is, in all persons, capable of determining the principles of action, and persons are capable of acting on such motivation, because such a principle holds for all rational agents. But of course, persons are not exclusively rational agents; they are creatures of sensibility, desire, and passion as well, and act, perhaps most of the time, on the basis of such passions and needs. They in effect allow themselves "to *be* determined"; they allow the course of their lives "to be set" by passions and interests that they do not "set" themselves, and so do not act freely in the fullest sense. Acting in a way that acknowledges the equal claim of all others to determine their own lives as well, and so according to a rational principle, and thereby in a self-determined way, thus came to be understood as a difficult moral ideal as well as an abstract principle.

Given the great power and influence of human passions and the human ego, we might think that the chances for the realization of such an ideal are slim to none. Although Kant himself believed in the possibility of some moral progress, his basic view was that "nothing straight could be made from such a crooked timber" as man, that we would remain "radically evil" (always inclined to give priority to our own case), and that the opposition between our capacity to direct our actions with reason and thereby freely, and our sensuous inclinations, allowed few opportunities for mediation and reconciliation. But Schiller, taking up some of Kant's own ideas about the symbolic importance of the beautiful, argued that our sensibilities should be understood as elements of a whole harmonious being, not as abstractly opposed to reason, and that when they are understood in this way, we can see how they could, in effect, change, be educated. They are subject to cultural training and habit, and Schiller tried to show that the most powerful vehicle both for evincing such a more harmonious human nature and for such moral education is art itself. There might be an "aesthetic education of mankind."

Schiller was not at all thinking about moralistic literature, or the Aesop's fable, lessons-for-life approach. His point was much more general and concerned the way in which all great art, apart from the issue of subject matter, can both demonstrate and help us experience the potential and real harmony between the ideal, rational, or formal elements of experience and the material or sensible elements. In such an aesthetic dimension, the material marble or sensible words are not simply the bearers of superimposed form, the stuff on which form is impressed; they express such formal elements in a kind of living harmony that Schiller took to be of immense moral as well as aesthetic significance. "Beauty," Schiller claimed, "is freedom in appearance."

On the face of it, there is no particular reason why aesthetic success of this sort—both the ability to embody what we can create in the matter of creation in a kind of seamless harmony, and our engaged, intense experience of such harmony—should have as much moral significance as Schiller insisted. The question of rational self-direction and sensible, egoistic opposition might be only a very general instance of the opposition between ideal and real, of no particular importance for moral experience or moral education. But not only did Schiller's apologia for art make a certain philosophical case; not only was he the first to express so clearly what would become an ardent hope of the emerging European middle classes— that their ever more routinized, regulated, alienated, money-dominated lives might still allow a moment of transcendent personal and universal meaning, a demonstration of higher cultural capacities and a redemption of sorts. The kind of importance that Schiller bestowed on certain elements of aesthetic experience, and the influence his position enjoyed, revealed a general anxiety in the age he addressed. The lack of common consensus about religious values, and the rapid dislocations, revolutions, and simply the pace of change characteristic of modernity had created a distinct kind of yearning for a sphere of meaning and a sense of importance not fulfilled by the secular standards of political or commercial success allowed by the emerging bourgeois world. That world was the world of "unfreedom," necessity, and control. The aesthetic world, on the other hand, was taken to represent the world of authenticity, integrity, and freedom. In the specific case of Schiller, it could even exhibit both a disinterested liberation from individual or egoistic interests, as well as a kind of reconciliation with such a sensible world. Beautiful art could evince and create a beautiful soul.

We have already seen in this brief survey that part of the answer to such questions as the nature of art, and its importance and value, seem to have a great deal to do with the kind of society in which such art is produced and appreciated. It might be expected that a culture that places a very high value on a kind of civic harmony, or on religious devotion, or on individual freedom and individual moral responsibility, or on commercial success, or on some recovery of meaning and purpose where such direction is experienced as threatened, might in effect turn to its artists with different sets of questions and hopes in such different circumstances. (Like all aesthetic issues, however, this is hardly an uncontroversial assumption and is much debated. Many critics see what is distinctive in all art as certain special formal properties and understand the history of alteration in attention to different properties as wholly internal to art history, as a matter of internal artistic experimentation among artists. Such critics point to our ability to appreciate art from all ages as proof of its formally transcendent nature. Still others, like Theodor Adorno, understand art in terms of its formal properties but see in art's formal properties precisely the locus of its historical and critical meaning.) If anything like such a general assumption about aesthetic social and historical meaning is true, though, it would especially help explain the altered status of the aesthetic realm when the official culture of European modernity began, in the latter half of the nineteenth century, to experience a series of profound crises of self-confidence and purpose.

One philosopher and culture critic above all others is associated with this crisis, Friedrich Nietzsche (who called it the problem of "nihilism"). Nietzsche published his first important book, *The Birth of Tragedy*, about the role that art, especially music (the opera of Richard Wagner most especially), should play in the light of that purported crisis. The modern secular movement of "enlightenment," Nietzsche claimed, had promised to allow only those claims to authority, whether political, moral, or intellectual, that could be securely defended by reason. This critically self-conscious culture would, so went the promise, allow us to foster a world of rational, self-reliant, diverse individuals, tolerant of each other's diversity and secure in the great universal authority of the claims of reason. Instead, Nietzsche said, such a rational criticism had become an all-encompassing skepticism, and, especially with Kant's philosophy, ultimately so critical even about its own enterprise that it had begun to "devour its own tail" and had produced intellectual confusion and lassitude, not confidence. Socially, instead of a race of self-reliant individuals, the European democratic enlightenment had produced, Nietzsche claimed, a race of timid sheep, conformist, anxious, and vulgar. This intellectual and social crisis amounted to a crisis of value, or the crisis of nihilism, the debilitating sense that "nothing is true; everything is allowed," that "the goal stands missing," that there is nothing worth wanting or striving for.

Nietzsche's early (1870) work, *The Birth of Tragedy out of the Spirit of Music*, is written largely in the form of a philological essay on the historical origins of Greek tragedy. But amid the historical details of his unusual claims about the role of the chorus and music, Nietzsche returned to the "ancient quarrel" between poetry and philosophy begun by Plato. For the first time in the history of Western thought, Nietzsche mounted a stinging attack on the West's greatest intellectual hero, Socrates, all in the name of, or as an advocate of, the tragic poets, especially Aeschylus and Sophocles. (Euripides was treated as already too much under the influence of Socrates' intellectualism.) Socrates was attacked for having created the kind of "false" or "naive" optimism about the possible role of reason and reflection in human life that, for Nietzsche, was to have such fateful consequences throughout the Western tradition. By contrast, "tragedy" was treated by Nietzsche not as a purely aesthetic criterion, but as a kind of ethical category. Tragic drama, treated as paradigmatic for all art, was analyzed not only as expressive of a violent, unstable, creative tension between human attempts at form-giving, clarity, and order (the Apollonian force) and the form-dissolving, intoxicating, even orgiastic materiality of the Dionysean (an opposition that owes more to Schiller than Nietzsche admits), but also as a powerful non-Socratic answer to the famous, core Socratic question: how should one live? The tragic point of view represented a "tragic pessimism," a kind of strength in the face of the failure of order and individuation and coherence, and affirmation of life in spite of such suffering, and without any appeal to a Socratic sort of "argument" or a rational "answer" to the question of "why life ought to be lived." The question itself, Nietzsche argued, already represented a hatred of life, a Socratic decadence that we need not accept as the necessary starting point of human affirmation.

Nietzsche's position raises many questions, and he himself very soon abandoned the call for a reanimation of the tragic point of view through the operatic music of Wagner. The idea of some failure in the Enlightenment version of modernity seemed to return us to the ancient quarrel and it reraised the question of whether a certain aesthetic stance toward life (or what Nietzsche continued to call an "aesthetic justification of existence") might prove superior in many ways to Enlightenment appeals to reason. Giving such an aesthetic form of sense-making and legitimacy a kind of priority might be truer to the unresolvability and ambiguities of life's tensions and it might provide a better, more adequate "affirmation of life." Such themes not only intensified with what had already proven to be powerful currents of European romanticism, but also helped intensify the enthusiasm in the late modern tradition for a "critical" view of art, for the avant-garde, the "modernist," the anti-bourgeois, and the revolutionary. In many ways, Nietzsche was the first avant-garde philosopher, the first modern philosopher who raised the question of whether he "belonged" in philosophy or in literature, whether he was writing philosophy or performing the parts of various philosophical characters. This was a deliberate confusion on his part, a consequence of his sense that the ascendancy of the Socratic or scientific point of view was over, and that a new era was at least possible, oriented from the creative, experimental, pessimistic but still affirmative potential of the aesthetic, and that he was to be its new "Socrates," the great historical turning point for what we now call such a "postmodern" age.

Of course, Nietzsche's stance is not the only way one might think about the continuity between the fate of art and the fate of the modern age. For many traditional Marxist critics, for whom artistic style and content were best understood as "ideological" reflections of class relations and class struggle, that is, as means by which ruling classes sought to legitimize themselves and determine the perceptions of others, the proper category of modernist art was also historical, but modernism was understood as "decadent" not liberating (as a reflection of the historically "contradictory" or dead-end or despair-filled state of modern capitalism).

Adorno's position is not crudely reductionist like this, and is connected with a revised new-Marxist analysis of modernity. For theorists like Adorno, the chief characteristic of modern capitalism is not class conflict as such but its enormous success at integrating individuals into its system of social organization, its ability to present a homogenizing and stultifying conformism as simply the neutral rationalizations of bureaucratic, efficient organization, and so its powerful ability to defuse, marginalize, and co-opt all opposition, its totalistic order. He called this the problem of "identity thinking" and, like others already discussed, he treated the aesthetic dimension as a form of negation of, or opposition to, such pervasive identity. ("Art is the social antithesis of society.") Adorno was much more sympathetic to the "negative" political potential in modernist and avant-garde artworks (especially in music), because he thought that the formal experimentation characteristic of such work could break the hold in some way of the dominant canons of rationalization and integration. He accordingly and somewhat paradoxically attributed a serious political importance to the autonomy of the artwork and developed a much more sympathetic social-critical position on modernist art than many other Marxist critics. The existence of art itself, especially formal experimental work, stood as a sign for a great dissatisfaction with reality as it was, for the need of a negation and reworking of social reality, an expression of rejection and negation that could itself have liberating effects.

For a much more optimistic, if nonstandard, modernist like John Dewey, the making and appreciating of all art was indeed connected with modern "experience," but not in the revolutionary or oppositional way suggested by Nietzsche and other avant-gardists, and not in the formally "negative" way proposed by Adorno. Art should be understood more as a continuous component of ordinary human experience, or understood functionally, in terms of the needs and goals of practical life within which the especially intense, formally ordered experiences of aesthetic appreciation could play their role and so could best be understood. These needs and goals include needs for depth of understanding and subtlety of communication and the stimulation of creative "energy" that art can satisfy, even across widely different historical periods. And finally, for all the differences between Dewey's account and many others here summarized, he ends his treatment with yet another expression of that great, persistent hope that art can make us better, that it can "remake" us, "redirect" our desire, and "insinuate possibilities of human relations not to be found in rules and precept."

Views like these, expressing the fear that art may corrupt us or the hope that art might educate our sensibilities or enrich or even redeem us, also recall a final contrary view, that the era of art's great significance and importance in human life is over, at an end. If the question is "what is the meaning of aesthetic experience—so-called high art or culture aspirations—in the late modern world?" the answer might be "there is no such meaning or role, that such experiences have been fatally marginalized." And if the question is "how might one differentiate genuinely aesthetic experience from the pleasurable entertainment provided by modern advertisers and mass market producers?" the answer might be "such a distinction no longer exists." The authors of these selections and many other philosophers and artists throughout history would clearly regard such a state of affairs as a catastrophe. Whether such a state of affairs has in fact come to pass, and if so, whether that judgment is correct, must be left here as open questions.

Having finished presenting an account of the perfectly just state, Socrates and his companions reflect upon it. Socrates begins a discussion with Glaucon about poetry, and why he has decreed that the poets must be exiled from the city.

Of the many excellences which I perceive in the order of our State, there is none which upon reflection pleases me better than the rule about poetry.

To what do you refer?

To the rejection of imitative poetry, which certainly ought not to be received; as I see far more clearly now that the parts of the soul have been distinguished.

What do you mean?

Speaking in confidence, for I should not like to have my words repeated to the tragedians and the rest of the imitative tribe—but I do not mind saying to you, that all poetical imitations are ruinous to the understanding of all hearers, and that the knowledge of their true nature is the only antidote to them.

Explain the purport of your remark.

Well, I will tell you, although I have always from my earliest youth had an awe and love of Homer, which even now makes the words falter on my lips, for he is the great captain and teacher of the whole of that charming tragic company; but a man is not to be reverenced more than the truth, and therefore I will speak out.

Very good, he said.

Listen to me then, or rather, answer me.

Put your question.

Can you tell me what imitation is? For I really do not know.

A likely thing, then, that I should know.

Why not? For the duller eye may often see a thing sooner than the keener.

Very true, he said; but in your presence, even if I had any faint notion, I could not muster courage to utter it. Will you enquire yourself?

Well then, shall we begin the enquiry in our usual manner: Whenever a number of individuals have a common name, we assume them to have also a corresponding idea or form. Do you understand me?

I do.

Let us take a common instance; there are beds and tables in the world—plenty of them, are there not?

Yes.

But there are only two ideas or forms of them—one the idea of a bed, the other of a table.

True.

And the maker of either of them makes a bed or he makes a table for our use, in accordance with the idea—that is our way of speaking in this and similar instances—but no artificer makes the ideas themselves: how could he?

Impossible.

And there is another artist,—I should like to know what you would say of him.

Who is he?

One who is the maker of all the works of all other workmen.

What an extraordinary man!

Wait a little, and there will be more reason for your saying so. For this is he who is able to make not only vessels of every kind, but plants and animals, himself and all other things—the earth and heaven, and the things which are in heaven or under the earth; he makes the gods also.

He must be a wizard and make no mistake.

Oh! You are incredulous, are you? Do you mean that there is no such maker or creator, or that in one sense there might be a maker of all these things but in another not? Do you see that there is a way in which you could make them all yourself?

What way?

An easy way enough; or rather, there are many ways in which the feat might be quickly and easily accomplished, none quicker than that of turning a mirror round and round—you would soon make the sun and the heavens, and the earth and yourself, and other animals and plants, and all the other things of which we were just now speaking, in the mirror.

Yes, he said; but they would be appearances only.

Very good, I said, you are coming to the point now. And the painter too is, as I conceive, just such another—a creator of appearances, is he not?

Of course.

But then I suppose you will say that what he creates is untrue. And yet there is a sense in which the painter also creates a bed?

Yes, he said, but not a real bed.

And what of the maker of the bed? Were you not saying that he too makes, not the idea which, according to our view, is the essence of the bed, but only a particular bed?

Yes, I did.

Then if he does not make the bed which exists he cannot make true existence, but only some semblance of existence; and if any one were to say that the work of the maker of the bed, or of any other workman, has real existence, he could hardly be supposed to be speaking the truth.

At any rate, he replied, philosophers would say that he was not speaking the truth.

No wonder, then, that his work too is an indistinct expression of truth.

No wonder.

Suppose now that by the light of the examples just offered we enquire who this imitator is?

If you please.

Well, then, here are three beds: one existing in nature, which is made by God, as I think that we may say—for no one else can be the maker?

No.

There is another which is the work of the carpenter?

Yes.

And the work of the painter is a third?

Yes.

Beds, then, are of three kinds, and there are three artists who superintend them: God, the maker of the bed, and the painter?

Yes, there are three of them.

God, whether from choice or from necessity, made one bed in

nature and one only; two or more such ideal beds neither ever have been nor ever will be made by God.

Why is that?

Because even if He had made but two, a third would still appear behind them which both of them would have for their idea, and that would be the ideal bed and not the two others.

Very true, he said.

God knew this, and He desired to be the real maker of a real bed, not a particular maker of a particular bed, and therefore He created a bed which is essentially and by nature one only.

So we believe.

Shall we, then, speak of Him as the natural author or maker of the bed?

Yes, he replied; inasmuch as by the natural process of creation He is the author of this and of all other things.

And what shall we say of the carpenter—is not he also the maker of the bed?

Yes.

But would you call the painter a creator and maker?

Certainly not.

Yet if he is not the maker, what is he in relation to the bed?

I think, he said, that we may fairly designate him as the imitator of that which the others make.

Good, I said; then you call him who is third in the descent from nature an imitator?

Certainly, he said.

And the tragic poet is an imitator, and therefore, like all other imitators, he is thrice removed from the king and from the truth?

That appears to be so.

The latter.

As they are or as they appear? You have still to determine this.

What do you mean?

I mean, that you may look at a bed from different points of view, obliquely or directly or from any other point of view, and the bed will appear different, but there is no difference in reality. And the same of all things.

Yes, he said, the difference is only apparent.

Now let me ask you another question: Which is the art of painting designed to be—an imitation of things as they are, or as they appear—of appearance or of reality?

Of appearance.

Then the imitator, I said, is a long way off the truth, and can do all things because he lightly touches on a small part of them, and that part an image. For example: A painter will paint a cobbler, carpenter, or any other artist, though he knows nothing of their arts; and, if he is a good artist, he may deceive children or simple persons, when he shows them his picture of a carpenter from a distance, and they will fancy that they are looking at a real carpenter.

Certainly.

And whenever any one informs us that he has found a man who knows all the arts, and all things else that anybody knows, and every single thing with a higher degree of accuracy than any other man— whoever tells us this, I think that we can only imagine him to be a simple creature who is likely to have been deceived by some wizard or actor whom he met, and whom he thought all-knowing, because be himself was unable to analyse the nature of knowledge and ignorance and imitation.

Most true.

And so, when we hear persons saying that the tragedians, and Homer, who is at their head, know all the arts and all things human, virtue as well as vice, and divine things too, for that the good poet cannot compose well unless he knows his subject, and that he who has not this knowledge can never be a poet, we ought to consider whether here also there may not be a similar illusion. Perhaps they may have come across imitators and been deceived by them; they may not have remembered when they saw their works that these were but imitations thrice removed from the truth, and could easily be made without any knowledge of the truth, because they are appearances only and not realities? Or, after all, they may be in the right, and poets do really know the things about which they seem to the many to speak so well?

The question, he said, should by all means be considered.

Now do you suppose that if a person were able to make the original as well as the image, he would seriously devote himself to the image-making branch? Would he allow imitation to be the ruling principle of his life, as if he had nothing higher in him?

I should say not.

The real artist, who knew what he was imitating, would be interested in realities and not in imitations; and would desire to leave as memorials of himself works many and fair; and, instead of being the author of encomiums, he would prefer to be the theme of them.

Yes, he said, that would be to him a source of much greater honour and profit.

Then, I said, we must put a question to Homer; not about medicine, or any of the arts to which his poems only incidentally refer: we are not going to ask him, or any other poet, whether he has cured patients like Asclepius, or left behind him a school of medicine such as the Asclepiads were, or whether he only talks about medicine and other arts at second hand; but we have a right to know respecting military tactics, politics, education, which are the chiefest and noblest subjects of his poems, and we may fairly ask him about them. "Friend Homer," then we say to him, "if you are only in the second remove from truth in what you say of virtue, and not in the third—not an image maker or imitator—and if you are able to discern what pursuits make men better or worse in private or public life, tell us what State was ever better governed by your help? The good order of Lacedaemon is due to Lycurgus, and many other cities great and small have been similarly benefited by others; but who says that you have been a good legislator to them and have done them any good? Italy and Sicily boast of Charondas, and there is Solon who is renowned among us; but what city has anything to say about you? Is there any city which he might name?

I think not, said Glaucon; not even the Homerids themselves pretend that he was a legislator.

Well, but is there any war on record which was carried on successfully by him, or aided by his counsels, when he was alive?

There is not.

Or is there any invention of his, applicable to the arts or to human life, such as Thales the Milesian or Anacharsis the Scythian, and other ingenious men have conceived, which is attributed to him?

There is absolutely nothing of the kind.

But, if Homer never did any public service, was he privately a guide or teacher of any? Had he in his lifetime friends who loved to associate with him, and who handed down to posterity an Homeric way of life, such as was established by Pythagoras who was so greatly beloved for his wisdom, and whose followers are to this day quite celebrated for the order which was named after him?

Nothing of the kind is recorded of him. For surely, Socrates, Creophylus, the companion of Homer, that child of flesh, whose name always makes us laugh, might be more justly ridiculed for his stupidity, if, as is said, Homer was greatly neglected by him and others in his own day when he was alive?

Yes, I replied, that is the tradition. But can you imagine, Glaucon, that if Homer had really been able to educate and improve mankind—if he had possessed knowledge and not been a mere imitator—can you imagine, I say, that he would not have had many followers, and been honoured and loved by them? Protagoras of Abdera, and Prodicus of Ceos, and a host of others, have only to whisper to their contemporaries: "You will never be able to manage either your own house or your own State until you appoint us to be your ministers of education"—and this ingenious device of theirs has such an effect in making men love them that their companions all but carry them about on their shoulders. And is it conceivable that the contemporaries of Homer, or again of Hesiod, would have allowed either of them to go about as rhapsodists, if they had really been able to make mankind virtuous? Would they not have been as unwilling to part with them as with gold, and have compelled them to stay at home with them? Or, if the master would not stay, then the disciples would have followed him about everywhere, until they had got education enough?

Yes, Socrates, that, I think, is quite true.

Then must we not infer that all these poetical individuals, beginning with Homer, are only imitators; they copy images of virtue and the like, but the truth they never reach? The poet is like a painter who, as we have already observed, will make a likeness of a cobbler though he understands nothing of cobbling; and his picture is good enough for those who know no more than he does, and judge only by colours and figures.

Quite so.

In like manner the poet with his words and phrases may be said to lay on the colours of the several arts, himself understanding their nature only enough to imitate them; and other people, who are as ignorant as he is, and judge only from his words, imagine that if he speaks of cobbling, or of military tactics, or of anything else, in metre and harmony and rhythm, he speaks very well—such is the sweet influence which melody and rhythm by nature have. And I think that you must have observed again and again what a poor appearance the tales of poets make when stripped of the colours which music puts upon them, and recited in simple prose.

Yes, he said.

They are like faces which were never really beautiful, but only blooming; and now the bloom of youth has passed away from them?

Exactly.

Here is another point: The imitator or maker of the image knows nothing of true existence; he knows appearances only. Am I not right?

Yes.

Then let us have a clear understanding, and not be satisfied with half an explanation.

Proceed.

Of the painter we say that he will paint reins, and he will paint a bit?

Yes.

And the worker in leather and brass will make them?

Certainly.

But does the painter know the right form of the bit and reins? Nay, hardly even the workers in brass and leather who make them; only the horseman who knows how to use them—he knows their right form.

Most true.

And may we not say the same of all things?

What?

That there are three arts which are concerned with all things: one which uses, another which makes, a third which imitates them?

Yes.

And the excellence or beauty or truth of every structure, animate or inanimate, and of every action of man, is relative to the use for which nature or the artist has intended them?

True.

Then the user of them must have the greatest experience of them, and he must indicate to the maker the good or bad qualities which develop themselves in use; for example, the flute-player will tell the flute-maker which of his flutes is satisfactory to the performer; he will tell him how be ought to make them, and the other will attend to his instructions?

Of course.

The one knows and therefore speaks with authority about the goodness and badness of flutes, while the other, confiding in him, will do what he is told by him?

True.

The instrument is the same, but about the excellence or badness of it the maker will only attain to a correct belief; and this he will gain from him who knows, by talking to him and being compelled to hear what he has to say, whereas the user will have knowledge?

True.

But will the imitator have either? Will he know from use whether or not his drawing is correct or beautiful? Or will he have right opinion from being compelled to associate with another who knows and gives him instructions about what he should draw?

Neither.

Then he will no more have true opinion than he will have knowledge about the goodness or badness of his imitations?

I suppose not.

The imitative artist will be in a brilliant state of intelligence about his own creations?

Nay, very much the reverse.

And still he will go on imitating without knowing what makes a thing good or bad, and may be expected therefore to imitate only that which appears to be good to the ignorant multitude?

Just so.

Thus far then we are pretty well agreed that the imitator has no knowledge worth mentioning of what he imitates. Imitation is only a kind of play or sport, and the tragic poets, whether they write in Iambic or in Heroic verse, are imitators in the highest degree?

Very true.

And now tell me, I conjure you, has not imitation been shown by us to be concerned with that thrice removed from the truth?

Certainly.

And what is the faculty in man to which imitation is addressed?

What do you mean?

I will explain: The body which is large when seen near, appears small when seen at a distance?

True.

And the same object appears straight when looked at out of the water, and crooked when in the water; and the concave becomes convex, owing to the illusion about colours to which the sight is liable. Thus every sort of confusion is revealed within us; and this is that weakness of the human mind on which the art of conjuring and of deceiving by light and shadow and other ingenious devices imposes, having an effect upon us like magic.

True.

And the arts of measuring and numbering and weighing come to the rescue of the human understanding—there is the beauty of them—and the apparent greater or less, or more or heavier, no longer have the mastery over us, but give way before calculation and measure and weight?

Most true.

And this, surely, must be the work of the calculating and rational principle in the soul?

To be sure.

And when this principle measures and certifies that some things are equal, or that some are greater or less than others, there occurs an apparent contradiction?

True.

But were we not saying that such a contradiction is impossible—the same faculty cannot have contrary opinions at the same time about the same thing?

Very true.

Then that part of the soul which has an opinion contrary to measure is not the same with that which has an opinion in accordance with measure?

True.

And the better part of the soul is likely to be that which trusts to measure and calculation?

Certainly.

And that which is opposed to them is one of the inferior principles of the soul?

No doubt.

This was the conclusion at which I was seeking to arrive when I said that painting or drawing, and imitation in general, when doing their own proper work, are far removed from truth, and the companions and friends and associates of a principle within us which is equally removed from reason, and that they have no true or healthy aim.

Exactly.

The imitative art is an inferior who marries an inferior, and has inferior offspring.

Very true.

And is this confined to the sight only, or does it extend to the hearing also, relating in fact to what we term poetry?

Probably the same would be true of poetry.

Do not rely, I said, on a probability derived from the analogy of painting; but let us examine further and see whether the faculty with which poetical imitation is concerned is good or bad.

By all means.

We may state the question thus:—Imitation imitates the actions of men, whether voluntary or involuntary, on which, as they imagine, a good or bad result has ensued, and they rejoice or sorrow accordingly. Is there anything more?

No, there is nothing else.

But in all this variety of circumstances is the man at unity with himself—or rather, as in the instance of sight there was confusion and opposition in his opinions about the same things, so here also is there not strife and inconsistency in his life? Though I need hardly raise the question again, for I remember that all this has been already admitted; and the soul has been acknowledged by us to be full of these and ten thousand similar oppositions occurring at the same moment?

And we were right, he said.

Yes, I said, thus far we were right; but there was an omission which must now be supplied.

What was the omission?

Were we not saying that a good man, who has the misfortune to lose his son or anything else which is most dear to him, will bear the loss with more equanimity than another?

Yes.

But will he have no sorrow, or shall we say that although he cannot help sorrowing, he will moderate his sorrow?

The latter, he said, is the truer statement.

Tell me: Will he be more likely to struggle and hold out against his sorrow when he is seen by his equals, or when he is alone?

It will make a great difference whether he is seen or not.

When he is by himself he will not mind saying or doing many things which he would be ashamed of any one hearing or seeing him do?

True.

There is a principle of law and reason in him which bids him resist, as well as a feeling of his misfortune which is forcing him to indulge his sorrow?

True.

But when a man is drawn in two opposite directions, to and from the same object, this, as we affirm, necessarily implies two distinct principles in him?

Certainly.

One of them is ready to follow the guidance of the law?

How do you mean?

The law would say that to be patient under suffering is best, and that we should not give way to impatience, as there is no knowing whether such things are good or evil; and nothing is gained by impatience; also, because no human thing is of serious importance, and grief stands in the way of that which at the moment is most required.

What is most required? he asked.

That we should take counsel about what has happened, and when the dice have been thrown order our affairs in the way which reason deems best; not, like children who have had a fall, keeping hold of the part struck and wasting time in setting up a howl, but always accustoming the soul forthwith to apply a remedy, raising up that which is sickly and fallen, banishing the cry of sorrow by the healing art.

Yes, he said, that is the true way of meeting the attacks of fortune.

Yes, I said; and the higher principle is ready to follow this suggestion of reason?

Clearly.

And the other principle, which inclines us to recollection of our troubles and to lamentation, and can never have enough of them, we may call irrational, useless, and cowardly?

Indeed, we may.

And does not the latter—I mean the rebellious principle—furnish a great variety of materials for imitation? Whereas the wise and calm temperament, being always nearly equable, is not easy to imitate or to appreciate when imitated, especially at a public festival when a promiscuous crowd is assembled in a theatre. For the feeling represented is one to which they are strangers.

Certainly.

Then the imitative poet who aims at being popular is not by

nature made, nor is his art intended, to please or to affect the rational principle in the soul; but he will prefer the passionate and fitful temper, which is easily imitated?

Clearly.

And now we may fairly take him and place him by the side of the painter, for he is like him in two ways: first, inasmuch as his creations have an inferior degree of truth—in this, I say, he is like him; and he is also like him in being concerned with an inferior part of the soul; and therefore we shall be right in refusing to admit him into a well-ordered State, because he awakens and nourishes and strengthens the feelings and impairs the reason. As in a city when the evil are permitted to have authority and the good are put out of the way, so in the soul of man, as we maintain, the imitative poet implants an evil constitution, for he indulges the irrational nature which has no discernment of greater and less, but thinks the same thing at one time great and at another small—he is a manufacturer of images and is very far removed from the truth.

Exactly.

But we have not yet brought forward the heaviest count in our accusation:—the power which poetry has of harming even the good (and there are very few who are not harmed), is surely an awful thing?

Yes, certainly, if the effect is what you say.

Hear and judge: The best of us, as I conceive, when we listen to a passage of Homer, or one of the tragedians, in which he represents some pitiful hero who is drawling out his sorrows in a long oration, or weeping, and smiting his breast—the best of us, you know, delight in giving way to sympathy, and are in raptures at the excellence of the poet who stirs our feelings most.

Yes, of course I know.

But when any sorrow of our own happens to us, then you may observe that we pride ourselves on the opposite quality—we would fain be quiet and patient; this is the manly part, and the other which delighted us in the recitation is now deemed to be the part of a woman.

Very true, he said.

Now can we be right in praising and admiring another who is doing that which any one of us would abominate and be ashamed of in his own person?

No, he said, that is certainly not reasonable.

Nay, I said, quite reasonable from one point of view.

What point of view?

If you consider, I said, that when in misfortune we feel a natural hunger and desire to relieve our sorrow by weeping and lamentation, and that this feeling which is kept under control in our own calamities is satisfied and delighted by the poets;—the better nature in each of us, not having been sufficiently trained by reason or habit, allows the sympathetic element to break loose because the sorrow is another's; and the spectator fancies that there can be no disgrace to himself in praising and pitying any one who comes telling him what a good man he is, and making a fuss about his troubles; he thinks that the pleasure is a gain, and why should he be supercilious and lose this and the poem too? Few persons ever reflect, as I should imagine, that from the evil of other men something of evil is communicated to themselves. And so the feeling of sorrow which has gathered strength at the sight of the misfortunes of others is with difficulty repressed in our own.

How very true!

And does not the same hold also of the ridiculous? There are jests which you would be ashamed to make yourself, and yet on the comic stage, or indeed in private, when you bear them, you are greatly amused by them, and are not at all disgusted at their unseemliness;—the case of pity is repeated;—there is a principle in human nature which is disposed to raise a laugh, and this which you once restrained by reason, because you were afraid of being thought a buffoon, is now let out again; and having stimulated the risible faculty at the theatre, you are betrayed unconsciously to yourself into playing the comic poet at home.

Quite true, he said.

And the same may be said of lust and anger and all the other affections, of desire and pain and pleasure, which are held to be inseparable from every action—in all of them poetry feeds and waters the passions instead of drying them up; she lets them rule, although they ought to be controlled, if mankind are ever to increase in happiness and virtue.

I cannot deny it.

Therefore, Glaucon, I said, whenever you meet with any of the eulogists of Homer declaring that he has been the educator of Hellas, and that he is profitable for education and for the ordering of human things, and that you should take him up again and again and get to know him and regulate your whole life according to him, we may love and honour those who say these things—they are excellent people, as far as their lights extend; and we are ready to acknowledge that Homer is the greatest of poets and first of tragedy writers; but we must remain firm in our conviction that hymns to the gods and praises of famous men are the only poetry which ought to be admitted into our State. For if you go beyond this and allow the honeyed muse to enter, either in epic or lyric verse, not law and the reason of mankind, which by common consent have ever been deemed best, but pleasure and pain will be the rulers in our State.

That is most true, he said.

And now since we have reverted to the subject of poetry, let this our defence serve to show the reasonableness of our former judgment in sending away out of our State an art having the tendencies which we have described; for reason constrained us. But that she may not impute to us any harshness or want of politeness, let us tell her that there is an ancient quarrel between philosophy and poetry; of which there are many proofs, such as the saving of "the yelping hound howling at her lord," or of one "mighty in the vain talk of fools," and the mob of sages circumventing Zeus," and the "subtle thinkers who are beggars after all"; and there are innumerable other signs of ancient enmity between them.

1.

I propose to treat of Poetry in itself and of its various kinds, noting the essential quality of each; to inquire into the structure of the plot as requisite to a good poem; into the number and nature of the parts of which a poem is composed; and similarly into whatever else falls within the same inquiry. Following, then, the order of nature, let us begin with the principles which come first.

Epic poetry and Tragedy, Comedy also and Dithyrambic poetry, and the music of the flute and of the lyre in most of their forms, are all in their general conception modes of imitation. They differ, however, from one another in three respects,—the medium, the objects, the manner or mode of imitation, being in each case distinct.

For as there are persons who, by conscious art or mere habit, imitate and represent various objects through the medium of colour and form, or again by the voice; so in the arts above mentioned, taken as a whole, the imitation is produced by rhythm, language, or "harmony," either singly or combined.

Thus in the music of the flute and of the lyre, "harmony" and rhythm alone are employed; also in other arts, such as that of the shepherd's pipe, which are essentially similar to these. In dancing, rhythm alone is used without "harmony"; for even dancing imitates character, emotion, and action, by rhythmical movement.

There is another art which imitates by means of language alone, and that either in prose or verse—which verse, again, may either combine different metres or consist of but one kind—but this has hitherto been without a name. For there is no common term we could apply to the mimes of Sophron and Xenarchus and the Socratic dialogues on the one hand; and, on the other, to poetic imitations in iambic, elegiac, or any similar metre. People do, indeed, add the word "maker" or "poet" to the name of the metre, and speak of elegiac poets, or epic (that is, hexameter) poets, as if it were not the imitation that makes the poet, but the verse that entitles them all indiscriminately to the name. Even when a treatise on medicine or natural science is brought out in verse, the name of poet is by custom given to the author; and yet Homer and Empedocles have nothing in common but the metre, so that it would be right to call the one poet, the other physicist rather than poet. On the same principle, even if a writer in his poetic imitation were to combine all metres, as Chaeremon did in his Centaur, which is a medley composed of metres of all kinds, we should bring him too under the general term poet. So much then for these distinctions.

There are, again, some arts which employ all the means above mentioned,—namely rhythm, tune, and metre. Such are Dithyrambic and Nomic poetry, and also Tragedy and Comedy; but between them the difference is, that in the first two cases these means are all employed in combination, in the latter, now one means is employed, now another.

Such, then, are the differences of the arts with respect to the medium of imitation.

2.

Since the objects of imitation are men in action, and these men must be either of a higher or a lower type (for moral character mainly answers to these divisions, goodness and badness being the distinguishing marks of moral differences), it follows that we must represent men either as better than in real life, or as worse, or as they are. It is the same in painting. Polygnotus depicted men as nobler than they are, Pauson as less noble, Dionysius drew them true to life.

Now it is evident that each of the modes of imitation above mentioned will exhibit these differences, and become a distinct kind in imitating objects that are thus distinct. Such diversities may be found even in dancing, flute-playing, and lyre-playing. So again in language, whether prose or verse unaccompanied by music. Homer, for example, makes men better than they are; Cleophon as they are; Hegemon the Thasian, the inventor of parodies, and Nicochares, the author of the Deiliad, worse than they are. The same thing holds good of Dithyrambs and Nomes; here too one may portray different types, as Timotheus and Philoxenus differed in representing their Cyclopes. The same distinction marks off Tragedy from Comedy, for Comedy aims at representing men as worse, Tragedy as better than in actual life.

3.

There is still a third difference—the manner in which each of these objects may be imitated. For the medium being the same, and the objects the same, the poet may imitate by narration—in which case he can either take another personality as Homer does, or speak in his own person, unchanged—or he may present all his characters as living and moving before us.

These, then, as we said at the beginning, are the three differences which distinguish artistic imitation,—the medium, the objects, and the manner. So that from one point of view, Sophocles is an imitator of the same kind as Homer—for both imitate higher types of character; from another point of view, of the same kind as Aristophanes—for both imitate persons acting and doing. Hence, some say, the name of "drama" is given to such poems, as representing action. For the same reason the Dorians claim the invention both of Tragedy and Comedy. The claim to Comedy is put forward by the Megarians,—not only by those of Greece proper, who allege that it originated under their democracy, but also by the Megarians of Sicily, for the poet Epicharmus, who is much earlier than Chionides and Magnes, belonged to that country. Tragedy too is claimed by certain Dorians of the Peloponnese. In each case they appeal to the evidence of language. The outlying villages, they say, are by them called κωμαι, by the Athenians δημοι: and they assume that Comedians were so named not from κφμάζειν, "to revel," but because they wandered from village to village (κατά κωμαζ), being excluded contemptuously from the city. They add also that the Dorian word for "doing" is δραν, and the Athenian, πράττειν.

This may suffice as to the number and nature of the various modes of imitation.

4.

Poetry in general seems to have sprung from two causes, each of them lying deep in our nature. First, the instinct of imitation is implanted in man from childhood, one difference between him and other animals being that he is the most imitative of living creatures, and through imitation learns his earliest lessons; and no less universal is the pleasure felt in things imitated. We have evidence of this in the facts of experience. Objects which in themselves we view with pain, we delight to contemplate when reproduced with minute fidelity: such as the forms of the most ignoble animals and of dead bodies. The cause of this again is, that to learn gives the liveliest pleasure, not only to philosophers but to men in general; whose capacity, however, of learning is more limited. Thus the reason why men enjoy seeing a likeness is, that in contemplating it they find themselves learning or inferring, and saying perhaps, "Ah, that is he." For if you happen not to have seen the original, the pleasure will be due not to the imitation as such, but to the execution, the colouring, or some such other cause.

Imitation, then, is one instinct of our nature. Next, there is the instinct for "harmony" and rhythm, metres being manifestly sections of rhythm. Persons, therefore, starting with this natural gift developed by degrees their special aptitudes, till their rude improvisations gave birth to Poetry.

Poetry now diverged in two directions, according to the individual character of the writers. The graver spirits imitated noble actions, and the actions of good men. The more trivial sort imitated the actions of meaner persons, at first composing satires, as the former did hymns to the gods and the praises of famous men. A poem of the satirical kind cannot indeed be put down to any author earlier than Homer; though many such writers probably there were. But from Homer onward, instances can be cited,—his own Margites, for example, and other similar compositions. The appropriate metre was also here introduced; hence the measure is still called the iambic or lampooning measure, being that in which people lampooned one another. Thus the older poets were distinguished as writers of heroic or of lampooning verse.

As, in the serious style, Homer is pre-eminent among poets, for he alone combined dramatic form with excellence of imitation, so he too first laid down the main lines of Comedy, by dramatising the ludicrous instead of writing personal satire. His Margites bears the same relation to Comedy that the Iliad and Odyssey do to Tragedy. But when Tragedy and Comedy came in to light, the two classes of poets still followed their natural bent: the lampooners became writers of Comedy, and the Epic poets were succeeded by Tragedians, since the drama was a larger and higher form of art.

Whether Tragedy has as yet perfected its proper types or not; and whether it is to be judged in itself, or in relation also to the audience,—this raises another question. Be that as it may, Tragedy—as also Comedy—was at first mere improvisation. The one originated with the authors of the Dithyramb, the other with those of the phallic songs, which are still in use in many of our cities. Tragedy advanced by slow degrees; each new element that showed itself was in turn developed. Having passed through many changes, it found its natural form, and there it stopped.

Aeschylus first introduced a second actor; he diminished the importance of the Chorus, and assigned the leading part to the dialogue. Sophocles raised the number of actors to three, and added scene-painting. Moreover, it was not till late that the short plot was discarded for one of greater compass, and the grotesque diction of the earlier satyric form for the stately manner of Tragedy. The iambic measure then replaced the trochaic tetrameter, which was originally employed when the poetry was of the satyric order, and had greater affinities with dancing. Once dialogue had come in, Nature herself discovered the appropriate measure. For the iambic is, of all measures, the most colloquial: we see it in the fact that conversational speech runs into iambic lines more frequently than into any other kind of verse: rarely into hexameters, and only when we drop the colloquial intonation. The additions to the number of "episodes" or acts, and the other accessories of which tradition tells, must be taken as already described; for to discuss them in detail would, doubtless, be a large undertaking.

5.

Comedy is, as we have said, an imitation of characters of a lower type,—not, however, in the full sense of the word bad, the Ludicrous being merely a subdivision of the ugly. It consists in some defect or ugliness which is not painful or destructive. To take an obvious example, the comic mask is ugly and distorted, but does not imply pain.

The successive changes through which Tragedy passed, and the authors of these changes, are well known, whereas Comedy has had no history, because it was not at first treated seriously. It was late before the Archon granted a comic chorus to a poet; the performers were till then voluntary. Comedy had already taken definite shape when comic poets, distinctively so called, are heard of. Who furnished it with masks, or prologues, or increased the number of actors,—these and other similar details remain unknown. As for the plot, it came originally from Sicily; but of Athenian writers Crates was the first who, abandoning the "iambic" or lampooning form, generalised his themes and plots.

Epic poetry agrees with Tragedy in so far as it is an imitation in verse of characters of a higher type. They differ, in that Epic poetry admits but one kind of metre, and is narrative in form. They differ, again, in their length: for Tragedy endeavours, as far as possible, to confine itself to a single revolution of the sun, or but slightly to exceed this limit; whereas the Epic action has no limits of time. This, then, is a second point of difference; though at first the same freedom was admitted in Tragedy as in Epic poetry.

Of their constituent parts some are common to both, some peculiar to Tragedy: whoever, therefore, knows what is good or bad Tragedy, knows also about Epic poetry. All the elements of an Epic poem are found in Tragedy, but the elements of Tragedy are not all found in the Epic poem.

6.

Of the poetry which imitates in hexameter verse, and of Comedy, we will speak hereafter. Let us now discuss Tragedy, resuming its formal definition, as resulting from what has been already said.

Tragedy, then, is an imitation of an action that is serious, complete, and of a certain magnitude; in language embellished with each kind of artistic ornament, the several kinds being found in separate parts of the play; in the form of action, not of narrative; through pity and fear effecting the proper purgation of these emotions. By "language embellished," I mean language into which rhythm, "harmony," and song enter. By "the several kinds in separate parts," I mean, that some parts are rendered through the medium of verse alone, others again with the aid of song.

Now as tragic imitation implies persons acting, it necessarily follows, in the first place, that Spectacular equipment will be a part of Tragedy. Next, Song and Diction, for these are the medium of imitation. By "Diction" I mean the mere metrical arrangement of the words: as for "Song," it is a term whose sense every one understands.

Again, Tragedy is the imitation of an action; and an action implies personal agents, who necessarily possess certain distinctive qualities both of character and thought; for it is by these that we qualify actions themselves, and these—thought and character—are the two natural causes from which actions spring, and on actions again all success or failure depends. Hence, the Plot is the imitation of the action:—for by plot I here mean the arrangement of the incidents. By Character I mean that in virtue of which we ascribe certain qualities to the agents. Thought is required wherever a statement is proved, or, it may be, a general truth enunciated. Every Tragedy, therefore, must have six parts, which parts determine its quality—namely, Plot, Character, Diction, Thought, Spectacle, Song. Two of the parts constitute the medium of imitation, one the manner, and three the objects of imitation. And these complete the list. These elements have been employed, we may say, by the poets to a man; in fact, every play contains Spectacular elements as well as Character, Plot, Diction, Song, and Thought.

But most important of all is the structure of the incidents. For Tragedy is an imitation, not of men, but of an action and of life, and life consists in action, and its end is a mode of action, not a quality. Now character determines men's qualities, but it is by their actions that they are happy or the reverse. Dramatic action, therefore, is not with a view to the representation of character: character comes in as subsidiary to the actions. Hence the incidents and the plot are the end of a tragedy; and the end is the chief thing of all. Again, without action there cannot be a tragedy; there may be without character. The tragedies of most of our modern poets fail in the rendering of character; and of poets in general this is often true. It is the same in painting; and here lies the difference between Zeuxis and Polygnotus. Polygnotus delineates character well: the style of Zeuxis is devoid of ethical quality. Again, if you string together a set of speeches expressive of character, and well finished in point of diction and thought, you will not produce the essential tragic effect nearly so well as with a play which, however deficient in these respects, yet has a plot and artistically constructed incidents. Besides which, the most powerful elements of emotional interest in Tragedy—Peripeteia or Reversal of the Situation, and Recognition scenes—are parts of the plot. A further proof is, that novices in the art attain to finish of diction and precision of portraiture before they can construct the plot. It is the same with almost all the early poets.

The Plot, then, is the first principle, and, as it were, the soul of a tragedy: Character holds the second place. A similar fact is seen in painting. The most beautiful colours, laid on confusedly, will not give as much pleasure as the chalk outline of a portrait. Thus Tragedy is the imitation of an action, and of the agents mainly with a view to the action.

Third in order is Thought,—that is, the faculty of saying what is possible and pertinent in given circumstances. In the case of oratory, this is the function of the political art and of the art of rhetoric: and so indeed the older poets make their characters speak the language of civic life; the poets of our time, the language of the rhetoricians. Character is that which reveals moral purpose, showing what kind of things a man chooses or avoids. Speeches, therefore, which do not make this manifest, or in which the speaker does not choose or avoid anything whatever, are not expressive of character. Thought, on the other hand, is found where something is proved to be or not to be, or a general maxim is enunciated.

Fourth among the elements enumerated comes Diction; by which I mean, as has been already said, the expression of the meaning in words; and its essence is the same both in verse and prose.

Of the remaining elements Song holds the chief place among the embellishments.

The Spectacle has, indeed, an emotional attraction of its own, but, of all the parts, it is the least artistic, and connected least with the art of Poetry. For the power of Tragedy, we may be sure, is felt even apart from representation and actors. Besides, the production of spectacular effects depends more on the art of the stage machinist than on that of the poet.

7.

These principles being established, let us now discuss the proper structure of the Plot, since this is the first and most important thing in Tragedy.

Now, according to our definition. Tragedy is an imitation of an action that is complete, and whole, and of a certain magnitude; for there may be a whole that is wanting in magnitude. A whole is that which has a beginning, a middle, and an end. A beginning is that which does not itself follow anything by causal necessity, but after which something naturally is or comes to be. An end, on the contrary, is that which itself naturally follows some other thing, either by necessity, or as a rule, but has nothing following it. A middle is that which follows something as some other thing follows it. A well constructed plot, therefore, must neither begin nor end at haphazard, but conform to these principles.

Again, a beautiful object, whether it be a living organism or any whole composed of parts, must not only have an orderly arrangement of parts, but must also be of a certain magnitude; for beauty depends on magnitude and order. Hence a very small animal organism cannot be beautiful; for the view of it is confused, the object being seen in an almost imperceptible moment of time. Nor, again, can one of vast size be beautiful; for as the eye cannot take it all in at once, the unity and sense of the whole is lost for the spectator; as for instance if there were one a thousand miles long. As, therefore, in the case of animate bodies and organisms a certain magnitude is necessary, and a magnitude which may be easily embraced in one view; so in the plot, a certain length is necessary, and a length which can be easily embraced by the memory. The limit length in relation to dramatic competition and sensuous presentment, is no part of artistic theory. For had it been the rule for a hundred Tragedies to compete together, the performance would have been regulated by the water-clock,—as indeed we are told was formerly done. But the limit as fixed by the nature of the drama itself is this:—the greater the length, the more beautiful will the piece be by reason of its size, provided that the whole be perspicuous. And to define the matter roughly, we may say that the proper magnitude is comprised within such limits, that the sequence of events, according to the law of probability or necessity, will admit of a change from bad fortune to good, or from good fortune to bad.

8.

Unity of plot does not, as some persons think, consist in the unity of the hero. For infinitely various are the incidents in one man's life which cannot be reduced to unity; and so, too, there are many actions of one man out of which we cannot make one action. Hence the error, as it appears, of all poets who have composed a Heracleid, a Theseid, or other poems of the kind. They imagine that as Heracles was one man, the story of Heracles must also be a unity. But Homer, as in all else he is of surpassing merit, here too—whether from art or natural genius—seems to have happily discerned the truth. In composing the Odyssey he did not include all the adventures of Odysseus—such as his wound on Parnassus, or his feigned madness at the mustering of the host—incidents between which there was no necessary or probable connexion: but he made the Odyssey, and likewise the Iliad, to centre round an action that in our sense of the word is one. As therefore, in the other imitative arts, the imitation is one when the object imitated is one, so the plot, being an imitation of an action, must imitate one action and that a whole, the structural union of the parts being such that, if any one of them is displaced or removed, the whole will be disjointed and disturbed. For a thing whose presence or absence makes no visible difference, is not an organic part of the whole.

9.

It is, moreover, evident from what has been said, that it is not the function of the poet to relate what has happened, but what may happen,—what is possible according to the law of probability or necessity. The poet and the historian differ not by writing in verse or in prose. The work of Herodotus might be put into verse, and it would still be a species of history, with metre no less than without it. The true difference is that one relates what has happened, the other what may happen. Poetry, therefore, is a more philosophical and a higher thing than history: for Poetry tends to express the universal, history the particular. By the universal I mean how a person of a certain type will on occasion speak or act, according to the law of probability or necessity; and it is this universality at which Poetry aims in the names she attaches to the personages. The particular is—for example—what Alcibiades did or suffered. In Comedy this is already apparent: for here the poet first constructs the plot on the lines of probability, and then inserts characteristic names;—unlike the lampooners who write about particular individuals. But tragedians still keep to real names, the reason being that what is possible is credible: what has not happened we do not at once feel sure to be possible: but what has happened is manifestly possible: otherwise it would not have happened. Still there are even some Tragedies in which there are only one or two well known names, the rest being fictitious. In others, none are well known,—as in Agathon's Antheus, where incidents and names alike are fictitious, and yet they give none the less pleasure. We must not, therefore, at all costs keep to the received legends, which are the usual subjects of Tragedy. Indeed, it would be absurd to attempt it; for even subjects that are known are known only to a few, and yet give pleasure to all. It clearly follows that the poet or "maker" should be the maker of plots rather than of verses; since he is a poet because he imitates, and what he imitates are actions. And even if he chances to take an historical subject, he is none the less a poet; for there is no reason why some events that have actually happened should not conform to the law of the probable and possible, and in virtue of that quality in them he is their poet or maker.

Of all plots and actions the episodic are the worst. I call a plot "episodic" in which the episodes or acts succeed one another without probable or necessary sequence. Bad poets compose such pieces by their own fault, good poets, to please the players; for, as they write show pieces for competition, they stretch the plot beyond its capacity, and are often forced to break the natural continuity.

But again, Tragedy is an imitation not only of a complete action, but of events inspiring fear or pity. Such an effect is best produced when the events come on us by surprise; and the effect is heightened when, at the same time, they follow as cause and effect. The tragic wonder will then be greater than if they happened of themselves or by accident; for even coincidences are most striking when they have an air of design. We may instance the statue of Mitys at Argos, which fell upon his murderer while he was a spectator at a festival, and killed him. Such events seem not to be due to mere chance. Plots, therefore, constructed on these principles are necessarily the best.

10.

Plots are either Simple or Complex, for the actions in real life, of which the plots are an imitation, obviously show a similar distinction. An action which is one and continuous in the sense above defined, I call Simple, when the change of fortune takes place without Reversal of the Situation and without Recognition.

A Complex action is one in which the change is accompanied by such Reversal, or by Recognition, or by both. These last should arise from the internal structure of the plot, so that what follows should be the necessary or probable result of the preceding action. It makes all the difference whether any given event is a case of *propter hoc* or *post hoc*.

11.

Reversal of the Situation is a change by which the action veers round to its opposite, subject always to our rule of probability or necessity. Thus in the Oedipus, the messenger comes to cheer Oedipus and free him from alarms about his mother, but by revealing who he is, he produces the opposite effect. Again in the Lynceus, Lynceus is being led away to his death and Danaus goes with him; meaning to slay him; but the outcome of the preceding incidents is that Danaus is killed and Lynceus saved.

Recognition, as the name indicates, is a change from ignorance to knowledge, producing love or hate between the persons destined by the poet for good or bad fortune. The best form of recognition is coincident with a Reversal of the Situation, as in the Oedipus. There are indeed other forms. Even inanimate things of the most trivial kind may in a sense be objects of recognition. Again, we may recognise or discover whether a person has done a thing or not. But the recognition which is most intimately connected with the plot and action is, as we have said, the recognition of persons. This recognition, combined with Reversal, will produce either pity or fear; and actions producing these effects are those which, by our definition, Tragedy represents. Moreover, it is upon such situations that the issues of good or bad fortune will depend. Recognition, then, being between persons, it may happen that one person only is recognised by the other—when the latter is already known—or it may be necessary that the recognition should be on both sides. Thus Iphigenia is revealed to Orestes by the sending of the letter; but another act of recognition is required to make Orestes known to Iphigenia.

Two parts, then, of the Plot—Reversal of the Situation and Recognition—turn upon surprises. A third part is the Scene of Suffering. The Scene of Suffering is a destructive or painful action, such as death on the stage, bodily agony, wounds and the like.

12.

[The parts of Tragedy which must be treated as elements of the whole have been already mentioned. We now come to the quantitative parts—the separate parts into which Tragedy is divided—namely, Prologue, Episode, Exode, Choric song; this last being divided into Parode and Stasimon. These are common to all plays: peculiar to some are the songs of actors from the stage and the Commoi.

The Prologue is that entire part of a Tragedy which precedes the Parode of the Chorus. The Episode is that entire part of a tragedy which is between complete Choric songs. The Exode is that entire part of a tragedy which has no Choric song after it. Of the Choric part the Parode is the first undivided utterance of the Chorus: the Stasimon is a Choric ode without anapaests or trochaic tetrameters: the Commos is a joint lamentation of Chorus and actors. The parts of a Tragedy which must be treated as elements of the whole have been already mentioned. The quantitative parts—the separate parts into which it is divided—are here enumerated.]

13.

As the sequel to what has already been said, we must proceed to consider what the poet should aim at, and what he should avoid, in constructing his plots; and by what means the specific effect of Tragedy will be produced.

A perfect Tragedy should, as we have seen, be arranged not on the simple but on the complex plan. It should, moreover, imitate actions which excite pity and fear, this being the distinctive mark of tragic imitation. It follows plainly, in the first place, that the change of fortune presented must not be the spectacle of a virtuous man brought from prosperity to adversity: for this moves neither pity nor fear; it merely shocks us. Nor, again, that of a bad man passing from adversity to prosperity: for nothing can be more alien to the spirit of Tragedy; it possesses no single tragic quality; it neither satisfies the moral sense nor calls forth pity or fear. Nor, again, should the downfall of the utter villain be exhibited. A plot of this kind would, doubtless, satisfy the moral sense, but it would inspire neither pity nor fear; for pity is aroused by unmerited misfortune, fear by the misfortune of a man like ourselves. Such an event, therefore, will be neither pitiful nor terrible. There remains, then, the character between these two extremes,—that of a man who is not eminently good and just, yet whose misfortune is brought about not by vice or depravity, but by some error or frailty. He must be one who is highly renowned and prosperous,—a personage like Oedipus, Thyestes, or other illustrious men of such families.

A well constructed plot should, therefore, be single in its issue, rather than double as some maintain. The change of fortune should be not from bad to good, but, reversely, from good to bad. It should come about as the result not of vice, but of some great error or frailty, in a character either such as we have described, or better rather than worse. The practice of the stage bears out our view. At first the poets recounted any legend that came in their way. Now, the best Tragedies are founded on the story of a few houses,—on the fortunes of Alcmaeon, Oedipus, Orestes, Meleager, Thyestes, Telephus, and those others who have done or suffered something terrible. A Tragedy, then, to be perfect according to the rules of art should be of this construction. Hence they are in error who censure Euripides just because he follows this principle in his plays, many of which end unhappily. It is, as we have said, the right ending. The best proof is that on the stage and in dramatic competition, such plays, if well worked out, are the most tragic in effect; and Euripides, faulty though he may be in the general management of his subject, yet is felt to be the most tragic of the poets.

In the second rank comes the kind of Tragedy which some place first. Like the Odyssey, it has a double thread of plot, and also an opposite catastrophe for the good and for the bad. It is accounted the best because of the weakness of the spectators; for the poet is guided in what he writes by the wishes of his audience. The pleasure, however, thence derived is not the true tragic pleasure. It is proper rather to Comedy, where those who, in the piece, are the deadliest enemies—like Orestes and Aegisthus—quit the stage as friends at the close, and no one slays or is slain.

14.

Fear and pity may be aroused by spectacular means; but they may also result from the inner structure of the piece, which is the better way, and indicates a superior poet. For the plot ought to be so constructed that, even without the aid of the eye, he who hears the tale told will thrill with horror and melt to pity at what takes place. This is the impression we should receive from hearing the story of Oedipus. But to produce this effect by the mere spectacle is a less artistic method, and dependent on extraneous aids. Those who employ spectacular means to create a sense not of the terrible but only of the monstrous, are strangers to the purpose of Tragedy; for we must not demand of Tragedy any and every kind of pleasure, but only that which is proper to it. And since the pleasure which the poet should afford is that which comes from pity and fear through imitation, it is evident that this quality must be impressed upon the incidents.

Let us then determine what are the circumstances which strike us as terrible or pitiful.

Actions capable of this effect must happen between persons who are either friends or enemies or indifferent to one another. If an enemy kills an enemy, there is nothing to excite pity either in the act or the intention,—except so far as the suffering in itself is pitiful. So again with indifferent persons. But when the tragic incident occurs between those who are near or dear to another—if, for example, a brother kills, or intends to kill, a brother, a son his father, a mother her son, a son his mother, or any other deed of the kind is done—these are the situations to be looked for by the poet. He may not indeed destroy the framework of the received legends—the fact, for instance, that Clytemnestra was slain by Orestes and Eriphyle by Alcmaeon—but he ought to show invention of his own, and skilfully handle the traditional material. Let us explain more clearly what is meant by skilful handling.

The action may be done consciously and with knowledge of the persons, in the manner of the older poets. It is thus too that Euripides makes Medea slay her children. Or, again, the deed of horror may be done, but done in ignorance, and the tie of kinship or friendship be discovered afterwards. The Oedipus of Sophocles is an example. Here, indeed, the incident is outside the drama proper; but cases occur where it falls within the action of the play: one may cite the Alcmaeon of Astydamas, or Teleconus in the Wounded Odysseus. Again, there is a third case,—to be about to act with knowledge of the persons and then not to act. The fourth case is when some one is about to do an irreparable deed through ignorance, and makes the discovery before it is done. These are the only possible ways. For the deed must either be done or not done,—and that wittingly or unwittingly. But of all these ways, to be about to act knowing the persons, and then not to act, is the worst. It is shocking without being tragic, for no disaster follows. It is, therefore, never, or very rarely, found in Poetry. One instance, however, is in the Antigone, where Haemon threatens to kill Creon. The next and better way is that the deed should be perpetrated. Still better, that it should be perpetrated in ignorance, and the discovery made afterwards. There is then nothing to shock us, while the discovery produces a startling effect. The last case is the best, as when in the Cresphontes Merope is about to slay her son, but, recognising who he is, spares his life. So in the Iphigenia, the sister recognises the brother just in time. Again in the Helle, the son recognises the mother when on the point of giving her up. This, then, is why a few families only, as has been already observed, furnish the subjects of Tragedy. It was not art, but happy chance, that led the poets in search of subjects to impress the tragic quality upon their plots. They are compelled, therefore, to have recourse to those houses whose history contains moving incidents like these.

Enough has now been said concerning the structure of the incidents, and the right kind of plot.

ON THE AESTHETIC EDUCATION OF MAN IN A SERIES OF LETTERS

by

FRIEDRICH SCHILLER

First Letter

1. I have, then, your gracious permission to submit the results of my inquiry concerning Art and Beauty in the form of a series of letters. Sensible as I am of the gravity of such an undertaking, I am also alive to its attraction and its worth. I shall be treating of a subject which has a direct connexion with all that is best in human happiness, and no very distant connexion with what is noblest in our moral nature. I shall be pleading the cause of Beauty before a heart which is as fully sensible of her power as it is prompt to act upon it, a heart which, in an inquiry where one is bound to invoke feelings no less often than principles, will relieve me of the heaviest part of my labours.

2. What I would have asked of you as a favour, you in your largesse impose upon me as a duty, thus leaving me the appearance of merit where I am in fact only yielding to inclination. The free mode of procedure you prescribe implies for me no constraint; on the contrary, it answers to a need of my own. Little practised in the use of scholastic modes, I am scarcely in danger of offending against good taste by their abuse. My ideas, derived from constant communing with myself rather than from any rich experience of the world or from reading, will be unable to deny their origin: the last reproach they are likely to incur is that of sectarianism, and they are more liable to collapse out of inherent weakness than to maintain themselves with the support of authority and borrowed strength.

3. True, I shall not attempt to hide from you that it is for the most part Kantian principles on which the following theses will be based.

But you must ascribe it to my ineptitude rather than to those principles if in the course of this inquiry you should be reminded of any particular philosophical school. No, the freedom of your mind shall, I can promise you, remain inviolable. Your own feeling will provide me with the material on which to build, your own free powers of thought dictate the laws according to which we are to proceed.

4. Concerning those ideas which prevail in the Practical part of the Kantian system only the philosophers are at variance; the rest of mankind, I believe I can show, have always been agreed. Once divested of their technical form, they stand revealed as the immemorial pronouncements of Common Reason, and as data of that moral instinct which Nature in her wisdom appointed Man's guardian until, through the enlightenment of his understanding, he should have arrived at years of discretion. But it is precisely this technical form, whereby truth is made manifest to the intellect, which veils it again from our feeling. For alas! intellect must first destroy the object of Inner Sense if it would make it its own. Like the analytical chemist, the philosopher can only discover how things are combined by analysing them, only lay bare the workings of spontaneous Nature by subjecting them to the torment of his own techniques. In order to lay hold of the fleeting phenomenon, he must first bind it in the fetters of rule, tear its fair body to pieces by reducing it to concepts, and preserve its living spirit in a sorry skeleton of words. Is it any wonder that natural feeling cannot find itself again in such an image, or that in the account of the analytical thinker truth should appear as paradox?

5. I too, therefore, would crave some measure of forbearance if the following investigations, in trying to bring the subject of inquiry closer to the understanding, were to transport it beyond reach of the senses. What was asserted above of moral experience, must hold even more of the phenomenon we call Beauty. For its whole magic resides in its mystery, and in dissolving the essential amalgam of its elements we find we have dissolved its very Being.

Second Letter

1. But should it not be possible to make better use of the freedom

you accord me than by keeping your attention fixed upon the domain of the fine arts? Is it not, to say the least, untimely to be casting around for a code of laws for the aesthetic world at a moment when the affairs of the moral offer interest of so much more urgent concern, and when the spirit of philosophical inquiry is being expressly challenged by present circumstances to concern itself with that most perfect of all the works to be achieved by the art of man: the construction of true political freedom?

2. I would not wish to live in a century other than my own, or to have worked for any other. We are citizens of our own Age no less than of our own State. And if it is deemed unseemly, or even inadmissible, to exempt ourselves from the morals and customs of the circle in which we live, why should it be less of a duty to allow the needs and taste of our own epoch some voice in our choice of activity?

3. But the verdict of this epoch does not, by any means, seem to be going in favour of art, not at least of the kind of art to which alone my inquiry will be directed. The course of events has given the spirit of the age a direction which threatens to remove it ever further from the art of the Ideal. This kind of art must abandon actuality, and soar with becoming boldness above our wants and needs; for Art is a daughter of Freedom, and takes her orders from the necessity inherent in minds, not from the exigencies of matter. But at the present time material needs reign supreme and bend a degraded humanity beneath their tyrannical yoke. Utility is the great idol of our age, to which all powers are in thrall and to which all talent must pay homage. Weighed in this crude balance, the insubstantial merits of Art scarce tip the scale, and, bereft of all encouragement, she shuns the noisy market-place of our century. The spirit of philosophical inquiry itself is wresting from the imagination one province after another, and the frontiers of art contract the more the boundaries of science expand.

4. Expectantly the gaze of philosopher and man of the world alike is fixed on the political scene, where now, so it is believed, the very fate of mankind is being debated. Does it not betray a culpable indifference to the common weal not to take part in this general debate? If this great action is, by reason of its cause and its consequences, of

urgent concern to every one who calls himself man, it must, by virtue of its method of procedure, be of quite special interest to every one who has learnt to think for himself. For a question which has hitherto always been decided by the blind right of might, is now, so it seems, being brought before the tribunal of Pure Reason itself, and anyone who is at all capable of putting himself at the centre of things, and of raising himself from an individual into a representative of the species, may consider himself at once a member of this tribunal, and at the same time, in his capacity of human being and citizen of the world, an interested party who finds himself more or less closely involved in the outcome of the case. It is, therefore, not merely his own cause which is being decided in this great action; judgment is to be passed according to laws which he, as a reasonable being, is himself competent and entitled to dictate.

5. How tempting it would be for me to investigate such a subject in company with one who is as acute a thinker as he is a liberal citizen of the world! And to leave the decision to a heart which has dedicated itself with such noble enthusiasm to the weal of humanity. What an agreeable surprise if, despite all difference in station, and the vast distance which the circumstances of the actual world make inevitable, I were, in the realm of ideas, to find my conclusions identical with those of a mind as unprejudiced as your own! That I resist this seductive temptation, and put Beauty before Freedom, can, I believe, not only be excused on the score of personal inclination, but also justified on principle. I hope to convince you that the theme I have chosen is far less alien to the needs of our age than to its taste. More than this: if man is ever to solve that problem of politics in practice he will have to approach it through the problem of the aesthetic, because it is only through Beauty that man makes his way to Freedom. But this cannot be demonstrated without my first reminding you of the principles by which Reason is in any case guided in matters of political legislation.

Third Letter

1. Nature deals no better with Man than with the rest of her works: she acts for him as long as he is as yet incapable of acting

for himself as a free intelligence. But what makes him Man is precisely this: that he does not stop short at what Nature herself made of him, but has the power of retracing by means of Reason the steps she took on his behalf, of transforming the work of blind compulsion into a work of free choice, and of elevating physical necessity into moral necessity.

2. Out of the long slumber of the senses he awakens to consciousness and knows himself for a human being; he looks about him, and finds himself—in the State. The force of his needs threw him into this situation before he was as yet capable of exercising his freedom to choose it; compulsion organized it according to purely natural laws before he could do so according to the laws of Reason. But with this State of compulsion, born of what Nature destined him to be, and designed to this end alone, he neither could nor can rest content as a Moral Being. And woe to him if he could! With that same right, therefore, by virtue of which he is Man, he withdraws from the dominion of blind necessity, even as in so many other respects he parts company from it by means of his freedom; even as, to take but one example, he obliterates by means of morality, and ennobles by means of beauty, the crude character imposed by physical need upon sexual love. And even thus does he, in his maturity, retrieve by means of a fiction the childhood of the race: he conceives, as idea, a state of nature, a state not indeed given him by any experience, but a necessary result of what Reason destined him to be; attributes to himself in this idealized natural state a purpose of which in his actual natural state he was entirely ignorant, and a power of free choice of which he was at that time wholly incapable; and now proceeds exactly as if he were starting from scratch, and were, from sheer insight and free resolve, exchanging a state of complete independence for a state of social contracts. However skilfully, and however firmly, blind caprice may have laid the foundations of her work, however arrogantly she may maintain it, and with whatever appearance of venerability she may surround it—Man is fully entitled in the course of these operations to treat it all as though it had never happened. For the work of blind forces possesses no authority before which Freedom need bow, and everything must accommodate itself to the highest end which Reason now decrees in him as Person. This is the origin and justification of any attempt on the part of a people

grown to maturity to transform its Natural State into a Moral one.

3. This Natural State (as we may term any political body whose organization derives originally from forces and not from laws) is, it is true, at variance with man as moral being, for whom the only Law should be to act in conformity with law. But it will just suffice for man as physical being; for he only gives himself laws in order to come to terms with forces. But physical man does in fact exist, whereas the existence of moral man is as yet problematic. If, then, Reason does away with the Natural State (as she of necessity must if she would put her own in its place), she jeopardizes the physical man who actually exists for the sake of a moral man who is as yet problematic, risks the very existence of society for a merely hypothetical (even though morally necessary) ideal of society. She takes from man something he actually possesses, and without which he possesses nothing, and refers him instead to something which he could and should possess. And if in so doing she should have counted on him for more than he can perform, then she would, for the sake of a humanity which he still lacks—and can without prejudice to his mere existence go on lacking—have deprived him of the means of that animal existence which is the very condition of his being human at all. Before he has had time to cleave unto the Law with the full force of his moral will, she would have drawn from under his feet the ladder of Nature.

4. What we must chiefly bear in mind, then, is that physical society in time must never for a moment cease to exist while moral society as idea is in the process of being formed; that for the sake of man's moral dignity his actual existence must never be jeopardized. When the craftsman has a timepiece to repair, he can let its wheels run down; but the living clockwork of the State must be repaired while it is still striking, and it is a question of changing the revolving wheel while it still revolves. For this reason a support must be looked for which will ensure the continuance of society, and make it independent of the Natural State which is to be abolished.

5. This support is not to be found in the natural character of man which, selfish and violent as it is, aims at the destruction of society rather than at its preservation. Neither is it to be found in his moral

character which has, *ex hypothesi*, first to be fashioned, and upon which, just because it is free, and because it never becomes manifest, the lawgiver could never exert influence, nor with any certainty depend. It would, therefore, be a question of abstracting from man's physical character its arbitrariness, and from his moral character its freedom; of making the first conformable to laws, and the second dependent upon sense-impressions; of removing the former somewhat further from matter, and bringing the latter somewhat closer to it; and all this with the aim of bringing into being a third character which, kin to both the others, might prepare the way for a transition from the rule of mere force to the rule of law, and which, without in any way impeding the development of moral character, might on the contrary serve as a pledge in the sensible world of a morality as yet unseen.

Fourth Letter

1. This much is certain: Only the predominance of such a character among a people makes it safe to undertake the transformation of a State in accordance with moral principles. And only such a character can guarantee that this transformation will endure. The setting up of a moral State involves being able to count on the moral law as an effective force, and free will is thereby drawn into the realm of cause and effect, where everything follows from everything else in a chain of strict necessity. But we know that the modes of determination of the human will must always remain contingent, and that it is only in Absolute Being that physical necessity coincides with moral necessity. If, therefore, we are to be able to count on man's moral behaviour with as much certainty as we do on natural effects, it will itself have to be nature, and he will have to be led by his very impulses to the kind of conduct which is bound to proceed from a moral character. But the will of man stands completely free between duty and inclination, and no physical compulsion can, or should, encroach upon this sovereign right of his personality. If, then, man is to retain his power of choice and yet, at the same time, be a reliable link in the chain of causality, this can only be brought about through both these motive forces, inclination and duty, producing completely identical results in the world of phenomena; through the

content of his volition remaining the same whatever the difference in form; that is to say, through impulse being sufficiently in harmony with reason to qualify as universal legislator.

2. Every individual human being, one may say, carries within him, potentially and prescriptively, an ideal man, the archetype of a human being, and it is his life's task to be, through all his changing manifestations, in harmony with the unchanging unity of this ideal. This archetype, which is to be discerned more or less clearly in every individual, is represented by the State, the objective and, as it were, canonical form in which all the diversity of individual subjects strives to unite. One can, however, imagine two different ways in which man existing in time can coincide with man as Idea, and, in consequence, just as many ways in which the State can assert itself in individuals: either by the ideal man suppressing empirical man, and the State annulling individuals; or else by the individual himself becoming the State, and man in time being ennobled to the stature of man as Idea.

3. It is true that from a one-sided moral point of view this difference disappears. For Reason is satisfied as long as her law obtains unconditionally. But in the complete anthropological view, where content counts no less than form, and living feeling too has a voice, the difference becomes all the more relevant. Reason does indeed demand unity; but Nature demands multiplicity; and both these kinds of law make their claim upon man. The law of Reason is imprinted upon him by an incorruptible consciousness; the law of Nature by an ineradicable feeling. Hence it will always argue a still defective education if the moral character is able to assert itself only by sacrificing the natural. And a political constitution will still be very imperfect if it is able to achieve unity only by suppressing variety. The State should not only respect the objective and generic character in its individual subjects; it should also honour their subjective and specific character, and in extending the invisible realm of morals take care not to depopulate the sensible realm of appearance.

4. When the artisan lays hands upon the formless mass in order to shape it to his ends, he has no scruple in doing it violence; for the natural material he is working merits no respect for itself, and his

concern is not with the whole for the sake of its parts, but with the parts for the sake of the whole. When the artist lays hands upon the same mass, he has just as little scruple in doing it violence; but he avoids showing it. For the material he is handling he has not a whit more respect than has the artisan; but the eye which would seek to protest the freedom of the material he will endeavour to deceive by a show of yielding to this latter. With the pedagogic or the political artist things are very different indeed. For him Man is at once the material on which he works and the goal towards which he strives. In this case the end turns back upon itself and becomes identical with the medium; and it is only inasmuch as the whole serves the parts that the parts are in any way bound to submit to the whole. The statesman-artist must approach his material with a quite different kind of respect from that which the maker of Beauty feigns towards his. The consideration he must accord to its uniqueness and individuality is not merely subjective, and aimed at creating an illusion for the senses, but objective and directed to its innermost being.

5. But just because the State is to be an organization formed by itself and for itself, it can only become a reality inasmuch as its parts have been tuned up to the idea of the whole. Because the State serves to represent that ideal and objective humanity which exists in the heart of each of its citizens, it will have to observe toward those citizens the same relationship as each has to himself, and will be able to honour their subjective humanity only to the extent that this has been ennobled in the direction of objective humanity. Once man is inwardly at one with himself, he will be able to preserve his individuality however much he may universalize his conduct, and the State will be merely the interpreter of his own finest instinct, a clearer formulation of his own sense of what is right. If, on the other hand, in the character of a whole people, subjective man sets his face against objective man with such vehemence of contradiction that the victory of the latter can only be ensured by the suppression of the former, then the State too will have to adopt towards its citizens the solemn rigour of the law, and ruthlessly trample underfoot such powerfully seditious individualism in order not to fall a victim to it.

6. But man can be at odds with himself in two ways: either as savage, when feeling dominates over principle; or as barbarian, when

principle destroys feeling. The savage despises Civilization, and acknowledges Nature as his sovereign mistress. The barbarian derides and dishonours Nature, but, more contemptible than the savage, as often as not continues to be the slave of his slave. The man of Culture makes a friend of Nature, and honours her freedom whilst curbing only her caprice.

7. Consequently, whenever Reason starts to introduce the unity of the moral law into any actually existing society, she must beware of damaging the variety of Nature. And whenever Nature endeavours to maintain her variety within the moral framework of society, moral unity must not suffer any infringement thereby. Removed alike from uniformity and from confusion, there abides the triumph of form. Wholeness of character must therefore be present in any people capable, and worthy, of exchanging a State of compulsion for a State of freedom.

Fifth Letter

1. Is this the character which the present age, which contemporary events present to us? Let me turn my attention at once to the object most in evidence on this enormous canvas.

2. True, the authority of received opinion has declined, arbitrary rule is unmasked and, though still armed with power, can no longer, even by devious means, maintain the appearance of dignity. Man has roused himself from his long indolence and self-deception and, by an impressive majority, is demanding restitution of his inalienable rights. But he is not just demanding this; over there, and over here, he is rising up to seize by force what, in his opinion, has been wrongfully denied him. The fabric of the natural State is tottering, its rotting foundations giving way, and there seems to be a physical possibility of setting law upon the throne, of honouring man at last as an end in himself, and making true freedom the basis of political associations. Vain hope! The moral possibility is lacking, and a moment so prodigal of opportunity finds a generation unprepared to receive it.

3. Man portrays himself in his actions. And what a figure he cuts in

the drama of the present time! On the one hand, a return to the savage state; on the other, to complete lethargy: in other words, to the two extremes of human depravity, and both united in a single epoch!

4. Amongst the lower and more numerous classes we are confronted with crude, lawless instincts, unleashed with the loosening of the bonds of civil order, and hastening with ungovernable fury to their animal satisfactions. It may well be that objective humanity had cause for complaint against the State; subjective humanity must respect its institutions. Can the State be blamed for having disregarded the dignity of human beings as long as it was still a question of ensuring their very existence? Or for having hastened to divide and unite by the [mechanical] forces of gravity and cohesion, while there could as yet be no thought of any [organic] formative principle from within? Its very dissolution provides the justification of its existence. For society, released from its controls, is falling back into the kingdom of the elements, instead of hastening upwards into the realm of organic life.

5. The cultivated classes, on the other hand, offer the even more repugnant spectacle of lethargy, and of a depravation of character which offends the more because culture itself is the source. I no longer recall which of the ancient or modern philosophers it was who remarked that the nobler a thing is, the more repulsive it is when it decays; but we shall find that this is no less true in the moral sphere. The child of Nature, when he breaks loose, turns into a madman; the creature of Civilization into a knave. That Enlightenment of the mind, which is the not altogether groundless boast of our refined classes, has had on the whole so little of an ennobling influence on feeling and character that it has tended rather to bolster up depravity by providing it with the support of precepts. We disown Nature in her rightful sphere only to submit to her tyranny in the moral, and while resisting the impact she makes upon our senses are content to take over her principles. The sham propriety of our manners refuses her the first say—which would be pardonable—only to concede to her in our materialistic ethics the final and decisive one. In the very bosom of the most exquisitely developed social life egotism has founded its system, and without ever acquiring therefrom a heart that is truly sociable, we suffer all the contagions and afflic-

tions of society. We subject our free judgment to its despotic opinion, our feeling to its fantastic customs, our will to its seductions; only our caprice do we uphold against its sacred rights. Proud self-sufficiency contracts the heart of the man of the world, a heart which in natural man still often beats in sympathy; and as from a city in flames each man seeks only to save from the general destruction his own wretched belongings. Only by completely abjuring sensibility can we, so it is thought, be safe from its aberrations; and the ridicule which often acts as a salutary chastener of the enthusiast is equally unsparing in its desecration of the noblest feeling. Civilization, far from setting us free, in fact creates some new need with every new power it develops in us. The fetters of the physical tighten ever more alarmingly, so that fear of losing what we have stifles even the most burning impulse towards improvement, and the maxim of passive obedience passes for the supreme wisdom of life. Thus do we see the spirit of the age wavering between perversity and brutality, between unnaturalness and mere nature, between superstition and moral unbelief; and it is only through an equilibrium of evils that it is still sometimes kept within bounds.

from

THE BIRTH OF TRAGEDY
AND THE GENEOLOGY OF MAN
by
FRIEDRICH NIETZSCHE

This selection is excerpted from "The Birth of Tragedy from the Spirit of Music."

I

Much will have been gained for esthetics once we have succeeded in apprehending directly—rather than merely *ascertaining*—that art owes its continuous evolution to the Apollonian-Dionysiac duality, even as the propagation of the species depends on the duality of the sexes, their constant conflicts and periodic acts of reconciliation. I have borrowed my adjectives from the Greeks, who developed their mystical doctrines of art through plausible *embodiments*, not through purely conceptual means. It is by those two art-sponsoring deities, Apollo and Dionysos, that we are made to recognize the tremendous split, as regards both origins and objectives, between the plastic, Apollonian arts and the non-visual art of music inspired by Dionysos. The two creative tendencies developed alongside one another, usually in fierce opposition, each by its taunts forcing the other to more energetic production, both perpetuating in a discordant concord that agon which the term *art* but feebly denominates: until at last, by the thaumaturgy of an Hellenic act of will, the pair accepted the yoke of marriage and, in this condition, begot Attic tragedy, which exhibits the salient features of both parents.

To reach a closer understanding of both these tendencies, let us begin by viewing them as the separate art realms of *dream* and *intoxication*, two physiological phenomena standing toward one another in much the same relationship as the Apollonian and Dionysiac. It was in a dream, according to Lucretius, that the marvelous gods and goddesses first presented themselves to the minds of men. That great sculptor, Phidias, beheld in a dream the entrancing bodies of more-than-human beings, and likewise, if anyone had asked the Greek poets about the mystery of poetic creation, they too would have referred him to dreams and instructed him much as Hans Sachs instructs us in *Die Meistersinger*:

> *My friend, it is the poet's work*
> *Dreams to interpret and to mark.*
> *Believe me that man's true conceit*
> *In a dream becomes complete:*
> *All poetry we ever read*
> *Is but true dreams interpreted.*

The fair illusion of the dream sphere, in the production of which every man proves himself an accomplished artist, is a precondition not only of all plastic art, but even, as we shall see presently, of a wide range of poetry. Here we enjoy an immediate apprehension of form, all shapes speak to us directly, nothing seems indifferent or redundant. Despite the high intensity with which these dream realities exist for us, we still have a residual sensation that they are illusions; at least such has been my experience—and the frequency, not to say normality, of the experience is borne out in many passages of the poets. Men of philosophical disposition are known for their constant premonition that our everyday reality, too, is an illusion, hiding another, totally different kind of reality. It was Schopenhauer who considered the ability to view at certain times all men and things as mere phantoms or dream images to be the true mark of philosophic talent. The person who is responsive to the stimuli of art behaves toward the reality of dream much the way the philosopher behaves toward the reality of existence: he observes exactly and enjoys his observations, for it is by these images that he interprets life, by these processes that he rehearses it. Nor is it by pleasant images only that such plausible connections are made: the whole divine comedy of life, including its somber aspects, its sudden balkings, impish accidents, anxious expectations, moves past him, not quite like a shadow play—for it is he himself, after all, who lives and suffers through these scenes—yet never without giving a fleeting sense of illusion; and I imagine that many persons have reassured themselves amidst the perils of dream by calling out, "It is a dream!

I want it to go on." I have even heard of people spinning out the causality of one and the same dream over three or more successive nights. All these facts clearly bear witness that our innermost being, the common substratum of humanity, experiences dreams with deep delight and a sense of real necessity. This deep and happy sense of the necessity of dream experiences was expressed by the Greeks in the image of Apollo. Apollo is at once the god of all plastic powers and the soothsaying god. He who is etymologically the "lucent" one, the god of light, reigns also over the fair illusion of our inner world of fantasy. The perfection of these conditions in contrast to our imperfectly understood waking reality, as well as our profound awareness of nature's healing powers during the interval of sleep and dream, furnishes a symbolic analogue to the soothsaying faculty and quite generally to the arts, which make life possible and worth living. But the image of Apollo must incorporate that thin line which the dream image may not cross, under penalty of becoming pathological, of imposing itself on us as crass reality: a discreet limitation, a freedom from all extravagant urges, the sapient tranquillity of the plastic god. His eye must be sunlike, in keeping with his origin. Even at those moments when he is angry and ill-tempered there lies upon him the consecration of fair illusion. In an eccentric way one might say of Apollo what Schopenhauer says, in the first part of *The World as Will and Idea*, of man caught in the veil of Maya: "Even as on an immense, raging sea, assailed by huge wave crests, a man sits in a little rowboat trusting his frail craft, so, amidst the furious torments of this world, the individual sits tranquilly, supported by the *principium individuationis* and relying on it." One might say that the unshakable confidence in that principle has received its most magnificent expression in Apollo, and that Apollo himself may be regarded as the marvelous divine image of the *principium individuationis*, whose looks and gestures radiate the full delight, wisdom, and beauty of "illusion."

In the same context Schopenhauer has described for us the tremendous awe which seizes man when he suddenly begins to doubt the cognitive modes of experience, in other words, when in a given instance the law of causation seems to suspend itself. If we add to this awe the glorious transport which arises in man, even from the very depths of nature, at the shattering of the *principium individuationis*, then we are in a position to apprehend the essence of

Dionysiac rapture, whose closest analogy is furnished by physical intoxication. Dionysiac stirrings arise either through the influence of those narcotic potions of which all primitive races speak in their hymns, or through the powerful approach of spring, which penetrates with joy the whole frame of nature. So stirred, the individual forgets himself completely. It is the same Dionysiac power which in medieval Germany drove ever increasing crowds of people singing and dancing from place to place; we recognize in these St. John's and St. Vitus' dancers the bacchic choruses of the Greeks, who had their precursors in Asia Minor and as far back as Babylon and the orgiastic Sacaea. There are people who, either from lack of experience or out of sheer stupidity, turn away from such phenomena, and, strong in the sense of their own sanity, label them either mockingly or pityingly "endemic diseases." These benighted souls have no idea how cadaverous and ghostly their "sanity" appears as the intense throng of Dionysiac revelers sweeps past them.

Not only does the bond between man and man come to be forced once more by the magic of the Dionysiac rite, but nature itself, long alienated or subjugated, rises again to celebrate the reconciliation with her prodigal son, man. The earth offers its gifts voluntarily, and the savage beasts of mountain and desert approach in peace. The chariot of Dionysos is bedecked with flowers and garlands; panthers and tigers stride beneath his yoke. If one were to convert Beethoven's "Paean to Joy" into a painting, and refuse to curb the imagination when that multitude prostrates itself reverently in the dust, one might form some apprehension of Dionysiac ritual. Now the slave emerges as a freeman; all the rigid, hostile walls which either necessity or despotism has erected between men are shattered. Now that the gospel of universal harmony is sounded, each individual becomes not only reconciled to his fellow but actually at one with him—as though the veil of Maya had been torn apart and there remained only shreds floating before the vision of mystical Oneness. Man now expresses himself through song and dance as the member of a higher community; he has forgotten how to walk, how to speak, and is on the brink of taking wing as he dances. Each of his gestures betokens enchantment; through him sounds a supernatural power, the same power which makes the animals speak and the earth render up milk and honey. He feels himself to be godlike and strides with the same elation and ecstasy as the gods he has seen in his dreams. No longer the *artist*, he has himself become a *work of art*: the productive power of the whole universe is now manifest in his transport, to the glorious satisfaction of the primordial One. The finest clay, the most precious marble—man—is here kneaded and hewn, and the chisel blows of the Dionysiac world artist are accompanied by the cry of the Eleusinian mystagogues: "Do you fall on your knees, multitudes, do you divine your creator?"

II

So far we have examined the Apollonian and Dionysiac states as the product of formative forces arising directly from nature without the mediation of the human artist. At this stage artistic urges are satisfied directly, on the one hand through the imagery of dreams, whose perfection is quite independent of the intellectual rank, the artistic development of the individual; on the other hand, through an ecstatic reality which once again takes no account of the individual and may even destroy him, or else redeem him through a mystical experience of the collective. In relation to these immediate creative conditions of nature every artist must appear as "imitator," either as the Apollonian dream artist or the Dionysiac ecstatic artist, or, finally (as in Greek tragedy, for example) as dream and ecstatic artist in one. We might picture to ourselves how the last of these, in a state of Dionysiac intoxication and mystical self-abrogation, wandering apart from the reveling throng, sinks upon the ground, and how there is then revealed to him his own condition—complete oneness with the essence of the universe—in a dream similitude.

Having set down these general premises and distinctions, we now turn to the Greeks in order to realize to what degree the formative forces of nature were developed in them. Such an inquiry will enable us to assess properly the relation of the Greek artist to his prototypes or, to use Aristotle's expression, his "imitation of nature." Of the dreams the Greeks dreamed it is not possible to speak with any certainty, despite the extant dream literature and the large number of dream anecdotes. But considering the incredible accuracy of their eyes, their keen and unabashed delight in colors, one can hardly be wrong in assuming that their dreams too showed a strict consequence of lines and contours, hues and groupings, a progression of scenes similar to their best bas-reliefs. The perfection of these dream scenes might almost tempt us to consider the dreaming Greek as a Homer and Homer as a dreaming Greek; which would be as though the modern man were to compare himself in his dreaming to Shakespeare.

Yet there is another point about which we do not have to conjecture at all: I mean the profound gap separating the Dionysiac Greeks from the Dionysiac barbarians. Throughout the range of ancient civilization (leaving the newer civilizations out of account for the moment) we find evidence of Dionysiac celebrations which stand to the Greek type in much the same relation as the bearded satyr, whose name and attributes are derived from the hegoat, stands to the god Dionysos. The central concern of such celebrations was, almost universally, a complete sexual promiscuity overriding every form of established tribal law; all the savage urges of the mind were unleashed on those occasions until they reached that paroxysm of lust and cruelty which has always struck me as the "witches' cauldron" *par excellence*. It would appear that the Greeks were for a while quite immune from these feverish excesses which must have reached them by every known land or sea route. What kept Greece safe was the proud, imposing image of Apollo, who in holding up the head of the Gorgon to those brutal and grotesque Dionysiac forces subdued them. Doric art has immortalized Apollo's majestic rejection of all license. But resistance became difficult, even impossible, as soon as similar urges began to break forth from the deep substratum of Hellenism itself. Soon the function of the Delphic god developed into something quite different and much more limited: all he could hope to accomplish now was to wrest the destructive weapon, by a timely gesture of pacification, from his opponent's hand. That act of pacification represents the most important event in the history of Greek ritual; every department of life now shows symptoms of a revolutionary change. The two great antagonists have been reconciled. Each feels obliged henceforth to keep to his bounds, each will honor the other by the bestowal of periodic gifts, while the cleavage remains fundamentally the same. And yet, if we examine what happened to the Dionysiac powers under the pressure of that treaty we notice a great difference: in the place of the Babylonian Sacaea, with their throwback of men to the condition of apes and tigers, we now see entirely new rites celebrated: rites of universal redemption, of glorious transfiguration. Only now has it become possible to speak

of nature's celebrating an *esthetic* triumph; only now has the abroga-
tion of the *principium individuationis* become an esthetic event.
That terrible witches' brew concocted of lust and cruelty has lost all
power under the new conditions. Yet the peculiar blending of emotions in the heart of the Dionysiac reveler—his ambiguity if you
will—seems still to hark back (as the medicinal drug harks back to
the deadly poison) to the days when the infliction of pain was experienced as joy while a sense of supreme triumph elicited cries of
anguish from the heart. For now in every exuberant joy there is
heard an undertone of terror, or else a wistful lament over an
irrecoverable loss. It is as though in these Greek festivals a sentimental trait of nature were coming to the fore, as though nature
were bemoaning the fact of her fragmentation, her decomposition
into separate individuals. The chants and gestures of these revelers,
so ambiguous in their motivation, represented an absolute *novum* in
the world of the Homeric Greeks; their Dionysiac music, in especial,
spread abroad terror and a deep shudder. It is true: music had long
been familiar to the Greeks as an Apollonian art, as a regular beat
like that of waves lapping the shore, a plastic rhythm expressly developed for the portrayal of Apollonian conditions. Apollo's music was
a Doric architecture of sound—of barely hinted sounds such as are
proper to the cithara. Those very elements which characterize
Dionysiac music and, after it, music quite generally: the heart-
shaking power of tone, the uniform stream of melody, the incomparable resources of harmony—all those elements had been carefully
kept at a distance as being inconsonant with the Apollonian norm.
In the Dionysiac dithyramb man is incited to strain his symbolic
faculties to the utmost; something quite unheard of is now clamor-
ing to be heard: the desire to tear asunder the veil of Maya, to sink
back into the original oneness of nature; the desire to express the
very essence of nature symbolically. Thus an entirely new set of symbols springs into being. First, all the symbols pertaining to physical
features: mouth, face, the spoken word, the dance movement which
coordinates the limbs and bends them to its rhythm. Then suddenly
all the rest of the symbolic forces—music and rhythm as such,
dynamics, harmony—assert themselves with great energy. In order
to comprehend this total emancipation of all the symbolic powers
one must have reached the same measure of inner freedom those
powers themselves were making manifest; which is to say that the

votary of Dionysos could not be understood except by his own kind. It is not difficult to imagine the awed surprise with which the Apollonian Greek must have looked on him. And that surprise would be further increased as the latter realized, with a shudder, that all this was not so alien to him after all, that his Apollonian consciousness was but a thin veil hiding from him the whole Dionysiac realm.

III

In order to comprehend this we must take down the elaborate edifice of Apollonian culture stone by stone until we discover its foundations. At first the eve is struck by the marvelous shapes of the Olympian gods who stand upon its pediments, and whose exploits, in shining bas-relief, adorn its friezes. The fact that among them we find Apollo as one god among many, making no claim to a privileged position, should not mislead us. The same drive that found its most complete representation in Apollo generated the whole Olympian world, and in this sense we may consider Apollo the father of that world. But what was the radical need out of which that illustrious society of Olympian beings sprang?

Whoever approaches the Olympians with a different religion in his heart, seeking moral elevation, sanctity, spirituality, loving-kindness, will presently be forced to turn away from them in ill-humored disappointment. Nothing in these deities reminds us of asceticism, high intellect, or duty: we are confronted by luxuriant, triumphant *existence*, which deifies the good and the bad indifferently. And the beholder may find himself dismayed in the presence of such overflowing life and ask himself what potion these heady people must have drunk in order to behold, in whatever direction they looked, Helen laughing back at them, the beguiling image of their own existence. But we shall call out to this beholder, who has already turned his back: Don't go! Listen first to what the Greeks themselves have to say of this life, which spreads itself before you with such puzzling serenity. An old legend has it that King Midas hunted a long time in the woods for the wise Silenus, companion of Dionysos, without being able to catch him. When he had finally caught him the king asked him what he considered man's greatest good. The daemon remained sullen and uncommunicative until finally, forced by the king, he broke into a shrill laugh and spoke: "Ephemeral wretch, begotten by accident and toil, why do you force me to tell you what it would be your greatest boon not to hear? What would be best for you is quite beyond your reach: not to have been born, not to *be*, to be *nothing*. But the second best is to die soon."

What is the relation of the Olympian gods to this popular wisdom? It is that of the entranced vision of the martyr to his torment. Now the Olympian magic mountain opens itself before us, showing us its very roots. The Greeks were keenly aware of the terrors and horrors of existence; in order to be able to live at all they had to place before them the shining fantasy of the Olympians. Their tremendous distrust of the titanic forces of nature: *Moira*, mercilessly enthroned beyond the knowable world; the vulture which fed upon the great philanthropist Prometheus; the terrible lot drawn by wise Oedipus; the curse on the house of Atreus which brought Orestes to the murder of his mother: that whole Panic philosophy, in short, with its mythic examples, by which the gloomy Etruscans perished, the Greeks conquered—or at least hid from view—again and again by means of this artificial Olympus. In order to live at all the Greeks had to construct these deities. The Apollonian need for beauty had to develop the Olympian hierarchy of joy by slow degrees from the original titanic hierarchy of terror, as roses are seen to break from a thorny thicket. How else could life have been borne by a race so hypersensitive, so emotionally intense, so equipped for suffering? The same drive which called art into being as a completion and consummation of existence, and as a guarantee of further existence, gave rise also to that Olympian realm which acted as a transfiguring mirror to the Hellenic will. The gods justified human life by living it themselves—the only satisfactory theodicy ever invented. To exist in the clear sunlight of such deities was now felt to be the highest good, and the only real grief suffered by Homeric man was inspired by the thought of leaving that sunlight, especially when the departure seemed imminent. Now it became possible to stand the wisdom of Silenus on its head and proclaim that it was the worst evil for man to die soon, and second worst for him to die at all. Such laments as arise now arise over short-lived Achilles, over the generations ephemeral as leaves, the decline of the heroic age. It is not unbecoming to even the greatest hero to yearn for an afterlife, though it be as a day laborer. So impetuously, during the Apollonian phase, does man's will desire to remain on earth, so identified does he become with existence, that even his lament turns to a song of praise.

It should have become apparent by now that the harmony with nature which we late-comers regard with such nostalgia, and for which Schiller has coined the cant term *naïve*, is by no means a simple and inevitable condition to be found at the gateway to every culture, a kind of paradise. Such a belief could have been endorsed only by a period for which Rousseau's Emile was an artist and Homer just such an artist nurtured in the bosom of nature. Whenever we encounter "naïveté" in art, we are face to face with the ripest fruit of Apollonian culture—which must always triumph first over titans, kill monsters, and overcome the somber contemplation of actuality, the intense susceptibility to suffering, by means of illusions strenuously and zestfully entertained. But how rare are the instances of true naïveté, of that complete identification with the beauty of appearance! It is this achievement which makes Homer so magnificent—Homer, who, as a single individual, stood to Apollonian popular culture in the same relation as the individual dream artist to the oneiric capacity of a race and of nature generally. The naïveté of Homer must be viewed as a complete victory of Apollonian illusion. Nature often uses illusions of this sort in order to accomplish its secret purposes. The true goal is covered over by a phantasm. We stretch out our hands to the latter, while nature, aided by our deception, attains the former. In the case of the Greeks it was the will wishing to behold itself in the work of art, in the transcendence of genius; but in order so to behold itself its creatures had first to view themselves as glorious, to transpose themselves to a higher sphere, without having that sphere of pure contemplation either challenge them or upbraid them with insufficiency. It was in that sphere of beauty that the Greeks saw the Olympians as their mirror images; it was by means of that esthetic mirror that the Greek will opposed suffering and the somber wisdom of suffering which always accompanies artistic talent. As a monument to its victory stands Homer, the naïve artist.

IV

We can learn something about that naïve artist through the analogy of dream. We can imagine the dreamer as he calls out to himself, still caught in the illusion of his dream and without disturbing it, "This is a dream, and I want to go on dreaming," and we can infer, on the one hand, that he takes deep delight in the contemplation of his dream, and, on the other, that he must have forgotten the day, with its horrible importunity, so to enjoy his dream. Apollo, the interpreter of dreams, will furnish the clue to what is happening here. Although of the two halves of life—the waking and the dreaming—the former is generally considered not only the more important but the only one which is truly lived, I would, at the risk of sounding paradoxical, propose the opposite view. The more I have come to realize in nature those omnipotent formative tendencies and, with them, an intense longing for illusion, the more I feel inclined to the hypothesis that the original Oneness, the ground of Being, ever-suffering and contradictory, time and again has need of rapt vision and delightful illusion to redeem itself. Since we ourselves are the very stuff of such illusions, we must view ourselves as the truly non-existent, that is to say, as a perpetual unfolding in time, space, and causality—what we label "empiric reality." But if, for the moment, we abstract from our own reality, viewing our empiric existence, as well as the existence of the world at large, as the *idea* of the original Oneness, produced anew each instant, then our dreams will appear to us as illusions of illusions, hence as a still higher form of satisfaction of the original desire for illusion. It is for this reason that the very core of nature takes such a deep delight in the naïve artist and the naïve work of art, which likewise is merely the illusion of an illusion. Raphael, himself one of those immortal "naïve" artists, in a symbolic canvas has illustrated that reduction of illusion to further illusion which is the original act of the naïve artist and at the same time of all Apollonian culture. In the lower half of his "Transfiguration," through the figures of the possessed boy, the despairing bearers, the helpless, terrified disciples, we see a reflection of original pain, the sole ground of being: "illusion" here is a reflection of eternal contradiction, begetter of all things. From this illusion there rises, like the fragrance of ambrosia, a new illusory world, invisible to those enmeshed in the first: a radiant vision of pure delight, a rapt seeing through wide-open eyes. Here we have, in a great symbol of art, both the fair world of Apollo and its substratum, the terrible wisdom of Silenus, and we can comprehend intuitively how they mutually require one another. But Apollo appears to us once again as the apotheosis of the *principium indi-viduationis*, in whom the eternal goal of the original Oneness, namely its redemption through illusion, accomplishes itself. With august gesture the god shows us how there is need for a whole world of torment in order for the individual to produce the redemptive vision and to sit quietly in his rocking rowboat in mid-sea, absorbed in contemplation.

If this apotheosis of individuation is to be read in normative terms, we may infer that there is one norm only: the individual—or, more precisely, the observance of the limits of the individual: *sophrosyne*. As a moral deity Apollo demands self-control from his people and, in order to observe such self-control, a knowledge of self. And so we find that the esthetic necessity of beauty is accompanied by the imperatives, "Know thyself," and "Nothing too much." Conversely, excess and *hubris* come to be regarded as the hostile spirits of the non-Apollonian sphere, hence as properties of the pre-Apollonian era—the age of Titans—and the extra-Apollonian world, that is to say the world of the barbarians. It was because of his Titanic love of man that Prometheus had to be devoured by vultures; it was because of his extravagant wisdom which succeeded in solving the riddle of the Sphinx that Oedipus had to be cast into a whirlpool of crime: in this fashion does the Delphic god interpret the Greek past.

The effects of the Dionysiac spirit struck the Apollonian Greeks as Titanic and barbaric; yet they could not disguise from themselves the fact that they were essentially akin to those deposed Titans and heroes. They felt more than that: their whole existence, with its temperate beauty, rested upon a base of suffering and *knowledge* which had been hidden from them until the reinstatement of Dionysos uncovered it once more. And lo and behold! Apollo found it impossible to live without Dionysos. The elements of Titanism and barbarism turned out to be quite as fundamental as the Apollonian element. And now let us imagine how the ecstatic sounds of the Dionysiac rites penetrated ever more enticingly into that artificially restrained and discreet world of illusion, how this clamor expressed the whole outrageous gamut of nature—delight, grief, knowledge—even to the most piercing cry; and then let us imagine how the Apollonian artist with his thin, monotonous harp music must have sounded beside the demoniac chant of the multitude! The muses

presiding over the illusory arts paled before an art which enthusias-
tically told the truth, and the wisdom of Silenus cried "Woe!"
against the serene Olympians. The individual, with his limits and
moderations, forgot himself in the Dionysiac vortex and became
oblivious to the laws of Apollo. Indiscreet extravagance revealed
itself as truth, and contradiction, a delight born of pain, spoke out
of the bosom of nature. Wherever the Dionysiac voice was heard,
the Apollonian norm seemed suspended or destroyed. Yet it is equally true that, in those places where the first assault was withstood, the
prestige and majesty of the Delphic god appeared more rigid and
threatening than before. The only way I am able to view Doric art
and the Doric state is as a perpetual military encampment of the
Apollonian forces. An art so defiantly austere, so ringed about with
fortifications—an education so military and exacting—a polity so
ruthlessly cruel—could endure only in a continual state of resistance
against the titanic and barbaric menace of Dionysos.

Up to this point I have developed at some length a theme which
was sounded at the beginning of this essay: how the Dionysiac and
Apollonian elements, in a continuous chain of creations, each
enhancing the other, dominated the Hellenic mind; how from the
Iron Age, with its battles of Titans and its austere popular philosophy, there developed under the aegis of Apollo the Homeric world
of beauty; how this "naïve" splendor was then absorbed once more
by the Dionysiac torrent, and how, face to face with this new power,
the Apollonian code rigidified into the majesty of Doric art and contemplation. If the earlier phase of Greek history may justly be
broken down into four major artistic epochs dramatizing the battle
between the two hostile principles, then we must inquire further
(lest Doric art appear to us as the acme and final goal of all these
striving tendencies) what was the true end toward which that evolution moved. And our eyes will come to rest on the sublime and
much lauded achievement of the dramatic dithyramb and Attic
tragedy, as the common goal of both urges; whose mysterious marriage, after long discord, ennobled itself with such a child, at once
Antigone and Cassandra.

V

We are now approaching the central concern of our inquiry, which has as its aim an understanding of the Dionysiac-Apollonian spirit, or at least an intuitive comprehension of the mystery which made this conjunction possible. Our first question must be: where in the Greek world is the new seed first to be found which was later to develop into tragedy and the dramatic dithyramb? Greek antiquity gives us a pictorial clue when it represents in statues, on cameos, etc., Homer and Archilochus side by side as ancestors and torch-bearers of Greek poetry, in the certainty that only these two are to be regarded as truly original minds, from whom a stream of fire flowed onto the entire later Greek world. Homer, the hoary dreamer, caught in utter abstraction, prototype of the Apollonian naïve artist, stares in amazement at the passionate head of Archilochus, soldierly servant of the Muses, knocked about by fortune. All that more recent esthetics has been able to add by way of interpretation is that here the "objective" artist is confronted by the first "subjective" artist. We find this interpretation of little use, since to us the subjective artist is simply the bad artist, and since we demand above all, in every genre and range of art, a triumph over subjectivity, deliverance from the self, the silencing of every personal will and desire; since, in fact, we cannot imagine the smallest genuine art work lacking objectivity and disinterested contemplation. For this reason our esthetic must first solve the following problem: how is the lyrical poet at all possible as artist—he who, according to the experience of all times, always says "I" and recites to us the entire chromatic scale of his passions and appetites? It is this Archilochus who most disturbs us, placed there beside Homer, with the stridor of his hate and mockery, the drunken outbursts of his desire. Isn't he—the first artist to be called subjective—for that reason the veritable non-artist? How, then, are we to explain the reverence in which he was held as a poet, the honor done him by the Delphic oracle, that seat of "objective" art, in a number of very curious sayings?

Schiller has thrown some light on his own manner of composition by a psychological observation which seems inexplicable to himself without, however, giving him pause. Schiller confessed that, prior to composing, he experienced not a logically connected series of images but rather a *musical mood*. "With me emotion is at the beginning without clear and definite ideas; those ideas do not arise until later on. A certain musical disposition of mind comes first, and after follows the poetical idea." If we enlarge on this, taking into account the most important phenomenon of ancient poetry, by which I mean that union—nay identity—everywhere considered natural, between musician and poet (alongside which our modern poetry appears as the statue of a god without a head), then we may, on the basis of the esthetics adumbrated earlier, explain the lyrical poet in the following manner. He is, first and foremost, a Dionysiac artist, become wholly identified with the original Oneness, its pain and contradiction, and producing a replica of that Oneness as music, if music may legitimately be seen as a repetition of the world; however, this music becomes visible to him again, as in a dream similitude, through the Apollonian dream influence. That reflection, without image or idea, of original pain in music, with its redemption through illusion, now produces a second reflection as a single simile or example. The artist had abrogated his subjectivity earlier, during the Dionysiac phase: the image which now reveals to him his oneness with the heart of the world is a dream scene showing forth vividly, together with original pain, the original delight of illusion. The "I" thus sounds out of the depth of being; what recent writers on esthetics speak of as "subjectivity" is a mere figment. When Archilochus, the first lyric poet of the Greeks, hurls both his frantic love and his contempt at the daughters of Lycambes, it is not his own passion that we see dancing before us in an orgiastic frenzy: we see Dionysos and the maenads, we see the drunken reveler Archilochus, sunk down in sleep—as Euripides describes him for us in the *Bacchae*, asleep on a high mountain meadow, in the midday sun—and now Apollo approaches him and touches him with his laurel. The sleeper's enchantment through Dionysiac music now begins to emit sparks of imagery, poems which, at their point of highest evolution, will bear the name of tragedies and dramatic dithyrambs.

The sculptor, as well as his brother, the epic poet, is committed to the pure contemplation of images. The Dionysiac musician, himself imageless, is nothing but original pain and reverberation of the image. Out of this mystical process of un-selving, the poet's spirit feels a whole world of images and similitudes arise, which are quite different in hue, causality, and pace from the images of the sculptor or narrative poet. While the last lives in those images, and only in them, with joyful complacence, and never tires of scanning them down to the most minute features, while even the image of angry Achilles is no more for him than an *image* whose irate countenance he enjoys with a dreamer's delight in appearance—so that this mirror of appearance protects him from complete fusion with his characters—the lyrical poet, on the other hand, himself becomes his images, his images are objectified versions of himself. Being the active center of that world he may boldly speak in the first person, only his "I" is not that of the actual waking man, but the "I" dwelling, truly and eternally, in the ground of being. It is through the reflections of that "I" that the lyric poet beholds the ground of being. Let us imagine, next, how he views himself too among these reflections—as non-genius, that is, as his own subject matter, the whole teeming crowd of his passions and intentions directed toward a definite goal; and when it now appears as though the poet and the nonpoet joined to him were one, and as though the former were using the pronoun "I," we are able to see through this appearance, which has deceived those who have attached the label "subjective" to the lyrical poet. The man Archilochus, with his passionate loves and hates, is really only a vision of genius, a genius who is no longer merely Archilochus but the genius of the universe, expressing its pain through the similitude of Archilochus the man. Archilochus, on the other hand, the subjectively willing and desiring human being, can never be a poet. Nor is it at all necessary for the poet to see only the phenomenon of the man Archilochus before him as a reflection of Eternal Being: the world of tragedy shows us to what extent the vision of the poet can remove itself from the urgent, immediate phenomenon.

Schopenhauer, who was fully aware of the difficulties the lyrical poet creates for the speculative esthetician, thought that he had found a solution, which, however, I cannot endorse. It is true that he alone possessed the means, in his profound philosophy of music, for solving this problem; and I think I have honored his achievement in these pages, I hope in his own spirit. Yet in the first part of *The World as Will and Idea* he characterizes the essence of song as follows: "The consciousness of the singer is filled with the subject of will, which is to say with his own willing. That willing may either be a released, satisfied willing (joy), or, as happens more commonly, an inhibited willing (sadness). In either case there is affect here: passion, violent commotion. At the same time, however, the singer is moved by the contemplation of nature surrounding him to experience himself as the subject of pure, un-willing ideation, and the unshakable tranquillity of that ideation becomes contrasted with the urgency of his willing, its limits, and its lacks. It is the experience of this contrast, or tug of war, which he expresses in his song. While we find ourselves in the lyrical condition, pure ideation approaches us, as it were, to deliver us from the urgencies of willing; we obey, yet obey for moments only. Again and again our willing, our memory of personal objectives, distracts us from tranquil contemplation, while, conversely, the next scene of beauty we behold will yield us up once more to pure ideation. For this reason we find in song and in the lyrical mood a curious mixture of willing (our personal interest in *purposes*) and pure contemplation (whose subject matter is furnished by our surroundings); relations are sought and imagined between these two sets of experiences. Subjective mood—the affection of the will—communicates its color to the purely viewed surroundings, and vice versa. All authentic song reflects a state of mind mixed and divided in this manner."

Who can fail to perceive in this description that lyric poetry is presented as an art never completely realized, indeed a hybrid whose essence is made to consist in an uneasy mixture of will and contemplation, i.e., the esthetic and the non-esthetic conditions? We, on our part, maintain that the distinction between subjective and objective, which even Schopenhauer still uses as a sort of measuring stick to distinguish the arts, has no value whatever in esthetics; the reason being that the subject—the striving individual bent on furthering his egoistic purposes—can be thought of only as an enemy to art, never as its source. But to the extent that the subject is an artist he is already delivered from individual will and has become a medium through which the True Subject celebrates His redemption in illusion. For better or worse, one thing should be quite obvious to all of us: the entire comedy of art is not played for our own sakes—for our betterment or education, say—nor can we consider ourselves the true originators of that art realm; while on the other hand we have every right to view ourselves as esthetic projections of the veritable creator and derive such dignity as we possess from our status as art works. Only as an esthetic product can the world be justified to all eternity—although our consciousness of our own significance does scarcely exceed the consciousness a painted soldier might have of the battle in which he takes part. Thus our whole knowledge of art is at bottom illusory, seeing that as mere *knowers* we can never be fused with that essential spirit, at the same time creator and spectator, who has prepared the comedy of art for his own edification. Only as the genius in the act of creation merges with the primal architect of the cosmos can he truly know something of the eternal essence of art. For in that condition he resembles the uncanny fairy tale image which is able to see itself by turning its eyes. He is at once subject and object, poet, actor, and audience.

XI

Greek tragedy perished in a manner quite different from the older sister arts: it died by suicide, in consequence of an insoluble conflict, while the others died serene and natural deaths at advanced ages. If it is the sign of a happy natural condition to die painlessly, leaving behind a fair progeny, then the decease of those older genres exhibits such a condition; they sank slowly, and their children, fairer than they, stood before their dying eyes, lifting up their heads in eagerness. The death of Greek tragedy, on the other hand, created a tremendous vacuum that was felt far and wide. As the Greek sailors in the time of Tiberius heard from a lonely island the agonizing cry "Great Pan is dead!" so could be heard ringing now through the entire Greek world these painful cries: "Tragedy is dead! And poetry has perished with it! Away with you, puny, spiritless imitators! Away with you to Hades, where you may eat your fill of the crumbs thrown you by your former masters!"

When after all a new genre sprang into being which honored tragedy as its parent, the child was seen with dismay to bear indeed the features of its mother, but of its mother during her long death struggle. The death struggle of tragedy had been fought by Euripides, while the later art is known as the New Attic comedy. Tragedy lived on there in a degenerate form, a monument to its painful and laborious death.

In this context we can understand the passionate fondness of the writers of the new comedy for Euripides. Now the wish of Philemon—who was willing to be hanged for the pleasure of visiting Euripides in Hades, providing he could be sure that the dead man was still in possession of his senses—no longer seems strange to us. If one were to attempt to say briefly and merely by way of suggestion what Menander and Philemon had in common with Euripides, and what they found so exemplary and exciting in him, one might say that Euripides succeeded in transporting the spectator onto the stage. Once we realize out of what substance the Promethean dramatists before Euripides had formed their heroes and how far it had been from their thoughts to bring onto the stage a true replica of actuality, we shall see clearly how utterly different were Euripides' intentions. Through him the common man found his way from the auditorium onto the stage. That mirror, which previously had shown only the great and bold features, now took on the kind of accuracy that reflects also the paltry traits of nature. Odysseus, the typical Greek of older art, declined under the hands of the new poets to the character of Graeculus, who henceforth held the center of the stage as the good-humored, cunning slave. The merit which Euripides, in Aristophanes' *Frogs* , attributes to himself, of having by his nostrum rid tragic art of its pompous *embonpoint*, is apparent in every one of his tragic heroes. Now every spectator could behold his exact counterpart on the Euripidean stage and was delighted to find him so eloquent. But that was not the only pleasure. People themselves learned to *speak* from Euripides—don't we hear him boast, in his contest with Aeschylus, that through him the populace had learned to observe, make transactions and form conclusions according to all the rules of art, with the utmost cleverness? It was through this revolution in public discourse that the new comedy became possible. From now on the stock phrases to represent everyday affairs were ready to hand. While hitherto the character of dramatic speech had been determined by the demigod in tragedy and the drunken satyr in comedy, that bourgeois mediocrity in which Euripides placed all his political hopes now came to the fore. And so the Aristophanic Euripides could pride himself on having portrayed life "as it really is" and shown men how to attack it: if now all members of the populace were able to philosophize, plead their cases in court and make their business deals with incredible shrewdness, the merit was really his, the result of that wisdom he had inculcated in them.

The new comedy could now address itself to a prepared,

enlightened crowd, for whom Euripides had served as choirmaster—only in this case it was the chorus of spectators who had to be
trained. As soon as this chorus had acquired a competence in the
Euripidean key, the new comedy—that chesslike species of play—
with its constant triumphs of cleverness and cunning, arose.
Meanwhile choirmaster Euripides was the object of fulsome praise;
in fact, people would have killed themselves in order to learn more
from him had they not known that the tragic poets were quite as
dead as tragedy itself. With tragedy the Greeks had given up the
belief in immortality: not only the belief in an ideal past, but also
the belief in an ideal future. The words of the famous epitaph
"Inconstant and frivolous in old age" apply equally well to the last
phase of Hellenism. Its supreme deities are wit, whim, caprice, the
pleasure of the moment. The fifth estate, that of the slaves, comes
into its own, at least in point of attitude, and if it is possible at all
now to speak of Greek serenity, then it must refer to the serenity of
the slave, who has no difficult responsibilities, no high aims, and to
whom nothing, past or future, is of greater value than the present.
It was this semblance of Greek serenity that so outraged the profound and powerful minds of the first four centuries after Christ.
This womanish escape from all seriousness and awe, this smug
embracing of easy pleasure, seemed to them not only contemptible
but the truly anti-Christian frame of mind. It was they who handed
on to later generations a picture of Greek antiquity painted entirely
in the pale rose hues of serenity—as though there had never been a
sixth century with its birth of tragedy, its Mysteries, its Pythagoras
and Heracleitus, indeed as though the art works of the great period
did not exist at all. And yet none of the latter could, of course, have
sprung from the soil of such a trivial ignoble cheer, pointing as they
do to an entirely different philosophy as their *raison d'être*.

When I said earlier that Euripides had brought the spectator on
the stage in order to enable him to judge the play, I may have created the impression that the older drama had all along stood in a false
relation to the spectator; and one might then be tempted to praise
Euripides' radical tendency to establish a proper relationship
between art work and audience as an advance upon Sophocles. But,
after all, *audience* is but a word, not a constant unchanging value.
Why should an author feel obliged to accommodate himself to a
power whose strength is merely in numbers? If he considers himself

superior in his talent and intentions to every single spectator, why should he show respect for the collective expression of all those mediocre capacities rather than for the few members of the audience who seem relatively the most gifted? The truth of the matter is that no Greek artist ever treated his audience with greater audacity and self-sufficiency than Euripides; who at a time when the multitude lay prostrate before him disavowed in noble defiance and publicly his own tendencies—those very tendencies by which he had previously conquered the masses. Had this genius had the slightest reverence for that band of Bedlamites called the public, he would have been struck down long before the mid-point of his career by the bludgeon blows of his unsuccess. We come to realize now that our statement, "Euripides brought the spectator on the stage"—implying that the spectator would be able henceforth to exercise competent judgment—was merely provisional and that we must look for a sounder explanation of his intentions. It is also generally recognized that Aeschylus and Sophocles enjoyed all through their lives and longer the full benefit of popular favor, and that for this reason it would be absurd to speak in either case of a disproportion between art work and public reception. What was it, then, that drove the highly talented and incessantly creative Euripides from a path bathed in the light of those twin luminaries—his great predecessors—and of popular acclaim as well? What peculiar consideration for the spectator made him defy that very same spectator? How did it happen that his great respect for his audience made him treat that audience with utter disrespect?

Euripides—and this may be the solution of our riddle—considered himself quite superior to the crowd as a whole; not, however, to two of his spectators. He would translate the crowd onto the stage but insist, all the same, on revering the two members as the sole judges of his art; on following all their directions and admonitions, and on instilling in the very hearts of his dramatic characters those emotions, passions and recognitions which had heretofore seconded the stage action, like an invisible chorus, from the serried ranks of the amphitheater. It was in deference to these judges that he gave his new characters a new voice, too, and a new music. Their votes, and no others, determined for him the worth of his efforts. And whenever the public rejected his labors it was their encouragement, their faith in his final triumph, which sustained him.

One of the two spectators I just spoke of was Euripides himself—the thinker Euripides, not the poet. Of him it may be said that the extraordinary richness of his critical gift had helped to produce, as in the case of Lessing, an authentic creative offshoot. Endowed with such talent, such remarkable intellectual lucidity and versatility, Euripides watched the performances of his predecessors' plays and tried to rediscover in them those fine lineaments which age, as happens in the case of old paintings, had darkened and almost obliterated. And now something occurred which cannot surprise those among us who are familiar with the deeper secrets of Aeschylean tragedy. Euripides perceived in every line, in every trait, something quite incommensurable: a certain deceptive clarity and, together with it, a mysterious depth, an infinite background. The clearest figure trailed after it a comet's tail which seemed to point to something uncertain, something that could not be wholly elucidated. A similar twilight seemed to invest the very structure of drama, especially the function of the chorus. Then again, how ambiguous did the solutions of all moral problems seem! How problematical the way in which the myths were treated! How irregular the distribution of fortune and misfortune! There was also much in the language of older tragedy that he took exception to, or to say the least, found puzzling: why all this pomp in the representation of simple relationships? Why all those tropes and hyperboles, where the characters themselves were simple and straightforward? Euripides sat in the theater pondering, a troubled spectator. In the end he had to admit to himself that he did not understand his great predecessors. But since he looked upon reason as the fountainhead of all doing and enjoying, he had to find out whether anybody shared these notions of his, or whether he was alone in facing up to such incommensurable features. But the multitude, including some of the best individuals, gave him only a smile of distrust; none of them would tell him why, notwithstanding his misgivings and reservations, the great masters were right nonetheless. In this tormented state of mind, Euripides discovered his second spectator—one who did not understand tragedy and for that reason spurned it. Allied with him he could risk coming out of his isolation to fight that tremendous battle against the works of Aeschylus and Sophocles; not by means of polemics, but as a tragic poet determined to make his notion of tragedy prevail over the traditional notions.

ART AS EXPERIENCE
by
JOHN DEWEY

Art and Civilization

A rt is a quality that permeates an experience; it is not, save by a figure of speech, the experience itself. Esthetic experience is always more than esthetic. In it a body of matters and meanings, not in themselves esthetic, *become* esthetic as they enter into an ordered rhythmic movement toward consummation. The material itself is widely human. The material of esthetic experience in being human—human in connection with the nature of which it is a part—is social. Esthetic experience is a manifestation, a record and celebration of the life of a civilization, a means of promoting its development, and is also the ultimate judgment upon the quality of a civilization. For while it is produced and is enjoyed by individuals, those individuals are what they are in the content of their experience because of the cultures in which they participate.

The Magna Carta is held up as the great political stabilizer of Anglo-Saxon civilization. Even so, it has operated in the meaning given it in imagination rather than by its literal contents. There are transient and there are enduring elements in a civilization. The enduring forces are not separate; they are functions of a multitude of passing incidents as the latter are organized into the meanings that form minds. Art is the great force in effecting this consolidation. The individuals who have minds pass away one by one. The works in which meanings have received objective expression endure. They become part of the environment, and interaction with this phase of the environment is the axis of continuity in the life of civilization. The ordinances of religion and the power of law are efficacious as they are clothed with a pomp, a dignity and majesty that are the work of imagination. If social customs are more than uniform external modes of action, it is because they are saturated with story and transmitted meaning. Every art in some manner is a medium of this transmission while its products are no inconsiderable part of the saturating matter.

"The glory that was Greece and the grandeur that was Rome" for most of us, probably for all but the historical student, sum up those civilizations; glory and grandeur are esthetic. For all but the anti-quarian, ancient Egypt is its monuments, temples and literature. Continuity of culture in passage from one civilization to another as well as within the culture, is conditioned by art more than by any other one thing. Troy lives for us only in poetry and in the objects of art that have been recovered from its ruins. Minoan civilization is today its products of art. Pagan gods and pagan rites are past and gone and yet endure in the incense, lights, robes, and holidays of the present. If letters devised for the purpose, presumably, of facilitating commercial transactions, had not developed into literature, they would still be technical equipments, and we ourselves might live amid hardly a higher culture than that of our savage ancestors. Apart from rite and ceremony, from pantomime and dance and the drama that developed from them, from dance, song and accompanying instrumental music, from the utensils and articles of daily living that were formed on patterns and stamped with insignia of community life that were akin to those manifested in the other arts, the inci-dents of the far past would now be sunk in oblivion.

It is out of the question to do more than suggest in bare outline the function of the arts in older civilizations. But the arts by which primitive folk commemorated and transmitted their customs and institutions, arts that were communal, are the sources out of which all fine arts have developed. The patterns that were characteristic of weapons, rugs and blankets, baskets and jars, were marks of tribal union. Today the anthropologist relies upon the pattern carved on a club, or painted on a bowl to determine its origin. Rite and cere-mony as well as legend bound the living and the dead in a common partnership. They were esthetic but they were more than esthetic. The rites of mourning expressed more than grief; the war and har-vest dance were more than a gathering of energy for tasks to be performed; magic was more than a way of commanding forces of nature to do the bidding of man; feasts were more than a satisfac-tion of hunger. Each of these communal modes of activity united the practical, the social, and the educative in an integrated whole having esthetic form. They introduced social values into experience in the way that was most impressive. They connected things that were overtly important and overtly done with the substantial life of the community. Art was *in* them, for these activities conformed to the needs and conditions of the most intense, most readily grasped and longest remembered experience. But they were more than just art, although the esthetic strand was ubiquitous.

In Athens, which we regard as the home par excellence of epic and lyric poetry, of the arts of drama, architecture and sculpture, the idea of art for art's sake would not, as I have already remarked, have been understood. Plato's harshness toward Homer and Hesiod seems strained. But they were the moral teachers of the people. His attacks upon the poets are like those which some critics of the present day bring against portions of Christian scriptures because of evil moral influence attributed to them. Plato's demand of censorship of poetry and music is a tribute to the social and even political influence exercised by those arts. Drama was enacted on holy-days; attendance was of the nature of an act of civic worship. Architecture in all its significant forms was public, not domestic, much less devoted to industry, banking, or commerce.

The decay of art in the Alexandrian period, its degeneracy into poor imitations of archaic models, is a sign of the general loss of civic consciousness that accompanied the eclipse of city-states and the rise of a conglomerate imperialism. Theories about art and the cultivation of grammar and rhetoric took the place of creation. And theories about art gave evidence of the great social change that had taken place. Instead of connecting arts with an expression of the life of the community, the beauty of nature and of art was regarded as an echo and reminder of some supernal reality that had its being outside social life, and indeed outside the cosmos itself—the ultimate source of all subsequent theories that treat art as something imported into experience from without.

As the Church developed, the arts were again brought into connection with human life and became a bond of union among men. Through its services and sacraments, the Church revived and adapted in impressive form what was most moving in all prior rites and ceremonies.

The Church, even more than the Roman Empire, served as the focus of unity amid the disintegration that followed the fall of Rome. The historian of intellectual life will emphasize the dogmas of the

Church; the historian of political institutions, the development of law and authority by means of the ecclesiastic institution. But the influence that counted in the daily life of the mass of the people and that gave them a sense of unity was constituted, it is safe to surmise, by sacraments, by song and pictures, by rite and ceremony, all having an esthetic strand, more than by any other one thing. Sculpture, painting, music, letters were found in the place where worship was performed. These objects and acts were much more than works of art to the worshipers who gathered in the temple. They were in all probability much less works of art to them than they are today to believers and unbelievers. But because of the esthetic strand, religious teachings were the more readily conveyed and their effect was the more lasting. By the art in them, they were changed from doctrines into living experiences.

That the Church was fully conscious of this extra-esthetic effect of art is evident in the care it took to regulate the arts. Thus in 787 A.D., the Second Council of Nicaea officially ordained the following:

"The substance of religious scenes is not left to the initiative of artists; it derives from the principles laid down by the Catholic Church and religious tradition. . . . The art alone belongs to the painter; its organization and arrangement belongs to the clergy." The censorship desired by Plato held full sway.

There is a statement of Machiavelli that has always seemed to me symbolic of the spirit of the Renascence. He said that when he was through with the business of the day, he retired into his study and lost himself in absorption of the classic literature of antiquity. This statement is doubly symbolic. On the one hand, ancient culture would not be lived. It could only be studied. As Santayana has well said, Greek civilization is now an ideal to be admired, not one to be realized. On the other hand, knowledge of Greek art, especially of architecture and sculpture, revolutionized the practice of the arts, including painting. The sense of naturalistic shapes of objects and of their setting in the natural landscape was recovered; in the Roman school painting was almost an attempt to produce the feelings occasioned by sculpture, while the Florentine school developed the peculiar values inherent in line. The change affected both esthetic form and substance. The lack of perspective, the flat and profile quality of Church art, its use of gold, and a multitude of other traits were not due to mere lack of technical skill. They were organically connected with the particular interactions in human experience that were desired as the consequence of art. The secular experiences that were emerging at the time of the Renascence and that fed upon antique culture involved of necessity the production of effects demanding new form in art. The extension of substance from Biblical subjects and the lives of saints to portrayal of scenes of Greek mythology and then to spectacles of contemporary life that were socially impressive inevitably ensued.

These remarks are intended merely to be a bare illustration of the fact that every culture has its own collective individuality. Like the individuality of the person from whom a work of art issues, this collective individuality leaves its indelible imprint upon the art that is produced. Such phrases as the art of the South Sea islands, of the North American Indian, of the Negro, Chinese, Cretan, Egyptian, Greek, Hellenistic, Byzantine, Moslem, Gothic, Renascence, art have a veridical significance. The undeniable fact of the collective cultural origin and import of works illustrates the fact, previously mentioned, that art is a strain in experience rather than an entity in itself. A problem has been made out of the fact, however, by a recent school of thought. It is contended that since we cannot actually reproduce the experience of a people remote in time and foreign in culture, we cannot have a genuine appreciation of the art it produced. Even of Greek art it is asserted that the Hellenic attitude toward life and the world was so different from ours that the artistic product of Greek culture must esthetically be a sealed book to us.

In part an answer to this contention has already been given. It is doubtless true that the total experience of the Greeks in presence of, say, Greek architecture, statuary, and painting is far from being identical with ours. Features of their culture were transient; they do not now exist, and these features were embodied in their experience of their works of art. But experience is a matter of the interaction of the artistic product with the self. It is not therefore twice alike for different persons even today. It changes with the same person at different times as he brings something different to a work. But there is no reason why, in order to be esthetic, these experiences should be identical. So far as in each case there is an ordered movement of the matter of the experience to a fulfillment, there is a dominant esthetic quality. *Au fond*, the esthetic quality is the same for Greek, Chinese and American.

This answer does not, however, cover the whole ground. For it does not apply to the total human effect of the art of a culture. The question, while wrongly framed with respect to the distinctively esthetic, suggests the question of what the art of another people may mean for our total experience. The contention of Taine and his school that we must understand art in terms of "race, milieu and time" touches the question, but hardly more than touches it. For such understanding may be purely intellectual, and so on the level of the geographical, anthropological and historical information with which it is accompanied. It leaves open the question of the significance of foreign art for the experience characteristic of present civilization.

The nature of the problem is suggested by Mr. Hulme's theory of the basic difference between Byzantine and Moslem art on one side and Greek and Renascence art on the other. The latter, he says, is vital and naturalistic. The former is geometric. This difference he goes on to explain is not connected with differences in technical capacity. The gulf is made by a fundamental difference of attitude, of desire and purpose. We are now habituated to one mode of satis-faction and we take our own attitude of desire and purpose to be so inherent in all human nature as to give the measure of all works of art, as constituting the demand which all works of art meet and should satisfy. We have desires that are rooted in longing for an increase of experienced vitality through delightful intercourse with the forms and movements of "nature." Byzantine art, and some other forms of Oriental art, spring from an experience that has no delight in nature and no striving after vitality. They "express a feel-ing of separation in the face of outside nature." This attitude characterizes objects as unlike as the Egyptian pyramid and the Byzantine mosaic. The difference between such art and that which is characteristic of the Western world is not to be explained by inter-est in abstractions. It manifests the idea of separation, of disharmony, of man and nature.

Mr. Hulme sums up by saying that "art cannot be understood by itself, but must be taken as one element in a general process of adjustment between man and the outside world." Irrespective of the truth of Mr. Hulme's explanation of the characteristic difference between much of Oriental and Occidental art (it hardly applies in any case to Chinese art), his way of stating the matter puts, to my mind, the general problem in its proper context and suggests the solution. Just because art, speaking from the standpoint of the influence of collective culture upon creation and enjoyment of works of art, is expressive of a deep-seated attitude of adjustment, of an underlying idea and ideal of generic human attitude, the art characteristic of a civilization is the means for entering sympathetically into the deepest elements in the experience of remote and foreign civilizations. By this fact is explained also the human import of their arts for ourselves. They effect a broadening and deepening of our own experience, rendering it less local and provincial as far as we grasp, by their means, the attitudes basic in other forms of experience. Unless we arrive at the attitudes expressed in the art of another civilization, its products are either of concern to the "esthete" alone, or else they do not impress us esthetically. Chinese art then seems "queer," because of its unwonted schemes of perspective; Byzantine art, stiff and awkward; Negro art, grotesque.

In the reference to Byzantine art, I put the term nature in quotation marks. I did so because the word "nature" has a special meaning in esthetic literature, indicated especially by the use of the adjective "naturalistic." But "nature" also has a meaning in which it includes the whole scheme of things—in which it has the force of the imaginative and emotional word "universe." In experience, human relations, institutions, and traditions are as much a part of the nature in which and by which we live as is the physical world. Nature in this meaning is not "outside." It is in us and we are in and of it. But there are multitudes of ways of participating in it, and these ways are characteristic not only of various experiences of the same individual, but of attitudes of aspiration, need and achievement that belong to civilizations in their collective aspect. Works of art are means by which we enter, through imagination and the emotions they evoke, into other forms of relationship and participation than our own.

The art of the late nineteenth century was characterized by "naturalism" in its restricted sense. The productions most characteristic of the early twentieth century were marked by the influence of Egyptian, Byzantine, Persian, Chinese, Japanese, and Negro art. This influence is marked in painting, sculpture, music, and literature. The effect of "primitive" and early medieval art is a part of the same general movement. The eighteenth century idealized the noble savage and the civilization of remote peoples. But aside from Chinoiseries and some phases of romantic literature, the *sense* of what is back of the arts of foreign people did not affect the actual art produced. Seen in perspective, the so-called pre-Raphaelite art of England is the most typically Victorian of all the painting of the period. But in recent decades, beginning in the nineties, the influence of the arts of distant cultures has entered intrinsically into artistic creation.

For many persons, the effect is doubtless superficial, merely providing a type of objects enjoyable in part because of their individual novelty, and in part because of an added decorative quality. But the idea that would account for the production of contemporary works by mere desire for the unusual, or eccentric or even charm is more superficial than this kind of enjoyment. The moving force is genuine participation, in some degree and phase, in the type of experience of which primitive, Oriental, and early medieval objects of art are the expression. Where the works are merely imitative of foreign works, they are transient and trivial. But at their best they bring about an organic blending of attitudes characteristic of the experience of our own age with that of remote peoples. For the new features are not mere decorative additions but enter into the *structure* of works of art and thus occasion a wider and fuller experience. Their enduring effect upon those who perceive and enjoy will be an expansion of *their* sympathies, imagination, and sense.

This new movement in art illustrates the effect of all genuine acquaintance with art created by other peoples. We understand it in the degree in which we make it a part of our own attitudes, not just by collective information concerning the conditions under which it was produced. We accomplish this result when, to borrow a term from Bergson, we install ourselves in modes of apprehending nature that at first are strange to us. To some degree we become artists ourselves as we undertake this integration, and, by bringing it to pass, our own experience is re-oriented. Barriers are dissolved, limiting prejudices melt away, when we enter into the spirit of Negro or Polynesian art. This insensible melting is far more efficacious than the change effected by reasoning, because it enters directly into attitude.

The possibility of the occurrence of genuine communication is a broad problem of which the one just dealt with is one species. It is a fact that it takes place, but the nature of community of experience is one of the most serious problems of philosophy—so serious that some thinkers deny the fact. The existence of communication is so disparate to our physical separation from one another and to the inner mental lives of individuals that it is not surprising that supernatural force has been ascribed to language and that communion has been given sacramental value.

Moreover, events that are familiar and customary are those that we are least likely to reflect upon; we take them for granted. They are also, because of their closeness to us, through gesture and pantomime, the most difficult to observe. Communication through speech, oral and written, is the familiar and constant feature of social life. We tend, accordingly, to regard it as just one phenomenon among others of what we must in any case accept without question. We pass over the fact that it is the foundation and source of all activities and relations that are distinctive of internal union of human beings with one another. A vast number of our contacts with one another are external and mechanical. There is a "field" in which they take place, a field defined and perpetuated by legal and political institutions. But the consciousness of this field does not enter our conjoint action as its integral and controlling force. Relations of nations to one another, relations of investors and laborers, of producers and consumers, are interactions that are only to a slight degree forms of communicative intercourse. There are interactions between the parties involved, but they are so external and partial that we undergo their consequences without integrating them into an experience.

We hear speech, but it is almost as if we were listening to a babel of tongues. Meaning and value do not come home to us. There is in such cases no communication and none of the result of community of experience that issues only when language in its full import breaks down physical isolation and external contact. Art is a more universal mode of language than is the speech that exists in a multitude of mutually unintelligible forms. The language of art has to be acquired. But the language of art is not affected by the accidents of history that mark off different modes of human speech. The power of music in particular to merge different individualities in a common surrender, loyalty and inspiration, a power utilized in religion and in warfare alike, testifies to the relative universality of the language of art. The differences between English, French and German speech create barriers that are submerged when art speaks.

Philosophically speaking, the problem with which we are confronted is the relation of the discrete and the continuous. Both of them are stubborn facts and yet they have to meet and blend in any human association that rises above the level of brute intercourse. In order to justify continuity, historians have often resorted to a falsely named "genetic" method, wherein there is no genuine genesis, because everything is resolved into what went before. But Egyptian civilization and art were not just a preparation for Greek, nor were Greek thought and art mere reedited versions of the civilizations from which they so freely borrowed. Each culture has its own individuality and has a pattern that binds its parts together.

Nevertheless, when the art of another culture enters into attitudes that determine our experience genuine continuity is effected. Our own experience does not thereby lose its individuality but it takes unto itself and weds elements that expand its significance. A community and continuity that do not exist physically are created. The attempt to establish continuity by methods which resolve one set of events and one of institutions into those which preceded it in time is doomed to defeat. Only an expansion of experience that absorbs into itself the values experienced because of life-attitudes, other than those resulting from our own human environment, dissolves the effect of discontinuity.

The problem in question is not unlike that we daily undergo in the effort to understand another person with whom we habitually associate. All friendship is a solution of the problem. Friendship and intimate affection are not the result of information about another person even though knowledge may further their formation. But it does so only as it becomes an integral part of sympathy through the imagination. It is when the desires and aims, the interests and modes of response of another become an expansion of our own being that we understand him. We learn to see with his eyes, hear with his ears, and their results give true instruction, for they are built into our own structure. I find that even the dictionary avoids defining the term "civilization." It defines civilization as the state of being civilized and "civilized" as "being in a state of civilization." However, the verb "to civilize" is defined as "to instruct in the arts of life and thus to raise in the scale of civilization." Instruction in the arts of life is something other than conveying information about them. It is a matter of communication and participation in values of life by means of the imagination, and works of art are the most intimate and energetic means of aiding individuals to share in the arts of living. Civilization is uncivil because human beings are divided into non-communicating sects, races, nations, classes and cliques.

The brief sketch of some historical phases of the connection of art with community life set forth earlier in this chapter suggests contrast with present conditions. It is hardly enough to say that the absence of obvious organic connection of the arts with other forms of culture is explained by the complexity of modern life, by its many specializations, and by the simultaneous existence of many diverse centres of culture in different nations that exchange their products but that do not form parts of an inclusive social whole. These things are real enough, and their effect upon the status of art in relation to civilization may be readily discovered. But the significant fact is widespread disruption.

We inherit much from the cultures of the past. The influence of Greek science and philosophy, of Roman law, of religion having a Jewish source, upon our present institutions, beliefs and ways of thinking and feeling is too familiar to need more than mention. Into the operation of these factors two forces have been injected that are distinctly late in origin and that constitute the "modern" in the present epoch. These two forces are natural science and its application in industry and commerce through machinery and the use of non-human modes of energy. In consequence, the question of the place and role of art in contemporary civilization demands notice of its relations to science and to the social consequences of machine industry. The isolation of art that now exists is not to be viewed as an isolated phenomenon. It is one manifestation of the incoherence of our civilization produced by new forces, so new that the attitudes belonging to them and the consequences issuing from them have not been incorporated and digested into integral elements of experience.

Science has brought with it a radically novel conception of physical nature and of our relation to it. This new conception stands as yet side by side with the conception of the world and man that is a heritage from the past, especially from that Christian tradition through which the typically European social imagination has been formed. The things of the physical world and those of the moral realm have fallen apart, while the Greek tradition and that of the medieval age held them in intimate union—although a union accomplished by different means in the two periods. The opposition that now exists between the spiritual and ideal elements of our historic heritage and the structure of physical nature that is disclosed by science, is the ultimate source of the dualisms formulated by philosophy since Descartes and Locke. These formulations in turn reflect a conflict that is everywhere active in modern civilization. From one point of view the problem of recovering an organic place for art in civilization is like the problem of reorganizing our heritage from the past and the insights of present knowledge into a coherent and integrated imaginative union.

The problem is so acute and so widely influential that any solution that can be proposed is an anticipation that can at best be realized only by the course of events. Scientific method as now practiced is too new to be naturalized in experience. It will be a long time before it so sinks into the subsoil of mind as to become an integral part of corporate belief and attitude. Till that happens, both method and conclusions will remain the possession of specialized experts, and will exercise their general influence only by way of external and more or less disintegrating impact upon beliefs, and by equally external practical application. But even now it is possible to exaggerate the harmful effect exercised by science upon imagination. It is true that physical science strips its objects of the qualities that give the objects and scenes of ordinary experience all their poignancy and preciousness, leaving the world, as far as scientific rendering of it is concerned, without the traits that have always constituted its immediate value. But the world of immediate experience in which art operates, remains just what it was. Nor can the fact that physical science presents us with objects that are wholly indifferent to human desire and aspiration be used to indicate that the death of poetry is imminent. Men have always been aware that there is much in the scene in which their lives are set that is hostile to human purpose. At no time would the masses of the disinherited have been surprised at the declaration that the world about them is indifferent to their hopes.

The fact that science tends to show that man is a part of nature has an effect that is favorable rather than unfavorable to art when its intrinsic significance is realized and when its meaning is no longer interpreted by contrast with beliefs that come to us from the past. For the closer man is brought to the physical world, the clearer it becomes that his impulses and ideas are enacted by nature within him. Humanity in its vital operations has always acted upon this principle. Science gives this action intellectual support. The sense of relation between nature and man in some form has always been the actuating spirit of art.

Moreover, resistance and conflict have always been factors in generating art; and they are, as we have seen, a necessary part of artistic form. Neither a world wholly obdurate and sullen in the face of man nor one so congenial to his wishes that it gratifies all desires is a world in which art can arise. The fairy tales that relate situations of this sort would cease to please if they ceased to be fairy tales. Friction is as necessary to generate esthetic energy as it is to supply the energy that drives machinery. When older beliefs have lost their grip on imagination—and their hold was always there rather than upon reason—the disclosure by science of the resistance that environment offers to man will furnish new materials for fine art. Even now we owe to science a liberation of the human spirit. It has aroused a more avid curiosity, and has greatly quickened in a few at least alertness of observation with respect to things of whose existence we were not before even aware. Scientific method tends to generate a respect for experience, and even though this new reverence is still confined to the few, it contains the promise of a new kind of experiences that will demand expression.

Who can foresee what will happen when the experimental outlook has once become thoroughly acclimatized in a common culture? The attainment of perspective with reference to the future is a most difficult task. We are given to taking features that are most prominent and most troublesome at a given time as if they were the clews to the future. So we think of the future effect of science in terms derived from the present situation in which it occupies a position of conflict and disruption with reference to great traditions of the western world, as if these terms defined its place necessarily and forever. But to judge justly, we have to see science as things will be when the experimental attitude is thoroughly naturalized. And art in particular will always be distracted or else soft and overrefined when it lacks familiar things for its material.

So far, the effect of science as far as painting, poetry, and the novel are concerned, has been to diversify their materials and forms rather than to create an organic synthesis. I doubt if there were at any time any large number of persons who "saw life steadily and saw it whole." And, at the very worst, it is something to have been freed from syntheses of the imagination that went contrary to the grain of things. Possession of a quickened sense of the value for esthetic experience of a multitude of things formerly shut out, is some compensation amid the miscellany of present objects of art. The bathing beaches, street corners, flowers and fruits, babies and bankers of contemporary painting are after all something more than mere diffuse and disconnected objects. For they are the fruits of a new vision.

I suppose that at all times a great deal of the "art" that has been produced has been trivial and anecdotal. The hand of time has winnowed much of this away, while in an exhibition today we are faced with it *en masse*. Nevertheless, the extension of painting and the other arts to include matter that was once regarded as either too common or too out of the way to deserve artistic recognition is a permanent gain. This extension is not directly the effect of the rise of science. But it is a product of the same conditions that led to the revolution in scientific procedure.

Such diffuseness and incoherence as exist in art today are the manifestation of the disruption of consensus of beliefs. Greater integration in the matter and form of the arts depends consequently upon a general change in culture in the direction of attitudes that are taken for granted in the basis of civilization and that form the subsoil of conscious beliefs and efforts. One thing is sure; the unity cannot be attained by preaching the need of returning to the past. Science is here, and a new integration must take account of it and include it.

The most direct and pervasive presence of science in present civilization is found in its applications in industry. Here we find a more serious problem regarding the relation of art to present civilization and its outlook than in the case of science itself. The divorce of useful and fine art signifies even more than does the departure of science from the traditions of the past. The difference between them was not instituted in modern times. It goes as far back as the Greeks when the useful arts were carried on by slaves and "base mechanics" and shared in the low esteem in which the latter were held. Architects, builders, sculptors, painters, musical performers were artisans. Only those who worked in the medium of words were esteemed artists, since their activities did not involve the use of hands, tools and physical materials. But mass production by mechanical means has given the old separation between the useful and fine a decidedly new turn. The split is reenforced by the greater importance that now attaches to industry and trade in the whole organization of society.

The mechanical stands at the pole opposite to that of the esthetic, and production of goods is now mechanical. The liberty of choice allowed to the craftsman who worked by hand has almost vanished with the general use of the machine. Production of objects enjoyed in direct experience by those who possess, to some extent, the capacity to produce useful commodities expressing individual values, has become a specialized matter apart from the general run of production. This fact is probably the most important factor in the status of art in present civilization.

There are, however, certain considerations that should deter one from concluding that industrial conditions render impossible an integration of art in civilization. I am not able to agree with those who think that effective and economical adaptation of the parts of an object to one another with respect to use automatically results in "beauty" or esthetic effect. Every well-constructed object and machine has form, but there is esthetic form only when the object having this external form fits into a larger experience. Interaction of the material of this experience with the utensil or machine cannot be left out of account. But adequate objective relationship of parts with respect to most efficient use at least brings about a condition that is *favorable* to esthetic enjoyment. It strips away the adventitious and superfluous. There is something clean in the esthetic sense about a piece of machinery that has a logical structure that fits it for its work, and the polish of steel and copper that is essential to good performance is intrinsically pleasing in perception. If one compares the commercial products of the present with those of even twenty years ago, one is struck by the great gain in form and color. The change from the old wooden Pullman cars with their silly encumbering ornamentations to the steel cars of the present is typical of what I mean. The external architecture of city apartments remains box-like but internally there is hardly less than an esthetic revolution brought about by better adaptation to need.

A more important consideration is that industrial surroundings work to create that larger experience into which particular products fit in such a way that they get esthetic quality. Naturally, this remark does not refer to the destruction of the natural beauties of the landscape by ugly factories and their begrimed surroundings, nor to the city slums that have followed in the wake of machine production. I mean that the habits of the eye as a medium of perception are being slowly altered in being accustomed to the shapes that are typical of industrial products and to the objects that belong to urban as distinct from rural life. The colors and planes to which the organism habitually responds develop new material for interest. The running brook, the greensward, the forms associated with a rural environment, are losing their place as the primary material of experience. Part at least of the change of attitude of the last score of years to "modernistic" figures in painting is the result of this change. Even the objects of the natural landscape come to be "apperceived" in terms of the spatial relations characteristic of objects the design of which is due to mechanical modes of production; buildings, furnishings, wares. Into an experience saturated with these values, objects having their own internal functional adaptations will fit in a way that yields esthetic results.

But since the organism hungers naturally for satisfaction in the material of experience, and since the surroundings which man has made, under the influence of modern industry, afford less fulfillment and more repulsion than at any previous time, there is only too evidently a problem that is still unsolved. The hunger of the organism for satisfaction through the eye is hardly less than its urgent impulsion for food. Indeed many a peasant has given more care to the cultivation of a flower plot than to producing vegetables for food. There must be forces at work that affect the mechanical means of production that are extraneous to the operation of machinery itself. These forces are found, of course, in the economic system of production for private gain.

The labor and employment problem of which we are so acutely aware cannot be solved by mere changes in wage, hours of work and sanitary conditions. No permanent solution is possible save in a radical social alteration, which affects the degree and kind of participation the worker has in the production and social disposition of the wares he produces. Only such a change will seriously modify the content of experience into which creation of objects made for use enters. And this modification of the nature of experience is the finally determining element in the esthetic quality of the experience of things produced. The idea that the basic problem can be solved merely by increase of hours of leisure is absurd. Such an idea merely retains the old dualistic division between labor and leisure.

The important matter is a change that will reduce the force of external pressure and will increase that of a sense of freedom and personal interest in the operations of production. Oligarchical control from the outside of the processes and the products of work is the chief force in preventing the worker from having that ultimate interest in what he does and makes that is an essential prerequisite of esthetic satisfaction. There is nothing in the nature of machine production *per se* that is an insuperable obstacle in the way of workers' consciousness of the meaning of what they do and enjoyment of the satisfactions of companionship and of useful work well done. The psychological conditions resulting from private control of the labor of other men for the sake of private gain, rather than any fixed psychological or economic law, are the forces that suppress and limit esthetic quality in the experience that accompanies processes of production.

As long as art is the beauty parlor of civilization, neither art nor civilization is secure. Why is the architecture of our large cities so unworthy of a fine civilization? It is not from lack of materials nor from lack of technical capacity. And yet it is not merely slums but the apartments of the well-to-do that are esthetically repellent, because they are so destitute of imagination. Their character is determined by an economic system in which land is used—and kept out of use—for the sake of gain, because of profit derived from rental and sale. Until land is freed from this economic burden, beautiful buildings may occasionally be erected, but there is little hope for the rise of general architectural construction worthy of a noble civilization. The restriction placed on building affects indirectly a large number of allied arts, while the social forces that affect the buildings in which we subsist and wherein we do our work operate upon all the arts.

Auguste Comte said that the great problem of our time is the organization of the proletariat into the social system. The remark is even truer now than when it was made. The task is impossible of achievement by any revolution that stops short of affecting the imagination and emotions of man. The values that lead to production and intelligent enjoyment of art have to be incorporated into the system of social relationships. It seems to me that much of the discussion of proletarian art is aside from the point because it confuses the personal and deliberate intent of an artist with the place and operation of art in society. What is true is that art itself is not secure under modern conditions until the mass of men and women who do the useful work of the world have the opportunity to be free in conducting the processes of production and are richly endowed in capacity for enjoying the fruits of collective work. That the material for art should be drawn from all sources whatever and that the products of art should be accessible to all is a demand by the side of which the personal political intent of the artist is insignificant.

The moral office and human function of art can be intelligently discussed only in the context of culture. A particular work of art may have a definite effect upon a particular person or upon a number of persons. The social effect of the novels of Dickens or of Sinclair Lewis is far from negligible. But a less conscious and more massed constant adjustment of experience proceeds from the total environment that is created by the collective art of a time. Just as physical life cannot exist without the support of a physical environment, so moral life cannot go on without the support of a moral environment. Even technological arts, in their sum total, do something more than provide a number of separate conveniences and facilities. They shape collective occupations and thus determine direction of interest and attention, and hence affect desire and purpose.

The noblest man living in a desert absorbs something of its harshness and sterility, while the nostalgia of the mountain-bred man when cut off from his surroundings is proof how deeply environment has become part of his being. Neither the savage nor the civilized man is what he is by native constitution but by the culture in which he participates. The final measure of the quality of that culture is the arts which flourish. Compared with their influence things directly taught by word and precept are pale and ineffectual. Shelley did not exaggerate when he said that moral science only "arranges the elements that poetry has created," if we extend "poetry" to include all products of imaginative experience. The sum total of the effect of all reflective treatises on morals is insignificant in comparison with the influence of architecture, novel, drama, on life, becoming important when "intellectual" products formulate the tendencies of these arts and provide them with an intellectual base. An "inner" rational check is a sign of withdrawal from reality unless it is a reflection of substantial environing forces. The political and economic arts that may furnish security and competency are no warrants of a rich and abundant human life save as they are attended by the flourishing of the arts that determine culture.

Words furnish a record of what has happened and give direction by request and command to particular future actions. Literature conveys the meaning of the past that is significant in present experience and is prophetic of the larger movement of the future. Only imaginative vision elicits the possibilities that are interwoven within the texture of the actual. The first stirrings of dissatisfaction and the first intimations of a better future are always found in works of art. The impregnation of the characteristically new art of a period with a sense of different values than those that prevail is the reason why the conservative finds such art to be immoral and sordid, and is the reason why he resorts to the products of the past for esthetic satisfaction. Factual science may collect statistics and make charts. But its predictions are, as has been well said, but past history reversed. Change in the climate of the imagination is the precursor of the changes that affect more than the details of life.

The theories that attribute direct moral effect and intent to art fail because they do not take account of the collective civilization that is the context in which works of art are produced and enjoyed. I would not say that they tend to treat works of art as a kind of sublimated Aesop's fables. But they all tend to extract particular works, regarded as especially edifying, from their milieu and to think of the moral function of art in terms of a strictly personal relation between the selected works and a particular individual. Their whole conception of morals is so individualistic that they miss a sense of the *way* in which art exercises its humane function.

Matthew Arnold's dictum that "poetry is criticism of life" is a case in point. It suggests to the reader a moral intent on the part of the poet and a moral judgment on the part of the reader. It fails to see or at all events to state *how* poetry is a criticism of life; namely, not directly, but by disclosure, through imaginative vision addressed to imaginative experience (not to set judgment) of possibilities that contrast with actual conditions. A sense of possibilities that are unrealized and that might be realized are when they are put in contrast with actual conditions, the most penetrating "criticism" of the latter that can be made. It is by a sense of possibilities opening before us that we become aware of constrictions that hem us in and of burdens that oppress.

Mr. Garrod, a follower of Matthew Arnold in more senses than one, has wittily said that what we resent in didactic poetry is not that it teaches, but that it does not teach, its incompetency. He added words to the effect that poetry teaches as friends and life teach, by being, and not by express intent. He says in another place, "Poetical values are, after all, values in a human life. You cannot mark them off from other values, as though the nature of man were built in bulkheads." I do not think that what Keats has said in one of his letters can be surpassed as to the way in which poetry acts. He asks what would be the result if every man spun from his imaginative experience "an airy Citadel" like the web the spider spins, "filling the air with a beautiful circuiting." For, he says, "man should not dispute or assert, but whisper results to his neighbour, and thus, by every germ of spirit sucking the sap from mould ethereal, every human being might become great, and Humanity instead of being a wide heath of Furze and Briars with here and there a remote Pine or Oak, would become a grand democracy of Forest Trees!"

It is by way of communication that art becomes the incomparable organ of instruction, but the way is so remote from that usually associated with the idea of education, it is a way that lifts art so far above what we are accustomed to think of as instruction, that we are repelled by any suggestion of teaching and learning in connection with art. But our revolt is in fact a reflection upon education that proceeds by methods so literal as to exclude the imagination and one not touching the desires and emotions of men. Shelley said, "The imagination is the great instrument of moral good, and poetry administers to the effect by acting upon the cause." Hence it is, he goes on to say, "a poet would do ill to embody his own conceptions of right and wrong, which are usually those of his own time and place, in his poetical creations. . . . By the assumption of this inferior office . . . he would resign participation in the cause"—the imagination. It is the lesser poets who "have frequently affected a moral aim, and the effect of their poetry is diminished in exact proportion as they compel us to advert to this purpose." But the power of imaginative projection is so great that he calls poets "the founders of civil society."

The problem of the relation of art and morals is too often treated as if the problem existed only on the side of art. It is virtually assumed that morals are satisfactory in idea if not in fact, and that the only question is whether and in what ways art should conform to a moral system already developed. But Shelley's statement goes to the heart of the matter. Imagination is the chief instrument of the good. It is more or less a commonplace to say that a person's ideas and treatment of his fellows are dependent upon his power to put himself imaginatively in their place. But the primacy of the imagination extends far beyond the scope of direct personal relationships. Except where "ideal" is used in conventional deference or as a name for a sentimental reverie, the ideal factors in every moral outlook and human loyalty are imaginative. The historic alliance of religion and art has its roots in this common quality. Hence it is that art is more moral than moralities. For the latter either are, or tend to become, consecrations of the *status quo*, reflections of custom, reenforcements of the established order. The moral prophets of humanity have always been poets even though they spoke in free verse or by parable. Uniformly, however, their vision of possibilities has soon been converted into a proclamation of facts that already exist and hardened into semi-political institutions. Their imaginative presentation of ideals that should command thought and desire have been treated as rules of policy. Art has been the means of keeping alive the sense of purposes that outrun evidence and of meanings that transcend indurated habit.

Morals are assigned a special compartment in theory and practice because they reflect the divisions embodied in economic and political institutions. Wherever social divisions and barriers exist, practices and ideas that correspond to them fix metes and bounds, so that liberal action is placed under restraint. Creative intelligence is looked upon with distrust; the innovations that are the essence of individuality are feared, and generous impulse is put under bonds not to disturb the peace. Were art an acknowledged power in human association and not treated as the pleasuring of an ideal moment or as a means of ostentatious display, and were morals understood to be identical with every aspect of value that is shared in experience, the "problem" or the relation of art and morals would not exist.

The idea and the practice of morality are saturated with conceptions that stem from praise and blame, reward and punishment. Mankind is divided into sheep and goats, the vicious and virtuous, the law-abiding and criminal, the good and bad. To be beyond good and evil is an impossibility for man, and yet as long as the good signifies only that which is lauded and rewarded, and the evil that which is currently condemned or outlawed, the ideal factors of morality are always and everywhere beyond good and evil. Because art is wholly innocent of ideas derived from praise and blame, it is looked upon with the eye of suspicion by the guardians of custom, or only the art that is itself so old and "classic" as to receive conventional praise is grudgingly admitted, provided, as with, say, the case of Shakespeare, signs of regard for conventional morality can be ingeniously extracted from his work. Yet this indifference to praise and blame because of preoccupation with imaginative experience constitutes the heart of the moral potency of art. From it proceeds the liberating and uniting power of art.

Shelley said, "The great secret of morals is love, or *a going out of our nature* and the identification of ourselves with the beautiful which exists in thought, action, or person, not our own. A man to be greatly good must imagine intensely and comprehensively." What is true of the individual is true of the whole system of morals in thought and action. While perception of the union of the possible with the actual in a work of art is itself a great good, the good does not terminate with the immediate and particular occasion in which it is had. The union that is presented in perception persists in the remaking of impulse and thought. The first intimations of wide and large redirections of desire and purpose are of necessity imaginative. Art is a mode of prediction not found in charts and statistics, and it insinuates possibilities of human relations not to be found in rule and precept, admonition and administration.

> But Art, wherein man speaks in no wise to man,
> Only to mankind—Art may tell a truth
> Obliquely, do the deed shall breed the thought.

from
AESTHETIC THEORY
by
THEODOR ADORNO

Art, Society, Aesthetics

It is self-evident that nothing concerning art is self-evident any-more, not its inner life, not its relation to the world, not even its right to exist. The forfeiture of what could be done spontaneously or unproblematically has not been compensated for by the open infinitude of new possibilities that reflection confronts. In many regards, expansion appears as contraction. The sea of the formerly inconceivable, on which around 1910 revolutionary art movements set out, did not bestow the promised happiness of adventure. Instead, the process that was unleashed consumed the categories in the name of that for which it was undertaken. More was constantly pulled into the vortex of the newly taboo; everywhere artists rejoiced less over the newly won realm of freedom than that they immedi-ately sought once again after ostensible yet scarcely adequate order. For absolute freedom in art, always limited to a particular, comes into contradiction with the perennial unfreedom of the whole. In it the place of art became uncertain. The autonomy it achieved, after having freed itself from cultic function and its images, was nour-ished by the idea of humanity. As society became ever less a human one, this autonomy was shattered. Drawn from the ideal of human-ity, art's constituent elements withered by art's own law of movement. Yet art's autonomy remains irrevocable. All efforts to restore art by giving it a social function—of which art is itself uncer-tain and by which it expresses its own uncertainty—are doomed. Indeed, art's autonomy shows signs of blindness. Blindness was ever an aspect of art; in the age of art's emancipation, however, this blind-ness has begun to predominate in spite of, if not because of, art's lost naïveté, which, as Hegel already perceived, art cannot undo. This binds art to a naïveté of a second order: the uncertainty over what purpose it serves. It is uncertain whether art is still possible; whether, with its complete emancipation, it did not sever its own preconditions. This question is kindled by art's own past. Artworks detach themselves from the empirical world and bring forth another world, one opposed to the empirical world as if this other world too were an autonomous entity. Thus, however tragic they appear, artworks tend a priori toward affirmation. The clichés of art's reconciling glow enfolding the world are repugnant not only because they parody the emphatic concept of art with its bourgeois version and class it among those Sunday institutions that provide solace. These clichés rub against the wound that art itself bears. As a result of its inevitable withdrawal from theology, from the unqualified claim to the truth of salvation, a secularization without which art would never have developed, art is condemned to provide the world as it exists with a consolation that—shorn of any hope of a world beyond—strengthens the spell of that from which the autonomy of art wants to free itself. The principle of autonomy is itself suspect of giving consolation: By undertaking to posit totality out of itself, whole and self-encompassing, this image is transferred to the world in which art exists and that engenders it. By virtue of its rejection of the empirical world—a rejection that inheres in art's concept and thus is no mere *escape*, but a law immanent to it—art sanctions the primacy of reality. In a work dedicated to the praise of art, Helmut Kuhn warranted that art's each and every work is a paean. His thesis would be true, were it meant critically. In the face of the abnormality into which reality is developing, art's inescapable affirmative essence has become insufferable. Art must turn against itself, in opposition to its own concept, and thus become uncertain of itself right into its innermost fiber. Yet art is not to be dismissed simply by its abstract negation. By attacking what seemed to be its foundation throughout the whole of its tradition, art has been qualitatively transformed; it itself becomes qualitatively other. It can do this because through the ages by means of its form, art has turned against the status quo and what merely exists just as much as it has come to its aid by giving form to its elements. Art can no more be reduced to the general formula of consolation than to its opposite.

The concept of art is located in a historically changing constellation of elements; it refuses definition. Its essence cannot be deduced from its origin as if the first work were a foundation on which everything that followed were constructed and would collapse if shaken.

The belief that the first artworks are the highest and purest is warmed-over romanticism; with no less justification it could be claimed that the earliest artistic works are dull and impure in that they are not yet separated from magic, historical documentation, and such pragmatic aims as communicating over great distances by means of calls or horn sounds; the classical conception of art gladly made use of such arguments. In bluntly historical terms, the facts blur. The effort to subsume the historical genesis of art ontologically under an ultimate motif would necessarily flounder in such disparate material that the theory would emerge empty-handed except for the obviously relevant insight that the arts will not fit into any gapless concept of art. In those studies devoted to the aesthetic ἀρχαί, positivistic sampling of material and such speculation as is otherwise disdained by the sciences flourish wildly alongside each other; Bachofen is the best example of this. If, nevertheless, one wanted in the usual philosophical fashion categorically to distinguish the so-called question of origin—as that of art's essence—from the question of art's historical origin, that would amount only to turning the concept of origin arbitrarily against the usual sense of the word. The definition of art is at every point indicated by what art once was, but it is legitimated only by what art became with regard to what it wants to, and perhaps can, become. Although art's difference from the merely empirical is to be maintained, this difference is transformed in itself qualitatively; much that was not art—cultic works, for instance—has over the course of history metamorphosed into art; and much that was once art is that no longer. Posed from on high, the question whether something such as film is or is no longer art leads nowhere. Because art is what it has become, its concept refers to what it does not contain. The tension between what motivates art and art's past circumscribes the so-called questions of aesthetic constitution. Art can be understood only by its laws of movement, not according to any set of invariants. It is defined by its relation to what it is not. The specifically artistic in art must be derived concretely from its other; that alone would fulfill the demands of a materialistic-dialectical aesthetics. Art acquires its specificity by separating itself from what it developed out of; its law of movement is its law of form. It exists only in relation to its other; it is the process that transpires with its other. Nietzsche's late insight, honed in opposition to traditional philosophy, that even what has become can be true, is axiomatic for a reoriented aesthetic. The traditional view, which he demolished, is to be turned on its head: Truth exists exclusively as that which has become. What appears in the artwork as its own lawfulness is the late product of an inner-technical evolution as well as art's position within progressive secularization; yet doubtless artworks became artworks only by negating their origin. They are not to be called to account for the disgrace of their ancient dependency on magic, their servitude to kings and amusement, as if this were art's original sin, for art retroactively annihilated that from which it emerged. Dinner music is not inescapable for liberated music, nor was dinner music honest service from which autonomous art outrageously withdrew. The former's miserable mechanical clattering is on no account improved because the overwhelming part of what now passes for art drowns out the echo of that clatter.

The Hegelian vision of the possible death of art accords with the fact that art is a product of history. That Hegel considered art transitory while all the same chalking it up to absolute spirit stands in harmony with the double character of his system, yet it prompts a thought that would never have occurred to him: that the substance of art, according to him its absoluteness, is not identical with art's life and death. Rather, art's substance could be its transitoriness. It is thinkable, and not merely an abstract possibility, that great music— a late development—was possible only during a limited phase of humanity. The revolt of art, teleologically posited in its "attitude to objectivity" toward the historical world, has become a revolt against art; it is futile to prophesy whether art will survive it. What reactionary cultural pessimism once vociferated against cannot be suppressed by the critique of culture: that, as Hegel ruminated a hundred and fifty years ago, art may have entered the age of its demise. Just as Rimbaud's stunning dictum one hundred years ago divined definitively the history of new art, his later silence, his stepping into line as an employee, anticipated art's decline. It is outside the purview of aesthetics today whether it is to become art's necrology; yet it must not play at delivering graveside sermons, certifying the end, savoring the past, and abdicating in favor of one sort of barbarism that is no better than the culture that has earned barbarism as recompense for its own monstrosity. Whether art is abolished, perishes, or despairingly hangs on, it is not mandated that the content [*Gehalt*] of past art perish. It could survive art in a society that had freed itself of the barbarism of its culture. Not just aesthetic forms but innumerable themes have already become extinct, adultery being one of them. Although adultery filled Victorian and early-twentieth-century novels, it is scarcely possible to empathize directly with this literature now, given the dissolution of the high-bourgeois nuclear family and the loosening of monogamy; distorted and impoverished, this literature lives on only in illustrated magazines. At the same time, however, what is authentic in *Madame Bovary* and was once embedded in its thematic content has long since outstripped this content and its deterioration. Obviously this is not grounds for historicophilosophical optimism over the invincibility of spirit. It is equally possible for the thematic material in its own demise to take with it that which is more than merely thematic. Art and artworks are perishable, not simply because by their heteronomy they are dependent, but because right into the smallest detail of their autonomy, which sanctions the socially determined splitting off of spirit by the division of labor, they are not only art but something foreign and opposed to it. Admixed with art's own concept is the ferment of its own abolition.

There is no aesthetic refraction without something being refracted; no imagination without something imagined. This holds true particularly in the case of art's immanent purposiveness. In its relation to empirical reality art sublimates the latter's governing principle of *sese conservare* as the ideal of the self-identity of its works; as Schoenberg said, one paints a painting, not what it represents. Inherently every artwork desires identity with itself, an identity that in empirical reality is violently forced on all objects as identity with the subject and thus travestied. Aesthetic identity seeks to aid the nonidentical, which in reality is repressed by reality's compulsion to identity. Only by virtue of separation from empirical reality, which sanctions art to model the relation of the whole and the part according to the work's own need, does the artwork achieve a heightened order of existence. Artworks are afterimages of empirical life insofar as they help the latter to what is denied them outside their own sphere and thereby free it from that to which they are condemned by reified external experience. Although the demarcation line between art and the empirical must not be effaced, and least of all by the glorification of the artist, artworks nevertheless have a life sui generis. This life is not just their external fate. Important artworks constantly divulge new layers; they age, grow cold, and die. It is a tautology to point out that as humanly manufactured artifacts they do not live as do people. But the emphasis on the artifactual element in art concerns less the fact that it is manufactured than its own inner constitution, regardless of how it came to be. Artworks are alive in that they speak in a fashion that is denied to natural objects and the subjects who make them. They speak by virtue of the communication of everything particular in them. Thus they come into contrast with the arbitrariness of what simply exists. Yet it is precisely as artifacts, as products of social labor, that they also communicate with the empirical experience that they reject and from which they draw their content [*Inhalt*]. Art negates the categorial determinations stamped on the empirical world and yet harbors what is empirically existing in its own substance. If art opposes the empirical through the element of form—and the mediation of form and content is not to be grasped without their differentiation—the mediation is to be sought in the recognition of aesthetic form as sedimented content. What are taken to be the purest forms (e.g., traditional musical forms) can be traced back even in the smallest idiomatic detail to content such as dance. In many instances ornaments in the visual arts were once primarily cultic symbols. Tracing aesthetic forms back to contents, such as the Warburg Institute undertook to do by following the afterlife of classical antiquity, deserves to be more broadly undertaken. The communication of artworks with what is external to them, with the world from which they blissfully or unhappily seal themselves off, occurs through noncommunication; precisely thereby they prove themselves refracted. It is easy to imagine that art's autonomous realm has nothing in common with the external world other than borrowed elements that have entered into a fully changed context. Nevertheless, there is no contesting the cliché of which cultural history is so fond, that the development of artistic processes, usually classed under the heading of style, corresponds to social development. Even the most sublime artwork takes up a determinate attitude to empirical reality by stepping outside of the constraining spell it casts, not once and for all, but rather ever and again, concretely, unconsciously polemical toward this spell at each historical moment. That artworks as windowless monads "represent" what they themselves are not can scarcely be understood except in that their own dynamic, their immanent historicity as a dialectic of nature and its domination, not only is of the same essence as the dialectic external to them but resembles it without imitating it. The aesthetic force of production is the same as that of productive labor and has the same teleology; and what may be called aesthetic relations of production—all that in which the productive force is embedded and in which it is active—are sedimentations or imprintings of social relations of production. Art's double character as both autonomous and *fait social* is incessantly reproduced on the level of its autonomy. It is by virtue of this relation to the empirical that artworks recuperate, neutralized, what once was literally and directly experienced in life and what was expulsed by spirit. Artworks participate in enlightenment because they do not lie: They do not feign the literalness of what speaks out of them. They are real as answers to the puzzle externally posed to them. Their own tension is binding in relation to the tension external to them. The basic levels of experience that motivate art are related to those of the objective world from which they recoil. The unsolved antagonisms of reality return in artworks as immanent problems of form. This, not the insertion of objective elements, defines the relation of art to society. The complex of tensions in artworks crystallizes undisturbed in these problems of form and through emancipation from the external world's factual facade converges with the real essence. Art, χωρίζ from the empirically existing, takes up a position to it in accord with Hegel's argument against Kant: The moment a limit is posited, it is overstepped and that against which the limit was established is absorbed. Only this, not moralizing, is the critique of the principle of *l'art pour l'art*, which by abstract negation posits the χωρισμό of art as absolute. The freedom of artworks, in which their self-consciousness glories and without which these works would not exist, is the ruse of art's own reason. Each and every one of their elements binds them to that over which, for their happiness, they must soar and back into which at every moment they threaten once again to tumble. In their relation to empirical reality, artworks recall the theologumenon that in the redeemed world everything would be as it is and yet wholly other. There is no mistaking the analogy with the tendency of the profane to secularize the realm of the sacred to the point that only as secularized does the latter endure; the realm of the sacred is objectified, effectively staked off, because its own element of untruth at once awaits secularization and through conjuration wards off the secular. Accordingly, the pure concept of art could not define the fixed circumference of a sphere that has been secured once and for all; rather, its closure is achieved only in an intermittent and fragile balance that is more than just comparable to the psychological balance between ego and id. The act of repulsion must be constantly renewed. Every artwork is an instant; every successful work is a cessation, a suspended moment of the process, as which it reveals itself to the unwavering eye. If artworks are answers to their own questions, they themselves thereby truly become questions. The tendency to perceive art either in extra-aesthetic or preaesthetic fashion, which to this day is undiminished by an obviously failed education, is not only a barbaric residue or a danger of regressive consciousness. Something in art calls for this response. Art perceived strictly aesthetically is art aesthetically misperceived. Only when art's other is sensed as a primary layer in the experience of art does it become possible to sublimate this layer, to dissolve the thematic bonds, without the autonomy of the artwork becoming a matter of indifference. Art is autonomous and it is not; without what is heterogeneous to it, its autonomy eludes it. The great epics, which have survived even their own oblivion, were in their own age intermingled with historical and geographical reportage; Valéry the artist took note of how much of their material had yet to be recast by the formal requirements of the Homeric, pagan-Germanic, and Christian epics, without this reducing their rank vis-à-vis drossless works. Likewise tragedy, which may have been the origin of the idea of aesthetic autonomy, was an afterimage of cultic acts that were intended to have real effects. The history of art as that of its progressive autonomy never succeeded in extirpating this element, and not just because the bonds were too strong. At the height of its form, in the nineteenth century, the realistic novel had something of what the theory of so-called socialist realism rationally plotted for its debasement: reportage, the anticipation of what social science would later ascertain. The fanatic linguistic perfection of *Madame Bovary* is probably a symptom of precisely this contrary element; the unity of both, of reportage and linguistic perfectionism, accounts for the book's unfaded actuality. In artworks, the criterion of success

ADORNO • *Aesthetic Theory*

is twofold: whether they succeed in integrating thematic strata and details into their immanent law of form and in this integration at the same time maintain what resists it and the fissures that occur in the process of integration. Integration as such does not assure quality; in the history of art, integration and quality have often diverged. For no single select category, not even the aesthetically central concept of the law of form, names the essence of art and suffices to judge its products. Essential to art are defining characteristics that contradict its fixed art-philosophical concept. Hegel's content-aesthetics [*Inhaltsästhetik*] recognized that element of otherness immanent to art and thus superseded formal aesthetics, which apparently operates with a so much purer concept of art and of course liberated historical developments such as nonrepresentational painting that are blocked by Hegel's and Kierkegaard's content-aesthetics. At the same time, however, Hegel's idealist dialectic, which conceives form as content, regresses to a crude, preaesthetic level. It confuses the representational or discursive treatment of thematic material with the otherness that is constitutive of art. Hegel transgresses against his own dialectical conception of aesthetics, with consequences he did not foresee; he in effect helped transform art into an ideology of domination. Conversely, what is unreal and nonexistent in art is not independent of reality. It is not arbitrarily posited, not invented, as is commonly thought; rather, it is structured by proportions between what exists, proportions that are themselves defined by what exists, its deficiency, distress, and contradictoriness as well as its potentialities; even in these proportions real contexts resonate. Art is related to its other as is a magnet to a field of iron filings. Not only art's elements, but their constellation as well, that which is specifically aesthetic and to which its spirit is usually chalked tip, refer back to its other. The identity of the artwork with existing reality is also that of the work's gravitational force, which gathers around itself its *membra disjecta*, traces of the existing. The artwork is related to the world by the principle that contrasts it with the world, and that is the same principle by which spirit organized the world. The synthesis achieved by means of the artwork is not simply forced on its elements; rather, it recapitulates that in which these elements communicate with one another; thus the synthesis is itself product of otherness. Indeed, synthesis has its foundation in the spirit-distant material dimension of works, in that in which synthesis is active. This unites the aesthetic element of form with noncoercion. By its difference from empirical reality the artwork necessarily constitutes itself in relation to what it is not, and to what makes it an artwork in the first place. The insistence on the nonintentional in art—which is apparent in art's sympathy with its lower manifestations beginning at a specific historical point with Wedekind's derision of the "art-artist," with Apollinaire, and indeed with the beginnings of cubism—points up art's unconscious self-consciousness in its participation in what is contrary to it; this self-consciousness motivated art's culture-critical turn that cast off the illusion of its purely spiritual being.

Art is the social antithesis of society, not directly deducible from it. The constitution of art's sphere corresponds to the constitution of an inward space of men as the space of their representation: A priori the constitution of this space participates in sublimation. It is therefore plausible to conceive of developing the definition of art out of a theory of psychic life. Skepticism toward anthropological theories of human invariants recommends psychoanalytic theory. But this theory is more productive psychologically than aesthetically. For psychoanalysis considers artworks to be essentially unconscious projections of those who have produced them, and, preoccupied with the hermeneutics of thematic material, it forgets the categories of form and, so to speak, transfers the pedantry of sensitive doctors to the most inappropriate objects, such as Leonardo da Vinci or Baudelaire. The narrow-mindedness, in spite of all the emphasis on sex, is revealed by the fact that as a result of these studies, which are often offshoots of the biographical fad, artists whose work gave uncensored shape to the negativity of life are dismissed as neurotics. Laforgue's book actually in all seriousness accuses Baudelaire of having suffered from a mother complex. The question is never once broached whether a psychically sound Baudelaire would have been able to write *The Flowers of Evil*, not to mention whether the poems turned out worse because of the neurosis. Psychological normalcy is outrageously established as the criterion even, as in Baudelaire, where aesthetic quality is bluntly predicated on the absence of *mens sana*. According to the tone of psychoanalytic monographs, art should deal affirmatively with the negativity of experience. The negative element is held to be nothing more than the mark of that process of repression that obviously goes into the artwork. For psychoanalysis, artworks are daydreams; it confuses them with documents and displaces them into the mind of a dreamer, while on the other hand, as compensation for the exclusion of the extramental sphere, it reduces artworks to crude thematic material, failing strangely short of Freud's own theory of the "dreamwork." As with all positivists, the fictional element in artworks is vastly overestimated by the presumed analogy with the dream. In the process of production, what is projected is only one element in the artist's relation to the artwork and hardly the definitive one; idiom and material have their own importance, as does, above all, the product itself; this rarely if ever occurs to the analysts. The psychoanalytic thesis, for instance, that music is a defense against the threat of paranoia, does indeed for the most part hold true clinically, yet it says nothing about the quality and content of a particular composition. The psychoanalytic theory of art is superior to idealist aesthetics in that it brings to light what is internal to art and not itself artistic. It helps free art from the spell of absolute spirit. Whereas vulgar idealism, rancorously opposed to knowledge of the artwork and especially knowledge of its entwinement with instinct, would like to quarantine art in a putatively higher sphere, psychoanalysis works in the opposite direction, in the spirit of enlightenment. Where it deciphers the social character that speaks from a work and in which on many occasions the character of its author is manifest, psychoanalysis furnishes the concrete mediating links between the structure of artworks and the social structure. But psychoanalysis too casts a spell related to idealism, that of an absolutely subjective sign system denoting subjective instinctual impulses. It unlocks phenomena, but falls short of the phenomenon of art. Psychoanalysis treats artworks as nothing but facts, yet it neglects their own objectivity, their inner consistency, their level of form, their critical impulse, their relation to nonpsychical reality, and, finally, their idea of truth. When a painter, obeying the pact of total frankness between analyst and patient, mocked the bad Viennese engravings that defaced his walls, she was informed by the analyst that this was nothing but aggression on her part. Artworks are incomparably less a copy and possession of the artist than a doctor who knows the artist exclusively from the couch can imagine. Only dilettantes reduce everything in art to the unconscious, repeating clichés. In artistic production, unconscious forces are one sort of impulse, material among many others.

They enter the work mediated by the law of form; if this were not the case, the actual subject portrayed by a work would be nothing but a copy. Artworks are not *Thematic Apperception Tests* of their makers. Part of the responsibility for this philistinism is the devotion of psychoanalysis to the reality principle: Whatever refuses to obey this principle is always merely "escape"; adaptation to reality becomes the *summum bonum*. Yet reality provides too many legitimate reasons for fleeing it for the impulse to be met by the indignation of an ideology sworn to harmony; on psychological grounds alone, art is more legitimate than psychology acknowledges. True, imagination is escape, but not exclusively so: What transcends the reality principle toward something superior is always also part of what is beneath it; to point a taunting finger at it is malicious. The image of the artist, as one of the tolerated, integrated as a neurotic in a society sworn to the division of labor, is distorted. Among artists of the highest rank, such as Beethoven or Rembrandt, the sharpest sense of reality was joined with estrangement from reality; this, truly, would be a worthwhile object for the psychology of art. It would need to decipher the artwork not just as being like the artist but as being unlike as well, as labor on a reality resisting the artist. If art has psychoanalytic roots, then they are the roots of fantasy in the fantasy of omnipotence. This fantasy includes the wish to bring about a better world. This frees the total dialectic, whereas the view of art as a merely subjective language of the unconscious does not even touch it.

Kant's aesthetics is the antithesis of Freud's theory of art as wish fulfillment. Disinterested liking is the first element of the judgment of taste in the "Analytic of the Beautiful." There interest is termed "the liking that we combine with the representation of the existence of an object." It is not clear, however, if what is meant by the "representation of the existence of an object" is its content, the thematic material in the sense of the object treated in the work, or the artwork itself; the pretty nude model or the sweet resonance of a musical tone can be kitsch or it can be an integral element of artistic quality. The accent on "representation" is a consequence of Kant's subjectivistic approach, which in accord with the rationalistic tradition, notably that of Moses Mendelssohn, tacitly seeks aesthetic quality in the effect the artwork has on the observer. What is revolutionary in the *Critique of Judgment* is that without leaving the circle of the older effect-aesthetics Kant at the same time restricted it through immanent criticism; this is in keeping with the whole of his subjectivism, which plays a significant part in his objective effort to save objectivity through the analysis of subjective elements. Disinterestedness sets itself at a distance from the immediate effect that liking seeks to conserve, and this initiates the fragmentation of the supremacy of liking. For, once shorn of what Kant calls interest, satisfaction becomes so indeterminate that it no longer serves to define beauty. The doctrine of disinterested satisfaction is impoverished vis-à-vis the aesthetic; it reduces the phenomenon either to formal beauty, which when isolated is highly dubious, or to the so-called sublime natural object. The sublimation of the work to absolute form neglects the spirit of the work in the interest of which sublimation was undertaken in the first place. This is honestly and involuntarily attested by Kant's strained footnote, in which he asserts that a judgment of an object of liking may indeed be disinterested, yet interesting; that is, it may produce interest even when it is not based on it. Kant divides aesthetic feeling—and thus, in accord with the whole of his model, art itself—from the power of desire, to which the "representation of the existence of an object" refers; the liking of such a representation "always has reference to the power of desire." Kant was the first to achieve the insight, never since forgotten, that aesthetic comportment is free from immediate desire; he snatched art away from that avaricious philistinism that always wants to touch it and taste it. Nevertheless, the Kantian motif is not altogether alien to psychoanalytic art theory: Even for Freud artworks are not immediate wish fulfillments but transform unsatisfied libido into a socially productive achievement, whereby the social value of art is simply assumed, with uncritical respect for art's public reputation. Although Kant emphasizes the difference between art and the power of desire—and thereby between art and empirical reality—much more energetically than does Freud, he does not simply idealize art: The separation of the aesthetic sphere from the empirical constitutes art. Yet Kant transcendentally arrested this constitution, which is a historical process, and simplistically equated it with the essence of the artistic, unconcerned that the subjective, instinctual components of art return metamorphosed even in art's maturest form, which negates them. The dynamic character of the artistic is much more fully grasped by Freud's theory of sublimation. But for this Freud clearly had to pay no smaller a price than did Kant. If in the latter's case, in spite of his preference for sensual intuition, the spiritual essence of the artwork originates in the distinction between aesthetic and practical, appetitive behavior, Freud's adaptation of the aesthetic to the theory of the instincts seems to seal itself off from art's spiritual essence; for Freud, artworks are indeed, even though sublimated, little more than plenipotentiaries of sensual impulses, which they at best make unrecognizable through a sort of dreamwork. The confrontation of these two heterogeneous thinkers—Kant not only rejected philosophical psychologism but in his old age increasingly rejected all psychology—is nevertheless permitted by a commonality that outweighs the apparently absolute difference between the Kantian construction of the transcendental subject, on the one hand, and the Freudian recourse to the empirically psychological on the other: Both are in principle subjectively oriented by the power of desire, whether it is interpreted negatively or positively. For both, the artwork exists only in relation to its observer or maker. By a mechanism to which his moral philosophy is subordinate, even Kant is compelled to consider the existing individual, the ontic element, more than is compatible with the idea of the transcendental subject. There is no liking without a living person who would enjoy it. Though it is never made explicit, the *Critique of Judgment* is as a whole devoted to the analysis of *constituta*. Thus what was planned as a bridge between theoretical and practical pure reason is vis-à-vis both an ἀλλογένοω. Indeed, the taboo on art—and so far as art is defined it obeys a taboo, for definitions are rational taboos—forbids that one take an animalistic stance toward the object, that is, that one dominate it by physically devouring it. But the power of the taboo corresponds to the power that it prohibits. There is no art that does not contain in itself as an element, negated, what it repulses. If it is more than mere indifference, the Kantian "without interest" must be shadowed by the wildest interest, and there is much to be said for the idea that the dignity of artworks depends on the intensity of the interest from which they are wrested. Kant denies this in favor of a concept of freedom that castigates as heteronomous whatever is not born exclusively of the subject. His theory of art is distorted by the insufficiency of the doctrine of practical reason. The idea of something beautiful, which possesses or has acquired some degree of autonomy in the face of the sovereign I, would, given the tenor of his philosophy, be disparaged as wandering off into intelligible realms. But along with that from which art antithetically originated, art is shorn of all content, and in its place he posits something as formal as aesthetic satisfaction. For Kant, aesthetics becomes paradoxically a castrated hedonism, desire without desire. An equal injustice is done both to artistic experience, in which liking is by no means the whole of it but plays a subordinate role, and to sensual interest, the suppressed and unsatisfied needs that resonate in their aesthetic negation and make artworks more than empty patterns. Aesthetic disinterestedness has broadened interest beyond particularity. The interest in the aesthetic totality wanted to be, objectively, an interest in a correct organization of the whole. It aims not at the fulfillment of the particular but rather at unbound possibility, though that would be no possibility at all without the presupposition of the fulfillment of the particular. Correlative to the weakness of Kant's aesthetics, Freud's is much more idealistic than it suspects. When artworks are translated purely into psychical immanence, they are deprived of their antithetic stance to the not-I, which remains unchallenged by the thorniness of artworks. They are exhausted in the psychical performance of gaining mastery over instinctual renunciation and, ultimately, in the achievement of conformity. The psychologism of aesthetic interpretation easily agrees with the philistine view of the artwork as harmoniously quieting antagonisms, a dream image of a better life, unconcerned with the misery from which this image is wrested. The conformist psychoanalytic endorsement of the prevailing view of the artwork as a well-meaning cultural commodity corresponds to an aesthetic hedonism that banishes art's negativity to the instinctual conflicts of its genesis and suppresses any negativity in the finished work. If successful sublimation and integration are made the end-all and be-all of the artwork, it loses the force by which it exceeds the given, which it renounces by its mere existence. The moment, however, the artwork comports itself by retaining the negativity of reality and taking a position to it, the concept of disinterestedness is also modified. Contrary to the Kantian and Freudian interpretation of art, artworks imply in themselves a relation between interest and its renunciation. Even the contemplative attitude to artworks, wrested from objects of action, is felt as the announcement of an immediate praxis and—to this extent itself practical—as a refusal to play along. Only artworks that are to be sensed as a form of comportment have a raison d'être. Art is not only the plenipotentiary of a better praxis than that which has to date predominated, but is equally the critique of praxis as the rule of brutal self-preservation at the heart of the status quo and in its service. It gives the lie to production for production's sake and opts for a form of praxis beyond the spell of labor. Art's *promesse du bonheur* means not only that hitherto praxis has blocked happiness but that happiness is beyond praxis. The measure of the chasm separating praxis from happiness is taken by the force of negativity in the artwork. Certainly Kafka does not awaken the power of desire. Yet the real fear triggered by prose works like *Metamorphosis* or *The Penal Colony*, that shock of revulsion and disgust that shakes the physis, has, as defense, more to do with desire than with the old disinterestedness canceled by Kafka and what followed him. As a response, disinterestedness would be crudely inadequate to his writings. Ultimately disinterestedness debases art to what Hegel mocked, a pleasant or useful plaything of Horace's *Ars Poetica*. It is from this that the aesthetics of the idealist age, contemporaneously with art itself, freed itself. Only once it is done with tasteful savoring does artistic experience become autonomous. The route to aesthetic autonomy proceeds by way of disinterestedness; the emancipation of art from cuisine or pornography is irrevocable. Yet art does not come to rest in disinterestedness. For disinterestedness immanently reproduces—and transforms—interest. In the false world all ηδονη is false. For the sake of happiness, happiness is renounced. It is thus that desire survives in art.

Pleasure masquerades beyond recognition in the Kantian disinterestedness. What popular consciousness and a complaisant aesthetics regard as the taking pleasure in art, modeled on real enjoyment, probably does not exist. The empirical subject has only a limited and modified part in artistic experience *tel quel*, and this part may well be diminished the higher the work's rank. Whoever concretely enjoys artworks is a philistine; he is convicted by expressions like "a feast for the ears." Yet if the last traces of pleasure were extirpated, the question of what artworks are for would be an embarrassment. Actually, the more they are understood, the less they are enjoyed. Formerly, even the traditional attitude to the artwork, if it was to be absolutely relevant to the work, was that of admiration that the works exist as they do in themselves and not for the sake of the observer. What opened up to, and overpowered, the beholder was their truth, which as in works of Kafka's type outweighs every other element. They were not a higher order of amusement. The relation to art was not that of its physical devouring; on the contrary, the beholder disappeared into the material; this is even more so in modern works that shoot toward the viewer as on occasion a locomotive does in a film. Ask a musician if the music is a pleasure, the reply is likely to be—as in the American joke of the grimacing cellist under Toscanini—"*I just hate music.*" For him who has a genuine relation to art, in which he himself vanishes, art is not an object; deprivation of art would be unbearable for him, yet he does not consider individual works sources of joy. Incontestably, no one would devote himself to art without—as the bourgeois put it— getting something out of it; yet this is not true in the sense that a balance sheet could be drawn up: "heard the Ninth Symphony tonight, enjoyed myself so and so much" even though such feeble-mindedness has by now established itself as common sense. The bourgeois want art voluptuous and life ascetic; the reverse would be better. Reified consciousness provides an ersatz for the sensual immediacy of which it deprives people in a sphere that is not its abode. While the artwork's sensual appeal seemingly brings it close to the consumer, it is alienated from him by being a commodity that he possesses and the loss of which he must constantly fear. The false relation to art is akin to anxiety over possession. The fetishistic idea of the artwork as property that can be possessed and destroyed by reflection has its exact correlative in the idea of exploitable property within the psychological economy of the self. If according to its own concept art has become what it is, this is no less the case with its classification as a source of pleasure; indeed, as components of ritual praxis the magical and animistic predecessors of art were not autonomous; yet precisely because they were sacred they were not objects of enjoyment. The spiritualization of art incited the rancor of the excluded and spawned consumer art as a genre, while conversely antipathy toward consumer art compelled artists to ever more reckless spiritualization. No naked Greek sculpture was a *pin-up*. The affinity of the modern for the distant past and the exotic is explicable on the same grounds: Artists were drawn by the abstraction from natural objects as desirable; incidentally, in the construction of "symbolic art" Hegel did not overlook the unsensuous element of the archaic. The element of pleasure in art, a protest against the universally mediated commodity character, is in its own fashion mediable: Whoever disappears into the artwork thereby gains dispensation from the impoverishment of a life that is always too little. This pleasure may mount to an ecstasy for which the meager concept of enjoyment is hardly adequate, other than to produce disgust for enjoying anything. It is striking, incidentally, that an aesthetic that constantly insists on subjective feeling, as the basis of all beauty never seriously analyzed this feeling. Almost without exception its descriptions were banausic, perhaps because from the beginning, the subjective approach made it impossible to recognize that something compelling can be grasped of aesthetic experience only on the basis of a relation to the aesthetic object, not by recurring to the fun of the art lover. The concept of artistic enjoyment was a bad compromise between the social and the socially critical essence of the artwork. If art is useless for the business of self-preservation—bourgeois society never quite forgives that—it should at least demonstrate a sort of use-value modeled on sensual pleasure. This distorts art as well as the physical fulfillment that art's aesthetic representatives do not dispense. That a person who is incapable of sensual differentiation—who cannot distinguish a beautiful from a flat sound, a brilliant from a dull color—is hardly capable of artistic experience, is hypostatized. Aesthetic experience does indeed benefit from an intensified sensual differentiation as a medium of giving form, yet the pleasure in this is always indirect. The importance of the sensual in art has varied; after an age of asceticism pleasure becomes an organ of liberation and vivaciousness, as it did in the Renaissance and then again in the anti-Victorian impulse of impressionism; at other moments creatural sadness has home witness to a metaphysical content by erotic excitement permeating the forms. Yet however powerful, historically, the force of pleasure to return may be, whenever it appears in art literally, undefracted, it has an infantile quality. Only in memory and longing, not as a copy or as an immediate effect, is pleasure absorbed by art. Ultimately, aversion to the crudely sensual alienates even those periods in which pleasure and form could still communicate in a more direct fashion; this not least of all may have motivated the rejection of impressionism.

Underlying the element of truth in aesthetic hedonism is the fact that in art the means and the ends are not identical. In their dialectic, the former constantly asserts a certain, and indeed mediated, independence. Through the element of sensuous satisfaction the work's sine qua non, its appearance, is constituted. As Alban Berg said, it is a prosaic matter to make sure that the work shows no nails sticking out and that the glue does not stink; and in many of Mozart's compositions the delicacy of expression evokes the sweetness of the human voice. In important artworks the sensuous illuminated by its art shines forth as spiritual just as the abstract detail, however indifferent to appearance it may be, gains sensuous luster from the spirit of the work. Sometimes by virtue of their differentiated formal language, artworks that are developed and articulated in themselves play over, secondarily, into the sensuously pleasing. Even in its equivalents in the visual arts, dissonance, the seal of everything modern, gives access to the alluringly sensuous by transfiguring it into its antithesis, pain: an aesthetic archetype of ambivalence. The source of the immense importance of all dissonance for new art since Baudelaire and *Tristan*—veritably an invariant of the modern—is that the immanent play of forces in the artwork converges with external reality: Its power over the subject intensifies in parallel with the increasing autonomy of the work. Dissonance elicits from within the work that which vulgar sociology calls its social alienation. In the meantime, of course, artworks have set a taboo even on spiritually mediated suavity as being too similar to its vulgar form. This development may well lead to a sharpening of the taboo on the sensual, although it is sometimes hard to distinguish to what extent this taboo is grounded in the law of form and to what extent simply in the failure of craft; a question, incidentally, that like many of its ilk becomes a fruitless topic of aesthetic debate. The taboo on the sensual ultimately encroaches on the opposite of pleasure because, even as the remotest echo, pleasure is sensed in its specific negation. For this aesthetic sensorium dissonance bears all too closely on its contrary, reconciliation; it rebuffs the semblance of the human as an ideology of the inhuman and prefers to join forces with reified consciousness. Dissonance congeals into an indifferent material; indeed, it becomes a new form of immediacy, without any memory trace of what it developed out of, and therefore gutted and anonymous. For a society in which art no longer has a place and which is pathological in all its reactions to it, art fragments on one hand into a reified, hardened cultural posses-sion and on the other into a source of pleasure that the customer pockets and that for the most part has little to do with the object itself. Subjective pleasure in the artwork would approximate a state of release from the empirical as from the totality of heteronomous. Schopenhauer may have been the first to realize this. The happiness gained from artworks is that of having suddenly escaped, not a morsel of that from which art escaped; it is accidental and less essen-tial to art than the happiness in its knowledge; the concept of aesthetic pleasure as constitutive of art is to be superseded. If in keeping with Hegel's insight all feeling related to an aesthetic object has an accidental aspect, usually that of psychological projection, then what the work demands from its beholder is knowledge, and indeed, knowledge that does justice to it: The work wants its truth and untruth to be grasped. Aesthetic hedonism is to be confronted with the passage from Kant's doctrine of the sublime, which he timidly excluded from art: Happiness in artworks would be the feel-ing they instill of standing firm. This holds true for the aesthetic sphere as a whole more than for any particular work.

PART FOUR
METAPHYSICS

INTRODUCTION

by

RICHARD VELKLEY

What Is Metaphysics?

M*etaphysics*—the term itself appears first in late antiquity—names the investigation of the ultimate principles, causes, origins, constituents, and categories of all things. Philosophy begins in ancient Greece as metaphysics, and from thence the tradition of metaphysical inquiry continues almost without break into the twentieth century. In our time *metaphysics* is thought by many as a thinking attending mostly to the supernatural, and superseded by the modern sciences to the extent that it addresses nature. The selected readings that follow and this introduction should help to correct this misinformed view.

Metaphysics is a prime instance of the essential stance of philosophy: the habitual refusal to accept the "reduction of the strange to the familiar." It exposes a troublesome fact: the arts, sciences, and all human activities employ fundamental notions that their practitioners cannot or will not clarify and justify. For example, all the sciences save mathematics employ some idea of *cause*. But what is a *cause*? This question must be pursued by an inquiry that is logically prior to particular causal investigations. What is meant by *law of nature*? Through such terms as *cause* and *law* we seek to identify fundamental connections, or unities, within the world. But what makes anything "one"? Is nature itself a "one" and a whole, of some sort? Is nature's unity grounded in a single unifying principle, or is it a mere aggregate of parts?

Beyond these questions there is the question of the "why" of the natural whole. Why does it, or anything at all, exist? To pursue this question one must address some logically primary questions: What does it mean to speak of *being* or *existence*? Do these words denote properties of things, so that *existing* is a property like *red*? If it is a property, is it then separable from the thing, as *red* is separable from *apple*? Or is the existence of the apple simply the apple itself, and nothing more? But if that is the case, how is it that we can think about *existence* or *being* in some universal sense? Is there a universal class or genus *being* denoting a reality that exists apart from particular beings?

There is a temptation to suppose that these notions (cause, law, unity, being, etc.) exist solely through linguistic convention, and hence it should be an easy matter to settle on agreed meanings. Yet these notions, or similar ones, do not emerge randomly and accidentally, like conventions; they naturally occur whenever humans think. Furthermore, reflection on these notions and what they mean will always, as Aristotle observes, evoke wonder: "Indeed the question which was raised of old and is raised now and always, and is always the subject of doubt—is what is a Being?" Metaphysics is not just the raising of questions about being; it is the discovery that being is questionable.

Aristotle and Ancient Metaphysics

Aristotle declares that "all humans by nature desire to know," and thereby helps justify the way that a relatively new human type, the "philosophers" or "lovers of wisdom," rank their activity: as the most choiceworthy way of life. What makes it most desirable is its contemplation of the primary objects of thought: the first causes of being that are not subject to human action but which make all human thought and action possible. To know such causes is therefore to have, in the highest sense, self-knowledge.

Beyond the "special" sciences, which examine particular regions of things, there must exist a science that inquires about their common principles and starting points. This science Aristotle terms *first philosophy* and *wisdom*; after him it is called *metaphysics* and the *queen of the sciences*. This science determines what causes the beings to come into being, and what makes them knowable. Through such inquiry it shows that the beings form various orders: (1) with respect to their causes of generation, as when lower causes, such as the generative powers in particular plants or animals, are dependent on higher causes, such as the first cause of motion in nature as a whole; (2) with respect to their purposes or finality, as when lower beings (or sciences) serve higher beings (or sciences); (3) with respect to their level of knowledge or knowability, as when a lower form of knowledge (optics) is dependent on a higher form (mathematics).

Finally, and most difficult, metaphysics as the "architectonic science" seeks to determine how these orders relate to each other: whether they are the same order and, if not, how they can be coordinated. Let us note some difficulties in this effort. One can ask: Are *to be* and *to be knowable* the same thing? It is plain that *knowability* is a feature of anything in the universe that can enter in some way into our knowledge. (*Knowing* is the capacity to relate the thought or perception of things to general principles.) *Being* is a feature of all things that in some way exist. One can ask: is *knowability* applicable only to the beings that are knowable to humans, as the one species in the whole that—to our knowledge—has knowledge?

If, however, one argues that being and knowability must be coextensive, this may have the disturbing consequence that both being and knowability are as finite as our species. To avoid this consequence while preserving the coextension of being and knowability, one can argue that there is a divine intellect that knows all beings or (as Aristotle argues) contains in itself the principle that makes all things knowable. Metaphysics, then, culminates in an account of the divine intellect, or theology. But the divine intellect still is only one being in the whole, although it is the one that accounts for the most important features of the whole. Theology, the study of that unique being, is distinguished from the study of being as being (the study of the features common to all beings), which in modern times bears the name *onology*. Metaphysics, it seems, is not one science, but at the minimum it is two.

Another difficulty is this: beings have motions of coming into being, passing away, and generating motion in other beings. Aristotle argues that the divine being, while unmoved, is in some way responsible for the motion in all beings. But is what makes beings knowable (the first principle of knowability) the same as what gives them motion (the first principle of generation)? The attempt to answer that question in the affirmative is the very heart of Aristotle's metaphysics. His metaphysical treatises are centrally engaged in a criticism of his predecessors, who had not answered this question or even formulated it properly. Aristotle shows that they progressively discovered the essential components of the true first philosophy, but they could not formulate the principles that unify generation, knowability, and being.

The early philosophers before Socrates speculated on the causes of nature as a whole, without much attention to the constitution of particular beings (species and individuals), but with a focus on natural change in a very abstract and general sense. They tended to give accounts of a unitary origination of all things, that is, doctrines of underlying enduring substances (most famously the water of Thales), modifications of which would in principle account for the manifold changes in nature. It did not take long for the philosophers to discover that they could now address change without having another cause beside the primary substance: a cause of motion, or "efficient cause," to bring about complex entities and their changes (thus the Love and Strife of Empedocles). But these two causes still left in the dark the tendency of nature to produce things with distinctive structures and forms. (To illustrate with an example from human art: the form of the sculpture is more crucial to its being than whether it is made of stone or wood.)

Aristotle credits Socrates with having seen the necessity for two further closely related causal principles: the form, which corresponds to the question "what is it?" and which comes into view through the "looks" of a thing as whole, and the final cause or purpose, which corresponds to the question "for the sake of what does it exist?" The two causes tend to coincide since the form embodies the essence by which the being of things is measured. We look to the form when we ask to what extent things are achieving their essence: how far does a given man achieve the form of man? Thereby it becomes possible to consider the Good as an explanatory principle. Nature as ordered toward the production of things that achieve (or resemble) the forms is not a goalless and mindless process. Goodness and mind are constitutive features of the whole. Aristotle notes that the turn to form enabled Socrates to begin to account for the nature of the ethical and political life of humans.

Yet Aristotle finds that none of his predecessors made adequate use of all four causes (material, efficient, formal, and final). None of them tried to answer this question: how do all four causes work together in the production of a being? Do they work together as independent agents or as aspects of one primary reality? Aristotle famously criticized his teacher Plato for having treated the forms and the Good (the final cause) as abstract "ideas" (universals such as "justice" and "humanity") separate from the sensible beings. The forms as prototypes were to explain the existence of the sensible beings as "imitations." But if the forms are unmoving, unchanging, suprasensible beings, how can they account for the motion and change of the sensible world? Actually it is doubtful that Plato ever held such a simplistic doctrine as Aristotle ascribes to him, and as Plato's pupil he must have known this. Indeed it is clear that Plato himself regarded the "doctrine of ideas" as a natural tendency of the human mind in its effort to solve the problem of being. For this reason the "doctrine" has to be aired and criticized.

At first Aristotle's approach to the causes of beings seems radically different from the Platonic. Aristotle underscores that the true being is not the "what" (life, justice, humanity, etc.) but the "this" (this living being, this just thing, this human being). Plato's "Good itself," the universal idea of goodness, is according to Aristotle only an abstraction Plato produced by thinking about the many kinds of concrete goodness that humans and other beings pursue. The concrete individual being, "this man" or "Socrates," has privileged ontological status. It cannot be the attribute of another being but subsists in itself. Only a "this," therefore, is a true "substance"—its attributes. Within attributes that cannot subsist on their own, but exist only in true beings (or in terms of speech, are predicated of their subjects), a distinction must be drawn. There are those that are accidental and can be removed (*white*, as in "Socrates is white") and those that are essential and cannot be removed (*rational*, as in "Socrates is rational"). Aristotle charges that Plato mistakenly treated the essential attributes as substances.

Even so, Aristotle shows he is Plato's student, for he says that among the various senses of being, the "what" or the essence most closely addressed the nature of the being. (See the reading from *Metaphysics*, Book Seven.) Competitors often note the tension in Aristotle between the priority of the "what" and priority of the "this." Aristotle is of course aware of the tension; he offers a resolution in the following way. The concrete individual ("this") is our experiential starting point, for the doctor does not treat "illness" but the patient who is ill. But the doctor approaches the individual through its essence (the "what" of humanity), for his medical art has knowledge of cures not solely for this individual, and not as separate. Indeed Aristotle goes farther: the essence or form as "immanent" is the active principle responsible for the being of the individual, and not solely for the knowledge of it. The Platonic forms come down from heaven to Earth, as "dynamic" principles that actualize the potential in a material substrate to become a certain being. (See *Metaphysics*, Book Nine.) The active form (the "what" as individualized) is the true being. Aristotle hereby claims to do justice to the Socratic-Platonic stress on the priority of form to matter, and also to the experiential or "commonsense" priority of the concrete individual.

Still this solution contains a profound ambiguity about what has ontological priority. The concrete individual is more than the active form or essence, as having a material aspect, and is what (unlike the form) clearly exists "on its own" in the world. But if we ask about what is most responsible for the coming into being of the individual, we have to turn to the form; this is what we have to think about in making the causality of the being intelligible. Mentally we must separate the form, in order to consider its causal action. This means that what we most understand about Socrates is "humanity" and not the unique individual Socrates. In our effort to make the individual intelligible, we have to regard it as the derivative product of active form and acted-upon matter. Accordingly there are two approaches to what is prior in being: for sense perception and to a great extent for practical action, the concrete individual ("this") is prior, and for thought and for most inquiry into causes, the form ("what") is prior. The point is not that Aristotle is confused but that this ontological ambiguity is, as he sees, the very nature of things. Further study of the *Metaphysics* and other writings reveals that this ambiguity runs through his inquiries and is connected to the duality of human nature as having both practical and speculative needs and inclinations. Philosophy in the genuine sense must be able to address both sides of that nature.

Descartes and the Beginning of Modern Metaphysics

After a long period of relative neglect, the philosophy of Aristotle attained preeminence in European society in the High Middle Ages, by way of translations and commentaries from Arabic scholars. Space does not allow us to discuss the vastly important and rich developments of Aristotelian and medieval philosophy leading to the modern period. A distinctively modern approach to questions of metaphysics and other sciences emerges in the sixteenth century. The names Niccolò Machiavelli, Martin Luther, and Nicolaus Copernicus will bring to mind that this was an era of great revolutions. Machiavelli initiates the approach to political life based on a bold unleashing of the passions and self-interest, abandoning the classical habituation of appetite to form civic virtue. His "realism" was appealing to many who sought effective means to end the miseries of conflict over religious doctrine. Sir Francis Bacon, the English philosopher and statesman, transcribes the lessons of Machiavellism into the study of nature. For just as the *politique* followers of Machiavelli seek to make the ground of political life neutral to doctrinal disputes and therefore metaphysics-free, Bacon thinks that natural philosophy can achieve hitherto unrealized certainty if "laws of action" governing natural processes can be established without the use of species and forms—those subjects of endless metaphysical perplexity.

Nature thus divested of formal perfections and ends is not primarily an object of contemplative interest. Like Machiavelli, Bacon doubts that reason has its own end, independent of the passions. Thus the new metaphysics-free "laws of nature" are viewed primarily as instruments for the practical advance of human power. Their "governance" of the phenomena enables our "mastery of nature." The rejection of formal and final causes (of "teleological" explanation) has immense theoretical and practical import. Modern physics and modern politics continue to this day to follow their parallel paths, in cooperative tandem, pursuing the satisfaction of the passions without concepts of the ultimate good and human perfection. In this we are also the heirs of Thomas Hobbes, the first thinker to develop a thoroughly nonteleological "physics" of moral and political life.

The question arose for René Descartes: what sort of metaphysics is compatible with the new account of nature? He earns the title "father of modern philosophy" through combining the new manner of investigating nature and human affairs with remarkable mathematical innovations, whereby he finds the way to new metaphysical principles of mind and body. His *Meditations of First Philosophy* (1640), written in the form of an Augustinian confessional treatise, gives the rather misleading impression that Descartes is chiefly a speculative thinker concerned with theological apologetics.

Doubtless he wanted the doctors of the Sorbonne to believe this, thereby to gain their stamp of approval for a new mode of thought whose real intent they did not see. But Descartes had given enough warnings a few years before, when he published some physical and mathematical treatises prefaced by an extraordinary autobiographical account of the origins and purpose of his philosophy, the *Discourse on Method.* Surely Descartes today would find it very amusing and even gratifying that scholars still tend to regard this *Discourse* as less "serious" philosophically than the *Meditations.* He was able to have his revolution without being seen (except by highly perceptive readers like Gottfried Wilhelm Leibniz and Jean d'Alembert) as a dangerous revolutionary.

The *Discourse*, especially when read in conjunction with the earlier unpublished "Rules for the Direction of the Mind," enables one to approach the metaphysical arguments of the *Meditations* with certain helpful points in mind. These include the intrinsic connection between metaphysical principles and two other fundamental concerns of Descartes: (1) the reduction of natural phenomena to the language of a new symbolic and constructive mathematics, the analytic geometry that supplies the basis for mathematicization of the motions of bodies in uniform homogeneous space ("extension"), which is the core of the famous Cartesian "method"; (2) the primacy of the resolve, or the steady willing, to undertake this reduction for the purpose of increasing human power or rendering us "like masters and possessors of nature." Once again the modern move toward nature divested of final causes in (1) is related to a new moral and political approach toward inquiry in (2). Metaphysics and physics (the roots and trunk of the tree of knowledge) are pursued for their practical fruits, as Descartes asserts in his *Principles of Philosophy*: these fruits are medicine, mechanics, and moral science which teaches us how to enjoy the passions.

The *Meditations* show how a new metaphysics of mind and body will support the project described. The revolution Descartes intends requires a drastic reorientation in thinking, away from the ordinary way we apprehend the world in terms of its sensible qualities. At the same time ancient philosophy is his target—above all, Aristotle, who found the evidence for the existence of species and form from the sensible appearance of things. The first act of Descartes in the *Meditations* is to place that sensible starting point in doubt; what he questions is the reliability of the body's mediation between thought and the world, a reliability assumed by both Aristotle and the ordinary man. This doubting is not a frivolous and gratuitous leap into extreme skepticism. It is a method for testing the reliability of beliefs and is motivated by the search for a foundation of knowledge that is immune to any possible defect: philosophical knowledge of the world and human beings must attain an ideal of mathematical certitude, an immovable "Archimedean point" forever impervious to the squabbles of disputatious metaphysicians. The presence of this ideal is indicated by the reflection on dreaming: even if Descartes cannot distinguish his waking thoughts about sensible objects from dream-images, he finds that mathematical propositions are still evidently true. Geometry can be pursued in one's sleep.

As another technique for testing the reliability of his opinions, Descartes introduces an omnipotent God who can cause him to be in error about all things, including mathematical truths. But immediately he replaces this deity with a less powerful "evil genius" who causes him to doubt all bodily things, but not mathematical truths. This is a significant shift and a clue to Descartes's purpose. Later in the *Meditations* Descartes proves the existence of God (which at one point he actually identifies with nature), whose primary function in the universe is to support Descartes's application of mathematics to the external world. Thus one can conclude that Descartes does not think there are any grounds for supposing the existence of a supreme power capable of undermining mathematical science.

Mathematical truth is "clear and distinct" knowledge, but it is not itself the end of inquiry. It says nothing about being. Descartes seeks an ontology that grounds the mathematical approach to the world as the sole legitimate approach. He needs to make propositions about "what is," propositions of a quite novel sort. It becomes evident through radical doubting that there is one proposition about being that cannot be doubted under any circumstances: "I think, therefore I exist." So long as I am thinking (even if the thinking is doubting), I as thinker must in some fashion exist. The soul—which in ancient-medieval philosophy combines cognitive, appetitive, and organic functions—is reduced to mere thinking, indeed the mere thought of "I." Yet the "I" as thinking on itself is able to generate mathematical ideas about nature. "Pure thought" reflecting on its possessions discovers the quantifiable notion of "extension" among its ideas: the infinite homogenous continuum to which the world of concrete sensible things can be reduced, stripped of all ordinary sensible qualities such as color, texture, and taste. The pure "I" contains the resources for the mathematical science of the world. Again one sees that Descartes's concerns are not merely speculative; the "I" thinking about itself is not an end in itself but the foundation for the expansive conquest of reality by mathematics.

Although the relation of the "I" to the body is initially unclear, Descartes is not uninterested in the body. In fact the doubt of the body's reliability is proof of Descartes's interest in attaining a better hold on it and other bodies. His point is that the mind as simply receptive to form (as is the Aristotelian intellect) is subject to the vicissitudes of nature or fortune; it is not master of its fate. Descartes's pure "I" is a new sort of intelligence: one in which thinking is identical with doing, even with making. "I think, I am, is necessarily true enough each time that I pronounce it, or that I mentally conceive it" (*Meditation II*). This is not timeless contemplation but temporally self-productive thinking. It is the core thought of modern metaphysics. The end or telos of thinking is not to remain separate from the world but to appropriate the world and reconstruct it on the mind's own terms. The mind superimposes on the "raw" matter of sensation its own self-generated plan of investigation. This was already Bacon's view of forcing nature to answer the questions we put to it in the "experiment"; later Kant takes this approach still farther.

Modernity, in rebellion against both Greek antiquity and revealed religion, is fundamentally seeking to free humanity from the fetters of nature, or at least to make nature's forces serve ends that humanity devises. To understand the motives for this epochal change, one must study the founders of modernity. Descartes's new account of the mind-body compound offers compensation, through its promise of mastery, for nature or God's failure to provide humankind with a good and beautiful cosmos.

Leibniz's Reform of Modern Metaphysics

Descartes's greatest critic is the German philosopher Leibniz, one of the most capacious intellects in human history. He grasps better than anyone in his age the intent of Descartes and addresses the true source of the difficulty in Descartes's project. At the same time Leibniz appreciates the virtues of the new mathematical science of nature, which he advances through his own pioneering work in infinitesimal analysis (calculus). The problem is not that Descartes neglects the body but that he misunderstands it. It is an error, Leibniz argues, to conceive the essence of body as extension, since extension is not anything remotely like a true being. It is lifeless, infinitely divisible, having merely mathematical qualities, and thus cannot have the unity of a genuine being, which must be grounded in some formal and purposive organization. Being or substance cannot exist where there is no unifying principle, and this requires a dynamic source of unification. In sum, Leibniz rediscovers the cogency of Aristotle's arguments for active form and even employs Aristotle's term *entelechy* (possessing within oneself the end or telos) to characterize substance.

Active form has to be reconciled with the new mathematical approach to nature. Since mathematical structure fails to account for the living *dynamis* directed toward more perfect states, it must be treated as derivative, not primary. Boldly Leibniz treats the entire realm of mathematicized nature as merely "phenomenal," and he grounds it in extensionless and imperceptible atomlike substances having active force, which he names monads. The relations between these—different from the causal relations that occur in space and time—give rise to the world of extended coporeality. The monads also contain the sources of perception and thought, since their active force seeks "expression" through achieving finer perceptions of other substances. Each monad reflects the entire universe and strives perpetually to amplify its relation with the infinity of substances composing the universe. Leibniz thus sees a way to conceive the world of bodies as akin in nature to thinking—something like "soul" gives form to matter—and to explain why the universe has more than quantitative features. Order and perfection are grounded in the dynamic essence of all things.

In this way Leibniz argues for a benevolent universe, against the grim visions of most of the leading thinkers of the new science of nature. The divine ground of things cannot be accused of negligence, ill will, or indifference toward the human desires for the good, the true, and the beautiful. An excellent plan for the order of the whole can be discerned through metaphysical inquiry (unassisted by revealed faith, it should be noted) and thus "theodicy," the justification of God's ways, is possible. "Reflections on the Common Concept of Justice" provides a popular statement of this theodicy, with a few glimpses of its metaphysical basis. Briefly it presents the central metaphysical idea: "The principle of action and of consciousness could not derive from a purely passive extended thing indifferent to all motion, as is matter. Therefore action and consciousness necessarily come from something simple and immaterial without extension and without parts, which is called the soul."

In this work Leibniz is most concerned with expounding the moral and political implications of his metaphysics. If nature or the principle that rules the whole (the "divine monarch") is not indifferent to goodness, justice has a natural ground besides the "right of the strongest." Human beings are then not, as in Hobbes, compelled by their solely self-preserving passions—the effect of nature as purely mechanical—to devise an artificial means for escaping the misery of the natural state of the "war of all against all." The rule of justice is that "one ought to prevent evil for another if it can be done conveniently." Justice includes charity as guided by prudent intellect: "Justice is the charity of the wise." In sum, Leibniz is the founder of the German speculative tradition endeavoring to reconcile the realms of matter and thought, nature and morality, and thus in important respects, antiquity and modernity.

Kant's Critical Restriction of Metaphysics

The next great metaphysical thinker after Leibniz is another German, Immanuel Kant, who is often regarded as the central figure in the entire modern philosophical epoch. Metaphysics is the problem at the heart of Kant's thought, in a peculiar double fashion. On the one hand, Kant seeks to restore the honor of metaphysics as the "architectonic science" after a series of powerful assaults on the possibility of metaphysic in the writings of John Locke and David Hume. The primary question is "whether metaphysics as a science is possible." The selected reading was written by Kant as an introduction to his great treatise on this problem, the *Critique of Pure Reason* (1781). On the other hand, Kant's renewal of metaphysics denies the possibility of knowledge of things in themselves, or things as they may exist apart from the framework of knowledge that the human mind supplies. This side of Kant's argument is directed against Plato and Leibniz, and denies that reason has access to any ultimate substances that ground the phenomenal world. Strictly speaking, we know only "phenomena": sensation as received by our sense organs and ordered by space, time, and categories of thought making possible the order in monadic substances Kant dismisses as illusion. Indeed all rational theology and rational psychology— knowledge of the essences of God and the soul—must be rejected as speculative failures.

Why, then, does Kant still call his inquiry a kind of metaphysics? Kant claims to have discovered that human reason possesses hither- to unknown sources for "pure" or "a priori" knowledge, that is, knowledge presupposed by any experience that makes use of notions such as space, time, causal connection, and substance as enduring substrate of change. This knowledge is grounded in something Kant terms "synthetic a priori judgments." Kant clearly distinguishes these from innate ideas, with which they are readily confused. He calls the mode of argument showing that such an a priori ground- ing of experience is possible a "transcendental argument."

One of the principal aims of Kant (as the reading selection makes plain) is to show that Hume's reduction of causal connection to a customary subjective association of impression is an error. Kant in opposing Hume could describe his own reasoning as a kind of meta- physics, for it establishes that causal connection, substance, and other metaphysical categories are objectively necessary, and not merely psychological facts, as they are for Hume. All the same, the metaphysics is based on a "Copernican revolution" wherein the cen- ter of cognition is moved from the object and placed in the synthetic activity of reason. "Hitherto it has been assumed that all our knowl- edge must conform to objects," but the transcendental philosophy shows that "objects must conform to our knowledge." Kant's enlargement of the synthetic powers of the mind to construct the general features of the world is also, not secondarily, employed in the moral realm. In addition to theoretical reason's legislation of the order of the laws of nature, there is practical reason's legislation of the laws of moral freedom, the principles under which the rational will exercises free causality unhindered by the laws of nature. Freedom is our one access to "things in themselves" ("noumena") beyond appearances. Indeed Kant claims that establishing the validity of moral reason is his most important accomplishment. Yet, as Kant avers in his personal papers, it was Jean-Jacques Rousseau who gave him the critical insight that moral freedom is the true "end of reason."

Hegel's Dialectical Completion of Metaphysics

Coming to maturity during the French Revolution and the new ascendancy of Kant's philosophy in the German universities, Georg Wilhelm Friedrich Hegel, together with some illustrious friends, sought to improve on the Kantian account of the synthetic power of reason by developing a more ambitious philosophy of freedom on its basis. Centrally he denies that reason has to limit itself to the knowledge of phenomena. Reason has insight into the Absolute, which combines features of the post-Cartesian subject-centered philosophy of the "I" with a more classical metaphysics that starts from being. Nearly all the leading minds of Hegel's generation were great enthusiasts of Greek antiquity and admired the "concreteness" of Hellenic education and culture, as contrasting favorably with the mathematical abstractness of modern thought and life. Hegel's mature philosophy could be characterized as a metaphysical working out of the tension between antiquity and modernity, and remains therefore a philosophy of profound interest to all persons reflecting on that tension and its meaning. But it is also one of the most difficult of all philosophies to make intelligible in a short introduction.

In Hegel's philosophy of the Absolute the characteristically modern opposition of subject and object is progressively overcome through a temporal process that at every level makes use of the Aristotelian notions of potentiality (*dynamis*) and actuality (*energeia*). But Aristotle's concepts are now understood, in a very un-Aristotelian way, as applying to the whole historical development of humanity, and not solely to natural beings. In the last analysis the Greeks for Hegel did not appreciate the true elevation of spirit above nature, which humanity (with crucial help from Christianity) had to discover through 'long and painful exertions. The realization of the truth of spirit takes the form of a dialectical logic radically unlike traditional formal logic. Its concepts unfold in a process of self-differentiation, wherein moments of experience or thought that appear initially as merely independent or immediate are discovered—through a special Hegelian sense of negation—to be actually dependent or mediated aspects of the whole. The entire development is one that moves from an abstract level of thought toward maximum concreteness. In other terms, the Absolute at the start is merely with itself in undifferentiated unity, but in producing the manifold distinction of reality in both nature and human history, it recognizes itself in the other which it has produced. When all distinctions have unfolded and the Absolute finds itself fully manifest in the world, it then fulfills its essence in "absolute knowing." No "otherness" remains outside itself to be overcome through further negations, and the complete reality of freedom—mind being at home with itself—is attained.

Hegel argues that this logical completion corresponds to the moment in human history when political and moral freedom attain stable recognition institutionally, and art, religion, and philosophy arrive at their definitive forms. This is the moment of the present age. The history of philosophy can show that all previous philosophies contribute to the completion of the system that embraces all reality. Thus in Hegel's conception of history the thought of any earlier epoch has limitations defined by its moment in the process. Hegel does not regard his own system, however, as subject to such a historical limitation, since it is the permanently valid expression of the final truth about being. All the same, Hegel's emphasis on the historical conditioning of the unfolding of truth was a major source of the historicism of many later thinkers, who no longer accept Hegel's metaphysics of the Absolute but regard all thought as bound to history without any suprahistorical remainder.

Metaphysics in the Twentieth Century

After Hegel there is no philosopher who presents such an impressive system of the whole of being. In fact, immediately after Hegel's death in 1831 German philosophy took a sharp turn toward anti-speculative and materialistic forms, a tendency that was only somewhat corrected by the revival of Kantian philosophy at mid-century, and some renewal of Hegelianism at the century's end. Outside academic philosophy there were isolated figures, such as the Dane Søren Kierkegaard and Friedrich Nietzsche, who rejected all forms of traditional argumentative and logical procedure in philosophy. These figures proved to be decisive for the twentieth century. There arose around 1900 the movement of phenomenology under the guidance of Edmund Husserl, which sought to give new vitality to philosophy by stressing the need to turn to the prescientific phenomena of ordinary life, and to describe them without reliance on scientific assumptions. This "suspension" of scientific thought allowed a new openness to problems and traditions considered dead or irrelevant, and after the First World War it inspired many remarkable inquiries in theology, ethics, political philosophy, aesthetics, and classical philology. But perhaps most striking and unexpected was its contribution to metaphysics in Martin Heidegger's renewal of the "question of Being." This combined in a startling fashion a deeply probing recovery of Greek philosophical texts with a radically anti-academic account of the human existential situation (as anxiety in the face of death) that was shaped by Heidegger's reading of Kierkegaard and Nietzsche, and by the mood of crisis following the disastrous world war.

We must limit ourselves to a few remarks on Heidegger, who no doubt is the greatest metaphysical thinker since Hegel. Heidegger understands Being in a radically temporal and historical way (recalling Hegel), but as lacking a logical and articulable structure (unlike Hegel's logic of the Absolute). As the unfolding "openness to beings" or "unconcealment of beings" constituting the humanness of human life, Being is the hidden and elusive ground of all that is speakable and thinkable. Being is the groundless ground. It is not groundable in any natures or essences of things, the emphasis on which in Western metaphysics has only concealed—or caused "forgetting" of—Being's act of unconcealment. But to the proper attunement of mind, Being is manifest in language, above all that of great poets who attest to the futility of mortal strivings—reaching their critical phase in modern technology—to ground permanent "dwellings."

We have not included any selection from Heidegger, since a short reading from him is unlikely to be very helpful. But another figure has been selected, Ludwig Wittgenstein, whose effect on twentieth-century philosophy, chiefly in the English-speaking countries, is almost as great as Heidegger's. Indeed his affinities with Heidegger are striking, although the two thinkers had no contact. After beginning as a leading figure in the logical positivist movement, which regarded scientific thought as disclosing that all metaphysics is nonsense, Wittgenstein pursued a very different philosophical path. He turned to ordinary language as an unsystematizable, never fully clarifiable realm of ritual-like practices ("language games") that determine meaning. Rather like Heidegger, the later Wittgenstein regards truth as manifest in particular and local languages that are not explicable in terms of general laws (sciences of linguistic or mental activity). In significant accord with the phenomenological movement, Wittgenstein sees physiological accounts of the mind as a prevalent form of error, reducing the complex activity of thinking to the presence of mental entities (images, etc.). For Wittgenstein the attraction of finding causal mechanisms to account for thought is the primary source of all metaphysics. "Philosophers constantly see the method of science before their eyes, and are irresistibly tempted to ask and answer questions in the way science does."

Heidegger and Wittgenstein have advanced our insight into the blindnesses and errors of scientific reductionism and modern thought, and they (especially Heidegger) have enabled us to read the great thinkers of the past with new questions. But it is questionable that they have also succeeded, as they claim, to overcome all previous metaphysics. Nevertheless, their thoughts have inspired the many "postmodernist" and "postphilosophical" movements of our time. We must resist the impulse to greet recent declarations of the "end of metaphysics" with approval. The questions of metaphysics remain, as ever, to be further examined. Indeed, they remain to be understood.

METAPHYSICS
by
ARISTOTLE

Book Four (Γ)

1. There is a science which investigates being as being and the attributes which belong to this in virtue of its own nature. Now this is not the same as any of the so-called special sciences; for none of these others deals generally with being as being. They cut out a part of being and investigate the attributes of this part—this is what the mathematical sciences for instance do. Now since we are seeking the first principles and the highest causes, clearly there must be some thing to which these belong in virtue of its own nature. If then our predecessors who sought the elements of existing things were seeking these same principles, it is necessary that the elements must be elements of being not by accident but just because it *is* being. Therefore it is of being as being that we also must grasp the first causes.

2. There are many senses in which a thing may be said to "be," but they are related to one central point, one definite kind of thing, and are not homonymous. Everything which is healthy is related to health, one thing in the sense that it preserves health, another in the sense that it produces it, another in the sense that it is a symptom of health, another because it is capable of it. And that which is medical is relative to the medical art, one thing in the sense that it possesses it, another in the sense that it is naturally adapted to it, another in the sense that it is a function of the medical art. And we shall find other words used similarly to these. So, too, there are many senses in which a thing is said to be, but all refer to one starting-point; some things are said to be because they are substances, others because they are affections of substance, others because they are a process towards substance, or destructions or privations or qualities of substance, or productive or generative of substance, or of things which are relative to substance, or negations of some of these things

or of substance itself. It is for this reason that we say even of non-being that it *is* non-being. As, then, there is one science which deals with all healthy things, the same applies in the other cases also. For not only in the case of things which have one common notion does the investigation belong to one science, but also in the case of things which are related to one common nature; for even these in a sense have one common notion. It is clear then that it is the work of one science also to study all things that are, *qua* being.—But everywhere science deals chiefly with that which is primary, and on which the other things depend, and in virtue of which they get their names. If, then, this is substance, it is of substances that the philosopher must grasp the principles and the causes.

Now for every single class of things, as there is one perception, so there is one science, as for instance grammar, being one science, investigates all articulate sounds. Therefore to investigate all the species of being *qua* being, is the work of a science which is generically one, and to investigate the several species is the work of the specific parts of the science.

If, now, being and unity are the same and are one thing in the sense that they are implied in one another as principle and cause are, not in the sense that they are explained by the same formula (though it makes no difference even if we interpret them similarly—in fact this would strengthen our case); for one man and a man are the same thing and existent man and a man are the same thing, and the doubling of the words in "one man" and "one existent man" does not give any new meaning (it is clear that they are not separated either in coming to be or in ceasing to be); and similarly with "one," so that it is obvious that the addition in these cases means the same thing, and unity is nothing apart from being; and if, further, the essence of each thing is one in no merely accidental way, and similarly is from its very nature something that *is*:—all this being so, there must be exactly as many species of being as of unity. And to investigate the essence of these is the work of a science which is generically one—I mean, for instance, the discussion of the same and the similar and the other concepts of this sort; and nearly all contraries are referred to this source; but let us take them as having been investigated in the "Selection of Contraries."—And there are as many parts of philosophy as there are kinds of substance, so that there must necessarily be among them a first philosophy and one which follows this. For being falls immediately into genera; and therefore the sciences too will correspond to these genera. For "philosopher" is like "mathematician"; for mathematics also has parts, and there is a first and a second science and other successive ones within the sphere of mathematics.

Now since it is the work of one science to investigate opposites, and plurality is opposite to unity, and it belongs to one science to investigate the negation and the privation because in both cases we are really investigating unity, to which the negation or the privation refers (for we either say simply that unity is not present, or that it is not present in some particular class; in the latter case the characteristic difference of the class modifies the meaning of "unity," as compared with the meaning conveyed in the bare negation; for the negation means just the absence of unity, while in privation there is also implied an underlying nature of which the privation is predicated),—in view of all these facts, the contraries of the concepts we named above, the other and the dissimilar and the unequal, and everything else which is derived either from these or from plurality and unity, must fall within the province of the science above-named.—And contrariety is one of these concepts, for contrariety is a kind of difference, and difference is a kind of otherness. Therefore, since there are many senses in which a thing is said to be one, these terms also will have many senses, but yet it belongs to one science to consider them all; for a term belongs to different sciences not if it has different senses, but if its definitions neither are identical nor can be referred to one central meaning. And since all things are referred to that which is primary, as for instance all things which are one are referred to the primary one, we must say that this holds good also of the same and the other and of contraries in general; so that after distinguishing the various senses of each, we must then explain by reference to what is primary in each term, saying how they are related to it; some in the sense that they possess it, others in the sense that they produce it, and others in other such ways. . . .

3. We must state whether it belongs to one or to different sciences to inquire into the truths which are in mathematics called axioms, and into substance. Evidently the inquiry into these also belongs to one science, and that is the science of the philosopher; for these truths hold good for everything that is, and not for some special

genus apart from others. And all men use them, for they are true of being *qua* being, and each genus has being. But men use them just so far as to satisfy their purposes; that is, as far as the genus, whose attributes they are proving, extends. Therefore since these truths clearly hold good for all things *qua* being (for this is what is common to them), he who studies being *qua* being will inquire into them too.—And for this reason no one who is conducting a special inquiry tries to say anything about their truth or falsehood,—neither the geometer nor the arithmetician. Some natural philosophers indeed have done so, and their procedure was intelligible enough; for they thought that they alone were inquiring about the whole of nature and of being. But since there is one kind of thinker who is even above the natural philosopher (for nature is only one particular genus of being), the discussion of these truths also will belong to him whose inquiry is universal and deals with primary substance. Natural science also is a kind of wisdom, but it is not the first kind.—And the attempts of some who discuss the terms on which truth should be accepted, are due to a want of training in logic; for they should know these things already when they come to a special study, and not be inquiring into them while they are pursuing it.— Evidently then the philosopher, who is studying the nature of all substance, must inquire also into the principles of deduction.

But he who knows best about each genus must be able to state the most certain principles of his subject, so that he whose subject is being *qua* being must be able to state the most certain principles of all things. This is the philosopher, and the most certain principle of all is that regarding which it is impossible to be mistaken; for such a principle must be both the best known (for all men may be mistaken about things which they do not know), and non-hypothetical. For a principle which every one must have who knows anything about being, is not a hypothesis; and that which every one must know who knows anything, he must already have when he comes to a special study. Evidently then such a principle is the most certain of all; which principle this is, we proceed to say. It is, that the same attribute cannot at the same time belong and not belong to the same subject in the same respect; we must presuppose, in face of dialectical objections, any further qualifications which might be added. This, then, is the most certain of all principles, since it answers to the definition given above. For it is impossible for any one to believe the same thing to be and not to be, as some think Heraclitus says; for what a man says he does not necessarily believe. If it is impossible that contrary attributes should belong at the same time to the same subject (the usual qualifications must be presupposed in this proposition too), and if an opinion which contradicts another is contrary to it, obviously it is impossible for the same man at the same time to believe the same thing to be and not to be; for if a man were mistaken in this point he would have contrary opinions at the same time. It is for this reason that all who are carrying out a demonstration refer it to this as an ultimate belief; for this is naturally the starting-point even for all the other axioms.

4. There are some who, as we have said, both themselves assert that it is possible for the same thing to be and not to be, and say that people can judge this to be the case. And among others many writers about nature use this language. But we have now posited that it is impossible for anything at the same time to be and not to be, and by this means have shown that this is the most indisputable of all principles.—Some indeed demand that even this shall be demonstrated, but this they do through want of education, for not to know of what things one may demand demonstration, and of what one may not, argues simply want of education. For it is impossible that there should be demonstration of absolutely everything; there would be an infinite regress, so that there would still be no demonstration. But if there are things of which one should not demand demonstration, these persons cannot say what principle they regard as more indemonstrable than the present one.

We can, however, demonstrate negatively even that this view is impossible, if our opponent will only say something; and if he says nothing, it is absurd to attempt to reason with one who will not reason about anything, in so far as he refuses to reason. For such a man, as such, is seen already to be no better than a mere plant. Now negative demonstration I distinguish from demonstration proper, because in a demonstration one might be thought to be assuming what is at issue, but if another person is responsible for the assumption we shall have negative proof, not demonstration. The starting-point for all such arguments is not the demand that our opponent shall say that something either is or is not (for this one might perhaps take to be assuming what is at issue), but that he shall say something which is significant both for himself and for another; for this is necessary, if he really is to say anything. For, if he means nothing, such a man will not be capable of reasoning, either with himself or with another. But if any one grants this, demonstration will be possible; for we shall already have something definite. The person responsible for the proof, however, is not he who demonstrates but he who listens; for while disowning reason he listens to reason. And again he who admits this has admitted that something is true apart from demonstration [so that not everything will be "so and not so"].

First then this at least is obviously true, that the word "be" or "not be" has a definite meaning, so that not everything will be so and not so.—Again, if "man" has one meaning, let this be "two-footed animal"; by having one meaning I understand this: if such and such is a man, then if anything is a man, that will be what being a man is. And it makes no difference even if one were to say a word has several meanings, if only they are limited in number; for to each formula there might be assigned a different word. For instance, we might say that "man" has not one meaning but several, one of which would be defined as "two-footed animal," while there might be also several other formulae if only they were limited in number; for a special name might be assigned to each of the formulae. If, however, they were not limited but one were to say that the word has an infinite number of meanings, obviously reasoning would be impossible; for not to have one meaning is to have no meaning, and if words have no meaning reasoning with other people, and indeed with oneself has been annihilated; for it is impossible to think of anything if we do not think of one thing; but if this *is* possible, one name might be assigned to this thing. Let it be assumed then, as was said at the beginning, that the name has a meaning and has one meaning; it is impossible, then, that being a man should mean precisely not being a man, if "man" is not only predicable of one subject but also has one meaning (for we do not identify "having one meaning" with "being predicable of one subject," since on that assumption even "musical" and "white" and "man" would have had one meaning, so that all things would have been one; for they would all have been synonymous).

And it will not be possible for the same thing to be and not to be, except in virtue of an ambiguity, just as one whom we call "man," others might call "not-man"; but the point in question is not this, whether the same thing can at the same time be and not be a man in name, but whether it can in fact. Now if "man" and "not-man" mean nothing different, obviously "not being a man" will mean nothing different from "being a man"; so that being a man will be not being a man; for they will be one. For being one means this— what we find in the case of "raiment" and "dress"—viz. that the definitory formula is one. And if "being a man" and "not being a man" are to be one, they must mean one thing. But it was shown earlier that they mean different things. Therefore, if it is true to say of anything that it is a man, it must be a two-footed animal; for this was what "man" meant; and if this is necessary, it is impossible that the same thing should not be a two-footed animal; for this is what "being necessary" means—that it is impossible for the thing not to be. It is then, impossible that it should be at the same time true to say the same thing is a man and is not a man.

The same account holds good with regard to not being man, for "being man" and "being not-man" mean different things, since even "being white" and "being man" are different; for the former terms are much more opposed, so that they must mean different things. And if any one says that "white" means one and the same thing as "man," again we shall say the same as what was said before, that it would follow that *all* things are one, and not only opposites. But if this is impossible, then what has been said will follow, if our opponent answers our question.

And if, when one asks the question simply, he adds the contradictories, he is not answering the question. For there is nothing to prevent the same thing from being both man and white and countless other things: but still if one asks whether it is true to call this a man or not our opponent must give an answer which means one thing, and not add that it is also white and large. For, besides other reasons, it is impossible to enumerate the accidents, which are infinite in number; let him, then, enumerate either all or none. Similarly, therefore, even if the same thing is a thousand times man and not-man, we must not add, in answering the question whether this is a man, that it is also at the same time not a man, unless we are bound to add also all the other accidents, all that the subject is or is not; and if we do this, we are not observing the rules of argument.

And in general those who use this argument do away with substance and essence. For they must say that all attributes are accidents, and that there is no such thing as being essentially man or animal. For if there is to be any such thing as being essentially man this will not be being not-man or not being man (yet these are negations of it); for there was some one thing which it meant, and this was the substance of something. And denoting the substance of a thing means that the essence of the thing is nothing else. But if its being essentially man is to be the same as either being essentially not-man or essentially not being man, then its essence *will* be something else. Therefore our opponents must say that there cannot be such a definition of anything, but that all attributes are accidental; for this is the distinction between substance and accident—white is accidental to man, because though he is white, whiteness is not his essence. But if *all* statements are accidental, there will be nothing primary about which they are made, if the accidental always implies predication about a subject. The predication, then, must go on *ad infinitum*. But this is impossible; for not even more than two terms can be combined. For an accident is not an accident of an accident, unless it be because both are accidents of the same subject. I mean, for instance, the white is musical and the latter is white, only because both are accidental to man. But Socrates is musical, not in this sense, that both terms are accidental to something else. Since then some predicates are accidental in this and some in that sense, those which are accidental in the latter sense, in which white is accidental to Socrates, cannot form an infinite series in the upward direction, e.g., Socrates the white has not yet another accident; for no unity can be got out of such a sum. Nor again will white have another term accidental to it, e.g., musical. For this is no more accidental to that than that is to this; and at the same time we have drawn the distinction, that while some predicates are accidental in this sense, others are so in the sense in which musical is accidental to Socrates; and the accident is an accident of an accident not in cases of the latter kind, but only in cases of the other kind, so that not *all* terms will be accidental. There must, then, even in this case be something which denotes substance. And it has been shown that, if this is so, contradictories cannot be predicated at the same time. . . .

Book Seven (Z)

1. There are several senses in which a thing may be said to be, as we pointed out previously in our book on the various senses of words; for in one sense it means what a thing is or a "this," and in another sense it means that a thing is of a certain quality or quantity or has some such predicate asserted of it. While "being" has all these senses, obviously that which is primarily is the "what," which indicates the substance of the thing. For when we say of what quality a thing is, we say that it is good or beautiful, but not that it is three cubits long or that it is a man; but when we say *what* it is, we do not say "white" or "hot" or "three cubits long," but "man" or "God." And all other things are said to be because they are, some of them, quantities of that which *is* in this primary sense, others qualities of it, others affections of it, and others some other determination of it. And so one might raise the question whether "to walk" and "to be healthy" and "to sit" signify in each case something that is, and similarly in any other case of this sort; for none of them is either self-subsistent or capable of being separated from substance, but rather, if anything, it is that which walks or is seated or is healthy that is an existent thing. Now these are seen to be more real because there is something definite which underlies them; and this is the substance or individual, which is implied in such a predicate; for "good" or "sitting" are not used without this. Clearly then it is in virtue of this category that each of the others *is*. Therefore that which is primarily and *is* simply (not is something) must be substance.

Now there are several senses in which a thing is said to be primary; but substance is primary in every sense—in formula, in order of knowledge, in time. For of the other categories none can exist independently, but only substance. And in formula also this is primary; for in the formula of each term the formula of its substance must be present. And we think we know each thing most fully, when we know what it is, e.g., what man is or what fire is, rather than when we know its quality, its quantity, or where it is; since we know each of these things also, only when we know *what* the quantity or the quality *is*.

And indeed the question which, both now and of old, has always been raised, and always been the subject of doubt, viz. what being is, is just the question, what is substance? For it is this that some assert to be one, others more than one, and that some assert to be limited in number, others unlimited. And so we also must consider chiefly and primarily and almost exclusively what that is which *is* in this sense.

2. Substance is thought to belong most obviously to bodies; and so we say that both animals and plants and their parts are substances, and so are natural bodies such as fire and water and earth and everything of the sort, and all things that are parts of these or composed of these (either of parts or of the whole bodies), e.g., the heaven and its parts, stars and moon and sun. But whether these alone are substances, or there are also others, or only some of these, or some of these and some other things are substances, or none of these but only some other things, must be considered. Some think the limits of body, i.e., surface, line, point, and unit, are substances, and more so than body or the solid. Further, some do not think there is anything substantial besides sensible things, but others think there are eternal substances which are more in number and more real, e.g., Plato posited two kinds of substance—the Forms and the objects of mathematics—as well as a third kind, viz. the substance of sensible bodies. And Speusippus made still more kinds of substance, beginning with the One, and making principles for each kind of substance, one for numbers, another for spatial magnitudes, and then another for the soul; and in this way he multiplies the kinds of substance. And some say Forms and numbers have the same nature, and other things come after them, e.g., lines and planes, until we come to the substance of the heavens and to sensible bodies.

Regarding these matters, then, we must inquire which of the common statements are right and which are not right, and what things are substances, and whether there are or are not any besides sensible substances, and how sensible substances exist, and whether there is a separable substance (and if so why and how) or there is no substance separable from sensible substances; and we must first sketch the nature of substance.

3. The word "substance" is applied, if not in more senses, still at least to four main objects; for both the essence and the universal and the genus are thought to be the substance of each thing, and fourthly the substratum. Now the substratum is that of which other things are

predicated, while it is itself not predicated of anything else. And so we must first determine the nature of this; for that which underlies a thing primarily is thought to be in the truest sense its substance. And in one sense matter is said to be of the nature of substratum, in another, shape, and in a third sense, the compound of these. By the matter I mean, for instance, the bronze, by the shape the plan of its form, and by the compound of these (the concrete thing) the statue. Therefore if the form is prior to the matter and more real, it will be prior to the compound also for the same reason. . . .

Book Nine (Θ)

1. We have treated of that which *is* primarily and to which all the other categories of being are referred—i.e., of substance. For it is in virtue of the formula of substance that the others are said to be— quantity and quality and the like; for all will be found to contain the formula of substance, as we said in the first part of our work. And since "being" is in one way divided into "what," quality, and quantity, and is in another way distinguished in respect of potentiality and fulfillment, and of function, let us discuss potentiality and fulfillment. First let us explain potentiality in the strictest sense, which is, however, not the most useful for our present purpose. For potentiality and actuality extend further than the mere sphere of motion. But when we have spoken of this first kind, we shall in our discussions of actuality explain the other kinds of potentiality.

We have pointed out elsewhere that "potentiality" and the word "can" have several senses. Of these we may neglect all the potentialities that are so called homonomously. For some are called so by analogy, as in geometry; and we say things can be or cannot be because in some definite way they are or are not.

But all potentialities that conform to the same type are starting-points, and are called potentialities in reference to one primary kind, which is a starting-point of change in another thing or in the thing itself *qua* other. For one kind is a potentiality for being acted on, i.e., the principle in the very thing acted on, which makes it capable of being changed and acted on by another thing or by itself regarded as other; and another kind is a state of insusceptibility to change for the worse and to destruction by another thing or by the thing itself *qua* other, i.e., by a principle of change. In all these definitions is contained the formula of potentiality in the primary sense.—And again these so-called potentialities are potentialities either of acting merely or of being acted on, or of acting or being acted on *well*, so that even in the formulae of the latter the formulae of the prior kinds of potentiality are somehow contained.

Obviously, then, in a sense the potentiality of acting and of being acted on is one (for a thing may be capable either because it can be acted on or because something else can be acted on by it), but in a sense the potentialities are different. For the one is in the thing acted on; it is because it contains a certain motive principle, and because even the matter is a motive principle, that the thing acted on is acted on, one thing by one, another by another; for that which is oily is inflammable, and that which yields in a particular way can be crushed; and similarly in all other cases. But the other potentiality is in the agent, e.g., heat and the art of building are present, one in that which can produce heat and the other in the man who can build. And so in so far as a thing is an organic unity, it cannot be acted on by itself; for it is one and not two different things. And want of potentiality, or powerlessness, is the privation which is contrary to potentiality of this sort, so that every potentiality belongs to the same subject and refers to the same process as a corresponding want of potentiality. Privation has several senses; for it means that which has not a certain quality and that which might naturally have it but has not got it, either in general of when it might naturally have it, and either in some particular way, e.g., when it *completely* fails to have it, or when it in any degree fails to have it. And in certain cases if things which naturally have a quality lose it by violence, we say they suffer privation.

2. Since some such principles are present in soulless things, and others in things possessed of soul, and in soul and in the rational part of the soul, clearly some potentialities will be non-rational and some will be accompanied by reason. This is why all arts, i.e., all productive forms of knowledge, are potentialities; they are principles of change in another thing or in the artist himself considered as other.

And each of those which are accompanied by reason is alike capable of contrary effects, but one non-rational power produces one effect; e.g., the hot is capable only of heating, but the medical art can produce both disease and health. The reason is that science is a rational formula, and the same rational formula explains a thing and its privation, only not in the same way; and in a sense it applies to both, but in a sense it applies rather to the positive fact. Therefore such sciences must deal with contraries, but with one in virtue of their own nature and with the other not in virtue of their nature; for the rational formula applies to one object in virtue of that object's nature, and to the other, in a sense, accidentally. For it is by denial and removal that it explains the contrary; for the contrary is the primary privation, and this is the entire removal of the positive term. Now since on the one hand contraries do not occur in the same thing, but on the other hand science is a potentiality which depends on the possession of a rational formula, and the soul possesses a principle of movement; therefore, on the other hand, the healthy produces only health and what can heat only heat and what can cool only cold, but the scientific man, on the other hand, produces both the contrary effects. For there is a rational formula which applies to both, though not in the same way, and it is in a soul which possesses a principle of movement; so that the soul will start both processes from the same principle, applying them to the same object. And so the things whose potentiality is according to a rational formula act contrariwise to the things whose potentiality is non-rational; for the products of the former are included under one principle, the rational formula.

It is obvious also that the potentiality of merely doing a thing or having it done to one is implied in that of doing it or having it done *well*, but the latter is not always implied in the former: for he who does a thing well must do it, but he who does it merely need not do it well.

3. There are some who say, as the Megaric school does, that a thing can act only when it is acting, and when it is not acting it cannot act, e.g., he who is not building cannot build, but only he who is building, when he is building; and so in all other cases. It is not hard to see the absurdities that attend this view.

For it is clear that on this view a man will not be a builder unless he is building (for to be a builder is to be able to build), and so with the other arts. If, then, it is impossible to have such arts if one has not at some time learnt and acquired them, and it is then impossible not to have them if one has not sometime lost them (either by forgetfulness or by some accident or by time; for it cannot be by the destruction of the object itself, for that lasts for ever), a man will not have the art when he has ceased to use it, and yet he may immediately build again; how then will he have got the art? And similarly with regard to lifeless things; nothing will be either cold or hot or sweet or perceptible at all if people are not perceiving it; so that the upholders of this view will have to maintain the doctrine of Protagoras. But, indeed, nothing will even have perception if it is not perceiving, i.e., exercising its perception. If, then, that is blind which has not sight though it would naturally have it, when it would naturally have it and when it still exists, the same people will be blind many times in the day—and deaf too.

Again, if that which is deprived of potentiality is incapable, that which is not happening will be incapable of happening; but he who says of that which is incapable of happening that it is or will be will say what is untrue; for this is what incapacity meant. Therefore these views do away with both movement and becoming. For that which stands will always stand, and that which sits will always sit; if it is sitting it will not get up; for that which cannot get up will be incapable of getting up. But we cannot say this, so that evidently potentiality and actuality are different; but these views make potentiality and actuality the same, so that it is no small thing they are seeking to annihilate.

Therefore it is possible that a thing may be capable of being and not *be*, and capable of not being and yet *be*, and similarly with the other kinds of predicate; it may be capable of walking and yet not walk, or capable of not walking and yet walk. And a thing is capable of doing something if there is nothing impossible in its having the actuality of that of which it is said to have the capacity. I mean for instance, if a thing is capable of sitting and it is open to it to sit, there will be nothing impossible in its actually sitting; and similarly if it is capable of being moved or moving or of standing or making to stand or of being or coming to be, or of not being or not coming to be. . . .

from

MEDITATIONS ON THE FIRST PHILOSOPHY IN WHICH THE EXISTENCE OF GOD AND THE DISTINCTION BETWEEN MIND AND BODY ARE DEMONSTRATED

by

RENÉ DESCARTES

Meditation I

Of the things which may be brought within the sphere of the doubtful

It is now some years since I detected how many were the false beliefs that I had from my earliest youth admitted as true, and how doubtful was everything I had since constructed on this basis; and from that time I was convinced that I must once for all seriously undertake to rid myself of all the opinions which I had formerly accepted, and commence to build anew from the foundation, if I wanted to establish any firm and permanent structure in the sciences. But as this enterprise appeared to be a very great one, I waited until I had attained an age so mature that I could not hope that at any later date I should be better fitted to execute my design. This reason caused me to delay so long that I should feel that I was doing wrong were I to occupy in deliberation the time that yet remains to me for action. To-day, then, since very opportunely for the plan I have in view I have delivered my mind from every care [and am happily agitated by no passions] and since I have procured for myself an assured leisure in a peaceable retirement, I shall at last seriously and freely address myself to the general upheaval of all my former opinions.

Now for this object it is not necessary that I should show that all of these are false—I shall perhaps never arrive at this end. But inasmuch as reason already persuades me that I ought no less carefully to withhold my assent from matters which are not entirely certain and indubitable from those which appear to me manifestly to be false, if I am able to find in each one some reason to doubt, this will suffice to justify my rejecting the whole. And for that end it will not be requisite that I should examine each in particular, which would be an endless undertaking; for owing to the fact that the destruction of the foundations of necessity brings with it the downfall of the rest of the edifice, I shall only in the first place attack those principles upon which all my former opinions rested.

All that up to the present time I have accepted as most true and certain I have learned either from the senses or through the senses; but it is sometimes proved to me that these senses are deceptive, and it is wiser not to trust entirely to any thing by which we have once been deceived.

But it may be that although the senses sometimes deceive us concerning things which are hardly perceptible, or very far away, there are yet many others to be met with as to which we cannot reasonably have any doubt, although we recognise them by their means. For example, there is the fact that I am here, seated by the fire, attired in a dressing gown, having this paper in my hands and other similar matters. And how could I deny that these hands and this body are mine, were it not perhaps that I compare myself to certain persons, devoid of sense, whose cerebella are so troubled and clouded by the violent vapours of black bile, that they constantly assure us that they think they are kings when they are really quite poor, or that they are clothed in purple when they are really without covering, or who imagine that they have an earthenware head or are nothing but pumpkins or are made of glass. But they are mad, and I should not be any the less insane were I to follow examples so extravagant.

At the same time I must remember that I am a man, and that consequently I am in the habit of sleeping, and in my dreams representing to myself the same things or sometimes even less probable things, than do those who are insane in their waking moments. How often has it happened to me that in the night I dreamt that I found myself in this particular place, that I was dressed and seated near the fire, whilst in reality I was lying undressed in bed! At this moment it does indeed seem to me that it is with eyes awake that I am looking at this paper; that this head which I move is not asleep, that it is deliberately and of set purpose that I extend my hand and perceive it; what happens in sleep does not appear so clear nor so distinct as does all this. But in thinking over this I remind myself that on many occasions I have in sleep been deceived by similar illusions, and in dwelling carefully on this reflection I see so manifestly that there are no certain indications by which we may clearly distinguish wakefulness from sleep that I am lost in astonishment. And my astonishment is such that it is almost capable of persuading me that I now dream.

Now let us assume that we are asleep and that all these particulars, e.g., that we open our eyes, shake our head, extend our hands, and so on, are but false delusions; and let us reflect that possibly neither our hands nor our whole body are such as they appear to us to be. At the same time we must at least confess that the things which are represented to us in sleep are like painted representations which can only have been formed as the counterparts of something real and true, and that in this way those general things at least, i.e., eyes, a head, hands, and a whole body, are not imaginary things, but things really existent. For, as a matter of fact, painters, even when they study with the greatest skill to represent sirens and satyrs by forms the most strange and extraordinary, cannot give them natures which are entirely new, but merely make a certain medley of the members of different animals; or if their imagination is extravagant enough to invent something so novel that nothing similar has ever before been seen, and that then their work represents a thing purely fictitious and absolutely false, it is certain all the same that the colours of which this is composed are necessarily real. And for the same reason, although these general things, to wit, [a body], eyes, a head, hands, and such like, may be imaginary, we are bound at the same time to confess that there are at least some other objects yet more simple and more universal, which are real and true; and of these just in the same way as with certain real colours, all these images of things which dwell in our thoughts, whether true and real or false and fantastic, are formed.

To such a class of things pertains corporeal nature in general, and its extension, the figure of extended things, their quantity or magnitude and number, as also the place in which they are, the time which measures their duration, and so on.

That is possibly why our reasoning is not unjust when we conclude from this that Physics, Astronomy, Medicine and all other sciences which have as their end the consideration of composite things, are very dubious and uncertain; but that Arithmetic, Geometry and other sciences of that kind which only treat of things that are very simple and very general, without taking great trouble to ascertain whether they are actually existent or not, contain some measure of certainty and an element of the indubitable. For whether I am awake or asleep, two and three together always form five, and the square can never have more than four sides, and it does not seem possible that truths so clear and apparent can be suspected of any falsity [or uncertainty].

Nevertheless I have long had fixed in my mind the belief that an all-powerful God existed by whom I have been created such as I am. But how do I know that He has not brought it to pass that there is no earth, no heaven, no extended body, no magnitude, no place, and that nevertheless [I possess the perceptions of all these things and that] they seem to me to exist just exactly as I now see them? And, besides, as I sometimes imagine that others deceive themselves in the things which they think they know best, how do I know that I am not deceived every time that I add two and three, or count the sides of a square, or judge of things yet simpler, if anything simpler can be imagined? But possibly God has not desired that I should be thus deceived, for He is said to be supremely good. If, however, it is contrary to His goodness to have made me such that I constantly deceive myself, it would also appear to be contrary to His goodness to permit me to be sometimes deceived, and nevertheless I cannot doubt that He does permit this.

There may indeed be those who would prefer to deny the existence of a God so powerful, rather than believe that all other things are uncertain. But let us not oppose them for the present, and grant that all that is here said of a God is a fable; nevertheless in whatever way they suppose that I have arrived at the state of being that I have reached—whether they attribute it to fate or to accident, or make out that it is by a continual succession of antecedents, or by some other method—since to err and deceive oneself is a defect, it is clear that the greater will be the probability of my being so imperfect as to deceive myself ever, as is the Author to whom they assign my origin the less powerful. To these reasons I have certainly nothing to reply, but at the end I feel constrained to confess that there is nothing in all that I formerly believed to be true, of which I cannot in some measure doubt, and that not merely through want of thought or through levity, but for reasons which are very powerful and maturely considered; so that henceforth I ought not the less carefully to refrain from giving credence to these opinions than to that which is manifestly false, if I desire to arrive at any certainty [in the sciences].

But it is not sufficient to have made these remarks, we must also be careful to keep them in mind. For these ancient and commonly held opinions still revert frequently to my mind, long and familiar custom having given them the right to occupy my mind against my inclination and rendered them almost masters of my belief; nor will I ever lose the habit of deferring to them or of placing my confidence in them, so long as I consider them as they really are, i.e., opinions in some measure doubtful, as I have just shown, and at the same time highly probable, so that there is much more reason to believe in than to deny them. That is why I consider that I shall not be acting amiss, if, taking of set purpose a contrary belief, I allow myself to be deceived, and for a certain time pretend that all these opinions are entirely false and imaginary, until at last, having thus balanced my former prejudices with my latter [so that they cannot divert my opinions more to one side than to the other], my judgment will no longer be dominated by bad usage or turned away from the right knowledge of the truth. For I am assured that there can be neither peril nor error in this course, and that I cannot at present yield too much to distrust, since I am not considering the question of action, but only of knowledge.

I shall then suppose, not that God who is supremely good and the fountain of truth, but some evil genius not less powerful than deceitful, has employed his whole energies in deceiving me; I shall consider that the heavens, the earth, colours, figures, sound, and all other external things are nought but the illusions and dreams of which this genius has availed himself in order to lay traps for my credulity; I shall consider myself as having no hands, no flesh, no blood, nor any senses, yet falsely believing myself to possess all these things; I shall remain obstinately attached to this idea, and if by this means it is not in my power to arrive at the knowledge of any truth, I may at least do what is in my power [i.e., suspend my judgment], and with firm purpose avoid giving credence to any false thing, or being imposed upon by this arch deceiver, however powerful and deceptive he may be. But this task is a laborious one, and insensibly a certain lassitude leads me into the course of my ordinary life. And just as a captive who in sleep enjoys an imaginary liberty, when he begins to suspect that his liberty is but a dream, fears to awaken, and conspires with these agreeable illusions that the deception may be prolonged, so insensibly of my own accord I fall back into my former opinions, and I dread awakening from this slumber, lest the laborious wakefulness which would follow the tranquillity of this repose should have to be spent not in daylight, but in the excessive darkness of the difficulties which have just been discussed.

from
LECTURES ON THE
HISTORY OF PHILOSOPHY
by
GEORG WILHELM FRIEDRICH HEGEL

The Notion of the History of Philosophy

The thought which may first occur to us in the history of Philosophy, is that the subject itself contains an inner contradiction. For Philosophy aims at understanding what is unchangeable, eternal, in and for itself: its end is Truth. But history tells us of that which has at one time existed, at another time has vanished, having been expelled by something else. Truth is eternal; it does not fall within the sphere of the transient, and has no history. But if it has a history, and as this history is only the representation of a succession of past forms of knowledge, the truth is not to be found in it, for the truth cannot be what has passed away.

It might be said that all this argument would affect not only the other sciences, but in like degree the Christian religion, and it might be found inconsistent that a history of this religion and of the other sciences should exist; but it would be superfluous further to examine this argument, for it is immediately contradicted by the very fact that there are such histories. But in order to get a better understanding of this apparent contradiction, we must distinguish between the outward history of a religion or a science and the history of the subject itself. And then we must take into account that the history of Philosophy because of the special nature of its subject-matter, is different from other histories. It is at once evident that the contradiction in question could not refer to the outward history, but merely to the inward, or that of the content itself. There is a history of the spread of Christianity and of the lives of those who have avowed it, and its existence has formed itself into that of a Church. This in itself constitutes an external existence such that being brought into contact with temporal affairs of the most diverse kind, its lot is a varied one and it essentially possesses a history. And of the Christian doctrine it is true that it, too, has its history, but it necessarily soon reached its full development and attained to its appointed powers. And this old creed has been an acknowledged influence to every age, and will still be acknowledged unchanged as the Truth, even though this acknowledgment were become no more than a pretence, and the words an empty form. But the history of this doctrine in its wider sense includes two elements: first the various additions to and deviations from the truth formerly established, and secondly the combating of these errors, the purification of the principles that remain from such additions, and a consequent return to their first simplicity.

The other sciences, including Philosophy, have also an external history like Religion. Philosophy has a history of its origin, diffusion, maturity, decay, revival; a history of its teachers, promoters, and of its opponents—often, too, of an outward relation to religion and occasionally to the State. This side of its history likewise gives occasion to interesting questions. Amongst other such, it is asked why Philosophy, the doctrine of absolute Truth, seems to have revealed itself on the whole to a small number of individuals, to special nations, and how it has limited itself to particular periods of time. Similarly with respect to Christianity, to the Truth in a much more universal form than the philosophical, a difficulty has been encountered in respect to the question whether there is a contradiction in the fact that this religion should have appeared so late in time, and that it should have remained so long and should still remain limited to special races of men. But these and other similar questions are too much a matter of detail to depend merely on the general conflict referred to, and when we have further touched upon the peculiar character of philosophic knowledge, we may go more specially into the aspects which relate to the external existence and external history of Philosophy,

But as regards the comparison between the history of Religion and that of Philosophy as to inner content, there is not in the latter as there is in Religion a fixed and fundamental truth which, as unchangeable, is apart from history. The content of Christianity, which is Truth, has, however, remained unaltered as such, and has therefore little history or as good as none. Hence in Religion, on account of its very nature as Christianity, the conflict referred to disappears. The errors and additions constitute no difficulty. They are transitory and altogether historical in character.

The other sciences, indeed, have also according to their content a History, a part of which relates to alterations, and the renunciation of tenets which were formerly current. But a great, perhaps the greater, part of the history relates to what has proved permanent, so that what was new, was not an alteration on earlier acquisitions, but an addition to them. These sciences progress through a process of juxtaposition. It is true that in Botany, Mineralogy, and so on, much is dependent on what was previously known, but by far the greatest part remains stationary and by means of fresh matter is merely added to without itself being affected by the addition. With a science like Mathematics, history has, in the main, only the pleasing task of recording further additions. Thus to take an example, elementary geometry in so far as it was created by Euclid, may from his time on be regarded as having no further history.

The history of Philosophy, on the other hand, shows neither the motionlessness of a complete, simple content, nor altogether the onward movement of a peaceful addition of new treasures to those already acquired. It seems merely to afford the spectacle of ever-recurring changes in the whole, such as finally are no longer even connected by a common aim.

Common Ideas Regarding the History of Philosophy

At this point appear these ordinary superficial ideas regarding the history of Philosophy which have to be referred to and corrected. As regards these very current views, which are doubtless known to you, gentlemen, for indeed they are the rejections most likely to occur in one's first crude thoughts on a history of Philosophy, I will shortly explain what requires explanation, and the explanation of the differences in philosophies will lead us further into the matter itself.

a. The History of Philosophy as an Accumulation of Opinions

History, at the first glance, includes in its aim the narration of the accidental circumstances of times, of races, and of individuals, treated impartially partly as regards their relation in time, and partly as to their content. The appearance of contingency in time-succession is to be dealt with later on. It is contingency of content which is the idea with which we have first to deal—the idea of contingent actions. But thoughts and not external actions, or griefs, or joys, form the content of Philosophy. Contingent thoughts, however, are nothing but opinions, and philosophical opinions are opinions relating to the more special content of Philosophy, regarding God, Nature and Spirit.

Thus we now meet the view very usually taken of the history of Philosophy which ascribes to it the narration of a number of philosophical opinions as they have arisen and manifested themselves in time. This kind of matter is in courtesy called opinions; those who think themselves more capable of judging rightly, call such a history a display of senseless follies, or at least of errors made by men engrossed in thought and in mere ideas. This view is not only held by those who recognize their ignorance of Philosophy. Those who do this, acknowledge it, because that ignorance is, in common estimation, held to be no obstacle to giving judgment upon what has to do with the subject; for it is thought that anybody can form a judgment on its character and value without any comprehension of it whatever. But the same view is even held by those who write or have written on the history of Philosophy. This history, considered only as the enumeration of various opinions, thus becomes an idle tale, or, if you will, an erudite investigation. For erudition is, in the main, acquaintance with a number of useless things, that is to say, with that which has no intrinsic interest or value further than being known. Yet it is thought that profit is to be derived from learning the various opinions and reflections of other men. It stimulates the powers of thought and also leads to many excellent reflections; this signifies that now and then it occasions an idea, and its art thus consists in the spinning one opinion out of the other.

If the history of Philosophy merely represented various opinions in array, whether they be of God or of natural and spiritual things existent, it would be a most superfluous and tiresome science, no matter what advantage might be brought forward as derived from such thought-activity and learning. What can be more useless than to learn a string of bald opinions, and what more unimportant? Literary works, being histories of Philosophy in the sense that they produce and treat the ideas of Philosophy as if they were opinions, need be only superficially glanced at to find how dry and destitute of interest everything about them is.

An opinion is a subjective conception, an uncontrolled thought, an idea which may occur to me in one direction or in another: an opinion is mine, it is in itself a universal thought which is existent in and for itself. But Philosophy possesses no opinions, for there is no such thing as philosophical opinions. When we hear a man speaking of philosophical opinions, even though he be an historian of philosophy itself, we detect at once this want of fundamental education. Philosophy is the objective science of truth, it is science of necessity, conceiving knowledge, and neither opinion nor the spinning out of opinions.

The more precise significance of this idea is that we get to know opinions only, thus laying emphasis upon the word Opinion. Now the direct opposite of opinion is the Truth; it is Truth before which mere opinion pales. Those who in the history of Philosophy seek mere theories, or who suppose that on the whole only such are to be found within it, also turn aside when that word Truth confronts them. Philosophy here encounters opposition from two different sides. On the one hand piety openly declares Reason or Thought to be incapable of apprehending what is true, and to lead only to the abyss of doubt; it declares that independent thought must be renounced, and reason held in bounds by faith in blind authority, if Truth is to be reached. Of the relation existing between Religion and Philosophy and of its history, we shall deal later on. On the other hand, it is known just as well, that so-called reason has maintained its rights, abandoning faith in mere authority, and has endeavoured to make Christianity rational, so that throughout it is only my personal insight and conviction which obliges me to make any admissions. But this affirmation of the right of reason is turned round in an astonishing manner, so that it results in making knowledge of the Truth through reason an impossibility. This so-called reason on the one hand has combated religious faith in the name and power of thinking reason, and at the same time it has itself turned against reason and is true reason's adversary. Instinct and feeling are maintained by it against the true reason, thus making the measure of true value the merely subjective—that is a particular conviction such as each can form in and for himself in his subjective capacity. A personal conviction such as this is no more than the particular opinion that has become final for men.

If we begin with what meets us in our very first conceptions, we cannot neglect to make mention of this aspect in the history of Philosophy. In its results it permeates culture generally, being at once the misconception and true sign of our times. It is the principle through which men mutually understand and know each other; an hypothesis whose value is established and which is the ground of all the other sciences. In theology it is not so much the creed of the church that passes for Christianity, as that every one to a greater or less degree makes a christianity of his own to tally with his conviction. And in history we often see theology driven into acquiring the knowledge of various opinions in order that an interest may thus be furnished to the science, and one of the first results of the attention paid them is the honour awarded to all convictions, and the esteem vouchsafed to what has been constituted merely by the individual. The endeavour to know the Truth is then of course relinquished. It is true that personal conviction is the ultimate and absolute essential which reason and its philosophy, from a subjective point of view, demand in knowledge. But there is a distinction between conviction when it rests on subjective grounds such as feelings, speculations and perceptions, or, speaking generally, on the particular nature of the subject, and when it rests on thought proceeding from acquaintance with the Notion and the nature of the thing. In the former case conviction is opinion.

This opposition between mere opinion and truth now sharply defined, we already recognize in the culture of the period of Socrates and Plato—a period of corruption in Greek life—as the Platonic opposition between opinion (δύξα) and Science (ἐπιστήμη). It is the same opposition as that which existed in the decadence of Roman public and political life under Augustus, and subsequently when Epicureanism and indifference set themselves up against Philosophy. Under this influence, when Christ said, "I came into the world that I should bear witness unto the Truth," Pilate answered, "What is Truth?" That was said in a superior way, and signifies that this idea of truth is an expedient which is obsolete: we have got further, we know that there is no longer any question about knowing the Truth, seeing that we have gone beyond it. Who makes this statement has gone beyond it indeed. If this is made our starting point in the history of Philosophy, its whole significance will consist in finding out the particular ideas of others, each one of which is different from the other: these individual points of view are thus foreign to me: my thinking reason is not free, nor is it present in them: for me they are but extraneous, dead historic matter, or so much empty content, and to satisfy oneself with empty vanity is mere subjective vanity itself.

To the impartial man, the Truth has always been a heart-stirring word and one of great import. As to the assertion that the Truth cannot be known, we shall consider it more closely in the history of Philosophy itself where it appears. The only thing to be here remarked is that if this assumption be allowed, as was the case with Tennemann, it is beyond conception why anyone should still trouble about Philosophy, since each opinion asserts falsely in its turn that it has found the truth. This immediately recalls to me the old belief that Truth consists in knowledge, but that an individual only knows the Truth in so far as he reflects and not as he walks and stands: and that the Truth cannot be known in immediate apprehension and perception, whether it be external and sensuous, or whether it be intellectual perception (for every perception as a perception is sensuous) but only through the labour of thought.

b. Proof of the Futility of Philosophical Knowledge Obtained Through the History of Philosophy Itself

From another point of view another consequence ensues from the above conception of the history of Philosophy which may at will be looked at as an evil or a benefit. In view of such manifold opinions and philosophical systems so numerous, one is perplexed to know which one ought to be accepted. In regard to the great matters to which man is attracted and a knowledge of which Philosophy would bestow, it is evident that the greatest minds have erred, because they have been contradicted by others. "Since this has been so with minds so great, how then can *ego homuncio* attempt to form a judgment?" This consequence, which ensues from the diversity in philosophical systems, is, as may be supposed, the evil in the matter, while at the same time it is a subjective good. For this diversity is the usual plea urged by those who, with an air of knowledge, wish to make a show of interest in Philosophy, to explain the fact that they, with this pretence of good-will, and, indeed, with added motive for working at the science, do in fact utterly neglect it. But this diversity in philosophical systems is far from being merely an evasive plea. It has far more weight as a genuine serious ground of argument against the zeal which Philosophy requires. It justifies its neglect and demonstrates conclusively the powerlessness of the endeavour to attain to philosophic knowledge of the truth. When it is admitted that Philosophy ought to be a real science, and one Philosophy must certainly be the true, the question arises as to which Philosophy it is, and when it can be known. Each one asserts its genuineness, each even gives different signs and tokens by which the truth can be discovered; sober reflective thought must therefore hesitate to give its judgment.

This, then, is the wider interest which the history of Philosophy is said to afford. Cicero (De natura Deorum I. 8 sq.) gives us from this point of view, a most slovenly history of philosophic thought on God. He puts it in the mouth of an Epicurean, but he himself knew of nothing more favourable to say, and it is thus his own view. The Epicurean says that no certain knowledge has been arrived at. The proof that the efforts of philosophy are futile is derived directly from the usual superficial view taken of its history; the results attendant on that history make it appear to be a process in which the most various thoughts arise in numerous philosophies, each of which opposes, contradicts and refutes the other. This fact, which cannot be denied, seems to contain the justification, indeed the necessity for applying to Philosophy the words of Christ, "Let the dead bury their dead; arise, and follow Me." The whole of the history of Philosophy becomes a battlefield covered with the bones of the dead; it is a kingdom not merely formed of dead and lifeless individuals, but of refuted and spiritually dead systems, since each has killed and buried the other. Instead of "Follow thou Me," here then it must indeed be said, "Follow thine own self"—that is, hold by thine own convictions, remain steadfast to thine own opinion, why adopt another?

It certainly happens that a new philosophy makes its appearance, which maintains the others to be valueless; and indeed each one in turn comes forth at first with the pretext that by its means all previous philosophies not only are refuted, but what in them is wanting is supplied, and now at length the right one is discovered. But following upon what has gone before, it would rather seem that other words of Scripture are just as applicable to such a philosophy—the words which the Apostle Peter spoke to Ananias, "Behold the feet of them that shall carry thee out are at the door." Behold the philosophy by which thine own will be refuted and displaced shall not tarry long as it has not tarried before.

c. Explanatory Remarks on the Diversity in Philosophies

Certainly the fact is sufficiently well established that there are and have been different philosophies. The Truth is, however, one; and the instinct of reason maintains this irradicable intuition or belief. It is said that only one philosophy can be true, and, because philosophies are different, it is concluded that all others must be erroneous. But, in fact, each one in turn gives every assurance, evidence and proof of being the one and true Philosophy. This is a common mode of reasoning and is what seems in truth to be the view of sober thought. As regards the sober nature of the word at issue— thought—we can tell from everyday experience that if we fast we feel hunger either at once or very soon. But sober thought always has the fortunate power of not resulting in hunger and desire, but of being and remaining as it is, content. Hence the thought expressed in such an utterance reveals the fact that it is dead understanding; for it is only death which fasts and yet rests satisfied. But neither physical life nor intellectual remains content with mere abstention; as desire it presses on through hunger and through thirst towards Truth, towards knowledge itself. It presses on to satisfy this desire and does not allow itself to feast and find sufficiency in a reflection such as this.

As to this reflection, the next thing to be said of it is that however different the philosophies have been, they had a common bond in that they were Philosophy. Thus whoever may have studied or become acquainted with a philosophy, of whatever kind, provided only that it is such, has thereby become acquainted with Philosophy. That delusive mode of reasoning which regards diversity alone, and from doubt of or aversion to the particular form in which a Universal finds its actuality, will not grasp or even allow this universal nature, I have elsewhere likened to an invalid recommended by the doctor to eat fruit, and who has cherries, plums or grapes, before him, but who pedantically refuses to take anything because no part of what is offered him is fruit, some of it being cherries, and the rest plums or grapes.

But it is really important to have a deeper insight into the bearings of this diversity in the systems of Philosophy. Truth and Philosophy known philosophically, make such diversity appear in another light from that of abstract opposition between Truth and Error. The explanation of how this comes about will reveal to us the significance of the whole history of Philosophy. We must make the fact conceivable, that the diversity and number of philosophies not only does not prejudice Philosophy itself, that is to say the possibility of a philosophy, but that such diversity is, and has been, absolutely necessary to the existence of a science of Philosophy and that it is essential to it.

This makes it easy to us to comprehend the aim of Philosophy, which is in thought and in conception to grasp the Truth, and not merely to discover that nothing can be known, or that at least temporal, finite truth, which also is an untruth, can alone be known and not the Truth indeed. Further we find that in the history of Philosophy we have to deal with Philosophy itself. The facts within that history are not adventures and contain no more romance than does the history of the world. They are not a mere collection of chance events, of expeditions of wandering knights, each going about fighting, struggling, purposelessly, leaving no results to show for all his efforts. Nor is it so that one thing has been thought out here, another there, at will; in the activity of thinking mind there is real connection, and what there takes place is rational. It is with this belief in the spirit of the world that we must proceed to history, and in particular to the history of Philosophy.

Explanatory Remarks upon the Definition of the History of Philosophy

The above statement, that the Truth is only one, is still abstract and formal. In the deeper sense it is our starting point. But the aim of Philosophy is to know this one Truth as the immediate source from which all else proceeds, both all the laws of nature and all the manifestations of life and consciousness of which they are mere reflections, or to lead these laws and manifestations in ways apparently contrary, back to that single source, and from that source to comprehend them, which is to understand their derivation. Thus what is most essential is to know that the single truth is not merely a solitary, empty thought, but one determined within itself. To obtain this knowledge we must enter into some abstract Notions which, as such, are quite general and dry, and which are the two principles of *Development* and of the *Concrete*. We could, indeed, embrace the whole in the single principle of development; if this were clear, all else would result and follow of its own accord. The product of thinking is the thought; thought is, however, still formal; somewhat more defined it becomes Notion, and finally Idea is Thought in its totality, implicitly and explicitly determined. Thus the Idea, and it alone is Truth. Now it is essentially in the nature of the Idea to develop, and only through development to arrive at comprehension of itself, or to become what it is. That the Idea should have to make itself what it is, seems like a contradiction; it may be said that it is what it is.

a. The Notion of Development

The idea of development is well known, but it is the special characteristic of Philosophy to investigate such matters as were formerly held as known. What is dealt with or made use of without consideration as an aid to daily life, is certainly the unknown to man unless he be informed in Philosophy. The further discussion of this idea belongs to the science of Logic.

In order to comprehend what development is, what may be called two different states must be distinguished. The first is what is known as capacity, power, what I call being-in-itself (*potentia*, δύναμιξ); the second principle is that of being-for-itself, actuality (*actus*, ενέργεια). If we say, for example, that man is by nature rational, we would mean that he has reason only inherently or in embryo: in this sense, reason, understanding, imagination, will, are possessed from birth or even from the mother's womb. But while the child only has capacities or the actual possibility of reason, it is just the same as if he had no reason; reason does not yet exist in him since he cannot yet do anything rational, and has no rational consciousness. Thus what man is at first implicitly becomes explicit, and it is the same with reason. If, then, man has actuality on whatever side, he is actually rational; and now we come to reason.

What is the real meaning of this word? That which is in itself must become an object to mankind, must arrive at consciousness, thus becoming for man. What has become an object to him is the same as what he is in himself; through the becoming objective of this implicit being, man first becomes for himself; he is made double, is retained and not changed into another. For example, man is thinking, and thus he thinks out thoughts. In this way it is in thought alone that thought is object; reason produces what is rational: reason is its own object. The fact that thought may also descend to what is destitute of reason is a consideration involving wider issues, which do not concern us here. But even though man, who in himself is rational, does not at first seem to have got further on since he became rational for himself—what is implicit having merely retained itself—the difference is quite enormous: no new content has been produced, and yet this form of being for self makes all the difference. The whole variation in the development of the world in history is founded on this difference. This alone explains how since all mankind is naturally rational, and freedom is the hypothesis on which this reason rests, slavery yet has been, and in part still is, maintained by many peoples, and men have remained contented under it. The only distinction between the Africans and the Asiatics on the one hand, and the Greeks, Romans, and moderns on the other, is that the latter know and it is explicit for them, that they are free, but the others are so without knowing that they are, and thus without existing as being free. This constitutes the enormous difference in their condition. All knowledge, and learning, science, and even commerce have no other object than to draw out what is inward or implicit and thus to become objective.

Because that which is implicit comes into existence, it certainly passes into change, yet it remains one and the same, for the whole process is dominated by it. The plant, for example, does not lose itself in mere indefinite change. From the germ much is produced when at first nothing was to be seen; but the whole of what is brought forth, if not developed, is yet hidden and ideally contained within itself. The principle of this projection into existence is that the germ cannot remain merely implicit, but is impelled towards development, since it presents the contradiction of being only implicit and yet not desiring so to be. But this coming without itself has an end in view; its completion fully reached, and its previously determined end is the fruit or produce of the germ, which causes a return to the first condition. The germ will produce itself alone and manifest what is contained in it, so that it then may return to itself once more thus to renew the unity from which it started. With nature it certainly is true that the subject which commenced and the matter which forms the end are two separate units, as in the case of seed and fruit. The doubling process has apparently the effect of separating into two things that which in content is the same. Thus in animal life the parent and the young are different individuals although their nature is the same.

In Mind it is otherwise: it is consciousness and therefore it is free, uniting in itself the beginning and the end. As with the germ in nature, Mind indeed resolves itself back into unity after constituting itself another. But what is in itself becomes for Mind and thus arrives at being for itself. The fruit and seed newly contained within it on the other hand, do not become for the original germ, but for us alone; in the case of Mind both factors not only are implicitly the same in character, but there is a being for the other and at the same time a being for self. That for which the "other" is, is the same as that "other"; and thus alone Mind is at home with itself in its "other." The development of Mind lies in the fact that its going forth and separation constitutes its coming to itself.

This being-at-home-with-self, or coming-to-self of Mind may be described as its complete and highest end: it is this alone that it desires and nothing else. Everything that from eternity has happened in heaven and earth, the life of God and all the deeds of time simply are the struggles for Mind to know itself, to make itself objective to itself, to find itself, be for itself, and finally unite itself to itself; it is alienated and divided, but only so as to be able thus to find itself and return to itself. Only in this manner does Mind attain its freedom, for that is free which is not connected with or dependent on another. True self-possession and satisfaction are only to be found in this, and in nothing else but Thought does Mind attain this freedom. In sense-perception, for instance, and in feeling, I find

myself confined and am not free; but I am free when I have a consciousness of this my feeling. Man has particular ends and interests
even in will; I am free indeed when this is mine. Such ends, however, always contain "another," or something which constitutes for me
"another," such as desire and impulse. It is in Thought alone that all
foreign matter disappears from view, and that Mind is absolute free.
All interest which is contained in the Idea and in Philosophy is
expressed in it.

b. The Notion of the Concrete

As to development, it may be asked, what does develop and what
forms the absolute content? Development is considered in the light
of a formal process in action and as destitute of content. But the act
has no other end but activity, and through this activity the general
character of the content is already fixed. For being-in-self and
being-for-self are the moments present in action; but the act is the
retention of these diverse elements within itself. The act thus is really one, and it is just this unity of differences which is the concrete.
Not only is the act concrete, but also the implicit, which stands to
action in the relation of subject which begins, and finally the product is just as concrete as the action or as the subject which begins.
Development in process likewise forms the content, the Idea itself;
for this we must have the one element and then the other: both
combined will form a unity as third, because the one in the other
is at home with, and not without, itself. Thus the Idea is in its content concrete within itself, and this in two ways: first it is concrete
potentially, and then it is its interest that what is in itself should be
there for it.

It is a common prejudice that the science of Philosophy deals
only with abstractions and empty generalities, and that sense-
perception, our empirical self-consciousness, natural instinct, and
the feelings of every-day life, lie, on the contrary, in the region of the
concrete and the self-determined. As a matter of fact, Philosophy is
in the region of thought, and has therefore to deal with universals;
its content is abstract, but only as to form and element. In itself the
Idea is really concrete, for it is the union of the different determinations. It is here that reasoned knowledge differs from mere

knowledge of the understanding, and it is the business of Philosophy, as opposed to understanding, to show that the Truth or the Idea does not consist in empty generalities, but in a universal; and that is within itself the particular and the determined. If the Truth is abstract it must be untrue. Healthy human reason goes out towards what is concrete; the reflection of the understanding comes first as abstract and untrue, correct in theory only, and amongst other things unpractical. Philosophy is what is most antagonistic to abstraction, and it leads back to the concrete.

If we unite the Notion of the concrete with that of development we have the motion of the concrete. Since the implicit is already concrete within itself, and we only set forth what is implicitly there, the new form which now looks different and which was formerly shut up in the original unity, is merely distinguished. The concrete must become for itself or explicit; as implicit or potential it is only differentiated within itself, not as yet explicitly set forth, but still in a state of unity. The concrete is thus simple, and yet at the same time differentiated. This, its inward contradiction, which is indeed the impelling force in development, brings distinction into being. But thus, too, its right to be taken back and reinstated extends beyond the difference; for its truth is only to be found in unity. Life, both that which is in Nature and that which is of the Idea, of Mind within itself, is thus manifested. Were the Idea abstract, it would simply be the highest conceivable existence, and that would be all that could be said of it; but such a God is the product of the understanding of modern times. What is true is rather found in motion, in a process, however, in which there is rest; difference, while it lasts, is but a temporary condition, through which comes unity, full and concrete.

We may now proceed to give examples of sensuous things, which will help us further to explain this Notion of the concrete. Although the flower has many qualities, such as smell, taste, form, colour, &c., yet it is one. None of these qualities could be absent in the particular leaf or flower: each individual part of the leaf shares alike all the qualities of the leaf entire. Gold similarly contains in every particle all its qualities unseparated and entire. It is frequently allowed with sensuous things that such varied elements may be joined together, but, in the spiritual, differentiation is supposed to involve opposition. We do not controvert the fact, or think it contradictory, that the smell and taste of the flower, although otherwise opposed, are yet clearly in one subject; nor do we place the one against the other. But the understanding and understanding thought find everything of a different kind, placed in conjunction, to be incompatible. Matter, for example, is complex and coherent, or space is continuous and uninterrupted. Likewise we may take separate points in space and break up matter dividing it ever further into infinity. It then is said that matter consists of atoms and points, and hence is not continuous. Therefore we have here the two determinations of continuity and of definite points, which understanding regards as mutually exclusive, combined in one. It is said that matter must be clearly either continuous or divisible into points, but in reality it has both these qualities. Or when we say of the mind of man that it has freedom, the understanding at once brings up the other quality, which in this case is necessity, saying, that if Mind is free it is not in subjection to necessity, and, inversely, if its will and thought are determined through necessity, it is not free—the one, they say, excludes the other. The distinctions here are regarded as exclusive, and not as forming something concrete. But that which is true, the Mind, is concrete, and its attributes are freedom and necessity. Similarly the higher point of view is that Mind is free in its necessity, and finds its freedom in it alone, since its necessity rests on its freedom. But it is more difficult for us to show the unity here than in the case of natural objects. Freedom can, however, be also abstract freedom without necessity, which false freedom is self-will, and for that reason it is self-opposed, unconsciously limited, an imaginary freedom which is free in form alone.

The fruit of development, which comes third, is a result of motion, but inasmuch as it is merely the result of one stage in development, as being last in this stage, it is both the starting point and the first in order in another such stage. Goethe somewhere truly says, "That which is formed ever resolves itself back into its elements." Matter—which as developed has form—constitutes once more the material for a new form. Mind again takes as its object and applies its activity to the Notion in which in going within itself, it has comprehended itself, which it is in form and being, and which has just been separated from it anew. The application of thought to this, supplies it with the form and determination of thought. This action thus further forms the previously formed, gives it additional determinations, makes it more determinate in itself, further developed and more profound. As concrete, this activity is a succession of processes in development which must be represented not as a straight line drawn out into vague infinity, but as a circle returning within itself, which, as periphery, has very many circles, and whose whole is a large number of processes in development turning back within themselves.

c. Philosophy as the Apprehension of the Development of the Concrete

Having thus generally explained the nature of the Concrete, I now add as regards its import, that the Truth thus determined within itself is impelled towards development. It is only the living and spiritual which internally bestirs and develops itself. Thus the Idea as concrete in itself, and self-developing, is an organic system and a totality which contains a multitude of stages and of moments in development. Philosophy has now become for itself the apprehension of this development, and as conceiving Thought, is itself this development in Thought. The more progress made in this development, the more perfect is the Philosophy.

This development goes no further out than into externality, but the going without itself of development also is a going inwards. That is to say, the universal Idea continues to remain at the foundation and still is the all-embracing and unchangeable. While in Philosophy the going out of the Idea in course of its development is not a change, a becoming "another," but really is a going within itself, a self-immersion, the progress forward makes the Idea which was previously general and undetermined, determined within itself. Further development of the Idea or its further determination is the same thing exactly. Depth seems to signify intensiveness, but in this case the most extensive is also the most intensive. The more intensive is the Mind, the more extensive is it, hence the larger is its embrace. Extension as development, is not dispersion or falling asunder, but a uniting bond which is the more powerful and intense as the expanse of that embraced is greater in extent and richer. In such a case what is greater is the strength of opposition and of separation; and the greater power overcomes the greater separation.

These are the abstract propositions regarding the nature of the Idea and of its development, and thus within it Philosophy in its developed state is constituted: it is one Idea in its totality and in all its individual parts, like one life in a living being, one pulse throbs throughout all its members. All the parts represented in it, and their systematization, emanate from the one Idea; all these particulars are but the mirrors and copies of this one life, and have their actuality only in this unity. Their differences and their various qualities are only the expression of the Idea and the form contained within it. Thus the Idea is the central point, which is also the periphery, the source of light, which in all its expansion does not come without itself, but remains present and immanent within itself. Thus it is both the system of necessity and its own necessity, which also constitutes its freedom.

from

REFLECTIONS ON THE
COMMON CONCEPT OF JUSTICE

by

GOTTFRIED WILHELM LEIBNIZ

It is generally agreed that whatever God wills is good and just. But there remains the question whether it is good and just because God wills it or whether God wills it because it is good and just; in other words, whether justice and goodness are arbitrary or whether they belong to the necessary and eternal truths about the nature of things, as do numbers and proportions. The former opinion has been held by certain philosophers and by theologians, both Roman and Reformed. But the Reformed theologians of today usually reject this teaching, as do also all our own theologians and most of those of the Roman church as well.

As a matter of fact it would destroy the justice of God. For why praise him for acting justly if the concept of justice adds nothing to his act? And to say, *Stat pro ratione voluntas*—"Let my will stand for the reason"—is definitely the motto of a tyrant. Moreover, this opinion would hardly distinguish God from the devil. For if the devil, that is, an intelligent, invisible power who is very great and very evil, were the master of the world, this devil or this god would still be evil even if we were forced to honor him, just as certain peoples honor imaginary gods of this kind in the hope of bringing them to do less evil. Consequently, some people, overly devoted to the absolute right of God, have believed that he could justly condemn innocent people and even that this may actually happen. This does violence to those attributes which make God love-worthy and destroys our love for God, leaving only fear. Those who believe, for example, that infants who die without baptism are cast into the eternal flames must in effect have a very weak idea of the goodness and the justice of God and thus thoughtlessly injure what is most essential to religion.

The Sacred Scriptures also give us an entirely different idea of this sovereign substance, speaking, as they so often and so clearly do, of the goodness of God and presenting him as a person who justifies himself against complaints. In the story of the creation of the world, the Scripture says that God considered all that he had done and found it good; that is, he was content with his work and had reason to be so. This is a human way of speaking which seems to be used explicitly to point out that the goodness of the acts and products of God does not depend on his will but on their nature. Otherwise he would only have to see what he willed and did to determine if it is good and to justify himself to himself as a wise sovereign. All our theologians, therefore, and most of those of the Roman church, as well as the ancient Church Fathers and the wisest and most esteemed philosophers, have favored the second view, which holds that goodness and justice have grounds independent of will and of force.

In his dialogues Plato introduces and refutes a certain Thrasymachus who tried to explain what justice is by a definition which, if acceptable, would strongly support the view which we are opposing. That is just, he says, which suits or pleases the most powerful. If this were true, the sentence of a sovereign court or a supreme judge would never be unjust, nor would an evil but powerful man ever deserve condemnation. What is more, the same action could be just and unjust depending on the judges who decide, which is ridiculous. It is one thing to *be* just, another to *pass* for just and to take the place of justice.

A celebrated English philosopher named Hobbes, who has a reputation for his paradoxes, has tried to maintain almost the same thing as Thrasymachus. He holds that God has the right to do anything because he is all-powerful. This fails to distinguish between *right* and *fact*. For what *can* be is one thing; what *ought* to be is another. This same Hobbes believes, for almost the same reason, that the true religion is that of the state. It would follow that if the emperor Claudius, who decreed in an edict that *"in libera re publica crepitus atque ructus liberos esse debere,"* had established the god Crepitus among the authorized gods, he would have been a true god worthy of worship.

This amounts to saying, in concealed terms, that there is no true religion and that religion is merely an invention of men. And in the same vein, the remark that justice is that which pleases the most powerful is nothing but saying that there is no certain and determined rule of justice which prevents our doing what we wish to do and can do with impunity, however evil it may be. Thus treason, assassination, poisoning, the torture of innocents, would all be just if they succeeded. This is essentially to change the meaning of terms and to speak a language different from that of other men. Until now we have meant by justice something different from that which always prevails. We have believed that a happy man can be evil and that an unpunished act can nevertheless be unjust, that is, it may deserve punishment, so that the issue is solely to know why it deserves punishment, without raising the question of whether the punishment will actually follow or not, or whether there is any judge to impose it.

There were once two tyrants in Sicily named Denis, father and son. The father was more evil than the son. He had established his tyranny by destroying many honorable men. His son was less cruel but more addicted to disorders and luxuries. The father was happy and kept himself in power; the son was overthrown and finally made himself schoolmaster at Corinth in order to have the pleasure of ruling always and of carrying a scepter, after a fashion at least, by wielding the switches used in punishing the children. Should we say that the actions of the father were more just than those of the son because he was happy and unpunished? Would such a view permit history to condemn a happy tyrant? We see too, every day, that men, whether interested or disinterested, complain of the actions of certain powerful people and find them unjust. So the question is only whether they have reason to complain and whether history can justly blame the inclinations and acts of any prince. If this be granted, we must acknowledge that men mean something else by justice and right than that which pleases a powerful being who remains unpunished because there is no judge capable of mending matters.

In the universe as a whole, or in the government of the world, it is fortunately true that he who is the most powerful is at the same time just and does nothing against which anyone has a right to complain. We must hold for certain that if we understood that universal order, we should find it impossible to do anything better than he has done it. Yet his power is not the formal reason which makes him just. Otherwise, if power were the formal reason for justice, all powerful beings would be just, each in proportion to his power, which is contrary to experience.

We must therefore search after this formal reason, that is, the "wherefore" of this attribute or the concept which should teach us what justice is and what men mean when they call an act just or unjust. And this formal reason must be common to God and man. Otherwise we should be wrong in seeking to ascribe the same attribute to both without equivocation. These are fundamental rules for reasoning and discourse.

I grant that there is a great difference between the way in which men are just and the way in which God is just, but this difference is only one of degree. For God is perfectly and entirely just, while the justice of men is mixed with injustice, with faults and sins, because of the imperfection of human nature. The perfections of God are infinite; ours are limited. Anyone, therefore, who tries to maintain that the justice and goodness of God have entirely different rules from those of men must at the same time admit that two entirely different concepts are involved and that to ascribe justice to both is either deliberate equivocation or gross self-deceit. But if we choose one of the two concepts as the proper conception of justice, it must follow either that there is no true justice in God or that there is none in man, or perhaps that there is none in either God or man, so that in the end we do not know what we are talking about when we speak of justice. This would in effect destroy justice and leave nothing but the name, as do those who make it arbitrary and dependent on the whim of a judge or ruler, since the same act will appear just and unjust to different judges.

This is somewhat as if we should try to maintain that our science—for example, arithmetic, or the science of numbers—does not agree with the science of God or the angels, or perhaps that all truth is arbitrary and based on a whim. For example, 1, 4, 9, 16, 25, etc., are square numbers produced by multiplying 1, 2, 3, 4, 5, etc., by themselves. Thus 1 times 1 is 1; 2 times 2 is 4; 3 times 3 is 9, etc. We discover that the successive odd numbers are the differences between successive square numbers. Thus the difference between 1 and 4 is 3, that between 4 and 9 is 5, between 9 and 16 is 7, etc. . . . Now would one have any reason to maintain that this is not true for God and the angels and that they see or discover something in numbers entirely contrary to what we find in them? Would we not be right in laughing at a man who maintained this and who did not know the difference between eternal and necessary truths, which must be the same for all, and truths that are contingent and changeable or arbitrary?

This same thing is true about justice. If it is a fixed term with determinate meaning—in a word, if it is not a simple sound without sense, like *blitiri*—the term or word *justice* will have some definition or intelligible meaning. And, by using the incontestable rules of logic, one can draw definite consequences from every definition. This is precisely what we do in building the necessary and demonstrative sciences which do not depend at all on facts but solely on reason; such are logic, metaphysics, arithmetic, geometry, the science of motion, and the and the science of Right [*droit*] as well, which are not at all based on experience or facts but serve rather to give reasons for facts and to control them in advance. This would be true in regard to Right, even if there were no law [*loi*] in the world. The error of those who have made justice depend upon power comes in part from their confusion of *Right* with *law*. Right cannot be unjust; this would be a contradiction. But law can be, for it is power which gives and maintains law; and if this power lacks wisdom or good will, it can give and maintain very bad laws. But happily for the world, the laws of God are always just, and he is in a position to maintain them, as he without a doubt does, even though this has not always happened visibly and at once—for which he assuredly has good reasons.

We must determine, then, the formal principle of justice and the measure by which we should judge acts to know if they are just or unjust. After what has been said we can already foresee what this must be. Justice is nothing but what conforms to wisdom and goodness combined. The end of goodness [*bonté*] is the greatest good [*bien*]. But to recognize this we need wisdom, which is merely the knowledge of the good, as goodness is merely the inclination to do good to all and to prevent evil, at least if evil is not necessary for a greater good or to prevent a greater evil. Thus wisdom is in the understanding, and goodness is in the will, and as a result justice is in both. Power is another matter. But if power is added, it brings to pass the Right and causes that which should be to exist really as well, insofar as the nature of things permits. And this is what God does in the world.

But since justice aims at the good, and wisdom and goodness together form justice and so refer to the good, we may ask what is the true good. I reply that it is merely whatever serves the perfection of intelligent substances. It is obvious, therefore, that order, contentment, joy, wisdom, goodness, and virtue are goods in an essential sense and can never be bad and that power is a good in a natural sense, that is, by itself, because, other things being equal, it is better to have it than not to have it. But power does not become an assured good until it is joined with wisdom and goodness. For the power of an evil man serves only sooner or later to plunge him further into misery, since it gives him the means of doing more evil and of earning a greater punishment, from which he will not escape, since the universe has a perfectly just monarch whose infinite penetration and sovereign power one cannot avoid.

Since experience shows us that God, for reasons unknown to us but surely very wise and based on a greater good, permits many evil persons to be happy in this life and many good persons to be unhappy, a fact which would not conform to the rules of a perfect government such as God's if it had not been corrected, it follows necessarily that there will be another life and that souls will not perish with the visible bodies. Otherwise there would be crimes unpunished and good deeds unrewarded, which is contrary to order.

There are demonstrative proofs, besides, of the immortality of the soul, for the principle of action and of consciousness could not derive from a purely passive extended thing indifferent to all motion, as is matter. Therefore action and consciousness must necessarily come from something simple or immaterial, without extension and without parts, which is called the soul. But whatever is simple and without parts is not subject to dissolution and as a result, cannot be destroyed. There are people who imagine that we are too small a thing in the sight of an infinite God for him to be concerned about us. It is thought that we are to God as are the worms which we crush without thinking, in relation to us. But this is to imagine that God is like man and that he cannot think of everything. God, according to this reasoning, being infinite, does things without work in a way that results from his will, just as it results from my will and that of my friend that we are in accord, without needing some action to produce the accord after our resolutions are made. But if mankind, or even the smallest thing, were not well governed, the whole universe would not be well governed, for the whole consists of its parts.

We also find order and wonders in the smallest whole things when we are capable of distinguishing their parts and at the same time of seeing the whole, as we do in looking at insects and other small things in the microscope. There are thus the strongest reasons for holding that the same craftsmanship and harmony would be found in great things if we were capable of seeing them as a whole. Above all, they would be found in the whole economy of the government of spirits, which are the substances most similar to God because they are themselves capable of recognizing and inventing order and craftsmanship. As a result we must conclude that the Author of things who is so inclined to order will be concerned for those creatures who are naturally sources of order in the measure of their perfection and who are alone capable of imitating his workmanship. But it is impossible that this should seem so to us, in this small portion of life which we live here below, which is but a small bit of the life without bounds which no spirit can fail to achieve. To consider this bit separately is to consider things like a broken stick or like the bits of flesh of an animal taken separately, so that the craftsmanship of its organs cannot be made apparent.

This is also true when one looks at the brain, which must undoubtedly be one of the greatest wonders of nature, since it contains the most immediate organs of sense. Yet one finds there only a confused mass in which nothing unusual appears but which nevertheless conceals some kind of filaments of a fineness much greater than that of a spider's web which are thought to be the vessels for that very subtle fluid called the animal spirits. Thus this mass of brain contains a very great multitude of passages—and of passages too small for us to overcome the labyrinth with our eyes, whatever microscope we may use. For the subtlety of the spirits contained in these passages is equal to that of light rays themselves. Yet our eyes and our sense of touch show us nothing extraordinary in the appearance of the brain.

We may say that it is the same in the government of intelligent substances under the kingship of God, in which everything seems confused to our eyes. Nevertheless, it must be the most beautiful and most marvelous arrangement of the world, since it comes from an Author who is the source of all perfection. But it is too great and too beautiful for spirits with our present range to be able to perceive it so soon. To try to see it here is like wishing to take a novel by the tail and to claim to have deciphered the plot from the first book; the beauty of a novel, instead, is great in the degree that order emerges from very great apparent confusion. The composition would thus contain a fault if the reader could divine the entire issue at once. But what is only suspense [*curiosité*] and beauty in novels, which imitate creation, so to speak, is also utility and wisdom in this great and true poem, this word-by-word creation, the universe. The beauty and justice of the divine government have been hidden in part from our eyes, not only because it could not be otherwise without changing the entire harmony of the world, but also because it is proper in order that there may be more exercise of free virtue, wisdom, and a love of God which is not mercenary, since the rewards and punishments are still outwardly invisible and appear only to the eyes of our reason or faith. This I find to be a good thing here, since the true faith is based on reason. And since the wonders of nature show us that God's operations are admirably beautiful whenever we can envisage a whole in its setting, even though this beauty is not apparent when we consider things detached or torn from their whole, we must likewise conclude that all that we cannot yet disentangle or envisage as a whole with all its parts must no less have justice and beauty. To recognize this point is to have a natural foundation for faith, hope, and the love of God, since these virtues are based on a knowledge of the divine perfections.

Now nothing better corroborates the incomparable wisdom of God than the structure of the works of nature, particularly the structure which appears when we study them more closely with a microscope. It is for this reason, as well as because of the great light which could be thrown upon bodies for the use of medicine, food, and mechanical ends, that it should be most necessary to push our knowledge further with the aid of microscopes. There are scarcely ten men in the world who are carefully at work on this, and if there were a hundred thousand, there would not be too many to discover the important wonders of this new world which makes up the interior of ours and which is capable of making our knowledge a hundred thousand times greater than it is. It is for this reason that I have more than once hoped that the great princes might be led to arrange for this and to induce men to work at it. Observatories have been founded for watching the stars, whose structures are spectacular and demand great apparatus, but telescopes are far from being as useful and from revealing the beauties and varieties of knowledge which microscopes reveal. A man in Delft has accomplished wonders at it, and if there were many others like him, our knowledge of physics would be advanced far beyond its present state. It behooves great princes to arrange this for the public welfare, in which they are most interested. And since this matter involves little cost and display, is very easy to direct, and needs very little but good will and attention to accomplish it, there is little reason to neglect it. As for me I have no other motive in recommending this research than to advance our knowledge of truth and the public good, which is strongly interested in the increase of the treasure of human knowledge.

Most of the questions of Right, but especially of the right of sovereigns and nations, are confused because they do not agree on a *common conception of justice*, with the result that we do not understand the same thing by the same word, and this opens the way to endless dispute. Everyone would agree, perhaps, on this nominal definition—that justice is a constant will to act in such a way that no person has reason to complain of us. But this is not enough unless the method is given for determining these reasons. Now I observe that some people restrict the reasons for human complaints very narrowly and that others extend them. There are those who believe that it is enough if no harm is done to them and if no one has deprived them of their possessions, holding that no one is obligated to seek the good of others or prevent evil for them, even if it should cost us nothing and give us no pain. Many who pass in the world for great judges keep themselves within these limits. They content themselves with harming no one, but they are not inclined to improve people's conditions. In a word, they believe one can be just without being charitable.

There are others in the world who have greater and more beautiful views and who would not wish anyone to complain of their lack of goodness. They would approve what I have said in my preface to the *Codex juris gentium*—that justice is the charity of the wise man, that is, a goodness toward others which ought to conform to wisdom. And wisdom, in my opinion, is nothing but the knowledge of happiness. Men may be permitted to vary in their use of words, and if anyone wants to insist on limiting the term *just* to what is the opposite of charitable, there is no way to force him to change his language, since names are arbitrary. Yet we have a right to learn the reasons which he has for being what he calls just, in order to see whether these same reasons will not bring him also to be good and to do good.

I believe we will agree that those who are charged with the conduct of others, like tutors, the directors of societies, and certain magistrates, are obligated not merely to prevent evil but also to secure the good. But it might perhaps be questioned whether a man free from commitments, or the sovereign of a state, has such obligations, the former in relation to others involved in the situation, the latter in relation to his subjects.

On top of this I shall ask that whoever can sustain a person must not do evil to others. One can give more than one reason for this. The most pressing will be the fear that someone will do the same thing to us. But are we not also subject to the fear that men will hate us if we refuse them aid which does not at all inconvenience us and if we neglect to prevent an evil which is about to crush them? Someone may say, "I am content that others should not harm me. I do not ask at all for their aid and their good deeds and have no wish either to give or to claim more." But can one sincerely maintain this? Let him ask himself what he would say or hope for if he should find himself actually on the point of falling into an evil which someone could help him avoid by a turn of his hand? Would one not hold him for a bad man and even for an enemy if he refused to save us in such a situation? . . . It will be granted, then, that one ought to prevent evil for another if it can be done conveniently. But perhaps it will not be granted that justice orders us to do positive good to others. I now ask if one is not at least obligated to relieve others' ills. And I return again to the proof, that is, to the rule, *quod tibi non vis fieri*. Suppose that you were plunged into misery. Would you not complain about someone who did not help you, if he could easily do so? You have fallen into the water. If he refuses to throw a rope to you to give you a way of saving yourself, would you not judge him to be an evil man and even an enemy? Suppose that you suffered from violent pains and that someone had in his house, under his lock and key, a healing fountain capable of relieving your ills. What would you say and what would you do if he refused to give you a few glasses of its water?

Led by degrees, people will agree not only that men ought to abstain from doing evil but also that they ought to prevent evil from being done and even to alleviate it when it is done, at least as far as they can without inconvenience to themselves. I am not now examining how far this inconvenience can go. Yet it will still be doubted, perhaps, that one is obligated to secure the good of another, even when this can be done without difficulty. Someone may say, "I am not obligated to help you achieve. Each for himself, God for all." But let me again suggest an intermediate case. A great good comes to you, but an obstacle arises, and I can remove that obstacle without pain. Would you not think it right to ask me to do so and to remind me that I would ask it of you if I were in a similar plight? If you grant this point, as you can hardly help doing, how can you refuse the only remaining request, that is, to procure a great good for me when you can do this without inconvenience of any kind to yourself and without being able to offer any reason for not doing it except a simple, "I do not want to"? You could make me happy, and you refuse to do so. I complain, and you would complain in the same circumstances; therefore, I complain with justice.

This gradation shows us that the same grounds for complaint subsist throughout. Whether one does evil or refuses to do good is a matter of degree, of more or less, but this does not alter the nature of the matter. It can also be said that the absence of the good is an evil and the absence of the evil a good. In general, if someone asks you to do something or not to do something, and you refuse his request, he has reason to complain if he can judge that you would make the same request if you were in his place. And this is the principle of *equity* or, what is the same thing, of equality or of the identity of reasons, which holds that one should grant to others whatever one would himself wish in a similar situation, without claiming any privilege contrary to reason or without claiming to be able to allege one's will as a reason.

Perhaps we can say, then, that not to do evil to another, *neminem laedere*, is the precept of the Law which is called strict Right [*jus strictum*] but that *equity* demands that one also do good when this is fitting and that it is in this that the precept consists which orders us to give each one his due, *suum cuique tribuere*. But what determines fitness [*covenance*] or what each one is due can be known by the rule of equity or of equality: *quod tibi non vis fieri aut quod tibi vis fieri, neque aliis facito aut negato*. This is the rule of reason and of our Master. Put yourself in the place of another, and you will have the true point of view to judge what is just or not.

Certain objections have been made against this great rule, but they come from the fact that it is not applied universally. For example, it has been objected that by virtue of this maxim a criminal can claim a pardon from the sovereign judge because the judge would wish the same thing if he were in a similar position. The reply is easy. The judge must put himself not only in the place of the criminal but also in that of the others whose interest lies in the crime being punished. And he must determine the greater good in which the lesser evil is included. The same is true of the objection that distributive justice demands an inequality among men, that a society ought to divide gains in proportion to what each has contributed, and that merit and lack of merit must be considered. Here the reply is also easy. Put yourself in the place of all and assume that they are well informed and enlightened. You will gather this conclusion from their votes: they will regard it fitting to their own interest that distinctions be made between one another. For example, if profits were not divided proportionally in a commercial society, some would not enter it at all, and others would quickly leave it, which is contrary to the interest of the whole society.

We may say, then, that *justice*, at least among men, is the constant will to act as far as possible in such a way that no one can complain of us if we would not complain of others in a similar situation. From this it is evident that when it is impossible to act so that the whole world is satisfied, we should try to satisfy people as much as possible. What is just thus conforms to the charity of the wise man.

So wisdom, which is a knowledge of our own good, brings us to justice, that is to say, to a reasonable advance toward the good of others. So far we have proposed as a reason for this the fear that we will be harmed if we do otherwise. But there is also the hope that others will do the same for us. Nothing is surer than the proverbs, *homo homini deus, homo homini lupus*. Nothing can contribute more to the happiness, or to the misery, of man than men themselves. If they were all wise and knew how to treat each other, they would all be happy, as far as happiness can be obtained by human reason. But we may be permitted to use fictions for a better insight into the nature of things. Assume a person who has nothing to fear from others; such a person as would be a superior power in relation to men—some higher spirit; some substance which pagans would have called a divinity; some immortal, invulnerable, invincible man—in short, a person who can neither hope for nor fear anything from us. Shall we say that such a person is nonetheless obligated to do us no harm and even to do us good? Mr. Hobbes would say "No." He would even add that this person would have an absolute right in making us his conquest, because we could not complain of such a conqueror on the grounds which we have just pointed out, since there is another condition which exempts him from all consideration for us. But without needing a fiction, what shall we say of the supreme divinity whom reason makes us recognize? Christians agree, and others should agree, that this great God is supremely just and supremely good. But it cannot be for his own repose or to maintain peace with us that he shows us so much goodness, for we should be unable to wage war against him. What then is the principle of his justice, and what is its law? It cannot be this equity or equality which exists among men and makes them envisage the common end of our human condition, "to do unto others what we wish others to do unto us."

One cannot envisage any other motive in God than that of perfection or if you like, of his pleasure. Assuming, according to my definition, that *pleasure* is nothing but the feeling of perfection, he has nothing to consider outside of himself; on the contrary, everything depends upon him. But his happiness would not be supreme if he did not aim at as much good and perfection as possible. But what will you say if I show that this same motive is found in truly virtuous and generous men, whose highest function is to imitate divinity so far as human nature is able? The earlier reasons of fear and hope can bring men to be just in public and when necessary for their own interest. They will even obligate them to exercise and practice the rules of justice from childhood in order to acquire habits, out of fear of betraying themselves too easily, and so harming themselves along with others. Yet if there were no other motive, this would merely be political at bottom. And if someone who is just in this sense should find opportunity to make a great fortune through a great crime which would remain unknown, or at least unpunished, he would say as did Julius Caesar, following Euripides:

> Si violandum est jus, regnandi gratia
> Violandum est.

But he whose justice is proof against such a temptation cannot have any motive but that of his own inclination, acquired by birth or exercise and regulated by reason, which makes him find so much pleasure in the practice of justice and so much ugliness in unjust acts that other pleasures and displeasures are compelled to give way.

One can say that this serenity of spirit, which finds the greatest pleasure in *virtue* and the greatest evil in *vice*, that is, in the perfection and imperfection of the will, would be the greatest good of which man is capable here below, even if he had nothing to expect beyond this life. For what can be preferred to this internal harmony, this continual pleasure in the purest and greatest, of which one is always master and which one need never abandon? Yet it must also be said that it is difficult to attain this disposition of spirit and that the number of those who have achieved it is small, most men remaining insensible to this motive, great and beautiful though it be. This seems to be why the Siamese believed that those who attain this degree of perfection receive divinity as a reward. The goodness of the Author of things has therefore provided for it through a motive more nearly within the reach of all men, by making himself known to the human race, as he has done by the eternal light of reason which he has given us and by the wonderful effects which he has placed before our eyes of his power, wisdom and infinite goodness. This knowledge should make us see God as the sovereign Monarch of the universe, whose government is the most perfect state conceivable, in which nothing is neglected, in which all the hairs on our heads are counted, in which everything right becomes a fact, either in itself or in some equivalent form, in such a way that justice coincides with the good pleasure of God and no divorce ever arises between the honorable [*l'honnête*] and the useful. After this it must be imprudent not to be just, because, according as he is just or unjust, a man will certainly experience good or bad for himself from what he has done.

But there is something still more beautiful than all this in the government of God. What Cicero has said allegorically of ideal justice is really true in reference to this substantial justice—that if we could see it, we should be inflamed by its beauty. One can compare the divine Monarchy to a kingdom whose sovereign would be a queen more spiritual and more learned than Queen Elizabeth; more judicious, more happy, and in a word, greater than Queen Anne; cleverer, wiser, and more beautiful than the Queen of Prussia—in short, as accomplished as it is possible to be. Conceive that the perfections of this queen make such an impression upon the minds of her subjects that it is their greatest pleasure to obey and to please her. In this case the whole world would be virtuous and just by inclination. It is this which occurs literally and beyond all description in relation to God and to those who know him. It is in him that wisdom, virtue, justice, and grandeur are accompanied by sovereign beauty. One cannot know God as one should without loving him above all things, and one cannot love him thus without willing what he wills. His perfections are infinite and cannot cease. This is why the pleasure which consists in the feeling of his perfections is the greatest and most durable possible; that is, it is the greatest felicity. And that which causes one to love him at the same time makes one happy and virtuous. . . .

This shows that justice can be taken in different ways. It can be opposed to charity, and then it is only the *jus strictum*. It can be opposed to the wisdom of him who must exercise justice, and then it conforms to the general good, but there will be cases in which the particular good will not be found in it. God and immortality would not enter into account. When one considers them, however, one always finds his own good in the general good.

While justice is merely a particular virtue, moreover, when we leave out of consideration God or a government which imitated that of God, and while this virtue so limited includes only what is called commutative and distributive justice, it can be said that as soon as it is based on God or on the imitation of God it becomes *universal justice* and contains all the virtues. For when we are vicious not only do we harm ourselves but we also diminish, so far as depends on us, the perfection of the great state of which God is the monarch. And although the evil is in fact redressed by the wisdom of the sovereign Lord this is partly through our punishment. Universal justice is distinguished by the supreme precept—*honeste (hoc est probe, pie) vivere*; as *suum cuique tribuere* conforms to particular justice, whether in general or taken more narrowly as the distributive justice which distinguishes men in particular; and as *neminem laedere* stands for commutative justice or for *jus strictum* as opposed to equity, as one takes these terms.

It is true that Aristotle has recognized this universal justice, though he has not related it to God; even so, I find it beautiful that he had so lofty an idea. But a well-formed government or state takes the place of God on earth for him, and this government will do what it can to require men to be virtuous. But as I have already said, one cannot compel men to be always virtuous by the principle solely of self-interest in this life; even less can one find the rare secret of lifting them up so that virtue constitutes their greatest pleasure, in the way I have just finished describing. Aristotle seems to have hoped for this rather than shown it. Yet I do not find it impossible that there should be times and places where one attains this, especially if piety is added.

We can still distinguish *jus strictum*, equity, and piety when we are considering the right of sovereigns and of peoples. Hobbes and Filmer seem to have considered only *jus strictum*. The Roman jurisconsults also sometimes adhere to this level of right alone. It can even be said that piety and equity regularly demand the *jus strictum* when they do not supply an exception to it. In insisting upon *jus strictum*, however, one must always add, "except for the demands of equity and of piety." Otherwise the proverb would hold: *summum jus summa est injuria.*

In examining the *jus strictum*, it is important to consider the origin of kingdoms or states. Hobbes seems to think that men were something like beasts at first and became more tractable little by little but that, as long as they were free, they were in a state of war of all against all and thus had no *jus strictum*, since each had a right in everything and was able, without injustice, to seize the possessions of his neighbor as he saw fit. For there was then no security or judge, and anyone had the right to forestall those whom one had grounds to fear greatly. But as this state of crude nature was a state of misery, men agreed upon the means to secure their safety, transferring their right to judge to the person of the state, represented by an individual or by some assembly. However, Hobbes acknowledges somewhere that a man has not, for this reason, lost the right to judge what is most agreeable to him and that a criminal is allowed to do what he can to save himself. But the citizens of a state must submit to the judgment of the state. The same author must also recognize, however, that these same citizens, who have not lost their power of judgment, also cannot let their own safety be endangered in some situation where many of them are mistreated. So in the end, in spite of what Hobbes says, each one has retained his right and his liberty regardless of the transfer to the state, and this transfer will be provisional and limited, that is, it will take place to the degree that we believe our safety is involved. The reasons which this illustrious author gives to prevent subjects from resisting their sovereign are nothing but plausible considerations based on the true principle that ordinarily such a remedy is worse than the evil itself. But what is ordinarily the case is not absolutely so. The one is like the *jus strictum*, the other like equity.

It seems to me also that this author makes the mistake of confusing right with its factual application. A man who has acquired a good, who has built a house or forged a sword, is the proprietary master of it, although someone else, in time of war, has the right to drive him from his house and to take away his sword. And although there are cases where one cannot enjoy his right for want of a judge and of enforcement the right does not cease to subsist. To try to destroy something because there is no way at once to prove it and to enjoy it is to confuse matters.

Mr. Filmer seems to me to have recognized rightly that there is a right, even a *jus strictum*, before the foundation of states. Whoever produces something new or gains possession of something already existing but which no one has possessed before, and improves and adapts it to his use, cannot as a rule be deprived of it without injustice. This is also true if one acquires a thing from such an owner, either directly or through intermediaries. The right of acquisition is a *jus strictum* which even equity approves. Hobbes believes that by virtue of this right children are the property of their mother unless society orders differently, and Filmer, assuming the superiority of the father, gives him the right of property over his children as well as over the children of his slaves. Since all men from the beginning until now are, according to sacred history, descended from Adam and also from Noah, it follows, according to Filmer, that if Noah were living, he would have the right of an absolute monarch over all men. In his absence fathers always are, or should be, the sovereign masters of their descendants. This paternal power is the origin of kings, who replace progenitors, in the last analysis, either by force or by consent. And since the power of fathers is absolute, that of kings is absolute also.

This conception ought not entirely to be condemned, but I think we can say that it has been pushed too far. We must admit that a father or a mother acquires a great power over children by their procreation and education. But I do not think that we can conclude from this that children are the property of their progenitors, as are the horses or dogs which are born to us and the works which we create. The objection may be raised that we can acquire slaves and that the children of slaves are also slaves. And according to the law of nations, slaves are the property of their masters, and no reason can be seen why children whom we have produced and nurtured by education should not be our slaves by an even juster title than those whom we have bought or captured.

To this I reply that even if I were to agree that there is a right of slavery among men which conforms to natural reason, and that according to *jus strictum* the bodies of slaves and their infants are under the power of their masters, it will always be true that another stronger right opposes the abuse of this one. This is the right of reasonable souls, which are naturally and inalienably free. It is the Law of God who is the sovereign master of bodies and souls and under whom masters are the fellow-citizens of their slaves, since slaves have the right of citizenship in the kingdom of God as well as their masters. So it can be said that a man's body is the property of his soul and ought not to be taken from him as long as he lives. Since a man's soul cannot be acquired, neither can ownership of his body be acquired, so that the right of a master over his slave can be in the nature only of what is called servitude to another, or a kind of usufruct. But usufruct has its limits; it must be practiced without destroying itself, *salva re*, so that this right cannot be extended to the point of making a slave evil or unhappy. But even if I were to agree, contrary to the nature of things, that an enslaved man is the property of another man, the right of the master, however rigorous, would be limited by *equity*, which demands that one man shall care for another as he would wish another to care for himself in a similar situation, and by *charity*, which orders us to work for the happiness of others. And these obligations are perfected by *piety*, that is, by what we owe to God. If we wished to stop with *jus strictum* alone, the American cannibals would have a right to eat their prisoners. There are those among them who demand even more; they use their prisoners to have children, then fatten and eat the children, and afterward, when she produces no more, the mother. Such are the consequences of a pretended right of masters over slaves and of fathers over children.

PROLEGOMENA TO ANY FUTURE METAPHYSICS THAT WILL BE ABLE TO COME FORWARD AS A SCIENCE

by

IMMANUEL KANT

Prologue

These prolegomena are not intended to be used by students, but rather by future teachers; they should not serve as a lecture for a science already present at hand, but as a guide for discovering this science itself for the first time.

There are scholars for whom the history of philosophy (the ancient as well as the modern) is itself philosophy; the present prolegomena are not written for these men. They must wait until those who toil at drawing it from the fountain of reason have completed their work. It will then be the work of these scholars to give to the world news of the event. Unfortunately, in their opinion nothing can be said which has not already been said, and this serves as a true prediction for all future time. Since human reason has speculated in various ways over innumerable objects throughout many centuries, one cannot fail to expect that many similarities to the ideas of the past can be found for every new idea discovered.

My intention is to convince all those who would seek to occupy themselves with metaphysics that it is essentially necessary to set aside all that has been done before and pause for a moment to look first at this preliminary question: is such a thing as metaphysics at all possible?

If metaphysics is a science, why does it not have the universal and permanent recognition accorded to the other sciences? And how can it appear to be a completed science if it taunts human reason with hopes never ceasing yet never satisfied? One may demonstrate knowledge or lack of knowledge in this alleged science, but first one must come, once and for all, to a certain conclusion concerning its nature. It cannot possibly remain on its present unsteady footing. It seems worthy of laughter that, while every other science marches proudly forward, this, which would be Wisdom itself, the Oracle to which every man puts his questions, goes in circles, constantly, in the same place, not moving forward a single step. And so it has lost its supporters. It does not find that those who feel strongly that they will shine in other sciences seek their glory here; for in this area, every person, however ignorant in all other areas, presumes to pass decisive judgment. In this land there is no standard weight and measure to distinguish thoroughness from empty prattling.

But it is not exactly unheard of that while arranging a science, one may begin to wonder how far one has already come, and then the question should at last occur concerning if and how in general such a science is possible. Human reason is so inclined toward construction that it repeatedly builds up towers and then wears them down in order to examine their foundation. It is never too late to become reasonable and wise, but it is always more difficult to begin a reformation if insight comes late.

To ask, therefore, if a science is a possibility, presupposes a doubt that the science exists in actuality. Such doubt insults the man who has put all he has in this supposed jewel, and so the one who raises this doubt is always greeted only with resistance from all sides. Some, in the proud awareness of all their ancient and therefore considered legitimate possessions, will take their metaphysical compendia in their hands and look on him with contempt. Others, who never see anything unless it is similar to something they have already seen somewhere else, will not understand him. And everything will remain for a time as if nothing had taken place to generate concern or the hope for an approaching change.

All the same, I dare to predict that the independent thinker who reads these prolegomena will do more than simply doubt his previous science. He will be fully persuaded that it cannot come to be unless the demands made here, on which its possibility is founded, are satisfied, and that this has never been done. At present, there is no such thing as metaphysics. For such a thing the demand can never cease, since the interests of general human understanding are deeply entwined with it. A full reform, a new birth of this science according to a wholly unknown plan, inevitably approaches, though men still struggle against it for a time.

Since the *Essays* of Locke and Leibniz, or rather since the origin of metaphysics so far as we know its history, there has been no event so decisive to its fate as the attack made upon it by David Hume. He shed no light on this sort of knowledge, but he struck a spark which could grow to give light, if it found something to support and develop its nascent glow.

Hume's initial principle was a single but important metaphysical concept, that of the combination of cause and effect (and with it the derivative concepts of force and action, etc.). He challenged reason, which pretends to have generated these concepts, to speak and give an answer by what right she thinks that something could be such that when it is posited, something else must also be posited, and that this is what is expressed in the concept of cause. He demonstrated irrefutably that it is entirely impossible for reason to think a priori and by means of concepts such as a connection that involves necessity. It is not possible to see how, because something is the case, something else must necessarily also be the case, and how therefore the concept of such connection can arise a priori. From this he inferred that reason has been quite deceived with this concept, which she falsely took for one of her children, when it is nothing other than a bastard of the imagination which, impregnated by experience, came to know representations under the law of association and had taken a subjective necessity (habit) for an objective necessity that arises out of insight. From this he inferred that reason has no capacity whatsoever for such connections, even generally, through thinking, because its concepts would then be fictions, and all of its professed a priori knowledge would be nothing but common experiences stamped falsely, which amounts to saying that there is no metaphysics at all, and there cannot be.

However hasty and incorrect his conclusions appear, they were at least grounded in an examination, and this examination united the attention of the great minds of his time in a search for a happier solution to the problem in the sense he proposed. All of this would have brought forth a complete reform of the science, only he met the usual unfortunate fate of metaphysicians—he was understood by no one. One cannot see without agony how his rivals (Reid, Oswals, Beattie and finally Priestley) so utterly missed the point of what he had put forward and, in always assuming that which he doubted, while proving with great ferocity and at times with great impudence that which it had never come into his head to doubt, they failed to recognize his signs for the betterment of the science, and everything remained as it was, as if nothing had happened. It was not a question of whether or not the concept of cause was right, useful, and indispensable for all our knowledge of nature. Hume never doubted any of this. Rather it was a question of whether the concept of cause could arise through reason alone, a priori, and in such a way contain inner truth, independent of all our experience, and therefore a much broader usefulness. The question was whether reason could discover a concept of cause that was not restricted in its use to objects of experience. This was the question Hume invited. It was solely a question of the origin of this concept, not of its indispensability in use. Determining the origin of the concept would be the determining of the conditions of its use and the perimeter in which it is valid.

But the rivals of the notorious man, in order to satisfy the problem, had to penetrate deeply into the nature of reason so far as it is concerned with pure thought, which was inconvenient for them. They found a more comfortable way to be defiant, without having any insight: the appeal to common sense. It is indeed a great gift of heaven to possess right (or as it is newly named, plain) common sense. But one must demonstrate common sense in deeds, through being well-considered and rational in what one thinks and says, not by appealing to it when one has no intelligent means of justifying oneself, as though it were an oracle. When insight and science fail—it is then and not sooner that they refer to common sense. This is one of the subtle discoveries of modern times, by means of which the most shallow prattler can stand with confidence among the greatest minds. But so long as the smallest remnant of insight is still present, no one would seize upon this deception. Seen in the light, this appeal is nothing more than an appeal to the judgment of the many. Their applause causes the philosopher to blush, while the popular clown stands triumphant and defiant in it. I should think that Hume had as sound a claim to common sense as Beattie, and over and above this that which Beattie did not have, namely a critical reason that can restrain common sense, keeping it from speculating, or, if the talk is of speculation, desires not to decide, because it understands that it cannot justify its own principles. It is only in this way that the understanding remains sound. Chisels and hammers are enough to work a piece of wood, but to etch one needs an etcher's needle. So common sense is as useful as speculative reason, but each is useful in its own way: the former, with judgments that are immediately applied to experience; the latter, when we judge universally, by means of mere concepts (e.g., in metaphysics, where common sense, in spite of being so named, cannot judge at all).

I confess freely that my remembering David Hume was that which many years ago first woke me from my dogmatic slumbers and gave my investigations in the field of speculative philosophy a wholly different direction. I was far from following him in the conclusions he gave, though, because he did not look at the whole of what he had put forward, but rather only at a part that fell from it, which, without taking the whole into consideration, can give no information. If we begin from a well-founded but undeveloped thought that another has left for us, we can hope that, by continued reflection, we can bring it further than the astute man whom we thank for the first spark of light.

I tried first, therefore, to see if Hume's objection could be put in more general form, and soon found that the concept of the combination of cause and effect was not the only concept through which the understanding takes a combination of things a priori, and that, moreover, it is precisely in this area that metaphysics is to be found. I sought to assure myself of their number, and I succeeded in this, starting from a single principle. I went on to deduce these concepts, which I was now assured did not come, as Hume had acquired them, through experience, but rather from pure understanding. This deduction had appeared impossible to my astute predecessor and had never come to anyone else, though everyone had used these concepts without asking where their objective validity was grounded. This deduction was the most important task that could ever be undertaken on behalf of metaphysics. What was worst of all was that metaphysics, as it was then present at hand, could not help me in the least, because only this deduction could make metaphysics possible in the first place. Now that I had dissolved Hume's problems, not simply in a particular instance but so far as they concerned the whole capacity of pure reason, I could go on safely, though always taking only slow steps, to determine (finally) the whole sphere of pure reason, its borders as well as its contents, completely and from general principles—which is what metaphysics needed in order to supply its system with a sure plan.

I am concerned, however, that my working out of Hume's problem in its greatest possible sense (namely, my critique of pure reason) should go just as far as the problem itself went when it was first put forward. It will be misjudged because it will not be understood. It will not be understood because it will only be skimmed, and men will not want to think it through. Men will not want to take the trouble to do this, because the work is dry, because it is obscure, because it opposes all their usual concepts, and because on top of all of this it is sprawling. Now I confess that I did not expect to hear from philosophers complaints concerning a lack of popularity, entertainment, or leisure, when it is the existence of indispensable human knowledge itself that I sought to find, which cannot be found unless the strictest rules of scholarly precision are agreed upon. Out of this, in time, popularity will come, but it should never be tolerated at the beginning. Yet concerning a certain obscurity that arises in part from the sprawling nature of the plan itself, into the darkness of which certain points of the investigation are lost, the complaint is correct. It is through the present prolegomena that I hope to correct it.

That work, which shows the capacity of pure reason, its whole sphere, and its boundaries, always remains the foundation, of which the prolegomena are only a preface—since that critique must, as a science, be systematic and stand complete down to its smallest parts, before we can even think of letting metaphysics appear, indeed, before we can have even only the most distant hope of doing so.

We have seen old knowledge passed off as new many times, taken out of its proper context, fitted into a systematic dress, and put under a new title; the greatest part of those who read this critique will expect nothing more from it. These prolegomena will on their own bring these readers to see that this is an entirely new science, which has never before been even considered, the very idea of which was unknown. Everything that has been given so far cannot be of use for it, with the possible exception that it can serve as a sign of Hume's doubt. And even Hume did not expect to find a possible formal science. He brought his ship to safety on the shores of skepticism, to let it lie there and decay, instead of giving it, as I intend, a pilot with a complete chart and compass, who, with the principles of the helmsman's art that provide knowledge of the globe, may steer the ship wherever it needs to go.

To begin a new science, one that is wholly isolated and the only representative of its kind, with the prejudice that we can only judge things through the mediation of putative knowledge already acquired (even though this is really what must be completely put in doubt), manages to bring about nothing other than the belief that we see only what we already know, because the expressions have a similar ring to them. Only that would make everything come forward disfigured, absurd, gibberish, because it is not the thought of the author, but rather always only our own thought, that we have as our foundation. It has become through long habit second nature to us. The sprawling dimension of the work (provided that it is part of the science itself and not merely its presentation), its inevitable dryness, its scholarly precision—these are features which are quite advantageous to the science itself, though they can be disadvantageous to the book that presents it.

It is not given to everyone to be so subtle and at the same time so attractive a writer as David Hume, or to have the thoroughness and still the elegance of Moses Mendelssohn; my presentation could have had its own popularity (how I flatter myself!) if I had only been sketching out a plan and leaving for others its execution, and my heart did not lie in the well-being of the science, if its health had not occupied me for so long. It required, by the way, much persistence, even self-denial, to set aside my attraction to immediate applause, having viewed the possibility of a more permanent approval that could come much later.

Plan making is most of the time a luxurious, boastful mind's occupation. Through it, one gives the appearance of creative genius; it demands what it cannot itself achieve, reprimanding what it cannot make better, making suggestions it does not know how to implement. Something more should belong to a competent plan for a general critique of reason than what one may merely suspect, if it is to be more than the simple, usual declamations of sanctimonious wishes. Pure reason, however, is so uniquely separate, such a thoroughly integrated sphere in itself, that it is impossible to infringe upon a part without incidentally touching the whole, and cannot organize the parts without first determining the place of each and its influence on all the others. There is nothing outside of it, our judgment can correct itself from within—the validity and use of every part depends upon the relation it has to everything else in reason itself, just as in the branches of any organized body, the function of each branch can only be derived from the concept of the whole. One can then say of such a critique that it is never reliable if it is not whole and complete down to the smallest elements of pure reason, and that in the sphere of this faculty one determines everything or nothing.

If a mere sketch that would precede a critique of pure reason would be unintelligible, unreliable, and useless coming before the critique itself, it would be exceedingly useful following it. For through what one had set down one could see the whole, the main points that emerge from the science, to examine and make the presentation stronger than it had been initially. Here is such a plan, now that the work is completed, calculated from this point on according to an analytic method. The work itself [the *Critique of Pure Reason*] had to be written in the synthetic style, with which the science could, as a branch of a particular cognitive faculty, place before our eyes all its articulations in their natural connections. Whoever finds this plan, which I put forward as a Prolegomena to any future metaphysics, still obscure itself, may consider the fact that it is not necessary for everyone to study metaphysics. Many are talented in the thorough and deep sciences which approximate intuition more closely; these men will have great success there, while they will not be successful in an inquiry that deals only with abstract concepts. In such cases, they must put their intellectual gifts to other uses. Those who judge metaphysics, or who are enterprising enough to write in this science, must satisfy the demands made here and accept my solution, or they must thoroughly refute it and set in its place another proposal—they cannot dismiss it. In conclusion, this maligned obscurity (which usually serves only to cover up mere laziness or idiocy) has its own use: all who observe cautious silence in other sciences speak with mastery and are bold and resolute in questions concerning metaphysics, because here their ignorance is free from opposition to the clarity of others. It is not free, however, from opposition to genuine critical principles, which one can therefore praise:

> Ignavum, fucos, pecus a praesepibus arcent.
> ["They keep out of the hives the drones, an indo-
> lent bunch." *Georgics*, IV 168.]

from
THE BLUE AND BROWN BOOKS
by
LUDWIG WITTGENSTEIN

L et us go back to the statement that thinking essentially consists in operating with signs. My point was that it is liable to mislead us if we say "thinking is a mental activity." The question what kind of an activity thinking is is analogous to this: "Where does thinking take place?" We can answer: on paper, in our head, in the mind. None of these statements of locality gives *the* locality of thinking. The use of all these specifications is correct, but we must not be misled by the similarity of their linguistic form into a false conception of their grammar. As, e.g., when you say: "Surely, the *real* place of thought is in our head." The same applies to the idea of thinking as an activity. It is correct to say that thinking is an activity of our writing hand, of our larynx, of our head, and of our mind, so long as we understand the grammar of these statements. And it is, furthermore, extremely important to realize how, by misunderstanding the grammar of our expressions, we are led to think of one in particular of these statements as giving the *real* seat of the activity of thinking.

There is an objection to saying that thinking is some such thing as an activity of the hand. Thinking, one wants to say, is part of our "private experience." It is not material, but an event in private consciousness. This objection is expressed in the question: "Could a machine think?" I shall talk about this at a later point, and now only refer you to an analogous question: "Can a machine have toothache?" You will certainly be inclined to say: "A machine can't have toothache." All I will do now is to draw your attention to the use which you have made of the word "can" and to ask you: "Did you mean to say that all our past experience has shown that a machine never had toothache?" The impossibility of which you speak is a logical one. The question is: What is the relation between thinking (or toothache) and the subject which thinks, has toothache, etc.? I shall say no more about this now.

If we say thinking is essentially operating with signs, the first question you might ask is: "What are signs?"—Instead of giving any kind of general answer to this question, I shall propose to you to look closely at particular cases which we should call "operating with signs." Let us look at a simple example of operating with words. I give someone the order: "fetch me six apples from the grocer," and I will describe a way of making use of such an order: The words "six apples" are written on a bit of paper, the paper is handed to the grocer, the grocer compares the word "apple" with labels on different shelves. He finds it to agree with one of the labels, counts from 1 to the number written on the slip of paper, and for every number counted takes a fruit off the shelf and puts it in a bag.—And here you have a case of the use of words. I shall in the future again and again draw your attention to what I shall call language games. These are ways of using signs simpler than those in which we use the signs of our highly complicated everyday language. Language games are the forms of language with which a child begins to make use of words. The study of language games is the study of primitive forms of language or primitive languages. If we want to study the problems of truth and falsehood, of the agreement and disagreement of propositions with reality, of the nature of assertion, assumption, and question, we shall with great advantage look at primitive forms of language in which these forms of thinking appear without the confusing background of highly complicated processes of thought. When we look at such simple forms of language the mental mist which seems to enshroud our ordinary use of language disappears. We see activities, reactions, which are clear-cut and transparent. On the other hand we recognize in these simple processes forms of language not separated by a break from our more complicated ones. We see that we can build up the complicated forms from the primitive ones by gradually adding new forms.

Now what makes it difficult for us to take this line of investigation is our craving for generality.

This craving for generality is the resultant of a number of tendencies connected with particular philosophical confusions. There is—

(*a*) The tendency to look for something in common to all the entities which we commonly subsume under a general term.—We are inclined to think that there must be something in common to all games, say, and that this common property is the justification for applying the general term "game" to the various games; whereas games form a *family* the members of which have family likenesses. Some of them have the same nose, others the same eyebrows and others again the same way of walking; and these likenesses overlap. The idea of a general concept being a common property of its particular instances connects up with other primitive, too simple, ideas of the structure of language. It is comparable to the idea that *properties* are *ingredients* of the things which have the properties; e.g., that beauty is an ingredient of all beautiful things as alcohol is of beer and wine, and that we therefore could have pure beauty, unadulterated by anything that is beautiful.

(*b*) There is a tendency rooted in our usual forms of expression, to think that the man who has learnt to understand a general term, say, the term "leaf," has thereby come to possess a kind of general picture of a leaf, as opposed to pictures of particular leaves. He was shown different leaves when he learnt the meaning of the word "leaf"; and showing him the particular leaves was only a means to the end of producing "in him" an idea which we imagine to be some kind of general image. We say that he sees what is in common to all these leaves; and this is true if we mean that he can on being asked tell us certain features or properties which they have in common. But we are inclined to think that the general idea of a leaf is something like a visual image, but one which only contains what is common to all leaves. (Galtonian composite photograph.) This again is connected with the idea that the meaning of a word is an image, or a thing correlated to the word. (This roughly means, we are looking at words as though they all were proper names, and we then confuse the bearer of a name with the meaning of the name.)

(*c*) Again, the idea we have of what happens when we get hold of the general idea "leaf," "plant," etc., etc., is connected with the confusion between a mental state, meaning a state of a hypothetical mental mechanism, and a mental state meaning a state of consciousness (toothache, etc.).

(*d*) Our craving for generality has another main source: our preoccupation with the method of science. I mean the method of reducing the explanation of natural phenomena to the smallest possible number of primitive natural laws; and, in mathematics, of unifying the treatment of different topics by using a generalization. Philosophers constantly see the method of science before their eyes, and are irresistibly tempted to ask and answer questions in the way science does. This tendency is the real source of metaphysics, and leads the philosopher into complete darkness. I want to say here that it can never be our job to reduce anything to anything, or to explain anything. Philosophy really *is* "purely descriptive." (Think of such questions as "Are there sense data?" and ask: What method is there of determining this? Introspection?)

Instead of "craving for generality" I could also have said "the contemptuous attitude towards the particular case." If, e.g., someone tries to explain the concept of number and tells us that such and such a definition will not do or is clumsy because it only applies to, say, finite cardinals I should answer that the mere fact that he could have given such a limited definition makes this definition extremely important to us. (Elegance is *not* what we are trying for.) For why should what finite and transfinite numbers have in common be more interesting to us than what distinguishes them? Or rather, I should not have said "why should it be more interesting to us?"— it *isn't*; and this characterizes our way of thinking.

The attitude towards the more general and the more special in logic is connected with the usage of the word "kind" which is liable to cause confusion. We talk of kinds of numbers, kinds of propositions, kinds of proofs; and, also, of kinds of apples, kinds of paper, etc. In one sense what defines the kind are properties, like sweetness, hardness, etc. In the other the different kinds are different grammatical structures. A treatise on pomology may be called incomplete if there exist kinds of apples which it doesn't mention. Here we have a standard of completeness in nature. Supposing on the other hand there was a game resembling that of chess but simpler, no pawns being used in it. Should we call this game incomplete? Or should we call a game more complete than chess if it in some way contained chess but added new elements? The contempt for what seems the less general case in logic springs from the idea that it is incomplete. It is in fact confusing to talk of cardinal arithmetic as something special as opposed to something more general. Cardinal arithmetic bears no mark of incompleteness; nor does an arithmetic which is cardinal and finite. (There are no subtle distinctions between logical forms as there are between the tastes of different kinds of apples.)

If we study the grammar, say, of the words "wishing," "thinking," "understanding," "meaning," we shall not be dissatisfied when we have described various cases of wishing, thinking, etc. If someone said, "surely this is not all that one calls 'wishing,'" we should answer, "certainly not, but you can build up more complicated cases if you like." And after all, there is not one definite class of features which characterize all cases of wishing (at least not as the word is commonly used). If on the other hand you wish to give a definition of wishing, i.e., to draw a sharp boundary, then you are free to draw it as you like; and this boundary will never entirely coincide with the actual usage, as this usage has no sharp boundary.

The idea that in order to get clear about the meaning of a general term one had to find the common element in all its applications has shackled philosophical investigation; for it has not only led to no result, but also made the philosopher dismiss as irrelevant the concrete cases, which alone could have helped him to understand the usage of the general term. When Socrates asks the question, "what is knowledge?" he does not even regard it as a *preliminary* answer to enumerate cases of knowledge.

PART FIVE
EPISTEMOLOGY

INTRODUCTION

by

JAAKKO HINTIKKA

Epistemology, otherwise known as *the theory of knowledge*, is best understood in the light of its history. That history involves several traditions. The sources of more than one of them can be witnessed in one of the most striking passages in the philosophical literature, perhaps in literature in general. It is the slave boy episode in Plato's dialogue *Meno*. The main character of the dialogue is Socrates, who is modeled on a real philosopher of the same name. In this episode, he engages an intelligent but uneducated slave boy in conversation to prove a philosophical point. Merely by putting questions to him, without giving him any new information, Socrates leads the boy to realize a nontrivial geometrical truth. Socrates' performance—or is it the boy's performance?—strikes one almost like a conjuring trick. Where did the knowledge of the theorem come from? The reader is witnessing an impressive and at the same time puzzling demonstration of the powers of the human mind. What is even more impressive, the particular mind in question is not that of a genius but of an uneducated slave.

One is tempted to see in the slave boy's achievement a small-scale example of the same kind of achievement as is attributed to Albert Einstein by C. P. Snow. In commenting on Einstein's articles (published in 1905) that revolutionized physics, Snow writes in a *Variety of Man* (1966): "All the papers are written in a style unlike any other theoretical physicist's. . . . The conclusions, the bizarre conclusions, emerge as though with the greatest ease: the reasoning is unbreakable. It looks as though he had reached the conclusions by pure thought, unaided, without listening to the opinions of others. To a surprisingly large extent, that is precisely what he had done."

Epistemology begins from this sense of wonder at the powers of the human knowledge-seeking mind.

Meno's slave boy episode marks the beginning of two traditions in epistemology. On the one hand, it illustrates the idea that there is a realm of truths that are independent of experience and hence reachable by pure thinking alone. Such truths are known as a priori truths. Their nature has been the subject of one of the research traditions in epistemology. This tradition will be discussed below.

On the other hand, the slave boy story brings out another line of thought about knowledge. How do we reach knowledge? Socrates did not deliver any new information to the slave boy; he only asked questions that the boy could have asked and got answered himself— if he had but known which questions to ask. Socrates' superiority does not lie in his knowing more answers than his interlocutors; it lies in his knowing what questions to ask. This suggests that the right method of reaching new knowledge is by raising the right questions. This idea is even imbedded in our vocabulary in that the English word *inquiry* means at one and the same time "the action of seeking for truth, knowledge or information" and "the action of asking or questioning; interrogation" (*Oxford English Dictionary*).

The Socratic idea of knowledge-seeking as questioning was developed by Plato into a method of philosophical training by means of questioning games. These games were studied and systematized by Aristotle, who thereby became the first systematic epistemologist as well the first logician in the Western tradition.

This tradition of questioning as the key epistemological method flourished again in the Middle Ages in the form of formal questioning games, called obligation games. In our days, it has been represented by such philosophers as R. G. Collingwood and H.-G. Gadamer, who have seen in "the logic of questions and answers" the crucial method of all inquiry.

Most philosophers nevertheless would not recognize this tradition of "inquiry as inquiry" as a part of the mainstream of modern epistemology. It is true that it has not often been discussed in so many words. It is, for instance, not until our own generation that a genuine systematic logic of questions and answers has been developed. However, in a more general perspective this tradition has been alive and well in science itself. For, as such philosophers as Sir Francis Bacon and Immanuel Kant have pointed out, experiments and observations can (and should) be considered as the scientist's questions to Nature.

One of the strengths of the questioning approach to epistemology is that it focuses our attention on the most important question that a scientist is likely to ask about knowledge-seeking in general. In presenting and defending his or her results, a scientist has to discuss the extent to which they are supported by available evidence. In other words, the scientist will have to ask: how well established are my results? But from the vantage point of the overall growth of science, an even more important question is: how can we obtain new and better evidence? In terms of the questioning approach, this question means: which new questions should we put to Nature? In other words, what new experiments and observations should we undertake?

One reason for the alienation of philosophers from the questioning tradition is that the questioning idea leads to problems. One of these problems figures already in the *Meno*. We cannot seek knowledge by asking questions unless we know what we are looking for. But if we know it, there is no need to look for it. This question is known as the *Meno* paradox.

Another problem is that it is clearly all right to rely on answers to questions in our quest of knowledge as long as one can trust all the answers one receives, but unfortunately such naive faith is not realistic either in ordinary life or in science. How can we cope with possibly mistaken or misleading answers? There are by and large two lines of thought that can be tried here. One possibility is for an inquirer to check answers to his or her questions by asking further questions and comparing the different answers with each other. Such a comparison procedure is what we find in a courtroom where lawyers try to discredit a witness's answers by showing that they contradict each other or contradict well-established answers from other witnesses or from other sources, such as physical evidence. Conversely, lawyers can seek to enhance the credibility of a witness by means of the testimony of other witnesses, for instance, so-called character witnesses. A similar procedure is found in science. Its success is guaranteed only if it can be argued that the method of questioning, or some equivalent method, is what is known as a self-correcting procedure, which ultimately leads to truth. This kind of line of thought has been represented among others by the great American pragmatist Charles S. Peirce. (Peirce did not identify the crucial steps in the self-correcting process of inquiry with questions, however, but with what he called abductive inferences.) The problem of coping with possibly false answers by means of further questions is a complicated one, however, and has been largely beyond the powers of philosophical epistemologists' logical tools till recently, even though scientists have in practice managed to cope with it.

Another way of attacking the problem of possibly false answers is to try to dispense with them altogether. In other words, one can try—and philosophers have tried—to find some truths, some answers, that are beyond any doubt and on which the rest of the structure of our knowledge can be based. This has been the most common type of approach to epistemology among philosophers. It is sometimes called epistemological *foundationalism*. It is wrought with formidable problems, however.

One problem is where to find the indubitable bases for our knowledge. A perennial candidate has been sense perception. But seeing should not always be believing, because it does not put us in direct touch with its objects. Perceptual illusions and hallucinations have been used as evidence to the contrary. With a modicum of ingenuity, a psychological experimenter can even make us "see" impossible objects. And even when no mistakes are involved, sense perception does not give us directly the information we spontaneously think that we receive from it. For instance, as George Berkeley urged especially forcefully, our depth (three-dimensional) seeing cannot, geometrically speaking, be automatic but is inevitably constructed from different clues, such as an unconscious comparison between the images on the retinas of one's two eyes. If anything, contemporary scientific study of perception has reinforced this indirectness and complexity of the process of sense perception, which makes its messages dependent on all sorts of different preconditions. For instance, according to one contemporary psychologist of perception, David Marr, the processing of visual information in the human central nervous system proceeds by stages. First, out of the visual input a primal sketch (as Marr calls it) is constructed, in which edges, boundaries, and regions of the visual field are distinguished. From this a two-and-a-half dimensional representation is constructed in which surfaces and shapes relative to the viewer are included. Finally, from those perspectival representations a truly three-dimensional object-centered model (representation) is created, according to Marr. Even if his theory is not accepted by all scientists, competing accounts are likely to be even more complex. Needless to say, all the processes described by Marr are unconscious. All of them involve neural processing and hence can in principle go wrong. Thus visual perception does not put us in direct contact with reality and is not infallible. Even one of philosophers' favorite examples of sense qualities, color, is not a simple matter of registrations of the kind of light that hits one's retina, but the end product of a complicated construction process in the brain.

In the philosophical literature the foundationalist approach is illustrated by the ideas of the British realists G. E. Moore and Bertrand Russell in the early years of the twentieth century. Moore argued in his famous article "The Refutation of Idealism" that in any experience I can in principle distinguish on the one hand the mere experience as a happening within my consciousness and on the other hand the object of that experience, that is, what is given to me in that experience. That "given" thing is not merely an appearance but something objective that is given to me in that experience. That something is the immediate object of that experience. It is directly given to me, and about it I cannot be mistaken. In perceptual experience, that object is called by Russell and Moore a sense datum. More generally, Russell called whatever is directly given to me an *object of acquaintance*, as distinguished from *objects of description* to which we do not have such a direct access. Accordingly, we can have knowledge either by acquaintance or by description. The reduction of the latter to the former is called by Russell reduction to acquaintance.

Sense data are among the Russellian objects of acquaintance, but they are not the only ones. Hence this object of direct perception, the *sense datum*, must be somehow closer to my consciousness than physical objects and yet belong to the world of physics. But what is it? Moore and Russell never gave a definitive answer, their best suggestion being that what is immediately given to me are the states of my own central nervous system.

Sense data are part of the physical world, but they are not themselves physical objects. The reason is that our perceptual experience can mislead us about physical objects, as attested to by perceptual illusions and hallucinations. But the difficulty of finding indubitable bases for our knowledge is not the only problem here. Even if direct perception provides us with such starting points, we still face the problem of showing how the rest of our knowledge rests on them. This looks like a serious problem. The testimony of the senses only provides us with particular truths. Yet much of our most important knowledge consists of general truths, such as scientific theories. Hence we need some way of either inferring general truths from particular ones or otherwise reducing the former to the latter.

Inferences from particular cases to a generalization (or to other particular cases) are usually known as *inductive inferences.* In view of what has been said, it is no surprise that the problem of induction has been one of the most prominent ones in epistemology. It was thrust to prominence in philosophy by David Hume. Hume was an empiricist who wanted to find the basis for all our "ideas" in the "impressions" with which experience provides us. With great ingenuity, Hume searches for the "impressions" that underlie such general beliefs as our trust in causal connections. In the end, he finds none. "The mind can never possibly find the effect in the supposed cause by the most accurate scrutiny and examination," he concludes. "For the effect is totally different from the cause, and consequently can never be discovered in it. Motion in the second billiard ball is a quite distinct event from the motion of the first, nor is there anything in the one to suggest the smallest hint of the other." Moreover, Hume argues even more cleverly that observing the cause should not on purely empirical grounds even make the effect more probable.

Hume certainly has logic on his side, in that from particular truths no nontrivial general truths (including probabilistic ones) can be inferred purely logically. Hence the structure of our knowledge apparently cannot be understood without postulating some strong a priori truths, such as would justify inductive inferences, for example. In our days, the same conclusion has apparently emerged from the heroic attempt by Rudolf Carnap to construct a probabilistic logic of induction based on purely logical principles. In the end Carnap, too, needs a priori principles in order to prefer one inductive method over others.

In this situation, many philosophers have been led to make, if not a virtue, then at least a philosophical theory out of necessity. They have defended a view that maintains we do not reach our general truths like scientific theories by inference or by any other process that is subject to rules. For instance, according to such philosophers, scientific discovery has no "logic." It is a matter of intuition or some other kind of insight, lucky guesses or whatnot, not of inference. Only afterward can a general truth be justified by comparing its consequences with the results of observations and experiments. This kind of view is known as the *hypothetico-deductive* model of scientific (and nonscientific) reasoning. It is sometimes expressed by distinguishing *contexts of discovery*, which allegedly are not subject to rules, and *contexts of justification*, for which a rational theory can be developed.

According to other philosophers, such a view is premature. Some have sought to look at general truths, and the rest of the structure of our indirect knowledge, not as being *inferred* from the basic data but as being *constructed* from them. As Russell formulated what he claims to be "the supreme maxim of scientific philosophizing": "whenever possible, logical constructions are to be substituted for inferred entities." Several major philosophers have sought to implement this idea of considering the entire structure of our knowledge as being constructed out of the given data of experience. Such attempts include Bertrand Russell's *Our Knowledge of the External World* (1914), Rudolf Carnap's *Logical Structure of the World* (1928), and Nelson Goodman's *The Structure of Appearance* (1951). These books are all major intellectual achievements, but as far as their ultimate success is concerned, the most favorable thing to be said is that the jury is perhaps still out.

One can also look at the original ambitious project of the phenomenological philosophy of Edmund Husserl in the same light. His famous "phenomenological reduction" may be compared with Russell's "reduction to acquaintance," and Russell's "acquaintance" can be thought of as a counterpart to what Husserl calls "intuition." An important example of Husserl's efforts in showing how concepts can be "constituted" on the basis of what is immediately given to one's consciousness is his discussion of the phenomenology of the internal awareness of time. The immediately given data include in this case one's spontaneous awareness of what has just happened ("retention") and one's spontaneous awareness of what is about to happen ("protention"). In a wider historical perspective, such a philosophical construction of time can perhaps be compared with the procedure of a modern novelist like Virginia Woolf, who does not present her readers with a ready-made chronology of events but instead forces them to construct the time sequence of her fictional world from the stream of consciousness of her characters.

A more conclusive rejoinder can be offered from the vantage point of the interrogative (questioning) approach to inquiry.

Whether or not some particular truths are indubitable, the actual input into our cognitive processes often consists of tentative general truths and not only of particular ones. For instance, a controlled experiment, the most important methodological weapon of actual science, can show as its result how one variable (the observed variable) depends on another one (the controlled variable). Such dependence, if true, is a general fact, even when it is restricted to certain limited values of the controlled variable. Of course we are no longer dealing with indubitable starting points for our knowledge. But if such general answers by Nature can be tested by further experiments and observations, there is no need to exclude them from the input that goes into the total structure of our knowledge.

In spirit, if not in the letter, such a view is close to the ideas of Charles S. Peirce. It is also among the ironies of history that Hume, who was restricting the input of our cognitive processes to particular "impressions," should have claimed to be following the methods of reasoning of the great scientist and mathematician Isaac Newton. For Newton's methodology relied essentially on using experiments and systematic observations that already possess some degree of generality. They can hence serve as the "phenomena" from which general laws can, according to Newton, be "deduced."

In recent decades, much of the specialized work in epistemology in English-speaking countries has concerned "contexts of justification" rather than "contexts of discovery." The topics that have been discussed include the definition of knowledge, the different kinds of evidential support ("warrants"), and what is known as belief dynamics. Of these subjects, the definition of knowledge was already discussed by Plato. In his dialogue *Theaetetus*, several attempted definitions of knowledge are examined and rejected, among them knowledge as perception (or should we say, in the light of hindsight, knowledge as acquaintance?), knowledge as true belief, and knowledge as true belief accompanied by an account (*logos*). In our time, other definitions of knowledge have likewise been criticized. The best-known case in point is Edmund Gettier's argument in 1963 to the effect that knowledge cannot be defined as justified true belief. Some others have tried to rely in their definitions of knowledge on the idea that in order to amount to knowledge a belief must not be defeasible, that is, that it would not be dislodged by any possible true information.

The best-known discussions of the warrant problem are Alvin Plantinga's books *Warrant: The Current Debate* (1993) and *Warrant and Proper Function* (1993). Belief revision theories deal with the justification, not of beliefs, but of belief changes. They are discussed, for instance, in Isaac Levi's book *The Fixation of Belief and Its Undoing* (1991).

But can knowledge be defined by reference only to the evidential support that a candidate for such a status has? Frank Ramsey suggested requiring also that the belief in question is formed by the right kind of method. More generally speaking, knowledge-seeking can be thought of as a "game" in the generalized sense of the mathematical theory of games. This viewpoint offers several interesting insights. For instance, from the theory of games it can be seen that what can in the last analysis be evaluated in knowledge-seeking are entire strategies governing an inquirer's choices in the entire knowledge-seeking process rather than particular "moves" or particular situations that may come about in the process. This makes it questionable whether it is worthwhile to try to define knowledge in purely evidential terms. This is because such a definition would involve evaluating the situation at some particular stage of the epistemic enterprise. At the same time, Ramsey's suggestion is vindicated insofar as we can identify what he called "methods" with strategies in the game-theoretical sense. Again, from the strategic viewpoint one can find certain remarkable connections between strategies of inquiry and strategies of logical deduction. These connections may be seen as justifying the widespread popular conception of logic and deduction as the secret of all good reasoning. Such a "Sherlock Holmes conception of logic and reasoning" would be viable only from a strategic viewpoint, however.

The kind of skeptical challenge exemplified by Hume was met head on even before Hume by another major thinker. The most resolute attempt to find an indubitable starting point for our knowledge was made by René Descartes. He turned the tables on the skeptics who doubted the possibility of knowledge by turning himself—or a part of his self—into a devil's or, rather, a skeptic's advocate.

> I resolved to pretend that all the things that had ever entered my mind were no more true than the illusions of my dreams. But immediately I noticed that while I was trying thus to think everything false, it

was necessary that I, who was thinking this, was
something. And observing that this truth, "I am
thinking, therefore I exist" [in Latin, cogito, ergo sum]
was so firm and sure that all the most extravagant
suppositions of the skeptics were incapable of shaking it, I decided that I could accept it without scruple
as the first principle of the philosophy I was seeking.

This is one of the most famous passages in epistemological literature. It has even more facets than *Meno*'s slave boy episode. First of
all, what is the nerve of Descartes's argument, and what does it
prove? Elsewhere, he formulates his conclusion as the impossibility
to deny his own existence. If René tries to tell his alter ego Descartes,
"I don't exist," by so doing he on the contrary shows that he does
exist, quite as much as (say) Mark Twain could have proved his existence by saying to a doubter "Mark Twain does not exist." Or not
quite, for the listener must for the purpose know that the speaker is
indeed Mark Twain. By the same token, a witness to Descartes's
experimental attempt to think to himself "I don't exist" must know
who that "I" is, and know it a priori because it is supposed to be the
first and foremost philosophical truth. Otherwise the only conclusion he could draw from "*I am thinking*" is, as the witty German
thinker Georg Christoph Lichtenberg put it, *es denkt* (*thinking is
going on*). But the only person who is witnessing Descartes's
thought-experiment and who can know for certain who Descartes's
"I" is is Descartes himself. In this sense, Descartes has proved his
existence only to himself. You cannot prove *Descartes's* existence to
yourself by the *cogito, ergo sum* argument, even though you can
hopefully prove *your* existence to yourself in the same way. In this
sense, Descartes's famous insight is subjective. In this respect, it has
set the tone of much of the later epistemology. For instance, the
grand projects of Husserl, Russell, and Carnap are attempts to show
how I can construct *my* knowledge of the world from *my* experiences. Descartes himself could not claim that his "clear and distinct"
ideas like the *cogito* insight gave him universally applicable knowledge until he had established by further arguments the existence of
a God who does not deceive us.

Descartes's controversial insight is not unrelated to yet another
tradition in epistemology. One of the most interesting aspects of the
cogito argument is that Descartes in it produces the grounds for his

conclusion by his own activity of thinking. This is reminiscent of the idea that we can have knowledge, and even particularly important knowledge, of what we ourselves make or otherwise produce—and perhaps only of such creations of ours. This idea of "genuine knowledge as maker's knowledge" is a double-edged one, however. It can be used—and has been used—to emphasize the exalted nature of humanistic and societal knowledge and to denigrate our knowledge of nature. For instance, Thomas Hobbes maintained that

> the science of every subject is derived from a precognition of the causes, generation, and construction of the same. . . . Geometry therefore is demonstrable for the lines and figures from which we reason are drawn and described by ourselves; and civil philosophy [i.e., political science] is demonstrable, because we make the commonwealth ourselves. But because of natural bodies we do not know the construction, but seek it from the effects, there lies no demonstration of what the causes be we seek for, but only what they may be.

On the other hand, the same idea could be used to emphasize the importance of acquiring knowledge of nature just because such knowledge gives us power over nature. Sir Francis Bacon's slogan "knowledge is power" is the best-known expression of this idea.

Hobbes's statement is controversial and arguably contains a confusion. In geometry, we may perhaps be said to argue by means of figures we "draw and describe" ourselves, but our arguments are not about self-constructed figures on paper but about what they signify, that is, geometric objects in space. However, the great Immanuel Kant took the bold step of correcting Hobbes's confusion by extending his ideas. As he put it in his famous *Critique of Pure Reason*: "Reason has insight only into that which it produces [itself] after a plan of its own." In particular, Kant maintained that we can have higher-grade knowledge (which he identified with what he called synthetic knowledge a priori) in mathematics because we have ourselves imposed a framework of mathematical concepts on reality. Kant thought that that imposition takes place in sense perception, a view which has been shown not to do justice to the facts. But his basic idea of focusing in epistemology on what we humans do in obtaining our knowledge of objects rather than on those objects is both interesting and promising, even though it has not been used very much in contemporary epistemological theorizing.

Kant's ideas can also be seen as echoing the interrogative approach to epistemology. It is not accidental that it was Kant who compared experiments to questions put to Nature. Another echo of Kantian activist ideas in epistemology can perhaps be seen in Ludwig Wittgenstein's idea that the relations of our language and our knowledge to the world are constituted by certain rule-governed human activities which he called language games.

But what about the kind of a priori knowledge that Socrates helped *Meno*'s slave boy to reach? The primary example of such a priori knowledge is mathematical knowledge. Kant's theory of mathematics as dealing with properties and relations that we ourselves unwittingly project on reality is essentially an attempt to answer this question. Much earlier, Plato assigned mathematical objects to a higher, supersensible reality of which we can have knowledge only by means of reason, not sense perception. A contemporary version of Plato's theory conceives of mathematics as dealing with an abstract realm of all possible structures, sometimes identified with the universe studied in the fundamental part of mathematics called set theory. In an apparent contrast to such views, a tradition in the epistemology of mathematics has tried to reduce mathematics to logic and even maintained that logical and hence presumably also mathematical truths are empty tautologies in the sense that they do not convey any information about reality.

There is no consensus in the epistemology of mathematics and more generally in the epistemology of a priori knowledge. But perhaps there is in the last analysis less real disagreement here than first meets the eye—or, rather, meets the mind. Just because mathematics is, according to the Platonists, about a different region or reality, it presumably does not convey any factual knowledge of the concrete reality. And perhaps that higher reality can be both objective and created by human thought. Bridges and highways are not made any less objective by the fact that they are made by us humans.

A subject often discussed under the heading of epistemology is the nature of truth. It might be suggested that this inclusion is based on a confusion, namely, a confusion of what it is for a proposition or belief *to be* true and what it is for it *to be known to be* true. But even if there is such a confusion—as there undoubtedly has been and still is—to make the proper distinction between the two is part of the business of epistemology.

Our naive pretheoretical idea of truth is undoubtedly something like a correspondence between a proposition and a fact. As Aristotle put this idea, "To say of what is that it is not, or of what is not that it is, is false, while to say of what is that it is, and of what is not that it is not, is true." Systematized and clarified, ideas of this kind are known as *correspondence theories of truth*. In view of their obvious plausibility, why should any philosopher have maintained anything different? Some have challenged the distinction between truth and known truth. What use can there be for an idea of truth unless its applicability to particular cases can be known? But in many cases we cannot decide once and for all whether a certain belief is true. The best we can do is to see how well it squares with other well-entrenched beliefs of ours. Sophisticated versions of such lines of thought have led some philosophers to maintain that the truth of a belief should be thought of in terms of its coherence with other beliefs. Views of this kind are known as *coherence theories of truth*.

Lines of thought of this kind are subject to charges of the confusion just mentioned. There is nevertheless a much deeper issue involved here. Maybe the nature of truth lies in correspondence between language and reality (or of thought and reality), but can we express such a correspondence in our language? Don't we have to use language to refer simultaneously to facts and also to itself? Is this possible? In brief, is truth expressible in language? Several of the greatest philosophers of the twentieth century (and perhaps of other centuries as well) have denied such expressibility. As Wittgenstein once put this claim, "The limit of language shows itself in the impossibility of describing the fact that corresponds to a sentence . . . without repeating that very sentence." On such a view, we cannot approach truth directly. We cannot define it. We cannot meaningfully ask what the truth is or look for truth. Philosophical truth has to reveal itself to us. Truth is not correspondence but openness, *Erschlossenheit,* as Martin Heidegger expressed it.

This line of thought leads to a view of the entire philosophical thinking, including epistemology, that is radically different from most of the traditional ones. According to this view we much approach reality not as an object of scientific investigation but as if it were a text that we have to decipher. This approach is known as *hermeneutical philosophy*. Its main representatives have been Heidegger and Gadamer.

But is truth ineffable, as hermeneutical philosophers assume? Here sober logical analysis suddenly becomes relevant to the major philosophical issues of our times. For a long time, the definitive answer was taken to be a result of the great logician Alfred Tarski first published in 1933. This result says that, given certain assumptions, the concept of truth for a language cannot be defined in the same language, but only in a richer one. Since there is no richer language over and above our actual working language, it seems to follow that a philosophically interesting concept of truth cannot be defined. Tarski's argument relies on a mathematically sophisticated version of the old chestnut known as the Paradox of the Liar. If I say, "What I am now saying is false," am I saying something true or false? Either answer seems to lead to a contradiction. Tarski argues that such paradoxes make it impossible to use the concept of truth coherently in our actual colloquial language. However, recent results have dramatically reversed the picture Tarski's result seems to suggest. The assumptions on which Tarski's theorem rests have been shown to be arbitrary and unnecessarily restrictive. The normal situation in a sufficiently rich language is that truth can be defined. The consequences of these new results for the different theories of truth and for epistemology largely remain to be worked out.

MENO
by
PLATO

Socrates is involved in a discussion with Meno about virtue. He wants to know what virtue is, and if it can be taught.

Socrates: Then answer me again from the beginning: what do both you and your associate say that virtue is?

Meno: Socrates, I used to be told, before I began to meet you, that yours was just such a case of being in doubt yourself and making others doubt also; and so now I find you are merely bewitching me with your spells and incantations, which have reduced me to utter perplexity. And if I am indeed to have my jest, I consider that both in your appearance and in other respects you are extremely like the flat torpedo sea-fish; for it benumbs anyone who approaches and touches it, and something of the sort is what I find you have done to me now. For in truth I feel my soul and my tongue quite benumbed, and I am at a loss what answer to give you. And yet on countless occasions I have made abundant speeches on virtue to various people—and very good speeches they were, so I thought—but now I cannot say one word as to what it is. You are well advised, I consider, in not voyaging or taking a trip away from home; for if you went on like this as a stranger in any other city you would very likely be taken up for a wizard.

Socrates: You are a rogue, Meno, and had almost deceived me.

Meno: How is that, Socrates?

Socrates: I perceive your aim in thus comparing me.

Meno: What was it?

Socrates: That I might compare you in return. One thing I know about all handsome people is this—they delight in being compared to something. They do well over it, since fine features, I suppose, must have fine similes. But I am not for playing your game. As for me, if the torpedo is torpid itself while causing others to be torpid,

I am like it, but not otherwise. For it is not from any sureness in myself that I cause others to doubt: it is from being in more doubt than anyone else that I cause doubt in others. So now, for my part, I have no idea what virtue is, whilst you, though perhaps you may have known before you came in touch with me, are now as good as ignorant of it also. But none the less I am willing to join you in examining it and inquiring into its nature.

Meno: Why, on what lines will you look, Socrates, for a thing of whose nature you know nothing at all? Pray, what sort of thing, amongst those that you know not, will you treat us to as the object of your search? Or even supposing, at the best, that you hit upon it, how will you know it is the thing you did not know?

Socrates: I understand the point you would make, Meno. Do you see what a captious argument you are introducing—that, forsooth, a man cannot inquire either about what he knows or about what he does not know? For he cannot inquire about what he knows, because he knows it, and in that case is in no need of inquiry; nor again can he inquire about what he does not know, since he does not know about what he is to inquire.

Meno: Now does it seem to you to be a good argument, Socrates?

Socrates: It does not.

Meno: Can you explain how not?

Socrates: I can; for I have heard from wise men and women who told of things divine that—

Meno: What was it they said?

Socrates: Something true, as I thought, and admirable.

Meno: What was it? And who were the speakers?

Socrates: They were certain priests and priestesses who have studied so as to be able to give a reasoned account of their ministry; and Pindar also and many another poet of heavenly gifts. As to their words, they are these: mark now, if you judge them to be true. They say that the soul of man is immortal, and at one time comes to an end, which is called dying, and at another is born again, but never perishes. Consequently one ought to live all one's life in the utmost holiness.

> For from whomsoever Persephone shall accept requital for ancient wrong, the souls of these she restores in the ninth year to the upper sun again;

>from them arise glorious kings and men of splendid
>might and surpassing wisdom, and for all remaining
>time are they called holy heroes amongst mankind.

Seeing then that the soul is immortal and has been born many times, and has beheld all things both in this world and in the nether realms, she has acquired knowledge of all and everything; so that it is no wonder that she should be able to recollect all that she knew before about virtue and other things. For as all nature is akin, and the soul has learned all things, there is no reason why we should not, by remembering but one single thing—an act which men call learning—discover everything else, if we have courage and faint not in the search; since, it would seem, research and learning are wholly recollection. So we must not hearken to that captious argument: it would make us idle, and is pleasing only to the indolent ear, whereas the other makes us energetic and inquiring. Putting my trust in its truth, I am ready to inquire with you into the nature of virtue.

Meno: Yes, Socrates, but what do you mean by saying that we do not learn, and that what we call learning is recollection? Can you instruct me that this is so?

Socrates: I remarked just now, Meno, that you are a rogue; and so here you are asking if I can instruct you, when I say there is no teaching but only recollection: you hope that I may be caught contradicting myself forthwith.

Meno: I assure you, Socrates, that was not my intention; I only spoke from habit. But if you can somehow prove to me that it is as you say, pray do so.

Socrates: It is no easy matter, but still I am willing to try my best for your sake. Just call one of your own troop of attendants there, whichever one you please, that he may serve for my demonstration.

Meno: Certainly. You, I say, come here.

Socrates: He is a Greek, I suppose, and speaks Greek?

Meno: Oh yes, to be sure—born in the house.

Socrates: Now observe closely whether he strikes you as recollecting or as learning from me.

Meno: I will.

Socrates: Tell me, boy, do you know that a square figure is like this?

Boy: I do.

Socrates: Now, a square figure has these lines, four in number, all equal?

Boy: Certainly.

Socrates: And these, drawn through the middle, are equal too, are they not?

Boy: Yes.

Socrates: And a figure of this sort may be larger or smaller?

Boy: To be sure.

Socrates: Now if this side were two feet and that also two, how many feet would the whole be? Or let me put it thus: if one way it were two feet, and only one foot the other, of course the space would be two feet taken once?

Boy: Yes.

Socrates: But as it is two feet also on that side, it must be twice two feet?

Boy: It is.

Socrates: Then the space is twice two feet?

Boy: Yes.

Socrates: Well, how many are twice two feet? Count and tell me.

Boy: Four, Socrates.

Socrates: And might there not be another figure twice the size of this, but of the same sort, with all its sides equal like this one?

Boy: Yes.

Socrates: Then how many feet will it be?

Boy: Eight.

Socrates: Come now, try and tell me how long will each side of that figure be. This one is two feet long: what will be the side of the other, which is double in size?

Boy: Clearly, Socrates, double.

Socrates: Do you observe, Meno, that I am not teaching the boy anything, but merely asking him each time? And now he supposes that he knows about the line required to make a figure of eight square feet; or do you not think he does?

Meno: I do.

Socrates: Well, does he know?

Meno: Certainly not.

Socrates: He just supposes it, from the double size required?

Meno: Yes.

Socrates: Now watch his progress in recollecting, by the proper use of memory. Tell me, boy, do you say we get the double space from the double line? The space I speak of is not long one way and short the other, but must be equal each way like this one, while being double its size—eight square feet. Now see if you still think we get this from a double length line.

Boy: I do.

Socrates: Well, this line is doubled, if we add here another of the same length?

Boy: Certainly.

Socrates: And you say we shall get our eight-foot space from four lines of this length?

Boy: Yes.

Socrates: Then let us describe the square, drawing four equal lines of that length. This will be what you say is the eight-foot figure, will it not?

Boy: Certainly.

Socrates: And here, contained in it, have we not four squares, each of which is equal to this space of four feet?

Boy: Yes.

Socrates: Then how large is the whole? Four times at space, is it not?

Boy: It must be.

Socrates: And is four times equal to double?

Boy: No, to be sure.

Socrates: But how much is it?

Boy: Fourfold.

Socrates: Thus, from the double-sized line, boy, we get a space, not of double, but of fourfold size.

Boy: That is true.

Socrates: And if it is four times four it is sixteen, is it not?

Boy: Yes.

Socrates: What line will give us a space of eight feet? This one gives us a fourfold space, does it not?

Boy: It does.

Socrates: And a space of four feet is made from this line of half the length?

Boy: Yes.

Socrates: Very well; and is not a space of eight feet double the size of this one, and half the size of this other?

Boy: Yes.

Socrates: Will it not be made from a line longer than the one of these, and shorter than the other?

Boy: I think so.

Socrates: Excellent: always answer just what you think. Now tell me, did we not draw this line two feet, and that four?

Boy: Yes.

Socrates: Then the line on the side of the eight-foot figure should be more than this of two feet, and less than the other of four?

Boy: It should.

Socrates: Try and tell me how much you would say it is.

Boy: Three feet.

Socrates: Then if it is to be three feet, we shall add on a half to this one, and so make it three feet? For here we have two, and here one more, and so again on that side there are two, and another one; and that makes the figure of which you speak.

Boy: Yes.

Socrates: Now if it be three this way and three that way, the whole space will be thrice three feet, will it not?

Boy: So it seems.

Socrates: And thrice three feet are how many?

Boy: Nine.

Socrates: And how many feet was that double one to be?

Boy: Eight.

Socrates: So we fail to get our eight-foot figure from this three-foot line.

Boy: Yes, indeed.

Socrates: But from what line shall we get it? Try and tell us exactly; and if you would rather not reckon it out, just show what line it is.

Boy: Well, on my word, Socrates, I for one do not know.

Socrates: There now, Meno, do you observe what progress he has already made in his recollection? At first he did not know what is the line that forms the figure of eight feet, and he does not know even now: but at any rate he thought he knew then, and confidently answered as though he knew, and was aware of no difficulty; whereas now he feels the difficulty he is in, and besides not knowing does not think he knows.

Meno: That is true.

Socrates: And is he not better off in respect of the matter which he did not know?

Meno: I think that too is so.

Socrates: Now, by causing him to doubt and giving him the torpedo's shock, have we done him any harm?

Meno: I think not.

Socrates: And we have certainly given him some assistance, it would seem, towards finding out the truth of the matter: for now he will push on in the search gladly, as lacking knowledge; whereas then he would have been only too ready to suppose he was right in saying, before any number of people any number of times, that the double space must have a line of double the length for its side.

Meno: It seems so.

Socrates: Now do you imagine he would have attempted to inquire or learn what he thought he knew, when he did not know it, until he had been reduced to the perplexity of realizing that he did not know, and had felt a craving to know?

Meno: I think not, Socrates.

Socrates: Then the torpedo's shock was of advantage to him?

Meno: I think so.

Socrates: Now you should note how, as a result of this perplexity, he will go on and discover something by joint inquiry with me, while I merely ask questions and do not teach him; and be on the watch to see if at any point you find me teaching him or expounding to him, instead of questioning him on his opinions.

Tell me, boy: here we have a square of four feet, have we not? You understand?

Boy: Yes.

Socrates: And here we add another square equal to it?

Boy: Yes.

Socrates: And here a third, equal to either of them?

Boy: Yes.

Socrates: Now shall we fill up this vacant space in the corner?

Boy: By all means.

Socrates: So here we must have four equal spaces?

Boy: Yes.

Socrates: Well now, how many times larger is this whole space than this other?

Boy: Four times.

Socrates: But it was to have been only twice, you remember?

Boy: To be sure.

Socrates: And does this line, drawn from corner to corner, cut in two each of these spaces?

Boy: Yes.

Socrates: And have we here four equal lines containing this space?

Boy: We have.

Socrates: Now consider how large this space is.

Boy: I do not understand.

Socrates: Has not each of the inside lines cut off half of each of these four spaces?

Boy: Yes.

Socrates: And how many spaces of that size are there in this part?

Boy: Four.

Socrates: And how many in this?

Boy: Two.

Socrates: And four is how many times two?

Boy: Twice.

Socrates: And how many feet is this space?

Boy: Eight feet.

Socrates: From what line do we get this figure?

Boy: From this.

Socrates: From the line drawn corner-wise across the four-foot figure?

Boy: Yes.

Socrates: The professors call it the diagonal: so if the diagonal is its name, then according to you, Meno's boy, the double space is the square of the diagonal.

Boy: Yes, certainly it is, Socrates.

Socrates: What do you think, Meno? Was there any opinion that he did not give as an answer of his own thought?

Meno: No, they were all his own.

Socrates: But you see, he did not know, as we were saying a while since.

Meno: That is true.

Socrates: Yet he had in him these opinions, had he not?

Meno: Yes.

Socrates: So that he who does not know about any matters, whatever they be, may have true opinions on such matters, about which he knows nothing?

Meno: Apparently.

Socrates: And at this moment those opinions have just been stirred up in him, like a dream; but if he were repeatedly asked these same questions in a variety of forms, you know he will have in the end as exact an understanding of them as anyone.

Meno: So it seems.

Socrates: Without anyone having taught him, and only through questions put to him, he will understand, recovering the knowledge out of himself?

Meno: Yes.

Socrates: And is not this recovery of knowledge, in himself and by himself, recollection?

Meno: Certainly.

Socrates: And must he not have either once acquired or always had the knowledge he now has?

Meno: Yes.

Socrates: Now if he always had it, he was always in a state of knowing; and if he acquired it at some time, he could not have acquired it in this life. Or has someone taught him geometry? You see, he can do the same as this with all geometry and every branch of knowledge. Now, can anyone have taught him all this? You ought surely to know, especially as he was born and bred in your house.

Meno: Well, I know that no one has ever taught him.

Socrates: And has he these opinions, or has he not?

Meno: He must have them, Socrates, evidently.

Socrates: And if he did not acquire them in this present life, is it not obvious at once that he had them and learnt them during some other time?

Meno: Apparently.

Socrates: And this must have been the time when he was not a human being?

Meno: Yes.

Socrates: So if in both of these periods—when he was and was not a human being—he has had true opinions in him which have only to be awakened by questioning to become knowledge, his soul must have had this cognisance throughout all time? For clearly he has always either been or not been a human being.

Meno: Evidently.

Socrates: And if the truth of all things that are is always in our soul, then the soul must be immortal; so that you should take heart and, whatever you do not happen to know at present—that is, what you do not remember—you must endeavour to search out and recollect?

Meno: What you say commends itself to me, Socrates, I know not how.

Socrates: And so it does to me, Meno. Most of the points I have made in support of my argument are not such as I can confidently assert; but that the belief in the duty of inquiring after what we do not know will make us better and braver and less helpless than the notion that there is not even a possibility of discovering what we do not know, nor any duty of inquiring after it—this is a point for which I am determined to do battle, so far as I am able, both in word and deed.

Meno: There also I consider that you speak aright, Socrates.

from

POSTERIOR ANALYTICS
by
ARISTOTLE

Now as for deduction and demonstration, it is evident both what each is and how it comes about—and at the same time this goes for demonstrative understanding too (for that is the same thing). But as for principles—how they become familiar and what is the state that becomes familiar with them—that will be clear from what follows, when we have first set down the puzzles.

Now, we have said earlier that it is not possible to understand through demonstration if we are not aware of the primitive, immediate, principles. But as to knowledge of the immediates, one might puzzle both whether it is the same or not the same—whether there is understanding of each, or rather understanding of the one and some other kind of thing of the other—and also whether the states are not present in us but come about in us, or whether they are present in us but escape notice.

Well, if we have them, it is absurd; for it results that we have pieces of knowledge more precise than demonstration and yet this escapes notice. But if we get them without having them earlier, how might we become familiar with them and learn them from no pre-existing knowledge? For that is impossible, as we said in the case of demonstration too. It is evidently impossible, then, both for us to have them to come about in us when we are ignorant and have no such state at all. Necessarily, therefore, we have some capacity, but do not have one of a type which will be more valuable than these in respect of precision.

And *this* evidently belongs to all animals; for they have a connate discriminatory capacity, which is called perception. And if perception is present in them, in some animals the retention of the percept comes about, but in others it does not come about. Now for those in which it does not come about, there is no knowledge outside perceiving (either none at all, or none with regard to that of which there is no retention); but for some perceivers, it is possible to grasp it in their minds. And when many such things come about, then a difference comes about, so that some come to have an account from the retention of such things, and others do not.

So from perception there comes memory, as we call it, and from memory (when it occurs often in connection with the same thing), experience; for memories that are many in number from a single experience. And from experience, or from the whole universal that has come to rest in the soul (the one apart from the many, whatever is one and the same in all those things), there comes a principle of skill and of understanding—of skill if it deals with how things come about, of understanding if it deals with what is the case.

Thus the states neither belong in us in a determinate form, nor come about from other states that are more cognitive; but they come about from perception—as in a battle when a rout occurs, if one man makes a stand another does and then another, until a position of strength is reached. And the soul is such as to be capable of undergoing this.

What we have just said but not said clearly, let us say again: when one of the undifferentiated things makes a stand, there is a primitive universal in the mind (for though one perceives the particular, perception is of the universal—e.g., of man but not of Callias the man); again a stand is made in these, until what has no parts and is universal stands—e.g., *such and such* an animal stands, until animal does, and in this a stand is made in the same way. Thus it is clear that it is necessary for us to become familiar with the primitives by induction; for perception too instills the universal in this way.

Since of the intellectual states by which we grasp truth some are always true and some admit falsehood (e.g., opinion and reasoning—whereas understanding and comprehension are always true), and no kind other than comprehension is more precise than understanding, and the principles of demonstrations are more familiar, and all understanding involves an account—there will not be understanding of the principles; and since it is not possible for anything to be truer than understanding, except comprehension, there will be comprehension of the principles—both if we inquire from these facts and because demonstration is not a principle of demonstration so that understanding is not a principle of understanding either—so if we have no other true kind apart from understanding, comprehension will be the principle of understanding. And the principle will be of the principle, and understanding as a whole will be similarly related to the whole object.

from

MEDITATIONS ON THE FIRST PHILOSOPHY IN WHICH THE EXISTENCE OF GOD AND THE DISTINCTION BETWEEN MIND AND BODY ARE DEMONSTRATED

by

RENÉ DESCARTES

Meditation II

Of the Nature of the Human Mind; and That It Is More Easily Known Than the Body

The Meditation of yesterday filled my mind with so many doubts that it is no longer in my power to forget them. And yet I do not see in what manner I can resolve them; and, just as if I had all of a sudden fallen into very deep water, I am so disconcerted that I can neither make certain of setting my feet on the bottom, nor can I swim and so support myself on the surface. I shall nevertheless make an effort and follow anew the same path as that on which I yesterday entered, i.e., I shall proceed by setting aside all that in which the least doubt could be supposed to exist, just as if I had discovered that it was absolutely false; and I shall ever follow in this road until I have met with something which is certain, or at least, if I can do nothing else, until I have learned for certain that there is nothing in the world that is certain. Archimedes, in order that he might draw the terrestrial globe out of its place, and transport it elsewhere, demanded only that one point should be fixed and immovable; in the same way I shall have the right to conceive high hopes if I am happy enough to discover one thing only which is certain and indubitable.

I suppose, then, that all the things that I see are false; I persuade myself that nothing has ever existed of all that my fallacious memory represents to me. I consider that I possess no senses; I imagine that body, figure, extension, movement and place are but the fictions of my mind. What, then, can be esteemed as true? Perhaps nothing at all, unless that there is nothing in the world that is certain.

But how can I know there is not something different from those things that I have just considered, of which one cannot have the slightest doubt? Is there not some God, or some other being by whatever name we call it, who puts these reflections into my mind? That is not necessary, for is it not possible that I am capable of producing them myself? I myself, am I not at least something? But I have already denied that I had senses and body. Yet I hesitate, for what follows from that? Am I so dependent on body and senses that I cannot exist without these? But I was persuaded that there was nothing in all the world, that there was no heaven, no earth, that there were no minds, nor any bodies: was I not then likewise persuaded that I did not exist? Not at all; of a surety I myself did exist since I persuaded myself of something [or merely because I thought of something]. But there is some deceiver or other, very powerful and very cunning, who ever employs his ingenuity in deceiving me. Then without doubt I exist also if he deceives me, and let him deceive me as much as he will, he can never cause me to be nothing so long as I think that I am something. So that after having reflected well and carefully examined all things, we must come to the definite conclusion that this proposition: I am, I exist, is necessarily true each time that I pronounce it, or that I mentally conceive it.

But I do not yet know clearly enough what I am, I who am certain that I am; and hence must be careful to see that I do not imprudently take some other object in place of myself, and thus that I do not go astray in respect of this knowledge that I hold to be the most certain and most evident of all that I have formerly learned. That is why I shall now consider anew what I believed myself to be before I embarked upon these last reflections; and of my former opinions I shall withdraw all that might even in a small degree be invalidated by the reasons which I have just brought forward, in order that there may be nothing at all left beyond what is absolutely certain and indubitable.

What then did I formerly believe myself to be? Undoubtedly I believed myself to be a man. But what is a man? Shall I say a reasonable animal? Certainly not; for then I should have to inquire what an animal is, and what is reasonable; and thus from a single question I should insensibly fall into an infinitude of others more difficult; and I should not wish to waste the little time and leisure remaining to me in trying to unravel subtleties like these. But I shall rather stop here to consider the thoughts which of themselves spring up in my mind, and which were not inspired by anything beyond my own nature alone when I applied myself to the consideration of my being. In the first place, then, I considered myself as having a face, hands, arms, and all that system of members composed of bones and flesh as seen in a corpse which I designated by the name of body. In addition to this I considered that I was nourished, that I walked, that I felt, and that I thought, and I referred all these actions to the soul: but I did not stop to consider what the soul was, or if I did stop, I imagined that it was something extremely rare and subtle like a wind, a flame, or an ether, which was spread throughout my grosser parts. As to body I had no manner of doubt about its nature, but thought I had a very clear knowledge of it; and if I had desired to explain it according to the notions that I had then formed of it, I should have described it thus: By the body I understand all that which can be defined by a certain figure: something which can be confined in a certain place, and which can fill a given space in such a way that every other body will be excluded from it; which can be perceived either by touch, or by sight, or by hearing, or by taste, or by smell: which can be moved in many ways not, in truth, by itself, but by something which is foreign to it, by which it is touched [and from which it receives impressions]: for to have the power of self-movement, as also of feeling or of thinking, I did not consider to appertain to the nature of body: on the contrary, I was rather astonished to find that faculties similar to them existed in some bodies.

But what am I, now that I suppose that there is a certain genius which is extremely powerful, and, if I may say so, malicious, who employs all his powers in deceiving me? Can I affirm that I possess the least of all those things which I have just said pertain to the nature of body? I pause to consider, I revolve all these things in my mind, and I find none of which I can say that it pertains to me. It would be tedious to stop to enumerate them. Let us pass to the attributes of soul and see if there is any one which is in me? What of nutrition or walking [the first mentioned]? But if it is so that I have no body it is also true that I can neither walk nor take nourishment. Another attribute is sensation. But one cannot feel without body, and besides I have thought I perceived many things during sleep that I recognised in my waking moments as not having been experienced at all. What of thinking? I find here that thought is an attribute that belongs to me; it alone cannot be separated from me. I am, I exist, that is certain. But how often? Just when I think; for it might possibly be the case if I ceased entirely to think, that I should likewise cease altogether to exist. I do not admit anything which is not necessarily true: to speak accurately I am not more than a thing which thinks, that is to say a mind or a soul, or an understanding, or a reason, which are terms whose significance was formerly unknown to me. I am, however, a real thing and really exist; but what thing? I have answered: a thing which thinks.

And what more? I shall exercise my imagination [in order to see if I am not something more]. I am not a collection of members which we call the human body: I am not a subtle air distributed through these members, I am not a wind, a fire, a vapour, a breath, nor anything at all which I can imagine or conceive; because I have assumed that all these were nothing. Without changing that supposition I find that I only leave myself certain of the fact that I am somewhat. But perhaps it is true that these same things which I supposed were non-existent because they are unknown to me, are really not different from the self which I know. I am not sure about this, I shall not dispute about it now; I can only give judgment on things that are known to me. I know that I exist, and I inquire what I am, I whom I know to exist. But it is very certain that the knowledge of my existence taken in its precise significance does not depend on things whose existence is not yet known to me; consequently it does not depend on those which I can feign in imagination. And indeed the very term *feign* in imagination proves to me my error, for I really do this if I image myself a something, since to imagine is nothing else than to contemplate the figure or image of a corporeal thing. But I already know for certain that I am, and that it may be that all these images, and, speaking generally, all things that relate to the nature of body are nothing but dreams [and chimeras]. For this reason I see clearly that I have as little reason to say, "I shall stimulate my imagination in order to know more distinctly what I am," than if I were to say, "I am now awake, and I perceive somewhat that is real and true: but because I do not yet perceive it distinctly enough, I shall go to sleep of express purpose, so that my dreams may represent the perception with greatest truth and evidence." And, thus, I know for certain that nothing of all that I can understand by means of my imagination belongs to this knowledge which I have of myself, and that it is necessary to recall the mind from this mode of thought with the utmost diligence in order that it may be able to know its own nature with perfect distinctness.

But what then am I? A thing which thinks. What is a thing which thinks? It is a thing which doubts. understands, [conceives], affirms, denies, wills, refuses, which also imagines and feels.

Certainly it is no small matter if all these things pertain to my nature. But why should they not so pertain? Am I not that being who now doubts nearly everything, who nevertheless understands certain things, who affirms that one only is true, who denies all the others, who desires to know more, is averse from being deceived, who imagines many things, sometimes indeed despite his will, and who perceives many likewise, as by the intervention of the bodily organs? Is there nothing in all this which is as true as it is certain that I exist, even though I should always sleep and though he who has given me being employed all his ingenuity in deceiving me? Is there likewise any one of these attributes which can be distinguished from my thought, or which might be said to be separated from myself? For it is so evident of itself that it is I who doubts, who understands, and who desires, that there is no reason here to add anything to explain it. And I have certainly the power of imagining likewise; for although it may happen (as I formerly supposed) that none of the things which I imagine are true, nevertheless this power of imagining does not cease to be really in use, and it forms part of my thought. Finally, I am the same who feels, that is to say, who perceives certain things, as by the organs of sense, since in truth I see light, I hear noise, I feel heat. But it will be said that these phenomena are false and that I am dreaming. Let it be so; still it is at least quite certain that it seems to me that I see light, that I hear noise and that I feel heat. That cannot be false; properly speaking it is what is in me called feeling; and used in this precise sense that is no other thing than thinking.

From this time I begin to know what I am with a little more clearness and distinction than before; but nevertheless it still seems to me, and I cannot prevent myself from thinking, that corporeal things, whose images are framed by thought, which are tested by the senses, are much more distinctly known than that obscure part of me which does not come under the imagination. Although really it is very strange to say that I know and understand more distinctly these things whose existence seems to me dubious, which are unknown to me, and which do not belong to me, than others of the truth of which I am convinced, which are known to me and which pertain to my real nature, in a word, than myself. But I see clearly how the case stands: my mind loves to wander, and cannot yet suffer itself to be retained within the just limits of truth. Very good, let us once more give it the freest rein, so that, when afterwards we seize the proper occasion for pulling up, it may the more easily be regulated and controlled.

Let us begin by considering the commonest matters, those which we believe to be the most distinctly comprehended, to wit, the bodies which we touch and see; not indeed bodies in general, for these general ideas are usually a little more confused, but let us consider one body in particular. Let us take, for example, this piece of wax: it has been taken quite freshly from the hive, and it has not yet lost the sweetness of the honey which it contains; it still retains somewhat of the odour of the flowers from which it has been culled; its colour, its figure, its size are apparent; it is hard, cold, easily handled, and if you strike it with the finger, it will emit a sound. Finally all the things which are requisite to cause us distinctly to recognise a body, are met with in it. But notice that while I speak and approach the fire what remained of the taste is exhaled, the smell evaporates, the colour alters, the figure is destroyed, the size increases, it becomes liquid, it heats, scarcely can one handle it, and when one strikes it, no sound is emitted. Does the same wax remain after this change? We must confess that it remains; none would judge otherwise. What then did I know so distinctly in this piece of wax? It could certainly be nothing of all that the senses brought to my notice, since all these things which fall under taste, smell, sight, touch, and hearing, are found to be changed, and yet the same wax remains.

Perhaps it was what I now think, viz. that this wax was not that sweetness of honey, nor that agreeable scent of flowers, nor that particular whiteness, nor that figure, nor that sound, but simply a body which a little while before appeared to me as perceptible under these forms, and which is now perceptible under others. But what, precisely, is it that I imagine when I form such conceptions? Let us alternatively consider this, and, abstracting from all that does not belong to the wax, let us see what remains. Certainly nothing remains excepting a certain extended thing which is flexible and movable. But what is the meaning of flexible and movable? Is it not that I imagine that this piece of wax being round is capable of becoming square and of passing from a square to a triangular figure? No, certainly it is not that, since I imagine it admits of an infinitude of similar chances, and I nevertheless do not know how to compass the infinitude by my imagination, and consequently this conception which I have of the wax is not brought about by the faculty of imagination. What now is this extension? Is it not also unknown? For it becomes greater when the wax is melted, greater when it is boiled, and greater still when the heat increases; and I should not conceive [clearly] according to truth what wax is, if I did not think that even this piece that we are considering is capable of receiving more variations in extension than I have ever imagined. We must then grant that I could not even understand through the imagination what this piece of wax is, and that it is my mind alone which perceives it. I say this piece of wax in particular, for as to wax in general it is yet clearer. But what is this piece of wax which cannot be understood excepting by the [understanding or] mind? It is certainly the same that I see, touch, imagine, and finally it is the same which I have always believed it to be from the beginning. But what must particularly be observed is that its perception is neither an act of vision, nor of touch, nor of imagination, and has never been such although it may have appeared formerly to be so, but only an intuition of the mind, which may be imperfect and confused as it was formerly, or clear and distinct as it is at present, according as my attention is more or less directed to the elements which are found in it, and of which it is composed.

Yet in the meantime I am greatly astonished when I consider [the great feebleness of mind] and its proneness to fall [insensibly] into error; for although without giving expression to my thoughts I consider all this in my own mind, words often impede me and I am almost deceived by the terms of ordinary language. For we say that we see the same wax, if it is present, and not that we simply judge that it is the same from its having the same colour and figure. From this I should conclude that I knew the wax by means of vision and not simply by the intuition of the mind; unless by chance I remember that, when looking from a window and saying I see men who pass in the street, I really do not see them, but infer that what I see is men, just as I say that I see wax. And yet what do I see from the window but hats and coats which may cover automatic machines? Yet I judge these to be men. And similarly solely by the faculty of judgment which rests in my mind, I comprehend that which I believed I saw with my eyes.

A man who makes it his aim to raise his knowledge above the common should be ashamed to derive the occasion for doubting from the forms of speech invented by the vulgar; I prefer to pass on and consider whether I had a more evident and perfect conception of what the wax was when I first perceived it, and when I believed I knew it by means of the external senses or at least by the common sense as it is called, that is to say by the imaginative faculty, or whether my present conception is clearer now that I have most carefully examined what it is, and in what way it can be known. It would certainly be absurd to doubt as to this. For what was there in this first perception which was distinct? What was there which might not as well have been perceived by any of the animals? But when I distinguish the wax from its external forms, and when, just as if I had taken from it its vestments, I consider it quite naked, it is certain that although some error may still be found in my judgment, I can nevertheless not perceive it thus without a human mind.

But finally what shall I say of this mind, that is, of myself, for up to this point I do not admit in myself anything but mind? What then, I who seem to perceive this piece of wax so distinctly, do I not know myself, not only with much more truth and certainty, but also with much more distinctness and clearness? For if I judge that the wax is or exists from the fact that I see it, it certainly follows much more clearly that I am or that I exist myself from the fact that I see it. For it may be that what I see is not really wax, it may also be that I do not possess eyes with which to see anything; but it cannot be that when I see, or (for I no longer take account of the distinction) when I think I see, that I myself who think am nought. So if I judge that the wax exists from the fact that I touch it, the same thing will follow, to wit, that I am; and if I judge that my imagination, or some other cause, whatever it is, persuades me that the wax exists, I shall still conclude the same. And what I have here remarked of wax may be applied to all other things which are external to me [and which are met with outside of me]. And further, if the [notion or] perception of wax has seemed to me clearer and more distinct, not only after the sight or the touch, but also after many other causes have rendered it quite manifest to me, with how much more [evidence] and distinctness must it be said that I now know myself, since all the reasons which contribute to the knowledge of wax, or any other body whatever, are yet better proofs of the nature of my mind! And there are so many other things in the mind itself which may contribute to the elucidation of its nature, that those which depend on body such as these just mentioned, hardly merit being taken into account.

But finally here I am, having insensibly reverted to the point I desired, for, since it is now manifest to me that even bodies are not properly speaking known by the senses or by the faculty of imagination, but by the understanding only, and since they are not known from the fact that they are seen or touched, but only because they are understood, I see clearly that there is nothing which is easier for me to know than my mind. But because it is difficult to rid oneself so promptly of an opinion to which one was accustomed for so long, it will be well that I should halt a little at this point, so that by the length of my meditation I may more deeply imprint on my memory this new knowledge.

from

AN ABSTRACT OF A BOOK LATELY PUBLISHED, ENTITULED, A TREATISE OF HUMAN NATURE, &C.

by

DAVID HUME

This book seems to be wrote upon the same plan with several other works that have had a great vogue of late years in England. The philosophical spirit, which has been so much improved all over Europe within these last fourscore years, has been carried to as great a length in this kingdom as in any other. Our writers seem even to have started a new kind of philosophy, which promises more both to the entertainment and advantage of mankind, than any other with which the world has been yet acquainted. Most of the philosophers of antiquity, who treated of human nature, have shewn more of a delicacy of sentiment, a just sense of morals, or a greatness of soul, than a depth of reasoning and reflection. They content themselves with representing the common sense of mankind in the strongest lights, and with the best turn of thought and expression, without following out steadily a chain of propositions, or forming the several truths into a regular science. But 'tis at least worth while to try if the science of *man* will not admit of the same accuracy which several parts of natural philosophy are found susceptible of. There seems to be all the reason in the world to imagine that it may be carried to the greatest degree of exactness. If, in examining several phenomena, we find that they resolve themselves into one common principle, and can trace this principle into another, we shall at last arrive at those few simple principles, on which all the rest depend. And tho' we can never arrive at the ultimate principles, 'tis a satisfaction to go as far as our faculties will allow us.

This seems to have been the aim of our late philosophers, and, among the rest, of this author. He proposes to anatomize human nature in a regular manner, and promises to draw no conclusions but where he is authorized by experience. He talks with contempt of hypotheses; and insinuates, that such of our countrymen as have banished them from moral philosophy, have done a more signal service to the world, than my Lord Bacon, whom he considers as the father of experimental physicks. He mentions, on this occasion, Mr. Locke, my Lord Schaftsbury, Dr. Mandeville, Mr. Hutchison, Dr. Butler, who, tho' they differ in many points among themselves, seem all to agree in founding their accurate disquisitions of human nature intirely upon experience.

Beside the satisfaction of being acquainted with what most nearly concerns us, it may be safely affirmed, that almost all the sciences are comprehended in the science of human nature, and are dependent on it. *The sole end of* logic *is to explain the principles and Operations of our reasoning faculty, and the nature of our ideas;* morals and criticism *regard our tastes and sentiments; and* politics *consider men as united in society, and dependent on each other.* This treatise therefore of human nature seems intended for a system of the sciences. The author has finished what regards logic, and has laid the foundation of the other parts in his account of the passions.

The celebrated Monsieur Leibniz has observed it to be a defect in the common systems of logic, that they are very copious when they explain the operations of the understanding in the forming of demonstrations, but are too concise when they treat of probabilities, and those other measures of evidence on which life and action intirely depend, and which are our guides even in most of our philosophical speculations. In this censure, he comprehends *the essay on human understanding, le recherche de la verité,* and *l'art de penser.* The author of the *treatise of human nature* seems to have been sensible of this defect in these philosophers, and has endeavoured, as much as he can, to supply it. As his book contains a great number of speculations very new and remarkable, it will be impossible to give the reader a just notion of the whole. We shall therefore chiefly confine ourselves to his explication of our reasonings from cause and effect. If we can make this intelligible to the reader, it may serve as a specimen of the whole.

Our author begins with some definitions. He calls a *perception* whatever can be present to the mind, whether we employ our senses, or are actuated with passion, or exercise our thought and reflection. He divides our perceptions into two kinds, *viz. impressions* and *ideas.*

When we feel a passion or emotion of any kind, or have the images of external objects conveyed by our senses; the perception of the mind is what he calls an *impression*, which is a word that he employs in a new sense. When we reflect on a passion or an object which is not present, this perception is an *idea. Impressions*, therefore, are our lively and strong perceptions; *ideas* are the fainter and weaker. This distinction is evident; as evident as that betwixt feeling and thinking.

The first proportion he advances, is, that all our ideas, or weak perceptions, are derived from our impressions, or strong perceptions, and that we can never think of any thing which we have not seen without us, or felt in our own minds. This proposition seems to be equivalent to that which Mr. Locke has taken such pains to establish, *viz. that no ideas are innate.* Only it may be observed, as an inaccuracy of that famous philosopher, that he comprehends all our perceptions under the term of idea, in which sense it is false, that we have no innate ideas. For it is evident our stronger perceptions or impressions are innate, and that natural affection, love of virtue, resentment, and all the other passions, arise immediately from nature. I am perswaded, whoever would take the question in this light, would be easily able to reconcile all parties. Father Malebranche would find himself at a loss to point out any thought of the mind, which did not represent something antecedently felt by it, either internally, or by means of the external senses, and must allow, that however we may compound, and mix, and augment, and diminish our ideas, they are all derived from these sources. Mr. Locke, on the other hand, would readily acknowledge, that all our passions are a kind of natural instincts, derived from nothing but the original constitution of the human mind.

Our author thinks, "that no discovery could have been made more happily for deciding all controversies concerning ideas than this, that impressions always take the precedency of them, and that every idea with which the imagination is furnished, first makes its appearance in a correspondent impression. These latter perceptions are all so clear and evident, that they admit of no controversy; tho' many of our ideas are so obscure, that 'tis almost impossible even for the mind, which forms them, to tell exactly their nature and composition." Accordingly, wherever any idea is ambiguous, he has always recourse to the impression, which must render it clear and precise. And when he suspects that any philosophical term has no idea annexed to it (as is too common) he always asks *from what impression that idea is derived?* And if no impression can be produced, he concludes that the term is altogether insignificant. 'Tis after this manner he examines our idea of *substance* and *essence*; and it were to be wished, that this rigorous method were more practiced in all philosophical debates.

'Tis evident, that all reasonings concerning *matter of fact* are founded on the relation of cause and effect, and that we can never infer the existence of one object from another, unless they be connected together, either mediately or immediately. In order therefore to understand these reasonings, we must be perfectly acquainted with the idea of a cause; and in order to that, must look about us to find something that is the cause of another.

Here is a billiard-ball lying on the table, and another ball moving towards it with rapidity. They strike; and the ball, which was formerly at rest, now acquires a motion. This is as perfect an instance of the relation of cause and effect as any which we know, either by sensation or reflection. Let us therefore examine it. 'Tis evident, that the two balls touched one another before the motion was communicated, and that there was no interval betwixt the shock and the motion. *Contiguity* in time and place is therefore a requisite circumstance to the operation of all causes. 'Tis evident likewise, that the motion, which was the cause, is prior to the motion, which was the effect. *Priority* in time, is therefore another requisite circumstance in every cause. But this is not all. Let us try any other balls of the same kind in a like situation, and we shall always find, that the impulse of the one produces motion in the other. Here therefore is a *third* circumstance, *viz.* that of a *constant conjunction* betwixt the cause and effect. Every object like the cause, produces always some object like the effect. Beyond these three circumstances of contiguity, priority, and constant conjunction, I can discover nothing in this cause. The first ball is in motion; touches the second; immediately the second is in motion: and when I try the experiment with the same or like balls, in the same or like circumstances, I find, that upon the motion and touch of the one ball, motion always follows in the other. In whatever shape I turn this matter, and however I examine it, I can find nothing farther.

This is the case when both the cause and effect are present to the senses. Let us now see upon what our inference is founded, when we conclude from the one that the other has existed or will exist. Suppose I see a ball moving in a straight line towards another, I immediately conclude, that they will shock, and that the second will be in motion. This is the inference from cause to effect; and of this nature are all our reasonings in the conduct of life: on this is founded all our belief in history: and from hence is derived all philosophy, excepting only geometry and arithmetic. If we can explain the inference from the shock of two balls, we shall be able to account for this operation of the mind in all instances.

Were a man, such as Adam, created in the full vigour of understanding, without experience, he would never be able to infer motion in the second ball from the motion and impulse of the first. It is not any thing that reason sees in the cause, which make us *infer* the effect. Such an inference, were it possible, would amount to a demonstration, as being founded merely on the comparison of ideas. But no inference from cause to effect amounts to a demonstration. Of which there is this evident proof. The mind can always *conceive* any effect to follow from any cause, and indeed any event to follow upon another: whatever we *conceive* is possible, at least in a metaphysical sense: but wherever a demonstration takes place, the contrary is impossible, and implies a contradiction. There is no demonstration, therefore, for any conjunction of cause and effect. And this is a principle, which is generally allowed by philosophers.

It would have been necessary, therefore, for Adam (if he was not inspired) to have had *experience* of the effect, which followed upon the impulse of these two balls. He must have seen, in several instances, that when the one ball struck upon the other, the second always acquired motion. If he had seen a sufficient number of instances of this kind, whenever he saw the one ball moving towards the other, he would always conclude without hesitation, that the second would acquire motion. His understanding would anticipate his sight, and form a conclusion suitable to his past experience.

It follows, then, that all reasonings concerning cause and effect, are founded on experience, and that all reasonings from experience are founded on the supposition, that the course of nature will continue uniformly the same. We conclude, that like causes, in like circumstances, will always produce like effects. It may now be worth while to consider, what determines us to form a conclusion of such infinite consequence.

'Tis evident, that Adam with all his science, would never have been able to *demonstrate*, that the course of nature must continue uniformly the same, and that the future must be conformable to the past. What is possible can never be demonstrated to be false; and 'tis possible the course of nature may change, since we can conceive such a change. Nay, I will go farther, and assert, that he could not so much as prove by any *probable* arguments, that the future must be conformable to the past. All probable arguments are built on the supposition, that there is this conformity betwixt the future and the past, and therefore can never prove it. This conformity is a *matter of fact*, and if it must be proved, will admit of no proof but from experience. But our experience in the past can be a proof of nothing for the future, but upon a supposition, that there is a resemblance betwixt them. This therefore is a point, which can admit of no proof at all, and which we take for granted without any proof.

We are determined by CUSTOM alone to suppose the future conformable to the past. When I see a billiard-ball moving towards another, my mind is immediately carry'd by habit to the usual effect, and anticipates my sight by conceiving the second ball in motion. There is nothing in these objects, abstractly considered, and independent of experience, which leads me to form any such conclusion: and even after I have had experience of many repeated effects of this kind, there is no argument, which determines me to suppose, that the effect will be conformable to past experience. The powers, by which bodies operate, are entirely unknown. We perceive only their sensible qualities: and what *reason* have we to think, that the same powers will always be conjoined with the same sensible qualities?

'Tis not, therefore, reason, which is the guide of life, but custom. That alone determines the mind, in all instances, to suppose the future conformable to the past. However easy this step may seem, reason would never, to all eternity, be able to make it.

This is a very curious discovery, but leads us to others, that are still more curious. *When I see a billiard-ball moving towards another, my mind is immediately carried by habit to the usual and anticipate my sight by conceiving the second ball in motion.* But is this all? Do I nothing but CONCEIVE the motion of the second ball? No surely. I also BELIEVE that it will move. What then is this *belief*? And how does it differ from the simple conception of any thing? Here is a new question unthought of by philosophers.

When a demonstration convinces me of any proposition, it not only makes me conceive the proposition, but also makes me sensible, that 'tis impossible to conceive any thing contrary. What is demonstratively false implies a contradiction; and what implies a contradiction cannot be conceived. But with regard to any matter of fact, however strong the proof may be from experience, I can always conceive the contrary, tho' I cannot always believe it. The belief, therefore, makes some difference betwixt the conception to which we assent, and that to which we do not assent.

To account for this, there are only two hypotheses. It may be said, that belief joins some new idea to those which we may conceive without assenting to them. But this hypothesis is false. For first, no such idea can be produced. When we simply conceive an object, we conceive it in all its parts. We conceive it as it might exist, tho' we do not believe it to exist. Our belief of it would discover no new qualities. We may paint out the entire object in imagination without believing it. We may set it, in a manner, before our eyes, with every circumstance of time and place. 'Tis the very object conceived as it might exist; and when we believe it, we can do no more.

Secondly, the mind has a faculty of joining all ideas together, which involve not a contradiction; and therefore if belief consisted in some idea, which we add to the simple conception, it would be in a man's power, by adding this idea to it, to believe any thing, which he can conceive.

Since therefore belief implies a conception, and yet is something more; and since it adds no new idea to the conception; it follows, that it is a different MANNER of conceiving an object; *something* that is distinguishable to the feeling, and depends not upon our will, as all our ideas do. My mind runs by habit from the visible object of one ball moving towards another, to the usual effect of motion in the second ball. It not only conceives that motion, but *feels* something different in the conception of it from a mere reverie of the imagination. The presence of this visible object, and the constant conjunction of that particular effect, render the idea different to the *feeling* from those loose ideas, which come into the mind without any introduction. This conclusion seems a little surprizing; but we are led into it by a chain of propositions, which admit of no doubt. To ease the reader's memory I shall briefly resume them. No matter of fact can be proved but from its cause or its effect. Nothing can be known to be the cause of another but by experience. We can give no reason for extending to the future our experience in the past; but are entirely determined by custom, when we conceive an effect to follow from its usual cause. But we also believe an effect to follow, as well as conceive it. This belief joins no new idea to the conception. It only varies the manner of conceiving, and makes a difference to the feeling or sentiment. Belief, therefore, in all matters of fact arises only from custom, and is an idea conceived in a peculiar *manner*.

Our author proceeds to explain the manner or feeling, which renders belief different from a loose conception. He seems sensible, that 'tis impossible by words to describe this feeling, which every one must be conscious of in his own breast. He calls it sometimes a *stronger* conception, sometimes a more *lively*, a more *vivid*, a *firmer*, or a more *intense* conception. And indeed, whatever name we may give to this feeling, which constitutes belief, our author thinks it evident, that it has a more forcible effect on the mind than fiction and mere conception. This he proves by its influence on the passions and on the imagination; which are only moved by truth or what is taken for such. Poetry, with all its art, can never cause a passion, like one in real life. It fails in the original conception of its objects, which never *feel* in the same manner as those which command our belief and opinion.

Our author presuming, that he had sufficiently proved, that the ideas we assent to are different to the feeling from the other ideas, and that this feeling is more firm and lively than our common conception, endeavours in the next place to explain the cause of this lively feeling by an analogy with other acts of the mind. His reasoning seems to be curious; but could scarce be rendered intelligible, or at least probable to the reader, without a long detail, which would exceed the compass I have prescribed to myself.

I have likewise omitted many arguments, which he adduces to prove that belief consists merely in a peculiar feeling or sentiment. I shall only mention one; our past experience is not always uniform. Sometimes one effect follows from a cause, sometimes another: In which case we always believe, that that will exist which is most common. I see a billiard-ball moving towards another. I cannot distinguish whether it moves upon its axis, or was struck so as to skim along the table. In the first cafe, I know it will not stop after the shock. In the second it may stop. The first is most common, and therefore I lay my account with that effect. But I also conceive the other effect, and conceive it as possible, and as connected with the cause. Were not the one conception different in the feeling or sentiment from the other, there would be no difference betwixt them.

We have confin'd ourselves in this whole reasoning to the relation of cause and effect, as discovered in the motions and operations of matter. But the same reasoning extends to the operations of the mind. Whether we consider the influence of the will in moving our body, or in governing our thought, it may safely be affirmed, that we could never foretel the effect, merely from the consideration of the cause, without experience. And even after we have experience of these effects, 'tis custom alone, not reason, which determines us to make it the standard of our future judgments. When the cause is presented, the mind, from habit, immediately passes to the conception and belief of the usual effect. This belief is something different from the conception. It does not, however, join any new idea to it. It only makes it be felt differently, and renders it stronger and more lively.

Having dispatcht this material point concerning the nature of the inference from cause and effect, our author returns upon his footsteps, and examines anew the idea of that relation. In the considering of motion communicated from one ball to another, we could find nothing but contiguity, priority in the cause, and constant conjunction. But, beside these circumstances, 'tis commonly suppos'd, that there is a necessary connexion betwixt the cause and effect, and that the cause possesses something, which we call a *power*, or *force*, or *energy*. The question is, what idea is annex'd to these terms? If all our ideas or thoughts be derived from our impressions, this power must either discover itself to our senses, or to our internal feeling. But so little does any *power* discover itself to the senses in the operations of matter, that the Cartesians have made no scruple to assert, that matter is utterly deprived of energy, and that all its operations are perform'd merely by the energy of the supreme Being. But the question still recurs, *What idea have we of energy or power even in the supreme Being?* All our idea of a Deity (according to those who deny innate ideas) is nothing but a composition of those ideas, which we acquire from reflecting on the operations of our own minds. Now our own minds afford us no more notion of energy than matter does. When we consider our will or volition a *priori*, abstracting from experience, we should never be able to infer any effect from it. And when we take the assistance of experience, it only shows us objects contiguous, successive, and constantly conjoined. Upon the whole, then, either we have no idea at all of force and energy, and these words are altogether insignificant, or they can mean nothing but that determination of the thought, acquir'd by habit, to pass from the cause to its usual effect. But who-ever would thoroughly understand this must consult the author himself. 'Tis sufficient, if I can make the learned world apprehend, that there is some difficulty in the case, and that who-ever solves the difficulty must say some thing very new and extraordinary; as new as the difficulty itself.

By all that has been said the reader will easily perceive, that the philosophy contain'd in this book is very sceptical, and tends to give us a notion of the imperfections and narrow limits of human understanding. Almost all reasoning is there reduced to experience; and the belief, which attends experience, is explained to be nothing but a peculiar sentiment, or lively conception produced by habit. Nor is this all, when we believe any thing of *external* existence, or suppose an object to exist a moment after it is no longer perceived, this belief is nothing but a sentiment of the same kind. Our author insists upon several other sceptical topics; and upon the whole concludes, that we assent to our faculties, and employ our reason only because we cannot help it. Philosophy wou'd render us entirely Pyrrhonian, were not nature too strong for it.

I shall conclude the logics of this author with an account of two opinions, which seem to be peculiar to himself, as indeed are most of his opinions. He asserts, that the soul, as far as we can conceive it, is nothing but a system or train of different perceptions, those of heat and cold, love and anger, thoughts and sensations; all united together, but without any perfect simplicity or identity. DesCartes maintained that thought was the essence of the mind; not this thought or that thought, but thought in general. This seems to be absolutely unintelligible, since everything, that exists, is particular: And therefore it must be our several particular perceptions, that compose the mind. I say, *compose* the mind, not *belong* to it. The mind is not a substance, in which the perceptions inhere. That notion is as unintelligible as the Cartesian, that thought or perception in general is the essence of the mind. We have no idea of substance of any kind, since we have no idea but what is derived from some impression, and we have no impression of any substance either material or spiritual. We know nothing but particular qualities and perceptions. As our idea of any body, a peach, for instance, is only that of a particular taste, colour, figure, size, consistence, &c. So our idea of any mind is only that of particular perceptions, without the notion of anything we call substance, either simple or compound.

The second principle, which I proposed to take notice of, is with regard to Geometry. Having denied the infinite divisibility of extension, our author finds himself obliged to refute those mathematical arguments, which have been adduced for it; and these indeed are the only ones of any weight. This he does by denying Geometry to be a science exact enough to admit of conclusions so subtle as those which regard infinite divisibility. His arguments may be thus explained. All Geometry is founded on the notions of equality and inequality, and therefore according as we have or have not an exact standard of that relation, the science itself will or will not admit of great exactness. Now there is an exact standard of equality, if we suppose that quantity is composed of indivisible points. Two lines are equal when the numbers of the points, that compose them, are equal, and when there is a point in one corresponding to a point in the other. But tho' this standard be exact, 'tis useless; since we can never compute the number of points in any line. It is besides founded on the supposition of finite divisibility, and therefore can never afford any conclusion against it. If we reject this standard of equality, we have none that has any pretensions to exactness. I find two that are commonly made use of. Two lines above a yard, for instance, are said to be equal, when they contain any inferior quantity, as an inch, an equal number of times. But this runs in a circle. For the quantity we call an inch in the one is supposed to be *equal* to what we call an inch in the other: And the question still is, by what standard we proceed when we judge them to be equal; or, in other words, what we mean when we say they are equal. If we take still inferior quantities we go on *in infinitum*. This therefore is no standard of equality. The greatest part of philosophers, when ask'd what they mean by equality, say, that the word admits of no definition, and that it is sufficient to place before us two equal bodies, such as two diameters of a circle, to make us understand that term. Now this is taking the *general appearance* of the objects for the standard of that proportion, and renders our imagination and senses the ultimate judges of it. But such a standard admits of no exactness, and can never afford any conclusion contrary to the imagination and senses. Whether this question be just or not, must be left to the learned world to judge. 'Twere certainly to be wish'd, that some expedient were fallen upon to reconcile philosophy and common sense, which with regard to the question of infinite divisibility have wag'd most cruel wars with each other.

We must now proceed to give some account of the second volume of this work, which treats of the PASSIONS. 'Tis of more easy comprehension than the first; but contains opinions, that are altogether as new and extraordinary. The author begins with pride and humility. He observes, that the objects which excite these passions, are very numerous and seemingly very different from each other. Pride or self-esteem may arise from the qualities of the mind; wit, good-sense, learning, courage, integrity: from those of the body; beauty, strength, agility, good mein, address in dancing, riding, fencing: from external advantages; country, family, children, relations, riches, houses, gardens, horses, dogs, cloaths. He afterwards proceeds to find out that common circumstance, in which all these objects agree, and which causes them to operate on the passions. His theory likewise extends to love and hatred, and other affections. As these questions, tho' curious, could not be rendered intelligible without a long discourse, we shall here omit them.

It may perhaps be more acceptable to the reader to be informed of what our author says concerning *free-will*. He has laid the foundation of his doctrine in what he said concerning cause and effect, as above explained. "'Tis universally acknowledged, that the operations of external bodies are necessary, and that in the communication of their motion in their attraction and mutual cohesion, there are not the least traces of indifference or liberty."——"Whatever therefore is in this respect on the same footing with matter, must be acknowledged to be necessary. That we may know whether this be the case with the actions of the mind, we may examine matter, and consider on what the idea of a necessity in its operations are founded, and why we conclude one body or action to be the infallible cause of another.

"It has been observed already, that in no single instance the ultimate connexion of any object is discoverable either by our senses or reason, and that we can never penetrate so far into the essence and construction of bodies, as to perceive the principle on which their mutual influence is founded. 'Tis their constant union alone, with which we are acquainted; and 'tis from the constant union the necessity arises, when the mind is determined to pass from one object to its usual attendant, and infer the existence of one from that of the other. Here then are two particulars, which we are to regard as essential to *necessity*, *viz.* the constant *union* and the *inference* of the mind, and wherever we discover these we must acknowledge a necessity." Now nothing is more evident than the constant union of particular actions with particular motives. If all actions be not constantly united with their proper motives, this uncertainty is no more than what may be observed every day in the actions of matter, where by reason of the mixture and uncertainty of causes, the effect is often variable and uncertain. Thirty grains of opium will kill any man that is not accustomed to it; tho' thirty grains of rhubarb will not always purge him. In like manner the fear of death will always make a man go twenty paces out of his road; tho' it will not always make him do a bad action.

And as there is often a constant conjunction of the actions of the will with their motives, so the inference from the one to the other is often as certain as any reasoning concerning bodies: and there is always an inference proportioned to the constancy of the conjunction. On this is founded our belief in witnesses, our credit in history, and indeed all kinds of moral evidence, and almost the whole conduct of life.

Our author pretends, that this reasoning puts the whole controversy in a new light, by giving a new definition of necessity. And, indeed, the most zealous advocates for free-will must allow this union and inference with regard to human actions. They will only deny, that this makes the whole of necessity. But then they must shew, that we have an idea of something else in the actions of matter; which, according to the foregoing reasoning, is impossible.

Thro' this whole book, there are great pretensions to new discoveries in philosophy; but if any thing can intitle the author to so glorious a name as that of an *inventor*, 'tis the use he makes of the principle of the association of ideas, which enters into most of his philosophy. Our imagination has a great authority over our ideas; and there are no ideas that are different from each other, which it cannot separate, and join, and compose into all the varieties of fiction. But notwithstanding the empire of the imagination, there is a secret tie or union among particular ideas, which causes the mind to conjoin them more frequently together, and makes the one, upon its appearance, introduce the other. Hence arises what we call the *apropos* of discourse: hence the connection of writing: and hence that thread, or chain of thought, which a man naturally supports even in the loosest *reverie*. These principles of association are reduced to three, *viz. Resemblance*; a picture naturally makes us think of the man it was drawn for. *Contiguity*; when St. Dennis is mentioned, the idea of Paris naturally occurs. *Causation*; when we think of the son, we are apt to carry our attention to the father. 'Twill be easy to conceive of what vast consequence these principles must be in the science of human nature, if we consider, that so far as regards the mind, these are the only links that bind the parts of the universe together, or connect us with any person or object exterior to ourselves. For as it is by means of thought only that any thing operates upon our passions, and as these are the only ties of our thoughts, they are really *to us* the cement of the universe, and all the operations of the mind must, in a great measure, depend on them.

QUESTIONING AS A
PHILOSOPHICAL METHOD
by
JAAKKO HINTIKKA

1. Questioning as a General Knowledge-Seeking Method

Questioning is not only an important philosophical method; it offers a useful model for many different types of knowledge-seeking. For the time being, I shall in fact treat questioning as a process of information-gathering in general. Only later, once the structure of information-seeking by questioning has been discussed, can we see how variants of this method are particularly adept to serve the purposes of philosophical thinking.

The best known historical paradigm of questioning as a philosophical method is the Socratic *elenchus*. It is of interest to see how several aspects of this celebrated technique can be understood and put into a perspective on the basis of my analysis of questioning as a philosophical method.

Before doing so, we nevertheless have to look at the logical structure of question-answer sequences. Here the first question that is likely to come up is probably going to be a skeptical one: What's so new about the idea of questioning, anyway, as a knowledge-seeking method? It is one of the first ideas likely to occur to anyone interested in philosophical or scientific or hermeneutical method, and it has in fact occurred to a number of philosophers, such as Plato, Francis Bacon, Kant, Collingwood, Gadamer, and Laudan. Moreover, a large number of different treatments of the logic of questions are on the market. It is surely not realistic to expect new insights to ensue from this old idea—or so it seems.

2. The Logical Structure of Questions

What is new and promising about the approach I am proposing is that it is based on an adequate analysis of the crucial question-answer relationship. Before we know what counts as an answer (intended, full, conclusive answer) to a given question, we cannot hope to understand how answers to questions one asks can yield information, for we don't really know what an answer to a given question is likely to be. Surprisingly, this crucial question-answer relationship is not analyzed satisfactorily in the earlier discussions of the logic of questions, in spite of the fact that the right analysis follows naturally from the basic idea of considering questions in informational terms. The line of thought—I shall call it, in analogy to Kant's "transcendental deductions," a "model-theoretical deduction"—which yields the right analysis is important enough to be sketched here. It relies on the idea that having information (knowing something) amounts to being able to eliminate certain alternative situations or courses of events ("possible worlds"). This is the true gist in the often-repeated idea of "information as elimination of uncertainty." What it means is that a person's, say b's, knowledge state in a "world" w_0 is characterized by reference to the set of all those "worlds" w_1 that are compatible with what b knows in w_0 (and by implication to the set of worlds that are excluded by b's knowledge). These will be called the epistemic b-alternatives to w_0. Then it will be the case that a sentence of the form

(1) b knows that p

is true in w_0 if and only if it is true that p in all the epistemic b-alternatives to w_0.

Furthermore, a wh-question like

(2) Who killed Roger Ackroyd?

is to be analysed for my purposes as a request for a certain item of information. What information? Obviously, the information the questioner has when she or he can truly say

(3) I know who killed Roger Ackroyd.

In general, a specification of the informational state that the questioner requests to be brought about is called the *desideratum* of the question in question. Thus (3) is the desideratum of (2).

Now (3) is naturally, not to say inevitably, analyzed as

(4) $(\exists x)$ I know that (x killed Roger Ackroyd)

where "x" ranges over persons. For what more could it conceivably mean to know *who* did it than to know *of some particular person x* that x did it?

In model-theoretical terms, (4) means that there is some individual x such that, in each world compatible with everything I know, x killed Roger Ackroyd. This is, of course, but saying that I have enough information to rule out x's not having done it.

3. Question-Answer Relation Analyzed

What is now going to count as a conclusive answer to (2)? Let's suppose someone tries to answer the question (2) by saying "d." (I am making no assumptions concerning the logical or grammatical nature of this response, as long as it makes (5) below grammatically acceptable. It may be a proper name, definite description, indefinite description, or what not.) This reply is a conclusive answer if and only if it provides the questioner with the information that was requested. For the sake of argument, I shall assume that the reply is true, honest, and backed up by sufficient information. What information does it then bring to the questioner? Clearly, the information that enables him or her to say, truly,

(5) I know that d killed Roger Ackroyd.

This is the state of knowledge (information), actually brought about by the reply "d." But it is not necessarily that state of information requested by the speaker, for this requested state is expressed by another proposition, viz. (4). Hence the reply "d" is a conclusive answer, i.e., it provides the requested information, *if and only if* (5) *implies* (4).

But when does this implication hold? First, why should it ever fail? The model-theoretical perspective provides an instant answer. What (5) says is that the term "d" picks out, from each world compatible with what I know, an individual who in that world killed

Roger Ackroyd. The reason why this does not imply knowing who did it is that those several references of "*d*" need not be the same person. We may put it as follows: my knowing that someone or other killed Roger Ackroyd means having enough information to rule out all courses of events under which someone or other did not kill him. But in order to know who did it, I need further information: I have to have enough information to guarantee that the killer of Roger Ackroyd is *one and the same person* in all the worlds my knowledge has not yet eliminated.

Thus the extra premise one needs to infer (4) from (5) will have to say that the term *d* picks out the same individual from all the worlds compatible with what I know, i.e., that there exists some one individual x such that in all those worlds $d = x$. But, according to our observation concerning (1), something is true in all the worlds my knowledge does not rule out if and only if I know that it is true. Hence the extra premise needed to restore the implication from (5) to (4) is

(6) $(\exists x)$ I know that $(d = x)$

This, then, is the criterion of conclusive answerhood. The reply "*d*" to (1) is a conclusive answer if and only if it satisfies (6).

What is remarkable about this result is not the particular condition (6). Indeed, it is precisely the condition one would expect. By the same token as the near synonymy of (3) and (4), (6) can be expressed more colloquially by

(7) I know who *d* is.

And this is obviously a necessary and sufficient condition for the reply "*d*" to satisfy the questioner. For if the questioner does not know who *d* is, this reply does not enable him or her to know who it was who killed Roger Ackroyd. Instead, it would prompt the further question, "But who is *d*?" or some equivalent response.

What is remarkable about the criterion (6) of conclusive answers to (1) is, first of all, that it is generalizable. Even though the technical details of some of the generalizations are messy, the leading idea is clear in all cases.

Even more remarkable is the fact that the aptness of my criterion of conclusive answerhood can be proved. The intuitive model-theoretical argument outlined above can be transformed into a formal argument, which relies on these principles of epistemic logic that codify my model-theoretical assumptions sketched above. Likewise, the generalizations of my criterion likewise can be proved to be correct in the strictest sense of the word in most of the relevant cases.

In view of the crucial importance of the question-answer relationship (criterion of conclusive answerhood) for any study of knowledge-seeking by questioning, a couple of further remarks are in order. The analysis of the question-answer relationship I have offered is an inevitable consequence of a certain way of conceptualizing knowledge (information). Hence those critics have been barking up the wrong tree who have tried to criticize it by reference to the surface phenomena of language, including unanalyzed and ill-understood "intuitions" that the critics profess to have about the logical implications between different natural-language sentences. The only relevant criticism would be to develop an alternative model-theoretical framework for (an alternative way of conceptualizing) information and knowledge, and an alternative way of codifying the idea that a question is a request of information. There is no need for me to respond to self-appointed critics who have not done this.

4. Further Problems

The outline account given above leads to further problems in virtually all directions. Here is a sample:

(i) Besides being a request for a certain item of information, a question implies certain restraints as to how this request is to be fulfilled. We need an account of these restraints.

(ii) It is not enough to use logicians' time-honored models as implementations of the idea of alternative states of altering or courses of events. For if we do so, we are led to the paradoxical conclusion that everyone always knows all the logical conclusions of everything he or she knows. What is the appropriate generalization we need here?

(iii) There is another way of taking a question like (1), viz. to take the requested state of knowledge to be expressible by

(8) (x) $(x$ killed Roger Ackroyd $\supset$ $(\exists z)$ $(z = x$ & I know that $(z$ killed Roger Ackroyd))).

In other words, the speaker wants to be aware of the identity, not just of one person who killed Roger Ackroyd, but of all of them. How are the two representations (4) and (8) related to each other?

(iv) What are the precise conditions on conclusive answers to more complicated questions? How are such complex questions to be analyzed in the first place?

(v) Many perfectly respectable responses to a question don't satisfy my condition of conclusive answerhood, but nevertheless contribute partial information towards a conclusive answer. How are such *partial answers* to be defined? How can we measure their distance from a conclusive answer?

(vi) Such representations as (4) or (8) assume that quantifiers and epistemic operators (e.g., "I know that") are informationally dependent on each other transitively, so that they can be represented in a linear fashion. Can this assumption fail? What happens if it does?

5. Strategic Aspects of Questioning— Presuppositions of Questions

Such questions can easily be multiplied.

It would be a serious mistake to take these new problems, and others like them, to constitute evidence against my approach. Here it is in order to anticipate the self-awareness that our discussion of knowledge-seeking by questioning can engender. One of the most important advantages, perhaps the most important advantage, of the questioning model is that by its means we can discuss and evaluate, not just someone's state of knowledge at a given time (vis-à-vis the evidence one has at the time) but also entire strategies of knowledge-seeking. Then the value of an answer A to a question Q of mine (or the value of conclusion I draw from such an answer A) cannot be measured in the sole terms of the knowledge (theory) this answer A yields. Rather, we must also consider the opportunities for further questions and answers that are opened by the original answer A. The basic reason for this is that questions cannot be asked in a vacuum. A question can only be asked after its presupposition has been established. Hence one may need answers to earlier "smaller" questions in order to be able to ask the crucial questions whose answers are likely to yield the information really desired.

Here we can also see the usefulness of game-theoretical conceptualizations. From game theory we know that utilities cannot be assigned to individual moves. Utilities, which in my information-seeking games depend essentially on the information (knowledge) sought, can only be assigned to entire strategies.

Likewise, we can see here the importance of another feature of my analysis of questions and answers, viz. the role of presuppositions. In the example above, the presupposition of (2) is

(9) $(\exists x)$ (x killed Roger Ackroyd),

that is

(10) Someone killed Roger Ackroyd.

Obviously, (2) can be sensibly asked only if (10) is true. Once again, my definition is generalizable beyond our particular example. In general the presupposition of a wh-question is obtained by omitting the outmost epistemic operator or operators "I know that" from the desderatum of the question.

The presupposition of a wh-question minus the quantifier is called the *matrix* of the question.

6. Significance of New Problems

Self-applied to the knowledge-seeking that is involved in my approach to questions, answers, and question-answer sequences, these observations imply that the approach should not be judged on the basis of the theory it has reached at one time. Even less should the open questions my approach prompts be counted against it. On the contrary, the ability of an approach to lead to interesting problems is a strong reason in its favor. These problems are evidence for its power to give rise to new questions whose answers are likely to essentially increase our knowledge of the subject matter.

This illustrates neatly how my general theory of knowledge-seeking by questioning can enhance our self-awareness of our own philosophical enterprise and its methods.

7. Meno Answered

The nature of the question-answer relation and of the presuppositions of questions deserves a few comments. Part of the philosophical relevance of my observations on these two subjects—especially on the former—can be expressed by saying that they provide a solution to Meno's puzzle. On the basis of what we have found, it is in fact easy to see how Meno's paradox comes about. Applied to *what is* questions, my criterion of answerhood yields the following result: Suppose Socrates asks the definitory question

(11) What is d?

The desideratum of (11) is

(12) I know what d is.

Then a reply, say "b," is a conclusive answer only if Socrates (i.e., the questioner) can truly say,

(13) $(\exists x)$ I know that $(b = x)$,

in other words, can truly say,

(14) I know what b is.

Thus it looks as if the question (11) can be answered conclusively only if the questioner already knows an answer. No wonder poor Meno was perplexed by this paradoxical-looking circularity.

The solution to Meno's problem lies in the fallaciousness of the word "already" in my formulation of the problem just given. The right conclusion to draw from my criterion of conclusive answerhood is not that the questioner must already know what the answer (in our example, the term "b") stands for prior to the reply, but rather that it is part of the task of that reply to provide the collateral information that enables the questioner to say, truly, (13) (= (14)). The right conclusion here is thus that an adequate response to a wh-question will have to serve two different functions. To put the point in the form of a paradox, it is not enough for a reply to provide (what is usually taken to be) an answer to the question (viz. a true substitution-instance of its matrix). It must also give to the questioner enough supplementary information to bring it about that the conclusiveness condition is satisfied, i.e., that the questioner knows what the reply term refers to *after* the reply has been given. This double function of replies to wh-questions is the true moral of Meno's paradox. It represents an important insight into the role of replies (answers) in discourse.

Speaking more generally, by spelling out the presuppositions for asking different kinds of questions as well as the conditions that conclusive answers to them have to satisfy, we can show just what a questioner has to know before he or she can ask a question and receive an answer to it, and thereby solve Meno's problem in its most general form.

All this highlights in turn a general truth about questions and answers. They are very much a discourse phenomena, and their theory must be developed as an integral part of the logic and semantics of discourse, as distinguished from the logic and semantics of (isolated) sentences.

8. Different Sources of Information

One feature of the conceptualizations expounded above is that they are independent of the specific nature of the answerer (source of information). For this reason, the theory of knowledge-seeking by questioning that is based on these conceptualizations is applicable to several different kinds of information-gathering. In order to see one of them, we may borrow a page from Kant's *Critique of Pure Reason* and think of the experimental inquiry of the physical sciences as a series of questions a scientist puts to nature. (The page in question is B xiii). In this application, we can once again see the crucial role of the question-answer relationship. For Kant's emphasis is on the way in which a scientist can actively guide the course of investigation by choosing correctly the questions put to nature. The mechanism of this control is of course precisely the question-answer relationship. A question Q predetermines its answers in that they have to be answers to this particular Q. I shall not pursue this application here, however.

Another interesting application along related lines is to construe observations—be they scientific, clinical, or pretheoretical—as answers to questions put to one's environment. This point is vividly illustrated in Sherlock Holmes's famed "deductions," which I have interpreted as so many questions put to a suitable source of information. (They will be discussed below.) Not only does Sherlock occasionally call his "Science of Deduction and Analysis" also a science of *observation* and deduction. He repeatedly speaks of the same conclusion as being obtained, now by deduction or "train of reasoning," now by observation or perception. Upon meeting Dr. Watson, Sherlock Holmes says: "You have been in Afghanistan, I *perceive*" (emphasis added). Yet he later describes a long train of thought (cf. below) he needed to reach that "conclusion." On another occasion, Sherlock is surprised that Watson "actually [was] not able to *see* [emphasis added] that that man was a sergeant of Marines," even though Dr. Watson had just referred to this conclusion as a deduction ("How in the world did you deduce that?") and even though Sherlock himself has to use no fewer than thirteen lines to explain the different steps of his train of thought.

Less anecdotally, assimilating observations to knowledge-seeking questions offers a natural framework for discussing some of the hottest problems in the contemporary philosophy of science, such as the concept-ladenness and theory-ladenness of observations. For instance, if an observation is construed as a question, then the information it yields depends on the concepts in terms of which the question is formulated. Likewise, the observation, being a question, depends on the antecedent availability of its presupposition, which ultimately depends on the theory one is presupposing. We are obviously dealing with an extremely promising line of investigation here.

9. Activating Tacit Knowledge

The applications I am primarily interested in here are nevertheless in a still different direction. The source of information need not be outside the questioner. It may be addressed to the questioner's own memory or to whatever other sources of "tacit knowledge" he or she may possess. Then the questioning process becomes a process of activating tacit knowledge. It seems to me that there is an especially dire need here of satisfactory semantical and logical analysis, for the process of bringing the relevant items of tacit information to bear on one's reasoning is practically never dealt with by philosophers and methodologists. Likewise, it seems to me that psychologists could profit from a better conceptual framework in dealing with this subject matter. Thus it is an extremely important subject in several respects. In earlier papers, I have argued that much that passes as "inference" or "deduction" in nonphilosophical jargon really consists in sequences of implicit questions and answers. In many of the most striking cases, such questions are answered on the basis of information that the questioner already has available to himself or herself but which the question serves to call attention to. It is precisely this quality of Sherlock Holmes's "deductions" that so frequently made them look "elementary" once they were spelled out. How did Sherlock Holmes know that the good Dr. Watson had been to Afghanistan when he was introduced to him? Here is a paraphrase of Holmes's "train of reasoning":[1]

> What is the profession of this gentleman? He is of a medical type, but with the air of a military man. Clearly an army doctor, then. Where has he been recently? In the tropics, for his face is dark, although it is not the natural tint of his skin, for his wrists are fair. But where in the tropics? He has undergone hardship and sickness, as his haggard face tells clearly. His left hand has been injured, for he holds it in a stiff and unnatural manner. Now where in the tropics could an English army doctor have recently seen so much hardship and got his arm wounded? Clearly in Afghanistan.

---

[1] The paraphrase is very close to the original. Essentially all that I have done is to use the interrogative mode more often than Doyle. See "A Study in Scarlet," in Baring-Gould 1967, vol. 1, pp. 160-62.

Apart from the observations that the famous detective is using, he is relying on perfectly commonplace knowledge about sun tan, medical clue's to one's past, and recent military history.

Actualization of tacit information is also the gist in philosophers' appeals, so prevalent in our days, to what are known as "intuitions." I have argued elsewhere that it is a serious mistake to construe them as the data that philosophical theory or explanation has to account for. If they are to have a legitimate role in philosophical reasoning, they must have some other role in philosophical argumentation. But what is that role? We don't find a satisfactory answer in the literature.

10. Analogy Between Interrogation and Deduction

On my model, what does guide the choice of questions that activate tacit knowledge? My answer is: largely the same strategic considerations as govern the choice of the best lines of questioning in general. But what are those strategic principles? It is hard to be specific, but a couple of relevant observations can nevertheless be made. The presuppositions of questions must be among the conclusions a questioner has reached. The crucial questions are typically wh-questions, and their presuppositions are existential sentences. (Cf. (9) above.) The decisive strategic consideration therefore is: Which of the available existential sentences should I use as presuppositions of wh-questions? An answer to such a question will instantiate the matrix of the question, which is an existential sentence. Hence the strategic choice just mentioned is nearly analogous to the choice faced by a deductive strategist. For it has been shown that the crucial consideration in the quest of optimal strategies is the choice of the existential formulas to be instantiated at each stage of the deduction, which is here assumed to be roughly a natural-deduction or *tableaux*-type procedure. In other words, the principles that govern the choice of optimal questioning strategies are extremely closely related to the choice of the principles that govern one's quest of the best deductive methods. In short, deductive logic is likely to yield the best clues to effective questioning. No wonder Sherlock Holmes called his art of investigation, which I have interpreted as a questioning method, "The Science of Deduction."

The same road can be traveled in the opposite direction. Because of the parallelism between deduction and questioning, suitable questions can trigger the right deductive conclusions by the answerer, and may thus serve inversely as heuristic guides to the right deductive strategies.

Hence a philosophical inquirer should discard the misleading positivistic generalization model and think of his or her task, not as a series of generalizations from the data offered by "intuitions," but on the model of Sherlock Holmes's "Science of Deduction and Analysis." In so far as my questioning model is applicable, i.e., insofar as Kant is right, such generalization from random data plays a much smaller role in science itself than philosophers seem to imagine these days, let alone in philosophical inquiry.

Another symptom of the insufficiency of the generalization model is that it does not offer any clues as to how our intuitions (the data) have to be changed if they prove unsatisfactory.

Here, then, we can see one of the main services that my questioning model can perform when thought of as a paradigm of philosophical method. It can guide a philosopher in activating the tacit knowledge that constitutes the raw materials of a philosopher's inquiry. In particular, it shows that important guidelines for this task are forthcoming from our familiar deductive logic. Successful thinking is colloquially referred to as "thinking logically." Philosophers might be well advised to take this idea more seriously than they are currently doing.

11. Trivial vs. Nontrivial Reasoning

Part of the force of the near analogy between questioning and deduction that I have argued for is brought out by the question: What characterizes nontrivial (synthetic) reasoning? I have argued on earlier occasions for an answer to this question applied to deductive reasoning. (It has turned out that this answer was not only anticipated but strongly emphasized by C. S. Peirce, even though no one had understood his idea in the interim.) Very briefly, and omitting all sorts of technicalities, the idea is that a logical inference is trivial ("corollarial," Peirce would have said) if it does not involve the introduction of any new entities into the argument. An inference is nontrivial ("theorematic," Peirce calls it) if it depends on the introduction of a new object into the purview of the reasoning. The more numerous such auxiliary objects are that a reasoner has to bring in, the more highly nontrivial is the reasoning. Historically, the paradigm case of such introductions of new objects into an argument have been the so-called auxiliary constructions of elementary geometry, a paradigm reflected by Peirce's choice of his terms.

The partial analogy between interrogation and deduction explained above allows us to generalize the trivial-nontrivial distinction to empirical reasoning relying on questioning over and above deductive reasoning in contemporary philosophers' narrow sense of the term. The extension is neatly illustrated by an example I have used before, viz. "the curious incident of the dog in the night-time" in Conan Doyle.[2] The famous racing horse *Silver Blaze* has been stolen from its stable in the middle of the night and its trainer, the stablemaster, has been found killed out in the heath. Everybody is puzzled till Sherlock Holmes directs our attention "to the curious incident of the dog in the night-time." "The dog did nothing in the night-time." "That was the curious incident." What Sherlock is doing here is in the first place to ask a few well-chosen questions. Was there a watchdog in the stable during the fateful night? Yes, we know that. Did the dog bark at the horse-thief? No, it did not. ("That was the curious incident.") Now who is it that a trained watchdog is not likely to bark at in the night-time? Its master, the trainer, of course. Each question and its answer may be "elementary," as Sherlock would say, but what makes the entire line of thought nontrivial is that Holmes brings, for the first time in the story, a new factor to bear on the solution of the mystery, viz. the dog. This introduction of a new object into the argument parallels an "auxiliary construction" by a geometer. It doesn't merely add a psychological twist to the tale; it is what logically speaking enables Holmes to carry out his "deduction."

The most famous deduction in the philosophical literature to be conducted in the form of a question-answer dialogue is Socrates's conversation with the slave boy in Plato's *Meno*. It illustrates forcefully the same power of auxiliary constructions (more generally, auxiliary individuals, in logicians' sense of individual) to facilitate

---

2 Arthur Conan Doyle, "Silver Blaze," in Baring-Gould 1967, pp. 261-81; see here p. 277.

nontrivial conclusions. In the *Meno*, Socrates extends the slave boy's purview by introducing three new squares adjoining the original one. (See *Meno* 84 d.) The original one is here:

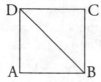

The completed one looks like this:

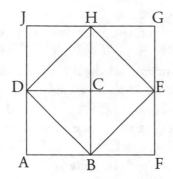

(The lines BE, EH, and HD are likewise introduced by Socrates in so many words in 84 e–85 a.) Once all these constructions have been carried out the conclusion is obvious: the square of BD can be seen to equal twice the square of AB. This argument depends crucially on the "auxiliary constructions" Socrates is allowed to carry out.

If the role and nature of such auxiliary constructions is not understood and appreciated, the power of philosophical questioning methods to yield nontrivial conclusions will be an intriguing puzzle. It is a small wonder, it seems to me, that this puzzle should have provoked Plato to hypothesize in his doctrine of *anamnesis*, i.e., of a memory-like knowledge of those unexpected conclusions. It would also be interesting to try to consider theories of innate ideas in the same light.

12. Thinking as Unspoken Discourse

One way of bringing out the crucial general significance of a suitable questioning model for the conceptual analysis of human thinking in general is the following: Time and again in the course of Western thought, philosophers have proposed to consider *thinking* on the model of *speaking*. Plato describes "thinking as discourse, and judgment as a statement pronounced, not aloud to someone else but silently to oneself."[3] Likewise C. S. Peirce asserts that "all thinking is dialogical in form. Your self of one instant appeals to your deeper self for his assent,"[4] and again, "One's thoughts are what he is 'saying to himself,' that is, saying to the other self that is just coming into life in the flow of time."[5] One reason why this idea is so suggestive is that, if it is right, the extensive and powerful logic that has been developed for the study of spoken or written *sentences* may be expected to help us understand the nature of *reasoning* and *thinking*.

Yet this suggestive idea has never led to major insights into the nature of thinking or reasoning. Why? In our days, Peter Geach has made an interesting effort to use the idea and construe the concept of thinking or "judging," as Geach calls it, "as an analogical extension of the concept *saying*." In spite of Geach's famous ingenuity, the results are rather meager. We can now see why, more generally, the suggestive idea of thinking as internal saying has not proved as useful so far as one might have hoped. The answer is implicit in Plato's and Peirce's formulations. They don't just compare thinking with saying, but with *discourse*—a discourse between several different selves. Hence it is not any old logic that can be hoped to be useful for understanding reasoning through the Plato-Peirce analogy; only a genuine logic of discourse as distinguished from logic done on the sentence level will do. We could call the latter "sentential logic" in contrast to discourse logic if the term had not been

---

[3] Plato, *Theaetetus* 190a; cf. *Sophist* 263e.

[4] C. S. Peirce, *Collected Papers*, vol. 2, sec. 26.

[5] Ibid., vol. 6, sec. 338.

pre-empted. What is striking about most of the usual logical conceptualizations and theories is that they move on the sentence level. They don't take into account differences between different speakers, for instance differences between what they know. Furthermore, most of the conceptualizations concerning the logic of questions in earlier literature have likewise been sentential.

Characteristically, Geach, too, tries to use the analogy between thinking and saying to examine, not different types of inferences one can make in one's thinking, but the various kinds of judgments one can make, such as "judgments of identification," "judgments about sensible particulars," etc. In other words, his conceptualizations remain predominantly on the sentence level.

Now questions and answers offer the simplest example of a discourse phenomenon that cannot be reduced to sentence-level phenomena. Indeed, there would not be any point in asking a question if the speaker and the hearer knew the same things or if epistemic differences between them did not matter. In view of the importance of the respective epistemic states of the parties in a question-answer dialogue, it is not surprising that my criterion of conclusive answerhood (cf. (16) above) is formulated in terms of what the questioner knows (i.e., knows after he or she has received a reply). If there is anything remarkable in my criterion, it lies in the fact that there is no need to refer to the other features of the dialogical situation.

Hence my theory of questions, answers, and question-answer dialogues offers a handy paradigm case for the study of characteristically discourse phenomena. According to what we have found, this implies that it also promises, via the Plato-Peirce analogy between discourse and thinking, to serve as an analogical model for at least some instructive sample cases of reasoning (thinking). In brief, it offers us the best hope that I can see of vindicating the Plato-Peirce analogy, at least in the case of selected sample problems. Only in terms of a dynamic theory like my theory of question-answer interaction can one hope to bring logical theorizing to bear on the study of reasoning and thinking in the way Plato and Peirce expected.

Several of the developments outlined, mentioned, or anticipated above receive their natural places in this overall perspective. It was for instance mentioned earlier that the process of calling the right items of tacit information to active duty can be approached as if it were a questioning procedure. This characteristically thinking process can in other words be handled by means of an analogy with explicit discourse. Likewise, the deep connections between actual deductive strategies in logic and the skills of a Sherlock Holmes–type practical cogitator uncovered above bear witness to the viability of the same analogy. In the last analysis, it is perhaps the capacity of the questioning model to throw light on the nature of thinking more generally that makes it so useful as a part of a philosopher's methodology. For a philosopher's last but not least task is to enhance our awareness of our own thinking. In philosophy only an examined thought is worth thinking.

PART SIX
PHILOSOPHY OF SCIENCE

INTRODUCTION:
TEN PHILOSOPHICAL
(AND CONTRADICTORY)
PREDICTIONS

by

GIAN-CARLO ROTA & JEFFREY THOMAS CRANTS

Editor's note: Professor Rota died shortly after the writing of this essay, and did not have the opportunity to see the edited version. As a result some discrepancies may exist.

Suppose that the future were to be disclosed to us like an open book. Would we like that? Probably not. We do not mind listening to predictions, as long as we feel confident that such predictions are unreliable. If ever there were an oracle who could predict the future with certainty, as happened to Cassandra in Troy, we would stay away from such a person. Rest assured that the present authors are not about to take Cassandra as a role model.

By and large, when we listen to predictions we expect our views about the future to be confirmed, except when we need advice about our investments. We then seek help from professional predictors, such as astrologers, soothsayers, and economists. Allow the senior author to begin with a personal story, taking my age as an excuse. My maternal grandfather, who was a baker in Italy, regularly sought the advice of a medium for predictions of the numbers he would bet on the Italian lotto, the oldest continuously running lottery in the world. The medium invariably recommended that he bet on the numbers 7-17-27. He did, and he lost. One week after his funeral, the numbers came up as the winning numbers. I take this episode as a warning that not all predictions need be wide of the mark.

Never before in history has science occupied as central a place in our culture, and never has the misunderstanding of science been as widespread as it is today. Our objective here is not to give a survey of the main academic fields of the philosophy of science. Rather, we will attempt to show from the point of view of a scientist the valid questions, the authentic problems that are found in today's science.

The German philosopher Georg Wilhelm Friedrich Hegel is blamed for the notorious statement "the real is rational and the rational is real." All efforts to give dispassionate descriptions of the world devastatingly disprove Hegel's assertion.

The present state of science confirms how hopelessly wrong Hegel was in his prescription of rationality for the real. The professional simplifiers of the twentieth century have found it expedient to follow in Hegel's footsteps (or what they believed Hegel ought to have said) and ignore the call to realism. We will take the bull by the horns and describe with as little comment as our lack of restraint allows us some of the puzzling features in today's science, those features that are likely to play a leading role in the fate of science in the next century.

As we take a philosophical stance toward science, we meet a host of seldom-mentioned phenomena that clash with our expectations. Realism must grapple with contradiction. As we peer within some scientific theory, we find that what purports to be the product of pure thought is instead a mixture of reason and myth. Fact and fiction play equiprimordial roles in scientific explanation. Only the never-ending and undreamed-of practical applications that improbable theoretical discoveries miraculously find provide the solace that we desperately seek after the collapse of Enlightenment rationalism.

Our task all but demands the rhetoric of the decalogue.

1. There Is Unity to the Sciences

We begin with an old and oft-repeated question: is there any reason to assert the unity of science? Is there a common thread of thought or method that runs from a theoretical science, such as mathematics, all the way to the descriptive sciences, such as the life sciences? Can the use of the word *science* be justified to include such different undertakings?

A positive answer to this question may become apparent, as we perform suitable thought experiments ("eidetic variations," as our teacher Edmund Husserl was wont to say), and thereby compare the profession of science to the more lucrative professions, such as banking or the law. We will then realize that the one word *science* does indeed suit the entire community of scientists.

A high officer of the CIA once remarked to the senior author that he benefited from personal consultations with scientists in their offices and labs more than he gleaned from interviews with astute businessmen or even from the top-secret reports of employees of his agency. I found his remark surprising, and I brought up a common objection. Scientists lack practical sense; they live in ivory towers; they are unaware of what goes on in the world. "But scientists are honest!" retorted my friend from the CIA.

Intellectual honesty is one trait that is shared by all scientists. The results of science are published in a way that is meant to be shared, verified, double-checked, and reproduced by scientists and engineers of any other time or culture. False statements and fraud are rare; whenever a fraudulent episode occurs, it gets wide reportage in the media. Such wide publicity given to scientific fraud is glaring proof of the fact that dishonesty in science is the exception.

A further confirmation of honesty is one trait that is shared by all scientists. The results of scientific experiment are tabulated and made available in journals that circulate all over the world. Anyone can assess the statistical accuracy of the numerical confirmation of a scientific hypothesis. Tentative results are pointed out and lead to further research, often carried out by other scientists. Ambiguous conclusions are drawn with caution, and in those rare instances when they are made in bad faith, they are spotted.

In some of the exact sciences, false statements are all but nonexistent. Either a proof of a mathematical theorem is correct, or else it is meaningless verbiage. A newfound chemical compound is eagerly reproduced by industry and made into a billion-dollar industry. A newly identified genetic trait will inexorably guide physicians to the discovery of a new medication. A morphological similarity between two vegetable species will lead to an improvement in agricultural production. An abstruse quirk of quantum mechanics is seized by engineers and leads to a revolution in computation.

Scientists are brought together by their belief that their work will result in the discovery of verifiable facts. Physics and chemistry, biology and mathematics may differ in method and in the objects of their investigations, but physicists and chemists, biologists and mathematicians close ranks when asked to agree that their work shares at least one feature: the discovery of the manifold properties of one and only one nature.

At the annual meeting of the National Academy of Sciences of the United States (which takes place in Washington, D.C., in April), there is seldom disagreement on matters of substance. No other meeting of individuals from such diverse backgrounds is as ready to provide a display of solidarity whenever one of the sciences is attacked. Such attacks are becoming frequent, orchestrated by powerful forces of obscurantism. Small but vocal anti-intellectual groups, livid with anger, disguise their loathing of scientific honesty in various ways and single out the sciences for periodic assaults.

2. There Is No Unity of the Sciences

Whoever casts a look at the varieties of science cultivated in our day will be struck by the disjointedness of scientific disciplines. Among research groups and laboratories all over the world one finds small, tightly knit communities brought together by shared presuppositions about their science that are exclusive and unique to them and their friends. These tiny research groups communicate awkwardly and rarely with one another. More often, they share their results by way of challenge.

Such secretive communities are found even within one and the same science. Particle physics, to take an outstanding instance, is cultivated by schools of physicists separated from one another not only by different research programs but by different beliefs in the structure of matter, and not infrequently by mutual suspicion and distrust.

If we include mathematics among the sciences—an opinion that is periodically reopened to debate—then we may ask whether the work of the mathematician and the work of the botanist can be viewed as having anything in common. A mathematical discovery is endowed with a definitiveness that no botanical classification can hope to achieve. A law of physics displays an invariability that is rarely found in any biological finding. The myriad striking but inconclusive facts discovered by psychologists have failed so far to lead to any theory that stands the test of time.

What reasons can be given for including such activities under one generic banner, other than a common interest?

3. We Are Living in One of the Great Ages of Science

Science, like Gaul, may be roughly divided into three parts. At the upper end one finds sciences like physics and chemistry, which make ample use of mathematics and whose futures are inextricable linked to the future of mathematics. In the middle there are those sciences, such as the life sciences, where experiment reigns supreme, and where mathematical theory is a latecomer, still looked upon with suspicion. At the bottom, we find those sciences that are sometimes called the new sciences, even though some of them have been around for quite a while. Three examples of new sciences are cosmology, economics, and the theory of evolution.

Three reasons lead us to surmise that the twenty-first century will be a golden age of science, at least as successful as the twentieth, and richer in achievement in each of these areas.

First, there are permanent conquests of science that have changed the face of the world. Two scientific theories will remain paradigms of success for all time: classical mechanics and electromagnetic theory. Both these theories exhibit a feature of scientific progress that tends to be passed over in silence.

The theoretical bases of classical mechanics and electromagnetism were stated in mathematical terms in the nineteenth century, in systems of differential equations that have changed little since that time. However, the definitive experimental confirmations and engineering applications of these theories were for a long time limited by the backwardness of technology. It took another fifty years, roughly to the middle of the twentieth century, before the full impact of the truth of these theories was felt.

Classical mechanics in its original frictionless formulation was triumphantly verified when the space age came along. Accurate predictions of the trajectories of missiles launched into space provided a definitive confirmation of the laws first stated by Isaac Newton and perfected by mathematicians and physicists for almost three centuries.

Electromagnetic theory underwent a similar evolution. The early applications of electricity did make use of James Clerk Maxwell's equations, but the inadequacy of technology made these applications unsatisfying. Only in the electronic age, with the advent of television and the computer, was electromagnetic theory to find its confirmation in its purest version, without concessions to approximation.

It is to the credit of scientists that they have held fast to their theories in the face of experimental adversities that seemed to cast a cloud on the perfection of their equations. Perhaps the outstanding episode of this triumph of theory over the adversity of experiment is Albert Einstein's. A few years after his special theory of relativity was published, an eminent American physicist—who was at the time the president of the American Physical Society—carried out an experiment that seemed to disprove Einstein's theory. Einstein held fast. Eventually, sometime in the 1920s, a flaw was found in the experiment, and Einstein was vindicated.

The greatest theoretical advance in science of all times is quantum mechanics. The basic ideas of quantum mechanics were developed over a period of some three years in the late 1920s, and they have not changed much since that time. But the applications of quantum mechanics have revolutionized physics.

Anyone who has ever studied quantum mechanics agrees that the different mode of thinking that is required in order to understand quantum mechanics is weird. "Nobody understands quantum mechanics," physicist Richard Feynman used to repeat. He was right. Even today, a student of quantum mechanics is given to master a set of mysterious kitchen recipes that work, and that he or she learns to apply without asking too many questions. No one has an "intuitive" grasp of quantum mechanics. What is worse, the sophisticated mathematics that quantum mechanics demands applies only imperfectly, and "close your eyes" cancellations in equations are often required to justify astonishing predictions that no present mathematical theory is able to account for.

Everyone who has worked in quantum mechanics knows that the space formalism of German mathematician David Hilbert that is presently of universal use is an approximation to what will one day be a more adequate mathematical theory. The discovery of such a theory is a challenge for the coming century.

Quantum mechanics calls for a new kind of logic that seems to run counter to the rules of ordinary logic, those rules that have survived unscathed for 2,000 years. Until a short while ago, no one was seriously worried about the subversion of logic that occurs in quantum mechanics, because quantum mechanics seemed to apply only to infinitely small phenomena, to electrons and photons and to other subatomic entities that are closer to fantasy than to our daily lives.

All this changed with the advent of quantum computation several years ago. Quantum computation will result in at least two dramatic changes, one in our daily lives and one in science.

Our daily lives will be affected as soon as quantum computation becomes a reality. This will probably happen sometime in the next ten years. Quantum computation will render all present methods of encryption obsolete. As soon as new programs are in place that factor large integers in a short time, which is what quantum computation promises to do, pin numbers, credit cards, and secure phone lines will become a thing of the past. One wonders how our grandchildren will manage to keep their secrets.

But the domino effect of quantum computation may be even more noticeable in the sciences. Thanks to quantum computation, the logic of quantum mechanics has been stripped of its subatomic hideaway. The needs of quantum computation are forcing mathematicians to spell out in simple mathematical terms the underlying reasoning process of the quantum theory, freed from appeals to the mysteries of the infinitely small. We are being retrained to think quantum mechanically. As scientists and mathematicians learn to think the quantum way, they will find new applications of this radically new way of thinking to the most diverse problems in all corners of science. A revolution has started.

Quantum mechanics is the first crack in the wall of the naive determinism going back to the French astronomer and mathematician Pierre-Simon Laplace. It opens the door to a new world that to this day we have not had the courage or the imagination to enter.

We now turn to the second reason for thinking the twenty-first century will be a golden age of science. The latter half of this century has ushered in an abundance of experimental techniques that were not previously available, and that provide data calling for precise theories to replace present-day speculations. Our understanding of space has been widened by measurements provided by the Hubble telescope and by sundry other optically accurate observations that are just now being made. The disclosure of the genetic structure of DNA is reaching dizzying levels of thoroughness and accuracy. Magnetic resonance imaging is allowing an insight into brain functions undreamed of only a few years ago.

These technical advances are providing a host of new and unforeseen facts that present a challenge for the development of theories in cosmology, in genetics, and in brain science that for the first time in history will meet the standards of exactness and reliability set by physics. We may surmise that scientists in the coming century will be kept busy by the development of such theories.

The third reason for anticipating a golden age of science is that we are witnessing the beginning of a restructuring of our idea of what a scientific theory should be. To this day, the model of scientific theory has been drawn from physics, and histories of science have been heavily slanted toward the history of physics. As the life sciences come into their own, thanks to some genial discoveries, the model of a scientific theory provided by physics is proving to be awkward and unsuitable. An eminent molecular biologist (Walter Fitch) made to one of us a startling remark—that whatever theories biologists will ever develop are more likely to resemble the narration of history than the statement of physical law.

The sciences are shaking themselves out of their physics-envy, and the opinion is taking hold that other modes of rigor are possible in the sciences that are as impeccable as and yet not reducible to physical rigor. The old prejudice that all science should be eventually "reduced" to physics (whatever such a statement may mean) was prodded by the simplistic positivism that truculently dominated the philosophy of science in the latter half of this century, and that we can now safely relegate to the dustbin of history.

4. Science Is Coming to an End

The mathematician John von Neumann used to say that the public may turn away from science, just as one day it turned away from classical music. A cynical observer of the scientific scene in the last fifty years will not fail to notice that support of science on the part of the federal government coincided with the arms race between the United States and the Soviet Union, a race in which most civilized countries felt they had to join.

With the demise of communism and the apparent triumph of a free market economy, the rationale for support of basic research in science is growing thin. Science is not a self-supporting enterprise;

it survives thanks to the largesse of governments and to the endowment of private benefactors. What is more worrying, the scientific community is a small constituency, unlikely to deliver a significant number of votes to a politician running for office.

The forces of anti-intellectualism are growing in strength and in voting power. Masses of disenfranchised poor are demanding their share of the economic pie. The resurgence of primitive scientific rites and of New Age mysticism conspire against the tenuous hold that scientific objectivity has managed with great effort to gain among the public. Few elected officials see it to their advantage to display appreciation of the contributions to science.

Only a new threat to civilization will save public support for science. The Congress of the United States stands ready to react swiftly and forcefully to a perceived threat. Most likely, the new threat is going to come from one of two sources. The first is the fragility of the manifold electrical networks upon which our daily survival is wholly dependent, an instability that has already been widely perceived by engineers, and that scientists might do well to publicize before a disaster of major proportions comes upon us.

The second threat is worse. The present ecological imbalance in both environment and nutrition, aided and abetted by the current frenzy for deregulation, will lead to widespread famines and to epidemics of panic proportions, which only a rapid, gigantic deployment of scientific know-how may hope to combat.

It is sad to pin the survival of what we hold most dear upon instability and disaster.

5. *Technology Cannot Survive Without Science*

Some five centuries ago, Leonardo da Vinci wrote: "*La teoria é il capitano e la pratica é il soldato.*" A widespread misunderstanding of the role of science has persisted through the centuries. Scientific research is mistakenly supposed to be spurred on by problems that arise in the practical needs of daily life. Scientists are looked upon as physicians hired to cure the ills of mankind and to satisfy the needs of the common man. The problems of sciences are believed to be inspired by the demands of the nation's economy.

A cursory look at the history of science provides the crushing refutation of this insidious prejudice. In each and every instance when a major application of science was discovered, the theory behind the application had been discovered first, and without apparent motivation. Applications were always found, but they came later and unexpectedly.

Engineers who are stuck on a technological problem do not turn to basic research. They do the opposite: they rush to the library and scan articles published years ago in whichever journals, in search of scientific facts that will help them. On rare occasions they may even turn to scientists for advice. Eventually, engineers will appropriate and adopt the scientist's work, often without acknowledgment, or after disguising it in their own jargon.

The miracle of science, which has repeated itself too often to be an accident, is that theoretical discoveries that are systematically denounced as devoid of conceivable application are later found to be the key to the advances in technology. We will give four instances of this phenomenon, but one could provide a hundred. The senior author has shamelessly drawn all four from his own field, namely, mathematics.

First: the notion of "spectrum," which is nowadays used all over science, and which most people believe to have originated in physics. The truth lies otherwise. The notion of spectrum was introduced by David Hilbert, one of the great mathematicians of this century, around 1910. It is not clear what Hilbert's motivation was in developing his theory of the spectrum, but it certainly did not come from physics. Some twenty years later, the discoverers of quantum mechanics found that Hilbert's special theory was what the doctor ordered, and proceeded to appropriate it and to make good use of it. Soon afterward, the idea of spectrum spread all over science.

Second: the discovery of infinite fields (you do not need to know what finite fields are), which was made by the American mathematician E. H. Moore at the beginning of this century. At that time, an eminent European scientist came out with the trouncing statement, "At last we have an instance of a mathematical idea for which we can be sure never to expect any applications whatsoever." Some fifty years later, courses in finite fields are being required of undergraduates in every electrical engineering department. Anyone who makes a telephone call or who uses an ATM machine is benefiting from codes that would be impossible without the application of the theory of finite fields.

Third: Brownian motion, or, to put it in deliberately abstruse terms, "integration in function space" (again, you do not need to know what these terms refer to), the work of MIT mathematician Norbert Wiener in the 1920s and 1930s. When Wiener's first articles on this subject were published, they were ridiculed for hitting "the utmost limit of abstraction," and even some mathematicians joined the chorus of condemnation. Wiener's insistence on a rigorous foundation of the theory (which even Einstein before him had not thought to be necessary) was dismissed as a mathematician's foible, as another instance of that morbid delectation in axiomatics that mathematicians are accused of wallowing in.

Nowadays, Wiener's foundations of Brownian motion, whose importance was at first cavalierly dismissed, has paid off. It has led to the theory of stochastic integrals, which is taught—would you believe it?—in economics departments and business schools. Specialists in stochastic integrals are handsomely rewarded on Wall Street.

Fourth: when the senior author was an undergraduate at Princeton, there was a lone mathematics professor on the faculty whose specialty was the mathematical theory of knots and links. He was not taken seriously because his research was thought to be extravagant. Today, the mathematical theory of knots is the talk of the town. In physics, it is believed to be the key to the innermost secrets of nature, hidden in what is now known as topological quantum field theory. In molecular biology, our understanding of the folding of molecules and proteins is essential in unraveling the enigmas of the genetic code. And as chemistry becomes more precise thanks to computer stimulation, the most amazing knots among atoms and molecules are disclosed to the human eye.

6. Technology Can Survive Without Science

The cutting edge in the applications of science lies nowadays in those areas of technology that have seen fit to misleadingly relabel themselves as sciences: computer science, information science, and even defense science. We will examine the claims that these self-styled sciences can now afford to dispense with the services of scientists.

Physics, chemistry, and biology call for separate arguments.

Even physicists throw up their hands nowadays when confronted with the puzzles of particle physics. A grudgingly accepted theory, called "the standard model," awkwardly fits the experimental facts as they are known in this day. However, most physicists agree that this theory is far from definitive, and everyone expects that it will be replaced by an aesthetically more satisfying theory. Except that the experiments required to make any small advance in particle physics are so costly (their cost exceeds the gross national product of several countries) that no government today is likely to foot the bill, especially now that competition between two superpowers has ceased to be an issue. Particle physics may join archaeology as one of the marginal sciences, proudly explained to the public in glossy articles in *Smithsonian* magazine, but shunned by talented young persons looking for a successful career in science.

Chemistry presents a different picture. It is a science overwhelmed by its own success. Organic chemists have developed a methodology of their own, whose rigor is confirmed by the success of whatever they decide to work on. However, the nature of the rigor of organic chemists is a puzzle to mathematicians and theoretical physicists, accustomed as they are to a rigor of an altogether different kind. The rigor of organic chemistry, whose description has been unforgivably neglected by philosophers of science, appears to be closer to the apprenticeship that makes a good artisan rather than to the laws of an exact science. *Intuition* is a catchall word that ill defines scientific creativity, but in organic chemistry it seems appropriate. The advent of the computer further rewards the deployment of tricks of the trade and places a premium on the free range of intuitive talent unsullied by any craving for generalities.

From artisanship to technology there is only one step.

Biology is "where the money is now," to put it in simple terms. The public recognizes the need for basic research in biology and is showering life scientists with a surfeit of funds. The consequences of this richness are not unlike those of the heyday of particle physics in the sixties: a rush to publication of dubious results, hasty formulation of questionable theories with an eye to the Nobel Prize, and even an occasional fraud. Together with these negative features, there goes an unquestioned wealth of findings of the most startling kind, in genetics, in molecular biology, in brain science.

Applications to medicine, to public health, and to our understanding of the phenomenon of life are a daily event.

The cross-fertilization of the life sciences and the computer has led to the improbable blossoming of a branch of mathematics that was once viewed as a poor cousin, namely, statistics. New statistical techniques stimulated by molecular biology and epidemiology yield a more reliable evaluation of experimental data than was ever thought possible. Yet the effects of the new lease on life for statistics will be felt not in the life sciences but in an altogether different area, namely, economics.

Despite brave efforts of the most talented minds, this abundance of data has so far failed to yield any stable theory of the kind that we have come to expect in the exact sciences. An eminent biologist once remarked to the senior author that the problem of inferring the structure of the human brain from a study of its anatomy is similar to the problem of inferring the working of the federal government from an examination of the buildings in Washington.

The numerous applications of biology to medicine will maintain a high level of funding for the life sciences, but the stress may remain on exploitation of scattered experimental findings, with a consequent veering away from traditional science toward cruder technology.

Yet, if we were to be asked which profession will make the greatest strides in years to come, our answer would unhesitatingly be: medicine. No one knows the causes of the infinity of diseases that plague mankind, and even a classification of diseases is missing. Most diseases, like schizophrenia, have been given a generic name out of desperation, to denote hundreds of conditions that may be attributed to different causes. Medicine is a profession that admittedly bears closer resemblance to African witchcraft than to scientific guesswork. The physician's magic touch will be enhanced by the availability of vast stores of data, and by the precision of measurement that has been made possible by the computer. Medication will still be prescribed on an empirical basis, but a more reliable one.

7. There Is Hope for the Soft Sciences

In days gone by, economics used to be labeled "the dismal science."

More recently, it has ceded this dubious distinction to more out-standing fellow travelers: psychology, sociology, linguistics, and other "sciences" of later vintage.

Haughty physicists used to dismiss these undertakings as "the slums of science," but such a rude exclusion is now believed to be unfair. Economics, psychology, sociology, and linguistics are abuzz with activity and with results of lasting value.

In economics, the adoption of sophisticated mathematical models has resulted in substantial progress. No trader on Wall Street today can dispense with computer programs that employ the latest findings in probability, statistics, and stochastic differential equations. While this increase in mathematical know-how puts a premium on fierce competition, it also betokens newly found predictive powers.

Psychology and sociology have been given a new lease on life by the pressing needs of predicting and controlling mass behavior. Whatever negative opinions one may have on such vulgar practices as focus groups, advertising, television commercials, and promotion of manufactured products, it cannot be denied that these business needs have resulted in the availability of financial resources for research in psychology and sociology. The prospect of a paying application works wonders on the development of science. The appellation "soft science," by which psychology and sociology were once confined to Building Twenty of MIT, will soon be a relic of a distant past.

Last but not least, linguistics has undergone a beneficial overhaul and has been given new life by the work of Noam Chomsky. The labyrinth of language has at last found Ariadne's thread, and the rebirth of linguistics is beginning to affect even the humanities.

Other new sciences, such as cosmology and the theory of evolution, have had a turbulent history. Experiment is all but impossible in these sciences. Instead, they have always relied on broad, speculative hypotheses. Because these hypotheses are difficult to verify, the confidence levels that were allowed in the interpretation of data were far more lax than the tight confidence levels that one has come to expect in biology or medicine, let alone chemistry. Theories about the origin and the evolution of the universe, for instance, were blithely and frequently revised on the basis of slim evidence. Rapid advances in instrumentation have changed this picture. Thanks to the new telescopes, our access to the skies now yields a bounty of data, more precise than ever before.

8. *There Is No Hope for the Soft Sciences*

As a consequence of this newfound wealth of evidence, a great many theories proposed in the past have fallen by the wayside, while few new theories have so far taken their place. We know less about the laws governing the functioning of the world economy today than economists thought they did fifty years ago. Cosmological speculations are grappling with a morass of data that do not fit any model of the universe ever dreamed of.

All corners of sciences are awash in a swelling sea of facts, made plentiful and precise by inexpensive data collection. Whether some sense will ever be made of such an abundance of facts, none of them pointing in a definite direction, is a question well worth pondering.

If Johannes Kepler's astronomical data had been too bountiful or more accurate, Newton might never have discovered the law of gravitation. Episodes in the history of science abound where a plethora of fact worked against the discovery of theory. The reason for this seeming contradiction is not hard to state. Fundamental scientific concepts are not obtained by scanning columns of data. They are the product of creative imagination; they are the children of daunting courage that dares conceive what is not before our eye, that sees what is not there. Galileo's idea of free fall was not to be found anywhere, and his detractors were right in labeling it the child of fantasy.

The embarrassing variety of facts that is swamping the soft sciences is a symptom of disarray, of lack of direction, of inability to take a creative leap that will disclose some hidden unity, some revealing law. Whether or not well-endowed minds will come along whose creative energy will take this leap is the cliff-hanger of today's science.

9. *Science Is Free from Ideological Prejudice*

Sometime ago, a *New Yorker* cartoon showed two members of a jury in a courtroom listening to an attorney who was pleading in favor of his client; one juror whispered to the other: "Logic! The last refuge of scoundrels."

This vignette vividly summarizes the characteristics of ordinary speech. Whether in conversation, in political peroration, or even in formal rhetoric, the process of conviction bears little relation to logical reasoning. Emotional considerations, appeals to prejudice, subconscious habits, and old customs are the tools whereby one person attempts to convince another. Listen to an audiotape of an ordinary conversation, larded with *I mean*'s and *you know*'s, and you will find confirmation of the absence of factual support, or worse yet, the appeal to imaginary events, which is called into play when one person is leading another into some private agenda.

In this world of irrational discourse, science has become the fortress of reason. Disunited as the sciences may appear, they stand together in their call to a reality that can and must be factually confirmed. It is no wonder that science comes periodically under attack. Science is the only bulwark against superstition.

Paradoxically, the advent of the Internet has increased the occurrence of imaginary and false rumors. A news item that may be devoid of any support, cynically planted by some hacker, spreads like wildfire through the Internet and reinforces itself as the news media find phony confirmation in circular referrals.

In the Manichaean world, we can only root for the victory of science. Science has one great advantage: the results of science benefit and improve the world. The periodic droning against the evils of technology is misleading. The society in which we live today is better and more congenial than that of our childhoods. Whatever ills are befalling mankind are brought about not by technology but by the misuse of technology by our narrow minds, always a step behind in appreciating the possibilities of whatever is new.

10. Science Is Laced with Ideology

The most alarming aspect in the progress of science is the reluctant acceptance of what Thomas Kuhn labeled *a new paradigm*. Perhaps the most striking occurrence of this phenomenon happened a few years ago in medicine. For years an obscure Australian physician asserted that stomach ulcers are caused by a virus. He was marginalized by the medical community, until someone mustered the courage to perform suitable experiments and found confirmation of the viral origin of ulcers. Soon enough, the new "viral paradigm" started to spread, and today we hear clamors for the viral origin of mental disorders.

This instance is by no means rare. An established scientific theory is protected by scientific communities, who see their interest and their livelihood depending on continuing acceptance. It is true that facts sooner or later make inroads into prejudice, but there is no more dangerous enemy than someone whose prejudice is being attacked.

Three thinkers who played key roles in shaping the world of today were Karl Marx, Sigmund Freud, and Charles Darwin. All three met the same fate. Each of them gave birth to a great new idea that was eventually altered beyond recognition. Marx was the first to clamor for the importance of economic factors in social phenomena. Freud initiated the study of the hidden layers of the mind. Darwin proposed the idea of evolution.

As these ideas blossomed, the original speculations of their inventors were rejected. Marxism is all but dead as an economic system. Contemporary psychiatry has gone beyond Freudian psychoanalysis, and practically none of Darwin's original assertions about evolution are still held to be scientific truths. Marx, Freud, and Darwin will be remembered not for their contributions but for the new horizons they opened up.

All scientific theories depend upon unstated ideological assumptions. These assumptions are only reluctantly brought out into the open, and philosophers of the twentieth century have been too condescending toward science to flatly criticize the underlying philosophical tenets that lie hidden within the roots of every science.

The need for a thorough critique of ill-formulated foundations is prominently found in evolutionary biology. Every exact scientist can tell his or her own stories of the defensive reactions of evolutionary biologists, whenever the slightest word of criticism is voiced about accepted dogmas. No physicist will feel irritated when someone, even a crackpot, walks into his office and begins to criticize the theory of relativity. Quite the contrary: the physicist will listen to the argument and offer tentative counterarguments. On rare occasions, the objector may be proved right. By contrast, an evolutionary biologist who hears the slightest criticism of Darwinian teleology will take offense, become red in the face, and retort by a stream of invective. If the offender is a student, he will see to it that the student is deprived of his fellowship (this is not a made-up story; it actually happened). This unusual sensitivity to criticism is a sign of weakness. A casual look at current debates among evolutionary biologists cannot fail to show a chasm of disagreement within the field.

Fortunately, giddying paleontological discoveries have provided evolutionary biologists with more food for thought than they ever expected to find, and to top it all, molecular biology is coming to play a major role in determining the sequence of events in the evolution of the species.

Only the support of genetic data, coming when all seems to be lost, will restore credibility, and, we dare predict, will overhaul a heap of unsupported assumptions. Despite some initial flops, such as the theory of an "African Eve" that was eventually disproved after finding a glitch in a computer program, the combined forces of genetics and computer science will provide us with a reliable picture of evolution. But a more accurate map of evolution is likely to deepen the mystery of our origins.

We will have to wait until certain persons die before this change of paradigms occurs.

A conspicuous instance of scientific failure due to ideological assumptions is macroeconomics. A recent article in *Fortune* magazine compares warring schools of macroeconomists, pointing out the inability of every one of them to make any predictions. *The Old Farmer's Almanac* is a more reliable economic predictor than macroeconomics.

Let there be no misunderstanding: science cannot be free of ideology, any more than it can be free of mathematics. What has been harmful is the acceptance of conceptual underpinnings uncritically drawn from so-called common sense. Modern chemistry was founded by discarding the commonsense notions of earth, air, fire, and water. Such mantras as *consciousness, creativity, information*, and even *time* are the earth, air, fire, and water of our day. Only a trenchant critique of the vague assumptions that lie behind these words will lead to a foundation, and hence to the success, of the newer sciences. Science and philosophy will supplement each other in attaining this difficult objective.

The twentieth century was a century of great discoveries and inventions: in science, relativity, and quantum mechanics; in technology, nuclear energy, and radar. The twentieth century was the century of big science. It was, if you allow the expression, the century of megalomania good and bad, all the way to the horrors of Nazism and the failed God of communism.

By contrast, the twenty-first century is likely to care a lot more for the small things. Tiny but powerful computers will enable scientists to carry out their work in their offices or in their garages. The life sciences, freed from teleological prejudice, will prosper thanks to scientific laws of local validity. The end of economic ideology, both socialist and capitalist, will pave the way for realistic economic theories. The planet Earth will receive more attention than distant planets.

The twenty-first century will be as much an age of philosophy as an age of science. As philosophy regains the autonomy that it lost to science in the twentieth century, it is likely to heed its calling to establish secure foundations for the sciences and thereby to become an equal partner in our project of understanding the world.

from
AGAINST METHOD
by
PAUL FEYERABEND

Ordnung ist heutzutage meistens dort,
wo nichts ist.
Es ist eine Mangelerscheinung.

         —Brecht

*Science is an essentially anarchic enterprise: theoretical anarchism
is more humanitarian and more likely to encourage progress than
its law-and-order alternatives.*

The following essay is written in the conviction that *anarchism*,
while perhaps not the most attractive *political* philosophy, is
certainly excellent medicine for *epistemology*, and for the *philosophy
of science.*

The reason is not difficult to find.

"History generally, and the history of revolution in particular, is
always richer in content, more varied, more many-sided, more lively
and subtle than even" the best historian and the best methodologist
can imagine.[1] History is full of "accidents and conjunctures and
curious juxtapositions of events"[2] and it demonstrates to us the
"complexity of human change and the unpredictable character of the
ultimate consequences of any given act or decision of men."[3] Are we

---

[1] "History as a whole, and the history of revolutions in particular, is always richer in
content, more varied, more multiform, more lively and ingenious than is imagined
by even the best parties, the most conscious vanguards of the most advanced classes"
(V. I. Lenin, "Left-Wing Communism—An Infantile Disorder," *Selected Works*,
Vol. 3, London, 1967, p. 401). Lenin is addressing parties and revolutionary vanguards rather than scientists and methodologists; the lesson, however, is the same.
Cf. footnote 5.

[2] Herbert Butterfield, *The Whig Interpretation of History*, New York, 1965, p. 66.

[3] Ibid., p. 21.

really to believe that the naive and simple-minded rules which methodologists take as their guide are capable of accounting for such a "Maze of interactions"?[4] And is it not clear that successful *participation* in a process of this kind is possible only for a ruthless opportunist who is not tied to any particular philosophy and who adopts whatever procedure seems to fit the occasion?

This is indeed the conclusion that has been drawn by intelligent and thoughtful observers. "Two very important practical conclusions follow from this [character of the historical process]," writes Lenin,[5] continuing the passage from which I have just quoted. "First, that in order to fulfil its task, the revolutionary class [i.e., the class of those who want to change either a part of society such as science, or society as a whole] must be able to master *all* forms or aspects of social activity without exception [it must be able to understand, and to apply, not only one particular methodology, but any methodology, and any variation thereof it can imagine] . . . ; second [it] must be ready to pass from one to another in the quickest and most unexpected manner."

---

[4] Ibid, p. 25, cf. Hegel, *Philosophie der Geschichte, Werke*, Vol. 9, ed. Edward Gans, Berlin, 1837, p. 9: "But what experience and history teach us is this, that nations and governments have never learned anything from history, or acted according to rules that might have derived from it. Every period has such peculiar circumstances, is in such an individual state, that decisions will have to be made, and decisions *can* only be made, in it and out of it."—"Very clever"; "shrewd and very clever"; "NB" writes Lenin in his marginal notes to this passage. (*Collected Works*, Vol. 38, London, 1961, p. 307.)

[5] Ibid. We see here very clearly how a few substitutions can turn a political lesson into a lesson for *methodology*. This is not at all surprising. Methodology and politics are both means for moving from one historical stage to another. We also see how an individual, such as Lenin, who is not intimidated by traditional boundaries and whose thought is not tied to the ideology of a particular profession, can give useful advice to everyone, philosophers of science included. In the 19th century the idea of an elastic and historically informed methodology was a matter of course. Thus Ernst Mach wrote in his book *Erkenntnis und Irrtum*, Neudruck, Wissenschaftliche Buchgesellschaft, Darmstadt, 1980, p. 200: "It is often said that research cannot be taught. That is quite correct, in a certain sense. The schemata of *formal* logic and of *inductive* logic are of little use for the intellectual situations are never exactly the same. But the examples of great scientists are very suggestive." They are not suggestive because we can abstract rules from them and subject future research to their jurisdiction; they are suggestive because they make the mind nimble and capable of inventing entirely new research traditions. For a more detailed account of Mach's philosophy see my essay *Farewell to Reason*, London, 1987, Chapter 7, as well as Vol. 2, Chapters 5 and 6 of my *Philosophical Papers*, Cambridge, 1981.

"The external conditions," writes Einstein,[6] "which are set for [the scientist] by the facts of experience do not permit him to let himself be too much restricted, in the construction of his conceptual world, by the adherence to an epistemological system. He, therefore, must appear to the systematic epistemologist as a type of unscrupulous opportunist. . . ." A complex medium containing surprising and unforeseen developments demands complex procedures and defies analysis on the basis of rules which have been set up in advance and without regard to the ever-changing conditions of history.

Now it is, of course, possible to simplify the medium in which a scientist works by simplifying its main actors. The history of science, after all, does not just consist of facts and conclusions drawn from facts. It also contains ideas, interpretations of facts, problems created by conflicting interpretations, mistakes, and so on. On closer analysis we even find that science knows no "bare facts" at all but that the "facts" that enter our knowledge are already viewed in a certain way and are, therefore, essentially ideational. This being the case, the history of science will be as complex, chaotic, full of mistakes, and entertaining as the ideas it contains, and these ideas in turn will be as complex, chaotic, full of mistakes, and entertaining as are the minds of those who invented them. Conversely, a little brainwashing will go a long way in making the history of science duller, simpler, more uniform, more "objective" and more easily accessible to treatment by strict and unchangeable rules.

Scientific education as we know it today has precisely this aim. It simplifies "science" by simplifying its participants: first, a domain of research is defined. The domain is separated from the rest of history (physics, for example, is separated from metaphysics and from theology) and given a "logic" of its own. A thorough training in such a "logic" then conditions those working in the domain; it makes *their actions* more uniform and it freezes large parts of the *historical process* as well. Stable "facts" arise and persevere despite the vicissitudes of history. An essential part of the training that makes such facts appear consists in the attempt to inhibit intuitions that might

---

[6] Albert Einstein, *Albert Einstein: Philosopher Scientist*, ed. P. A. Schilpp, New York, 1951, pp. 683f.

lead to a blurring of boundaries. A person's religion, for example, or his metaphysics, or his sense of humour (his *natural* sense of humour and not the inbred and always rather nasty kind of jocularity one finds in specialized professions) must not have the slightest connection with his scientific activity. His imagination is restrained, and even his language ceases to be his own. This is again reflected in the nature of scientific "facts" which are experienced as being independent of opinion, belief, and cultural background.

It is thus *possible* to create a tradition that is held together by strict rules, and that is also successful to some extent. But is it *desirable* to support such a tradition to the exclusion of everything else? Should we transfer to it the sole rights for dealing in knowledge, so that any result that has been obtained by other methods is at once ruled out of court? And did scientists ever remain within the boundaries of the traditions they defined in this narrow way? These are the questions I intend to ask in the present essay. And to these questions my answer will be a firm and resounding NO.

There are two reasons why such an answer seems to be appropriate. The first reason is that the world which we want to explore is a largely unknown entity. We must, therefore, keep our options open and we must not restrict ourselves in advance. Epistemological prescriptions may look splendid when compared with other epistemological prescriptions, or with general principles—but who can guarantee that they are the best way to discover, not just a few isolated "facts," but also some deep-lying secrets of nature? The second reason is that a scientific education as described above (and as practised in our schools) cannot be reconciled with a humanitarian attitude. It is in conflict "with the cultivation of individuality which alone produces, or can produce, well-developed human beings";[7] it "maims by compression, like a Chinese lady's foot, every part of human nature which stands out prominently, and tends to make a person markedly different in outline"[8] from the ideals of rationality that happen to be fashionable in science, or in the philosophy of sci-

---

[7] John Stuart Mill, "On Liberty," in *The Philosophy of John Stuart Mill*, ed. Marshall Cohen, New York, 1961, p. 258.

[8] Ibid., p. 265.

ence. The attempt to increase liberty, to lead a full and rewarding life, and the corresponding attempt to discover the secrets of nature and of man, entails, therefore, the rejection of all universal standards and of all rigid traditions. (Naturally, it also entails the rejection of a large part of contemporary science.)

It is surprising to see how rarely the stultifying effect of "the Laws of Reason" or of scientific practice is examined by professional anarchists. Professional anarchists oppose any kind of restriction and they demand that the individual be permitted to develop freely, unhampered by laws, duties or obligations. And yet they swallow without protest all the severe standards which scientists and logicians impose upon research and upon any kind of knowledge-creating and knowledge-changing activity. Occasionally, the laws of scientific method, or what are thought to be the laws of scientific method by a particular writer, are even integrated into anarchism itself. "Anarchism is a world concept based upon a mechanical explanation of all phenomena," writes Kropotkin.[9] "Its method of investigation is that of the exact natural sciences . . . the method of induction and deduction." "It is not so clear," writes a modern "radical" professor at Columbia,[10] "that scientific research demands an absolute freedom of speech and debate. Rather the evidence suggests that certain kinds of unfreedom place no obstacle in the way of science. . . ."

There are certainly some people to whom this is "not so clear." Let us, therefore, start with our outline of an anarchistic methodology and a corresponding anarchistic science. There is no need to fear that the diminished concern for law and order in science and society that characterizes an anarchism of this kind will lead to chaos.

---

[9] Peter Alexander Kropotkin, "Modern Science and Anarchism," *Kropotkin's Revolutionary Pamphlets*, ed. R. W. Baldwin, New York, 1970, pp. 150–2. "It is one of Ibsen's great distinctions that nothing was valid for him but science." B. Shaw, *Back to Methuselah*, New York, 1921, p. xcvii. Commenting on these and similar phenomena Strindberg writes (*Antibarbarus*): "A generation that had the courage to get rid of God, to crush the state and church, and to overthrow society and morality, still bowed before Science. And in Science, where freedom ought to reign, the order of the day was 'believe in the authorities or off with your head.'"

[10] R. P. Wolff, *The Poverty of Liberalism*, Boston, 1968, p. 15. For a criticism of Wolff see footnote 52 of my essay "Against Method," in *Minnesota Studies in the Philosophy of Science*, Vol. 4, Minneapolis, 1970.

The human nervous system is too well organized for that."[11] There may, of course, come a time when it will be necessary to give reason a temporary advantage and when it will be wise to defend its rules to the exclusion of everything else. I do not think that we are living in such a time today.[12]

> *This is shown both by an examination of historical episodes and by an abstract analysis of the relation between idea and action. The only principle that does not inhibit progress is: anything goes.*

The idea of a method that contains firm, unchanging, and absolutely binding principles for conducting the business of science meets considerable difficulty when confronted with the results of historical research. We find, then, that there is not a single rule, however plausible, and however firmly grounded in epistemology, that is not violated at some time or other. It becomes evident that such violations are not accidental events, they are not results of insufficient knowledge or of inattention which might have been avoided. On the contrary, we see that they are necessary for progress. Indeed, one of the most striking features of recent discussions in the history and philosophy of science is the realization that events and developments, such as the invention of atomism in antiquity, the Copernican Revolution, the rise of modem atomism (kinetic theory; dispersion theory; stereochemistry; quantum theory), the gradual emergence of the wave theory of light, occurred only because some thinkers either *decided* not to be bound by certain "obvious" methodological rules, or because they *unwittingly broke* them.

---

[11] Even in undetermined and ambiguous situations, uniformity of action is soon achieved and adhered to tenaciously. See Muzafer Sherif, *The Psychology of Social Norms*, New York, 1964.

[12] This was my opinion in 1970 when I wrote the first version of this essay. Times have changed. Considering some tendencies in U.S. education ("politically correct," academic menus, etc.), in philosophy (postmodernism) and in the world at large I think that reason should now be given greater weight not because it is and always was fundamental but because it seems to be needed, in circumstances that occur rather frequently today (but may disappear tomorrow), to create a more humane approach.

This liberal practice, I repeat, is not just a *fact* of the history of science. It is both reasonable and *absolutely necessary* for the growth of knowledge. More specifically, one can show the following: given any rule, however "fundamental" or "rational," there are always circumstances when it is advisable not only to ignore the rule, but to adopt its opposite. For example, there are circumstances when it is advisable to introduce, elaborate, and defend *ad hoc* hypotheses, or hypotheses which contradict well-established and generally accepted experimental results, or hypotheses whose content is smaller than the content of the existing and empirically adequate alternative, or self-inconsistent hypotheses, and so on.

There are even circumstances—and they occur rather frequently—when *argument* loses its forward-looking aspect and becomes a hindrance to progress. Nobody would claim that the teaching of *small children* is exclusively a matter of argument (though argument may enter into it, and should enter into it to a larger extent than is customary), and almost everyone now agrees that what looks like a result of reason—the mastery of a language, the existence of a richly articulated perceptual world, logical ability—is due partly to indoctrination and partly to a process of *growth* that proceeds with the force of natural law. And where arguments do seem to have an effect, this is more often due to their *physical repetition* than to their *semantic content*.

Having admitted this much, we must also concede the possibility of non-argumentative growth in the *adult* as well as in (the theoretical parts of) *institutions* such as science, religion, prostitution, and so on. We certainly cannot take it for granted that what is possible for a small child—to acquire new modes of behaviour on the slightest provocation, to slide into them without any noticeable effort—is beyond the reach of his elders. One should rather expect that catastrophic changes in the physical environment, wars, the breakdown of encompassing systems of morality, political revolutions, will transform adult reaction patterns as well, including important patterns of argumentation. Such a transformation may again be an entirely natural process and the only function of a rational argument may lie in the fact that it increases the mental tension that preceded *and caused* the behavioural outburst.

Now, if there are events, not necessarily arguments, which *cause* us to adopt new standards, including new and more complex forms of argumentation, is it then not up to the defenders of the *status quo* to provide, not just counter-arguments, but also contrary *causes*? ("Virtue without terror is ineffective," says Robespierre.) And if the old forms of argumentation turn out to be too weak a cause, must not these defenders either give up or resort to stronger and more "irrational" means? (It is very difficult, and perhaps entirely impossible, to combat the effects of brainwashing by argument.) Even the most puritanical rationalist will then be forced to stop reasoning and to use *propaganda* and *coercion*, not because some of his *reasons* have ceased to be valid, but because the *psychological conditions* which make them effective, and capable of influencing others, have disappeared. And what is the use of an argument that leaves people unmoved?

Of course, the problem never arises quite in this form. The teaching of standards and their defence never consists merely in putting them before the mind of the student and making them as *clear* as possible. The standards are supposed to have maximal *causal efficacy* as well. This makes it very difficult indeed to distinguish between the *logical force* and the *material effect* of an argument. Just as a well-trained pet will obey his master no matter how great the confusion in which he finds himself, and no matter how urgent the need to adopt new patterns of behaviour, so in the very same way a well-trained rationalist will obey the mental image of *his* master, he will conform to the standards of argumentation he has learned, he will adhere to these standards no matter how great the confusion in which he finds himself, and he will be quite incapable of realizing that what he regards as the "voice of reason" is but a *causal after-effect* of the training he had received. He will be quite unable to discover that the appeal to reason to which he succumbs so readily is nothing but a *political manoeuvre*.

That interests, forces, propaganda and brainwashing techniques play a much greater role than is commonly believed in the growth of our knowledge and in the growth of science, can also be seen from an analysis of the *relation between idea and action*. It is often taken for granted that a clear and distinct understanding of new ideas precedes, and should precede, their formulation and their institutional expression. *First*, we have an idea, or a problem, *then* we act, i.e., either speak, or build, or destroy. Yet this is certainly not the way in which small children develop. They use words, they combine them, they play with them, until they grasp a meaning that has so far been beyond their reach. And the initial playful activity is an essential prerequisite of the final act of understanding. There is no reason why this mechanism should cease to function in the adult. We must expect, for example, that the *idea* of liberty could be made clear only by means of the very same actions, which were supposed to *create* liberty. Creation of a *thing*, and creation plus full understanding of a *correct idea* of the thing, *are very often parts of one and the same indivisible process* and cannot be separated without bringing the process to a stop. The process itself is not guided by a well-defined programme, and cannot be guided by such a programme, for it contains the conditions for the realization of all possible programmes. It is guided rather by a vague urge, by a "passion" (Kierkegaard). The passion gives rise to specific behaviour which in turn creates the circumstances and the ideas necessary for analysing and explaining the process, for making it "rational."

The development of the Copernican point of view from Galileo to the twentieth century is a perfect example of the situation I want to describe. We start with a strong belief that runs counter to contemporary reason and contemporary experience. The belief spreads and finds support in other beliefs which are equally unreasonable, if not more so (law of inertia; the telescope). Research now gets deflected in new directions, new kinds of instruments are built, "evidence" is related to theories in new ways until there arises an ideology that is rich enough to provide independent arguments for any particular part of it and mobile enough to find such arguments whenever they seem to be required. We can say today that Galileo was on the right track, for his persistent pursuit of what once seemed to be a silly cosmology has by now created the material needed to defend it against all those who will accept a view only if it is told in a certain way and who will trust it only if it contains certain magical phrases, called "observational reports." And this is not an exception—it is the normal case: theories become clear and "reasonable" only *after* incoherent parts of them have been used for a long time. Such unreasonable, nonsensical, unmethodical foreplay thus turns out to be an unavoidable precondition of clarity and of empirical success.

Now, when we attempt to describe and to understand developments of this kind in a general way, we are, of course, obliged to appeal to the existing forms of speech which do not take them into account and which must be distorted, misused, beaten into new patterns in order to fit unforeseen situations (without a constant misuse of language there cannot be any discovery, any progress). "Moreover, since the traditional categories are the gospel of everyday thinking (including ordinary scientific thinking) and of everyday practice, [such an attempt at understanding] in effect presents rules and forms of false thinking and action—false, that is, from the standpoint of (scientific) common sense."[13] This is how *dialectical thinking* arises as a form of thought that "dissolves into nothing the detailed determinations of the understanding",[14] formal logic included.

(Incidentally, it should be pointed out that my frequent use of such words as "progress," "advance," "improvement," etc., does not mean that I claim to possess special knowledge about what is good and what is bad in the sciences and that I want to impose this knowledge upon my readers. *Everyone can read the terms in his own way* and in accordance with the tradition to which he belongs. Thus for an empiricist, "progress" will mean transition to a theory that provides direct empirical tests for most of its basic assumptions. Some people believe the quantum theory to be a theory of this kind. For others, "progress" may mean unification and harmony, perhaps even at the expense of empirical adequacy. This is how Einstein viewed the general theory of relativity. *And my thesis is that anarchism helps to achieve progress in any one of the senses one cares to choose*. Even a law-and-order science will succeed only if anarchistic moves are occasionally allowed to take place.)

It is clear, then, that the idea of a fixed method, or of a fixed theory of rationality, rests on too naive a view of man and his social surroundings. To those who look at the rich material provided by history, and who are not intent on impoverishing it in order to please their lower instincts, their craving for intellectual security in the form of clarity, precision, "objectivity," "truth," it will become clear that there is only one principle that can be defended under *all* circumstances and in all stages of human development. It is the principle: *anything goes*.

---

[13] Herbert Marcuse, *Reason and Revolution*, London, 1941, p. 130.

[14] Hegel, *Wissenschaft der Logik*, Vol. 1, Hamburg, 1965, p. 6.

THE STRUCTURE
OF SCIENTIFIC REVOLUTIONS
by
THOMAS KUHN

The Nature and Necessity of Scientific Revolutions

These remarks permit us at last to consider the problems that provide this essay with its title. What are scientific revolutions, and what is their function in scientific development? Many of the answers to these questions have been anticipated in earlier sections. In particular, the preceding discussion has indicated that scientific revolutions are here taken to be those non-cumulative developmental episodes in which an older paradigm is replaced in whole or in part by an incompatible new one. There is more to be said, however, and an essential part of it can be introduced by asking one further question. Why should a change of paradigm be called a revolution? In the face of the vast and essential differences between political and scientific development, what parallelism can justify the metaphor that finds revolutions in both?

One aspect of the parallelism must already be apparent. Political revolutions are inaugurated by a growing sense, often restricted to a segment of the political community, that existing institutions have ceased adequately to meet the problems posed by an environment that they have in part created. In much the same way, scientific revolutions are inaugurated by a growing sense, again often restricted to a narrow subdivision of the scientific community, that an existing paradigm has ceased to function adequately in the exploration of an aspect of nature to which that paradigm itself had previously led the way. In both political and scientific development the sense of malfunction that can lead to crisis is prerequisite to revolution. Furthermore, though it admittedly strains the metaphor, that parallelism holds not only for the major paradigm changes, like those attributable to Copernicus and Lavoisier, but also for the far smaller ones associated with the assimilation of a new sort of phenomenon, like oxygen or X-rays. Scientific revolutions need seem revolutionary only to those whose paradigms are affected by them. To outsiders they may, like the Balkan revolutions of the early twentieth century, seem normal parts of the developmental process. Astronomers, for example, could accept X-rays as a mere addition to knowledge, for their paradigms were unaffected by the existence of the new radiation. But for men like Kelvin, Crookes, and Roentgen, whose research dealt with radiation theory or with cathode ray tubes, the emergence of X-rays necessarily violated one paradigm as it created another. That is why these rays could be discovered only through something's first going wrong with normal research.

This genetic aspect of the parallel between political and scientific development should no longer be open to doubt. The parallel has, however, a second and more profound aspect upon which the significance of the first depends. Political revolutions aim to change political institutions in ways that those institutions themselves prohibit. Their success therefore necessitates the partial relinquishment of one set of institutions in favor of another, and in the interim, society is not fully governed by institutions at all. Initially it is crisis alone that attenuates the role of political institutions as we have already seen it attenuate the role of paradigms. In increasing numbers individuals become increasingly estranged from political life and behave more and more eccentrically within it. Then, as the crisis deepens, many of these individuals commit themselves to some concrete proposal for the reconstruction of society in a new institutional framework. At that point the society is divided into competing camps or parties, one seeking to defend the old institutional constellation, the others seeking to institute some new one. And, once that polarization has occurred, *political recourse fails*. Because they differ about the institutional matrix within which political change is to be achieved and evaluated, because they acknowledge no supra-institutional framework for the adjudication of revolutionary difference, the parties to a revolutionary conflict must finally resort to the techniques of mass persuasion, often including force. Though revolutions have had a vital role in the evolution of political institutions, that role depends upon their being partially extrapolitical or extrainstitutional events.

The remainder of this essay aims to demonstrate that the historical study of paradigm change reveals very similar characteristics in the evolution of the sciences. Like the choice between competing political institutions, that between competing paradigms proves to be a choice between incompatible modes of community life. Because it has that character, the choice is not and cannot be determined merely by the evaluative procedures characteristic of normal science, for these depend in part upon a particular paradigm, and that paradigm is at issue. When paradigms enter, as they must, into a debate about paradigm choice, their role is necessarily circular. Each group uses its own paradigm to argue in that paradigm's defense.

The resulting circularity does not, of course, make the arguments wrong or even ineffectual. The man who premises a paradigm when arguing in its defense can nonetheless provide a clear exhibit of what scientific practice will be like for those who adopt the new view of nature. That exhibit can be immensely persuasive, often compellingly so. Yet, whatever its force, the status of the circular argument is only that of persuasion. It cannot be made logically or even probabilistically compelling for those who refuse to step into the circle. The premises and values shared by the two parties to a debate over paradigms are not sufficiently extensive for that. As in political revolutions, so in paradigm choice—there is no standard higher than the assent of the relevant community. To discover how scientific revolutions are effected, we shall therefore have to examine not only the impact of nature and of logic, but also the techniques of persuasive argumentation effective within the quite special groups that constitute the community of scientists.

To discover why this issue of paradigm choice can never be unequivocally settled by logic and experiment alone, we must shortly examine the nature of the differences that separate the proponents of a traditional paradigm from their revolutionary successors. That examination is the principal object of this section and the next. We have, however, already noted numerous examples of such differences, and no one will doubt that history can supply many others. What is more likely to be doubted than their existence—and what must therefore be considered first—is that such examples provide essential information about the nature of science. Granting that paradigm rejection has been a historic fact, does it illuminate more than human credulity and confusion? Are there intrinsic reasons why the assimilation of either a new sort of phenomenon or a new scientific theory must demand the rejection of an older paradigm?

First notice that if there are such reasons, they do not derive from the logical structure of scientific knowledge. In principle, a new phenomenon might emerge without reflecting destructively upon any part of past scientific practice. Though discovering life on the moon would today be destructive of existing paradigms (these tell us things about the moon that seem incompatible with life's existence there), discovering life in some less well-known part of the galaxy would not. By the same token, a new theory does not have to conflict with any of its predecessors. It might deal exclusively with phenomena not previously known, as the quantum theory deals (but, significantly, not exclusively) with subatomic phenomena unknown before the twentieth century. Or again, the new theory might be simply a higher level theory than those known before, one that linked together a whole group of lower level theories without substantially changing any. Today, the theory of energy conservation provides just such links between dynamics, chemistry, electricity, optics, thermal theory, and so on. Still other compatible relationships between old and new theories can be conceived. Any and all of them might be exemplified by the historical process through which science has developed. If they were, scientific development would be genuinely cumulative. New sorts of phenomena would simply disclose order in an aspect of nature where none had been seen before. In the evolution of science new knowledge would replace ignorance rather than replace knowledge of another and incompatible sort.

Of course, science (or some other enterprise, perhaps less effective) might have developed in that fully cumulative manner. Many people have believed that it did so, and most still seem to suppose that cumulation is at least the ideal that historical development would display if only it had not so often been distorted by human idiosyncrasy. There are important reasons for that belief. In Section X we shall discover how closely the view of science-as-cumulation is entangled with a dominant epistemology that takes knowledge to be a construction placed directly upon raw sense data by the mind. And in Section XI we shall examine the strong support provided to the same historiographic schema by the techniques of effective science pedagogy. Nevertheless, despite the immense plausibility of that ideal image, there is increasing reason to wonder whether it can possibly be an image of *science*. After the pre-paradigm period the assimilation of all new theories and of almost all new sorts of phenomena has in fact demanded the destruction of a prior paradigm and a consequent conflict between competing schools of scientific thought. Cumulative acquisition of unanticipated novelties proves to be an almost non-existent exception to the rule of scientific development. The man who takes historic fact seriously must suspect that science does not tend toward the ideal that our image of its cumulativeness has suggested. Perhaps it is another sort of enterprise.

If, however, resistant facts can carry us that far, then a second look at the ground we have already covered may suggest that cumulative acquisition of novelty is not only rare in fact but improbable in principle. Normal research, which *is* cumulative, owes its success to the ability of scientists regularly to select problems that can be solved with conceptual and instrumental techniques close to those already in existence. (That is why an excessive concern with useful problems, regardless of their relation to existing knowledge and technique, can so easily inhibit scientific development.) The man who is striving to solve a problem defined by existing knowledge and technique is not, however, just looking around. He knows what he wants to achieve, and he designs his instruments and directs his thoughts accordingly. Unanticipated novelty, the new discovery, can emerge only to the extent that his anticipations about nature and his instruments prove wrong. Often the importance of the resulting discovery will itself be proportional to the extent and stubbornness of the anomaly that foreshadowed it. Obviously, then, there must be a conflict between the paradigm that discloses anomaly and the one that later renders the anomaly lawlike. The examples of discovery through paradigm destruction examined in Section VI did not confront us with mere historical accident. There is no other effective way in which discoveries might be generated.

The same argument applies even more clearly to the invention of new theories. There are, in principle, only three types of phenomena about which a new theory might be developed. The first consists of phenomena already well explained by existing paradigms, and these seldom provide either motive or point of departure for theory construction. When they do, as with the three famous anticipations discussed at the end of Section VII, the theories that result are seldom accepted, because nature provides no ground for discrimination. A second class of phenomena consists of those whose nature is indicated by existing paradigms but whose details can be understood only through further theory articulation. These are the phenomena to which scientists direct their research much of the time, but that research aims at the articulation of existing paradigms rather than at the mention of new ones. Only when these attempts at articulation fail do scientists encounter the third type of phenomena, the recognized anomalies whose characteristic feature is their stubborn refusal to be assimilated to existing paradigms. This type alone gives rise to new theories. Paradigms provide all phenomena except anomalies with a theory-determined place in the scientist's field of vision.

But if new theories are called forth to resolve anomalies in the relation of an existing theory to nature, then the successful new theory must somewhere permit predictions that are different from those derived from its predecessor. That difference could not occur if the two were logically compatible. In the process of being assimilated, the second must displace the first. Even a theory like energy conservation, which today seems a logical superstructure that relates to nature only through independently established theories, did not develop historically without paradigm destruction. Instead, it emerged from a crisis in which an essential ingredient was the incompatibility between Newtonian dynamics and some recently formulated consequences of the caloric theory of heat. Only after the caloric theory had been rejected could energy conservation become part of science.[1] And only after it had been part of science for some time could it come to seem a theory of a logically higher type, one not in conflict with its predecessors. It is hard to see how new theories could arise without these destructive changes in beliefs about nature. Though logical inclusiveness remains a permissible view of the relation between successive scientific theories, it is a historical implausibility.

A century ago it would, I think, have been possible to let the case for the necessity of revolutions rest at this point. But today, unfortunately, that cannot be done because the view of the subject devel-

---

[1] Silvanus P. Thompson, *Life of William Thomson Baron Kelvin of Largs* (London, 1910), I, 266–81.

oped above cannot be maintained if the most prevalent contemporary interpretation of the nature and function of scientific theory is accepted. That interpretation, closely associated with early logical positivism and not categorically rejected by its successors, would restrict the range and meaning of an accepted theory so that it could not possibly conflict with any later theory that made predictions about some of the same natural phenomena. The best-known and the strongest case for this restricted conception of a scientific theory emerges in discussions of the relation between contemporary Einsteinian dynamics and the older dynamical equations that descend from Newton's *Principia*. From the viewpoint of this essay these two theories are fundamentally incompatible in the sense illustrated by the relation of Copernican to Ptolemaic astronomy: Einstein's theory can be accepted only with the recognition that Newton's was wrong. Today this remains a minority view.[2] We must therefore examine the most prevalent objections to it.

The gist of these objections can be developed as follows. Relativistic dynamics cannot have shown Newtonian dynamics to be wrong, for Newtonian dynamics is still used with great success by most engineers and, in selected applications, by many physicists. Furthermore, the propriety of this use of the older theory can be proved from the very theory that has, in other applications, replaced it. Einstein's theory can be used to show that predictions from Newton's equations will be as good as our measuring instruments in all applications that satisfy a small number of restrictive conditions. For example, if Newtonian theory is to provide a good approximate solution, the relative velocities of the bodies considered must be small compared with the velocity of light. Subject to this condition and a few others, Newtonian theory seems to be derivable from Einsteinian, of which it is therefore a special case.

But, the objection continues, no theory can possibly conflict with one of its special cases. If Einsteinian science seems to make Newtonian dynamics wrong, that is only because some Newtonians were so incautious as to claim that Newtonian theory yielded entirely

---

[2] See, for example, the remarks by P. P. Wiener in *Philosophy of Science*, XXV (1958), 298.

precise results or that it was valid at very high relative velocities. Since they could not have had any evidence for such claims, they betrayed the standards of science when they made them. In so far as Newtonian theory was ever a truly scientific theory supported by valid evidence, it still is. Only extravagant claims for the theory—claims that were never parts of science—can have been shown by Einstein to be wrong. Purged of these merely human extravagances, Newtonian theory has never been challenged and cannot be.

Some variant of this argument is quite sufficient to make any theory ever used by a significant group of competent scientists immune to attack. The much-maligned phlogiston theory, for example, gave order to a large number of physical and chemical phenomena. It explained why bodies burned—they were rich in phlogiston—and why metals had so many more properties in common than did their ores. The metals were all compounded from different elementary earths combined with phlogiston, and the latter, common to all metals, produced common properties. In addition, the phlogiston theory accounted for a number of reactions in which acids were formed by the combustion of substances like carbon and sulphur. Also, it explained the decrease of volume when combustion occurs in a confined volume of air—the phlogiston released by combustion "spoils" the elasticity of the air that absorbed it, just as fire "spoils" the elasticity of a steel spring.[3] If these were the only phenomena that the phlogiston theorists had claimed for their theory, that theory could never have been challenged. A similar argument will suffice for any theory that has ever been successfully applied to any range of phenomena at all.

But to save theories in this way, their range of application must be restricted to those phenomena and to that precision of observation with which the experimental evidence in hand already deals.[4]

---

[3] James B. Conant, *Overthrow of the Phlogiston Theory* (Cambridge, 1950), pp. 13–16; and J. R. Partington, *A Short History of Chemistry* (2d ed.; London, 1951), pp. 85–88. The fullest and most sympathetic account of the phlogiston theory's achievements is by H. Metzger, *Newton, Stahl, Boerhaave et la doctrine chimique* (Paris, 1930), Part II.

[4] Compare the conclusions reached through a very different sort of analysis by R. B. Braithwaite, *Scientific Explanation* (Cambridge, 1953), pp. 50–87, esp. p. 76.

Carried just a step further (and the step can scarcely be avoided once the first is taken), such a limitation prohibits the scientist from claiming to speak "scientifically" about any phenomenon not already observed. Even in its present form the restriction forbids the scientist to rely upon a theory in his own research whenever that research enters an area or seeks a degree of precision for which past practice with the theory offers no precedent. These prohibitions are logically unexceptionable. But the result of accepting them would be the end of the research through which science may develop further.

By now that point too is virtually a tautology. Without commitment to a paradigm there could be no normal science. Furthermore, that commitment must extend to areas and to degrees of precision for which there is no full precedent. If it did not, the paradigm could provide no puzzles that had not already been solved. Besides, it is not only normal science that depends upon commitment to a paradigm. If existing theory binds the scientist only with respect to existing applications, then there can be no surprises, anomalies, or crises. But these are just the signposts that point the way to extraordinary science. If positivistic restrictions on the range of a theory's legitimate applicability are taken literally, the mechanism that tells the scientific community what problems may lead to fundamental change must cease to function. And when that occurs, the community will inevitably return to something much like its pre-paradigm state, a condition in which all members practice science but in which their gross product scarcely resembles science at all. Is it really any wonder that the price of significant scientific advance is a commitment that runs the risk of being wrong?

More important, there is a revealing logical lacuna in the positivist's argument, one that will reintroduce us immediately to the nature of revolutionary change. Can Newtonian dynamics really be *derived* from relativistic dynamics? What would such a derivation look like? Imagine a set of statements, $E_1, E_2, \ldots, E_n$, which together embody the laws of relativity theory. These statements contain variables and parameters representing spatial position, time, rest mass, etc. From them, together with the apparatus of logic and mathematics, is deducible a whole set of further statements including some that can be checked by observation. To prove the adequacy of Newtonian dynamics as a special case, we must add to the E_1's additional statements, like $(v/c)^2 < < 1$, restricting the range of the parameters and variables. This enlarged set of statements is then manipulated to yield a new set, $N_1, N_2, \ldots, N_m$, which is identical in form with Newton's laws of motion, the law of gravity, and so on. Apparently Newtonian dynamics has been derived from Einsteinian, subject to a few limiting conditions.

Yet the derivation is spurious, at least to this point. Though the N_1's are a special case of the laws of relativistic mechanics, they are not Newton's Laws. Or at least they are not unless those laws are reinterpreted in a way that would have been impossible until after Einstein's work. The variables and parameters that in the Einsteinian E_1's represented spatial position, time, mass, etc., still occur in the N_1's; and they there still represent Einsteinian space, time, and mass. But the physical referents of these Einsteinian concepts are by no means identical with those of the Newtonian concepts that bear the same name. (Newtonian mass is conserved; Einsteinian is convertible with energy. Only at low relative velocities may the two be measured in the same way, and even then they must not be conceived to be the same.) Unless we change the definitions of the variables in the N_1's, the statements we have derived are not Newtonian. If we do change them, we cannot properly be said to have *derived* Newton's Laws, at least not in any sense of "derive" now generally recognized. Our argument has, of course, explained why Newton's Laws ever seemed to work. In doing so it has justified, say, an automobile driver in acting as though he lived in a Newtonian universe. An argument of the same type is used to justify teaching earth-centered astronomy to surveyors. But the argument has still not done what it purported to do. It has not, that is, shown Newton's Laws to be a limiting case of Einstein's. For in the passage to the limit it is not only the forms of the laws that have changed. Simultaneously we have had to alter the fundamental structural elements of which the universe to which they apply is composed.

This need to change the meaning of established and familiar concepts is central to the revolutionary impact of Einstein's theory. Though subtler than the changes from geocentrism to heliocentrism, from phlogiston to oxygen, or from corpuscles to waves, the resulting conceptual transformation is no less decisively destructive of a previously established paradigm. We may even come to see it as a prototype for revolutionary reorientations in the sciences. Just because it did not involve the introduction of additional objects or concepts, the transition from Newtonian to Einsteinian mechanics illustrates with particular clarity the scientific revolution as a displacement of the conceptual network through which scientists view the world.

These remarks should suffice to show what might, in another philosophical climate, have been taken for granted. At least for scientists, most of the apparent differences between a discarded scientific theory and its successor are real. Though an out-of-date theory can always be viewed as a special case of its up-to-date successor, it must be transformed for the purpose. And the transformation is one that can be undertaken only with the advantages of hindsight, the explicit guidance of the more recent theory. Furthermore, even if that transformation were a legitimate device to employ in interpreting the older theory, the result of its application would be a theory so restricted that it could only restate what was already known. Because of its economy, that restatement would have utility, but it could not suffice for the guidance of research.

Let us, therefore, now take it for granted that the differences between successive paradigms are both necessary and irreconcilable. Can we then say more explicitly what sorts of differences these are? The most apparent type has already been illustrated repeatedly. Successive paradigms tell us different things about the population of the universe and about that population's behavior. They differ, that is, about such questions as the existence of subatomic particles, the materiality of light, and the conservation of heat or of energy. These are the substantive differences between successive paradigms, and they require no further illustration. But paradigms differ in more than substance, for they are directed not only to nature but also back upon the science that produced them. They are the source of the methods, problem-field, and standards of solution accepted by any mature scientific community at any given time. As a result, the reception of a new paradigm often necessitates a redefinition of the corresponding science. Some old problems may be relegated to another science or declared entirely "unscientific." Others that were previously non-existent or trivial may, with a new paradigm, become the very archetypes of significant scientific achievement. And as the problems change, so, often, does the standard that distinguishes a real scientific solution from a mere metaphysical speculation, word game, or mathematical play. The normal-scientific tradition that emerges from a scientific revolution is not only incompatible but often actually incommensurable with that which has gone before.

The impact of Newton's work upon the normal seventeenth-century tradition of scientific practice provides a striking example of these subtler effects of paradigm shift. Before Newton was born the "new science" of the century had at last succeeded in rejecting Aristotelian and scholastic explanations expressed in terms of the essences of material bodies. To say that a stone fell because its "nature" drove it toward the center of the universe had been made to look a mere tautological word-play, something it had not previously been. Henceforth the entire flux of sensory appearances, including color, taste, and even weight, was to be explained in terms of the size, shape, position, and motion of the elementary corpuscles of base matter. The attribution of other qualities to the elementary atoms was a resort to the occult and therefore out of bounds for science. Molière caught the new spirit precisely when he ridiculed the doctor who explained opium's efficacy as a soporific by attributing to it a dormitive potency. During the last half of the seventeenth century many scientists preferred to say that the round shape of the opium particles enabled them to soothe the nerves about which they moved.

In an earlier period explanations in terms of occult qualities had been an integral part of productive scientific work. Nevertheless, the seventeenth century's new commitment to mechanico-corpuscular explanation proved immensely fruitful for a number of sciences, ridding them of problems that had defied generally accepted solution and suggesting others to replace them. In dynamics, for example, Newton's three laws of motion are less a product of novel experiments than of the attempt to reinterpret well-known observations in terms of the motions and interactions of primary neutral corpuscles. Consider just one concrete illustration. Since neutral corpuscles could act on each other only by contact, the mechanico-corpuscular view of nature directed scientific attention to a brand-new subject of study, the alteration of particulate motions by collisions. Descartes announced the problem and provided its first putative solution. Huygbens, Wren, and Wallis carried it still further, partly by experimenting with colliding pendulum bobs, but mostly by applying previously well-known characteristics of motion to the new problem. And Newton embedded their results in his laws of motion. The equal "action" and "reaction" of the third law are the changes in quantity of motion experienced by the two parties to a collision. The same change of motion supplies the definition of dynamical force implicit in the second law. In this case, as in many others during the seventeenth century, the corpuscular paradigm bred both a new problem and a large part of that problem's solution.[5]

Yet, though much of Newton's work was directed to problems and embodied standards derived from the mechanico-corpuscular world view, the effect of the paradigm that resulted from his work was a further and partially destructive change in the problems and standards legitimate for science. Gravity, interpreted as an innate attraction between every pair of particles of matter, was an occult quality in the same sense as the scholastics' "tendency to fall" had been. Therefore, while the standards of corpuscularism remained in effect, the search for a mechanical explanation of gravity was one of the most challenging problems for those who accepted the *Principia* as paradigm. Newton devoted much attention to it and so did many of his eighteenth-century successors. The only apparent option was to reject Newton's theory for its failure to explain gravity, and that alternative, too, was widely adopted. Yet neither of these views ultimately triumphed. Unable either to practice science without the *Principia* or to make that work conform to the corpuscular standards of the seventeenth century, scientists gradually accepted the view that gravity was indeed innate. By the mid-eighteenth century that interpretation had been almost universally accepted, and the result was a genuine reversion (which is not the same as a retrogression) to a scholastic standard. Innate attractions and repulsions joined size, shape, position, and motion as physically irreducible primary properties of matter.[6]

The resulting change in the standards and problem-field of physical science was once again consequential. By the 1740s, for example, electricians could speak of the attractive "virtue" of the

---

[5] R. Dugas, *La mécanique au XVIIe siècle* (Neuchatel, 1954), pp. 177–85, 284–98, 345–56.

[6] I. B. Cohen, *Franklin and Newton: An Inquiry into Speculative Newtonian Experimental Science and Franklin's Work in Electricity as an Example Thereof* (Philadelphia, 1956), chaps. vi–vii.

electric fluid without thereby inviting the ridicule that had greeted Molière's doctor a century before. As they did so, electrical phenomena increasingly displayed an order different from the one they had shown when viewed as the effects of a mechanical effluvium that could act only by contact. In particular, when electrical action-at-a-distance became a subject for study in its own right, the phenomenon we now call charging by induction could be recognized as one of its effects. Previously, when seen at all, it had been attributed to the direct action of electrical "atmospheres" or to the leakages inevitable in any electrical laboratory. The new view of inductive effects was, in turn, the key to Franklin's analysis of the Leyden jar and thus to the emergence of a new and Newtonian paradigm for electricity. Nor were dynamics and electricity the only scientific fields affected by the legitimization of the search for forces innate to matter. The large body of eighteenth-century literature on chemical affinities and replacement series also derives from this supramechanical aspect of Newtonianism. Chemists who believed in these differential attractions between the various chemical species set up previously unimagined experiments and searched for new sorts of reactions. Without the data and the chemical concepts developed in that process, the later work of Lavoisier and, more particularly, of Dalton would be incomprehensible.[7] Changes in the standards governing permissible problems, concepts, and explanations can transform a science. In the next section I shall even suggest a sense in which they transform the world.

Other examples of these nonsubstantive differences between successive paradigms can be retrieved from the history of any science in almost any period of its development. For the moment let us be content with just two other and far briefer illustrations. Before the chemical revolution, one of the acknowledged tasks of chemistry was to account for the qualities of chemical substances and for the changes these qualities underwent during chemical reactions. With the aid of a small number of elementary "principles"—of which phlogiston was one—the chemist was to explain why some substances are acidic, others metalline, combustible, and so forth. Some

---

[7] For electricity, see *ibid*, chaps. viii-ix. For chemistry, see Metzger, *op. cit.*, Part I.

success in this direction had been achieved. We have already noted that phlogiston explained why the metals were so much alike, and we could have developed a similar argument for the acids. Lavoisier's reform, however, ultimately did away with chemical "principles," and thus ended by depriving chemistry of some actual and much potential explanatory power. To compensate for this loss, a change in standards was required. During much of the nineteenth century failure to explain the qualities of compounds was no indictment of a chemical theory.[8]

Or again, Clerk Maxwell shared with other nineteenth-century proponents of the wave theory of light the conviction that light waves must be propagated through a material ether. Designing a mechanical medium to support such waves was a standard problem for many of his ablest contemporaries. His own theory, however, the electromagnetic theory of light, gave no account at all of a medium able to support light waves, and it clearly made such an account harder to provide than it had seemed before. Initially, Maxwell's theory was widely rejected for those reasons. But, like Newton's theory, Maxwell's proved difficult to dispense with, and as it achieved the status of a paradigm, the community's attitude toward it changed. In the early decades of the twentieth century Maxwell's insistence upon the existence of a mechanical ether looked more and more like lip service, which it emphatically had not been, and the attempts to design such an ethereal medium were abandoned. Scientists no longer thought it unscientific to speak of an electrical "displacement" without specifying what was being displaced. The result, again, was a new set of problems and standards, one which, in the event, had much to do with the emergence of relativity theory.[9]

These characteristic shifts in the scientific community's conception of its legitimate problems and standards would have less significance to this essay's thesis if one could suppose that they always occurred from some methodologically lower to some higher type. In that case their effects, too, would seem cumulative. No

---

[8] E. Meyerson, *Identity and Reality* (New York, 1930), chap. x.

[9] E. T. Whittaker, *A History of the Theories of Aether and Electricity*, II (London, 1953), 28–30.

wonder that some historians have argued that the history of science records a continuing increase in the maturity and refinement of man's conception of the nature of science.[10] Yet the case for cumulative development of science's problems and standards is even harder to make than the case for cumulation of theories. The attempt to explain gravity, though fruitfully abandoned by most eighteenth-century scientists, was not directed to an intrinsically illegitimate problem; the objections to innate forces were neither inherently unscientific nor metaphysical in some pejorative sense. There are no external standards to permit a judgment of that sort. What occurred was neither a decline nor a raising of standards, but simply a change demanded by the adoption of a new paradigm. Furthermore, that change has since been reversed and could be again. In the twentieth century Einstein succeeded in explaining gravitational attractions, and that explanation has returned science to a set of canons and problems that are, in this particular respect, more like those of Newton's predecessors than of his successors. Or again, the development of quantum mechanics has reversed the methodological prohibition that originated in the chemical revolution. Chemists now attempt, and with great success, to explain the color, state of aggregation, and other qualities of the substances used and produced in their laboratories. A similar reversal may even be underway in electromagnetic theory. Space, in contemporary physics, is not the inert and homogenous substratum employed in both Newton's and Maxwell's theories; some of its new properties are not unlike those once attributed to the ether; we may someday come to know what an electric displacement is.

By shifting emphasis from the cognitive to the normative functions of paradigms, the preceding examples enlarge our understanding of the ways in which paradigms give form to the scientific life. Previously, we had principally examined the paradigm's role as a vehicle for scientific theory. In that role it functions by telling the scientist about the entities that nature does and does not contain and about the ways in which those entities behave. That

---

[10] For a brilliant and entirely up-to-date attempt to fit scientific development into this Procrustean bed, see C. C. Gillispie, *The Edge of Objectivity: An Essay in the History of Scientific Ideas* (Princeton, 1960).

information provides a map whose details are elucidated by mature scientific research. And since nature is too complex and varied to be explored at random, that map is as essential as observation and experiment to science's continuing development. Through the theories they embody, paradigms prove to be constitutive of the research activity. They are also, however, constitutive of science in other respects, and that is now the point. In particular, our most recent examples show that paradigms provide scientists not only with a map but also with some of the directions essential for map-making. In learning a paradigm the scientist acquires theory, methods, and standards together, usually in an inextricable mixture. Therefore, when paradigms change, there are usually significant shifts in the criteria determining the legitimacy both of problems and of proposed solutions.

That observation returns us to the point from which this section began, for it provides our first explicit indication of why the choice between competing paradigms regularly raises questions that cannot be resolved by the criteria of normal science. To the extent, as significant as it is incomplete, that two scientific schools disagree about what is a problem and what a solution, they will inevitably talk through each other when debating the relative merits of their respective paradigms. In the partially circular arguments that regularly result, each paradigm will be shown to satisfy more or less the criteria that it dictates for itself and to fall short of a few of those dictated by its opponent. There are other reasons, too, for the incompleteness of logical contact that consistently characterizes paradigm debates. For example, since no paradigm ever solves all the problems it defines and since no two paradigms leave all the same problems unsolved, paradigm debates always involve the question: Which problems is it more significant to have solved? Like the issue of competing standards, that question of values can be answered only in terms of criteria that lie outside of normal science altogether, and it is that recourse to external criteria that most obviously makes paradigm debates revolutionary.

from
THE CRISIS OF
EUROPEAN SCIENCES
by
EDMUND HUSSERL

Idealization and the Science of Reality—
The Mathematization of Nature

Science has its origin in Greek philosophy with the discovery of the idea and of the exact science which determines by means of ideas. It leads to the development of pure mathematics as pure science of ideas, science of possible objects in general as objects determined by ideas. Science is confronted with the problem of that which is, as the real which exists in itself, existing in itself over against the multiplicity of subjective manners of givenness belonging to the particular knowing subject; [it is confronted with] the question concerning the flux of being in becoming and concerning the conditions of the possibility of the identity of being in becoming, of the identical determinablity of an existing real [entity] as the determinability of intuitively given continuity through the mathematization of continua. But this must be independent of accidental subjectivity, and this means, first of all, independent of the accidental character of the particular sensibility [which apprehends it].

Confronted with the task of resolving these questions, the process leads to the *development of the logic of being as the logic of reality,* and first of all of natural reality, and to the development of apophantic logic as the formal logic of predicative determination.

As for the latter, it deals with entities in general as identical substrates of identical determinations; furthermore, it has to do with the multiplicity of forms of judgment, with the forms of substrates as determined, with the forms of determining predicates, and with the possibilities of hypothetical, disjunctive manners of determination, the modal variations, etc., which belong to determination. Something identical is the correlate of [the act of] identifying; to determine is to judge, and something determined is as such the correlate of [the act of] judging.

To this belong also the norms for possible judgments which are capable of being truths, as norms for possible ways of inferential derivation, of the deduction of truths out of truths (the mediate production of truths), or the attainment of hypothetical truths from hypothetical stipulations (stipulated truths, hypotheses); further, there is the consideration of the forms of thought, the forms of possible productions in thought, of the possible forms of the ways of production, or of the thoughts derived from deductive productions, and the critique of thoughts according to the possible forms of true thoughts; also, there is the problem of the identity of the "object," the "meant" [*das Vermeinte*], being carried over into self-evidence. And through self-evidence, the necessities belonging to the possible maintenance of identity become generally known; while that which is identical undergoes only those variations which maintain its identity. Here one is led to an identity of the forms of thought which run through all determinations and which do not break the identity of the determined objects.

Against the first seeds of the development of science there arose the skeptical critique of science and of all practical norms which lay claim to objective validity. The Socratic return to self-evidence represents a reaction; and specifically this is making clear to oneself, by means of example, the fields of pure possibilities, the free variation which upholds the identity of meaning, identity of the object as substrate of determination, and makes it possible to discern this identity. Over against these alterations are others which break the identity. The variations are accomplished in the transition to the pure "in general," to the general forms of possibilities and the essential possibilities and essential impossibilities belonging to them. There arise norm-concepts of the good, the beautiful, the truly good statesman, the genuine judge, true honor, true courage and justice, and the fundamental concepts of criticism itself: just, unjust, true, false, etc.

Thus skepticism forces the critique of the skeptical critique, and since this critique concerns the possibility of truth and of knowable being in general, it forces a radical consideration of the conditions of possible truth and possible being; and it forces the recognition that not vague thinking and talking but only radical thinking, aimed at the ultimate showing of possible being, carried out in self-evidence, [indeed] only self-evidence itself, can help in assuring ourselves of truth and being. I must not talk vaguely on, must not follow vague traditional concepts or the sediments of passively accumulated experiential residues, analogies, etc.; rather, I must create my concepts anew in autonomous thinking through pure intuition; then I shall attain truths which are destined to be norms. Every truth derived from pure self-evidence is a genuine truth and is a norm. On the other hand, it does not need to contain any normative concepts within itself, i.e., none of the variational forms of "genuine," "correct"; these themselves, when grasped conceptually, result in concepts and predications about genuineness, truth; such predications must themselves be derived from self-evidence—they must [be shown to] be true, and they can be false.

Science is not naïve knowledge in the theoretical interest; rather, to its essence there belongs from now on a certain critique—a critique based on principle, a critique which justifies every step of the knowing activity through "principles," which at every step involves the consciousness that any step of such a form is necessarily a correct one, that in this way the path of cognitive grounding, of the progress of that which grounds and that which is grounded upon it, is a correct path aimed at the goal, so that [the resulting] knowledge is a genuine knowledge and that the being known is not merely supposed [*vermeintes*] but known in the pregnant sense, true being itself, exhibiting its legitimacy in the knowledge itself. Now this is true first of all of present [*aktuelle*] knowledge in its progress through thoroughgoing self-evidence. But science makes use of the cognitive results of earlier knowledge. The norm-consciousness involved in such knowledge implies [a present] consciousness referring back to [such] earlier groundings [and having] the real capacity to reestablish the [earlier] grounding, to trace the [present] conviction of its legitimacy back to its origin, and to justify it anew.

What has antiquity offered us here? What path has it thus opened up? [It has offered] in part seminal beginnings and impulses, in part fragments of science actually set upon its way.

The path that it indicates is that of the development of the principle of self-evidence which is general and based on principle:

Singular experience, experience of individual existence, results in no assertion that can be justified objectively. But then how can singular judgments of fact be valid at all? How can the *experienced* world even be in truth? Being reveals itself to be an ideal pole for "infinities" of presumptive self-evidences with self-evidently given sense-adumbrations ("sides," appearances) through which the same being is adumbrated in self-evident manner but is [merely] presumptive in every finite series [of adumbrations]—though this is a legitimate presumption.[1] Real truth is the correlate of real being, and just as real being is an infinitely distant idea, the idea of a pole for systematic infinities of appearances, of "experiences" in constantly legitimate presumption, so real truth is an infinitely distant idea, [that of] what is identical in the agreement of experiential judgments, in each of which truth "appears," achieves legitimate subjective givenness. The infinitely distant idea is determinable a priori in the pure form of generality which contains all possibilities, and in accord with this form one can construct, out of the finitely closed total experience (that is, out of its relatively "closed-off appearance," out of the realm of determined sensible things, out of the sensible experiential predicates) an anticipation of an appropriate idea required by this experience and implied in it.

Included in the form of the idea of something real are one-sided, partial ideas, just as, in the full truth which determines the entity (the totality of the predicates belonging to it which determine it as itself), there is a multiplicity of individual predicable determinations, of individual truths which leave the being still undetermined in other directions. Insofar as every experience can a priori contain elements of discrepancy which will be separated out in further experience and its synthesis, the idea-determination which is to be gained from it is capable of being not only one-sided but also in part false, though required, for the sake of truth, by this experience up to now. To the idea of the real [entity] itself, and to the idea as a pure form, there belongs correlatively an infinite system of experiences which set up a system of pure harmony (through the continued exclusion of what is experienced as discrepant and the adoption of what agrees) and which characterize themselves *as* [possible] experiences. And then there belongs a priori to every experience, or every appropriately delimited experience, an idea which is proper to it but

---

[1] But here it is always merely nature which is in view, and an idea of reality is thereby presupposed for the world, whose correlate is the idea of a truth-in-itself, the idea of a mathematically constructible truth, even though it is [given only] in any number of approximations.

appropriately delimited experience, an idea which is proper to it but which is never the last idea but rather a starting point, in a certain way a representation of the infinitely distant and unattainable idea, of which only the form, as an absolute norm for the construction of all starting points, is given.

To make all these things clear and to outline a priori the form of a possible determination of what is in itself true of nature, a determination which is relatively true and relatively necessary for every stage of experience—this is the theory of natural science; as method: the theory of natural-scientific method. Yet a twofold distinction must be made:

1. Ontology of nature "in itself": what is necessary for a nature in general, the necessary form, the ideal essence, of a nature and the necessary forms of determinations of every individual which *idealiter* and "in itself" can belong to nature. Such considerations of the *pure idea* are accomplished by the sciences of the pure mathematics of nature.

2. A priori methodology of a possible knowledge of nature in itself, through truths in themselves: if, instead of pure nature as an idea (as a mathematical, supersensible idea), we think of a *nature as experienced* by experiencing beings, or, if we take a mathematical nature as an ideal in-itself belonging to nature-experiences (ontically: sensibly intuited natures), then we have *another pure idea*. We attain then a science of the possibility of knowledge of a nature in itself through nature-experience, and this is the a priori science of the possibility of a mathematical natural science, or the science of the method of natural-scientific determination of nature through the data of experience.

In a more limited sense: we allow only "normal experience" to count as experience, normal sensibility in relation to normal "understanding." How can mathematical, true nature be determined through normal appearances? This occurs through the methods of rendering the continua exact, through the transformation of sensible causalities into mathematical causalities, etc. Only then must one take the psychophysically abnormal into account.

But can one really distinguish in this way between an a priori *ontology of nature* and an a priori *methodology* of a possible determination of a nature in itself through the experiences of it? How do I, the knower, attain the a priori ontological knowledge of nature? I live then in possible experiences, in possible perceptions and possible perceptual judgments. What belongs to the identical itself, throughout all the alteration of the sensible manners of appearance, when it is precisely the latter which, whatever else they may do, are supposed to be able to go together into identity-agreement and to make identical determinations possible?

Not every *change* in the sensible stock of characteristics disturbs identity, and not every one maintains it under the title of a "change in the object." Anomalous changes of appearance are not apperceived or need not be apperceived as "changes [in the object]." If they are so apperceived, they are later suspended under the title of "illusions." If I am living in experience (in its apperceptions, through which I have experience as [being that of] sensibly intuited reality), and if I hold the lines of agreement secure, all anomalies are separated out, and every intuitively given change is a real change for *me* in the framework of the synthesis of my own experiences. If I now enter into relation with *another*, I may find that he (in his normality—but he is color-blind) differs from me in his judgments about samenesses, differences, etc., while we are experiencing the same thing. (He can also have a finer sense than I—he has good eyes, I bad, etc.—and the relation changes with each different human being.) Here, in terms of possibility, very many and, ideally, infinitely many differences—and also contradictions—are open. What can help us here?

If we look to developed natural science, the answer is: Every sensible difference experienced by the single subject is an index of a true difference, and what is true is determined by measurement in the sphere of the κοινά. Hand in hand with the qualitative differences, in a certain rough way, go quantitative differences. In the quantitative sphere, in the realm of extension, everything true expresses itself.

On the other hand, not everything that can be established quantitatively, by way of magnitudes and dependencies of magnitudes, is "noticeable" to me or to anyone in the same way. Through measuring methods, I can convince myself that certain quantitative relations and laws are valid, relations and laws that I know about as persistently obtaining and as valid only through the method, whereas before using the method I am dependent upon sensibility and "perceptual judgments."

Could natural science arrive at such a view any other way than through general reflections about a method—reflections about how, in the face of the relativity of the appearances, something true which appears in them is to be determined, and first of all through reflections about how, in the alteration of the appearances, true being is able to announce itself, manifest itself? But clearly such reflections, carried out purely eidetically, lead to an ontology of nature.

Thus we can also say: *How could I arrive at an a priori ontology* other than by rendering self-evident [the following]:

I. If I have nature as harmoniously experienced, and if I remain within the framework of this harmony and specifically within the framework of certain harmoniously experienced things or processes; and if in any number of other cases I have experienced the same things, etc., or if another has experienced them (as I become convinced through understanding him): the possibility of the knowledge of the same [thing or process] through the experiences on the two sides necessarily presupposes the *res extensa*, the spatiotemporal *skeleton* of the qualities perceived on the two sides, the identity of the shape-distribution through communal time, identity of the temporal sequences and thus also of the causal dependency of the corresponding configurations. By contrast, the alteration of the qualities perceived and of the judgments about these qualities is "accidental." In this sense, that is, even if contradictions arise from them, they do not damage the identity. (Even in solitary experience, the identity of what is experienced in different modalities of sense is necessarily the identity of the "spatiotemporal" skeleton. It is the latter that is necessarily identical, a necessarily identical content of determination throughout all differences of sensible "manner of appearance.") The first separating-out of what essentially—i.e., of necessity—belongs to the identical [object] leads to geometry, phoronomy, and could also have led to a priori mechanics, to disciplines of the possible forms of functional dependences among changes or to a discipline of the forms of possible quantitative causality and its possible causal laws. The real is in itself determined if it is lawfully fixed not only in respect to its geometrical form but also in respect to its possible changes in form. Something real has real properties, its empirically causal properties. In order to be identical in itself, it must have empirically knowable quantitative-causal properties.

Thus, the new natural science is distinguished by the fact that it first of all elevated to the central point of concern what is in a determined sense necessary by contrast to the alteration of (legitimate) sensible appearance, and [it] recognized that quantitative causal laws belong to this necessary element.

A *second* element [in the development of an a priori ontology] was made up of such observations as: I hear a tone and see a vibrating motion [of a string], and the tone is qualitatively the same, independently of color, of the sensibly qualitative, but it is dependent on the strength of tension, the thickness [of the string]—and the latter are all measurable factors. The quantitative is not merely [what is found] in the appearing extensional processes [as such]; the quantitative is also something indicated by what is merely qualitative. And it is possible that the quantitative [in the latter sense] be subsequently exhibited sensibly through sensible manners of appearance (somehow "clothed" qualitatively).

Conversely: every qualitative change, every qualitative being-such [*Sosein*], should, if the quality belongs to a normal appearance, be a property of the real itself. But quality (secondary quality) cannot belong to the object in itself; possibly it is a subjectively altering quality, [differing among] subjects, each of whom, for himself, experiences harmoniously the reality in question. If every experienced quality shall have its right to objectivity, this is possible only if it is an index for something mathematical and indicates the mathematical for one person as well as another only in differing degrees of perfection: methodically, everyone must be able to attain the quantitative on the basis of the indications, perhaps with the help of another; whereas he can determine the qualitative himself. Thus every "in-itself" is a mathematical in-itself, and all causal laws must be mathematical laws. Real properties are causal properties which are determined on the basis of causal laws.

Yet we would have to make a twofold distinction here:

1. The recognition, discussed in detail above, that in harmonious experience (as sensible manner of appearance) one must distinguish between the accidental and the necessary, i.e., between primary characteristics, which necessarily run through all sensible experience, and the specifically sensible, the secondary characteristics; the recognition, that is, that the "common" sense-characteristics are not accidentally but necessarily common.

2. The perceived, the experienced as such, is thoroughly "vague"; it always stands, taken in harmonious experience, under the essential law of a certain gradation of perfection which always exists as an ideal possibility. Accordingly I can have the same characteristic given more or less "clearly"; and, no matter how clear it is, yet another gradation is still thinkable. It is always thinkable that what I clearly find to be undifferentiated will, given greater clarity, exhibit differentiations, both for me and intersubjectively. Belonging correlatively to the differentiations of perfection are free "can"-possibilities of approximation to the absolutely perfect, the true self [of the object]—though, to be sure, the latter is forever receding. Our talk of the "manners of appearance" of the same thing also applies thus in respect to the graduality of clarity. But behind this lies the idea of an identical self, the in-itself. The true characteristics are the limit-points of possible gradation. But since only mathematical characteristics are "true" ones, the true mathematical characteristics are mathematical limits.

Explicated more distinctly: in the continuing synthesis of experience the primary as well as the secondary characteristics have their differentiations of perfection. Corresponding to this in the case of the primary characteristics is the graduality of the perfection of measurement and of approximation through measurement, and what proceeds from this, or is carried out in connection with it, namely, quantification through geometrical and similar concepts. This leads to the limit-idealization of the exact mathematics of nature with its determinations of thought. Whereas the primary characteristics are intersubjective as long as harmonious identification can take place at all, and have only [the above-mentioned] relativity of perfection and approximation (and also the relativity of interreal causality), the secondary characteristics are relative in another way, namely, relative to the normality and abnormality of experience and thus "accidentally" to the subjects, and can change with the subjects.[2] In addition, the perfection-limit of the secondary qualities is not measurable; it is

---

[2] We have two kinds of normality: (1) The presupposition of communication, [i.e., that there is a] communal nature, and the necessary here is the quantitative; (2) as opposed to this, the accidental—that is, agreement on secondary qualities is "accidental."

only "intuitable." But it is intersubjectively determined and determinable through relation to the mathematical limits of the primary characteristics.

3. To determine is to predicate; to determine originally and self-evidently is to form perceptual judgments, and to determine mediately is to form empirically general judgments (inductive, experiential judgments) and empirically causal judgments, etc. Determininative thinking, judging, inferring, generalizing, particularizing, which are accomplished in the actual sphere of experience, take the appearing things, characteristics, regularities as the true ones; but this truth is a relative and "subjectively conditioned" truth. A *new sort of thinking*, or a peculiar *method*, is required in order to relate what results here (which suffices for lower-level practical ends) to its "objectivity,"[3] to extract from it, by technique, truth in itself and true reality in itself. The consideration of the conditions in principle of the possibility of something identical that gives itself (harmoniously) in flowing and subjectively changing manners of appearance[4] leads to the mathematization of the appearances as a necessity which is immanent in them, or to the necessity of a constructive method, in order to construct out of the appearances the identical and its identical determinations.[5]

But can appearances of different senses contain something identical? And in what sense can they? Manifolds of appearances which harmoniously belong together and which constitute something identical must correspond to the conditions of the possibility of the identical (true) object [*Gegenständlichkeit*], and all the laws of mathematics as applied to the real [*reale Mathematik*] must be particularizations of the laws of formal ontology, of formal mathematics (theory of manifolds). They are particularizations because formal mathematics teaches us how to construct and constructively determine the infinitely many forms, indeed all possible forms of objects and infinities of objects; and every given system of appearances, every unity of experiences, outlines an objective totality or nature: in respect to its form.

---

[3] This objectivity is the idea of a "nonrelative" truth in itself.

[4] But also which in principle gives itself only in this way.

[5] This identical is necessarily a substruction.

In ancient philosophy the focus of interest is first of all upon the compelling necessity of reason, whose denial is absurdity. This necessity first entered the scene purely in the mathematical sphere as geometrical and arithmetical necessity. In this sphere of magnitudes, and initially of spatial magnitudes—first of all in classes of privileged cases (straight lines, limited plane figures, and the corresponding cases of spatial magnitudes), first of all in the empirical intuition that magnitudes divide into equal parts and are composed again of equal parts—or of aggregates [*Mengen*] of like elements which decompose into partial aggregates and can be expanded into new aggregates through the addition of elements or of aggregates of such elements—in this sphere, there arose the "exact" comparisons of magnitudes which led back to the comparison of numbers. Upon the vague "greater," "smaller," "more," "less," and the vague "equal" one could determinately superimpose the exact "so much" greater or less, or "how many times" greater or less, and the exact "equal." Every such exact consideration presupposed the possibility of stipulating an equality which excluded the greater and the smaller and of stipulating units of magnitude which were strictly substitutable for one another, were identical as magnitudes, i.e., which stood under an identical concept or essence of magnitude. Belonging to [the essence of] the spatial magnitudes, as objects of empirical intuition, is the fact that one can come nearer to them, can look at them with more "exactness." In practical life the "exact" is determined by the [particular] end in view; the "equal" is that which counts equally for this end, for which there can also be irrelevant differences which do not count. Here, with the exclusion of all practical limitation, the idea of the absolutely equal, the mathematically exactly equal, could be developed.

Here, then, first began the thought process of the idealizing development of concepts, that logicization which makes possible "rigorous" truths, logical truths, and makes it possible, in this logical sphere, to think with the rigorous necessity and universal validity which was able to mark every negation, and insightfully so, with the sign of absurdity. The naturally developing significations of words are vague and flowing, such that it is not determinately fixed what comes under the "concept," the general sense. Logical signification is exact. The logically general, the concept, is absolutely identical with itself, and subsumption is absolutely unambiguous. But logical concepts are not concepts taken from what is simply intuitive; they arise through a rational activity proper to them, the development of ideas, *exact* development of concepts, e.g., through that sort of idealization which produces, out of the empirically straight and curved, the geometrical straight line and circle.

The practical needs of field-measurement force one at first only vaguely, i.e., in the realm of the sensibly typical, to distinguish what typically counts as equal (for the particular practical needs) from what typically counts as not equal. What counted as being equal for certain sorts of practical ends was posited as being equal, and differences of characteristics within the equality were "indifferent" differences, i.e., they were regarded as not disturbing the equal validity and could be ignored. Thus it was possible to establish measurement and calculation, to express and even prove "geometrical" propositions—with certain reservations, to be sure. For when a thousand "equal" lengths were laid in a row, each of which differed from the following only by a finger's breadth (an indifferent difference), the measurement could give the result that 1000 yards = 1001. That is, different measurements with the same standard could give different results, i.e., not indifferently different. It was only the conception of pure mathematical "ideas" as ideal norms and the development of approximative methods of application that led to a pure material mathematics and a mathematical technique. It was of the nature of spatial experience that one had to recognize, in comparing things in experience, possible differences of perfection in equality: for example, what was seen from a certain distance to be fully "equal" could be seen, when approached more closely, to be different after all; what remained equal could be looked at even more closely, etc.

Thus it was possible to conceive of processes converging *idealiter* through which an absolute equal could be constructed ideally as the limit of the constant approach to equality, provided that one member [of the system] was thought of as absolutely fixed, as absolutely identical with itself in magnitude. In this exact thinking with ideas one operated with ideal concepts of the unchanging, of rest, of lack of qualitative change, with ideal concepts of equality and of the general (magnitude, shape) that gives absolute equalities in any number of ideally unchanged and thus qualitatively identical instances; every change was constructed out of phases which were looked upon as momentary, exact, and unchanging, having exact magnitudes, etc.

Platonic idealism, through the fully conscious discovery of the "idea" and of approximation, opened up the path of logical thinking, "logical" science, rational science. Ideas were taken as archetypes, in which everything singular participates more or less "ideally," which everything approaches, which everything realizes more or less fully; the ideal truths belonging to the ideas were taken as the absolute norms for all empirical truths. If we designate as rationalism the conviction that all reasonable knowing must be rational—whether purely rationally, in the thinking that investigates the essential relations between the purely rational concepts (or rather, the thinking that investigates, in terms of laws, everything that is possible, insofar as it stands under purely rational ideas, or is thought in an exactly determinate way) or else in such a way that it measures the empirical against the pure ideals through methods of approximation and other norms for judging the empirical according to corresponding pure ideas—then the whole modern conviction is rationalistic.

A true object in the sense of logic is an object which is absolutely identical "with itself," that is, which is, absolutely identically, what it is; or, to express it in another way: an object *is* through its determinations, its quiddities [*Washeiten*], its predicates, and it is identical if these quiddities are identical as belonging to it or when their belonging absolutely excludes their not belonging. But only ideals have a rigorous identity; the consequence would be that an individual is truly something identical—i.e., an entity—if it is the ideally identical substrate for general absolute ideas. But how can something individual participate in the general, not only approximately but exactly? How can the subsumption-relation be exact?

Purely mathematical thinking is related to possible objects which are thought determinately through ideal-"exact" mathematical (limit-) concepts, e.g., spatial shapes of natural objects which, as experienced, stand in a vague way under shape-concepts and [thus] have their shape-determinations; but it is of the nature of these experiential data that one can and by rights must posit, beneath the identical object which exhibits itself in harmonious experience as existing, an ideally identical object which is ideal in all its determinations; all [its] determinations are exact—that is, whatever [instances] fall under their generality are equal—and this equality excludes inequality; or, what is the same thing, an exact determination, in belonging to an object, excludes the possibility that this determination not belong to the same object. And for every particular [kind of] determination, as delimited by the "general nature" of the object—within the [particular] domain, that is; e.g., spatial shape in the case of natural objects—one [such determination] belongs [to the object], and every other [such determination] does not belong. (Principle of the excluded middle.)

An object has spatial shape generally. Empirically experienced spatial shapes have their different empirical types. But it can happen that an object has a (lowest) type—that is, I experience that it has this particular shape—and that it does not have it—that is, I see upon further experience that it does not have it (without [its] having changed). (In the empirical sphere the principle of the excluded middle does not hold.) I can take no empirical determination as actually belonging to the object; I can only say that it is experienced under this determination. Even in thought I cannot hold fast to the determination in an absolutely identical way; I can never, in approaching the experienced object, say that the determination I experience now is absolutely the same as the one I have experienced.

But I can posit, beneath every spatial shape I experience, the idea of a pure spatial shape in which the seen shape "participates"; and spatial shape in general becomes an empirical genus which has behind it a pure genus of purely exact spatial shapes. Every empirical object is empirically shaped (is necessarily experienceable and is equipped in experience with an intuited shape), but it also has a true shape, the exact shape. Exact ideas of shapes are absolutely distinguished; if an object has a particularization of one [such shape], then every other, different one is excluded. Of two exact shapes (lowest differences of spatial shapes), to any object there belongs one and not the other. (Principle of the excluded middle.)

THE CONCEPT
OF BIOLOGICAL PROGRESS

by

FRANCISCO J. AYALA

Change, Evolution, Direction and Progress

The notion that living organisms can be classified in a hierarchy going from lower to higher forms goes back to Aristotle, and indeed to even earlier times. The creation of the world as described in the book of Genesis contains the explicit notion that some organisms are higher than others, and implies that living things can be arranged in a continuous sequence from the lowest to the highest, which is man. The Bible's narrative of the creation reflects the common-sense impression that earthworms are in some sense lower than fish or birds, and the latter lower than man. The idea of a "ladder of life" rising from amoeba to man is present, explicitly or implicitly, in all preevolutionary biology.

The theory of evolution adds the dimension of time, or history, to the classification of living things into lower and higher. The transition from amoeba to man can now be seen as a natural, progressive development from simple to gradually more complex organisms. The expansion and diversification of life can also be judged as progress; some form of advance seems obvious in the transition from one or only a few kinds of living things to the more than two million different species living today.

It is not immediately clear, however, what is meant by statements like "The evolution of organisms is progressive," or "Progress has occurred in the evolutionary sequence leading from amoeba to man." Such expressions may simply mean that evolutionary sequences have a time direction, or even more simply that they are accompanied by change. The term "progress" needs to be distinguished from other terms commonly used in biological discourse with which it shares areas of common meaning. These terms are "change," "evolution," and "direction."

Change means alteration, whether in the position, the state or the nature of a thing. Progress implies change, but not *vice versa*; not all changes are progressive. The positions of the molecules of oxygen and nitrogen in the air of a room are changing continuously; such change would not generally be labelled as progressive. The mutation of a gene from a functional allelic state to a non-functional one is a change, but definitely not a progressive one.

The terms "evolution" and "progress" can also be distinguished, although both imply that sustained change has occurred. Evolutionary change is not necessarily progressive. The evolution of a species may lead to its extinction, a change which is not progressive, at least not for that species. Progress also can occur without evolutionary change. Assume that in a given region of the world the seeds of a certain species are dormant because of a prolonged drought; after a burst of rain the seeds germinate and give origin to a population of plants. This change might be labeled progressive for the species, even though no evolutionary change need have taken place.

The concept of direction implies that a series of changes have occurred that can be arranged in a linear sequence such that elements in the later part of the sequence are further apart from early elements of the sequence than intermediate elements are, according to some property or feature under consideration. Directional change may be uniform or not, depending on whether every later member of the sequence is further displaced than every earlier member, or whether directional change occurs only on the average. This distinction will also be made later when defining progress. If the elements in the sequence are plotted on a two-dimensional graph with time on one axis and some property or feature of the elements of the sequence on the other axis, and all the elements are connected by a line, directional change is uniform when the slope of that line is at every point positive or at every point negative. The line connecting all the elements in the sequence may be straight or curved but should go up or down monotonously. Non-uniform ("net"; see below) directional change occurs when the line connecting all the elements in the sequence does not change monotonously but its regression on time is either significantly positive or significantly negative. Some elements in the sequence may represent a change of direction with respect to the immediately previous elements, but later elements in the sequence are further displaced than earlier ones on the average.

In evolutionary writings, "directionality" is sometimes equated with "irreversibility." The process of evolution is said to have a direction because it is irreversible. Biological evolution is irreversible (except perhaps in some trivial sense, like when a previously mutated gene mutates back to its former allelic state). Direction, however, implies more than irreversibility. Consider a new pack of cards with each suit arranged from ace to ten, then knave, queen, king, and with the suits arranged in the sequence spades, clubs, hearts, diamonds. If we shuffle the cards thoroughly, the order of the cards will change, and the changes will be irreversible by shuffling. We may shuffle again and again until the cards are totally worn out, without ever restoring the original sequence. The change of order in the pack of cards is irreversible but not directional. Irreversible and directional changes both occur in the inorganic as well as in the organic world. The second law of thermodynamics, which applies to all processes in nature, describes sequential changes which are irreversible but are also directional, and indeed uniformly directional. Within a closed system, entropy always increases; that is, a closed system passes continuously from less to more probable states.

The concept of direction is used in paleontology to describe what are called "evolutionary trends." A trend occurs in a phylogenetic sequence when there is a feature which gradually increases or gradually decreases in the members of the sequence. Trends are common occurrences in all fossil sequences which are sufficiently long to be called "sustained."

The concept of direction and the concept of progress can be distinguished. Consider the trend in the whole evolutionary sequence from fish to man towards a gradual reduction with paleontological time of the number of dermal bones in the skull roof; or the trend towards increased molarisation of the last premolars which occurred in the phylogeny of the *Equidae* from early Eocene (*Hyracotherium*) to early Oligocene (*Haplohippus*). These trends represent indeed directional change, but it is not obvious that they should be labeled progressive. To label them progressive we would need to agree that the directional change had been in some sense for the better. That is, to consider a sequence as progressive we need to add to the knowledge of the directionality of change an evaluation, namely that the condition in the latter members of the sequence represents, according to some standard, a betterment or improvement. The directionality of the sequence can be recognised and accepted without the added evaluation. Progress implies directional change, but not *vice versa*.

The Concept of Progress

Evolution, direction and progress all imply a historical sequence of events which exhibits a systematic alteration of a property or state of the elements in the sequence. Progress occurs when there is directional change towards a *better* state or condition. The concept of progress, then, contains two elements: one descriptive—that directional change has occurred; the other axiological—that the change represents an improvement or betterment. The notion of progress requires that a value judgment be made of what is better and what is worse, or what is higher and what is lower, according to some axiological standard. Contrary to the belief of some authors (Ginsberg, 1944; Lewontin, 1968), the axiological standard of reference need not be a moral one. Moral progress is possible, but not all forms of progress are moral. The evaluation required for progress is one of better *vs.* worse, of higher *vs.* lower, but not necessarily one of right *vs.* wrong. Better may simply mean more efficient, or more abundant, or more complex, without connotating any reference to moral goals or standards.

Progress can be defined as systematic change in at least one feature belonging to all the members of a historical sequence, which is such that later members of the sequence exhibit an improvement of that feature. More simply, it could be defined as directional change towards the better. Similarly, regression is directional change for the worse. The two elements of the definition, namely directional change and improvement according to some standard, are jointly necessary and sufficient for the occurrence of progress.

To clarify further the concept of progress I want to distinguish several kinds of progress. The distinctions which follow relate to the descriptive element of the definition, that is, to the requirement of directional change. Therefore, the distinctions also apply to the concept of direction. Attending to the *continuity* of the direction of change in the members of the sequence, progress can be of two kinds—uniform and net.

Uniform progress takes place whenever according to a certain standard every later member of the sequence is better than every earlier member of the sequence. Let m_i be the members of the sequence, temporally ordered from 1 to n, and let p_i measure the state of the feature evaluated according to a given axiological standard of reference. There is uniform progress if, given any m_i with a certain p_i, every m_j is such that $p_j > p_i$ if $j > i$, and $p_j < p_i$, if $j < i$.

Net progress does not require that every member of the sequence be better than all previous members of the sequence and worse than all its successors; it requires rather that later members of the sequence be better, *on the average*, than earlier members of the sequence. Net progress permits temporary fluctuations of value. Formally, if the members of the sequence, m_i, are linearly arranged over time, net progress has occurred whenever the regression of p on time is significantly positive. Some authors have argued that progress has not occurred in evolution because, no matter what standard is chosen, fluctuations of value are always found to have occurred. This argument is valid against the occurrence of uniform but not of net evolutionary progress.

The distinction between uniform and net progress is similar to, but not identical with, the distinction proposed by Broad (1925) and also Goudge (1961) between uniform and perpetual progress. Perpetual progress, as defined by Broad, requires that the maxima of value increase and the minima do not decrease with time. In the formulation given above, Broad's perpetual progress requires that for every m_i there is at least one m_j $(j > i)$ such that $p_j > p_i$, and that there is at least one m_k $(k < i)$ such that $p_k < p_i$. This definition encounters some difficulties in its applications, and has the undesirable feature of requiring that the first element in the sequence be the worst one and the last element the best one. None of these two requirements are made in my definition of net progress. Also the term "perpetual" has connotations which are undesirable in the discussion of progress. The distinction between uniform and net progress is implicit, although never formally established, in Simpson (1949), who applies terms like "universal," "invariable," "constant" and "continuous" to the kind of progress that I have called uniform, but also uses them with other meanings.

Note that neither uniform nor net progress require that progress be unlimited, or that any specified goal will be surpassed if the sequence continues for a sufficiently long period of time. Progress requires a gradual improvement in the members of the sequence, but the rate of improvement may decrease with time. According to the definition given here, it is possible that the sequence tends asymptotically towards a finite goal, which is continuously approached but never reached.

Another distinction is possible in the concept of progress. Attending to the *scope* of the sequence which is being considered, progress can be either general or particular. *General* progress is that which occurs in all historical sequences of a given domain of reality and from the beginning of the sequences until their end, or if they are not finished, until the present time. *Particular* progress is that which occurs in one or several, but not in all, historical sequences of a given domain of reality, or progress which takes place during part but not all the duration of the sequence or sequences.

In biological evolution, general progress is any kind of progress, if such exist, that can be predicated of the evolution of all life from its origin to the present. If a type of progress is predicated of only one or several, but not all, lines of evolutionary descent, it is a particular kind of progress. Progress which embraces a limited span only of the time going from the origin of life to the present is also a particular kind of progress.

It is obvious that other relevant distinctions of the concept of progress are possible. The two distinctions given above have been made having in mind a discussion of evolutionary progress, and are considered sufficient for the present purposes.

Can "Progress" Be Defined as a Purely Biological Term?

Can we find in biology any criterion by which progress could be defined and measured by an absolute standard without involving judgments of value? Some authors believe that we can. Thoday (1953, 1958) has pointed out the obvious fact that survival is essential to life. Therefore, he argues, progress is increase in fitness for survival, "provided only that fitness and survival be defined as generally as possible." According to Thoday, fitness must be defined in reference to groups of organisms which can have common descendants; these groups he calls *units of evolution*. A unit of evolution is what population geneticists call a Mendelian population; the most inclusive Mendelian population is the species. The fitness of a unit of evolution is defined by Thoday as "the probability that such a unit of evolution will survive for a long period of time, such as 10^8 years, that is to say will have descendants after the lapse of that time." According to Thoday, evolutionary changes, no matter what other results may have been produced, are progressive only if they have increased the probability of leaving descendants after long periods of time. He correctly points out that this definition has the advantage of not assuming that progress has in fact occurred, an assumption which vitiates other attempts to define progress as a purely biological concept.

Thoday's definition of progress has been criticised because it apparently leads to the paradox that progress is impossible, in fact that regress is necessary since any group of organisms will be more progressive than any of their descendants. Assume that we are concerned with ascertaining whether progress has occurred in the evolutionary transition from a Cretaceous mammal to its descendants of 100 million (10^8) years later. It is clear that if the present-day mammal population M_1 has a probability P of having descendants 10^8 years from now, the ancestral mammal populations M_0 will have a probability no smaller than P of leaving descendants after 2×10^8 years from the time of their existence (Ayala, 1969). In fact the probability that the ancestral population M_0 will leave descendants 2×10^8 years after their existence will be greater than P if it has any other living descendants besides M_1. As Thoday (1970) himself has pointed out, such criticism is mistaken, since it confuses the probability of survival with the fact of survival. The *a priori* probability that a given population will have descendants after a given lapse of time may be smaller than the *a priori* probability that any of its descendants will leave progeny after the same length of time.

There is, however, a legitimate criticism of Thoday's definition of progress, namely that it is not operationally valid. Suppose that we want to find out whether M_1 is more progressive than M_0. We should have to estimate, first, the probability that M_1 will leave descendants after a given long period of time; then we should have to estimate the same probability for M_0. Thoday has enumerated a variety of components which contribute to the fitness of a population as defined by him. These components are adaptation, genetic stability, genetic flexibility, phenotypic flexibility and the stability of the environment. But it is by no means clear how these components could be quantified, nor by what sort of function they could be integrated into a single parameter. In any case, there seems to be no conceivable way in which the appropriate observations and measurements could be made for the ancestral population. Thoday's definition of progress is extremely ingenious, but lacks operational validity. If we accept his definition there seems to be no way in which we could ascertain whether progress has occurred in any one line of descent or in the evolution of life as a whole.

Another attempt to consider evolutionary progress as a purely biological notion has been made by defining biological progress as an increase in the amount of genetic information stored in the organism. This information is encoded, at least for the most part, in the DNA of the nucleus. The DNA contains the information which in interaction with the environment directs the development and behaviour of the organism. By making certain assumptions, Kimura (1961) has estimated the rate at which genetic information accumulates in evolution. He calculates that in the evolution of "higher" organisms genetic information has accumulated from the Cambrian to the present at an average rate of 0.29 bits per generation.

Kimura's method of measuring progressive evolution by the accumulation of genetic information is vitiated by several fundamental flaws. First, since the average rate of accumulation of information is allegedly constant *per generation*, it follows that organisms with a shorter generation time will have accumulated more information, and therefore are more progressive, than organisms with a longer generation time. In the evolution of mammals, moles and bats would necessarily be more progressive than horses, whales and men.

A second, more basic, flaw is that Kimura is not measuring how much genetic information has been accumulated in any given organism. Rather, he assumes that genetic information gradually accumulates with time and then proceeds to estimate the rate at which genetic information could have accumulated. The assumption that more recent organisms have more genetic information, and that therefore they are more progressive than their ancestors, is unwarranted and completely invalidates Kimura's attempt to measure evolutionary progress. There is, at least at present, no way of measuring the amount of genetic information present in any one organism.

Julian Huxley (1942, 1953) has argued that the biologist should not attempt to define progress *a priori*, but rather he should "proceed inductively to see whether he can or cannot find evidence of a process which can be legitimately called progressive." He believes that evolutionary progress can be defined without any reference to values. Huxley proposes first to investigate the features which mark off the "higher" from the "lower" organisms. Any evolutionary process in which the features which characterise higher organisms are achieved is considered progressive. Like Kimura, Huxley assumes that progress has in fact occurred, and that certain living organisms, especially man, are more progressive than others. But to classify organisms as "higher" or "lower" requires an evaluation. Huxley has not succeeded in avoiding reference to an axiological standard. The terms that he uses in his various definitions of progress, such as "improvement," "general advance," "level of efficiency," etc., are all in fact evaluative.

The Expansion and Diversification of Life

The concept of progress is axiological. To discuss evolutionary progress a choice must be made of the kind of value in reference to which organisms and evolutionary events can be assessed. Two decisions are required. First, we must choose the objective feature according to which the events or objects are to be ordered. Second, a decision must be made as to what pole of the ordered elements represents improvement. These divisions involve, admittedly, a subjective element, but they should not be arbitrary. Biological knowledge should guide them. There is a criterion by which the validity of the standards of reference can be chosen. A standard is valid if it enables us to say meaningful things about the evolution of life. How much of the required information is available, and whether the evaluation can be made more or less exactly, should also influence the choice of values.

What we know about the evolution of life enables us to decide immediately that there is no standard by which *uniform* progress has taken place in the process of evolution. Changes of direction, slackening and reversals have occurred in all evolutionary sequences, at least temporarily (Simpson, 1949, 1953). We must, then, concern ourselves exclusively with the question whether *net* progress has occurred, and in which sense, in the evolution of life.

Is there any criterion of progress by which net progress is a general feature of evolution? One conceivable standard of progress is the increase in the amount of genetic information stored in the organisms. Net progress would have occurred if organisms living at a later time would have, on the average, greater content of genetic information than their ancestors. One difficulty, insuperable at least for the present, is that there is no way in which genetic information can be measured. We do not even know how information is stored in organisms. We could choose the Shannon-Weaver solution, as Kimura has done, by regarding the DNA as a linear sequence of messages made up of groups of three-letter words (codons) with a four-letter alphabet (the four nucleotides, adenine, cytosine, guanine and thymine). Even so, a large fraction of the nuclear DNA probably does not encode information in such a way, and much DNA may have nonsense messages.

Accumulation of genetic information as a standard of progress can be understood in a different way. Progress can be measured by an increase in the *kinds* of ways in which the information is stored and as an increase in the *number* of different messages encoded. Different species represent different kinds of messages; individuals are messages or units of information. Thus understood, whether an increase in the amount of information has occurred reduces to the question whether life has diversified and expanded. This has been recognised by Simpson as the standard by which what I call general progress has occurred. According to Simpson (1949), in evolution as a whole we can find "a tendency for life to expand, to fill in all the available spaces in the livable environments, including those created by the process of that expansion itself."

The expansion of life can be measured by at least four different though related criteria of expansion: (1) expansion in the number of kinds of organisms, that is, species; (2) expansion in the number of individuals, or (3) of the total bulk of living matter; and (4) expansion in the total rate of flow of energy. Increases in the number of individuals or of their bulk may not be an unmixed blessing, as is the case now for the human species, but they can be a measure of biological success. By any one of the four standards of progress enumerated, it appears that net progress has been a general feature of the evolution of life.

Living organisms have a tendency to multiply exponentially without intrinsically imposed bounds. This is simply a consequence of the process of biological reproduction. The rate of increase in numbers is a net result of the balance between the rate of births and the rate of deaths of the population. In the absence of environmentally imposed restrictions, that balance is positive; populations have an intrinsic capacity to grow *ad infinitum*. Since the ambit in which life can exist is limited, and since the resources to which a population has access are even more limited, the rate of expansion of a population rapidly decreases to zero, or becomes negative.

Genetic differences between organisms of the same species result in natural selection of genotypes capable of a higher rate of expansion under the conditions in which the organisms live. Some genotypes are eliminated; others increase in frequency. The process of natural selection is creative in the non-trivial sense expounded by Dobzhansky. For the present purposes, natural selection is relevant in that it leads to the diversification of species, and this process in turn often leads to a further expansion of the number of individuals and their bulk.

The expansion of life is a tendency which encounters constraints of various sorts. Once a certain species has come to exist, its expansion is limited by the environment in at least two ways: first, because as stated above the resources accessible to the organisms are limited; second, because favourable conditions for increase in numbers, even when resources such as food and living space are available, do not always occur—at times the rate of growth of the population becomes negative, because deaths exceed births. The various parameters of the environment embodied by the term "weather" are the main factors interfering with the multiplication of organisms even when resources are available. Drastic and secular changes in the weather plus geological events lead at times to vast decreases in the size of some populations and even of the whole of life. Because of these constraints the tendency of life to expand has not always succeeded. That it has, on the average, expanded throughout most of the evolutionary process appears nevertheless certain.

Estimates of the number of living species vary from author to author. Probably there are more than two million but less than five million living species at present. Plant fossils are rare, but reasonable estimates of the number of animal species through paleontological history exist. Approximately 150,000 animal species live in the seas, a larger number than existed in the Cambrian (600 million years ago). Nevertheless, the present number of animal species may have been exceeded in the past, but if so it was certainly not by much. Life on land began in the Devonian (400 million years ago). The number of animal land species is probably at a maximum now, even if we exclude the insects. Insects make about three-quarters of all animal species, and about half of all species if plants are included. Insects did not appear until the early Carboniferous, some 350 million years ago. More species of insects exist now than at most, probably all, times in the past. This brief summary indicates that the number of living species is probably greater in recent times than was ever before, and that, in any case, a gradual increase in the number of species has characterised, at least on the average, the evolution of life. (Further details concerning the number of species, and also of genera, families, order, classes and phyla, through paleontological history can be found in the works of Simpson, particularly [1949] and [1953], from which the facts given in this paragraph are taken.)

The number of individuals living on the earth cannot be estimated with any reasonable approximation, even if we exclude microorganisms. It is a staggering number. I have estimated the number of individuals of a successful Neotropical insect species, *Drosophila willistoni*, as between 10^{10} and 10^{11}, that is, between 10 and 100 billions (Ayala *et al.*, 1972). The number of individual animals and plants living today and their bulk are doubtless greater than they were in the Cambrian. Very likely they are also greater than they have been throughout most of the time since the beginning of life. This is even more so if we include the large number and enormous bulk of the human population, and of all the plants and animals cultivated by man for his own use. Even if we include microorganisms, it is probable that the number of living individuals has increased, on the average, through the evolution of life. That the total bulk of living matter has also increased with the succession of time is even more likely.

The expansion of life operates as a positive feedback mechanism.

The more species appear, the more environments are created for new species to exploit. A trivial example is that once plants came into existence it was possible for animals to exist; and the animals themselves sustain large numbers of species of other animals, and of parasites and symbionts. T. H. Huxley likened the expansion of life to the filling of a barrel. First, the barrel is filled with apples until they overflow; then pebbles are added up to the brim; the space between the apples and the pebbles can be packed with sand; water is finally poured until it overflows. With many kinds of organisms the environment can be filled in more effectively than with only one kind. Huxley's analogy neglects one important aspect of life. A more appropriate analogy would have been that of an expanding barrel. The space available is increased rather than decreased by some additions.

The total flow of energy in the living world has probably increased through evolution even faster than the total bulk of matter. Johnstone (1921) pointed out that the influence of living things is to retard the dissipation of energy. Green plants do, indeed, store radiant energy from the sun which would otherwise be converted into heat. The influence of animals goes, however, in the opposite direction. The living activities of animals dissipate energy, since their catabolism exceeds their anabolism (Lotka, 1945). This apparently paradoxical situation results in fact in an increase in the rate at which energy flows through the whole of life. Animals do not simply provide a new path through which energy can flow, but rather their interactions with plants increase the total rate of flow through the system. An analogy can be used to illustrate this outcome. Suppose that a modern highway with three lanes in each direction connects two large cities. A need to accommodate an increase in the rate of traffic flow can be accomplished either by adding more lanes to the highway or by increasing the speed at which the traffic moves in the highway. In terms of the "carrying capacity" of the highway, these two approaches appear, at first sight, to work in opposite directions. However, together they increase the total flow of traffic through the highway.

Information About the Environment

There are many criteria by which net progress has occurred in some evolutionary sequences but not in others. One of the most meaningful of such criteria is the ability of the organism to obtain and process information about the environment. This criterion is of considerable biological interest, because such ability notably contributes to the biological success of the organisms which possess it. The criterion is particularly interesting in reference to man, since among the differences which mark off man from all other animals, his greatly developed ability to perceive the environment, and to react flexibly to it, is perhaps the most fundamental one. While organisms other than man become genetically adapted to their environments, man artificially creates environments to fit his genes.

Increased ability to gather and process information about the environment is sometimes expressed as evolution toward "independence from the environment." This latter expression is misleading. No organism can be truly independent of the environment. The evolutionary sequence fish → amphibian → reptile allegedly provides an example of evolution towards independence from an aqueous environment. Reptiles, birds and mammals are indeed free of need for water as an external living medium, but their lives depend on the conditions of the land. They have not become independent of the environment, but rather have exchanged dependence on one environment for dependence on another.

"Control over the environment" has been linked to the ability to gather and use information about the state of the environment. However, true control over the environment occurs to any large extent only in the human species. All organisms interact with the environment, but they do not control it. Burrowing a hole in the ground, or building a nest on a tree, like the construction of a beehive or of a beaver dam, do not represent control over the environment except in a trivial sense. The ability to control the environment started with the australopithecines, the first group of organisms which can be called human. They are considered to be men precisely because they were able to produce devices to manipulate the environment in the form of rudimentary pebble and bone tools. The ability to obtain and process information about the conditions of the environment does not provide control over the environment but rather it enables the organisms to avoid unsuitable environments and to seek suitable ones. It has developed in many organisms because it is a useful adaptation.

All organisms interact selectively with the environment. The cell membrane of a bacterium permits certain molecules but not others to enter the cell. Selective molecular exchange occurs also in the inorganic world; but this can hardly be called a form of information processing. Certain bacteria when placed on an agar plate move about in a zig-zag pattern which is almost certainly random. The most rudimentary ability to gather and process information about the environment can be found in certain single-celled eukaryotes. A *Paramecium* swims following a sinuous path ingesting the bacteria that it encounters as it swims. Whenever it meets unfavourable conditions, like unsuitable acidity or salinity in the water, the *Paramecium* checks its advance, turns and starts in a new direction. Its reaction is purely negative. The *Paramecium* apparently does not seek its food or a favourable environment, but simply avoids unsuitable conditions.

A somewhat greater ability to process information about the environment occurs in the single-celled *Euglena*. This organism has a light-sensitive spot by means of which it can orient itself towards the direction in which the light originates. *Euglena*'s motions are directional; it not only avoids unsuitable environments but it also actively seeks suitable ones. An amoeba represents further progress in the same direction; it reacts to light by moving away from it, and also actively pursues food particles.

Progress as increase in the ability to gather and process information about the environment is not a general characteristic of the evolution of life. Progress occurred in certain evolutionary lines of descent but not in others. Today's bacteria are not more progressive by this criterion than their ancestors of one billion years ago. In many evolutionary sequences some very limited progress took place in the early stages, without further progress through the rest of their history. In general, animals are more advanced than plants; vertebrates are more advanced than invertebrates; mammals more advanced than reptiles, which are more advanced than fish. The most advanced organism by this criterion is doubtless man.

The ability to obtain and to process information about the environment has progressed little in the plant kingdom. Plants generally react to light and to gravity. The geotropism is positive in the root, but negative in the stem. Plants also grow towards the light; some plants like the sunflower have parts which follow the course of the sun through its daily cycle. Another tropism in plants is the tendency of roots to grow towards water. The response to gravity, to water and to light is basically due to differential growth rates; a greater elongation of cells takes place on one side of the stem or of the root than on the other side. Gradients of light, gravity or moisture are the clues which guide these tropisms. Some plants react also to tactile stimuli. Tendrils twine around what they touch; *Mimosa* and carnivorous plants like the Venus flytrap (*Dionaea*) have leaves which close rapidly upon being touched.

In multicellular animals, the ability to obtain and process information about the environment is mediated by the nervous system. All major groups of animals, except the sponges, have nervous systems. The simplest nervous system among living animals occurs in coelenterates like hydra, corals and jellyfishes. Each tentacle of a jellyfish reacts only if it is individually and directly stimulated. There is no coordination of the information gathered by different parts of the animal. Jellyfishes are besides unable to learn from experience. A limited form of coordinated behaviour occurs in the echinoderms which comprise the starfishes and sea urchins. The coelenterates possess an undifferentiated nerve net; the echinoderms possess, besides a nerve net, a nerve ring and radial nerve cords. When the appropriate stimulus is encountered, a starfish reacts with direct and unified actions of the whole body. The most primitive form of a brain occurs in certain organisms like planarian flatworms, which also have numerous sensory cells and eyes without lenses. The information gathered by these sensory cells and organs is processed and coordinated by the central nervous system and the rudimentary brain; a planarian worm is capable of some variability of responses and of some simple learning. That is, the same stimuli will not necessarily produce always the same response.

Planarian flatworms have progressed farther than starfishes in the ability to gather and process information about the environment, and the starfishes have progressed farther than sea anemones and other coelenterates. But none of these organisms has gone very far by this criterion of progress. The most progressive group of organisms among the invertebrates are the arthropods, but the vertebrates have progressed much farther than any invertebrates.

It seems certain that among the ancestors of both the arthropods and the vertebrates there were organisms that, like the sponges, lacked a nervous system, and that their evolution went through a stage with only a simple network, with later stages developing a central nervous system and later a rudimentary brain. With further development of the central nervous system and of the brain, the ability to obtain and process information from the outside progressed much farther. The arthropods, which include the insects, have complex forms of behaviour. Precise visual, chemical and acoustic signals are obtained and processed by many arthropods, particularly in their search for food and in their selection of mates.

The vertebrates are generally able to obtain and process much more complicated signals and to produce a much greater variety of responses than the arthropods. The vertebrate brain has an enormous number of associative neurons with an extremely complex arrangement. Among the vertebrates, progress in the ability to deal with environmental information is correlated with increase in the size of the cerebral hemispheres and with the appearance and development of the "neopallium." The neopallium is involved in association and coordination of all kinds of impulses from all receptors and brain centres. The neopallium appeared first in the reptiles. In the mammals it has expanded to become the cerebral cortex, which covers most of the cerebral hemispheres. The larger brain of vertebrates compared to invertebrates permits them also to have a large amount of neurons involved in information storage or memory.

The ability to perceive the environment, and to integrate, coordinate and react flexibly to what is perceived, has attained its highest degree of development in man. Man is by this measure of biological progress the most progressive organism on the planet. That such ability is a sound criterion of biological progress was indicated earlier by pointing out that it is useful as an adaptation to the environment. Extreme advance in the ability to perceive and react to the environment is perhaps the most fundamental characteristic which marks off *Homo sapiens* from all other animals. Symbolic language, complex social organisation, control over the environment, the ability to envisage future states and to work towards them, values and ethics, are developments made possible by man's greatly developed capacity to obtain and organise information about the state of the environment.

Concluding Remarks

There is an abundant literature dealing with the subject of biological progress. Simpson (1949) has examined several criteria of progress and has stated in which sequences and for how long progress has occurred according to each one of the standards. The criteria of evolutionary progress explored by Simpson include dominance; invasion of new environments; replacement; improvement in adaptation; adaptability and possibility of further progress; increased specialisation; control over the environment; increasing structural complication; increase in general energy or maintained level of vital processes; and increase in the range and variety of adjustments to the environment. Rensch (1947) and Huxley (1942, 1953) have examined other lists of characteristics which can be used as standards of progressive evolution. Stebbins (1969) has written a provocative study of the law of "conservation of organisation" as a principle which accounts for evolutionary progress in the sense of a small bias towards increased complexity of organisation. Williams (1966) has examined, mostly critically, several criteria of progress. Two brief but incisive discussions of the concept of progress can be found in Herrick (1956) and Dobzhansky (1970). A philosophical study of the concept of progress has been made by Goudge (1961).

There is no need to examine here all the standards of progress which have been formulated by the authors just mentioned, nor to explore additional criteria. This paper was written primarily to clarify the notion of progress and its use in biology. Writings about biological progress have involved much disputation concerning (1) whether the notion of progress belongs in the realm of scientific discourse, (2) what criterion of progress is "best," and (3) whether progress has indeed taken place in the evolution of life. These controversies can be solved once the notion of progress is clearly established. First, the concept of progress involves an evaluation of good *vs.* bad, or of better *vs.* worse. The choice of a standard by which to evaluate organisms or their features is to a certain extent subjective. However, once a criterion of progress has been chosen, decisions concerning whether progress has occurred in the living world, and what organisms are more or less progressive, can be made following the usual standards and methods of scientific discourse. Second, there is no criterion of progress which is "best" in the abstract or for all purposes. The validity of any one criterion of progress depends on whether the use of that criterion leads to meaningful statements concerning the evolution of life. Which criterion or criteria are preferable depends on the particular context in which they are discussed. Third, the distinction between uniform and net progress makes it possible to recognise the occurrence of biological progress even though every member of a sequence or of a group of organisms may not always be more progressive than every previous member of the sequence or than every member of some other group of organisms. The distinction between general and particular progress makes it possible to study progress in particular groups of organisms, or during limited periods in the evolution of life.

Once it is recognised that an evaluation needs to be made, discussions of evolutionary progress can provide valuable insights for the understanding of life. That statement provides the clue to justify writing about evolutionary progress for this conference. Discussions of progress can be illuminating in biology, but are not so in the realm of the inorganic world. The only nontrivial processes in which sustained directional change has occurred outside the world of life are the increase of entropy, the expansion of the universe, the evolution of stars, and perhaps some geological processes. Nothing is gained, however, by labeling these processes progressive. Progress has occurred in nontrivial senses in the living world because of the creative character of the process of natural selection.

The basic components of organisms are the same physicochemical elements of the inorganic world. In living matter, these elements obey the same fundamental physicochemical laws which govern their behaviour in nonliving matter. Evolutionary progress, however, cannot be discussed purely in terms of the physicochemical components of living matter. The ability to gather and to process information about the environment, for instance, is an important biological parameter. It is clear that it cannot be analysed by reference only to physicochemical elements and laws. In fact, evolutionary progress measured by that standard can be interpreted as a gradual departure from the importance of physicochemical laws in determining the relevant aspects of the behaviour of organisms.

References

Ayala, F. J. (1969) An evolutionary dilemma; fitness of genotypes *versus* fitness of populations. *Canad. J. Genetics and Cytology,* 11, 439-56.

Ayala, F. J., Powell, J. R., Tracey, M. L., Mourao, C. A. and Perez-Salas, S. (1972). Enzyme variability in the *Drosophilia willistoni* group: IV. Genic variation in natural populations of *Drosophilia willistoni. Genetics,* 70, 113-39.

Broad, C. D. (1925). *The Mind and Its Place in Nature.* Kegan Paul, London.

Dobzhansky, Th. (1970). *Genetics of the Evolutionary Process.* Columbia University Press, New York and London.

Dobzhansky, Th. (1974). Chance and creativity in evolution. *Studies in the Philosophy of Biology.* University of California Press, Berkeley and Los Angeles.

Ginsberg, M. (1944). *Moral progress.* Frazer Lecture at the University of Glasgow. Glasgow University Press.

Goudge, T. A. (1961). *The Ascent of Life.* University of Toronto Press.

Herrick, G. J. (1956). *The Evolution of Human Nature.* University of Texas Press, Austin.

Huxley, J. S. (1942). *Evolution: the Modern Synthesis.* Harper, New York.

Huxley, J. S. (1953). *Evolution in Action.* Harper, New York.

Johnstone, J. (1921). *The Mechanism of Life.* Edward Arnold, London.

Kimura, M. (1961). Natural selection as the process of accumulating genetic information on adaptive evolution. *Genet. Research,* 2. 127-40.

Lewontin, R. C. (1968). The concept of evolution. *International Encyclopedia of the Social Sciences* (ed. D. L. Sills). Macmillan Co. and Free Press, London and New York.

Lotka, A. J. (1945). The law of evolution as a maximal principle. *Human Biology,* 17, 167-94.

Rensch, B. (1947). *Evolution above the Species Level.* Columbia University Press, New York.

Simpson, G. G. (1949). *The Meaning of Evolution.* Yale University Press, New Haven.

Simpson, G. G. (1953). *The Major Features of Evolution.* Columbia University Press, New York.

Stebbins. G. L. (1969). *The Basis of Progressive Evolution.* University of North Carolina Press, Chapel Hill.

Thoday, J. M. (1953). Components of fitness. *Symposia of the Society for the Study of Experimental Biology,* 7 (Evolution), 96-113.

Thoday, J. M. (1958). Natural selection and biological progress. In *A Century of Darwin* (ed. S. A. Barnet). Allen and Unwin, London.

Thoday, J. M. (1970). Genotype *versus* population fitness. *Canad. J. Genetics and Cytology,* 2, 674-5.

Williams, G. C. (1966) *Adaptation by Natural Selection.* Princeton University Press.

SCIENCE AND THE SCIENTIST
by
HENRI POINCARÉ

The Choice of Facts

Tolstoy somewhere explains why "science for its own sake" is in his eyes an absurd conception. We can not know *all* facts, since their number is practically infinite. It is necessary to choose; then we may let this choice depend on the pure caprice of our curiosity; would it not be better to let ourselves be guided by utility, by our practical and above all by our moral needs; have we nothing better to do than to count the number of ladybugs on our planet?

It is clear the word utility has not for him the sense men of affairs give it, and following them most of our contemporaries. Little cares he for industrial applications, for the marvels of electricity or of automobilism, which he regards rather as obstacles to moral progress; utility for him is solely what can make man better.

For my part, it need scarce be said, I could never be content with either the one or the other ideal; I want neither that plutocracy grasping and mean, nor that democracy goody and mediocre, occupied solely in turning the other cheek, where would dwell sages without curiosity, who, shunning excess, would not die of disease, but would surely die of ennui. But that is a matter of taste and is not what I wish to discuss.

The question nevertheless remains and should fix our attention; if our choice can only be determined by caprice or by immediate utility, there can be no science for its own sake, and consequently no science. But is that true? That a choice must be made is incontestable; whatever be our activity, facts go quicker than we, and we can not catch them; while the scientist discovers one fact, there happen milliards of milliards in a cubic millimeter of his body. To wish to comprise nature in science would be to want to put the whole into the part.

But scientists believe there is a hierarchy of facts and that among them may be made a judicious choice. They are right, since otherwise there would be no science, yet science exists. One need only open the eyes to see that the conquests of industry which have enriched so many practical men would never have seen the light, if these practical men alone had existed and if they had not been preceded by unselfish devotees who died poor, who never thought of utility, and yet had a guide far other than caprice.

As Mach says, these devotees have spared their successors the trouble of thinking. Those who might have worked solely in view of an immediate application would have left nothing behind them, and, in face of a new need, all must have been begun over again. Now most men do not love to think, and this is perhaps fortunate when instinct guides them, for most often, when they pursue an aim which is immediate and ever the same, instinct guides them better than reason would guide a pure intelligence. But instinct is routine, and if thought did not fecundate it, it would no more progress in man than in the bee or ant. It is needful then to think for those who love not thinking, and, as they are numerous, it is needful that each of our thoughts be as often useful as possible, and this is why a law will be the more precious the more general it is.

This shows us how we should choose: the most interesting facts are those which may serve many times; these are the facts which have a chance of coming up again. We have been so fortunate as to be born in a world where there are such. Suppose that instead of sixty chemical elements there were sixty milliards of them, that they were not some common, the others rare, but that they were uniformly distributed. Then, every time we picked up a new pebble there would be great probability of its being formed of some unknown substance; all that we knew of other pebbles would be worthless for it; before each new object we should be as the newborn babe; like it we could only obey our caprices or our needs. Biologists would be just as much at a loss if there were only individuals and no species and if heredity did not make sons like their fathers.

In such a world there would be no science; perhaps thought and even life would be impossible, since evolution could not there develop the preservational instincts. Happily it is not so; like all good fortune to which we are accustomed, this is not appreciated at its true worth.

Which then are the facts likely to reappear? They are first the simple facts. It is clear that in a complex fact a thousand circumstances are united by chance, and that only a chance still much less probable could reunite them anew. But are there any simple facts? And if there are, how recognize them? What assurance is there that a thing we think simple does not hide a dreadful complexity? All we can say is that we ought to prefer the facts which *seem* simple to those where our crude eye discerns unlike elements. And then one of two things: either this simplicity is real, or else the elements are so intimately mingled as not to be distinguishable. In the first case there is chance of our meeting anew this same simple fact, either in all its purity or entering itself as element in a complex manifold. In the second case this intimate mixture has likewise more chances of recurring than a heterogeneous assemblage; chance knows how to mix, it knows not how to disentangle, and to make with multiple elements a well-ordered edifice in which something is distinguishable, it must be made expressly. The facts which appear simple, even if they are not so, will therefore be more easily revived by chance. This it is which justifies the method instinctively adopted by the scientist, and what justifies it still better, perhaps, is that oft-recurring facts appear to us simple, precisely because we are used to them.

But where is the simple fact? Scientists have been seeking it in the two extremes, in the infinitely great and in the infinitely small. The astronomer has found it because the distances of the stars are immense, so great that each of them appears but as a point, so great that the qualitative differences are effaced, and because a point is simpler than a body which has form and qualities. The physicist on the other hand has sought the elementary phenomenon in fictively cutting up bodies into infinitesimal cubes, because the conditions of the problem, which undergo slow and continuous variation in passing from one point of the body to another, may be regarded as constant in the interior of each of these little cubes. In the same way the biologist has been instinctively led to regard the cell as more interesting than the whole animal, and the outcome has shown his wisdom, since cells belonging to organisms the most different are more alike, for the one who can recognize their resemblances, than are these organisms themselves. The sociologist is more embarrassed; the elements, which for him are men, are too unlike, too variable, too capricious, in a word, too complex; besides, history never begins over again. How then choose the interesting fact, which is that which begins again? Method is precisely the choice of facts; it is needful then to be occupied first with creating a method, and many have been imagined, since none imposes itself, so that sociology is the science which has the most methods and the fewest results.

Therefore it is by the regular facts that it is proper to begin; but after the rule is well established, after it is beyond all doubt, the facts in full conformity with it are erelong without interest since they no longer teach us anything new. It is then the exception which becomes important. We cease to seek resemblances; we devote ourselves above all to the differences, and among the differences are chosen first the most accentuated, not only because they are the most striking, but because they will be the most instructive. A simple example will make my thought plainer: Suppose one wishes to determine a curve by observing some of its points. The practician who concerns himself only with immediate utility would observe only the points he might need for some special object. These points would be badly distributed on the curve; they would be crowded in certain regions, rare in others, so that it would be impossible to join them by a continuous line, and they would be unavailable for other applications. The scientist will proceed differently; as he wishes to study the curve for itself, he will distribute regularly the points to be observed, and when enough are known he will join them by a regular line and then he will have the entire curve. But for that how does he proceed? If he has determined an extreme point of the curve, he does not stay near this extremity, but goes first to the other end; after the two extremities the most instructive point will be the mid-point, and so on.

So when a rule is established we should first seek the cases where this rule has the greatest chance of failing. Thence, among other reasons, come the interest of astronomic facts, and the interest of the geologic past; by going very far away in space or very far away in time, we may find our usual rules entirely overturned, and these grand overturnings aid us the better to see or the better to understand the little changes which may happen nearer to us, in the little corner of the world where we are called to live and act. We shall better know this corner for having traveled in distant countries with which we have nothing to do.

But what we ought to aim at is less the ascertainment of resemblances and differences than the recognition of likenesses hidden under apparent divergences. Particular rules seem at first discordant, but looking more closely we see in general that they resemble each other; different as to matter, they are alike as to form, as to the order of their parts. When we look at them with this bias, we shall see them enlarge and tend to embrace everything. And this it is which makes the value of certain facts which come to complete an assemblage and to show that it is the faithful image of other known assemblages.

I will not further insist, but these few words suffice to show that the scientist does not choose at random the facts he observes. He does not, as Tolstoy says, count the lady-bugs, because, however interesting lady-bugs may be, their number is subject to capricious variations. He seeks to condense much experience and much thought into a slender volume; and that is why a little book on physics contains so many past experiences and a thousand times as many possible experiences whose result is known beforehand.

But we have as yet looked at only one side of the question. The scientist does not study nature because it is useful; he studies it because he delights in it, and he delights in it because it is beautiful. If nature were not beautiful, it would not be worth knowing, and if nature were not worth knowing, life would not be worth living. Of course I do not here speak of that beauty which strikes the senses, the beauty of qualities and of appearances; not that I undervalue such beauty, far from it, but it has nothing to do with science; I mean that profounder beauty which comes from the harmonious order of the parts and which a pure intelligence can grasp. This it is which gives body, a structure so to speak, to the iridescent appearances which flatter our senses, and without this support the beauty of these fugitive dreams would be only imperfect, because it would be vague and always fleeting. On the contrary, intellectual beauty is sufficient unto itself, and it is for its sake, more perhaps than for the future good of humanity, that the scientist devotes himself to long and difficult labors.

It is, therefore, the quest of this especial beauty, the sense of the harmony of the cosmos, which makes us choose the facts most fitting to contribute to this harmony, just as the artist chooses from among the features of his model those which perfect the picture and give it character and life. And we need not fear that this instinctive and unavowed prepossession will turn the scientist aside from the search for the true. One may dream a harmonious world, but how far the real world will leave it behind! The greatest artists that ever lived, the Greeks, made their heavens; how shabby it is beside the true heavens, ours!

And it is because simplicity, because grandeur, is beautiful, that we preferably seek simple facts, sublime facts, that we delight now to follow the majestic course of the stars, now to examine with the microscope that prodigious littleness which is also a grandeur, now to seek in geologic time the traces of a past which attracts because it is far away.

We see too that the longing for the beautiful leads us to the same choice as the longing for the useful. And so it is that this economy of thought, this economy of effort, which is, according to Mach, the constant tendency of science, is at the same time a source of beauty and a practical advantage. The edifices that we admire are those where the architect has known how to proportion the means to the end, where the columns seem to carry, gaily, without effort, the weight placed upon them, like the gracious caryatids of the Erechtheum.

Whence comes this concordance? Is it simply that the things which seem to us beautiful are those which best adapt themselves to our intelligence, and that consequently they are at the same time the implement this intelligence knows best how to use? Or is there here a play of evolution and natural selection? Have the peoples whose ideal most conformed to their highest interest exterminated the others and taken their place? All pursued their ideals without reference to consequences, but while this quest led some to destruction, to others it gave empire. One is tempted to believe it. If the Greeks triumphed over the barbarians and if Europe, heir of Greek thought, dominates the world, it is because the savages loved loud colors and the clamorous tones of the drum which occupied only their senses, while the Greeks loved the intellectual beauty which hides beneath sensuous beauty, and this intellectual beauty it is which makes intelligence sure and strong.

Doubtless such a triumph would horrify Tolstoy, and he would not like to acknowledge that it might be truly useful. But this disinterested quest of the true for its own beauty is sane also and able to make man better. I well know that there are mistakes, that the thinker does not always draw thence the serenity he should find therein, and even that there are scientists of bad character. Must we, therefore, abandon science and study only morals? What! Do you think the moralists themselves are irreproachable when they come down from their pedestal?

SCIENCE AND HYPOTHESIS
by
HENRI POINCARÉ

Nature: Hypotheses in Physics

The Role of Experiment and Generalisation.—Experiment is the sole source of truth. It alone can teach us something new; it alone can give us certainty. These are two points that cannot be questioned. But then, if experiment is everything, what place is left for mathematical physics? What can experimental physics do with such an auxiliary—an auxiliary, moreover, which seems useless, and even may be dangerous?

However, mathematical physics exists. It has rendered undeniable service, and that is a fact which has to be explained. It is not sufficient merely to observe; we must use our observations, and for that purpose we must generalise. This is what has always been done, only as the recollection of past errors has made man more and more circumspect, he has observed more and more and generalised less and less. Every age has scoffed at its predecessor, accusing it of having generalised too boldly and too naively. Descartes used to commiserate the Ionians. Descartes in his turn makes us smile, and no doubt some day our children will laugh at us. Is there no way of getting at once to the gist of the matter, and thereby escaping the raillery which we foresee? Cannot we be content with experiment alone? No, that is impossible; that would be a complete misunderstanding of the true character of science. The man of science must work with method. Science is built up of facts, as a house is built of stones; but an accumulation of facts is no more a science than a heap of stones is a house. Most important of all, the man of science must exhibit foresight. Carlyle has written somewhere something after this fashion. "Nothing but facts are of importance. John Lackland passed by here. Here is something that is admirable. Here is a reality for which I would give all the theories in the world" [in *Past and Present*, 1843]. Carlyle was a compatriot of Bacon, and, like him, he wished to proclaim his worship of *the God of Things as they are.*

But Bacon would not have said that. That is the language of the historian. The physicist would most likely have said: "John Lackland passed by here. It is all the same to me, for he will not pass this way again."

We all know that there are good and bad experiments. The latter accumulate in vain. Whether there are a hundred or a thousand, one single piece of work by a real master—by a Pasteur, for example—will be sufficient to sweep them into oblivion. Bacon would have thoroughly understood that, for he invented the phrase *experimentum crucis*; but Carlyle would not have understood it. A fact is a fact. A student has read such and such a number on his thermometer. He has taken no precautions. It does not matter: he has read it, and if it is only the fact which counts, this is a reality that is as much entitled to be called a reality as the peregrinations of King John Lackland. What, then, is a good experiment? It is that which teaches us something more than an isolated fact. It is that which enables us to predict, and to generalise. Without generalisation, prediction is impossible. The circumstances under which one has operated will never again be reproduced simultaneously. The fact observed will never be repeated. All that can be affirmed is that under analogous circumstances an analogous fact will be produced. To predict it, we must therefore invoke the aid of analogy—that is to say, even at this stage, we must generalise. However timid we may be, there must be interpolation. Experiment only gives us a certain number of isolated points. They must be connected by a continuous line, and this is a true generalisation. But more is done. The curve thus traced will pass between and near the points observed; it will not pass through the points themselves. Thus we are not restricted to generalising our experiment, we correct it; and the physicist who would abstain from these corrections, and really content himself with experiment pure and simple, would be compelled to enunciate very extraordinary laws indeed. Detached facts cannot therefore satisfy us, and that is why our science must be ordered, or, better still, generalised.

It is often said that experiments should be made without preconceived ideas. That is impossible. Not only would it make every experiment fruitless, but even if we wished to do so, it could not be done. Every man has his own conception of the world, and this he cannot so easily lay aside. We must, for example, use language, and our language is necessarily steeped in preconceived ideas. Only they are unconscious preconceived ideas, which are a thousand times the most dangerous of all. Shall we say, that if we cause others to intervene of which we are fully conscious, that we shall only aggravate the evil? I do not think so. I am inclined to think that they will serve as ample counterpoises—I was almost going to say antidotes. They will generally disagree, they will enter into conflict one with another, and *ipso facto*, they will force us to look at things under different aspects. This is enough to free us. He is no longer a slave who can choose his master.

Thus, by generalisation, every fact observed enables us to predict a large number of others; only, we ought not to forget that the first alone is certain, and that all the others are merely probable. However solidly founded a prediction may appear to us, we are never *absolutely* sure that experiment will not prove it to be baseless if we set to work to verify it. But the probability of its accuracy is often so great that practically we may be content with it. It is far better to predict without certainty, than never to have predicted at all. We should never, therefore, disdain to verify when the opportunity presents itself. But every experiment is long and difficult, and the labourers are few, and the number of facts which we require to predict is enormous; and besides this mass, the number of direct verifications that we can make will never be more than a negligible quantity. Of this little that we can directly attain we must choose the best. Every experiment must enable us to make a maximum number of predictions having the highest possible degree of probability. The problem is, so to speak, to increase the output of the scientific machine. I may be permitted to compare science to a library which must go on increasing indefinitely; the librarian has limited funds for his purchases, and he must, therefore, strain every nerve not to waste them. Experimental physics has to make the purchases, and experimental physics alone can enrich the library. As for mathematical physics, her duty is to draw up the catalogue. If the catalogue is well done the library is none the richer for it; but the reader will be enabled to utilise its riches; and also by showing the librarian the gaps in his collection, it will help him to make a judicious use of his funds, which is all the more important, inasmuch as those funds are entirely inadequate. That is the rôle of mathematical physics.

It must direct generalisation, so as to increase what I called just now the output of science. By what means it does this, and how it may do it without danger, is what we have now to examine.

The Unity of Nature.—Let us first of all observe that every generalisation supposes in a certain measure a belief in the unity and simplicity of Nature. As far as the unity is concerned, there can be no difficulty. If the different parts of the universe were not as the organs of the same body, they would not re-act one upon the other; they would mutually ignore each other, and we in particular should only know one part. We need not, therefore, ask if Nature is one, but how she is one.

As for the second point, that is not so clear. It is not certain that Nature is simple. Can we without danger act as if she were?

There was a time when the simplicity of Mariotte's law was an argument in favour of its accuracy: when Fresnel himself, after having said in a conversation with Laplace that Nature cares naught for analytical difficulties, was compelled to explain his words so as not to give offence to current opinion. Nowadays, ideas have changed considerably; but those who do not believe that natural laws must be simple, are still obliged to act as if they did believe it. They cannot entirely dispense with this necessity without making all generalisation, and therefore all science, impossible. It is clear that any fact can be generalised in an infinite number of ways, and it is a question of choice. The choice can only be guided by considerations of simplicity. Let us take the most ordinary case, that of interpolation. We draw a continuous line as regularly as possible between the points given by observation. Why do we avoid angular points and inflexions that are too sharp? Why do we not make our curve describe the most capricious zigzags? It is because we know beforehand, or think we know, that the law we have to express cannot be so complicated as all that. The mass of Jupiter may be deduced either from the movements of his satellites, or from the perturbations of the major planets, or from those of the minor planets. If we take the mean of the determinations obtained by these three methods, we find three numbers very close together, but not quite identical. This result might be interpreted by supposing that the gravitation constant is not the same in the three cases; the observations would be certainly much better represented. Why do we reject this interpretation? Not because it is absurd, but because it is uselessly complicated. We shall only accept it when we are forced to, and it is not imposed upon us yet. To sum up, in most cases every law is held to be simple until the contrary is proved.

This custom is imposed upon physicists by the reasons that I have indicated, but how can it be justified in the presence of discoveries which daily show us fresh details, richer and more complex? How can we even reconcile it with the unity of nature? For if all things are interdependent, the relations in which so many different objects intervene can no longer be simple.

If we study the history of science we see produced two phenomena which are, so to speak, each the inverse of the other. Sometimes it is simplicity which is hidden under what is apparently complex; sometimes, on the contrary, it is simplicity which is apparent, and which conceals extremely complex realities. What is there more complicated than the disturbed motions of the planets, and what more simple than Newton's law? There, as Fresnel said, Nature playing with analytical difficulties, only uses simple means, and creates by their combination I know not what tangled skein. Here it is the hidden simplicity which must be disentangled. Examples to the contrary abound. In the kinetic theory of gases, molecules of tremendous velocity are discussed, whose paths, deformed by incessant impacts, have the most capricious shapes, and plough their way through space in every direction. The result observable is Mariotte's simple law. Each individual fact was complicated. The law of great numbers has re-established simplicity in the mean. Here the simplicity is only apparent, and the coarseness of our senses alone prevents us from seeing the complexity.

Many phenomena obey a law of proportionality. But why? Because in these phenomena there is something which is very small. The simple law observed is only the translation of the general analytical rule by which the infinitely small increment of a function is proportional to the increment of the variable. As in reality our increments are not infinitely small, but only very small, the law of proportionality is only approximate, and simplicity is only apparent. What I have just said applies to the law of the superposition of small movements, which is so fruitful in its applications and which is the foundation of optics.

And Newton's law itself? Its simplicity, so long undetected, is perhaps only apparent. Who knows if it be not due to some complicated mechanism, to the impact of some subtle matter animated by irregular movements, and if it has not become simple merely through the play of averages and large numbers? In any case, it is difficult not to suppose that the true law contains complementary terms which may become sensible at small distances. If in astronomy they are negligible, and if the law thus regains its simplicity, it is solely on account of the enormous distances of the celestial bodies. No doubt, if our means of investigation became more and more penetrating, we should discover the simple beneath the complex, and then the complex from the simple, and then again the simple beneath the complex, and so on, without ever being able to predict what the last term will be. We must stop somewhere, and for science to be possible we must stop where we have found simplicity. That is the only ground on which we can erect the edifice of our generalisations. But, this simplicity being only apparent, will the ground be solid enough? That is what we have now to discover.

For this purpose let us see what part is played in our generalisations by the belief in simplicity. We have verified a simple law in a considerable number of particular cases. We refuse to admit that this coincidence, so often repeated, is a result of mere chance, and we conclude that the law must be true in the general case.

Kepler remarks that the positions of a planet observed by Tycho are all on the same ellipse. Not for one moment does he think that, by a singular freak of chance, Tycho had never looked at the heavens except at the very moment when the path of the planet happened to cut that ellipse. What does it matter then if the simplicity be real or if it hide a complex truth? Whether it be due to the influence of great numbers which reduces individual differences to a level, or to the greatness or the smallness of certain quantities which allow of certain terms to be neglected—in no case is it due to chance. This simplicity, real or apparent, has always a cause. We shall therefore always be able to reason in the same fashion, and if a simple law has been observed in several particular cases, we may legitimately suppose that it still will be true in analogous cases. To refuse to admit this would be to attribute an inadmissible rôle to chance. However, there is a difference. If the simplicity were real and profound it would bear the test of the increasing precision of our methods of measurement. If, then, we believe Nature to be profoundly simple, we must conclude that it is an approximate and not a rigorous simplicity. This is what was formerly done, but it is what we have no longer the right to do. The simplicity of Kepler's laws, for instance, is only apparent; but that does not prevent them from being applied to almost all systems analogous to the solar system, though that prevents them from being rigorously exact.

Rôle of Hypothesis.—Every generalisation is a hypothesis. Hypothesis therefore plays a necessary rôle, which no one has ever contested. Only, it should always be as soon as possible submitted to verification. It goes without saying that, if it cannot stand this test, it must be abandoned without any hesitation. This is, indeed, what is generally done; but sometimes with a certain impatience. Ah well! This impatience is not justified. The physicist who has just given up one of his hypotheses should, on the contrary, rejoice, for he found an unexpected opportunity of discover. His hypothesis, I imagine, had not been lightly adopted. It took into account all the known factors which seem capable of intervention in the phenomenon. If it is not verified, it is because there is something unexpected and extra-ordinary about it, because we are on the point of finding something unknown and new. Has the hypothesis thus rejected been sterile? Far from it. It may be even said that it has rendered more service than a true hypothesis. Not only has it been the occasion of a deci-sive experiment, but if this experiment had been made by chance, without the hypothesis, no conclusion could have been drawn; nothing extraordinary would have been seen; and only one fact the more would have been catalogued, without deducing from it the remotest consequence.

Now, under what conditions is the use of hypothesis without danger? The proposal to submit all to experiment is not sufficient. Some hypotheses are dangerous,—first and foremost those which are tacit and unconscious. And since we make them without know-ing them, we cannot get rid of them. Here again, there is a service that mathematical physics may render us. By the precision which is its characteristic, we are compelled to formulate all the hypotheses that we would unhesitatingly make without its aid. Let us also notice that it is important not to multiply hypotheses indefinitely. If we construct a theory based upon multiple hypotheses, and if experiment condemns it, which of the premisses must be changed? It is impossible to tell. Conversely, if the experiment succeeds, must we suppose that it has verified all these hypotheses at once? Can several unknowns be determined from a single equation?

We must also take care to distinguish between the different kinds of hypotheses. First of all, there are those which are quite natural and necessary. It is difficult not to suppose that the influence of very distant bodies is quite negligible that small movements obey a linear law, and that effect is a continuous function of its cause. I will say as much for the conditions imposed by symmetry. All these hypotheses affirm, so to speak, the common basis of all the theories of mathematical physics. They are the last that should be abandoned. There is a second category of hypotheses which I shall qualify as indifferent. In most questions the analyst assumes, at the beginning of his calculations, either that matter is continuous, or the reverse, that it is formed of atoms. In either case, his results would have been the same. On the atomic supposition he has a little more difficulty in obtaining them—that is all. If, then, experiment confirms his conclusions, will he suppose that he has proved, for example, the real existence of atoms?

In optical theories two vectors are introduced, one of which we consider as a velocity and the other as a vortex. This again is an indifferent hypothesis, since we should have arrived at the same conclusions by assuming the former to be a vortex and the latter to be a velocity. The success of the experiment cannot prove, therefore, that the first vector is really a velocity. It only proves one thing—namely, that it is a vector; and that is the only hypothesis that has really been introduced into the premises. To give it the concrete appearance that the fallibility of our minds demands, it was necessary to consider it either as a velocity or as a vortex. In the same way, it was necessary to represent it by an x or a y, but the result will not prove that we were right or wrong in regarding it as a velocity; nor will it prove we are right or wrong in calling it x and not y.

These indifferent hypotheses are never dangerous provided their characters are not misunderstood. They may be useful, either as artifices for calculation, or to assist our understanding by concrete images, to fix the ideas, as we say. They need not therefore be rejected. The hypotheses of the third category are real generalisations. They must be confirmed or invalidated by experiment. Whether verified or condemned, they will always be fruitful; but, for the reasons I have given, they will only be so if they are not too numerous.

Origin of Mathematical Physics.—Let us go further and study more closely the conditions which have assisted the development of mathematical physics. We recognise at the outset that the efforts of men of science have always tended to resolve the complex phenomenon given directly by experiment into a very large number of elementary phenomena, and that in three different ways.

First, with respect to time. Instead of embracing in its entirety the progressive development of a phenomenon, we simply try to connect each moment with the one immediately preceding. We admit that the present state of the world only depends on the immediate past, without being directly influenced, so to speak, by the recollection of a more distant past. Thanks to this postulate, instead of studying directly the whole succession of phenomena, we may confine ourselves to writing down its *differential equation*; for the laws of Kepler we substitute the law of Newton.

Next, we try to decompose the phenomenon in space. What experiment gives us is a confused aggregate of facts spread over a scene of considerable extent. We must try to deduce the elementary phenomenon, which will still be localised in a very small region of space.

A few examples perhaps will make my meaning clearer. If we wished to study in all its complexity the distribution of temperature in a cooling solid, we could never do so. This is simply because, if we only reflect that a point in the solid can directly impart some of its heat to a neighbouring point, it will immediately impart that heat only to the nearest points, and it is but gradually that the flow of heat will reach other portions of the solid. The elementary phenomenon is the interchange of heat between two contiguous points. It is strictly localised and relatively simple if, as is natural, we admit that it is not influenced by the temperature of the molecules whose distance apart is small.

I bend a rod: it takes a very complicated form, the direct investigation of which would be impossible. But I can attack the problem, however, if I notice that its flexure is only the resultant of the deformations of the very small elements of the rod, and that the deformation of each of these elements only depends on the forces which are directly applied to it, and not in the least on those which may be acting on the other elements.

In all these examples, which may be increased without difficulty, it is admitted that there is no action at a distance or at great distances. That is an hypothesis. It is not always true, as the law of gravitation proves. It must therefore be verified. If it is confirmed, even approximately, it is valuable, for it helps us to use mathematical physics, at any rate by successive approximations. If it does not stand the test, we must seek something else that is analogous, for there are other means of arriving at the elementary phenomenon. If several bodies act simultaneously, it may happen that their actions are independent, and may be added one to the other, either as vectors or as scalar quantities. The elementary phenomenon is then the action of an isolated body. Or suppose, again, it is a question of small movements, or more generally of small variations which obey the well-known law of mutual or relative independence. The movement observed will then be decomposed into simple movements—for example, sound into its harmonics, and white light into its monochromatic components. When we have discovered in which direction to seek for the elementary phenomena, by what means may we reach it? First, it will often happen that in order to predict it, or rather in order to predict what is useful to us, it will not be necessary to know its mechanism. The law of great numbers will suffice. Take for example the propagation of heat. Each molecule radiates towards its neighbour—we need not inquire according to what law; and if we make any supposition in this respect, it will be an indifferent hypothesis, and therefore useless and unverifiable. In fact, by the action of averages and thanks to the symmetry of the medium, all differences are levelled, and, whatever the hypothesis may be, the result is always the same.

The same feature is presented in the theory of elasticity, and in that of capillarity. The neighbouring molecules attract and repel each other, we need not inquire by what law. It is enough for us that this attraction is sensible at small distances only, and that the molecules are very numerous, that the medium is symmetrical, and we have only to let the law of great numbers come into play.

Here again the simplicity of the elementary phenomenon is hidden beneath the complexity of the observable resultant phenomenon; but in its turn this simplicity was only apparent and disguised a very complex mechanism. Evidently the best means of reaching the elementary phenomenon would be experiment. It would be necessary by experimental artifices to dissociate the complex system which nature orders for our investigations and carefully to study the elements as dissociated as possible; for example, natural white light would be decomposed into monochromatic lights by the aid of the prism, and into polarised lights by the aid of the polariser. Unfortunately, that is neither always possible nor always sufficient, and sometimes the mind must run ahead of experiment. I shall only give one example which has always struck me rather forcibly. If I decompose white light, I shall be able to isolate a portion of the spectrum, but however small it may be, it will always be a certain width. In the same way the natural lights which are called *monochromatic* give us a very fine array, but [a ray] which is not, however, infinitely fine. It might be supposed that in the experimental study of the properties of these natural lights, by operating with finer and finer rays, and passing on at last to the limit, so to speak, we should eventually obtain the properties of a rigorously monochromatic light. That would not be accurate. I assume that two rays emanate from the same source, that they are first polarised in planes at right angles, that they are then brought back again to the same plane of polarisation, and that we try to obtain interference. If the light were *rigorously* monochromatic, there would be interference; but with our nearly monochromatic lights, there will be no interference, and that, however narrow the ray may be. For it to be otherwise, the ray would have to be several million times finer than the finest known rays.

Here then we should be led astray by proceeding to the limit. The mind has to run ahead of the experiment, and if it has done so with success, it is because it has allowed itself to be guided by the instinct of simplicity. The knowledge of the elementary fact enables us to state the problem in the form of an equation. It only remains to deduce from it by combination the observable and verifiable complex fact. That is what we call *integration*, and it is the province of the mathematician. It might be asked, why in physical science generalisation so readily takes the mathematical form. The reason is now easy to see. It is not only because we have to express numerical laws; it is because the observable phenomenon is due to the superposition of a large number of elementary phenomena which are *all similar to each other*; and in this way differential equations are quite naturally introduced. It is not enough that each elementary phenomenon should obey simple laws: all those that we have to combine must obey the same law; then only is the intervention of mathematics of any use. Mathematics teaches us, in fact, to combine like with like. Its object is to divine the result of a combination without having to reconstruct that combination element by element. If we have to repeat the same operation several times, mathematics enables us to avoid this repetition by telling the result beforehand by a kind of induction. This I have explained before in the chapter on mathematical reasoning. But for that purpose all these operations must be similar; in the contrary case we must evidently make up our minds to working them out in full one after the other, and mathematics will be useless. It is therefore, thanks to the approximate homogeneity of the matter studied by physicists, that mathematical physics came into existence. In the natural sciences the following conditions are no longer to be found:—homogeneity, relative independence of remote parts, simplicity of the elementary fact; and that is why the student of natural science is compelled to have recourse to other modes of generalisation.

LOGIC AND MATHEMATICS

by

STEPHEN G. SIMPSON

1. Logic

Logic is the science of formal principles of reasoning or correct inference. Historically, logic originated with the ancient Greek philosopher Aristotle. Logic was further developed and systematized by the Stoics and by the medieval scholastic philosophers. In the late nineteenth and twentieth centuries, logic saw explosive growth, which has continued up to the present.

One may ask whether logic is part of philosophy or independent of it. According to Bocheński [2, §10B], this issue is nowhere explicitly raised in the writings of Aristotle. However, Aristotle did go to great pains to formulate the basic concepts of logic (terms, premises, syllogisms, etc.) in a neutral way, independent of any particular philosophical orientation. Thus Aristotle seems to have viewed logic not as part of philosophy but rather as a tool or instrument[1] to be used by philosophers and scientists alike. This attitude about logic is in agreement with the modern view, according to which the predicate calculus (see 1.2 below) is a general method or framework not only for philosophical reasoning but also for reasoning about any subject matter whatsoever.

Logic is the science of correct reasoning. What, then, is reasoning? According to Aristotle [13, Topics, 100a25], reasoning is any argument in which certain assumptions or *premises* are laid down and then something other than these necessarily follows. Thus logic is the science of necessary inference. However, it is important to note that when logic is applied to specific subject matter, not all logical inference constitutes a scientifically valid demonstration. This is because a piece of formally correct reasoning is not scientifically valid unless it is based on a true and primary starting

---

[1] The Greek word for instrument is *organon*. The collection of Aristotle's logical writings is known as the *Organon*.

point. Furthermore, any decisions about what is true and primary do not pertain to logic but rather to the specific subject matter under consideration. In this way we limit the scope of logic, maintaining a sharp distinction between logic and the other sciences. All reasoning, both scientific and nonscientific, must take place within the logical framework, but it is only a framework, nothing more. This is what is meant by saying that logic is a *formal* science.

For example, consider the following inference:

> Some real estate will increase in value.
> Anything that will increase in value is a good investment.
> Therefore, some real estate is a good investment.

This inference is logically correct, because the conclusion "some real estate is a good investment" necessarily follows once we accept the premises "some real estate will increase in value" and "anything that will increase in value is a good investment." Yet this same inference may not be a demonstration of its conclusion, because one or both of the premises may be faulty. Thus logic can help us to clarify our reasoning, but it can only go so far. The real issue in this particular inference is ultimately one of finance and economics, not logic.

I shall now briefly indicate the basics of Aristotelean logic.

1.1. Aristotelean Logic

Aristotle's collection of logical treatises is known as the *Organon*. Of these treatises, the *Prior Analytics* contains the most systematic discussion of formal logic. In addition to the *Organon*, the *Metaphysics* contains relevant material.[2] See Aristotle [13] and Ross [19].

1.1.1. Subjects and Predicates

Aristotelean logic begins with the familiar grammatical distinction

---

[2] The *Metaphysics* is Aristotle's treatise on the science of existence, that is, being as such. It includes a detailed analysis of the various ways in which a thing can be said to be.

between subject and predicate. A *subject* is typically an individual entity, for instance a man[3] or a house or a city. It may also be a class of entities, for instance all men. A *predicate* is a property or attribute or mode of existence that a given subject may or may not possess. For example, an individual man (the subject) may or may not be skillful (the predicate), and all men (the subject) may or may not be brothers (the predicate).

The fundamental principles of predication are:

1. Identity. Everything is what it is and acts accordingly. In symbols:

$$A \text{ is } A.$$

For example, an acorn will grow into an oak tree and nothing else.

2. Noncontradiction. It is impossible for a thing both to be and not to be. A given predicate cannot both belong and not belong to a given subject in a given respect at a given time. Contradictions do not exist. Symbolically:

$$A \text{ and non-}A \text{ cannot both be the case.}$$

For example, an honest man cannot also be a thief.

3. Either-or. Everything must either be or not be. A given predicate either belongs or does not belong to a given subject in a given respect at a given time. Symbolically:

$$\text{Either } A \text{ or non-}A.$$

For example, a society must be either free or not free.

These principles have exercised a powerful influence on subsequent

---

[3] I use *man* in the traditional sense, equivalent to "human being." There is no intention to exclude persons of the female gender.

thinkers. For example, the twentieth-century intellectual Ayn Rand titled the three main divisions of her best-selling philosophical novel *Atlas Shrugged* after the three principles above, in tribute to Aristotle.[4]

1.1.2. Syllogisms

According to Aristotelean logic, the basic unit of reasoning is the *syllogism*. For example, the real estate inference that was presented above is a syllogism. It is of the form

> Some A is B.
> All B is C.
> Therefore, some A is C.

Here A denotes real estate, B denotes increase in value, and C denotes a good investment. Just as in this example, every syllogism consists of two premises and one conclusion. Each of the premises and the conclusion is of one of four types:

> universal affirmative: All A is B.
> universal negative: No A is B.
> particular affirmative: Some A is B.
> particular negative: Some A is not B.

The letters A, B, C are known as *terms*. Every syllogism contains three terms. The two premises always share a term that does not appear in the conclusion. This is known as the *middle term*. In our real estate example, the middle term is B, that is, that which increases in value.

In order to classify the various types of syllogisms, one must take account of certain symmetries. In particular, "no A is B" and "no B is A" are equivalent, as are "some A is B" and "some B is A." Furthermore, the order of the two premises in a syllogism does not matter. Allowing for these symmetries, we can enumerate a total of

---

[4] A survey conducted for the Book-of-the-Month Club and the Library of Congress in 1991 found that *Atlas Shrugged* is the most influential book in the United States, second only to the Bible. See http://www.lcweb.loc.gov/loc/cfbook/bklists.html.

126 possible syllogistic forms. Of these 126, only 11 represent correct inferences. For example, the form

all *A* is *B*, all *B* is *C*, therefore all *A* is *C*

represents a correct inference, while

all *A* is *B*, all *C* is *B*, therefore some *A* is *C*

does not.

The classification of syllogisms leads to a rather complex theory. Medieval thinkers perfected it and developed ingenious mnemonics to aid in distinguishing the correct forms from the incorrect ones. This culminated in the famous *pons asinorum* ("bridge of asses"), an intricate diagram which illustrates all of the syllogistic forms by means of a contrast between the good and the pleasurable. See Bocheński [2, §24H, §32F].

1.2. The Predicate Calculus

In 1879 the German philosopher Gottlob Frege published a remarkable treatise, the *Begriffsschrift* ("concept script") [22]. This brilliant monograph is the origin of modern logical theory. However, Frege's account was defective in several respects, and notationally awkward to boot. Instead of Frege's system, I shall present a streamlined system known as *first-order logic* or the *predicate calculus*.

The predicate calculus dates from the 1910s and 1920s. It is basic for all subsequent logical research. It is a very general system of logic which accurately expresses a huge variety of assertions and modes of reasoning. We shall see that it is much more flexible than the Aristotelean syllogistic.

1.2.1. Predicates and Individuals

In the predicate calculus, the subject/predicate distinction is drawn somewhat differently from the way it is drawn in Aristotelean logic. The main point here is that, in the predicate calculus, a subject is always an individual entity, never a class of entities. For example, an individual man can be treated as a subject, but the class of all men must be treated as a predicate. Since a subject in the predicate calculus is always an individual entity, it is usual to speak of *individuals* rather than subjects. I shall follow this customary practice.

The predicate calculus makes heavy use of symbolic notation. Lowercase letters a, b, c, . . . x, y, z, . . . are used to denote individuals. Uppercase letters M, N, P, Q, R, . . . are used to denote predicates. Simple assertions may be formed by juxtaposing a predicate with an individual.

For example, if M is the predicate "to be a man" and a is the individual "Socrates," then Ma denotes the assertion "Socrates is a man." The symbol a is called an *argument* of M. The predicate M may be applied to any individual, and that individual is then an argument of M. If b is the individual "New York," then Mb asserts, falsely, that New York is a man. In general, if x is any individual whatsoever, then Mx is the assertion that x is a man. This assertion may or may not be true, depending on what x is. The expression Mx is called an *atomic formula* of the predicate calculus.

Some predicates require more than one argument. For example, if B is the predicate "bigger than," then Bxy denotes the assertion "x is bigger than y." Thus B requires two arguments, and Bxy is an atomic formula. If we try to use B with only one argument, we obtain something like Bx, that is, "x is bigger than." This is not an atomic formula or any other kind of assertion. It is only a meaningless combination of symbols. In analogy with English grammar, we could say that Bxy is like a grammatically correct sentence, while Bx is merely a sentence fragment. Such fragments play no role in the predicate calculus.

Let us now go into more detail about the role of individuals in the predicate calculus. We shall divide the lowercase letters, which denote individuals, into two groups: a, b, c, . . . near the beginning of the alphabet, and x, y, z, . . . near the end of the alphabet. There is an important grammatical or logical distinction between these two groups. Letters of the first group are known as *individual constants* or simply *constants*. As in the above examples, we think of them as denoting specific individuals, such as Socrates or New York. Letters of the second group are known as *individual variables* or simply *variables*. For example, x is a variable. We think of x as denoting not a specific individual but rather an arbitrary or unspecified individual.[5]

1.2.2. Formulas and Logical Operators

In addition to the lowercase letters for individuals (constants and variables) and uppercase letters for predicates, the predicate calculus employs seven special symbols known as *logical operators*.[6]

$$ \& \quad \vee \quad \sim \quad \supset \quad \equiv \quad \forall \quad \exists $$

The names and meanings of the logical operators are given by

symbol	name	usage	meaning
&	conjunction	...&...	"both ... and ..."
∨	disjunction	...∨...	"either ... or ... (or both)"
~	negation	~...	"it is not the case that ..."
⊃	implication[7]	...⊃...	"if ... then ..."
≡	bi-implication[8]	...≡...	"... if and only if ..."
∀	universal quantifier	∀x...	"for all x, ..."
∃	existential quantifier	∃x...	"there exists x such that ..."

---

[5] The idea of using letters such as x and y as variables is of great value. Historically, the creators of the predicate calculus borrowed this idea from the mathematical discipline known as *algebra*. Recall that algebra is a kind of generalized arithmetic. In algebra there are constants, that is, specific quantities such as 2, the square root of 10, et cetera, but there are also variables such as x, y, et cetera. The key idea of algebra is that a variable x represents an unspecified or unknown quantity. It always stands for *some* quantity, but it *may* stand for *any* quantity. The use of variables makes algebra much more powerful than arithmetic. Variables help us to express and solve equations such as $2x + 3y = 11$ involving one or more unknown quantities. Variables can also be used to express arithmetical laws such as $x + y = y + x$.

[6] The first five logical operators (&, ∨, ~, ⊃, ≡) are equivalent to so-called Boolean logic gates of electrical engineering. Formulas built from them may be viewed as representations of the binary switching circuits that control the operation of modern digital computers. See Mendelson [14, 15].

[7] This is the so-called material implication: $\Phi_1 \supset \Phi_2$ is equivalent to $\sim (\Phi_1 \;\&\; \sim \Phi_2)$.

[8] This is called bi-implication because $\Phi_1 \equiv \Phi_2$ is equivalent to $(\Phi_1 \supset \Phi_2) \;\&\; (\Phi_2 \supset \Phi_1)$.

Here x is any variable.

A *formula* is a meaningful expression built up from atomic formulas by repeated application of the logical operators. In the above table, an ellipsis mark (. . .) stands for a formula within a larger formula.

For example, suppose we have a predicate M meaning "is a man," another predicate T meaning "is a truck," and another predicate D meaning "drives." Here M and T are predicates that require only one argument apiece. The predicate D requires two arguments: the driver, and the vehicle being driven. Thus Mx, Ty, and Dxy are atomic formulas meaning "x is a man," "y is a truck," and "x drives y," respectively. A typical formula built from these atomic formulas is

$$\forall x \, (Mx \supset \exists y \, (Ty \,\&\, Dxy))$$

which we can translate as "for all x, if x is a man, then there exists y such that y is a truck and x drives y." In other words,

Every man drives at least one truck.

Similarly, the formula

$$\forall y \, (Ty \supset \exists x \, (Mx \,\&\, Dxy))$$

translates to

Every truck is driven by at least one man.

In writing formulas, we often use parentheses as punctuation marks to indicate grouping and thereby remove ambiguity. If parentheses were not used, one could construe the formula $\sim Ty \,\&\, Dxy$ in two logically inequivalent ways: as $(\sim Ty) \,\&\, Dxy$ ("y is not a truck, and x drives y"), or as $\sim (Ty \,\&\, Dxy)$ ("y is not a truck that x drives"). The parentheses allow us to choose the meaning that we intend.

The predicate calculus is very rich in expressive power. For example, the four Aristotelean premise types discussed in 1.1.2 can easily be rendered as formulas of the predicate calculus. Letting A and B be predicates that require one argument apiece, we have

universal affirmative	all A is B	$\forall x \, (Ax \supset Bx)$
universal negative	no A is B	$\forall x \, (Ax \supset \sim Bx)$
particular affirmative	some A is B	$\exists x \, (Ax \ \& \ Bx)$
particular negative	some A is not B	$\exists x \, (Ax \ \& \sim Bx)$

In the second line of this table, the universal negative "no A is B" could have been rendered equivalently as $\sim \exists x \, (Ax \ \& \ Bx)$, or as $\forall x$ $(Bx \supset \sim Ax)$.

The above table may tend to gloss over a subtle but philosophically significant difference between Aristotelean logic and the predicate calculus. Namely, where Aristotelean logic views A as a subject and B as a predicate, the predicate calculus views both A and B as predicates. This is typical of the different perspectives involved. Aristotelean logic emphasizes the universal essences of subjects or entities, while the predicate calculus elevates predicates to a position of supreme importance.

1.2.3. Logical Validity and Logical Consequence

A formula of the predicate calculus is said to be *logically valid* if it is necessarily always true, regardless of the specific predicates and individuals involved. For example, the three fundamental principles of Aristotelean logic (see 1.1.1 above) correspond to formulas as follows:

Identity:	$\forall x \, (Ax \equiv Ax)$.
Noncontradiction:	$\sim \exists x \, (Ax \ \& \sim Ax)$.
Either-or:	$\forall x \, (Ax \vee \sim Ax)$.

These formulas are logically valid, because they are "necessarily" or "automatically" or "formally" true, no matter what predicate may be denoted by the symbol A.

The predicate calculus concept of logical validity subsumes the Aristotelean syllogism. Each syllogism corresponds to a logically valid implication

$$(\Phi_1 \ \& \ \Phi_2) \supset \Psi$$

where Φ_1 and Φ_2 are formulas expressing the two premises and Ψ expresses the conclusion. For example, the syllogism

Some A is B, all B is C, therefore some A is C

has a predicate calculus rendition

$$((\exists x \, (Ax \,\&\, Bx)) \,\&\, (\forall x \, (Bx \supset Cx))) \supset (\exists x \, (Ax \,\&\, Cx))$$

and this formula is logically valid.

More generally, a formula Ψ is said to be a *logical consequence* of a set of formulas $\Phi_1, \ldots, \Phi_n$ just in case

$$(\Phi_1 \,\&\, \ldots \,\&\, \Phi_n) \supset \Psi$$

is logically valid. Here $\Phi_1, \ldots, \Phi_n$ are premises and Ψ is a conclusion. This is similar to the Aristotelean syllogism, but it is of wider applicability, because the premises and the conclusion can be more complex. As an example, the nineteenth-century logician Augustus De Morgan noted[9] that the inference

All horses are animals,
 therefore, the head of a horse is the head of an animal

is beyond the reach of Aristotelean logic. Yet this same inference may be paraphrased as "if all horses are animals, then for all x, if x is the head of some horse then x is the head of some animal," and this corresponds to a logically valid formula

$$(\forall y \, (Hy \supset Ay)) \supset (\forall x \, ((\exists y \, (Rxy \,\&\, Hy)) \supset (\exists y \, (Rxy \,\&\, Ay))))$$

of the predicate calculus. Here H, A, R denote "is a horse," "is an animal," "is the head of," respectively. Thus De Morgan's conclusion is indeed a logical consequence of his premise.

---

[9] See, however, Bocheński [2, §10B].

1.2.4. The Completeness Theorem

Formulas of the predicate calculus can be exceedingly complicated. How, then, can we distinguish the formulas that are logically valid from the formulas that are not logically valid? It turns out that there is an algorithm for recognizing logically valid formulas.[10] We shall now examine this algorithm.

In order to recognize that a formula Φ is logically valid, we can construct what is known as a *proof tree* for Φ, or equivalently a *refutation tree* for Φ. This is a tree that carries $\sim \Phi$ at the root. Each node of the tree carries a formula. The growth of the tree is guided by the meaning of the logical operators appearing in Φ. New nodes are added to the tree depending on what nodes have already appeared. For example, if a node carrying $\sim (\Phi_1 \& \Phi_2)$ has appeared, we create two new nodes carrying $\sim \Phi_1$ and $\sim \Phi_2$ respectively. The thought behind these new nodes is that the only way for $\sim (\Phi_1 \& \Phi_2)$ to be the case is if at least one of $\sim \Phi_1$ and $\sim \Phi_2$ is the case. Similarly, if a node carrying $\sim \forall x\, \Psi$ has already appeared, we create a new node carrying $\sim \Psi'$, where Ψ' is the result of substituting a new constant a for the variable x throughout the formula Ψ. The idea here is that the only way for the universal statement $\forall x\, \Psi$ to be false is if Ψ is false for some particular x. Since a is a new constant, Ψ' is a formula that may be considered as the most general false instance of Ψ. Corresponding to each of the seven logical operators, there are prescribed procedures for adding new nodes to the tree. We apply these procedures repeatedly until they cannot be applied anymore. If explicit contradictions[11] are discovered along each and every branch of the tree, then we have a refutation tree for $\sim \Phi$. Thus $\sim \Phi$ is seen to be logically impossible. In other words, Φ is logically valid.

The adequacy of proof trees for recognizing logically valid formulas is a major insight of twentieth-century logic. It is a variant of the

---

10 The details of this algorithm are explained in modern logic textbooks. Variants of it have been programmed to run on digital computers. They form the basis of a system of computer logic. See Fitting [4].

11 An *explicit contradiction* is a pair of formulas of the form Ψ, $\sim \Psi$.

famous *completeness theorem*, first proved in 1930 by the great logician Kurt Gödel [5, 22].

On the other hand, the class of logically valid formulas is known
to be extremely complicated. Indeed, this class is *undecidable*: there
is no algorithm[12] that accepts as input an arbitrary formula Φ and
outputs "yes" if Φ is logically valid and "no" if Φ is not logically
valid. In this sense, the concept of logical validity is too general and
too intractable to be analyzed thoroughly. There will never be a
predicate calculus analog of the *pons asinorum*.

1.2.5. Formal Theories

The predicate calculus is a very general and flexible framework for
reasoning. By choosing appropriate predicates, one can reason about
any subject whatsoever. These considerations lead to the notion of a
formal theory.

In order to specify a formal theory, one first chooses a small collection of predicates that are regarded as basic for a given field of
study. These predicates are the *primitives* of the theory. They delim-
it the scope of the theory. Other predicates must be defined in terms
of the primitives. Using them, one writes down certain formulas
that are regarded as basic or self-evident within the given field of
study. These formulas are the *axioms* of the theory. It is crucial to
make all of our underlying assumptions explicit as axioms. Once
this has been done, *theorem* is any formula that is a logical consequence of the axioms. A *formal theory* is this structure of primitives,
axioms, and theorems.

As a frivolous example, we could envision a theory of cars, trucks,
and drivers. We would begin with some primitives such as C ("is a
car"), T ("is a truck"), D ("drives"), M ("is a man"), and so forth. We
could then write down certain obvious or self-evident axioms such
as $\forall x\,(Mx \supset \sim Cx)$ ("no man is a car"), $\forall x\,((\exists y\,Dxy) \supset Mx)$ ("every
driver is a man"), and so forth. Then, within the constraints

---

[12] The algorithms in question may be implemented as computer programs (Turing
machine programs). This undecidability result is known as *Church's theorem*. See
Mendelson [15].

imposed by the axioms, we could investigate the logical consequence relationships among various nonobvious assertions, such as

$$\sim \exists x \; (Mx \; \& \; \exists y \; (Dxy \; \& \; Cy) \; \& \; \exists z \; (Dxz \; \& \; Tz))$$

("nobody drives both a car and a truck"). Additional predicates V ("is a vehicle") and P ("is a driver") can be defined in terms of the primitives. The defining axioms for V and P would be $\forall y \; (Vy \equiv (Cy \vee Ty))$ and $\forall x \; (Px \equiv \exists y \; Dxy)$, respectively. In this fashion, we could attempt to codify all available knowledge about vehicles and drivers.

More seriously, one could try to write down formal theories corresponding to various scientific disciplines, such as mechanics or statistics or law. In this way one could hope to analyze the logical structure of the respective disciplines.

The process of codifying a scientific discipline by means of primitives and axioms in the predicate calculus is known as *formalization*. The key issue here is the choice of primitives and axioms. They cannot be chosen arbitrarily. The scientist who chooses them must exercise a certain aesthetic touch. They must be small in number; they must be basic and self-evident; and they must account for the largest possible number of other concepts and facts.

To date, this kind of formal theory-building has been convincingly carried out in only a few cases. A survey is in Tarski [21]. The most notable successes have been in mathematics.

2. Foundations of Mathematics

Mathematics is the science of quantity. Traditionally there were two branches of mathematics, arithmetic and geometry, dealing with two kinds of quantities: numbers and shapes. Modern mathematics is richer and deals with a wider variety of objects, but arithmetic and geometry are still of central importance.

Foundations of mathematics is the study of the most basic concepts and logical structure of mathematics, with an eye to the unity of human knowledge. Among the most basic mathematical concepts are: number, shape, set, function, algorithm, mathematical axiom, mathematical definition, mathematical proof.

The reader may reasonably ask why mathematics appears at all in this volume. Isn't mathematics too narrow a subject? Isn't the philosophy of mathematics of rather specialized interest, all the more so in comparison to the broad humanistic issues of philosophy proper, issues such as the good, the true, and the beautiful?

There are three reasons for discussing mathematics in a volume on general philosophy:

1. Mathematics has always played a special role in scientific thought. The abstract nature of mathematical objects presents philosophical challenges that are unusual and unique.

2. Foundations of mathematics is a subject that has always exhibited an unusually high level of technical sophistication. For this reason, many thinkers have conjectured that foundations of mathematics can serve as a model or pattern for foundations of other sciences.

3. The philosophy of mathematics has served as a highly articulated test-bed where mathematicians and philosophers alike can explore how various general philosophical doctrines play out in a specific scientific context.[13]

The purpose of this section is to indicate the role of logic in the foundations of mathematics. I begin with a few remarks on the geometry of Euclid, then describe some modern formal theories for mathematics.

2.1. The Geometry of Euclid

Above the gateway to Plato's academy appeared a famous inscription:

Let no one who is ignorant of geometry enter here.

In this way Plato indicated his high opinion of geometry. According to Heath [9, page 284], Plato regarded geometry as "the first essential

---

[13] For example, philosophical intrinsicism may play out as mathematical Platonism. Philosophical subjectivism may play out as mathematical constructivism. Nominalism may play out as formalism.

[14] The modern notion of a formal theory (see 1.2.5 above) is a variant of Aristotle's concept of scientific method.

in the training of philosophers," because of its abstract character. See also Plato [17, Republic, 527B].

In the *Posterior Analytics* [13], Aristotle laid down the basics of the scientific method.[14] The essence of the method is to organize a field of knowledge logically by means of primitive concepts, axioms, postulates, definitions, and theorems. The majority of Aristotle's examples of this method are drawn from arithmetic and geometry [1, 7, 9].

The methodological ideas of Aristotle decisively influenced the structure and organization of Euclid's monumental treatise on geometry, the *Elements* [8]. Euclid begins with twenty-one definitions, five postulates, and five common notions. The rest of the *Elements* is an elaborate deductive structure consisting of hundreds of propositions. Each proposition is justified by its own demonstration. The demonstrations are in the form of chains of syllogisms. In each syllogism, the premises are identified as coming from among the definitions, postulates, common notions, and previously demonstrated propositions. For example, in book 1 of the *Elements*, the demonstration of proposition 16 ("in any triangle, if one of the sides be produced, the exterior angle is greater than either of the interior and opposite angles") is a chain of syllogisms with postulate 2, common notion 5, and propositions 3, 4, and 15 ("if two straight lines cut one another, they make the vertical angles equal to one another") occurring as premises. It is true that the syllogisms of Euclid do not always conform strictly to Aristotelean templates. However, the standards of rigor are very high, and Aristotle's influence is readily apparent.

The logic of Aristotle and the geometry of Euclid are universally recognized as towering scientific achievements of ancient Greece.

2.2. Formal Theories for Mathematics

2.2.1. A Formal Theory for Geometry

With the advent of calculus in the seventeenth and eighteenth centuries, mathematics developed very rapidly and with little attention to logical foundations. Euclid's geometry was still regarded as a model of logical rigor, a shining example of what a well-organized scientific discipline ideally ought to look like. But the prolific Enlightenment mathematicians such as Leonhard Euler showed almost no interest in trying to place calculus on a similarly firm foundation. Only in the last half of the nineteenth century did scientists begin to deal with this foundational problem in earnest. The resulting crisis had far-reaching consequences. Even Euclid's geometry itself came under critical scrutiny. Geometers such as Moritz Pasch discovered what they regarded as gaps or inaccuracies in the *Elements*. Great mathematicians such as David Hilbert entered the fray.

An outcome of all this foundational activity was a thorough reworking of geometry, this time as a collection of formal theories within the predicate calculus. Decisive insights were obtained by Alfred Tarski. I shall now sketch Tarski's formal theory for Euclidean[15] plane geometry.[16]

As his primitive predicates, Tarski takes P ("point"), B ("between"), D ("distance"), I ("identity"). The atomic formulas Px, $Bxyz$, $Dxyuv$, and Ixy mean "x is a point," "y lies between x and z," "the distance from x to y is equal to the distance from u to v," and "x is identical to y," respectively. Geometrical objects other than points, such as line segments, angles, triangles, circles, are handled by means of the primitives. For example, the circle with center x and radius uv consists of all points y such that $Dxyuv$ holds.

In geometry, two points x and y are considered identical if the distance between them is zero. Tarski expresses this by means of an axiom

$$\forall x \, \forall y \, \forall z \, (Dxyzz \supset Ixy).$$

Another axiom

$$\forall w \, \forall x \, \forall y \, \forall z \, ((Bwxy \;\&\; Bwyz) \supset Bxyz)$$

---

[15] Here *Euclidean geometry* refers to the familiar geometry in which the angles of a triangle sum to 180 degrees, as distinct from the *non-Euclidean* (i.e., hyperbolic) geometry developed by Farkas Bolyai and Nikolay Lobachevsky in the nineteenth century.

[16] Tarski also showed how to handle non-Euclidean plane geometry, as well as Euclidean and non-Euclidean geometries of higher dimension, in a similar fashion.

expresses the fact that, given any four points, if the second is between the first and the third, and if the third is between the first and the fourth, then the third is between the second and the fourth. A noteworthy axiom is

$$\forall x \, \forall y \, \forall z \, \forall u \, \forall v \, ((Dxuxv \,\&\, Dyuyv \,\&\, Dzuzv \,\&\, \sim Iuv)$$
$$\supset (Bxyz \lor Bxzy \lor Byxz))$$

which says: any three points x, y, z equidistant from two distinct points u, v must be collinear. This axiom is typical of two-dimensional (i.e., plane) geometry and does not apply to geometries of dimension greater than two.

Altogether Tarski presents twelve axioms, plus an additional collection of axioms expressing the idea that a line is continuous. The full statement of Tarski's axioms for Euclidean plane geometry is given at [10, pages 19–20] Let T_g be the formal theory based on Tarski's axioms.

Remarkably, Tarski has demonstrated that T_g is *complete*. This means that, for any purely geometrical[17] statement Ψ, either Ψ or $\sim \Psi$ is a theorem of T_g. Thus we see that the axioms of T_g suffice to answer all yes/no questions of Euclidean plane geometry. Combining this with the completeness theorem of Gödel, we find that T_g is *decidable*: there is an algorithm that accepts as input an arbitrary statement of plane Euclidean geometry, and outputs "true" if the statement is true, and "false" if it is false.[18] This is a triumph of modern foundational research.

2.2.2. A Formal Theory for Arithmetic

By arithmetic we mean elementary school arithmetic, that is, the study of the positive whole numbers 1, 2, 3, . . . along with the

---

[17] This means that all occurrences of variables x within the formula Ψ are within subformulas of the form $\forall x \, (Px \supset \ldots)$ or $\exists x \, (Px \,\&\, \ldots)$. Thus we are restricting attention to the realm of geometry and excluding everything else.

[18] Such algorithms have been implemented as computer programs. They are useful in robotics and other artificial intelligence applications.

familiar operations of addition (+) and multiplication (×). This part of mathematics is obviously fundamental, yet it turns out to be surprisingly complicated. Let us now write down some of the axioms that go into a formal theory of arithmetic.[19]

Our primitive predicates for arithmetic are N ("number"), A ("addition"), M ("multiplication"), I ("identity"). The atomic formulas Nx, $Axyz$, $Mxyz$, Ixy mean "x is a number," "$x + y = z$," "$x \times y = z$," "$x = y$," respectively. Our axioms will use the predicates N, A, M, I to assert that for any given numbers x and y, the numbers $x + y$ and $x \times y$ always exist and are unique. We shall also have axioms expressing some well-known arithmetical laws:

substitution laws: if $x = y$ and x is a number then y is a number, etc.

commutative laws: $x + y = y + x$ and $x \times y = y \times x$.

associative laws: $(x + y) + z = x + (y + z)$ and $(x \times y) \times z = x \times (y \times z)$.

distributive law: $x \times (y + z) = (x \times y) + (x \times z)$.

comparison law: $x \neq y$ if and only if, for some z, $x + z = y$ or $x = y + z$.

unit law: $x \times 1 = x$.

Our formal axioms for arithmetic are as follows.

substitution laws:
$\forall x\, Ixx$
$\forall x\, \forall y\, (Ixy \equiv Iyx)$
$\forall x\, \forall y\, \forall z\, ((Ixy \;\&\; Iyz) \supset Ixz)$
$\forall x\, \forall y\, (Ixy \supset (Nx \equiv Ny))$

existence and uniqueness of $x + y$:
$\forall x\, \forall y\, \forall z\, \forall u\, \forall v\, \forall w\, ((Ixu \;\&\; Iyv \;\&\; Izw) \supset (Axyz \equiv Auvw))$
$\forall x\, \forall y\, \forall z\, (Axyz \supset (Nx \;\&\; Ny \;\&\; Nz))$
$\forall x\, \forall y\, ((Nx \;\&\; Ny) \supset \exists w\, \forall z\, (Iwz \equiv Axyz))$

---

[19] Two recent studies of formal arithmetic are Hájek / Pudlák [6] and Simpson [20].

existence and uniqueness of $x \times y$:

$\forall x \, \forall y \, \forall z \, \forall u \, \forall v \, \forall w \, ((Ixu \, \& \, Iyv \, \& \, Izw) \supset (Mxyz \equiv Muvw))$

$\forall x \, \forall y \, \forall z \, (Mxyz \supset (Nx \, \& \, Ny \, \& \, Nz))$

$\forall x \, \forall y \, ((Nx \, \& \, Ny) \supset \exists w \, \forall z \, (Iwz \equiv Mxyz))$

commutative laws:

$\forall x \, \forall y \, \exists z \, (Axyz \, \& \, Ayxz)$

$\forall x \, \forall y \, \exists z \, (Mxyz \, \& \, Myxz)$

associative laws:

$\forall x \, \forall y \, \forall z \, \exists u \, \exists v \, \exists w \, (Axyu \, \& \, Auzw \, \& \, Ayzv \, \& \, Axvw)$

$\forall x \, \forall y \, \forall z \, \exists u \, \exists v \, \exists w \, (Mxyu \, \& \, Muzw \, \& \, Myzv \, \& \, Mxvw)$

distributive law:

$\forall x \, \forall y \, \forall z \, \exists t \, \exists u \, \exists v \, \exists w \, (Ayzt \, \& \, Mxtw \, \& \, Mxyu \, \& \, Mxzv \, \&$
$Auvw)$

comparison law:

$\forall x \, \forall y \, ((Nx \, \& \, Ny) \supset (Ixy \equiv \sim \exists z \, (Axzy \vee Ayzx)))$

unit law:

$\exists z \, (Nz \, \& \, (\sim \exists x \, \exists y \, Axyz) \, \& \, \forall w \, (Nw \supset Mwzw))$

Let T_a be the formal theory specified by the above primitives and axioms.

It is known that T_a suffices to derive many familiar arithmetical facts. For example, $2 + 2 = 4$ may be expressed, awkwardly to be sure,[20] as $(1 + 1) + (1 + 1) = ((1 + 1) + 1) + 1$ or

$$\exists x \, \exists y \, \exists z \, \exists w \, (Mxxx \, \& \, Axxy \, \& \, Axyz \, \& \, Axzw \, \& \, Ayyw)[21]$$

---

[20] This kind of awkwardness can be alleviated by means of various devices. In particular, standard mathematical notation such as $x + 2$ can be incorporated into the predicate calculus.

[21] In this formula, the variables x, y, z, w play the role of 1, 2, 3, 4 respectively.

and this formula is indeed a theorem of T_a, that is, a logical consequence of the axioms of T_a. Another theorem of T_a is

$$\forall x \; \forall y \; \forall z \; \forall w \; (((Axzw \; \& \; Ayzw) \vee (Mxzw \; \& \; Myzw)) \supset Ixy)$$

expressing a familiar cancellation law: if either $x + z = y + z$ or $x \times z = y \times z$, then $x = y$.

On the other hand, the axioms of T_a are by no means exhaustive. They can be supplemented with other axioms expressing the *mathematical induction* or *least number* principle: if there exists a number having some well-defined property, then among all numbers having the property there is a smallest one. The resulting formal theory is remarkably powerful, in the sense that its theorems include virtually all known arithmetical facts. But it is not so powerful as one might wish. Indeed, any formal theory that includes T_a is necessarily either inconsistent[22] or incomplete. Thus there is no hope of writing down enough axioms or developing an algorithm to decide all arithmetical facts. This is a variant of the famous 1931 *incompleteness theorem* of Gödel [5, 22]. There are several methods of coping with the incompleteness phenomenon, and this constitutes a currently active area of research in foundations of mathematics.

The contrast between the completeness of formal geometry and the incompleteness of formal arithmetic is striking. Both sides of this dichotomy are of evident philosophical interest.

2.2.3. A Formal Theory of Sets

One of the aims of modern logical research is to devise a single formal theory that will unify all of mathematics. Such a theory will necessarily be subject to the Gödel incompleteness phenomenon, because it will incorporate not only T_g but also T_a.

One approach to a unified mathematics is to straightforwardly embed arithmetic into geometry, by identifying whole numbers with evenly spaced points on a line. This idea was familiar to the

---

[22] A formal theory is said to be inconsistent if its axioms logically imply an explicit contradiction. Such theories are of no scientific value.

ancient Greeks. Another approach is to explain geometry in terms of arithmetic and algebra, by means of coordinate systems, like latitude and longitude on a map. This idea goes back to the seventeenth-century mathematician and philosopher René Descartes and the nineteenth-century mathematician Karl Weierstrass. Both approaches give rise to essentially the same formal theory, known as *second-order arithmetic*.[23] This theory includes both T_a and T_g and is adequate for the bulk of modern mathematics. Thus the decision about whether to make geometry more fundamental than arithmetic or vice versa seems to be mostly a matter of taste.

A very different approach to a unified mathematics is via *set theory*. This peculiarly twentieth-century approach is based on one very simple-looking concept: sets. Remarkably, this one concept leads directly to a vast structure that encompasses all of modern mathematics.

A *set* is a collection of objects called the *elements* of the set. We sometimes use informal notations such as $x = \{y, z, \ldots\}$ to indicate that x is a set consisting of elements y, z, ... The number of elements in a set can be arbitrarily large or even infinite. A basic principle of set theory is that a set is determined by its elements. Thus two sets are identical if and only if they have the same elements. This principle is known as *extensionality*. For example, the set $\{a, b, c\}$ is considered to be the same set as $\{c, a, b\}$ because the elements are the same, even though written in a different order.

Much of the complexity of set theory arises from the fact that sets may be elements of other sets. For instance, the set $\{a, b\}$ is an element of the set $\{\{a, b\}, c\}$ and this is distinct from the set $\{a, b, c\}$.

For a formal theory of sets, we use three primitives: S ("set"), I ("identity"), E ("element"). The atomic formulas Sx, Ixy, Exy mean "x is a set," "x is identical to y," "x is an element of y," respectively. One of the ground rules of set theory is that only sets may have elements. This is expressed as an axiom $\forall w\, \forall x\, (Ewx \supset Sx)$. In addition there is an axiom of extensionality

$$\forall x\, \forall y\, ((Sx\ \&\ Sy) \supset (Ixy \equiv \forall w\, (Ewx \equiv Ewy)))$$

---

[23] A recent study of second-order arithmetic is Simpson [20].

and an axiom $\exists x$ (Sx & ~ $\exists w$ Ewx) expressing the existence of the *empty set*, that is, a set { } having no elements. A list of all the axioms of set theory may be found in textbooks [11, 15]. Let T_s be the formal theory of sets based on these axioms.

The set theory approach to arithmetic is in terms of the non-negative whole numbers 0, 1, 2, 3, ... These numbers are identified with specific sets. Namely, we identify 0 with the empty set { }, 1 with {{}}, 2 with {{},{{}}}, 3 with {{},{{}},{{},{{}}}}, and so forth. In general, we identify the number n with the set of smaller numbers {0, 1, . . . , n − 1}. Among the axioms of T_s is an *axiom of infinity* asserting the existence of the infinite set $\omega = \{0, 1, 2, 3, . . .\}$. One can use the set ω to show that T_s includes a theory equivalent to T_a. After that, one can follow the ideas of Descartes and Weierstrass to see that T_s also includes a theory equivalent to T_g. It turns out that the rest of modern mathematics can also be emulated within T_s. This includes an elaborate theory of infinite sets that are much larger than ω.

The set-theoretical approach to arithmetic and geometry is admittedly somewhat artificial. However, the idea of basing all of mathematics on one simple concept, sets, has exerted a powerful attraction.[24] The implications of this idea are not yet fully understood and are a topic of current research.

3. Philosophy of Mathematics

This section covers some issues and trends in the philosophy of mathematics.

3.1. Plato and Aristotle

The objects that are studied in mathematics tend to be somewhat abstract and remote from everyday perceptual experience. Therefore, the existence and nature of mathematical objects present

---

[24] The idea of set-theoretical foundations gave rise to the "new math" pedagogy of the 1960s. For a lively discussion, see Kline [12].

special philosophical challenges. For example, is a geometrical square different from a square floor tile? If so, then where is the geometrical square? Is it on the floor, in our minds, or somewhere else? And what about sets? Is a set of fifty-two cards something other than the cards themselves?

The ancient Greek philosophers took such questions very seriously. Indeed, many of their general philosophical discussions were carried on with extensive reference to geometry and arithmetic. Plato seemed to insist that mathematical objects, like the Platonic forms or essences, must be perfectly abstract and have a separate, nonmaterial kind of existence. Aristotle [1, 7, 13, 19] dissected and refuted this view in books *M* and *N* of the *Metaphysics*. According to Aristotle, the geometrical square is a significant aspect of the square floor tile, but it can only be understood by discarding other irrelevant aspects such as the exact measurements, the tiling material, and so on. Clearly these questions provide much food for philosophical analysis and debate.

3.2. The Twentieth Century

In the twentieth century, the advent of the predicate calculus and the digital computer profoundly affected our view of mathematics. The discovery that all of mathematics can be codified in formal theories created a huge stir. One expression of this excitement was the rise of an extreme philosophical doctrine known as *formalism*.[25]

According to formalism, mathematics is only a formal game, concerned solely with algorithmic manipulation of symbols. Under this view, the symbols of the predicate calculus do not denote predicates or anything else. They are merely marks on paper or bits and bytes in the memory of a computer. Therefore, mathematics cannot claim to be any sort of knowledge of mathematical objects. Indeed, mathematical objects do not exist at all, and the profound questions debated by Plato and Aristotle become moot. Mathematics is nothing but a kind of blind calculation.

---

[25] See, for example, Curry [3].

The formalist doctrine fits well with certain modern trends in computer science, such as artificial intelligence. However, formalism has proved inadequate as an integrated philosophy of mathematics, because it fails to account for human mathematical understanding, not to mention the spectacular applications of mathematics in fields like physics and engineering.

By way of reaction against formalism, several alternative doctrines have been advocated. One of these is *constructivism*, the idea that mathematical knowledge can be obtained by means of a series of purely mental constructions. Under this view, mathematical objects exist solely in the mind of the mathematician, so mathematical knowledge is absolutely certain. However, the status of mathematics vis-à-vis the external world becomes doubtful. An extreme version of constructivism is so solipsistic that it does not even allow for the possibility of mathematical communication from one mind to another.

An additional disturbing feature of constructivism is that it entails rejection of the basic laws of logic. To see how this comes about, consider some specific mathematical problem or question of a yes/no nature, for which the answer is currently unknown.[26] (Mathematics abounds with such questions, and the Gödel incompleteness phenomenon suggests that such questions will always exist.) Express the "yes" answer as a formula Ψ and the "no" answer as the negated formula $\sim\Psi$. Since the answer is unknown, neither Ψ nor $\sim\Psi$ is in the mind of the mathematician. Therefore, according to the constructivists, the disjunction $\Psi \vee \sim\Psi$ is not a legitimate mathematical assumption. Thus Aristotle's either-or principle (see 1.1.1 and 1.2.3 above) must be abandoned.[27]

Constructivism has the merit of allowing human beings to possess mathematical knowledge. However, the constructivist rejection of the external world and of Aristotelean logic are highly unpalatable to most mathematicians and mathematically oriented scientists. For

---

[26] For example, we could consider the following difficult question of Christian Goldbach. Can every even number greater than 2 be expressed as the sum of two prime numbers?

[27] See the essays of Luitzen Brouwer and Andrey Kolmogorov in [22].

this reason, constructivism remains a fringe movement on the twentieth-century mathematical landscape.

Another twentieth-century philosophical doctrine has arisen from set-theoretical foundations. The reliance on infinite sets suggests many perplexing questions. What do such sets correspond to in reality? Where are they, and how can the human mind grasp them? In order to boldly answer these questions, and as a reaction against formalism, many researchers in axiomatic set theory have subscribed to what is known as *set-theoretical Platonism*. According to this variant of the Platonic doctrine, infinite sets exist in a non-material, purely mathematical realm. By extending our intuitive understanding of this realm, we will be able to cope with chaos issuing from the Gödel incompleteness phenomenon. The most prominent and frequently cited authority for this kind of Platonism is Gödel himself [5].

There is a good fit between set-theoretical Platonism and certain aspects of twentieth-century mathematical practice. However, as a philosophical doctrine, set-theoretical Platonism leaves much to be desired. Many of Aristotle's objections to the Platonic forms are still cogent. There are serious questions about how a theory of infinite sets can be applicable to a finite world.

We have discussed three competing twentieth-century doctrines: formalism, constructivism, set-theoretical Platonism. None of these doctrines are philosophically satisfactory, and they do not provide much guidance for mathematically oriented scientists and other users of mathematics. As a result, late-twentieth-century mathematicians have developed a split view, a kind of Kantian schizophrenia, which is usually described as "Platonism on weekdays, formalism on weekends." In other words, they accept the existence of infinite sets as a working hypothesis in their mathematical research, but when it comes to philosophical speculation, they retreat to a formalist stance. Thus they have given up hope of an integrated view that accounts for both mathematical knowledge and the applicability of mathematics to physical reality. In this respect, the philosophy of mathematics is in a sorry state.

3.3. The Future

From the Renaissance through the twentieth century, Aristotle's ideas about the nature of mathematical objects have been neglected and ignored. Now the time seems ripe for a renovation of the philosophy of mathematics, based on Aristotelean and neo-Aristotelean [16] ideas and bolstered by the techniques of modern logic, including the predicate calculus.

The great mathematician David Hilbert anticipated such a renovation in his 1925 essay, "On the Infinite" [22]. Hilbert was aware that, according to modern physics, the physical universe is finite. Yet infinite sets were playing an increasingly large role in the mathematics of the day. Hilbert therefore recognized that the most vulnerable chink in the armor of mathematics was the infinite. In order to defend what he called "the honor of human understanding," Hilbert proposed to develop a new foundation of mathematics, in which formal theories of infinite sets, such as T_s, would be rigorously justified by reference to the finite. This is Hilbert's program of *finitistic reductionism*.[28]

Although Hilbert did not cite Aristotle, we can imagine that Hilbert would have profited from an examination of Aristotle's distinction between actual and potential infinity. An *actual infinity* is something like an infinite set regarded as a completed totality. A *potential infinity* is more like a finite but indefinitely long, unending series of events. According to Aristotle, actual infinities cannot exist, but potential infinities exist in nature and are manifested to us in various ways, for instance, the indefinite cycle of the seasons or the indefinite divisibility of a piece of gold.

In any case, it turned out that Hilbert had stated his program in too sweeping a fashion. The wholesale finitistic reduction that Hilbert desired cannot be carried out. This follows from Gödel's incompleteness theorem [5, 22]. The remarkable results obtained by Gödel in 1931 caused the philosophical ideas of Hilbert's 1925 essay

---

[28] Hilbert is often inaccurately described as a formalist. The details of Hilbert's program will not be presented here but see [20, 22]. Roughly speaking, a formal theory is said to be *finitistically reducible* if it can be embedded into some very restricted formal theory such as T_a which is physically meaningful and makes absolutely no reference to actual infinity.

to fall into disrepute. Hilbert's grand foundational program appeared to be dead, broken beyond hope of repair.

The last twenty years have seen a revival of Hilbert's program. Recent foundational research [20] has revealed that, although T_s is not finitistically reducible, there are other formal theories that *are* finitistically reducible, in the precise sense envisioned by Hilbert. Moreover, these other formal theories turn out to be adequate for a very large portion of mathematics. They do not encompass actual infinities such as ω, but they do include the main results of arithmetic and geometry and allied disciplines.

This new research has not yet had an impact on the philosophy of mathematics or on mathematical practice. Philosophers and mathematicians are free to choose which directions to pursue and which techniques to emphasize. Only time will reveal the future evolution of the philosophy of mathematics.

References

[1] Hippocrates G. Apostle, *Aristotle's Philosophy of Mathematics*, University of Chicago Press, 1952, x + 228 pages.

[2] I. M. Bocheński, *A History of Formal Logic*, 2nd ed., Chelsea Publishing Company, New York, 1970, translated and edited by Ivo Thomas, xxii + 567 pages.

[3] Haskell B. Curry, *Outlines of a Formalist Philosophy of Mathematics*, Studies in Logic and the Foundations of Mathematics, North-Holland, 1951, vii + 75 pages.

[4] Melvin Fitting, *First Order Logic and Automated Theorem Proving*, 2nd ed., Graduate Texts in Computer Science, Springer-Verlag New York Inc., 1996, xvi + 326 pages.

[5] Kurt Gödel, *Collected Works*, Oxford University Press, 1986–1995, three volumes.

[6] Petr Hájek and Pavel Pudlák, *Metamathematics of First-Order Arithmetic*, Perspectives in Mathematical Logic, Springer-Verlag, 1993, xiv + 460 pages.

[7] Thomas Heath, *Mathematics in Aristotle*, Clarendon Press, Oxford, 1949, xiv + 291 pages.

[8] ———, *The Thirteen Books of Euclid's Elements*, 2nd revised ed., Dover Publications, Inc., New York, 1956, three volumes.

[9] ———, *A History of Greek Mathematics*, Dover Publications, Inc., New York, 1981, volume I, xv + 446 pages, volume II, xi + 586 pages.

[10] Leon Henkin, Patrick Suppes, and Alfred Tarski (eds.), *The Axiomatic Method, With Special Reference to Geometry and Physics*, Studies in Logic and the Foundations of Mathematics, North-Holland, 1959, xi + 488 pages.

[11] Thomas J. Jech, *Set Theory*, Pure and Applied Mathematics, Academic Press, New York, 1978, xi + 621 pages.

[12] Morris Kline, *Why Johnny Can't Add*, St. Martin's Press, 1973, 173 pages.

[13] Richard McKeon (ed.), *The Basic Works of Aristotle*, Random House, 1941, xxxix + 1487 pages.

[14] Elliott Mendelson, *Boolean Algebra and Switching Circuits*, Schaum's Outline Series, 1970, 213 pages.

[15] ———, *Introduction to Mathematical Logic*, 3rd ed., Wadsworth, 1987, ix + 341 pages.

[16] Leonard Peikoff, *Objectivism: The Philosophy of Ayn Rand*, Dutton, New York, 1991, xv + 493 pages.

[17] Plato, *Dialogues*, 4th ed., Oxford, Clarendon Press, 1964, translated by Benjamin Jowett.

[18] Ayn Rand, *Atlas Shrugged*, Random House, New York, 1957, v + 1168 pages.

[19] David Ross, *Aristotle*, 5th revised ed., Barnes and Noble, 1964, xiv + 300 pages.

[20] Stephen G. Simpson, *Subsystems of Second Order Arithmetic*, Perspectives in Mathematical Logic, Springer-Verlag, 1998, xiv + 445 pages.

[21] Alfred Tarski, *Introduction to Logic and to the Methodology of Deductive Sciences*, 4th ed., Oxford University Press, New York, 1994, xxii + 229 pages.

[22] Jean van Heijenoort (ed.), *From Frege to Gödel: A Source Book in Mathematical Logic, 1879–1931*, Harvard University Press, 1967, xii + 660 pages.

CONTRIBUTORS

STANLEY ROSEN is the Borden Parker Bowne Professor of Philosophy at Boston University and the Evan Pugh Professor Emeritus at Penn State University. He received his B.A. from the University of Chicago and his doctorate at the Committee on Social Thought at the University of Chicago. He holds a Doctor Honoris Causa from the New University of Lisbon (Portugal) and is a past president of the Metaphysical Society of America. He pursued postdoctoral work at the American School of Classical Studies in Athens, the University of Paris, the Humanities Research Institute at the University of Wisconsin, Heidelberg University, and the London School of Economics. Professor Rosen has delivered some 200 lectures at universities in North America and Europe and is the author of thirteen books, including *Plato's Symposium, The Limits of Analysis, Hermeneutics as Politics, The Quarrel Between Philosophy and Poetry, The Question of Being, Metaphysics in Ordinary Language* and, most recently, *The Elusiveness of the Ordinary*. His work has been translated into French, Catalan, Japanese, Polish, and Chinese.

PAUL RAHE is Jay P. Walker Professor of History at the University of Tulsa, where he specializes in the history of ancient Greece and Rome and that of early modern Europe and revolutionary America. He received his B.A. in History, the Arts, and Letters and his Ph.D. in ancient history from Yale University and holds a second B.A. from Oxford University, where he read *Litterae Humaniores* on a Rhodes Scholarship. He has been awarded research fellowships by the Center for Hellenic Study; the National Humanities Center; the Institute of Current World Affairs; the Olin Foundation; Washington University's Center for the History of Freedom; the National Endowment for the Humanities; the Woodrow Wilson International Center for Scholars in Washington, D.C.; and Clare Hall at Cambridge University. Professor Rahe is the author of the three-volume study *Republics Ancient and Modern: Classical Republicanism and the American Revolution* and is co-editor of *Montesquieu's Science of Politics: Essays on the Spirit of Laws* and editor of the forthcoming volume *Machiavelli's Republican Legacy*.

WILLIAM DESMOND received his B.A. at the National University of Ireland and his Ph.D. from Pennsylvania State University. He is a professor of philosophy at the Institute of Philosophy at the Katholieke Universiteit Leuven. Professor Desmond has held the John N. Findlay Chair of Philosophy at Boston University, the Thomas Higgins Chair of Philosophy at Loyola College in Maryland, and has been a Senior Fulbright Research Fellow at the Katholieke Universiteit Leuven. He has been the president of the Hegel Society of America and the Metaphysical Society of America and is a founding fellow of the Society of Philosophers in America. Some of Professor Desmond's publications include *Art and the Absolute: A Study of Hegel's Aesthetics*; *Being and the Between; Philosophy and Its Others: Ways of Being and Mind*; *Perplexity and Ultimacy: Metaphysical Thoughts from the Middle*; *Hegel and His Critics: Philosophy in the Aftermath of Hegel*, and *Ethics and the Between*.

ROBERT PIPPIN is the Raymond W. and Martha Hilpert Gruner Distinguished Service Professor in the Committee on Social Thought and the Department of Philosophy at the University of Chicago. He received his B.A. in English at Trinity College and his Ph.D. in Philosophy at Pennsylvania State University. Professor Pippin is on the editorial board of the *Journal of the History of Philosophy* and *Philosophical Explorations* and was the series editor for *Modern European Philosophy*. Some of Professor Pippin's publications include *Kant's Theory of Form: Essays on the Critique of Pure Reason*; *Hegel's Idealism: The Satisfactions of Self-Consciousness*; *Idealism As Modernism: Hegelian Variations*; and *Henry James and Modern Moral Life*.

RICHARD VELKLEY received a B.A. in European history from Cornell University and a Ph.D. in philosophy from Pennsylvania State University. He has been associate professor of philosophy in the School of Philosophy, the Catholic University of America, since 1997. He is also the associate editor of the *Review of Metaphysics*. Professor Velkley's publications include *Freedom and the End of Reason: On the Moral Foundations of Kant's Critical Philosophy*, *Being After Rousseau: Philosophy and Culture in Question*, and several articles on Kant, Rousseau, Schelling, Husserl, Gadamer, and other topics in the history of philosophy.

JAAKKO (KAARLO JAAKKO JUHANI) HINTIKKA received his Ph.D. at the University of Helsinki in Finland. He is a member of the Norwegian Academy of Science and Letters, a fellow of the American Academy of Arts and Sciences, a scientific adviser and foreign member of the Internationales Forschungszentrum Salzburg, and a fellow of Societas Scientiarum Fennica. He is the editor in chief of the international journal

Synthese as well as the managing editor of the Synthese Library. Some of Professor Hintikka's publications include *Distributive Normal Forms in the Calculus of Predicates*; *Time and Necessity: Studies in Aristotle's Theory of Modality*; *The Semantics of Questions and the Questions of Semantics*; *Ludwig Wittgenstein: Half-Truths and One-and-a-Half Truths*; and *Paradigms for Language Theory and Other Essays in the Foundations of Language*. He has been discussed or honored in the books *Essays in Honour of Jaakko Hintikka*; *Profiles: Jaakko Hintikka*; *Investigating Hintikka*; and *Knowledge and Inquiry: Essays on Jaakko Hintikka's Epistemology and Philosophy of Science*.

GIAN-CARLO ROTA was a Professor of Applied Mathematics and Philosophy at the Massachusetts Institute of Technology from 1975 until 1999. He had been a member of the Comitato Scientifico, the National Academy of Sciences Committee on Women in Science and Engineering, and the Committee on Mathematics Advisory to the Office of Naval Research. His books included *On the Foundations of Combinatorial Theory*: *Combinatorial Geometries*; *Discrete Thoughts*; and *Finite Operator Calculus*. He also published numerous articles, including "On models for Linear Operators," "On the eigenvalues of positive operators," "An 'alternierendes Verfahren' for general positive operators," and "Baxter Algebras and Combinatorial Identities, I." Professor Rota died in 1999.

STEPHEN G. SIMPSON received his B.A. from Lehigh University and his Ph.D. in mathematics from MIT. He is an adjunct professor of mathematics at the University of Tennessee. He has been invited to speak at mathematics departments in England, France, Venezuela, Germany, the Netherlands, Japan, Taiwan, and Italy. Professor Simpson has published articles in *Annals of Mathematical Logic, Journal of Symbolic Logic, Advances in Mathematics, Annals of Pure and Applied Logic, Archiv fur mathematische Logik und Grundlagen der Mathematik, Journal of Combinatorial Theory,* and the *Archive for Mathematical Logic*.

SOURCES

Section One

Plato. *Symposium*. Selection from *The Dialogues of Plato*, vol. 2, 2nd edition, translated into English with analyses and introductions by B. Jowett. Oxford: Clarendon Press, 1875.

Plato. *Gorgias*. Selection from *The Dialogues of Plato*, vol. 2, 2nd edition, translated into English with analyses and introductions by B. Jowett. Oxford: Clarendon Press, 1875.

Plato. *Republic*. Selection from *The Republic of Plato*, translated by Benjamin Jowett. Oxford: Clarendon Press, 1888.

Aristotle. Selection from *The Politics and Economics of Aristotle*, translated, with notes and analyses, by Edward Walford. London: Bell & Daldy, 1871.

Machiavelli, Niccolò. Selection from *The Prince*, translated by Paul Rahe.

Hobbes, Thomas. Selection from *Leviathan*, edited, with an introduction and notes, by Edwin Curley. Indiana: Hackett Publishing, 1994. Copyright © 1994 by Hackett Publishing Company. Reprinted by permission of Hackett Publishing Company, Inc. All rights reserved.

Rousseau, Jean-Jacques. Selection from *The First and Second Discourses*, translated by Roger D. Masters. New York: Bedford/St. Martin's, 1969. Copyright © 1969 by St. Martin's Press, Inc. Reprinted by permission of Bedford/St. Martin's Press, Inc.

Section Two

Augustine. Selection from *Confessions*, translated by Edward B. Pusey. New York: P. F. Collier & Son, 1909.

Maimonides, Moses. Selection from *The Guide for the Perplexed*, 2nd edition, translated by M. Friedlander. New York: Dover, 1950, Copyright © 1950 by Dover. Reprinted by permission.

Sources

Pascal, Blaise. Selection from *Pensées*, translated by A. J. Krailsheimer. London: Penguin, 1966. Copyright © 1966 by Penguin Books. Reprinted by permission.

Hegel, Georg Wilhelm Friedrich. Selection from *Lectures on the Philosophy of Religion*, vol. 1, translated by E. B. Speirs and J. Burdon Sanderson. London: Kegan Paul, Trench, Trubner, 1895.

Kierkegaard, Søren. Selection from *Fear and Trembling*, edited and translated by Howard V. Hong and Edna H. Hong. Princeton: Princeton University Press, 1983. Copyright © 1983 by Princeton University Press. Reprinted by permission of Princeton University Press.

Section Three

Plato. *Republic*. Selection from *The Republic of Plato*, translated by Benjamin Jowett. Oxford: Clarendon Press, 1888.

Aristotle. Selection from *Aristotle's Theory of Poetry and Fine Art*, translated by S. H. Butcher. London: Macmillan, 1907.

Schiller, Friedrich. Selection from *On the Aesthetic Education of Man in a Series of Letters*, translated by Elizabeth Wilkinson and L. A. Willoughby. Oxford: Clarendon Press, 1967. Reprinted by permission of Oxford University Press.

Nietzsche, Friedrich Wilhelm. Selection from *The Birth of Tragedy and the Genealogy of Morals*, translated by Francis Golffing. New York: Doubleday Anchor Books, 1956. Copyright © 1956 by Doubleday, a division of Bantam Doubleday Dell Publishing Group, Inc. Reprinted by permission of Doubleday, a division of Random House, Inc.

Dewey, John. Selection from *John Dewey: The Later Works, 1925–1953*, vol. 10: 1934. *Art as Experience*, edited by Jo Ann Boydston. Carbondale and Edwardsville: Southern Illinois University Press, 1989. Reprinted by permission.

Adorno, Theodor W. Selection from *Aesthetic Theory*, edited by Gretel Adorno and Rolf Tiedemann, translated by Robert Hullot-Kentor. Minneapolis: University of Minnesota Press, 1997. Copyright © 1997 by the Regents of the University of Minnesota. Reprinted by permission.

Section Four

Aristotle. Selection from *Metaphysics*, from *The Complete Works of Aristotle*, the revised Oxford translation edited by Jonathan Barnes. Princeton: Princeton University Press, 1984. Copyright © 1984 by the Jowett Copyright Trustees. Reprinted by permission of Princeton University Press.

Descartes, René. Selection from *Meditations*, from *The Philosophical Works of Descartes*, vol. 1, translated by Elizabeth S. Haldane and G. R. T. Ross. Cambridge: Cambridge University Press, 1968. Reprinted by permission of Cambridge University Press.

Hegel, Georg Wilhelm Friedrich. Selection from *Lectures on the History of Philosophy: Greek Philosophy to Plato*, vol. 1, translated by E. S. Haldane. Lincoln and London: University of Nebraska Press, 1892.

Leibniz, Gottfried Wilhelm. Selection from *Philosophical Papers and Letters*, 2nd edition, translated and edited by Leroy E. Loemker. Dordrecht: Reidel, 1969. Reprinted by permission of Kluwer Academic Publishers.

Kant, Immanuel. Selection from *Prolegomena to Any Future Metaphysics*, 1783, translated by Lawrence G. Horsburgh.

Wittgenstein, Ludwig. Selection from *The Blue and Brown Books*. New York: Harper & Row, 1958. Copyright © 1958 by Basil Blackwell, Ltd. Copyright © renewed 1986 by Basil Blackwell, Ltd. Reprinted by permission of HarperCollins Publishers, Inc.

Section Five

Plato. Selection from *Meno*, from *Plato: Laches. Protagoras. Meno. Euthydemus*, vol. 2, translated by W. R. M. Lamb, Cambridge, Mass.: Harvard University Press, 1924. Reprinted by permission of the publishers and the Loeb Classical Library.

Aristotle. Selection from *Posterior Analytics*, from *The Complete Works of Aristotle*, vol. 1, edited by Jonathan Barnes. Oxford: Clarendon Press, 1994. Reprinted by permission of Princeton University Press.

Sources

Descartes, René. Selection from *Meditations*, from *The Philosophical Works of Descartes*, vol. 1, translated by Elizabeth S. Haldane and G.R.T. Ross. Cambridge: Cambridge University Press, 1968. Reprinted by permission of Cambridge University Press.

Hume, David. Selection from *An Abstract of a Book Lately Published, Entituled A Treatise of Human Nature, &c.*, 1740.

Hintikka, Jaakko. Selection from *Principles of Philosophical Reasoning*, edited by James H. Fetzer. Totowa, N.J.: Rowman & Allanheld, 1984.

Section Six

Feyerabend, Paul. Selection from *Against Method*. New York: Verso, 1993. Reprinted by permission.

Kuhn, Thomas. Selection from *The Structure of Scientific Revolutions*, 3rd edition. Chicago and London: University of Chicago Press, 1962. Reprinted by permission of the University of Chicago Press.

Husserl, Edmund. Selection from *The Crisis of European Sciences*, translated by David Carr, Northwestern University Press, 1970.

Ayala, Francisco J. Selection from *Studies in the Philosophy of Biology*, edited by Francisco J. Ayala and Theodosius Dobzhansky. Berkeley: University of California Press, 1974. Copyright © 1974 by the Macmillan Press, Ltd. Reprinted by permission.

Poincaré, Henri. Selection from *Science and Method*, translated by Francis Maitland. New York: Dover, 1952. Reprinted by permission.

Poincaré, Henri. Selection from *Science and Hypothesis*. New York: Dover, 1952. Reprinted by permission.

INDEX

Abraham (biblical), 172–79, 181–82
Absolute, the, 166–67, 324–25
  See also God
absolute monarchy, 20
abstraction, human tendency to, 394–97
  See also reason
action and ideas, 194, 500–501
actuality vs. capacity, 359–62
adaptability and evolutionary biology,
  548–51
Adorno, Theodor, 196, 199, 289–308
Aeschylus, 197, 221
aesthetics and religion, 105, 122, 188
  See also art and culture; beauty
agriculture, origins of, 22, 98–100
altruism, argument for, 376, 377, 378,
  379
ambition, political, 19–20, 34, 62, 101
anarchism in science, 493–502
anti-intellectualism, 481
anxiety, existential, 20–21, 195–96
Apollonian-Dionysiac duality of art,
  245–62
appetites. *See* passion and appetites
a priori knowledge
  Aristotle on, 425–27
  attempts to discover, 406
  definition, 402
  vs. innate ideas, 323
  mathematics as, 412, 532–34
  Platonic path to, 412, 415–24
  in science, 523–28
Aquinas, Saint Thomas, 16, 110, 112
Archilochus, 258, 259, 260
architectonic science, metaphysics as, 313
argumentation, political basis for, 500
Aristophanes, 7–9
Aristotle
  and Aquinas, 16
  on art, 185–86
  doctrine of mean, 17
  on justice, 381–82
  on knowledge, 140, 425–27, xiii, xv,
    xvi–xvii
  on logic, 577–81, 585

vs. Machiavelli, 17–18
  and mathematics, 591, 599
  on metaphysics, 312–16, 329–42
  on monotheism, 6
  on poetry, 217–32
  on politics, 14–16, 73–75
arithmetic, formal theory for, 593–98
Arnold, Matthew, 285–86
art and culture
  art and cultural development, 267–88
  art and truth, xxiv
  art as opposition to culture, 289–308
  collective individuality of, 271–74
  idea-based vs. emotionally based,
    245–66
  introduction, 185–200
  moral imperative of education in,
    233–44
  objectivist explanation for art, xiv–xv
  value of, 210–15
  See also beauty; poetry
atheism, 121
audience of Greek comedy, 263–66
Augustine of Hippo, Saint, 108, 109,
  125–33
authoritarianism, 20
auxiliary constructions, 466–67
axiological standard. *See* normative
  standards
Ayala, Francisco J., 535–53

Bacon, Sir Francis, 317, 566
beauty
  and appeal of science, 561–63
  experience of, 191–92, 193
  as freedom, 193–94, 195, 196
  Greek view of, 253–54, 256
  ideal form of, 35–37
  of justice, 380–81
  love of, 27–28, 31, 32, 33, 186
  modern status of, 188–89
  pursuit of, 185–86
  requirements for, 225
  subjective nature of, 189–90
  See also art and culture

construction, epistemological, 407
constructivism in mathematics, 600–601
contiguity and cause/effect relationships,
    442, 452
contingency of content, 352
cooperative action and exclusion, 15
    See also society
correspondence theories of truth, 413
cosmology, 486–87
Creation as designed, 110–11, 113, 116,
    137
    See also nature
Critique of Judgment (Kant), 189–93,
    300–301, 302
Critique of Pure Reason (Kant), 322–23
culture. *See* art and culture; society
cumulative, scientific knowledge as,
    506–7, 517–18
custom as basis for predictions of future
    effects, 444, 446–48
    See also society

deduction, logical, and inquiry strategies,
    407, 409, 454–58, 463–65
democracy, 24, 25, 70
demonstration of cause and effect, impos-
    sibility of, 443–45
demonstrative understanding, 425–27
Descartes, René
    on arithmetic, 597
    on foundation of knowledge, 409–11,
        429–37
    Hume's critique of, 448–49
    self-knowledge, 108–9, 316–20, 343–48
    vs. Socrates, 10
design, argument for God from, 110–11,
    113, 116, 137
desire
    and art, 301, 304
    gratification as strength, 43
    vs. ideation, 261
    for immortality, 32–34
    for power, 19, 20, 82–89
    and prophecy, 140
    Rousseau on, 22
    See also happiness; passion and appetites
Dewey, John, 199–200, 267–88
dialectical thinking, 118, 120, 123, 502
Dionysiac-Apollonian duality of art,
    245–62
direction of change and evolutionary
    progress, 536–38

discursive vs. sentential thinking, 461–62,
    464–65, 468–70
diversification of biological life, 543–47
divine, the
    and ambiguity of revelation, xvii
    Christian intimacy with, 121–22
    enigma of, 106
    experience of, 247–49
    inspiration for intelligence, 141–43
    mindfulness of, 122–23
    in nature, 157–60
    and paganism, 176
    permanence of, 34
    See also God
drama
    comedic, 217, 219, 220–22, 227,
        262–66
    definition of, 219
    emotional impact of, 229–32
    tragic, 197–98, 227
dreams
    analogy for naïve artist, 254–55, 259
    and Greek art, 245–47, 249
    life as, xxiv
    ontology of, 344–45
    and prophecy, 139
dualism (duality)
    in aesthetic dimension, 245–62, 278–83
    and God, 114–15, 126–27
    in human nature, 147–55, 191
duty, 23, 176
    See also morality

earth as separate from God, 126–27
    See also nature
ecological issues, 481
economics, 485–86, 487
education
    aesthetic, 186, 193–96, 233–44, 286
    Hobbesian, 82
    vs. imitation, 207
    Machiavelli's view, 17
    oversimplification of scientific, 495–96
    of philosophers, 13
    pleasure through, 220
    Rousseau's view, 23
    Socratic view, 54–56
efficient cause of being, 314–15
ego, 171–82, 247, 260, 319–20
    See also reason; self; self-knowledge
Einstein, Albert
    experimental verification of, 478

Index